LAW &
INTERNATIONAL
BUSINESS

2nd Edition

Seth E. Lipner

**Professor of Law
Zicklin School of Business
Bernard Baruch College, CUNY**

Linus
Publications, Inc.

Published by Linus Publications, Inc.

Deer Park, NY 11729

ISBN 1-934188-50-6

Printed in the United States of America.

10 9 8 7 6 5 4 3 2 1

Dedication

This book is dedicated to:

Elliot Axelrod and my colleagues in the Law Department

- They are the best

Table of Contents

CHAPTER 3

JURISDICTION TO ADJUDICATE

CHAPTER 4

CHOICE OF FORUM AND INTERNATIONAL ARBITRATION

CHAPTER 5

JURISDICTION TO PRESCRIBE: THE PUBLIC LAW TABOO

CHAPTER 6

JURISDICTION TO PRESCRIBE - THE ANTITRUST EXAMPLE

TABLE OF CASES

Preface

"Law and International Business" book grows out of lessons I learned from Prof. Andreas Lowenfeld of the New York University School of Law between 1980 until 1982, when I was a student in his courses. When asked to define "international law", Prof. Lowenfeld replied that it was "the kind of law international lawyers practice". My own mission since leaving NYU however has been educating BBA and MBA students, my reply to the question would be: "it is the kind of law people in international business must know." That phrase also best describes the scope and purpose of this book.

This book is designed as a guide to the study of law as it relates to international business. It is designed for a course whose objectives are to (1) immerse students in the language and methods of international business; (2) provide practical and in-depth knowledge of the legal principles that affect business in an international setting; and (3) enable students to improve and apply their analytical and business skills by studying in detail a wide variety of international transactions, businesses and industries . The book is appropriate for those pursuing executive and / or entrepreneurial education or careers, as well as for those studying international business at a law school. It is intended for use in a 14-week course that meets 2 ½ hours per week.

The orientation of the book is admittedly US-centric, since it assumes that the users of the book will be involved in international business that involves the foreign trade of the United States. While many of the subjects studied are universal, and cases from England, Australia, Canada are examined, the focus of the book is on the way US law interacts with domestic and foreign businesses, courts and governments.

In Chapters 1 and 2, the student is introduced to the nature of international trade. The subject is the relationships between sellers, buyers and banks as these entities engage in wealth-creating international transactions. The special risks of international business are exposed in a series of dramatic and famous cases from courts in England and the U.S. Students are taught, through a detailed study of the "business stuff" out of which these cases arose, to understand international contracts and risk allocation in a global economy. The main goal is to enable students to use effectively the methodologies and institutions that enable and facilitate international trade. As students gain an understanding of the structure and terms of a basic international trade contract, they are exposed to increasingly complex and "modern" business arrangements, including technology transfers, construction contracts, import and export financing, stand-by letters of credit, and the like. While the cases, court decisions and statutes are the centerpiece about which this table is set, the servings have large pieces of business heaped on every plate, and the lessons are "international" in the truest sense.

Chapters 3 and 4 deal with dispute resolution in international transactions. The focus here is on the jurisdiction (or competence) of courts and the question of where disputes will be resolved. Cases ranging from product liability (tort) to contract to trademark infringement on the internet are presented, raising issues of judicial power and the enforcement of foreign default judgments. Here especially, the US "view" is the focus, but the lessons are again global. As students read about "due process", "long-arm jurisdiction", "forum choice" and "international arbitration", they obtain a view of issues and problems that most international businesses don't see until it is too late.

Chapters 5 and 6 turn to a set of still different but equally important jurisdictional issues - those involving what some would call "jurisdiction to prescribe", and that others would call "conflict of laws" or even "private international law". In two sequences of cases (one in each chapter), the history and problems associated with the regulation of international business are revealed and analyzed. In Chapter 5, students meet Lord Mansfield and his so-called "revenue rule", and the chapter traces the development and mutation of that principle. Students watch as international jurisprudence evolves from "protectionist" to "international" and modern. In Chapter 6, students see how the United States abandoned the revenue rule, even as its foreign vestiges continue to interfere with U.S. attempts to regulate foreign business that affects our economy. The focus of Chapter 6 is US antitrust law (in considerable detail), but the chapter's application is broader; antitrust is the model for a broader paradigm for the legal regulation of international business. These last two chapters also teach important lessons about a variety of businesses and industries, ranging from manufacturing to licensing to insurance and even to smuggling. Students are challenged to consider the meaning and consequences of both sovereign power and economic reality on the legal environment in which international business functions.

Throughout the book, each case is followed by "Notes and Questions" that are designed to highlight important points and direct students' inquiries. These Notes and Questions function as a guide to the cases and business issues. In addition, at the end of each chapter (except Chapter 4) there are multiple choice review questions, essay/discussion problems; and references for additional studies.

A course taught using these materials will not be an easy one for students. They will be asked to read cases in full (or nearly-full) text. (The English cases may be especially difficult because of their style.) Yet among these cases and materials the reader will find the words and thoughts of great and influential legal thinkers and jurists, and the real-life stories of corporations and businesses large and small. The paucity of explanatory text may frustrate some at times, even as others are challenged by the open-ended questions that are posed. But the readings are rich and diverse, and all who dedicate themselves to the task will find great rewards.

I hope that you enjoy it.

Acknowledgments

First, this book would not exist if not for the seeds planted by Prof. Lowenfeld. In addition, I received help and inspiration, over the years, from my wife Judi and daughter Zoe, from my uncle Leon Lipner, for getting me stared in academia, from my colleagues in the Law Department at the Zicklin School of Business at Baruch College, from Prof. Jean Boddewyn, Lena Skou and my colleagues teaching international business at Baruch, from Dean Elliot, from Barbara Froehlich and Carmel Amero and my partner Herb Deutsch, from Ron Naane and Aysa Erguner for some of the sample documents, and from my "international" students of 25 years, each of whom taught me something. Sharsul Choudury and Susan Deng, especially, helped proofread the manuscript. I'm also grateful to Jay Herath and his staff for taking my electrons and making beautiful hard copies.

The International Sale of Goods: The Meaning of CIF

INTRODUCTION

International transactions today take many forms. While these transactions may involve technology transfers, joint ventures, the rendition of services, intellectual property licensing or electronic commerce, the oldest and simplest form of international trade is the sale of goods.

The law that governs the international sale of goods is truly international, in the sense that it is basically the same in all parts of the world. This degree of uniformity is rare in international legal fields, but its development is not an accident; it is largely the result of mercantile practice and reality, although the influence of those with economic power (sellers and banks, for example) is not to be discounted. It is also not an accident that, at least in the first instance, we look to the courts of Great Britain for the development and enunciation of the applicable legal rules. Great Britain not only was a major center of economic power at the time these rules were developing, but, perhaps more importantly it was, and remains today, a leading center of international adjudication.

Before looking at the law of international sales of goods, it's useful to place these types of transactions in the context of sales generally, and to compare international transactions with their domestic counterparts. For example, the differences in the nationality of the parties in the international transaction raise certain special considerations. Also:

1. in whose currency will the parties deal? Because in every international transaction, one (or both) parties will be dealing in the currency of a foreign country, the risks inherent in currency conversion necessarily come into play;

2.   in the event that there is a dispute between the parties, what country's law will govern? And where will the dispute be resolved?

These questions, and others, must be faced in nearly every international transaction, but they are rarely considerations domestically. More important, however, is the fact that performance of the international transaction is likely to take greater time, and involve greater distances (and hazards), than does performance of the domestic one. The result is that international events, such as war and blockade, which often have minimal effect domestically, sometimes have great effect internationally. This phenomenon exists not simply with respect to disputes involving the countries whose nationals are involved in the transactions, but it can also occur as a result of third-country disputes, some foreseeable, others not so foreseeable. And not unexpectedly, times of war and international upheaval are likely to coincide with the times where there are dramatic movements in the cost of commodities, raw materials, transport and insurance. It is, therefore, not an accident that the cases presented in this chapter and the next arise out of, inter alia, the beginning of World War II, the 1956 war in the mid-east, the takeover the US embassy in Iran, and the war in the Persian Gulf.

The lesson one should learn from these cases is not simply to beware international trade in times of international turmoil, even if such a lesson could at all be put to use. Rather, the purpose is to demonstrate the standard (or "conventional") method of international trade, so that a participant can intelligently assess (and hopefully deal with) the allocation of risks in these transactions. These risks, as stated, are best displayed at times of international turmoil. It is thus to these cases we look.

The principal issue these first cases address is performance, i.e. they seek to define the obligations of the parties to an international sale. From our domestic experiences, we know that in a sales contract, the seller's obligation is to deliver conforming goods, and the buyer's obligation is to pay for them. The type of goods which "conform" will be defined in the contract, although a good written description does not guarantee that there will not be a dispute over whether the seller's goods are "up to the contract" or not. The contract is also likely to state the time (and permissible methods) for the buyer's payment, and it might range from advance payment, to COD, to 30, 60 or 90 days credit.

It is unlikely, however, that the parties to a domestic transaction necessarily pay great attention to the "method" of the seller's performance; the seller is expected to deliver the goods at the designated time (or to make them available for pick-up), and, ordinarily, the buyer will have the right to conduct an inspection of the goods before he accepts the delivery and pays for them (unless he has paid in advance). Internationally, however, the method of the seller's performance will be quite different, and it is a difference borne of both necessity and economics.

Needless to say, in the international trade transaction, the fact that the parties are operating at a distance from eachother makes the precise definition of the method of the seller's performance important. The result is that international custom and usage has developed some simple, albeit important, rules defining the seller's obligations in an international sale.

Law and practice in this area makes an initial important distinction, between so-called (a) "shipment contracts" and (b) "destination" contracts. When the seller's contract falls into the first category, the seller has simply promised to ship the goods to the buyer by delivering them to (and making a contract of "affreightment" with) a shipping company; he has not promised to deliver them. Thus the term "shipment contract". By contrast, in a "destination contract", the seller does not merely promise to make a conforming shipment, he promises to deliver the goods, safe and sound, to the buyer.

It is easy to see why destination contracts are rare breeds in international trade - sellers rarely want to take the risks inherent in a guarantee of safe delivery in a foreign country. Indeed, much of international trade law, and many of the well-understood "conventional usages" in international trade are designed with an eye toward protecting the average seller from this very risk.

Among the "conventional usages" that are frequently seen are the shipping terms "CIF" and "FOB". Most students of international trade know that the initials "CIF" stand for "cost, insurance and freight," and that "FOB" stands for "free on board," but few know what these terms really mean in the way they allocate risks in international trade.

On their simplest level, these terms (and the less frequently seen "FAS" (free along side) and "ex-factory") describe components of the price. Thus, in a CIF contract, the price agreed to by the parties includes the shipping costs and insurance, while with FOB it does not. But in actuality, these conventional terms mean much more; an educated businessperson needs to know what the "much more" is, so that he may accurately assess the risks and obligations inherent in the contract he is making.

Of course, the letters CIF and FOB are always followed by a geographic point; in an FOB contract, it is the point of shipment, in a CIF contract, it is the point to which the shipment is destined. But a crucial principle that must be learned is that, in the absence of other language in the contract, a CIF designation, though always followed by the place to which the shipment is headed, is a shipment contract and not a destination contract. Thus, it must be understood that a seller selling CIF is not guaranteeing delivery to the stated point; he is simply saying that the cost of the freight and insurance to that point are included in the contract price.

3

Another important fact concerning the seller's obligations is that once he has delivered the goods to the shipping company, the seller is no longer in physical possession of them. Upon delivery to the carrier, the seller was given a receipt, called a "bill of lading". The bill of lading describes the shipment (or recites the description of the shipment provided to the carrier by the seller, followed by the term "shippers load and count"), and it recites the point of departure and the point of destination and the "Terms of Carriage". (A sample Bill of Lading is appended in the Documents Supplement at the end of this chapter.)

A "bill of lading" is thus much more than just a receipt, although that is one of its functions; the document contains the shipping company's obligations, and it must be used by the buyer at the other end of the voyage to secure possession of the goods from the carrier. Bills of Lading, because of these characteristics, are so widely recognized as being representative of the goods that they can be sold to another party even before the goods arrive.

Nearly all international sales are "documentary sales", meaning that the intention of the parties is that the seller will tender to the buyer the bill of lading in advance of the arrival of the goods (usually by sending the bill of lading by airmail to an agent of the seller near the buyer's place of business). The buyer will, upon tender, inspect the bill of lading (and any other documents required to be presented by the contract); if the documents "conform", i.e. they show the shipment called for in the contract of sale, the buyer is expected that day to pay the agreed price. If the buyer fails to do so in the face of conforming documents, the buyer is in breach.

Notice that the effect of this procedure is to require that the buyer pay "blind", i.e. without having had the opportunity to inspect the goods prior to payment. In a domestic transaction, such a procedure is virtually unheard of, but in international trade it is very much the unvaried norm. Why is that so? What are the consequences for the parties? Why would the buyer agree to such a practice? And what, if anything, can the buyer do to protect himself against having paid for a defective shipment?

The answers to these questions will be explored through study of the seminal case, Biddell Brothers v. E. Clemens Horst Co. In that case, the parties failed expressly to designate their international sales contract as one where the buyer must pay upon the seller's presentation of conforming documents. The buyer thus argued that it was not required to make payment at that time, and that it was entitled to wait for the goods to arrive before having to pay. Faced with an uncertain prospect for payment (and no doubt fearing that payment would not be made even if the goods conformed), the seller preferred not to ship the goods, and the law suit followed.

I. CIF AND DOCUMENTARY SALES

BIDDELL BROTHERS
v.
E. CLEMENS HORST COMPANY

Court of Appeal
(1911) K.B. 934

APPEAL from the judgement of Hamilton J. in an action tried by him without a jury.

The action was brought to recover damages for alleged breaches of two contracts, dated respectively October 13, 1904 ,and December 21, 1904.

The first contract, which was made at Sunderland between the defendants, of San Francisco and London, parties of the first part, and Vaux & Sons, Limited, of the city of Sunderland, parties of the second part, provided that "the parties of the first part agree to sell to the parties of the second part one hundred (100) bales. equal to or better than choice brewing Pacific Coast hops of each of the crops of the years 1905 to 1912 inclusive.

"The said hops to be shipped to Sunderland.

"The parties of the second part shall pay for the said hops at the rate of ninety (90) shillings sterling per 112 lbs., c.i.f. to London, Liverpool, or Hull (tare 5 lbs. per bale).

"Terms net cash.

"It is agreed that this contract is severable as to each bale.

"The sellers may consider entire unfulfilled portion of this contract violated by the buyers in case of refusal by them to pay for any hops delivered and accepted hereunder or if this contract or any part of it is otherwise violated by the buyers.

"Time of shipment to place of delivery, or delivery at place of delivery, during the months (inclusive) of October to March following the harvest of each year's crop.

"If for any reason the parties of the second part shall be dissatisfied with or object to all or any part of any lots of hops delivered hereunder, the parties ship or deliver other choice hops in place of those objected to."

The second contract was between the same parties, and in the same terms, except that it provided for the sale by the defendants to Vaux & Sons, Limited, of fifty bales of British Columbia hops equal to or better than choice Pacific Coast hops of each of the crops of the years 1906 to 1912 inclusive,; c.i.f. to London.

Upon August 11, 1908, Vaux & Sons, Limited, assigned for value to the plaintiffs all their rights and benefits under the two contracts, and express notice thereof in writing was given by the plaintiffs to the defendants.

Correspondence passed between the parties as to the shipment of the 150 bales of the 1909 crop and on January 29,1910, the defendants wrote to the plaintiffs stating that they were ready to make shipment of the 150 bales of the 1909 crop of the contracted quality, and that "for the invoice price less freight we will value on your good selves at sight with negotiable bills of lading and insurance certificate attached to draft, and if you wish we will also attach certificates of quality of the Merchant's Exchange, San Francisco, or other competent authority to cover the shipment." On February 1 the plaintiffs replied that they were prepared to take delivery on the terms of the contracts, and that it was in accordance with the universal practice of the trade and custom adopted by you in your dealings with other purchasers of your hops, and it has also been your custom with our assignors to submit samples, and the samples having been accepted to give delivery in bulk in accordance with the samples; but if you decline to adopt the usual and undoubtedly most convenient course, we can only pay for the hops against delivery and examination of each bale. We cannot fall in with your suggestion of accepting the certificate of quality of the Merchants' Exchange, San Francisco." On February 5 the defendants' solicitors wrote to the plaintiffs' solicitors that the refusal of the plaintiffs to pay for the hops except upon terms which were not in accordance with the contracts was a clear breach of the contracts by the plaintiffs, and, that being so, the defendants would not now ship to the plaintiffs the bales of the 1909 crop, and they reserved all their rights in respect of the breach of the contract by the plaintiffs.

Upon March 11, 1910, the plaintiffs issued the writ in this action claiming damages for breach of contract in refusing to ship or deliver the 150 bales of hops. The defence, after stating that the defendants raised no defence with reference to the assignment of the agreements, alleged that, by reason of the plaintiffs' violation of the entire unfulfilled portion of the agreements in refusing to pay for the hops in accordance with the terms of the agreements, the defendants were entitled to refuse to further perform the agreements, and they counterclaimed against the plaintiffs for the damages for the breach of contract in refusing to take and pay for the 150 bales of hops.

Hamilton J. gave judgment for the defendants.

VAUGHN·WILLIAMS L.J. I am going in the first instance deal with this case quite apart from any difficulties which arises on the construction of the peculiar conditions of this particular contract, and as if the words were simply, "the parties of the second part shall pay for the said hops at the rate of ninety (90) shillings sterling per 112 lbs c.i.f. to London, terms net cash."

It was argued before Hamilton J. on behalf of the defendants that the terms "net cash" in a c.i.f. contract necessarily means "cash against documents," and that a c.i.f. contract is performed by the vendor shipping goods of the description specified in the contract, effecting a proper insurance thereon, and then tendering to the buyer the documents representing the goods, namely, the indorsed bill of lading, invoice and policy, and that thereupon the buyer has to pay for the goods whether they have arrived or not. Hamilton J. affirmed the proposition just set forth as to performance of a c.i.f. contract by the seller, but in no way based his conclusion on the assumption that "terms net cash" means "cash against documents "and expressed his opinion that the words "terms net cash" in themselves mean only, in the absence of proof of trade custom or trade meaning, no credit and no deduction by way of discount or rebate or otherwise, which the law would have implied.

The judgment of the learned judge is based primarily ... upon the proposition that the terms c.i.f. "are now settled and, I hope I may add, well understood." Those are the words of the learned judge, and he goes on to say that it is not and cannot be contended but,"that the seller under a c.i.f. contract has first of all to arrange to put on board a ship at port of shipment goods of the description contained in the contract; secondly to arrange for a contract of affreightment under which they will be delivered at the destination contemplated in the contract; thirdly to arrange for an insurance upon the usual terms current in the trade, available for the benefit of the buyer; to make out an invoice;...and, finally, he has to tender to the buyer those documents so that the buyer may know what freight he has to pay in order to obtain delivery of the goods,if they are intact,or so that he may recover for the loss of them if they have gone to the bottom."

The plaintiffs contended that, in the absence of words providing for the payment against shipping documents, unless they accepted a transfer of the bill of lading, the price was not to be paid until they had the opportunity of examining the shipment, which could not be done until after the arrival of the ship in this country.

It is said that in the case of a c.i.f. contract an implication ought to be made that the payment must be made against tender of shipping documents, and this whether the ship and goods have arrived or not. It is suggested, as one of the reasons why this implication should be made, that the goods under a c.i.f. contract are carried at the risk of the buyer, and must be paid for whether the goods are lost at sea or not, because the policy is taken out on behalf and in the interest of the buyer. I do not think that any such implication ought to be made, seeing that "cash against documents" is a term which is frequently included in a c.i.f. contract by express words, and moreover, because, I do not think that the admitted fact that an object of the c.i.f. policy is to enable the goods at sea to be commercially dealt with before the ship arrives compels the buyer to take advantage of this opportunity, if for any reasons he is not disposed to do so.

There is no evidence in the present case of any law merchant or custom which reads such words as "payment to be made against shipping documents," or words to that effect, into the contract. The judgement of Hamilton J. does not rest on any such basis; what he says is that, because it is now well settled and well understood that the meaning of the terms "cost freight and insurance" is that, the seller having tendered the bill of lading, invoice, and policy, which completed the delivery of the goods in accordance with the agreement in the contract, the buyer is bound to pay the price of the goods, against shipping documents, before the arrival of the goods in this country.

The appeal, therefore, must be allowed, and judgement entered for the plaintiffs.

FARWELL L.J.... At common law the delivery of goods by the seller and acceptance and payment by the buyer are regarded as concurrent acts, the buyer being entitled to a reasonable opportunity for inspections before he accepts and pays...

... The general rule, therefore, is payment against inspected goods; and this is simple enough where both parties and the goods are together in the same place. But when the goods are shipped from across the seas, the contract becomes complicated by the fact that the delivery, although not complete until acceptance commences on a c.i.f. contract on shipment, and the property passes, subject to certain qualifications not necessary now to consider, when the goods are shipped; if the seller fails to ship, or ships goods not according to contract, the breach by him is committed there and then... But the buyer's acceptance and duty to pay is not shipment. The c.i.f. contract usually provides for payment against documents, a practice convenient for both parties, as the bill of lading enables financial dealings on the credit of the goods to be carried out before the arrival of the goods; but no one has ever suggested that on a c.i.f. contract, silent as to time of payment, the buyer is bound to pay on shipment of the goods. The result must therefore be that the ordinary rule of law is not displaced, namely, payment against examined goods. It is said that this cannot be so, because under the contract in common form "c.i.f. payment against documents" the buyer has to unload and warehouse the goods at his own expense; whereas the seller would not have to bear such expense if he has to afford the buyer an opportunity of inspection before payment can be required. But this is only to state the different consequences flowing from two contracts expressed in different terms; there is no necessity for any implication as to justify the Court in altering the usual incidence of burdens under a contract silent as to this particular burden; and actual physical necessity is not suggested....

I will assume that as a matter of usage the seller is bound to tender the bill of lading to the buyer when it arrives, and, if the buyer accepts it, he must of course, pay for such goods on acceptance, because the delivery of the bill of lading is a symbolic delivery of the goods, and, if the goods are accepted, the right of antecedent (though not of subsequent) inspection before payment is thereby waived, just as it would be in the case of acceptance without inspection. But I fail to follow the consequence said by the learned judge to ensue. The duty on A. to tender to B. a document before he can require payment does not impose on B. a duty to accept such document as equivalent to goods, if he has the right to inspect such goods before accepting and paying for them. B. has the option of choosing between two alternative rights: he may accept symbolic delivery or actual delivery, but in the absence of express contract it is at his option, not at the seller's. In the great majority of cases, it suits both buyer and seller better to give and accept symbolic delivery by the bill of lading and the existence and exercise of this option explains why in case where the c.i.f. contract does not contain the words "cash against documents" or the like, the contract is in fact so often so carried out. But this is no evidence of the buyer to accept in all cases, or, in other words, to waive the option. If the goods were lost at sea, the option at once ceases because inspection would have been rendered impossible, and the buyer would be bound to pay against documents.

The basis of my judgement is that the buyer has a common law right (now embodied in the Sale of Goods Act) to have inspected goods against payment, and this cannot be taken away from him without some contract express or implied, and here I can find neither. In this particular, and ill-drawn, contract there are words, especially in the clause referring to refusal to pay "for any hops delivered and accepted hereunder," which bear out the conclusion that I have arrived, but I prefer to rest my judgment on the general grounds above stated. It is said that this decision will upset mercantile practice, but I fail to see any difficulty in parties who desire it adding " against documents" to their contracts-a course hitherto adopted in the majority of c.i.f. contracts.

In my opinion, the appeal should be allowed and judgment entered for the plaintiffs.

KENNEDY L.J....

So far as regards the claim of the plaintiffs, which Hamilton J. has dismissed, his judgement was in my opinion right, and but for the contrary opinion of the other members of this Court, from whom I have the misfortune to differ, I should venture to think this case a reasonably simple one.

The plaintiffs'-that is the appellants'- argument, apart from a reference to certain subordinate and subsidiary printed clauses to which I shall advert after dealing with the main question, hangs upon considerations arising from (a) the absence, after the words "net cash," of such words as "against documents," or in exchange for documents";(b) the provisions of s.28 and s.34a of the Sale of Goods Act, 1893, in respect of the buyer's right to have delivery in exchange for the price and to have an opportunity to examined goods tendered for acceptance.

In regards to the wording of the contract, I do not think that the comment that the terms might have been more fully expressed helps one way or the other to the interpretation of the contract as it stands. All that can be said is that, the condition of payment not being expressly stated except in so far as the words "net cash" negative payment by acceptance and the allowance of deduction or discount, it must be settled by the interpretation of the documents according to the established principles of mercantile law. If any implication is necessary, the law....desires to give such business efficacy to the transactions as must have been intended at all events by both parties, who are business men. This is not a case, as it seems to me, of a contract, the terms of which present ambiguity or conflict. There is no contriety between "cost freight and insurance, net cash" or a contract "cost freight and insurance, net cash against documents." Both the fuller and the shorter form are, I believe, in everyday use, examples of both can be found within the covers of the modern law reports and, although it is probable, I should think, - and the present litigation certainly vindicates its expediency,- that the fuller form is the more common, it has, so far as I am aware, never before this case been suggested that a contract "cost fright and insurance, net cash" or a contract " cost freight and insurance, payment by acceptance" may not imply "against documents" in each case ...

Let us however, leave out of sight altogether for the present all question of usage or judicial recognition of usage. The application of the principles and rules of the common law now embodied in the Sale of Goods Act, 1893, to the business transactions embodied in the c.i.f. contract appears to me to be decisive of the issue between these parties. Let us see, step by step, how according to those principles and rules the transactions specified in the such a c.i.f. contract as that before us is and, I think, must be carried out in order to fulfill its terms.

At the port of shipment-in this case San Francisco- the vendor ships the goods intended for the purchaser under the contract. Under the Sale of Goods Act, 1893, s. 18c, by such shipment the goods are appropriated by the vendor to the fulfillment of the contract, and by virtue of s.32 the delivery of the goods to the carrier - whether named by the purchaser or not- for the purpose of transmission to the purchaser is prima facie to be deemed to be a delivery of the goods to the purchaser. Two further legal results arise out of the shipment. The goods are at risk of the purchaser, against which he has protected himself by the stipulation in his c.i.f. contract that the vendor shall at his own cost, provide him with a proper policy of the marine insurance intended to protect the buyer's interest, and available for his use, if the goods should be lost in transit; and the property in the goods has passed to the purchaser, either conditionally or unconditionally. It passes conditionally where the bill of lading for the goods, for the purpose of securing payment of the price, is made out in favour of the vendor or his agent or representative.... It passes unconditionally where the bill of lading is made out in favour of the purchaser or his agent or representative as consignee. But the vendor in absence of special agreement, is not yet in a position to demand payment from the purchaser; his delivery of the goods to the carrier is, according to the express terms of s.32, only "prima facie deemed to be a delivery of the goods to the buyer"; and under s.28 of the Sale of Goods Act, as under the common law...a tender of delivery entitling the vendor of the payment of the price must, in the absence of contractual stipulation to the contrary, be a tender of possession. How is such a tender to be made of goods afloat under a c.i.f. contract? By tender of the bill of lading, accompanied in the case the goods have been lost in transit by the policy of insurance. The bill of lading in law and in fact represents the goods. Possession of the bill of lading places the goods at the disposal of purchaser. "A cargo at sea," says Brown L.J. in Sanders v. Maclean, "while in the hands of the carrier, is necessarily incapable of physical delivery. During this period of transit and voyage, the bill of lading by the law merchant is universally recognized as it symbol, and the indorsement and delivery of the bill of lading operates as symbolic delivery of the cargo. Property in goods passes by such indorsement and delivery of the bill of lading, whenever it is the intention of the parties that the property should pass by an actual delivery of the goods. And for the purpose of passing such property in the goods and completing the title of the indorsee to full possession thereof, the bill of lading, until complete delivery of the cargo has been made on shore to some one rightfully claiming under it, remains in force as a symbol, and carries with it not only the full ownership of the goods but also all the rights created by the contract of carriage between the shipper and the shipowner. It is a key which in the hands of the rightful owner is intended to unlock the door of the warehouse, floating or fixed, in which the goods may chance to be." The meaning of "delivery" under the Sale od Goods Act is defined in s. 62 to be "voluntary transfer of the possession from one person to another." Such delivery, as the learned draftsman of the Act and its editor remarks in his note to this section may be either actual or constructive delivery of the bill of lading operates as a symbolical delivery of the goods. But then I understand it to be objected on behalf of the plaintiffs: "Granted that the purchaser might, if he pleased, take this constructive delivery and pay against it the price of the goods; what is there in the 'cost freight and insurance' contract which compels him to do so? Why may he not insist on an option of waiting for a tender of delivery of the goods themselves after having an opportunity of examining them after their arrival?"

There are, I think, several sufficient answers to such a proposition. In the first place, an option of a time of payment is not a term which can be inferred, where the contract itself is silent. So far as I am aware, there is no authority for the inference of an option as to the times of payment to be found either in the law books or in the Sale of Goods Act. Secondly, if there is a duty on the vendor to tender the bill of lading, there must, it seems to me, be a corresponding duty on the part of the purchaser to pay when such tender is made. Very relevant on this point is the language of Brett L.J. in his judgement in Sanders v. Maclean which applies to this class of contract the same principle as was expounded by Bowen L.J. in The Moorcock. He said: "The stipulations which are inferred in mercantile contracts are always that the party will do what is mercantilely reasonable"; and, if it be the duty implied in the c.i.f. contract, as held by Brett L.J. in that case, that the vendor shall make every reasonable exertion to send forward and tender the bill of lading as soon as possible after he has destined the cargo to the particular vendee, it is, I venture to think, "mercantilely reasonable" that the purchaser should be held bound to make the agreed payment when delivery of the goods is constructively tendered to him by the tender of the bill of lading, either drawn originally in his favour or indorsed to him, and accompanied in case of loss by the policy of insurance. For thereunder, as the bill of lading with its accompanying documents comes forward by mail, the purchaser obtains the privilege and absolute power of profitably dealing with the goods days or weeks, or, perhaps, in the case of shipments from a distant port, months, before the arrival of the goods themselves. This is, indeed, the essential and peculiar advantage which the buyer of imported goods intends to gain under the c.i.f. contract according to the construction which I put upon it.

But, in truth, the duty of the purchasers to pay against the shipping documents, under such a contract as the present, does not need the application of that doctrine of the inference in mercantile contracts that each party will do what is "mercantile reasonable," for which we have the great authority of Lord Esher. The plaintiffs' assertion of the right under a cost freight and insurance contract to withhold payment until delivery of the goods themselves, and until after an opportunity of examining them, cannot possibly be effectuated except in one of two ways. Landing and delivery can rightfully be given only to the holder of the bill of lading. Therefore, if the plaintiffs' contention is right, one of two things must happen. Either the seller must surrender to the purchaser the bill of lading, whereunder the delivery can be obtained, without receiving payment, which, as the bill of lading carries with it an absolute power of disposition, is, in the absence of a special agreement in the contract of sale, so unreasonable as to be absurd; or, alternatively, the vendor must himself retain the bill of lading, himself land and take delivery of the goods, and himself store the goods on the quay (if the rules of the port permit), or warehouse the goods, for such time as may elapse before the purchaser has an opportunity of examining them. But this involves a manifest violation of the express terms of the contract "90s per 112 lbs. of cost freight and insurance." The parties have in terms agreed that for the buyer's benefit the price shall include freight and insurance, and for his benefit nothing beyond freight and insurance. But, if the plaintiffs' contention were to prevail, the vendor must be saddled with the further payment of those charges at the port of discharge which ex necessitate rei would be added to the freight and insurance premium which alone he has by the terms of the contract undertaken to defray.

Finally, let me test the soundness of the plaintiffs' contention that according to the true meaning of this contract their obligation to pay arises only when delivery of the goods has been tendered to them after they have had an opportunity of examination, in this way. Suppose the goods to have been shipped, the bill of lading taken, and the insurance for the benefit of the buyer duly effected by the seller, as expressly stipulated in the contract. Suppose the goods then during the ocean transit to have been lost by the perils of the sea. The vendor tenders the bill of lading, with the insurance policy and the other shipping documents (if any) to the purchaser, to whom form the moment of shipment the property has passed, and at whose risk, covered by the insurance, the goods were at the time of loss. Is it, I ask myself, arguable that the purchaser could be heard to say," I will not pay because I cannot have delivery of and an examination of the goods"? But it is just this which is necessarily involved in the contention of these plaintiffs. The seller's answer, and I think conclusive answer, is, "You have the bill of lading and the policy of insurance." It is noticeable that in the course of the argument in Tregelles v. Sewell, Martin B. observes, "The purchaser was to have a policy of insurance, which is usually considered as equivalent to the goods of and earlier in the same argument Wilde B. asked, "If the meaning is 'to be delivered at Harburgh,' what necessity is there for insurance?" The contract in that case was a contract in the fuller form, namely, against documents, but it does not seem to me that that affects the value of those observations as to the relative rights of the buyer and the seller.

I have only to add as to this, the main question in the present case, a few words in regards to ss. 28 and 34 of the Sale of Goods Act. As I have already said, my own view as to s.28 is that the section is satisfied by the readiness and willingness of the seller to give possession of the bill of lading. I am, however, far from saying that the view which is suggested in the course of the judgement of Hamilton J., namely, that when the parties have entered into a c.i.f. contract they have "otherwise agreed," is not one which can be supported, as I hold that a similar view is the true view also in regards to s.34, sub-s.2. As to s.34, sub-s.1, there is no difficulty. No one suggests that the plaintiffs, if they pay against documents, be thereby precluded from rejecting the goods if, on examination after their arrival, they are found to be not goods in accordance with the contract, or from recovering damages for breach of contract if they prefer that course.

In my judgment, the judgment of Hamilton J. was right, and this appeal, so far as relates to the plaintiff's claim, should be dismissed.

Appeal allowed.

E. CLEMENS HORST COMPANY
V.
BIDDELL BROS.

House of Lords
(1912) A.C. 18

EARL LOREBURN L.C. My Lords, in this case there has been a remarkable divergence of judicial opinion, Hamilton J. and Kennedy L.J. holding one view, and Vaughn Williams and Farwell L.J.J. entertaining another. There is no doubt that the contract is of rather an exceptional and peculiar kind, as might have been inferred from the judicial difference to which I have alluded. For my part I think it is reasonably clear that this appeal ought to be allowed; and the remarkable judgement of Kennedy L.J., illuminating as it does, the whole field of controversy, relieves me from the necessity of saying much upon the subject.

This is a contract usually called a c.i.f. contract, under which the seller is to ship a cargo of hops and is to contract for freight and to effect insurance; and he is to receive 90s per 112 lbs. of hops. The buyer is to pay cash. But when is he to pay cash? The contract does not say. The buyer says that he is to pay cash against physical delivery and acceptance of the goods when they have come to England.

Now s.28 of the Sales of Goods Act says in effect that payment is to be made against delivery. Accordingly we have supplied by the general law an answer to the question when this cash is to be paid. But when is there delivery of the goods which are on board ship? That may be quite a different thing from delivery on shore. The answer is that the delivery of a bill of lading when the goods are at sea can be treated as delivery of the goods themselves, this law being so old that I think it is quite unnecessary to refer to authority for it.

Now in this contract there is no time fixed at which the seller is entitled to tender the bill of lading. He therefore may do so at any reasonable time; and it is wrong to say that he must defer the tender of bill of lading until the ship has arrived; and it is still more wrong to say that he must defer the tender of the bill of lading until after the goods have been landed, inspected and accepted.

Upon the question of the counter-claim, I think the Court of Appeals was right, and that there must be only one shilling damages upon the counter-claim.

Accordingly, Hamilton J.'s order ought to be restored so far as the claim is concerned. As regards the counter-claim, I think there ought to be judgment for the defendants with one shilling damages, and no cost on either side.

LORD ATKINSON. My Lords, I concur.

LORD GORELL. My Lords, I also concur.

LORD SHAW OF DUNFERMLINE. My Lords, I desire to express my adherence to the opinion delivered by Kennedy L.J. the value of which has not been overstated by the noble Earl on the woolsack.

> Order of the Court of the Appeals reversed. Judgment to be entered for the appellants, the defendants, on the claim with cost here and below, including the costs of the action.
> Judgment to be entered for the appellants, the defendants, on the counterclaim for one shilling damages with no costs upon either side.

NOTES AND QUESTIONS

1. The buyers' position is that in a normal sale, the buyer has the right to inspect the goods prior to payment. That right is removed when the parties expressly agree to a documentary sale. Since no such words appear in the contract, the buyers argued they had not given up the right to inspect the goods prior to payment. The seller obviously differed, arguing that the bill of lading represents the goods, and that the universal practice is to "deal in documents rather than goods". The seller thus asserts that while the buyer can inspect the *documents* prior to payment, they cannot decline to pay if the documents conform to the contract.

   A. There is no doubt that had the parties expressly used the designation "payment against documents", the buyer could not take the position it took; that omission made the case troubling, but note that all the judges agree that it would have been better for everyone if the contract was more clear. Even though the case might thus be deemed unusual, much can be learned about the ordinary case by looking at the extraordinary ones. Thus, as the debate among the judges turns contentious as to the meaning of the oft-used term "CIF", it is almost funny that the lower court judge (Hamilton) wrote that the term CIF was "settled and, I hope I may add, well understood."

   B. The first two judges in the Court of Appeals sided with the buyer. They declined to interpret the contract as a documentary sale, and would have held the seller in breach for having not shipped the goods and permitted inspection prior to payment. Lord Kennedy, by contrast, sided with the seller, holding that the documentary nature of the sale was dictated by the term "CIF". What is it about "CIF" that dictates a documentary sale?

15

2. The best answer to that important question begins with the definition of the seller's obligations in a CIF contract, and Lord Vaughn Williams thus recites the five (5) basic elements of the seller's obligations in a shipment contract:

    1. to deliver conforming goods to the carrier;

    2. to make a contract of affreightment;

    3. to procure a policy of marine insurance for the benefit of the buyer;

    4. to prepare a commercial invoice showing the amount due; and

    5. to present these documents to the buyer in a reasonable time.

    A. Note that as to this definition, all the judges are in agreement. The debate thus turns to the nature of the *buyers'* obligations. The first two judges would give the buyer the option either of paying for the bill of lading upon presentation, or waiting for delivery and inspection. Lord Kennedy observes that such a construction would expose the seller to the whim of the buyer, leaving the seller uncertain as to which course the buyer will choose. Under such a circumstance, the buyer would have all the advantage, since he could choose to pay against the bill of lading when it suits him, and to wait until arrival of the goods in other situations. But the other two judges point out that the seller could have avoided these eventualities by agreeing only to an express contractual provision for a documentary sale. Having failed to negotiate for itself such a bargain, it was argued that the court should not "remake" the agreement for the seller. Were you convinced by this logic? Or do you prefer the view of Lord Kennedy, that the failure to better word the contract does not "help[] one way or the other."

    B. Thus, at bottom, the first two judges do not find any contractual obligation on the part of the buyer to pay at the time of presentation of the documents. Lord Kennedy, however, disagrees. What exactly is the basis for that disagreement?

        1. One potential basis for Lord Kennedy's ruling is his observation that by agreeing to a CIF transaction, buyer and seller defined the items to be paid by the seller (cost, insurance and freight to London), and those items did not include the cost of making the goods available for inspection at London. Should that fact be dispositive? If you think the answer to that

question is "yes", how do you think Judge Kennedy would have ruled if the buyer, in his telex in advance of the shipment, offered to pay that expense? Probably, it would have made no difference to Lord Kennedy. Therefore, the real basis for his decision must lie elsewhere. But where is it?

2. According to Lord Kennedy, we should focus more on how a CIF contract is performed. As we observed at the outset, a CIF contract is a shipment contract, and in a shipment contract, the seller's obligations are discharged at the point of shipment. (It is thus often said that the seller's risks and duties end "when the goods pass the ship's rail.") Because the contract in <u>Biddell</u> was obviously a shipment contract (there was absolutely nothing in the contract from which the court could imply a destination contract), according to Lord Kennedy, it would be wrong to impose on the seller (a) the duty to land the goods and make them available for inspection and (2) to impose on the seller the risk of non-arrival of the goods. Put differently, Lord Kennedy is trying to demonstrate that the buyers were arguing that the parties had made a destination contract, an argument that could not withstand the test of logic and contract interpretation. Do you agree?

3. In his opinion, after reviewing the Sale of Goods Act, Lord Kennedy addresses the fundamental dispute: "Why may [the buyer] not insist on the option of waiting. . .?" Aside from his hesitation to imply such a term, Lord Kennedy notes:

    > if there is a duty on the vendor to tender the bill of lading, there must, it seems to me, be a corresponding duty on the part of the purchaser to pay when such tender is made.

    Is Justice Kennedy favoring the seller, or is he just trying to be even-handed?

4. If you said "even-handed", what did the buyer get out of it? He was forced to pay blind, after all. Lord Kennedy has an answer for him:

    > as the bill of lading with its accompanying documents comes forward by mail, the purchaser obtains the privilege and absolute power of profitably dealing with the goods days or weeks, or, perhaps, in the case of shipments from a distant port, months, before the arrival of the goods themselves. This is, indeed, the essential and peculiar advantage which the buyer of imported goods intends to gain under the c.i.f. contract according to the construction which I put upon it.

3. The House of Lords, Britain's highest court, reversed the decision of the Court of Appeals and adopted the principles and result advocated by Lord Kennedy. The result was not simply a victory for the sellers; its impact is felt in many ways.

    A. One effect of <u>Biddell</u> is the principle that even if they do not expressly provide in their contract, the parties to an international sale "deal in documents not in goods." The concept of the documentary sale is thus implied from the shipping term. Does that mean that the parties to a CIF (or FOB) contract cannot agree to a transaction in goods rather than documents? Does it mean they cannot agree to permit the buyer to conduct a physical inspection of the goods before paying? The answer is "of course not." They can agree to anything they want, but there may a shifting of risks and burdens way from what is conventional. We deal here with the law's "default provisions", <u>i.e.</u> the rules that come into effect when the parties do not specifically provide for something in the contract, or when they make use of the conventional terms.

    B. A very important side effect of <u>Biddell</u> is the establishment of the seller's ability to force the buyer to pay "blind," <u>i.e.</u> without first inspecting the goods. Consider how this phenomenon affects the buyer's risk. Is the buyer's risk of inadequate performance by the seller increased by the fact that these transactions are documentary sales? If you think the answer is yes, consider what happens in a domestic sale.

        1. Suppose B makes a goods contract with S in March, calling for August delivery COD. S makes his delivery in August, but, upon inspection, B discovers a defect. What happens? B will refuse to pay and will not take delivery. B will normally then arrange to buy substitute goods elsewhere (he does, after all, have a duty to "mitigate damages"); if he pays more, he might consider a lawsuit if the increase sufficiently high; if the difference was small, B would probably let it go. Note, however, that under this scenario, the buyer can use the money he did not pay S to purchase the substitute goods.

        2. Now instead suppose that the transaction was an international CIF sale. B was required to pay without an inspection, and he might wind up in possession of defective goods. If the defect is significant and B cannot use the goods, B will have little choice but to sue S. Not only is out the money he paid S, but he has to dip into his own pocket to buy substitute goods. S will be in the (relatively) comfortable position of having had the use of B's money for a substantial period, <u>i.e.</u> for the

pendency of the lawsuit. Thus, in the documentary sale, an aggrieved buyer is not without a legal remedy; he is, however, deprived the power to reject and not pay. Why would B agree to such a transaction? Were there any advantages? And is there any way for B to protect himself? For an answer to this last question, see Note 4, infra.

C. Perhaps the most important principle inherent in <u>Biddell</u> is Lord Kennedy's rejection of the "buyer has alternatives" approach of the majority in the Court of Appeal. Recall that Lord Kennedy explained that the law of international trade abhors options - that a party to a sale cannot be left hanging while the other party decides what he wants to do.

   1. As Lord Kennedy explained, if the seller is obligated to tender the bill of lading, the buyer must have a concomitant obligation to take it up and pay for it. In this manner, the smoothness of the transaction is assured; if the documents conform, nothing will prevent the seller from promptly receiving payment. That principle becomes crucial, because the seller is often a middle-man who must meet commitments to his suppliers, who may, in turn, have to meet commitments to the manufacturer of the goods. Permitting the buyer the option to either pay upon presentation or wait might well damage the fabric of international trade by throwing a monkey wrench into the works.

   2. Since the law should encourage, not discourage, international trade, the House of Lords sided with Lord Kennedy and the seller. Assuring a smooth transaction is important; disputes can, of course, be resolved later. The international legal principle abhorring options in the trade transaction will also be seen to be at work in other cases in this chapter.

4. After reading <u>Biddell,</u> are you troubled by the "buyer pays blind" regime in international trade? If so, what can an international buyer to minimize the risk of paying for defective goods and having to sue?

   A. One approach is to include in the contract of sale a provision that a sample of the shipment must accompany the documents, and that the buyer be afforded the opportunity to test the sample prior to paying. Of course, the buyer must endeavor to assure himself that the sample was fairly drawn, but, that aside, the provision of a random sample is quite helpful to the buyer.

      1. Note, however, that the seller in <u>Biddell</u> declined to send a sample. One might infer that seller feared that the buyer would discover a defect and not pay. But the real reason is

probably different. Seller may have feared that the buyer would say the sample was defective even if it was perfect; the seller would then be in the terrible position of having goods destined for a foreign port with no ready buyer available. Note that the seller in <u>Biddell</u> preferred not to ship, and face the vagaries of a lawsuit, rather than face the risk just described. What does that tell you about the importance of the principle abhorring options?

B.   Another approach to the buyer's problem, often used in commodity transactions, is for the contract to provide that the buyer will pay, say, 95% of the price upon presentation, the balance after delivery and inspection. In this way, both parties are satisfied - the buyer gets some leverage, but the seller gets the bulk of his contract price "blind", and is thus able to satisfy his obligations to his suppliers.

C.   A third approach, indeed the one most commonly used, is a provision in the contract of sale that one of the documents which must accompany the bill of lading is a testing certificate from an independent laboratory. That approach should satisfy the buyer (who will get his assurance that a sample was inspected at the point of shipment, and that it passed a test of quality), and it will satisfy the honest seller, who had no fears about the quality of his merchandise, but who feared subterfuge on the part of the buyer. Note that the seller in <u>Biddell</u> offered to provide such a certificate, but the buyer refused. Is it no wonder the seller smelled a rat? Or is it just something about the subjective qualities of a commodity such as hops? Perhaps there are just some problems that can't be worked out after the contract was made, as was the case here. That, too, is an important lesson.

5.   Independent testing labs exist in every major port, so they are not hard to find. Indeed, these organizations play an integral part in international trade because of their neutrality.

A.   What other "neutral organizations" play a role in international trade? Aside from the testing agency, did <u>Biddell</u> involve any "neutrals", <u>i.e.</u> individuals or organizations trusted by each side to be an honest player? Did any "neutrals" issue any documents upon which the buyer will rely in making payment? Consider this question as you read the case which follows, <u>The Julia</u>.

B.   Of course, the "neutral" referred to in the last point was the captain of the ship, and the document on which the parties were to rely was the bill of lading. By paying "against presentation" of a bill of lading, the buyer is assured (1) that the shipment is on its way (or at least that the goods have been received from the seller), and (2) that the goods will be delivered to the buyer when the ship arrives. That the buyer have these assurance from a "neutral" is important. But why is that so? Consider that question as you read The Julia.

II. CIF: THE SELLER'S OBLIGATION AND DOCUMENTS OF TITLE

COMPTOIR D'ACHAT ET DE VENTE DU BOERENBOND BELGE S/A
v.
LUIS DE RIDDER, LTDA.
(*THE JULIA*)

House of Lords
[1949] A.C. 293: 82 Ll.L. *Rep.* 270

This was an appeal by Comptoir d'Achat et de Vente du Boerenbond Belge, S.A., an Antwerp firm of grain importers, from a majority order of the Court of Appeal (80 Ll.L.Rep. 653) affirming a judgment of Mr. Justice Morris (80 Ll.L.Rep. 140) upholding an award made by Mr. Arthur Edward Cartwright as umpire in an arbitration between the appellants and the respondents, Luis de Ridder, Limitada, a firm of Argentine exporters of grain, and dismissing a claim by the appellants for the repayment of £1243 12s. 2d., with interest from Apr. 30, 1940, in respect of 500 tons of rye sold to them by the respondents and not delivered at Antwerp in May, 1940, as per contract.

According to the award, by a contract entered into at Antwerp on Apr. 24, 1940, between the buyers and sellers (acting by their Antwerp agents, the Belgian Grain & Produce Company, Ltd.) the buyers agreed to buy and the sellers agreed to sell about 500 tons of

> Plate Rye F.A.Q. Rye Terms Corp. 1939/40...for shipment per steamer...*Julia* afloat as per bill or bills of lading dated or to be dated accordingly at the price of $4,025 U.S.A. currency per 100 kos. c.i.f. Antwerp on the terms, conditions and rules contained in Form No. 41 of the London Corn Trade Association...and the details above and on the back given shall be taken as having been written into such Form in their appropriate place. Any special condition applying hereto shall be treated as if written on such Form.

The contract further provided (*inter alia*) as follows:

> Payment to be made by net cash on first presentation of and in exchange for first arriving copy/ies of bill/s of lading...and/or delivery order/s and policy/ies and/or certificate/s and/or letter/s of insurance at Antwerp by first rate cable transfer on New York, unless the vessel carrying the goods arrives before the said time, in which case payment is to be made on arrival of vessel at port of discharge.

Before entering into the contract, that is to say, on Feb. 27, 1940, the sellers had entered into a charter-party with Messrs. Rethymnis & Kulukundis, Ltd., as agents for the owners of a Greek vessel, the steamer *Julia*, whereby the vessel was to load at Bahia Blanca a full cargo of wheat and/or maize and/or rye for carriage to and delivery at Antwerp; the charter-party contained the clauses known as the "Chamber of Shipping War Risks Clauses."

The *Julia* duly loaded at Bahia Blanca a full cargo of grain which included a quantity of 1,120,000 kilos (equivalent to 1120 tons) of rye in bulk. The rye was loaded in bulk in the vessel's No. 5 hold. In respect of this parcel of rye the master of the vessel on Apr. 18, 1940, at Bahia Blanca signed a bill of lading acknowledging the shipment of the parcel by the sellers and providing for its delivery at Antwerp to the order of the Belgian Grain & Produce Company, Ltd. (who were the sellers' agents at Antwerp) on payment of freight in accordance with the charter-party, all the terms and conditions of which were expressed to be incorporated in the bill of lading.

On Apr. 29, 1940, the Belgian Grain & Produce Company, Ltd., as agents at Antwerp for the sellers, sent to the buyers a provisional invoice dated in Antwerp, Apr. 29, 1940, and requesting payment by the buyers by cable transfer to New York of the sum of 4999.33 U.S. dols. therein referred to.

On Apr. 30, 1940, the sellers presented to the buyers a delivery order signed by the Belgian Grain & Produce Company, Ltd., and addressed to F. van Bree, S.A., of Antwerp, instructing them to release to the buyers or to the bearer 500,000 kilos rye in bulk ex bill of lading for 1,120,000 kilos rye in bulk shipped by the sellers on the *Julia* to be received under the terms of the bill of lading of Apr. 18. The delivery order also contained the following statement (in translation):

> We give a share to the bearer of the present delivery order of $4973 in a certificate of insurance for $7117 covering 700,000 kilos rye in bulk (War and S.R. and C.C. Risks Clause included),[1]

and at the foot thereof a note stating that it was to be presented on arrival of the vessel to F. van Bree, S.A., for signature and release after payment of the freight of 15,250 dols. (being the amount of freight shown payable by the provisional invoice) at the offices of the Belgian Grain & Produce Company, Ltd. On Apr. 30, 1940, the buyers duly paid the sum of 4999.33 U.S. dols. (equivalent to £1243 12s. 2d.) to or for the account of the sellers in the manner requested by them.

On or about the same date the sellers delivered to F. van Bree, S.A., two certificates of insurance (one in respect of marine risks and the other in respect of war risks) signed by a firm of insurance brokers at Antwerp and certifying that insurance had been effected with certain named companies for account of the sellers in the sum of 7117 dols. on 700,000 kilos rye in bulk so valued per steamship *Julia* from Bahia Blanca to Antwerp, bill of lading dated Bahia Blanca, Apr. 18, 1940. Each of the certificates provided that it represented the original policies and conveyed all the rights of the original policy-holder for the purpose of collecting any claims; also that it might be exchanged for a stamped policy if and when required. It contained also a footnote stating: "This certificate not valid unless countersigned by Belgian Grain & Produce Company, Ltd.," followed by a space for the countersignature. The originals of these certificates were not available and there was no evidence tendered which enabled the umpire to find whether or not the certificates were in fact countersigned by the Belgian Grain & Produce Company, Ltd.

The *Julia* did not proceed to Antwerp on the chartered voyage, because on or about May 10, 1940, while she was at sea in the course of the voyage, Belgium was invaded by the Germans and shortly after that date Antwerp was occupied by the German Army. Accordingly, the *Julia*, by arrangement between her owners and the sellers (as charterers), went to Lisbon, where she discharged her cargo, and the parcel of rye in question was in June, 1940, sold there by the sellers ex ship for a price less than the sum which the buyers had paid.

The umpire found that at any rate for ten years prior to the date of the contract here in question these parties had been doing business (the sellers as sellers, and the buyers as buyers) in La Plata cereals, upon contracts made in the form used in this case, the business being known to them as "c.i.f. business" and the form of contract as a "c.i.f. contract." The course of business followed in these cases (of which it was admitted by the buyers' witness that there might have been not less than some 900 instances during the period) was that in the first place the Belgian Grain & Produce Company, Ltd., sent to the buyers a provisional invoice (similar in form to that sent in the present case) showing the amount payable for the goods, less the freight. Soon afterwards the Belgian Grain & Produce Company, Ltd., sent to the buyers a delivery order (again in the same form as that used in the present case) addressed to F. van Bree, S.A. Thereupon the buyers paid to the Belgian

---

[1] "Strikes, riots, and civil commotion."

Grain & Produce Company, Ltd., the amount named in the provisional invoice. On arrival of the vessel carrying the cargo or shipment the subject of the transaction, the buyers handed the delivery order together with a cheque in favour of the Belgian Grain & Produce Company, Ltd., for the freight shown due by the provisional invoice, to a firm named Carga. S.A., who were their own cargo superintendents at Antwerp for cereals bought by the buyers for delivery at that port. Carga. S.A., then handed to the Belgian Grain & Produce Company, Ltd., the cheque for the freight and at the same time presented to them the delivery order, and the Belgian Grain & Produce Company, Ltd., signed the note at the foot thereof, acknowledging receipt of the freight. Carga. S.A., then presented the delivery order to F. van Bree, S.A., who retained it and issued against it a release (or *laissez-suivre*) addressed to themselves and authorizing the delivery to Carga. S.A., of the parcel or of the required quantity ex bulk. Before, however, physical delivery of the goods to Carga. S.A., could be obtained, it was necessary that F. van Bree, S.A., should have received from the ship's agents a further release, known as the "captain's *laissez-suivre*," and this was not issued until the chartered freight had been paid by the sellers (as charterers) to the agents of the ship or until these agents were satisfied that it would be paid concurrently with the discharge of the cargo. This might take place either before or after Carga. S.A., having paid the buyers' freight to the Belgian Grain & Produce Company, Ltd., obtained from them their receipt for the amount on the delivery order issued by them. As soon as Carga. S.A., had this *laissez-suivre*, and in some cases before the issue of the captain's *laissez-suivre*, the representatives of Carga. S.A., and of F. van Bree, S.A., attended together on board the steamer and drew samples of the cargo or shipment, the parcel in question being indicated to Carga. S.A., by F. van Bree, S.A. The captain's *laissez-suivre* was addressed to his staff or superintendents on board the ship and instructed them to deliver the goods mentioned in the bill of lading. It was thus the effective document upon which F. van Bree, S.A., obtained physical possession of the goods; it was issued to F. van Bree, S.A., and was never physically in the buyers' hands. The goods were weighed in the elevator, which transferred them from the ship's hold to the lighter. There was very little evidence offered as to the difference (if any) in the procedure in cases where the buyers obtained a bill of lading and not a delivery order; the witness called from the buyers' office stated that the larger firms of shippers from La Plata (including the sellers here concerned) always tendered delivery orders, and he only named one small shipper (Pablo Hadra) from whom he had experience of a bill of lading being tendered under this form of contract. He stated that in this case the buyers paid the bill of lading freight direct to the ship's agents, and this was not disputed, and the umpire found accordingly. He further found that where the buyers received a bill of lading, the captain's *laissez-suivre* would in the normal course be issued to them on payment of the bill of lading freight.

As regards the position of F. van Bree, S.A., and how the transaction would have been dealt with by the parties had the *Julia* arrived at Antwerp on the chartered voyage, the umpire said that F. van Bree. S.A., were a firm of cargo superintendents at Antwerp who were regularly employed as such and paid by the sellers (or by the Belgian Grain & Produce Company, Ltd., on behalf of the sellers) and handle shipments of cereals from La Plata; their name formed part of the printed form of delivery orders issued by the Belgian Grain & Produce Company, Ltd., as described above, such delivery orders being addressed to them. They were so employed by the Belgian Grain & Produce Company, Ltd., in connection with the shipment here in question. On behalf of the Belgian Grain & Produce Company, Ltd., they would (had the *Julia* arrived) have received the buyers' cheque for the freight and would have issued to Carga, S.A., the *laissez-suivre* or release, addressed to their own staff on the wharf, and in the same capacity they would have received from the ship's agents the captain's *laissez-suivre* when the chartered freight was paid or when the ship's agents were satisfied that it would be paid concurrently with discharge...

The umpire said that he was invited by the buyers to find as a fact that it was the intention of the parties when making the contract that it should be implemented in the manner above described and would in the normal course of events have been so implemented. On the evidence before him as to the course of business followed by these parties under a great many contracts in the same form and for a long period of years, he had no hesitation in so finding.

The umpire said that he was also invited by the sellers to find as a fact that the parties in making the contract intended to make a c.i.f. contract. Unless the contract was ambiguous or incomplete, the intention of the parties had to be gathered from the contract itself, and no evidence of some other intention was admissible, and in so far as it was open to him to make any finding as to the intention of the parties when they made this contract, the umpire found that they intended to make a contract of the type which both parties knew and described in the ordinary course of their business as a "c.i.f. contract" or "c.i.f. business."
. . . . .

The question of law for the decision of the Court was whether upon the facts as found and upon a true construction of the contract the buyers were entitled to recover from the sellers the sum of £1243 12s. 2d. together with interest thereon at the rate of 4 per cent per annum from Apr. 30, 1940.

Subject to the decision of the Court upon this question, the umpire held that the sellers' contentions prevailed. He held that the written contract was upon its face a c.i.f. contract to be performed by the sellers by the tender of documents in accordance with the terms thereof, and the expression "c.i.f." could not be regarded as expressing merely the constituent elements in the contract price . . . .

Subject to the decision of the Court, therefore, the umpire awarded that the buyers were not entitled to recover from the sellers the sum of £1243 12s. 2d. paid by the buyers on Apr. 30, 1940, nor any interest thereon.

Mr.Justice Morris held that the contract was basically one on c.i.f. terms, and that the buyers in accepting the particular delivery order had received a document for which they had agreed to pay and that the risk had passed to them. There was accordingly no total failure of consideration, and his Lordship upheld the award in sellers' favour.

On appeal by the buyers, the Court of Appeal (Lord GREENE, M.R., and CROOM JOHNSON, J., ASQUITH, L.J., dissenting) held that the delivery order tendered by the sellers' agents on payment by the buyers was an appropriate document contemplated by the provisions in the sold note, and took the place of the usual documents under a c.i.f. contract; that the delivery order in addition gave the buyers direct and independent contractual rights against the sellers' cargo superintendents; and that therefore the buyers had failed to show that there was a total failure of consideration for the payment.

The buyers appealed.

LORD PORTER....

My Lords, the obligations imposed upon a seller under a c.i.f. contract are well known, and in the ordinary case include the tender of a bill of lading covering the goods contracted to be sold and no others, coupled with an insurance policy in the normal form and accompanied by an invoice which shows the price and, as in this case, usually contains a deduction of the freight which the buyer pays before delivery at the port of discharge. Against tender of these documents the purchaser must pay the price. In such a case the property may pass either on shipment or on tender, the risk generally passes on shipment or as from shipment, but possession does not pass until the documents which represent the goods are handed over in exchange for the price. In the result the buyer after receipt of the documents can claim against the ship for breach of the contract of carriage and against the underwriter for any loss covered by the policy. The strict form of c i.f. contract may, however, be modified: a provision that a delivery order may be substituted for a bill of lading or a certificate of insurance for a policy would not, I think, make the contract concluded upon something other than c.i.f. terms, but in deciding whether it comes within that category or not all the permutations and combinations of provision and circumstance must be taken into consideration. Not every contract which is expressed to be a c.i.f contract is such. Sometimes...terms are introduced into contracts so described which conflict with c.i.f. provisions. In the present case therefore it is not as if a usual form of delivery order had been given and accepted or an insurance certificate covering the parcel was in the hands of Van Bree as agents for the buyers, nor can a solution be found in the mere designation of the contract as c.i.f. This is not a case in which the overriding provision is the term c.i.f. under which antagonistic terms can be neglected on the ground that they are repugnant to the transaction, as was done by Rowlatt J. in <u>Law & Bonar Ld. v. British American Tobacco Co. Ld.</u>[2] The true effect of all its terms must be taken into account, though, of course, the description c.i.f. must not be neglected. It is true, no doubt, to say that some steps had been taken towards the performance of this contract, e.g., the goods had been shipped, an invoice sent, the customary so-called delivery order had been transmitted and that delivery order amongst its provisions contained a declaration by the sellers' agents, Belgian Grain and Produce Co. Ld. that they gave a share of the present delivery order of $4,973 in a certificate of insurance. But the taking of steps towards performance is not necessarily a part performance of a contract. The question is whether the purchaser has got what he is entitled to in return for the price. Of course, if the buyers paid the sum claimed in order to obtain the delivery order and the share purported to be given by it in the certificate of insurance, the contract would have been performed in part at least, but I do not so construe the contract, even when illuminated by the practice adopted by the parties. That practice seems to me rather to show that the payment was not made for the documents but as an advance payment for a contract afterwards to be performed. With all due respect to the learned judge and the Master of the Rolls, I can see no sufficient reason for supposing either that the delivery order had some commercial value or that Van Bree undertook a personal liability by their indorsement of the document. There was no evidence of commercial value and the document itself was merely an instruction by one agent of the sellers to another. In my view, if the Belgian Grain and Produce Co. Ld. were sued upon the document they would rightly reply that they were acting only as agents and Van Bree could make the same defence. The document appears to me to be no more than an indication that a promise already made by the sellers would be carried out in due course, but in no way increases their obligations or adds to the security of the buyers.

In my opinion, the method by which the contract was customarily carried out supports this view. No doubt the contract could have been so performed as to make it subject to the ordinary principles which apply to a c.i.f. contract. The tender of a bill of lading or even of a delivery order upon the ship, at any rate if attorned to by the master, and a policy or a certificate of insurance delivered to or even held for them might well put it in that category. But the type of delivery order tendered in the present case was a preliminary step only. A complicated procedure had to be followed before the goods would be released. The buyers had to hand the sum due for freight to their agents; those

---

[2] (1916) 2 K.B. 605. [In that case, the court held inapplicable as repugnant to a c.i.f. contract a clause providing that the goods were to be at seller's risk until actual delivery to buyer.]

agents would then pay the freight and present the delivery order to the Belgian Grain and Produce Co. Ld.; who would sign a note on it acknowledging receipt of the freight: the agents thereupon would hand the delivery order to Van Bree who would retain it and issue a "laissez suivre" or release to themselves authorizing delivery to the agents. But before physical delivery of the goods could take place Van Bree must have received a "Captain's laissez suivre" authorizing delivery to them. "It was thus," as the umpire says, "the effective document upon which Van Bree obtained physical possession of the goods; it was issued to Van Bree and was never physically in the buyers' hands." . . .

My Lords, the object and the result of a c.i.f. contract is to enable sellers and buyers to deal with cargoes or parcels afloat and to transfer them freely from hand to hand by giving constructive possession of the goods which are being dealt with. Undoubtedly the practice of shipping and insuring produce in bulk is to make the process more difficult, but a ship's delivery order and a certificate of insurance transferred to or held for a buyer still leaves it possible for some, though less satisfactory, dealing with the goods whilst at sea to take place. The practice adopted between buyers and sellers in the present case renders such dealing well nigh impossible. The buyer gets neither property nor possession until the goods are delivered to him at Antwerp, and the certificate of insurance, if it enures to his benefit at all, except on the journey from ship to warehouse, has never been held for or delivered to him. Indeed, it is difficult to see how a parcel is at the buyers' risk when he has neither property nor possession...

The vital question in the present case, as I see it, is whether the buyers paid for the documents as representing the goods or for delivery of the goods themselves. The time and place of payment are elements to be considered but by no means conclusive of the question: such considerations may, on the one hand, indicate a payment in advance or, on the other, they may show a payment postponed until the arrival of the ship, though the property in the goods or the risk have passed to the buyer whilst the goods are still at sea.... But the whole circumstances have to be looked at and where, as, in my opinion, is the case here, no further security beyond that contained in the original contract passed to the buyers as a result of payment, where the property and possession both remained in the sellers until delivery in Antwerp, where the sellers were to pay for deficiency in bill of lading weight, guaranteed condition on arrival and made themselves responsible for all averages, the true view, I think, is that it is not a c.i.f. contract even in a modified form but a contract to deliver at Antwerp. Nor do I think it matters that payment is said to be not only on presentation but "in exchange for" documents. There are many ways of carrying out the contract to which that expression would apply, but in truth whether the payment is described as made on presentation of or in exchange for a document, the document was not a fulfillment or even a partial fulfillment of the contract: it was but a step on the way. What the buyers wanted was delivery of the goods in Antwerp. What the sellers wanted was payment of the price before that date, and the delivery of the documents furnished the date for payment, but had no effect on the property or possession of the goods or the buyers' rights against the sellers. If this be the view there was plainly a frustration of the adventure—indeed the sellers admit so much in their pleadings—and no part performance and the consideration had wholly failed. The buyers are accordingly entitled to recover the money which they have paid. I would allow the appeal and pronounce for the alternative award with costs in your Lordships' House and in the courts below.

LORD SIMONDS.... The contract entitled the respondents as sellers to require payment "on first presentation of and in exchange for first arriving copy/ies of bill/s of lading .... and/or delivery order/s and policy/ies and/or certificate/s and/or letter/s of insurance at Antwerp," etc., etc. Therefore, it was urged, the sellers had done all, and I emphasize the word "all," they were bound to do if and when they handed over a delivery order and certificates of insurance. I do not pause to examine the factual basis of this contention, for it seems to me to be wholly unsound in law. The fact that a seller at a certain stage in the carrying out of his contract is entitled by its terms to demand payment does not mean that at that stage he has fully performed his contract. Confusion, as I think, has arisen from the fact that, had the sellers been in a position and elected to tender shipping documents by virtue of which the property in the goods passed to the buyers, then the latter could not have contended that there had been failure of consideration. But this result would have ensued not because a clause in the contract provided for payment against documents, but because in law there cannot be failure of consideration if the property has passed. It is in fact, as Asquith L.J. pointed out [dissenting in the court below], a part of the machinery by which the contract is carried out that payment should be made against, for instance, a delivery order and it is as little relevant to the question whether there has been failure of consideration as would be a provision that payment should be made, for example, on notification that the ship had left New York or had arrived at Cherbourg...

But then, it was said, assuming that the sellers did not perform all that they were required to do under the contract, yet they performed at least a part of what they were required to do. This contention had, I think, two slightly different aspects. In the first place it was said that there could not be total failure of consideration if the sellers had done something towards carrying out this contract and that they had done something, viz., handed over a delivery order. In the second place it was said that that something was itself of value, therefore there was not total failure of consideration. In its first aspect this contention appears to suffer from the same fallacy as that which I have already tried to expose. It is a confusion of the consideration for the contract with the mode in which it is to be carried out. But in its second aspect it demands closer attention, for here it has the support of the learned judges in the courts below.

My Lords, there is, in my opinion, no finding of fact by the umpire which would justify your Lordships in holding that the delivery order which was handed to the buyers had any commercial value in the ordinary sense. That it was not a document of title by itself entitling the buyers to delivery of the goods was expressly found. It is a matter of conjecture whether in these circumstances it had any commercial value, and your Lordships cannot found on conjecture.... I come, then, to the conclusion that the sellers performed neither all nor, in any material sense, a part of what they were required to do under the contract and that the buyers obtained no part of that which they had contracted to buy. There was therefore total failure of consideration.

. . . .

LORD NORMAND.

. . . .

What then is the basis of the contention that the buyers received consideration for the part of the price paid by them? The main proposition advanced by the sellers was that the delivery order must be treated as equivalent to the goods, though neither the property nor the risk passed, because the contract so provides. But there were independent and subsidiary contentions that the risk of marine loss had passed to the buyers, and, failing all else, that the delivery order was valuable consideration on one of two grounds, either that it was a document of commercial value or that it contained a promise by Van Bree that they personally would honour the delivery order in accordance with the terms of the bill of lading which they held for the inspection of the bearer.

I propose to consider first whether these subordinate contentions have any validity and relevance. Whether the passing of the marine risk under the contract would be relevant to the issue in the appeal may well be doubted. The agreement of parties that the buyers should bear the risk of a loss against which the insurance was provided for by the contract is not evidence of an intention that the buyers were also to take the risk of a frustration which was not within the contemplation of the contract. I have also difficulty in attaching any intelligible meaning in this case to the proposition that the marine risk passed though the property did not pass.

It may be conceded that the parties can agree to some purely artificial allocation of the risk and if they express that agreement in suitable language in the contract it must somehow be given effect. But the parties to commercial contracts are practical people and in those cases in which it has been held that the risk without the property has passed to the buyer it has been because the buyer rather than the seller was seen to have an immediate and practical interest in the goods, as for instance when he has an immediate right under the storekeeper's delivery warrant to the delivery of a portion of an undivided bulk in store or an immediate right under several contracts with different persons to the whole of a bulk not yet appropriated to the several contracts. But in the present case the buyers had no more than a promise to deliver a part of the bulk cargo and the case is typically one for the general rule res perit domino. The sellers' practical and real interest in the goods at risk is also evidenced by clauses in the contract by which they assumed liability for deficiency at discharge on bill of lading weight and guaranteed condition on arrival, and by a clause providing that all average should be for sellers' account. Nor is it immaterial to observe that if the contract had been completely performed the buyers would never have had in their hands any document entitling them to sue underwriters. The fact that on two occasions when there was a total loss the sellers collected the insured value and remitted it to the buyers less a small charge for collection is of no importance, because that was done without the buyers' instructions and, since the sum remitted was not less than the price paid, the buyers had no interest to question the sellers conduct. The clause obliging the sellers to give to the buyers all policies and certificates of insurance and, if and when called upon for the purpose of claiming upon underwriters, to give a letter certifying that there were no other insurances effected by them and to exchange certificates of insurance for duly stamped policies is not in harmony with a contract intended to be performed as this contract was. It seems, indeed, that this clause and perhaps some others, though appropriate where it was intended that the sale should be implemented by tender of shipping documents or by tender of a delivery order accepted by one in physical possession of the goods and by a policy or certificate of insurance, do not fit the course of dealing by the parties which by imposing a special meaning on "delivery order" required the sellers to accept a document which was not in law a symbol of the goods. It is not necessary to deny all effect to the clause dealing with policies of insurance and certificates. The buyers had a double interest in the insurance. First, the cost of the policies was a component of the price and they therefore had an interest to know that proper insurance had been effected and at what cost. Second, the marine risk policies would cover the risk from the time the rye was delivered to them by the ship till it reached their warehouse. Beyond these two interests I think that the buyers had no concern with the insurance, unless it is established by other terms of the contract that the parties were agreed that the delivery order was to be inter se equivalent to delivery of the goods.

The other subsidiary arguments for the sellers all depend on the attribution of some value to the delivery order. I again question the relevance of the line of argument. It is agreed that the delivery order was not the equivalent of the goods in the sense that its possession conferred on the holder the right of property in the goods valid against all the world. But the consideration for the price is nothing less than that right, unless there are special terms in the contract. If the delivery order had some value otherwise than as the equivalent of the goods the fact has not been proved, and if proved it would be without relevance. If, as is I think plain on the facts found, the delivery order is merely a cogwheel in the machinery for enabling the sellers to transfer the property, it cannot be treated as to any extent consideration for the price, for the consideration for the price is not what the seller does in order to effect the transfer but the actual transfer of the property itself. It is not therefore necessary to consider whether Van Bree intended to bind themselves personally by their signature to any of the undertakings contained in the delivery order. But I can find no evidence of such an intention and I can find no consideration moving from the buyers to Van Bree.

These subsidiary arguments by themselves therefore avail nothing, and the sellers must rely on their contention that the contract by its special terms provides that between the sellers and the buyers the delivery order shall be treated as equivalent to the goods. The sellers laid weight on the description of the price as a c.i.f. price and on the description of the business as c.i.f. business. They also founded on the clause dealing with payment which, they said, treated the delivery order as the equivalent of the bill of lading and the price as paid for it. I think, however, that the explanation of the description c.i.f. in relation to the price and the business carried on by these two parties is that the contract stipulates for a price the components of which were cost, insurance and freight, and that the printed form of the contract used was one which was suitable for an orthodox c.i.f. transaction though also for other transactions not conforming to the c.i.f. model. The use of the label c.i.f. was therefore not significant and I agree with Asquith L.J. that the question is not whether the label was appropriate but what was the effect of the terms of the contract when it was not intended or possible to perform it as an orthodox c.i.f. contract is performed. The stipulation that the price or part of it was to be paid in exchange for a bill of lading and policy or in exchange for a delivery order and certificate does not carry with it the implication that in relation to the rights of the parties inter se the delivery order is to have the effect of a bill of lading, and I can see no reason for reading into the words "in exchange for" anything more than their literal meaning or to read "payment.... in exchange for .... delivery order" as meaning "payment for the delivery order." But I think that if the words "delivery order" had had to be construed without the aid of the previous course of dealing, it would have been held to mean a document addressed to and accepted by one in physical possession of the goods. The sellers would then have been bound to tender a document which was in fact the legal equivalent of the goods. The effect of the course of dealing was to release the sellers from that obligation and to entitle them to payment on tender of a document which contains no more than a personal obligation. I do not find evidence in the contract that the parties have undertaken to treat this document as a document of title as between themselves. I would therefore allow the appeal, with costs, both here and in the courts below.

Appeal allowed.

NOTES AND QUESTIONS

1. The contract and procedures followed by the parties in <u>The Julia</u> appear convoluted; yet we have been admonished time and again by the judges in these cases that the parties are merchants, and that they are "practical people." Why then are they here engaged in such an unusual transaction?

A.   The seller (Luis de Ridder) shipped 1120 tons of rye, via the steamer Julia. While the vessel was in transit to Belgium, the seller made a contract with the buyer (Comptoir D'Achat) to sell 500 tons of that grain CIF Antwerp. While the goods were in transit, the seller, as provided in the contract of sale, presented to the buyer a commercial invoice (for the goods less the price of the freight, which had been sent "freight collect") and a "Delivery Order" made out by the seller's local agent, the Belgian Grain & Produce Co. The Delivery Order was addressed one F. Van Bree, it authorized the delivery of 500 tons of rye "ex-bill of lading" to the holder of the Delivery Order provided the holder paid the freight when the ship arrived, and it was signed by Belgian Grain as agents for the seller. Upon receipt of this "Delivery Order" from Belgian Grain, the buyer paid the cost of the goods less the freight, and went home awaiting notice that the shipment had arrived.

B.   The shipment, of course, did not arrive. Before the Julia got to Belgium, the Germans invaded the country; the port was closed, and the buyers apparently went into hiding. The seller, as charterers of the Julia, instructed the captain to proceed to Lisbon, where the cargo was sold for a fraction of the contract price. When the war ended, the buyers resurfaced, and sued the sellers for return of the $5,000 they had paid for the grain when they received the Delivery Order. The seller does not want return the $5,000 but is prepared to turn over the proceeds of the sale at Lisbon.

2.   Note first the unusual nature of the lawsuit. The buyer has no recourse against the marine insurer because the risk insured against did not result in the loss. The risk insured against is the ship going to the bottom, not the risk of inability to deliver. Thus, the buyer seeks recourse from the seller.

A.   As to the inability to deliver, the seller claims that, because this was a shipment contract (it was "CIF Antwerp"), he had not promised to deliver the goods, only to tender the documents representing the goods. The seller argued that tender to the buyer of the "Delivery Order" satisfied this obligation, and that seller was thus discharged.

1.   What is the buyer's argument? Is it that the contract was not a shipment contract? If the contract is not a shipment contract, what is it? Could it be a destination contract? Do you think the buyer must establish that the contract was a destination contract in order to succeed? Or can the buyer win with some other argument?

2.   What arguments, if any, can be marshalled to show that the parties intended a destination contract? As the members of the House of Lords each acknowledged, even though the

contract was a CIF contract, and that **normally** means a shipment contract, it is possible for the parties to have so varied the basic form of that contract so as to turn it into something else.

(a) Consider, for example, the fact that the buyers and Van Bree were (if the ship had arrived) to attend on board to draw a sample for testing. Does that fact mean that, under <u>Biddell</u>, the seller has agreed to permit an after-arrival inspection in violation of the basic principles of shipment contracts? Or was the taking of a sample different from what the buyer wanted in <u>Biddell</u>. The answer lies not in the plan for an inspection, but rather on the time for payment. Since, in <u>The Julia</u>, the payment was to have been made before arrival of the ship, any argument by the buyer that the provision for sampling made this case different from <u>Biddell</u> must fail. The conformity of the sample was not a condition on the buyer's obligation to pay, nor was it a guarantee of delivery. Why, then, did the buyer want to draw a sample?

(b) What about the fact that the seller instructed the captain to go to Lisbon, who there sold the cargo for less. Does the fact that the seller exercised control over the shipment at that point affect the outcome. After all, by the time of the diversion, the seller had already given the "Delivery Order" to the buyer. If, as the seller argues, that event transferred ownership of the goods to the seller, how can the seller be exercising control over those goods? Or do you think the Seller might credibly offer some other (legally valid) explanation for the order to the captain - such as that he (the seller) was the charterer of the ship, and that he was acting as agent for the buyer, who could not be contacted?

3. The buyer in this case is suing for breach of contract (the British call it "failure of consideration"). He will prevail if he can show that the seller did not do all that the contract obligated the seller to do. Did the seller perform fully? We know that the contract stated that the seller could present to the buyer either a bill of lading or a Delivery Order (in the form used); the seller chose the latter course, and in fact tendered the delivery order. How then can it be argued that the seller breached?

A. As in <u>Biddell</u>, part of the answer lies in the meaning of CIF, and the obligations inherent in such a contract. In this case the issue turns on defining the seller's obligation, rather than the buyer's (as it did in <u>Biddell</u>). Can you use the "symmetry" approach to support the buyer's case in <u>The Julia</u>?

B.   We saw in <u>Biddell</u> that the seller's obligation in a CIF contract is, inter alia, to present a bill of lading to the buyer. If that had been done here, the buyer would certainly have lost. But the bill of lading was not given to the buyer. Why? And who is in possession of that bill, anyway?

1.   As we hinted at the outset, the answer to that question uncovers certain crucial facts. Assume that Van Bree has the bill of lading (as the parties apparently anticipated). Who is Van Bree? What is his role? He is described by the Court as the agent of the seller. But who is he, really? Why is he in this transaction? Why didn't the parties simply allow the Belgian Grain and Produce Company to perform the role of Van Bree?

2.   In all probability, the answer to that last querry is that the buyer did not trust Belgian Grain. But trust it to do what? Why did the buyer insist that Van Bree, not, Belgian Grain, hold the Bill of Lading and arrange delivery from the ship? Notwithstanding the description of Van Bree as the agent of the seller, isn't Van Bree really acting as a neutral "escrowee" in the sale between buyer and seller? If indeed Van Bree is acting as a neutral, does that indicate to you anything about how to argue that the seller did not perform all his obligations under a CIF contract?

4.   As we have stated, under a CIF contract, the seller normally delivers a bill of lading. The delivery of that document is, we know, important to the buyer not only because it is his assurance that the goods have been shipped, but also because, once in possession of the bill of lading, he can "deal commercially with the goods while they are at sea." Why is that so? Obviously, it is because those in the "industry" are prepared to treat these documents (when combined with an inspection certificate and an insurance policy) as equivalent to the goods; simply put, one in possession of these documents is in a position that is commercially equivalent to having the goods (understanding that the goods are at sea).

A.   Why isn't the Delivery Order involved here the equivalent of a bill of lading? What does Lord Porter mean when he wrote that, here, the buyer had "neither property nor possession"? What does Lord Norman mean when he calls the Delivery Order "a mere cogwheel in the machinery"?

B.   The nature of the Delivery Order was the subject of the most intensive debate in the House of Lords. One Lord says it had no commercial value; another says, if that's so, why did the buyer pay $5,000 for it; the third accuses the other two of improper speculation. What is going on? Is the Delivery Order a document of title? Can the buyer use it as the trade equivalent of the goods? If not, why not? Compare the delivery order and sample bill of lading in the Document Supplement at the end of chapter 1.

C. Despite the differences between a bill of lading and the Delivery Order, the contract here gave the seller the option of tendering either a bill of lading or a delivery order, and the buyer was required to pay in either event. For reasons of practicality, the seller here chose to tender a Delivery Order. At that moment, the seller was entitled to (and did) get paid. What more did he have to? Put differently, if he was required to tender a delivery order, and he did so, what more was he supposed to do? If you think there was something else the seller must do, where in the contract does it say that?

D. Think, again, about the CIF term. Doesn't the fact that the seller made a CIF contract means he agreed to undertake five (5) specific duties. He has completed most of these obligations (delivery of goods to carrier, making a contract with the shipper, securing insurance and tendering an invoice.) But what about his last obligation under a CIF contract -the obligation to tender a document of title to the goods? Here, the seller tendered only the Delivery Order. Does that really fulfill the seller's obligation under a CIF contract? If not, why not? What differences are there between the Delivery Order and a typical bill of lading?

1. A bill of lading is issued by a ship's captain (or his agent). The Delivery Order here was issued by Belgian Grain as agents for the seller. Why is that difference significant? What right does the holder of a bill of lading have that the holder of the delivery order here does not have? Why is this difference in rights important?

2. Why is a bill of lading universally deemed to be the equivalent of the goods? We know that one reason is that "the trade" is prepared to accept the certification of the captain that he is in possession of the goods and will deliver them to the holder of the bill of lading upon arrival as being the equivalent of the goods. Do you think the trade looks at the Delivery Order from Belgian Grain that way? Why not? Is it because Belgian Grain isn't a ship's captain, because they are the agents of the seller (and thus not neutral), or because they cannot certify that they are in possession of the cargo?

3. If you say, in response to the previous question, that it is because Belgian Grain is not neutral, what about Van Bree? Isn't he a neutral "escrowee"? Assume that he is in possession of the bill of lading, having received it from the seller. Why isn't that, combined with possession of the Delivery Order addressed to him, the same as the buyer having received the

bill of lading? Is it because "the trade" doesn't know, and thus trust, Van Bree? Or is it because Van Bree hasn't signed anything (except the agreement to act as escrowee)? Why isn't that enough?

4.   Perhaps the reason the Delivery Order isn't the equivalent of the Bill of Lading is because Van Bree isn't in possession of the goods? Thus, even if Van Bree signed an agreement as escrowee (thus becoming obligated to buyer for non-delivery under certain circumstances) he still could not certify that he was in possession of the cargo, and would deliver it upon arrival of the goods. Consider, in this regard, our **Uniform Commercial Code 1-201(15)**, where the term Document of Title is defined to include:

(a)   bill of lading, dock warrant, dock receipt, warehouse receipt or order for the delivery of goods, and also any other document which in the regular course of business or financing is treated as adequately evidencing that the person in possession of it is entitled to receive, hold and dispose of the document and the goods it covers. To be a Document of Title a document must purport to be issued or addressed to a bailee and purport to cover goods in the bailee's possession . . . .

Does the Delivery Order in <u>The Julia</u> meet the definition of document of title in the UCC? Why not? Would it matter if it had been signed by Van Bree? Lord Porter mentions that tender by sellers of a "ship's delivery order" would produce a different result. Why? What is the difference btween the two? Why does a "ship's delivery order" meet the UCC definition, but Belgian Grain's does not?

5.   If, then, seller was bound by the CIF term to tender a document of title to the buyer, has the seller done all he was obligated to do? The answer given by the Court is no. Seller still must tender either the goods themselves or a document of title representing the goods. Here he has done neither. The mere fact that the buyer was obligated to pay at the moment the seller tendered the Delivery Order does not conclusively mean that the seller has completed the contract. Because of the war, the seller here had neither tendered the required document nor did he tender the goods. The buyer was thus entitled to get his money back. As Lord Porter says, the contract "was not a CIF contract even in a modified form but a contract to deliver at Antwerp." What, exactly, does that mean?

5. The lessons to be learned from <u>The Julia</u> are numerous, although not everyone would agree on what they are. But one obvious lesson, now demonstrated for the second time, is the way international trade law deals with variations from the conventional contract of sale. In <u>The Julia</u>, the seller obviously wanted to claim the advantages of a CIF contract, but he was concerned about his inability to perform it in the conventional way. He thought that by varying the terms of the typical CIF contract (allowing for tender of his Delivery Order rather than a bill of lading), the seller could remain protected from the risks inherent in the voyage. The buyer was prepared to accept this arrangement because of the role of Van Bree.

    A. But the Seller, in the end, was unable to accomplish all he desired, <u>i.e.</u>, solving his practical problem while at the same time not taking on added risk. Does that strike you as fair?

        1. In <u>Biddell</u>, when we concluded that CIF meant a documentary sale because of principles of symmetry. Seller was obligated to tender certain documents, and Buyer was obligated to take them up and pay for them. It was a fair bargain - seller got what he wanted, buyer did likewise, and trade was encouraged. As we complete our discussion of <u>The Julia</u>, note that <u>Biddell</u> addressed the second part of the formula recited above; One can say that <u>The Julia</u> demonstrates that the first part is true.

        2. In <u>Biddell</u>, we observed that that methodolgy of the documentary sale had benefits for both sides: seller could discharge his risks early on, while buyer (who would have the bill of lading) would have effective control over the goods while they were at sea. In <u>The Julia</u>, the seller wanted a CIF contract, but he could not bestow on the buyer the benefit inherent to which he (the buyer) was entitled. It wouldn't be fair, the argument goes, to allow the seller to claim for himself the contra-benefits of a CIF sale. And of course, absent those benefits, seller is obligated to deliver the goods or return the buyer's money. How is that for symmetry?

    B. Aside from demonstrating the practical difficulties inherent in shipping grain in bulk and selling off parcels along the way, and how even the best laid plans can sometimes go awry, this case thus demonstrates that when the parties to a contract adopt the "code words" of international trade, they (sometimes unconsciously) adopt all of the meaning given to those terms, not just the part that is to their liking. Occasionally there are consequences, sometimes consequences the parties never envisioned.

1. Of course, 900 times before this one, the practice adopted by the parties here worked just fine; Buyer got his goods, seller got their money, and Van Bree fulfilled the role that was designed for him. When an unforeseen event occurred, however, what had previously been a wonderful practical solution became a nightmare of confusion.

2. In the end, the court found that seller had made a contract that may have solved his practical problem (i.e the inability to tender the bill of lading), but he had not passed the risks of the voyage on to the buyer. The contract language calling for payment against the delivery order was narrowly construed, and the seller incurred a great loss. It is easy to argue he should have made a better contract, and undoubtedly he now has one. What does it say?

III. CIF: RISK ALLOCATION AND "FORCE MAJEURE"

As we have stated from the outset, it is not unheard of (even if it is unusual) that unforeseen world events will derail a party's performance under a contract, as it did in The Julia. It is thus quite common for the parties to include in the contract a provision known as a "force majeure clause" which excuses performance in the event performance is prevented by an event beyond the control of the parties. Tsakiroglou, one of the so-called Suez Canal cases, is such a case. In the end, however, the decision in that case seems more influenced by the meaning of CIF than by the force majeure clause in the contract. Consider why that is so as you read Tsakiroglou v. Noblee Thorl.

TSAKIROGLOU & CO. LTD.
v.
NOBLEE THORL G.M.B.H.

House of Lords
[1962] A.C. 93

By a contract in writing dated Hamburg, October 4, 1956, between Tsakiroglou & Co. Ltd., of Khartoum as sellers, and respondents, Noblee Thorl G.m.b.H. of Hamburg/Harburg as buyers, through agents, the sellers agreed to sell and the buyers to buy about 300 tons of Sudanese groundnuts in the shell basis 3 per cent admixture new crop 1956/57 at £50 per 1,000 kilos including bags c.i.f. Hamburg. Shipment November/December, 1956, with payment cash against documents on the first presentation for 95 per cent of the amount of provisional invoice, balance to be paid after the analysis on final invoice. The contract form was to be the Incorporated Oil Seed

Association Contract No. 38 (hereinafter called "I.O.S.A. Contract No. 38") with arbitration in London, and that contract was signed by the Hamburg agents. Clause 1 of I.O.S.A. Contract No. 38 provided for "Shipment from an East African port...by steamer or steamers (tankers excluded) direct or indirect with or without transshipment." It was found as a fact in the case stated that both parties contracted on the basis that the goods would be shipped from Port Sudan. Clause 6 of the contract provided: "In case of prohibition of import or export, blockade or war, epidemic or strike, and in all cases of force majeure preventing the shipment within the time fixed, or the delivery, the period allowed for shipment or delivery shall be extended by not exceeding two months. After that, if the case of force majeure be still operating, the contract shall be cancelled."

On October 29, 1956, the Israelis invaded Egypt; on November 1 Britain and France commenced military operations, and on November 2 the Suez Canal was blocked to shipping and remained blocked until April 9, 1957.

No goods were shipped under the contract, the sellers claiming that they were prevented from doing so by events which had occurred in the Middle East.

When the contract of October 4, 1956, was entered into the usual and normal route for the shipment of Sudanese groundnuts for Port Sudan to Hamburg was via the Suez Canal. After the closing of the Canal the shortest and a practicable route to Hamburg was via the Cape of Good Hope. The sea route via Suez to Hamburg was approximately 4,386 miles, and via the Cape 11,137 miles.

From November 10, 1956, a 25 per cent. freight surcharge was placed on goods shipped on vessels proceeding via the Cape of Good Hope and this was increased to 100 per cent. on December 13, 1956.

The sellers' claim that the contract was at an end because of the closure of the Suez Canal was not accepted by the buyers.

In arbitration proceedings, the umpire, by an award dated February 20, 1957, awarded that the sellers were in default and should pay to the buyers as damages the sum of £5.625 together with £79 15s. costs of the award. The sellers were dissatisfied with the award, and a board of appeal appointed to hear the appeal on January 28, 1958, dismissed the appeal and upheld the umpire's award.

The following findings of fact are relevant: "1. Sudanese groundnuts are harvested at the end of October or beginning of November and the customary port for shipment of such groundnuts is Port Sudan. All groundnuts exported from Sudan to Europe are shipped from Port Sudan which is the only suitable port." Paragraph 2: "At the date when the contract was entered into the usual and normal route for the shipment of Sudanese groundnuts from Port Sudan to Hamburg was via the Suez Canal. It would be unusual and rare for any substantial parcel of Sudanese groundnuts from Port Sudan to Europe to be shipped via the Cape at all times when the Suez Canal was open." Paragraph 6: "The closure of the Suez Canal prevented transport of the contract goods from Port Sudan to Hamburg via the Suez Canal and the impossibility of transportation by that route continued until April, 1957. The sellers could have transported the goods from Port Sudan to Hamburg via the Cape during November or December, 1956. Paragraph 7: The distance from Port Sudan to Hamburg via the Suez Canal is approximately 4,386 miles and the distance from Port Sudan to Hamburg via the Cape of Good Hope is approximately 11,137 miles. The distance from Port Sudan to Suez is 694 miles. Paragraph 8. The freight ruling at the time of the contract for the shipment of groundnuts from Port Sudan to Hamburg via the Suez Canal was about £7 10s. per ton. After the closure of the Canal the Port Sudan—U.K. Conference imposed the following surcharges for goods shipped on vessels proceeding via the Cape of Good Hope, viz., as from November 10, 1956, 25 per cent, and as from December 13, 1956, 100 per cent." Paragraph 10: "At the date when the contract was made both parties contemplated that shipment would be made via the Suez Canal."

The board of appeal's award was in these terms:

"So far as it is a question of fact we find and as far as it is a question of law we hold:

"(i) There were hostilities but not war in Egypt at the material time.

"(ii) Neither war nor force majeure prevented shipment of the contract goods during the contract period if the word 'shipment' means placing the goods on board a vessel destined for the Port of Hamburg.

"(iii) If the word 'shipment' includes not only the placing of the contract goods on board a vessel but also their transportation to the contract destination then shipment via the Suez Canal

was prevented during the contract period of shipment by reason of force majeure but shipment via the Cape was not so prevented.

"(iv) It was not an implied term of the contract that shipment or transportation should be made via the Suez Canal.

"(v) The performance of the contract by shipping the goods on a vessel routed via the Cape of Good Hope was not commercially or fundamentally different from its being performed by shipping the goods on a vessel routed via the Suez Canal."

VISCOUNT SIMONDS...I find two questions interlocked: (1) What does the contract mean? In other words, is there an implied term that the goods shall be carried by a particular route? (2) Is the contract frustrated?

It is convenient to examine the first question first, though the answer may be inconclusive. For it appears to me that it does not automatically follow that, because one term of a contact, for example, that the goods shall be carried by a particular route, becomes impossible of performance, the whole contract is thereby abrogated. Nor does it follow, because as a matter of construction a term cannot be implied, that the contract may not be frustrated by events. In the instant case, for example, the impossibility of the route via Suez, if that were assumed to be the implied contractual obligation, would not necessarily spell the frustration of the contract.

It is put in the forefront of the appellants' case that the contract was a contract for the shipment of goods via Suez. This contention can only prevail if a term is implied, for the contract does not say so. To say that that is nevertheless its meaning is to say in other words that the term must be implied. For this I see no ground...A variant of this contention was that there should be read into the contract by implication the words "by the usual and customary route" and that, as the only usual and customary route at the date of the contract was via Suez, the contractual obligation was to carry the goods via Suez. Though this contention has been viewed somewhat differently, I see as little ground for the implication. In this I agree with Harman L.J. [in the Court of Appeal] for it seems to me that there are precisely the same grounds for rejecting the one as the other. Both of them assume that sellers and buyers alike intended and would have agreed that, if the route via Suez became impossible, the goods should not be shipped at all. Inasmuch as the buyers presumably wanted the goods and might well have resold them, the assumption appears wholly unjustified. Freight charges may go up or down. If the parties do not specifically protect themselves against change, the loss must lie where it falls.

For the general proposition that in c.i.f. contract the obligation, in absence of express terms, is to follow the usual or customary route there is a significant absence of authority... The appellants relied on a passage in Kennedy on C.I.F. Contracts, 1st ed., p. 39: "In the absence of express terms in the contract the customary or usual route must be followed." I cannot accept this general proposition without some qualification. In particular, since it is, in any case, clear that it is not the date of the contract but the time of performance that determines what is customary, the proposition must be qualified by adding to it some such words as "unless at the time of performance there is no customary or usual route." If those words are implied, the question arises: "What then?" The answer must depend on the circumstances of each case. This leads me directly to section 32(2) of the Sale of Goods Act, 1893, which provides that "Unless otherwise authorized by the buyer, the seller must make such contract with the carrier on behalf of the buyer as may be reasonable having regard to the nature of the goods and the other circumstances of the case." If there is no customary route, that route must be chosen which is reasonable. If there is only one route, that must be taken if it is practicable.

I turn now to what was the main argument for the appellants: that the contract was frustrated by the closure of the Canal from November 2, 1956, till April 1957. Were it not for the decision of McNair J. in Green's case I should not have thought this contention arguable and I must say with the greatest respect to that learned judge that I cannot think he has given full weight to the decisions old and new of this House upon the doctrine of frustration. He correctly held upon the authority of Reardon Smith Line Ltd. v. Black Sea and Baltic General Insuransc Co. Ltd that "where a contract, expressly or by necessary implication, provides that performance, or a particular part of the performance, is to be carried out in a customary manner, the performance must be carried out in a manner which is customary at the time when the performance is called for." But he concluded that the continued availability of the Suez route was a fundamental assumption at the time when the contract was made and that to impose upon the sellers the obligation to ship by an emergency route via the Cape would be to impose upon them a fundamentally different obligation which neither party could at the time when the contract was performed have dreamed that the sellers would be required to perform. Your Lordships will observe how similar this line of argument is to that which supports the implication of a term that the route should be via Suez and no other. I can see no justification for it. We are concerned with a c.i.f. contract for the sale of goods, not a contract of affreightment, though part of the sellers' obligation will be to procure a contract of affreightment. There is no evidence that the buyers attached any importance to the route. They were content that the nuts should be shipped at any date in November or December. There was no evidence, and I suppose could not be, that the nuts would deteriorate as the result of a longer voyage and a double crossing of the Equator, nor any evidence that the market was seasonable. In a word, there was no evidence that the buyers cared by what route, or within reasonable limits, when the nuts arrived. What, then, of the sellers? I recall the well-known passage in the speech of Lord Atkinson in Johnson v. Taylor Bros. & Co. Ltd. where he states the obligations of the vendor of goods under a c.i.f. contract, and asks which of these obligations is (to use McNair J.'s word) "fundamentally" altered by a change of route. Clearly the contract of affreightment will be different and so may be the terms of insurance. In both these respects the sellers may be put to greater cost: their profit may be reduced or even disappear. But it hardly needs reasserting that an increase of expense is not a ground of frustration.... I venture to say what I have said myself before and others more authoritatively have said before me: that the doctrine of frustration must be applied within very narrow limits. In my opinion this case falls far short of satisfying the necessary conditions.... In my opinion the appeal should be dismissed with costs.

LORD REID.... Counsel for the appellants rightly did not argue that this increase in the freight payable by the appellants was sufficient to frustrate the contract and I need not therefore consider what the result might be if the increase had reached an astronomical figure. The route by the Cape was certainly practicable. There could be, on the findings in the case, no objection to it by the buyers and the only objection to it from the point of view of the sellers was that it cost them more and it was not excluded by the contract. Where, then, is there any basis for frustration?

It appears to me that the only possible way of reaching a conclusion that this contract was frustrated would be to concentrate on the altered nature of the voyage. I have no means of judging whether, looking at the matter from the point of view of a ship whose route from Port Sudan was altered from via Suez to via the Cape, the difference would be so radical as to involve frustration and I express no opinion about that. As I understood the argument it was based on the assumption that the voyage was the manner of performing the sellers' obligations and that therefore its nature was material. I do not think so. What the sellers had to do was simply to find a ship proceeding by what was a practicable and now a reasonable route—if perhaps not yet a usual route—to pay the freight and obtain a proper bill of lading, and to furnish the necessary documents to the buyers. That was their manner of performing their obligations, and for the reasons which I have given I think that such changes in these matters as were made necessary fell far short of justifying a finding of frustration. I agree that the appellants cannot rely on the provisions of clause 6 of the contract regarding prevention of shipment. I therefore agree that this appeal should be dismissed.

I should, perhaps, add a few words about the finding in the case that performance by shipping via the Cape of Good Hope was "not commercially or fundamentally different" from performance by shipping via Suez. This cannot be intended to mean that it was neither different commercially nor different fundamentally. Plainly there is a commercial difference between paying £7 10s. and paying £15 per ton freight. It must mean that performance was not fundamentally different in a commercial sense. But all commercial contracts ought to be interpreted in light of commercial considerations. I cannot imagine a commercial case where it would be proper to hold that performance is fundamentally different in a legal though not in a commercial sense. Whichever way one takes it the ultimate question is whether the new method of performance is fundamentally different and that is a question of law. The commercial importance of the various differences involved in the change of route—delay, risk to the goods, cost, etc.—is fact on which specific findings by arbitrators are entirely appropriate. But the inference to be drawn on a consideration of all the relevant factors must, in my view, be a matter of law —was there or was there no frustration.

LORD RADCLIFFE. My Lords, I think that the outcome of this appeal depends upon a short point. The real issue, as I see it, is to determine how to define the obligation of the appellants, the vendors, under the sale contract of October 4, 1956, so far as it related to shipment of the goods sold and the provision of shipping documents. Once it is settled what that definition should be, there is not much difficulty in seeing what are the legal consequences that should follow, having regard to the facts found for us by the special case.

This is a sale of goods on c.i.f. terms. Such a sale involves a variety of obligations, both those written out in the contract itself and those supplied by implication of law for the business efficacy of the transaction. The only sector of these obligations that is relevant for the purpose of this case is the vendors' duty "to procure a contract of affreightment under which the goods will be delivered at the destination contemplated by the contract" (see <u>Biddell Brothers v. E. Clemens Horst Co.</u>, per Hamilton, J.). Even within this sector, however, there are gaps which the law has to fill in: for instance, what form of contract of affreightment will meet the needs of the transaction, and what route or routes are permissible for the carrying vessel selected? In the present case nothing turns on the form of the bill of lading, which is not in evidence: everything turns on the question of route. The written contract makes no condition about this, its only stipulation being that shipment is to be from an East African port, by which we are asked to assume that the parties in fact meant Port Sudan. So the voyage was to begin at Port Sudan and to end at Hamburg. The primary duty under this part of the contract was to dispatch the groundnuts by sea from one port to the destination of the other.

Now in these circumstances were the appellants under obligation to procure a bill of lading for the transport of the goods by the Cape route, the Suez Canal not being available? That depends on how their obligation is defined. It is said on their behalf that the duty of shipment is a duty to ship by the "customary or usual route," a route which can be ascertained as that followed by settled and established practice. Failing express provision on the point by the terms of the contract, that is, in my opinion, a correct general statement of what the law would imply; but I do not accept the further proposition which the appellants' argument requires, namely that, given the existence of such a route at the date of the contract, the whole of the vendor's obligation with regard to shipment is contained in this phrase, "the customary or usual route." . . .

In my opinion there is no magic in the introduction of the formula "customary or usual route" to describe the term implied by law. It is only appropriate because it is in ordinary circumstances the test of what it is reasonable to impose upon the vendor in order to round out the imperfect form of the contract into something which, as mercantile men, the parties may be presumed to have intended. The corpus of commercial law has been built up largely by this process of supplying from the common usage of the trade what is the unexpressed intention of the parties. It is necessary first to ascertain what is the commercial nature or purpose of the adventure that is the subject of the contract; that ascertained, it has next to be asked what within this scope are the essential terms which, so far as not expressed, must be implied in order to make the contract efficacious as a business instrument.... The basic proposition is therefore that laid down by Brett M.R. in <u>Sanders v. .MacLean</u> "The stipulations which are inferred in mercantile contracts are always that the party will do what is mercantilely reasonable."

Applying that proposition to the present case, I do not think that it is enough for the appellants to point out that the usual and customary route for the transport of groundnuts from Port Sudan to Hamburg was via the Suez Canal, and that at the date of the sale contract both parties contemplated that shipment would be by that route. This contract was a sale of goods, which involved dispatching the goods from Port Sudan to Hamburg; but, of course, the transport was not the whole but only one of the incidents of the contract, in which particular incident neither vendors nor buyers were directly implicated. There was nothing to prevent the vendors from dispatching the goods as contracted, unless they were impliedly bound as a term of the contract to use no other route than that of the Suez Canal. I do not see why that term should be implied and, if it is not implied, the true question seems to me to be, since shipment was due to be made by some route during November/December, whether it was a reasonable action for a mercantile man to perform his contract by putting the goods on board a ship going round the Cape of Good Hope and obtaining a bill of lading on this basis. A man may habitually leave his house by the front door to keep his appointments; but, if the front door is stuck, he would hardly be excused for not leaving by the back. The question, therefore, is what is the reasonable mercantile method of performing the contract at a time when the Suez Canal is closed, not at a time when it is open. To such a question the test of "the usual and customary route" is ex hypothesi inapplicable.

On the facts found by the special case I think that the answer is inevitable. The voyage would be a much longer one in terms of miles; but length reflects itself in such matters as time of arrival, condition of goods, increase of freight rates. A change of route may, moreover, augment the sheer hazard of the transport. There is nothing in the circumstances of the commercial adventure represented by the appellants' contract which suggests that these changes would have been material. Time was plainly elastic. Not only did the vendors have the option of choosing any date within a two-month period for shipment, but also there was a wide margin within which there might be variations of the speed capacity of the carrying vessel or vessels selected. There was no stipulated date for arrival at Hamburg. Nothing appears to suggest that the Cape voyage would be prejudicial to the condition of the goods or would involve special packing or stowing, nor does there seem to have been any seasonal market to be considered. With all these facts before them, as well as the measure of freight surcharge that would fall to the vendors' account, the board of appeal made their finding that performance by shipping on the Cape route was not "commercially or fundamentally different" from shipping via the Suez Canal. We have no material which would make it possible for us to differ from that conclusion....

I would dismiss the appeal.

LORD GUEST.... The sellers' obligation is governed by section 32(2) of the Sale of Goods Act, 1893, whereby he has to make such contract with the carrier on behalf of the buyer as may be reasonable having regard to the nature of the goods and the other circumstances of the case. He must therefore procure a reasonable contract of affreightment. The appellants contended that the sellers' obligation was to procure a contract of affreightment which he could tender to the buyer whereunder the goods would be conveyed by the usual and customary route to the contractual destination, and that the usual and customary route must be ascertained at the date when the contract was made. The argument further proceeded that when this contract was entered into the usual and customary route was via the Suez Canal and that as that route had been closed by the time shipment fell to be made the contract had been frustrated. The first and critical matter to ascertain is the date when the sellers' obligation in regard to the contract of affreightment is to be judged. Under the present contract the sellers' obligation was shipment by a bill of lading to be dated November/December 1956. They could therefore fulfil their contractual obligation by shipping at any date up to December 31. By the date when performance was called for the Suez Canal was closed and the only available route was by the Cape of Good Hope. In my opinion the sellers' obligation is to be determined by the circumstances prevailing at the date when he chooses to ship the goods and not when the contract was made.... In my opinion, all that the seller has to do is to procure a reasonable contract of affreightment. In judging whether it was a reasonable contract of affreightment the question whether the route given is the usual or customary route may be of importance for consideration with all other relevant circumstances. Whether or not such a term is implied in the present case at the time when performance was called for there was no usual or customary route because the Suez Canal was closed and the only practicable route was via the Cape of Good Hope. The sellers could have fulfilled their obligation by a bill of lading via the Cape. There was accordingly no frustration because there was no change of circumstances to justify the application of the doctrine.

The cases dealing with contracts of affreightment are in my view not helpful because in such contracts very different considerations apply from those in a contract of sale. In a c.i.f. contract the seller does not have to deliver the goods. He only has to ship them at the port indicated with a contract of affreightment to the port of destination. An example of the frustration of a contract of affreightment is <u>Societe Franco Tunisienne D'Armament v. Sidermar S.P.A.</u>, where Pearson J. held that a charterparty was frustrated by the blocking of the Suez Canal on the ground that it was a term of the contract (express or implied) that the vessel was to go by the Suez Canal, and he was able to hold that the route via the Cape was so different that it was a fundamentally different voyage. There are no circumstances in the present case to justify the implication of a term that the route should be via the Suez Canal....

I would dismiss the appeal.

Appeal dismissed.

NOTES AND QUESTIONS

1. In <u>Tsakiroglou</u>, the seller sought to be excused from his CIF contract because the Suez Canal had been closed. But what, exactly, is the basis for his claim? Is it that the contract itself excused his non-performance, or is it that it is unfair to require him to perform despite the contract terms?

    A. Most contracts contain broad "force majeure" clauses. Read the clause in this contract closely. Is it sufficiently broad to excuse the seller's non-performance here? Doesn't the answer to that question depend on how one defines "the seller's performance"? How should that performance be defined? Is there any term in the contract that will help?

    B. Putting the contract aside momentarily, how much should considerations of fairness influence a court's decision in a case such as this? That question is not susceptible of easy answer.

        1. Most domestic legal systems provide an excuse for non-performance where the non-performance arises from an unforeseen and unprovided for event which renders performance impossible, especially when the impossibility places an unfair financial burden on one of the parties. In such a case, most courts in domestic cases would try to fashion a remedy that minimizes or seeks to vitiate that undue burden. Does the fact that <u>Tsakiroglou</u> is an international case change the way the law should look at the problem? If you think change is in order, would you suggest getting stricter or more lenient in deciding whether to excuse non-performance?

        2. The argument for being more lenient is that in international trade there are more, indeed, there are an infinite number of uncertainties. Since it is, as a practical matter, impossible to anticipate and provide for these uncertainties, the law should assume the role of arbiter, and do what would be fair and reasonable (such as trying to decide what the parties would have done had they foreseen the particular event. The argument for a stricter rule is that the role of law in international trade should be to reduce uncertainty; that one judge (or culture's) view of fairness might be different from another's, and that the court's role should be to simply interpret the contract, not change it or emend it. Which do you feel is jurisprudentially preferable? Where do you think the Law Lords came out?

3. In the end, only Lord Reid really addresses the case from a "fairness" approach. He says he will rule for the buyer, but that he need not consider what the result should be if the increase in the freight had been "astronomical." What does he mean by that? Is it the point at which the transaction becomes unprofitable to the seller? Presumably the increase surpassed that level here because the buyer preferred not to ship (the increase in freight having sopped up all his profit and rendered the transaction a loss). How high, then, is "astronomical". Like Lord Reid, we can be happy we don't have to decide, but not because it has not been reached in this case.

2. The question just posed (astronomical?) need not be answered because the other Lords took the stricter "contract interpretation" approach. They endeavored to interpret the contract in order to decide how that document allocated the risk. So what did the contract say?

    A. The contract was a CIF contract. The House of Lords uses that term, as it had in the past, as a benchmark for definition of the seller's obligations. The judges then test those obligations against the force majeure clause to see if performance had been prevented. Were any of the seller's obligations "prevent[ed]" because of Suez Canal closing?

    B. Viewed in this way, the weaknesses in the seller's case are exposed. He can only complain that the force majeure prevented him from shipping "via the Suez Canal"; since the contract is silent as to the route, he has no claim, even if the parties, at the time of contracting, had a particular route in mind. The question was thus whether such a route should be "implied".

        1. As can be seen from the discussion of the Noble Lords, that route is a dead end for the seller. They all declined to imply the "Suez Canal" route. They also reject the seller's arguments about a "reasonable and customary route". Why?

        2. The answer may again lie in the abhorrence of options. Suppose, for example, that despite the closing of the Suex Canal, the seller was prepared to ship via the southern route, and seller tendered documents. Could buyer refuse the tender? Which of the Law Lords consider this issue? How do they resolve it? Is that what Viscount Simonds means when he says: "the loss must lie where it falls"?

C.   Another problem for the seller is that when one asks who, under the contract, agreed to bear the risk of an increase in the price of the freight, the answer, of course, is the seller. The "CIF" term expresses the components of the price, and one of those components is the cost of freight. Put another way, if the cost of freight were to fall, the benefit would go to the seller. Why shouldn't he bear the risk of a freight increase?

1.   As it has been in the other cases, at first, one reflexively faults the seller for having not made a better contract. If seller did not want the risk of increases in the price of the freight, he could have quoted an equivalent FOB price, and placed that risk on the buyer. Do you think the buyer would have agreed? Why not? The answer is that the buyer doesn't want the risk either, and _he_ need not take it. He can buy the goods from Mississippi, or the Far East, or from a seller in western Africa. Simply put, the buyer has alternatives; the seller, by contrast has none - he cannot move from Khartoum.

2.   How about providing, expressly, that shipment would be "via the Suez Canal." Do you think the buyer would have agreed to such a clause? Can you think of some intermediate approach that the buyer might agree to?

3.   Before one goes about criticizing the seller and lauding the buyer in this case, consider the buyer's position if the seller had shipped the goods around the Cape of Good Hope. The shipment was supposed to be made in November/December 1956. Assuming a two month voyage (at the maximum), the ship would have arrived no later than the end of February. Suppose, in reliance on that expectation, the buyer made a contract with a salad oil company to sell them the imported nuts in January/February. Only now, the goods won't arrive until at least March, because the Suez Canal is closed. Note that now **the buyer** would be seeking to avoid the contract. What if the seller had shipped?

A.   Shouldn't the decision go the same way? The seller's obligation was to ship, and he did so. The buyer's obligation is to pay against documents. So, therefore, the buyer would lose. Symmetry.

B.   How can the buyer protect himself? Again, it is easy to criticize, but hard to achieve the result. Do you think the seller would "guarantee" January/February delivery? Why not?

C.   Suppose the buyer got the seller to agree, in the contract, that the shipment was "to arrive January/February 1957." Would that solve the hypothethical reseller's problem? Would it create a destination contract?

D.   The answer to the previous question is "no", a "to arrive" term is simply (a) an instruction to the seller as to what type of contract of affreightment will satisfy the contract and (b) an advice to the buyer when to expect the ship to arrive. So suppose the contract in <u>Tsakiroglou</u> said the shipment was "to arrive January/February 1957."

1.   What would the result be if the seller shipped the goods via the Cape, and the bill of lading showed that the ship was scheduled to arrive in March? Would the seller be liable to the buyer for damages for breach of contract? Would the buyer have an excuse for not paying?

2.   Now suppose that the contract said the shipment was "to arrive January/February 1957", but that the seller does not ship because he is unable to find a ship sailing from Port Sudan in November/December that is scheduled to arrive before March because of the extended route. Would the seller be excused from performing, or would he be in breach? Why? Answering these questions may help you understand <u>Tsakiroglou</u>.

3.   Of course, that is not the contract the buyer made. That is why the Lord Radcliffe says that "time was plainly elastic." Seller, after all, gave himself great flexibility in the manner of shipment (Shipment was to be "from an East African port...by steamer or steamers (tankers excluded) direct or indirect with or without transshipment." Given the flexibility, seller found it hard to complain that he was "prevented from shipping", and buyer was entitled to the benefit of the bargain. But note that the chips fall where they may - if seller had shipped the goods and buyer didn't want them (because they were to arrive late), buyer would be stuck. Put another way, if time wasn't elastic for the buyer, he could have protected himself with a "to arrive" clause - but note that, under that circumstance, such a clause, on these facts, might well have benefitted the seller. Is that irony? Or is it just more symmetry?

FINAL NOTES AND QUESTIONS ON THE MEANING OF CIF

1. As has been demonstrated in the cases we have reviewed, the shipping term in an international sales contract (usually "CIF") has much greater meaning than simply stating the components of the price. It defines the seller's obligations, and thus, under the symmetry principle, it defines the buyer's obligations, as we saw in <u>Biddell</u> and <u>The Julia</u>. It also is a "risk allocator," as we saw in <u>Tsakiroglou</u>. But we also saw that while it is used frequently, traders, lawyers and sometimes judges do not appreciate all that it involves. Of these three groups, interestingly enough, it is "the traders" who need to know it the best.

2. We also saw that traders sometimes, consciously or unconsciously, vary the standard form of the CIF contract. Sometimes the variation is trivial and inconsequential, as in <u>Biddell</u>, and sometimes it is critical, as it was in <u>The Julia</u>. There is often the matter of the interplay between the shipping term and other provisions in the contract, as took place in <u>The Julia</u> and <u>Taskiroglou</u>.

3. Finally, we considered issues of interpretation and implication. While it is easy to say that merchants are presumed to be reasonable people, acting in a commercial reasonable manner, gaps in a contract sometimes require a court to engage in thorny task of implying terms that were not expressed by the parties. One lesson of these cases is that courts are (rightfully) loath to do so, at least in small part because it rarely leads to a dispositive result, and in large part because it leads to uncertainty of results.

4. In studying this chapter, a student should thus appreciate the importance of the contract in international sales, the meaning of certain conventional terminology, the mechanics of the documentary sale, the role of the bill of lading and other documents in minimizing risk, and the general allocation of burdens and risks in international trade. The goal of the chapter, indeed of the entire book, is not simply to provide the student with an understanding of the legal concepts, but also to cause the student to think critically about how "the rules" of international trade impact and affect the business of international trade, and vice versa. The desired product is a better businessperson, able to assess risk intelligently, and armed with knowledge about how to protect against risk when possible, and to appreciate the times that circumstances make such protection impossible.

MULTIPLE CHOICE REVIEW QUESTIONS

1. If an international contract says "CIF New York":

    A. It contains a promise to ship from New York

    B. The freight is pre-paid as far as New York

    C. The seller's risks end when the goods were delivered to the carrier

    D. none of the above

2. In the case of *The Julia*, seller lost because:

    A. He made a destination contract

    B. He made an affreightment contract

    C. He had a business problem he couldn't solve

    D. He did not perform a CIF contract

3. A garage ticket is not a Document of Title under the UCC because:

    A. it is not issued by a bailee

    B. it is not addressed to a bailee

    C. it is not recognized in business as evidencing that the possessor is entitled to sell the goods

    D. it was unknown to the common law

4. If a CIF contract contains a "to arrive" term:

    A. the contract is treated as a destination contract

    B. the seller has promised that the goods will arrive on time

    C. the shipping company is liable if the goods arrive late

    D. none of the above

5. "Force Majeure" excuses a party if:

    A. an event was unforeseen

    B. an event was unforeseeable

    C. an event was beyond the control of the parties

    D. an event makes performance impossible

PROBLEMS FOR ANALYSIS

PROBLEM 1

Weng Heng Investment Co. Ltd. ("Weng Heng") is a Hong Kong corporation with its principal place of business in Hong Kong. CWJ International Trading, Inc. is a New York corporation with its principal place of business in New York City.

Weng Heng is an importer and distributor of various raw materials. On approximately February 16, 1995, through its agent Success Universal Limited, Weng Heng entered into a contract to purchase 800 metric tons of polyester chips from CWJ for $1.92 per kilogram, C & F Hong Kong, or a total of $1,536,000.00.

The Contract provided that the time of shipment for the first 400 metric tons was to be between February and May 1995. The second 400 metric tons was to be shipped in July 1995. The goods were to be shipped from Mexico (where they were made) to Hong Kong. The contract was silent as to the route to be taken, nor did it contain a time is of the essence clause or any provision as to arrival or delivery.

The first shipment of goods, however, were sent by CWJ in such a manner that they were transhipped through Rotterdam (Netherlands), and did not arrive in Hong Kong until June 29, 1995.

Prior to the arrival of the goods in Hong Kong, CWJ requested Weng Heng's payment for the first lot of goods. At that time, CWJ either knew or should have known that the goods were being transhipped, and CWJ deliberately concealed this fact from Weng Heng. That the goods were being transhipped was not apparent from the documents presented for payment. On approximately May 6, 1995, CWJ was paid for the shipment of the first lot of polyester chips.

The goods arrived in Hong Kong on June 23, 1995. On July 1, 1995, Weng Heng's attorney in Hong Kong notified CWJ that Weng Heng would not take delivery of the first lot of goods and would reject the second lot of goods if it was transhipped from Rotterdam, and for which payment had not yet been made. CWJ did not make the second shipment.

Weng Heng sued CWJ in New York for breach of contract. CWJ counterclaims. What result would you expect?

See Success Universal Limited v. CWJ International Trading, 1996 WL 535541 (S.D.N.Y.)

PROBLEM 2

You are an importer of sporting goods from China. On May 1, you received a purchase order from a Buy-Right, a potential customer in Pennsylvania interested in purchasing 5,000 leather footballs for $2.00 per item. Your customer's purchase order states that they must have the goods before September 1, when football season begins.

You have located a seller in Shanghai named Li Enterprises who has said he has the merchandise in stock. In a phone call today, Li Enterprises offered to ship the merchandise to New York right away at their expense, but that arranging the shipment to Pennsylvania would be your responsibility. The price would be $7,000 cash against documents. Shipments from China normally take 1-2 months.

You can arrange to have a tractor-trailer meet the container at the port in NY; it will cost you $1,000 for the pick-up and delivery to Pennsylvania. Anticipating a 20% gross profit, you immediately fax Buy-Right confirming their order.

Draft an e-mail to Li Enterprises, the seller in China, accepting their offer. Be sure to include all the terms that are important to you, but don't put in anything that might cause Li Enterprises to decline the deal. Be sure to use appropriate business terminology.

SUBJECTS FOR RESEARCH AND FURTHER LEARNING

1. Conduct research into the marine insurance business. How does the industry function? What are the standard policy terms? What limitations exist on the extent of coverage, and what "riders" (i.e. additional coverages) are available? How are premiums determined? How is the insurance obtained, and how are "brokers" compensated? How are claims handled? How are disputes resolved?

2. What documents other than those studied here (bills of lading, inspection certificates) are common in international transactions? When is an Export License required? What is the purpose of a Certificate of Origin? What is the role of a Customs Broker?

3. What are the liability limitations in the standard contract of carriage for ocean freight? How are ocean freight rates determined? What documents of title, other than bills of lading, do shipping companies issue, and how do they differ?

4. Research the ICC's "InCoTerms" on CIF contracts, FOB contracts, FAS contracts and ex-factory contracts. Compare the ICC definitions to the UCC definitions. You'll find the UCC and other statutes at www.law.cornell.edu. The ICC's web-site has less publicly-available information. Where would you go to find information about the ICC's InCoTerms?

DOCUMENTS SUPPLEMENT

BILL OF LADING FOR COMBINED TRANSPORT SHIPMENT OR PORT TO PORT SHIPMENT

Shipper

B L No.

Reference

Consignee or Order

Nedlloyd

Incorporated in The Netherlands at
Nedlloyd Lijnen B.V. Rotterdam

Notify Party Address "It is agreed that no responsibility shall attach to the Carrier or his Agents for failure to notify (see clause 20 on the reverse)

Place of Receipt | (Applicable only when this document is used as a Combined Transport Bill of Lading

Ocean Vessel

Place of Delivery | (Applicable only when this document is used as a Combined Transport Bill of Lading

Port of Loading

Port of Discharge

Marks and Nos; Container Nos:	Number and kind of Packages; Description of Goods	Gross Weight (kg)	Measurement

CONT NO.	SEAL NO.	TY/SZ	PKGS	NWT (LBS)	TWT (LBS)	GWT (LBS)	MEAS (CBM)

ABOVE PARTICULARS AS DECLARED BY SHIPPER

*Total No. of Containers/Packages received by the Carrier

Movement

Freight and Charges (indicate whether prepaid or collect):

Origin Inland Haulage Charge

Origin Terminal Handling/LCL Service Charge

Ocean Freight

Destination Terminal Handling/LCL Service Charge

Destination Inland Haulage Charge

RECEIVED by the Carrier from the Shipper in apparent good order and condition (unless otherwise noted herein) the total number or quantity of Containers or other packages or units indicated in the box opposite entitled "*Total No. Of Containers/Packages receive by the Carrier" for Carriage subject to all the terms hereof (INCLUDING THE TERMS ON THE REVERSE HEREOF AND THE TERMS OF THE CARRIER'S APPLICABLE TARIFF) from the Place of Receipt or the Port of Loading, whichever is applicable, to the Place of Discharge or the Place of Delivery, whichever is applicable. One original Bill of Lading must be surrendered, duly endorsed, in exchange for the Goods. In accepting this Bill of Lading the Merchant expressly accepts and agrees to all its terms and conditions Whether printed, stamped or written otherwise incorporated, notwithstanding the non-signing of this Bill of Lading by the Merchant.

Freight payable at	Place and Date of Issue
Number of Original Bills of Lading	IN WITNESS of the contract herein contained the number

BILL OF LADING FOR COMBINED TRANSPORT SHIPMENT OR PORT TO PORT SHIPMENT

Shipper

PANEAST GENERAL TRADING EST.
P.O. BOX 2359
AJMAN, U.A.E.

B L No.

DXB-A-3107
Reference

Consignee or Order

J & C INTERNATIONAL
175 27TH STREET
BROOKLYN, NY 11232

Nedlloyd

Incorporated in The Netherlands at
Nedlloyd Lijnen B.V. Rotterdam

Notify Party Address "It is agreed that no responsibility shall attach to the Carrier or his Agents for failure to notify (see clause 20 on the reverse)

SAME AS CONSIGNEE

Place of Receipt

(Applicable only when this document is used as a Combined Transport Bill of Lading)

Ocean Vessel

AL IHSA A/5444

Place of Delivery

(Applicable only when this document is used as a Combined Transport Bill of Lading)

Port of Loading
DUBAI

Port of Discharge
NEW YORK VIA FELIXSTOWE

Marks and Nos; Container Nos:	Number and kind of Packages; Description of Goods	Gross Weight (kg)	Measurement
	CY/CY SHIPPERS LOAD & COUNT *FREIGHT PREPAID* *SHIPPED ON BOARD* *1X20' CONTAINER STC* *468 CARTONS 18720 LBS OF FROZEN* *LOBSTER TAILS IQF/IWP* *OMAN ORIGIN* *BRAND: OCEANCREST* *TEMP - 18 DEG C* *NEW YORK THC : USD 320 PER 20' CONTAINER* *TO COLLECT*		

CONT NO.	SEAL NO.	TY/SZ	PKGS	NWT (LBS)	TWT (LBS)	GWT (LBS)	MEAS (CBM)
KNLU2785573	*0056174* *003631*	*2DC*	*468*	*.000*	*2000.000*		*21528.000*

TOTAL CONTAINERISED:
TWT: 2000.000 LBS. NWT: .000 LBS
GWT: 21528.000 LBS.

ABOVE PARTICULARS AS DECLARED BY SHIPPER

*Total No. of Containers/Packages received by the Carrier

1.20' R/CONTR

Movement

CY/CY
of

RECEIVED by the Carrier from the Shipper in apparent good order and condition (unless otherwise noted herein) the total number or quantity of Containers or other packages or units indicated in the box opposite entitled "*Total No. Of Containers/Packages received Carrier "for Carriage subject to all the terms hereof (INCLUDING THE TERMS ON THE REVERSE HEREOF AND THE TERMS OF THE CARRIER'S APPLICABLE TARIFF) from the Place of Receipt or the Port of Loading, whichever is applicable, to the Place of Discharge or the Place of Delivery, whichever is applicable. One original Bill

Lading must be surrendered, duly endorsed, in exchange for the Goods. In accepting this Bill of Lading the Merchant expressly accepts and agrees to all its terms and conditions whether printed, stamped or written otherwise incorporated, notwithstanding the non-signing of this Bill of Lading by the Merchant.

Freight and Charges (indicate whether prepaid or collect):

Origin Inland Haulage Charge   *N/A*

Origin Terminal Handling/LCL Service Charge   *PREPAID*

Ocean Freight   *PREPAID*

Destination Terminal Handling/LCL Service Charge   *COLLECT*

Destination Inland Haulage Charge   *N/A*

Freight payable at *DUBAI*	Place and Date of Issue *DUBAI* **08 DEC 1995**
Number of Original Bills of Lading *THREE (3)*	IN WITNESS of the contract herein contained the number */S/*

59

DELIVERY ORDER

To: F. Van Bree, S. A.
    Antwerp

You are hereby instructed to release to buyer or to bearer 500,000 kilos of rye in bulk ex bill of lading for 1,120,000 kilos rye in bulk shipped by sellers on the Julia under terms of the bill of lading dated Apr. 18.

We give a share to the bearer of the present delivery order of $4,973 in a certificate of insurance for $7117 covering 700 tons of rye in bulk (War and S.R. and C.C. Risks clauses included).

\s\ Belgian Grain & Produce Co., Ltd.
as agents for Louis de Ridder, S.A.

To be presented to F. Van Bree on arrival of the vessel, for signature and release to buyer or bearer after payment of the freight at the offices of the Belgian Grain and Produce Co., Ltd.

————
Freight
Paid

Letters of Credit in International Trade

INTRODUCTION

We observed in the last chapter that the parties to an international transaction face several risks - buyer faces receiving no performance, or inadequate performance, from the seller, and the seller faces the risk of not being paid, either because the buyer is unwilling to pay (for valid or fictitious reasons), or because the buyer is unable to pay, <u>i.e.</u> he is insolvent when the time for payment arrives.

After we identified these risks and came to understand how they relate to a domestic transaction, we examined the procedure generally followed in international trade, <u>i.e.</u> that the seller's obligation is to ship the goods and tender documents, and that the buyer is required, assuming the documents are in order, to pay before the cargo arrives and thus before an inspection can be conducted. We saw that this system addresses a major concern of the seller - that if the buyer is given an opportunity to inspect the goods prior to payment, the buyer might discover a defect and use that as an excuse not to pay at all, or at a miminum the buyer might use the inspection to gain some leverage over a distant seller. The documentary procedure is designed, in part, to assure the seller that that will not happen. At the same time, however, we observed how the documentary procedure gives the buyer the assurances he needs, first, that the goods have been shipped, and second (because it is usually required under the contract of sale), that they were certified by an inspector to be of the quality required.

Yet, even in the standard documentary sale as we have styled it, there is still a major risk facing the seller. Since one of the seller's greatest fears in international trade is to have goods bound for a foreign port with no ready buyer in hand, a risk-averse seller wants even further assurance that payment will be made upon presentation, and that nothing, not even the buyer's insolvency, will prevent it. Remember, as we saw in <u>Biddell</u>, that at least some sellers will prefer not to ship, rather than risk being confronted with the fate of having shipped goods and not getting paid.

The assurance that such a seller will seek is a guarantee from a bank that <u>it</u> (and not just the buyer) will pay the seller upon presentation of conforming documents. The guarantee is called a "letter of credit"; it is a letter, written on the stationery of the bank and addressed to the seller, who is called the beneficiary. The letter states that the bank will pay the seller directly under certain conditions, namely, that it is presented with certain documents before the date on which the letter of credit will expire.

The list of documents that trigger the bank's obligation to pay the seller will be identical to the documents listed in the contract; in this way, the seller is assured that payment <u>will be made</u> when conforming documents are presented, but the buyer is assured that payment <u>will not be made</u> if the documents do not conform. Based upon the assurance of payment received from the issuing bank, the seller will ship the goods, because he is no longer doing so solely on the trustworthiness and creditworthiness of the buyer; unlike the sales contract, <u>the bank's</u> credit and reputation stand behind the the letter of credit, and banks tend to be (a) more solvent than buyers, and (b) they tend to be more trustworthy. If the bank does not pay when it should, it is directly liable to the seller for "wrongful dishonor". (By contrast, if the bank pays when it shouldn't, the bank becomes liable to its customer, <u>i.e.</u> the buyer, for "wrongful honor".)

The main question which this chapter seeks to answer is: how good an assurance of payment is a letter of credit? Of course, one obvious answer is: it is as good as the credit and trustworthiness of the bank. For this reason, the contract of sale is likely to provide parameters for what type of "issuing bank" will be satisfactory. Terms like "reputable New York commercial bank" are common, and should satisfy most sellers; a designation of a specific bank is less common, but not unheard of. And, of course, the seller, as the last sentence indicates, will require an "LC" from a bank it trusts, one with a good international reputation, and an office close by (to sue, in case there is a problem).

But aside from questions about which bank is acceptable (a problem that is easily solved at the contract stage), there is another problem. Almost by definition, the buyer is a "customer" of the bank that will issue the letter of credit. In most cases, the issuing bank is the buyer's bank, <u>i.e.</u> the two have a longstanding professional relationship that goes beyond this specific credit. The result is that the buyer is likely to have some influence over the acts of the banker, and that the banker will be eager to please the buyer because of their business relationship. The danger, then, is that the buyer may, when conditions suit him, try to induce the banker to not pay on a letter of credit, even though the documents might conform. And there is the danger that the banker will comply, favoring his "customer" over the seller, who is a virtual stranger. The banker is, after all, used to following his customer's instructions.

That, then, is a major issue: can the buyer make a "stop payment" order on an LC, the way he can on even a "certified" check? The problem posed is far from simple, and the solution is equally complex. It involves 60-odd years of tortured legal history, but the resolution, it is submitted, is both logical and fair. Before turning to the problem and its solution, however, it is useful to look a little more deeply into the mechanics of letters of credit.

THE MECHANICS

Once the contract of sale is made, the buyer will be expected to apply for the letter of credit. He goes to his bank, fills out a letter of credit application, and pays a processing fee. The bank will review the application with a view toward "establishing" the credit.

Before the bank will issue a letter of credit putting its money behind a promise to pay, the bank will require that the buyer give the bank "security." The security could be in the form of cash or its equivalent. The money is deposited at the bank with a "hold" on the funds; the bank will use those funds to pay the seller when the time comes. In such a case, the bank is satisfied that it is not exposed to undue risk because it has cash on hand from the buyer to complete the transaction with the seller.

It is of course common that the buyer does not have sufficient cash or other liquid collateral to give to the bank. In such a case, the buyer will be seeking financing, i.e. a loan from the bank to cover the cost of the shipment. Naturally, banks are in the lending business, and they charge nice fees for that service (points, interest, etc.) But banks don't lend money willy nilly; with the exception of perhaps their very best customers, the bank will demand some "security" from the buyer before agreeing to lend him or her the money. But what "security" could the buyer offer, if it does not have the cash?

The answer is that the buyer has a contract to purchase goods; these goods have value, and the buyer will be able to exploit that value at the moment he (or his bank) comes into possession of the shipping documents. But goods in transit from a distant port is hardly the security upon which banks like to lend, so the buyer will likely need more. What can that be? How about a contract to resell the goods at a higher price, a contract that is itself backed by a letter of credit conditioning payment on an identical set of shipping documents? In such a case, the bank will feel secure in lending the purchase price to the buyer and establishing the credit in favor of the seller. The importer's

63

bank knows that the moment it comes into possession of the documents of title, it can "flip" those documents to the bank that issued the LC to the end-user, and that it will be paid. The bank's risk is minimal, and the reward (in fees and interest) is not insubstantial.[1]

Either situation is fine with the seller since he got what he wanted, a bank guarantee of payment. As stated, his only concern is with the quality of the bank. If he is not satisfied simply with a credit established by the buyer's bank (perhaps because they are unknown, or too close to the buyer to be trusted, or too distant from the seller to be an easy target of suit in the event of dishonor), he can, in the contract, make provision for a guarantee from a bank that is satisfactory to him. The typical way that is done is by requiring that the credit be established "or confirmed" by an appropriate bank. In such a case, the "confirming bank" becomes liable "as though it were the issuer", and the seller will be satisfied.

In our hypothetical, the buyer had a relationship with his home-town bank, and he was going to use it to establish the credit. To satisfy the terms of the sales contract, however, buyer is required to have the LC "confirmed" by a big, international bank like Chase, or Midland, or Hongkong & Shanghai. The buyer, however, has no relationship with these banks, so how does he proceed? The answer is that *his bank* has a relationship with these other banks. While these other banks may not be willing to lend on the credit of the buyer, they will lend on the credit of their sister banking institution, or, in any event, they can take deposit of the funds at the time the credit is established.

I. HOW GOOD AN ASSURANCE? THE INDEPENDENCE PRINCIPLE

Once the credit is established or confirmed in accordance with the contract of sale, the seller will be comfortable shipping the goods, because he is confident that nothing (at least not problems with the buyer's ability or willingness to pay) will prevent him from being paid if the documents conform. But, again, how good an assurance is it, or, put another way, what level of confidence is justified? The cases which follow attempt to answer this question.

---

1. This method of "import financing" is termed a "back-to-back" letter of credit. The importer-middleman will, of course, want to "substitute" his invoice for that of the original seller, so that he can hide that information from his buyer to assure himself future business. For this reason, even though it costs more, the back-to-back letter of credit is preferred to the practice of "assigning" the end-buyer's LC to the seller. In such a situation, the exporter-seller will learn the identity of the end-buyer (and the importer's profit margin), facts that the middleman needs to keep secret in order to survive in business.

MAURICE O'MEARA COMPANY
v.
THE NATIONAL PARK BANK OF NEW YORK

Court of Appeals of New York
239 N.Y. 386; 146 N.E. 636; 39 A.L.R. 747
January 27, 1925

McLaughin, S

This action was brought to recover damages alleged to have been sustained by the plaintiff's assignor, Ronconi & Millar, by defendant's refusal to pay three sight drafts against a confirmed irrevocable letter of credit. The letter of credit was in the following form:

"The National Park Bank

"of New York.

"Our Credit No. 14956 October 28, 1920.

"Messrs. Ronconi & Millar,

"49 Chambers Street,

"New York City, N.Y.:

"Dear Sirs. — In accordance with instructions received from the Sun-Herald Corporation of this City, we open a confirmed or irrevocable credit in your favor for account of themselves, in amount of $224,853.30, covering the shipment of 1322 2/3 tons of newsprint paper in 72 1/2" and 36 1/2" rolls to test 11-12, 32 lbs. at 8 1/2 cents per pound net weight — delivery to be made in December 1920 and January 1921.

"Drafts under this credit are to be drawn at sight on this Bank, and are to be accompanied by the following documents of a character which must meet with our approval:

"Commercial Invoice in triplicate

"Weight Returns

"Negotiable Dock Delivery Order actually carrying with it control of the goods.

"This is a confirmed or irrevocable credit, and will remain in force to and including February 15th, 1921, subject to the conditions mentioned herein.

"When drawing drafts under this credit, or referring to it please quote our number as above.

"Very truly yours,

"R. STUART,

"Assistant Cashier.

"(R.C.)"

The complaint alleged the issuance of the letter of credit; the tender of three drafts, the first on the 17th of December, 1920, for $46,301.71, the second on January 7, 1921, for $41,416.34, and the third on January 13, 1921, for $32,968.35. Accompanying the first draft were the following documents:

"1. Commercial invoice of the said firm of Ronconi and Millar in triplicate, covering three hundred (300) thirty-six and one-half (36 1/2) inch rolls of newsprint paper and three hundred (300) seventy-two and one-half (72 1/2) inch rolls of newsprint paper, aggregating a net weight of Five Hundred and forty-four thousand seven hundred and twenty-six pounds (544,726), to test eleven (11), twelve (12), thirty-two (32) pounds.

"2. Affidavit of Elwin Walker, verified December 16, 1920, to which were annexed samples of newsprint paper, which the said affidavit stated to be representative of the shipment covered by the accompanying invoices and to test twelve (12) points, thirty-two (32)pounds.

"3. Full weight returns in triplicate.

"4. Negotiable dock delivery order on the Swedish American Line, directing delivery to the order of the National Park Bank of three hundred (300) rolls of newsprint paper seventy-two and one-half (72 1/2) inches long and three hundred (300) half rolls of newsprint paper."

The documents accompanying the second draft were similar to those accompanying the first, except as to the number of rolls, weight of paper, omission of the affidavit of Walker, but with a statement: "Paper equal to original sample in test 11/12-32 pounds;" and a negotiable dock delivery order on the Seager Steamship Co., Inc.

The complaint also alleged defendant's refusal to pay; a statement of the amount of loss upon the resale of the paper due to a fall in the market price; expenses for lighterage, cartage, storage and insurance amounting to $3,045.02; an assignment of the cause of action by Ronconi & Millar to the plaintiff; and a demand for judgment.

The answer denied, upon information and belief, many of the allegations of the complaint, and set up (a) as an affirmative defense, that plaintiff's assignor was required by the letter of credit to furnish to the defendant "evidence reasonably satisfactory" to it that the paper shipped to the Sun-Herald Corporation was of a bursting or tensile strength of eleven to twelve points at a weight of paper of thirty-two pounds; that neither the plaintiff nor its assignor, at the time the drafts were presented, or at any time thereafter, furnished such evidence; (b) as a partial defense, that when the draft for $46,301.71 was presented, the defendant notified the plaintiff there had not been presented "evidence reasonably satisfactory" to it, showing that the newsprint paper referred to in the documents accompanying said drafts was of the tensile or bursting strength specified in the letter of credit; that thereupon an agreement was entered into between plaintiff and defendant that the latter should cause a test to be made of the paper represented by the documents then presented and if such test showed that the paper was up to the specifications of the letter of credit, defendant would make payment of the draft; (c) for a third separate and distinct defense that the paper tendered was not, in fact, of the tensile or bursting strength specified in the letter of credit.

After issue had been joined the plaintiff moved, upon the pleadings and affidavits, pursuant to rule 113 of the Rules of Civil Practice, to strike out the answer and for summary judgment.

The claim for damages for the non-payment of the third draft was, apparently, abandoned at or prior to the time the motion was made. It is unnecessary, therefore, to further consider that and it will not be again referred to in the discussion as to the first two drafts.

The motion for summary judgment was denied and the defendant appealed to the Appellate Division, where the order denying the same was unanimously affirmed, leave to appeal to this court granted, and the following question certified: "Should the motion of the plaintiff for summary judgment herein have been granted?"

I am of the opinion that the order of the Appellate Division and the Special Term should be reversed and the motion granted. The facts set out in defendant's answer and in the affidavits used by it in opposition to the motion are not a defense to the action.

The bank issued to plaintiff's assignor an irrevocable letter of credit, a contract solely between the bank and plaintiff's assignor, in and by which the bank agreed to pay sight drafts to a certain amount on presentation to it of the documents specified in the letter of credit. This contract was in no way involved in or connected with, other than the presentation of the documents, the contract for the purchase and sale of the paper mentioned. That was a contract between buyer and seller, which in no way concerned the bank. The bank's obligation was to pay sight drafts when presented if accompanied by genuine documents specified in the letter of credit. If the paper when delivered did not correspond to what had been purchased, either in weight, kind or quality, then the purchaser had his remedy against the seller for damages. Whether the paper were what the purchaser contracted to purchase did not concern the bank and in no way affected its liability. It was under no obligation to ascertain, either by a personal examination or otherwise, whether the paper conformed to the contract between the buyer and seller. The bank was concerned only in the drafts and the documents accompanying them. This was the extent of its interest. If the drafts, when presented, were accompanied by the proper documents, then it was absolutely bound to make the payment under the letter of credit, irrespective of whether it knew, or had reason to believe, that the paper was not of the tensile strength contracted for. This view, I think, is the one generally entertained with reference to a bank's liability under an irrevocable letter of credit of the character of the one here under consideration.

The defendant had no right to insist that a test of the tensile strength of the paper be made before paying the drafts. Nor did it even have a right to inspect the paper before payment, to determine whether it in fact corresponded to the description contained in the documents. The letter of credit did not so provide. All that the letter of credit provided was that documents be presented which described the paper shipped as of a certain size, weight and tensile strength. To hold otherwise is to read into the letter of credit something which is not there, and this the court ought not to do, since it would impose upon a bank a duty which in many cases would defeat the primary purpose of such letters of credit. This primary purpose is an assurance to the seller of merchandise of prompt payment against documents.

It has never been held, so far as I am able to discover, that a bank has the right or is under an obligation to see that the description of the merchandise contained in the documents presented is correct. A provision giving it such right, or imposing such obligation, might, of course, be provided for in the letter of credit. The letter under consideration contains no such provision. If the bank had the right to determine whether the paper were of the tensile strength stated, then it might be pertinent to inquire how much of the paper must it subject to the test? If it had to make a test as to tensile strength, then it was equally obligated to measure and weigh the paper. No such thing was intended by the parties and there was no such obligation upon the bank. The documents presented were sufficient. The only reason stated by defendant in its letter of December 18, 1920, for refusing to pay the draft, was that "there has arisen a reasonable doubt regarding the quality of the newsprint paper. Until such time as we can have a test made by an impartial and unprejudiced expert we shall be obliged to defer payment." This being the sole objection, the only inference to be drawn therefrom is that otherwise the documents presented conformed to the requirements of the letter of credit. All other objections were thereby waived.

There was a loss on the resale of the paper called for under the first draft of $5,447.26, and under the second draft of $14,617.53, making a total loss of $20,064.79, for which amount judgment should be directed in favor of the plaintiff.

The orders appealed from should, therefore, be reversed and the motion granted, with costs in all courts. The question certified is answered in the affirmative.

CARDOZO, J. (dissenting). I am unable to concur in the opinion of the court. I assume that no duty is owing from the bank to its depositor which requires it to investigate the quality of the merchandise (*Laudisi v. American Ex. National Bank*, 239 N.Y. 234). I dissent from the view that if it chooses to investigate and discovers thereby that the merchandise tendered is not in truth the merchandise which the documents describe, it may be forced by the delinquent seller to make payment of the price irrespective of its knowledge. We are to bear in mind that this controversy is not one between the bank on the one side and on the other a holder of the drafts who has taken them without notice and for value. The controversy arises between the bank and a seller who has misrepresented the security upon which advances are demanded. Between parties so situated, payment may be resisted if the documents are false.

I think we lose sight of the true nature of the transaction when we view the bank as acting upon the credit of its customer to the exclusion of all else. It acts not merely upon the credit of its customer, but upon the credit also of the merchandise which is to be tendered as security. The letter of credit is explicit in its provision that documents sufficient to give control of the goods shall be lodged with the bank when drafts are presented. I cannot accept the statement of the majority opinion that the bank was not concerned with any question as to the character of the paper. If that is so, the bales tendered might have been rags instead of paper, and still the bank would have been helpless, though it had knowledge of the truth, if the documents tendered by the seller were sufficient on their face. A different question would be here if the defects had no relation to the description in the documents. In such circumstances, it would be proper to say that a departure from the terms of the contract between the vendor and the vendee was of no moment to the bank. That is not the case before us. If the paper was of the quality stated in the defendant's answer, the documents were false.

I think the conclusion is inevitable that a bank which pays a draft upon a bill of lading misrepresenting the character of the merchandise may recover the payment when the misrepresentation is discovered, or at the very least the difference between the value of the thing described and the value of the thing received. If payment might have been recovered the moment after it was made, the seller cannot coerce payment if the truth is earlier revealed.

We may find persuasive analogies in connection with the law of sales. One who promises to make payment in advance of delivery and inspection may be technically in default if he refuses the promised payment before inspection has been made. None the less, if the result of the inspection is to prove that the merchandise is defective, the seller must fail in an action for the recovery of the price. The reason is that "the buyer would have been entitled to recover back the price if he had paid it without inspection of the goods" (2 Williston on Sales [2d ed.], §§479, 576).

I think the defendant's answer and the affidavits submitted in support of it are sufficient to permit a finding that the plaintiff's assignors misrepresented the nature of the shipment. The misrepresentation does not cease to be a defense, partial if not complete, though it was innocently made (*Bloomquist v. Farson*, 222 N.Y. 375; 2 Williston on Sales [2d ed.], §632).

The order should be affirmed and the question answered "no."

NOTES AND QUESTIONS

1. The majority opinion of Judge McLaughlin is founded on the principle of the *independence* of the letter of credit. The bank's obligation to pay is independent of the contract of sale, and it is thus independent of all questions of whether the seller complied with his obligations thereunder (such as delivering conforming goods to the carrier). The result of the "independence principle" is that it renders irrelevant the type of claim that the bank is making here.

   A. According to Judge McLaughlin, the independence principle is grounded in the principle that the bank, as a matter of law, is "unconcerned" with the quality of the goods. Do you agree? Can you think of a situation where the bank is concerned, as a matter of economics, if not law?

   B. In his dissent, Judge Cardozo takes issue with the majority's conclusion that the bank is not concerned with the underlying transaction. On what basis does he do so? Who is right?

2. While McLaughlin and Cardozo obviously disagree on some fundamental issues in the case, before looking at those issues it is useful to observe that there are some things on which they do agree. Both Judges state that the bank has no duty to inspect the goods, and they seem to agree that, indeed, the bank is not even privileged to do so if it wants to. They also agree that if the bank pays not knowing about a defect in the merchandise being sold, it is not liable to its customer for wrongful honor.

   A. But in this case, Judge Cardozo points out, apparently the bank did know that the goods were defective. Cardozo would hold that in such a circumstance, the innocent bank may refuse to pay the guilty seller. Cardozo analogizes the situation to a buyer who refused to pay for goods when payment was due. The buyer, Cardozo tells us, can defend a suit by the seller for breach by demonstrating that the goods to be tendered were defective, because, according to the authorities "the buyer would have been entitled to recover back the price if he had paid it without inspection of the goods."

1. Why, Cardozo reasons, should the seller be any better off here? Why indeed? Cardozo says "if payment might have been recovered the moment after it was made, the seller cannot coerce payment if the truth is earlier revealed." Is that statement jurisprudentially correct, or does it lose sight of an important aspect of international trade? Of letters of credit?

2. Should there be any limits on the seller's abilty to invoke the independence principle? It is, after all, clearly a good principle. Is Cardozo telling the majority he doesn't agree with that principle, or does he instead assert that the principle has limits, that it should apply generally, just not here?

B. Cardozo's answer is to characterize the shipping documents themselves as "false", thus sidestepping the independence principle. What does it mean to say the documents are "false"? It is obviously different from "forged" or "fake" documents. Presumably, Judge McLaughlin would agree that the bank should not pay if it knows the shipping documents are not genuine. How, though, are "ungenuine" documents different from documents which are "false"? Put differently, is there a difference between a seller who presents fraudulent documents and a fraudulent presentation of genuine documents? If so, what is the difference?

C. Has Judge Cardozo convinced you that the majority opinion is wrong? Or is the great Cardozo wrong, having lost sight of the fundamental nature of the transaction in favor of an overzealous attempt to do justice for the parties before him? Is there any way to accommodate the views of both Cardozo and the majority?

3. The simple "bank must pay" approach of the Maurice O'Meara majority is undoubtedly beneficial to international trade. Because it makes the bank liable for wrongful dishonor, it serves to minimize the influence that buyer-customers have over banks issuing letters of credit. It also assures the seller of hassle-free payment against conforming documents, thus fulfilling one of the basic purposes which LCs serve. But some (following Cardozo) would argue that it goes too far in protecting an unscrupulous seller against an innocent buyer and his bank, and that it can lead to an injustice that the law should avoid. Were it not for the fact that Benjamin Nathan Cardozo penned the dissent in Maurice O'Meara, the entire issue might have been settled there. But a Cardozo opinion is, as you might know, a force with which to be reckoned, so it cannot be dismissed. The reckoning begins with the Sztejn case.

II. CARDOZO'S LEGACY: THE FRAUD-IN-THE-TRANSACTION DOCTRINE

SZTEJN
v.
J. HENRY SCHRODER BANKING CORPORATION,
Robert Schwarz Bristle Corp.,
Transea Traders, Ltd., and
The Chartered Bank of India, Australia and China

Supreme Court of New York, Special Term, New York County
177 Misc. 719; 31 N.Y.S.2d 631
July 1, 1941

Sheintag, J.

This is a motion by the defendant The Chartered Bank of India, Australia and China (hereafter referred to as The Chartered Bank), made pursuant to subdivision 5 of rule 106 of the Rules of Civil Practice to dismiss the supplemental complaint on the ground that it fails to state facts sufficient to constitute a cause of action against the moving defendant. The plaintiff brings this action to restrain the payment or presentment for payment of drafts under a letter of credit issued to secure the purchase price of certain merchandise, bought by the plaintiff and his coadventurer, one Schwarz, who is a party defendant in this action. The plaintiff also seeks a judgment declaring the letter of credit and drafts thereunder null and void. The complaint alleges that the documents accompanying the drafts are fraudulent in that they do not represent actual merchandise but instead cover boxes fraudulently filled with worthless material by the seller of the goods. The moving defendant urges that the complaint fails to state a cause of action against it because The Chartered Bank is only concerned with the documents and on their face these conform to the requirements of the letter of credit.

On January 7, 1941, the plaintiff and his coadventurer contracted to purchase a quantity of bristles from the defendant Transea Traders, Ltd. (hereafter referred to as Transea), a corporation having its place of business in Lucknow, India. In order to pay for the bristles, the plaintiff and Schwarz contracted with the defendant J. Henry Schroder Banking Corporation (hereafter referred to as Schroder), a domestic corporation, for the issuance of an irrevocable letter of credit to Transea which provided that drafts by the latter for a specified portion of the purchase price of the bristles would be paid by Schroder upon shipment of the described merchandise and presentation of an invoice and a bill of lading covering the shipment, made out to the order of Schroder.

The letter of credit was delivered to Transea by Schroder's correspondent bank in India; Transea placed fifty cases of material on board a steamship, procured a bill of lading from the steamship company and obtained the customary invoices. These documents describe the bristles called for by the letter of credit. However, the complaint alleges that in fact Transea filled the fifty crates with cowhair, other worthless material and rubbish with intent to simulate genuine merchandise and defraud the plaintiff and Schwarz. The complaint then alleges that Transea drew a draft under the letter of credit to the order of The Chartered Bank and delivered the draft and the fraudulent documents to the "Chartered Bank at Cawnpore, India, for collection for the account of said defendant Transea." The Chartered Bank has presented the draft along with the documents to Schroder for payment. The plaintiff prays for a judgment declaring the letter of credit and draft thereunder void and for injunctive relief to prevent the payment of the draft. For the purposes of this motion the allegations of the complaint must be deemed established and "every intendment and fair inference is in favor of the pleading." Therefore, it must be assumed that Transea was engaged in a scheme to defraud the plaintiff and Schwarz, that the merchandise shipped by Transea is worthless rubbish and that The Chartered Bank is not an innocent holder of the draft for the value but is merely attempting to procure payment of the draft for Transea's account.

It is well established that a letter of credit is independent of the primary contract of sale between the buyer and seller. The issuing bank agrees to pay upon presentation of documents, not goods. This rule is necessary to preserve the efficiency of the letter of credit as an instrument for the financing of trade. One of the chief purposes of the letter of credit is to furnish the seller with a ready means of obtaining prompt payment for his merchandise. It would be a most unfortunate interference with business transactions if a bank before honoring drafts drawn upon it was obliged or even allowed to go behind the documents, at the request of the buyer, and enter into controversies between the buyer and the seller regarding the quality of the merchandise shipped. If the buyer and the seller intended the bank to do this they could have so provided in the letter of credit itself, and in the absence of such a provision the court will not demand or even permit the bank to delay paying drafts which are proper in form.

However, I believe that a different situation is presented in the instant action. This is not a controversy between the buyer and seller concerning a mere breach of warranty regarding the quality of the merchandise; on the present motion, it must be assumed that the seller has intentionally failed to ship any goods ordered by the buyer. In such a situation, where the seller's fraud has been called to the bank's attention before the drafts and documents have been presented for payment, the principle of the independence of the bank's obligation under the letter of credit should not be extended to protect the unscrupulous seller. It is true that even though the documents are forged or fraudulent, if the issuing bank has already paid the draft before receiving notice of the seller's fraud, it will be protected if it exercised reasonable diligence before making such payment. However, in the instant action Schroder has received notice of Transea's active fraud before it accepted or paid the draft. The Chartered Bank, which under the allegations of the complaint stands in no better position than Transea, should not be heard to complain because Schroder is not forced to pay the draft accompanied by documents covering a transaction which it has reason to believe is fraudulent.

Although our courts have used broad language to the effect that a letter of credit is independent of the primary contract between the buyer and seller, that language was used in cases concerning alleged breaches of warranty; no case has been brought to my attention on this point involving an intentional fraud on the part of the seller which was brought to the bank's notice with the request that it withhold payment of the draft on this account. The distinction between a breach of warranty and active fraud on the part of the seller is supported by authority and reason. As one court has stated: "Obviously, when the issuer of a letter of credit knows that a document, although correct in form, is, in point of fact, false or illegal, he cannot be called upon to recognize such a document as complying with the terms of a letter of credit." [citation omitted]

No hardship will be caused by permitting the bank to refuse payment where fraud is claimed, where the merchandise is not merely inferior in quality but consists of worthless rubbish, where the draft and the accompanying documents are in the hands of one who stands in the same position as the fraudulent seller, where the bank has been given notice of the fraud before being presented with the drafts and documents for payment, and where the bank itself does not wish to pay pending an adjudication of the rights and obligations of the other parties. While the primary factor in the issuance of the letter of credit is the credit standing of the buyer, the security afforded by the merchandise is also taken into account. In fact, the letter of credit requires a bill of lading made out to the order of the bank and not the buyer. Although the bank is not interested in the exact detailed performance of the sales contract, it is vitally interested in assuring itself that there are some goods represented by the documents.

On this motion only the complaint is before me and I am bound by its allegation that The Chartered Bank is not a holder in due course but is a mere agent for collection for the account of the seller charged with fraud. Therefore The Chartered Bank's motion to dismiss the complaint must be denied. If it had appeared from the face of the complaint that the bank presenting the draft for payment was a holder in due course, its claim against the bank issuing the letter of credit would not be defeated even though the primary transaction was tainted with fraud. This I believe to be the better rule despite some authority to the contrary.

The plaintiff's further claim that the terms of the documents presented with the draft are at substantial variance with the requirements of the letter of credit does not seem to be supported by the documents themselves.

Accordingly, the defendant's motion to dismiss the supplemental complaint is denied.

NOTES AND QUESTIONS

1. As we predicted in the last segment, the law could not easily dismiss Cardozo's dissent. Indeed, in <u>Sztejn</u>, much of Cardozo's logic (and sense of justice) is adopted by Justice Sheintag. But is it all adopted? What distinctions can you find between the Cardozo dissent and the decision in Sztejn?

   A. One difference is in the posture of the law suit. <u>Maurice O'Meara</u> was an action by the seller against the bank that issued the letter of credit? Who is suing whom in <u>Sztejn</u>? Why? What relief is the buyer seeking? Is it the same relief (in essence) that the buyer (and its bank) wanted in <u>Maurice O'Meara</u>? What is different?

   B. Judge Sheintag does not make a final ruling that the sellers committed fraud, and that they thus do not get paid. Rather, he issued a "preliminary injunction", temporarily freezing the money until the goods arrive and the issue of fraud of could be conclusively determined. From the seller's standpoint, that is better than a court permanantly enjoining payment, but it is hardly what the seller bargained for. What use, then, was the letter of credit?

   C. One answer to that question is that the letter of credit in fact limited the buyer's ability to make frivolous claims to avoid payment. The buyer, because <u>Maurice O'Meara</u> is still the law, found his bank unwilling to accede to the request to stop payment. The buyer had to go to court, and get a judge to approve the application for an injunction. Does that layer of judicial review address the concerns of the seller? Of the bank? Are there any concerns that remain?

2. Not only does Justice Sheintag place himself between the buyer and bank, he also sets a high standard of proof if the buyer is to secure an injunction.

   A. Judge Sheintag cunningly weaves a fine line between his decision and <u>Maurice O'Meara</u>. He states that <u>Maurice O'Meara</u> involved only a simple breach of warranty, while <u>Sztejn</u> involved fraud. What is the difference? Didn't both cases involve documents which were, in Cardozo's words, "false"? In setting a high standard for the buyer to meet, Judge Sheintag is limiting the number of cases where the buyer can secure an injunction. He is requiring not simply an allegation that the goods are not in conformity with the contract, but a higher degree of defect. What purpose does that serve? As a seller are you satisfied with the state of the law?

   B. In considering the seller's viewpoint, note that the buyer's ability to influence the bank has been eliminated; a "stop payment" will only issue after a <u>judge</u> (as opposed to the buyer's bank) is convinced that there is a probability of <u>fraud</u> (as opposed to ordinary breach of contract). The requirement of proof of fraud is a high standard; most disappointed buyers will not be able to meet it. As a seller, are you satisfied that you have adequate protection?

3. It was not clear in 1941 that the rule articulated by Justice Sheintag would indeed become U.S. law, let alone "international" law. Even if one were prepared to adopt it, however, there are still questions to answer:

    A. For example, one should ask - exactly what is meant by the term "fraud"? How does it differ from breach of contract or breach of warranty, and how does the buyer go about proving it?

    B. Another potential problem with the Sheintag approach is that even if we are prepared to accept the notion that one who commits fraud cannot reap the benefits of the guarantee in the letter of credit, we must still face the potential "domino effect" that would result? Remember, the seller is likely to also be a buyer, and the buyer to be a seller. Does that fact affect your view of the Sheintag approach? Does the approach need to be adjusted? Is that, perhaps, why Justice Sheintag (and Cardozo before him) assumed that the presenter of the drafts was not an innocent "holder" of the drafts? Who are they talking about, anyway when they invoke that caveat?

    C. And finally, what about the banks? How does the availability of an injunction in the case of fraud affect position, and their risks, and their business? The answer to all these questions is considered in the cases and materials which follow.

MORE ON THE ROLE OF BANKS IN INTERNATIONAL TRADE

Banks play many roles in international trade. First, they play the role of postmaster. When shipping documents are sent internationally, they are often transported by bank couriers. In addition, whether there is a letter of credit or not, banks play act as collection agents for sellers and also act as payment agents for buyers. Banks also play the role of currency converters, because, of necessity, at least one party to every international transaction will have to change currency.

We have also seen that banks also play an important part as "guarantors" of payment whenever they issue and/or confirm letters of credit. When issuing or confirming Letters of Credit, banks serve as trusted neutrals, similar to the way we looked at those who issue documents of title. Indeed, one significant effect of the interplay between <u>Maurice O'Meara</u> and <u>Sztejn</u> is that it keeps banks in their proper place.

Banks also play a major role financing import transactions, as we saw in our discussion of Maurice O'Meara and "back to back" letters of credit. They also, obviously, play an important role financing **export** transactions, a subject we have not yet discussed. Learning about that role, however, first requires introduction of another important "device" in international trade - the draft.

A draft, sometimes called a "bill of exchange",[2] is one of the documents that must be presented to the buyer along with the bill of lading. A draft is best understood when it is compared to a check; indeed a check is a form of draft. When a buyer makes out a check, he is instructing his bank (as his agent) to pay the stated sum to the seller. In commercial parlance, the buyer is the maker (he wrote up the instrument) and drawer, his bank is the drawee, and the seller is the payee. The buyer signs the instrument, and he thus agrees to pay it according to its terms in the event it is "dishonored" by the bank. The seller takes the written instrument to his bank, which will act as his "collection agent." The seller's bank "presents" the instrument to the drawee bank, and, because a check is payable on demand, the bank will pay it (assuming, of course, that (a) payment hasn't been stopped and (b) there are sufficient funds to cover the item).

The draft used in international trade has some differences and some similarities to the check. The first difference is that is made out by the seller rather than the buyer - recall that it is one of the documents seller presents to buyer when seller presents the bill of lading. As such, at the moment of presentment, it is not signed by the buyer. Nevertheless, a bank being presented with such a draft (or the buyer, if there is to be no bank) must act is it would with a check - it must either honor the draft or dishonor it. The wrong decision, of course, can create liability.

The second difference is that all checks are, by definition, payable on demand, meaning that the bank must decide either to honor or dishonor the draft by midnight of the day following presentment. By contrast, a draft in an international sale **may** be payable "at sight" (the equivalent of "on demand"), but *it also may* be payable at a time in the future - a so-called "time draft." A time draft payable after, say, 60 days would thus read, "pay 60 days from sight."

When presented with a time draft, even though payment is not yet due, the bank (or the buyer, if no bank is involved) must nevertheless honor or dishonor it just as it would a demand instrument. But, because payment will not be due at that moment, the act of honoring a time draft takes a different form. A time draft is honored by an act called "acceptance" - the party to whom it is presented (bank or buyer) will sign it and give it back to the presenter. The seller then holds an instrument containing an unconditional promise to pay, i.e. it makes no mention of the goods, and the acceptor, by signing, became contractually liable to pay. If the acceptor does not pay when the stated time expires, the seller is legally better off than one holding just a promise to pay against delivery of goods of a certain quality, because the acceptor's obligation to pay can, through a process known as "negotiation" (discussed infra), become totally independent of the quality of the contracted-for goods.

Clearly, a seller willing to sell against time draft is more attractive to a buyer than a seller who insists on being paid in cash at the time of presentment. (You should think about why that is so.) But do not confuse a seller selling against a time draft with one selling on open credit. The seller in the time draft scenario has far greater protection. If he sold against a so-called "trade acceptance" (<u>i.e.</u> where the buyer, and not the bank, was "acceptor"), and the buyer accepted the instrument but did not pay, the buyer is now liable on the instrument as well as the contract. If the bank has agreed to accept such a draft (for example, by issuing a letter of credit) and the bank fails to make timely acceptance (assuming all the other documents are in order), the bank will liable for wrongful dishonor.

Of course, only the buyer's credit is behind the instrument when it bears only a "trade acceptance"; a seller wanting greater assurance will make contracts requiring a "banker's acceptance". The advantage is clear: the bank's credit is behind the latter instrument, and since the acceptor's promise to pay is conditioned only on the passage of time, a seller selling against a time draft with banker's acceptance has reasonably good assurance it will be paid when the instrument becomes due.

All of this is of no small benefit to the seller. Consider his situation: as the holder of a draft containing a banker's acceptance, the seller has piece of paper, signed by a bank, unconditionally guaranteeing payment on a specific date in the future. Obviously, there are banks that "buy" such instruments, discounting them by an appropriate interest and time factor (legally, the process is known as "negotiation"; thus the term "negotiable instrument" to describe the draft). The seller holding such an instrument can thus obtain the ready cash he needs to finance his operations, at least so long as banks (and other export financers) recognize the value of the bank guarantee that underlies the instrument.

In fact, the exporter needing cash need not even wait until the instrument is accepted; his bank will probably be willing to provide (discounted) cash when the seller hands the bank the shipping documents and the (unsigned) draft, along with the buyer's letter of credit stating that the issuing bank will pay (or accept) drafts upon presentment when accompanied by the shipping documents. The seller's bank will be willing to pay cash to the exporter at that moment because it knows that it has in its possession all that is needed to get paid by the bank that issued the letter of credit.

---

2. "Bill of Exchange" is the older term; it is used infrequently in the United States, but it still appears in the British lexicon.

In this scenario, because the issuing bank is honest and a good credit risk, the risk to the export-financing bank is low, because nothing can prevent it from being paid. Nothing except, perhaps, Judge Sheintag and his brethren who may issue injunctions and restraining orders, and who may eventually rule that the seller's fraud means the issuing bank is prevented from paying on the letter of credit. The way the law deals with that problem is explored in the case which follows.

III. PROMOTING TRADE: THE *HOLDER IN DUE COURSE* RULE

UNITED BANK LIMITED ET AL.,
v.
CAMBRIDGE SPORTING GOODS CORP.,

Court of Appeals of New York
41 N.Y.2d 254; 360 N.E.2d 943; 392 N.Y.S.2d 265;
December 28, 1976

Gabrielli, J.

On this appeal, we must decide whether fraud on the part of a seller-beneficiary of an irrevocable letter of credit may be successfully asserted as a defense against holders of drafts drawn by the seller pursuant to the credit. If we conclude that this defense may be interposed by the buyer who procured the letter of credit, we must also determine whether the courts below improperly imposed upon appellant buyer the burden of proving that respondent banks to whom drafts were made payable by the seller-beneficiary of the letter of credit, were not holders in due course. The issues presented raise important questions concerning the application of the law of letters of credit and the rules governing proof of holder in due course status set forth in article 3 of the Uniform Commercial Code.

In April, 1971 appellant Cambridge Sporting Goods Corporation (Cambridge) entered into a contract for the manufacture and sale of boxing gloves with Duke Sports (Duke), a Pakistani corporation. Duke committed itself to the manufacture of 27,936 pairs of boxing gloves at a sale price of $42,576.80; and arranged with its Pakistani bankers, United Bank Limited (United) and The Muslim Commercial Bank (Muslim), for the financing of the sale. Cambridge was requested by these banks to cover payment of the purchase price by opening an irrevocable letter of credit with its bank in New York, Manufacturers Hanover Trust Company (Manufacturers). Manufacturers issued an irrevocable letter of credit obligating it, upon the receipt of certain documents indicating shipment of the merchandise pursuant to the contract, to accept and pay, 90 days after acceptance, drafts drawn upon Manufacturers for the purchase price of the gloves.

Following confirmation of the opening of the letter of credit, Duke informed Cambridge that it would be impossible to manufacture and deliver the merchandise within the time period required by the contract, and sought an extension of time for performance until September 15, 1971 and a continuation of the letter of credit, which was due to expire on August 11. Cambridge replied on June 18 that it would not agree to a postponement of the manufacture and delivery of the gloves because of its resale commitments and, hence, it promptly advised Duke that the contract was canceled and the letter of credit should be returned. Cambridge simultaneously notified United of the contract cancellation.

Despite the cancellation of the contract, Cambridge was informed on July 17, 1971 that documents had been received at Manufacturers from United purporting to evidence a shipment of the boxing gloves under the terms of the canceled contract. The documents were accompanied by a draft, dated July 16, 1971, drawn by Duke upon Manufacturers and made payable to United, for the amount of $21,288.40, one half of the contract price of the boxing gloves. A second set of documents was received by Manufacturers from Muslim, also accompanied by a draft, dated August 20, and drawn upon Manufacturers by Duke for the remaining amount of the contract price.

An inspection of the shipments upon their arrival revealed that Duke had shipped old, unpadded, ripped and mildewed gloves rather than new gloves to be manufactured as agreed upon. Cambridge then commenced an action against Duke in Supreme Court, New York County, joining Manufacturers as a party, and obtained a preliminary injunction prohibiting the latter from paying drafts drawn under the letter of credit; subsequently, in November, 1971 Cambridge levied on the funds subject to the letter of credit and the draft, which were delivered by Manufacturers to the Sheriff in compliance therewith. Duke ultimately defaulted in the action and judgment against it was entered in the amount of the drafts, in March, 1972.

The present proceeding was instituted by the Pakistani banks to vacate the levy made by Cambridge and to obtain payment of the drafts on the letter of credit. The banks asserted that they were holders in due course of the drafts which had been made payable to them by Duke and, thus, were entitled to the proceeds thereof irrespective of any defenses which Cambridge had established against their transferor, Duke, in the prior action which has terminated in a default judgment. The banks' motion for summary judgment on this claim was denied and the request by Cambridge for a jury trial was granted. Cambridge sought to depose the petitioning banks, but its request was denied and, as an alternative, written interrogatories were served on the Pakistani banks to learn the circumstances surrounding the transfer of the drafts to them. At trial, the banks introduced no evidence other than answers to several of the written interrogatories which were received over objection by Cambridge to the effect that the answers were conclusory, self-serving and otherwise inadmissible. Cambridge presented evidence of its dealings with Duke including the cancellation of the contract and uncontested proof of the subsequent shipment of essentially worthless merchandise.

The trial court concluded that the burden of proving that the banks were not holders in due course lay with Cambridge, and directed a verdict in favor of the banks on the ground that Cambridge had not met that burden; the court stated that Cambridge failed to demonstrate that the banks themselves had participated in the seller's acts of fraud, proof of which was concededly present in the record. The Appellate Division affirmed, agreeing that while there was proof tending to establish the defenses against the seller, Cambridge had not shown that the seller's acts were "connected to the petitioners [banks] in any manner."

We reverse and hold that it was improper to direct a verdict in favor of the petitioning Pakistani banks. We conclude that the defense of fraud in the transaction was established and in that circumstance the burden shifted to petitioners to prove that they were holders in due course and took the drafts for value, in good faith and without notice of any fraud on the part of Duke (Uniform Commercial Code, § 3-302).

This case does not come before us in the typical posture of a lawsuit between the bank issuing the letter of credit and presenters of drafts drawn under the credit seeking payment (see, generally, White and Summers, Uniform Commercial Code, § 18-6, pp 619-628). Because Cambridge obtained an injunction against payment of the drafts and has levied against the proceeds of the drafts, it stands in the same position as the issuer, and, thus, the law of letters of credit governs the liability of Cambridge to the Pakistani banks.[3] Article 5 of the Uniform Commercial Code, dealing with letters of credit, and the Uniform Customs and Practice for Documentary Credits promulgated by the International Chamber of Commerce set forth the duties and obligations of the issuer of a letter of credit.[4] A letter of credit is a

---

3. Cambridge has no direct liability on the drafts because it is not a party to the drafts which were drawn on Manufacturers by Duke as drawer; its liability derives from the letter of credit which authorizes the drafts to be drawn on the issuing banks. Since Manufacturers has paid the proceeds of the drafts to the Sheriff pursuant to the levy obtained in the prior proceeding, it has discharged its obligation under the credit and is not involved in this proceeding.

4. It should be noted that the Uniform Customs and Practice controls, in lieu of article 5 of the code, where, unless otherwise agreed by the parties, a letter of credit is made subject to the provisions of the Uniform Customs and Practice by its terms or by agreement, course of dealing or usage of trade (Uniform Commercial Code, §5-102, subd [4]). No proof was offered that there was an agreement that the Uniform Customs and Practice should apply, nor does credit so state. Neither do the parties otherwise contend that their rights should be resolved under the Uniform Customs and Practice. However, even if the Uniform Customs and Practice were deemed applicable to this case, it would not, in the absence of a conflict, abrogate the precode case law (now codified in Uniform Commercial Code, §5-114) and that authority continues to govern even where article 5 is not controlling (see White and Summers, op. cit., pp 613-614, 624-625). Moreover, the Uniform Customs and Practice provisions are not in conflict nor do they treat with the subject matter of section 5-114 which is dispositive of the issues presented on this appeal. Thus, we are of the opinion that the Uniform Customs and Practice, where applicable, does not bar the relief provided for in section 5-114 of the code.

commitment on the part of the issuing bank that it will pay a draft presented to it under the terms of the credit, and if it is a documentary draft, upon presentation of the required documents of title (see Uniform Commercial Code, § 5-103). Banks issuing letters of credit deal in documents and not in goods and are not responsible for any breach of warranty or nonconformity of the goods involved in the underlying sales contract (see Uniform Commercial Code, § 5-114, subd [1]; Uniform Customs Practice, General Provisions and Definitions [c] and article 9; O'Meara Co. v. National Park Bank of N.Y., 239 NY 386. Subdivision (2) of section 5-114, however, indicates certain limited circumstances in which an issuer may properly refuse to honor a draft drawn under a letter of credit or a customer may enjoin an issuer from honoring such a draft.[5] Thus, where "fraud in the transaction" has been shown and the holder has not taken the draft in circumstances that would make it a holder in due course, the customer may apply to enjoin the issuer from paying drafts drawn under the letter of credit. This rule represents a codification of precode case law most eminently articulated in the landmark case of Sztejn v. Schroder Banking Corp. (177 Misc 719, Shientag, J.) where it was held that the shipment of cowhair in place of bristles amounted to more than mere breach of warranty but fraud sufficient to constitute grounds for enjoining payment of drafts to one not a holder in due course. Even prior to the Sztejn case, forged or fraudulently procured documents were proper grounds for avoidance of payment of drafts drawn under a letter of credit; and cases decided after the enactment of the code have cited Sztejn with approval.

The history of the dispute between the various parties involved in this case reveals that Cambridge had in a prior, separate proceeding successfully enjoined Manufacturers from paying the drafts and has attached the proceeds of the drafts. It should be noted that the question of the availability and the propriety of this relief is not before us on this appeal.[6] The petitioning banks do not dispute the validity of the prior injunction nor do they dispute the delivery of worthless merchandise. Rather, on this appeal they contend that

---

5. Subdivision (2) of section 5-114 of the Uniform Commercial Code provides that,

"[unless] otherwise agreed when documents appear on their face to comply with the terms of a credit but if . . . there is fraud in the transaction

(a) the issuer must honor the draft or demand for payment if honor is demanded by a . . . holder of the draft . . . . which has taken the draft . . . under the credit and under circumstances which would make it a holder in due course (Section 3-302) . . . ; and

"(b) in all other cases as against its customer, an issuer acting in good faith may honor the draft . . . despite notification from the customer of fraud, forgery or other defect not apparent on the face of the documents but a court of appropriate jurisdiction may enjoin such honor."

6. It is not necessary, therefore, for us to reach the difficult question whether the Pakistani banks were indispensable parties in the first action.

as holders in due course they are entitled to the proceeds of the drafts irrespective of any fraud on the part of Duke (see Uniform Commercial Code, § 5-114, subd [2], par [b]). Although precisely speaking there was no specific finding of fraud in the transaction by either of the courts below, their determinations were based on that assumption. The evidentiary facts are not disputed and we hold upon the facts as established, that the shipment of old, unpadded, ripped and mildewed gloves rather than the new boxing gloves as ordered by Cambridge, constituted fraud in the transaction within the meaning of subdivision (2) of section 5-114. It should be noted that the drafters of section 5-114, in their attempt to codify the Sztejn case and in utilizing the term "fraud in the transaction", have eschewed a dogmatic approach and adopted a flexible standard to be applied as the circumstances of a particular situation mandate.[7] It can be difficult to draw a precise line between cases involving breach of warranty (or a difference of opinion as to the quality of goods) and outright fraudulent practice on the part of the seller. To the extent, however, that Cambridge established that Duke was guilty of fraud in shipping, not merely nonconforming merchandise, but worthless fragments of boxing gloves, this case is similar to Sztejn.

If the petitioning banks are holders in due course they are entitled to recover the proceeds of the drafts but if such status cannot be demonstrated their petition must fail. The parties are in agreement that section 3-307 of the code governs the pleading and proof of holder in due course status and that section provides:

"(1) Unless specifically denied in the pleadings each signature on an instrument is admitted. When the effectiveness of a signature is put in issue

   "(a)   the burden of establishing it is on the party claiming under the signature; but

   "(b)   the signature is presumed to be genuine or authorized except where the action is to enforce the obligation of a purported signer who has died or become incompetent before proof is required.

"(2) When signatures are admitted or established, production of the instrument entitles a holder to recover on it unless the defendant establishes a defense.

"(3) After it is shown that a defense exists a person claiming the rights of a holder in due course has the burden of establishing that he or some person under whom he claims is in all respects a holder in due course."

Even though section 3-307 is contained in article 3 of the code dealing with negotiable instruments rather than letters of credit, we agree that its provisions should control in the instant case. Section 5-114 (subd [2], par [a]) utilizes the

---

7. In its original version section 5-114 contained the language "fraud in a required document".

holder in due course criteria of section 3-302 of the code to determine whether a presenter may recover on drafts despite fraud in the sale of goods transaction. . . . Thus, a presenter of drafts drawn under a letter of credit must prove that it took the drafts for value, in good faith and without notice of the underlying fraud in the transaction (Uniform Commercial Code, § 3-302).

Turning to the rules of section 3-307 as they apply to this case, Cambridge failed to deny the effectiveness of the signatures on the draft in its answer and, thus, these are deemed admitted and their effectiveness is not an issue in the case. However, this does not entitle the banks as holders to payment of the drafts since Cambridge has established "fraud in the transaction". The courts below erroneously concluded that Cambridge was required to show that the banks had participated in or were themselves guilty of the seller's fraud in order to establish a defense to payment. But, it was not necessary that Cambridge prove the United and Muslim actually participated in the fraud, since merely notice of the fraud would have deprived the Pakistani banks of holder in due course status.

In order to qualify as a holder in due course, a holder must have taken the instrument "without notice . . . of any defense against . . . it on the part of any person" (Uniform Commercial Code, § 3-302, subd [1], par [c]). Pursuant to subdivision (2) of section 5-114 fraud in the transaction is a valid defense to payment of drafts drawn under a letter of credit. Since the defense of fraud in the transaction was shown, the burden shifted to the banks by operation of subdivision (3) of section 3-307 to prove that they were holders in due course and took the drafts without notice of Duke's alleged fraud. As indicated in the Official Comment to that subdivision, when it is shown that a defense exists, one seeking to cut off the defense by claiming the rights of a holder in due course "has the full burden of proof by a preponderance of the total evidence" on this issue. This burden must be sustained by "affirmative proof" of the requisites of holder in due course status (see Official Comment, McKinney's Cons Laws of NY, Book 62 1/2, Uniform Commercial Code, § 3-307, p 212). It was error for the trial court to direct a verdict in favor of the Pakistani banks because this determination rested upon a misallocation of the burden of proof; and we conclude that the banks have not satisfied the burden of proving that they qualified in all respects as holders in due course, by any affirmative proof. The only evidence introduced by the banks consisted of conclusory answers to the interrogatories which were improperly admitted by the Trial Judge. The failure of the banks to meet their burden is fatal to their claim for recovery of the proceeds of the drafts and their petition must therefore be dismissed.

Accordingly, the order of the Appellate Division should be reversed, with costs, and the petition dismissed.

NOTES AND QUESTIONS

1. The procedural context of <u>Cambridge</u> is different from both <u>Maurice O'Meara</u> and <u>Sztejn</u>. In the case just reprinted, the issuing bank, Manufacturer's Hanover, accepted a time draft under the letter of credit. Before payment, however, the buyer secured the desired preliminary injunction against payment by the bank, and the seller then defaulted at the hearing. The bank paid the money in dispute over to the Sheriff (an officer of the court), and Cambridge is trying to get it back by way of "levy". United Bank intervenes, claiming it is holding a draft accepted by the bank, and that it, rather than Cambridge, is entitled to the proceeds of the letter of credit.

2. The issue before the Court of Appeals is the role being played by United Bank. If it is acting merely as "collection agent" for the seller, it cannot collect because its principal, the seller, committed fraud. Simply stated, the bank will be charged with the sins of its principal, and will not be entitled to collect. But if United Bank acted as an innocent export financer, **purchasing the draft without knowledge of problems with the underlying transaction**, it should be protected. Why is that so?

   A. Why should the law favor the innocent bank over the equally-innocent purchaser in cases where the bank provided export financing? And why should it be disfavored when it did not?

   B. The answer to the first question lies in the law's desire to encourage international trade. If the bank that innocently extended financing (<u>i.e.</u> laid out its money in reliance on the fact that (a) the shipping documents were in order and (b) there was a bank guarantee of payment at a specified time in the future if those documents were presented) was forced to suffer the loss because of the exporter's fraud, the bank would be discouraged from financing exports. That result must, obviously, be avoided.

   C. On the other hand, if the bank didn't lay out its own money, if it is merely appearing to collect on the time draft, it has no real stake, and cannot assert any reason it should be paid aside from its principal's right to be paid. And if it's principal (the seller) is not entitled to be paid because it committed fraud, the bank must lose.

   D. Of course, the bank must, at the time, it bought the instrument ("gave value", in legal parlance), have no knowledge that there are problems with the instrument. If it meets this two-part test (value and lack of notice), the bank is categorized as "**holder in due course**" of the instrument, and it is entitled to be paid regardless of the fraud. If, on the other hand, the bank does not qualify as a holder in due course, the bank will not defeat the buyer's fraud claim.

85

3. Once this distinction (and the terminolgy) is digested, it is easy to understand the Court's decision. The draft is a "negotiable instrument"; it was indorsed over to the bank (the seller signed the back), and the bank is trying to collect on it. If the bank is a holder in due course, it will win; if not, it will lose.

   A. The court rules that United is not a holder in due course. Why? Is it because they had notice of the problems, or is it because they didn't pay value? Or can't you tell?

   B. In fact, the decision does not say. Why is that? The reason is that the Court assigns the "burden of proof" of "due course" status to the bank, and the bank never came forward with the proof of either element. The bank's failure even to try to prove its case indicates to the Court that it was not a holder in due course. Was it fair for the law to put that burden on the bank? After all, they are seeking "special treatment", so it does seem fair to require them to prove their status. And they are the ones in possession of the proof.

   C. The foregoing, at least, is true as to the payment of value. But what of the lack of notice? How does one prove the negative? And how "innocent" does the bank have to be? Does the bank have to show it conducted a diligent inquiry that showed no problems, or can it establish its holder in due course status without an inquiry. The answer is that the bank needs to conduct no inquiry, it need only show that no one notified it of problems, and there was no hint of problems on the face of the documents.

      1. Is that rule, the so-called "white heart, empty head" test, wise? Don't we encourage fraud by not making banks responsible for conducting a diligent inquiry into the underlying transaction (and the goods) before lending money? Or would requiring inquiry discourage something else, a thing we want to encourage? What could that be?

      2. Note that the buyer in <u>Cambridge</u>, as soon as it suspected fraud, notified not only the seller, but also United Bank, that it was cancelling the contract. Why did it do that? What effect does such notice have? Suppose, for example, that United extended financing to Duke (the seller) after it received the notice from Cambridge by discounting the drafts. Would the bank have been able to win? Since that is what happened here (at best), United cannot win.

4. Note where we have come. If we are going to have an exception to the "independence principle" for cases where the seller is trying to defraud the buyer, we need an exception to the exception for those who, without notice of problems, provide export financing by discounting drafts. We have done all that.

A. Are you satisfied that we have reached an acceptable compromise between the interests of sellers, buyers and banks? The issuing bank is happy because it is not stuck in the middle, as it was in <u>Maurice O'Meara</u>. And banks that provide export financing are protected from the "fraud in the transaction" defense to letter of credit payments by their holder in due course status. Buyers (and banks) are protected against those who would defraud, and the court will protect the seller by demanding a plausible allegation of fraud before enjoining payment even preliminarily. Who could be unhappy?

B. How about a seller who doesn't get paid (as he bargained for), who is being dragged into court in the buyer's jurisdiction to defend an injunction action. The court that granted the preliminary injunction made its order "ex parte", without the seller being present. The seller has not even had a chance to dispute the charge of fraud (which, at this stage, is not well-defined), and he has not yet been found guilty, yet he doesn't have his money, and he is looking at cost, and perhaps some time, at a minimum, before he gets it. Does he think this is fair? Can anything further be done to satisfy him?

5. One answer to the question posed at the end of 4.B. (above) regarding the general wisdom and fairness of issuing these injunctions is that the bar has set been high enough to protect him from nearly all his legitimate concerns. The buyer's influence with the bank has been removed. A judge, a public servant, will review the allegations before ordering payment stopped. And the standard that must be met is "fraud", not mere breach of contract. Isn't that enough?

A. What, by the way, is meant by fraud? How is it distinguished from breach of warranty or breach of contract? Is it simply a really-bad breach, or is it something more? We need to establish a good definition.

B. Even with a good definition of fraud, is the bar still set too low? How can it be raised without damaging the level of justice we have acheived for the buyer?

C. The answer to these two questions is explored in the case which follows. Both arise out of recent geo-political events, underscoring our earlier comment that international contracts can be affected by such events, and that the law of international trade is likely to be made in such cases. The first case involves the revolution in Iran, and it is highly informative about the way courts look, today, at letter of credit cases.

IV. GETTING THE INJUNCTION: IRREPARABLE HARM AND A LIKELIHOOD OF SUCCESS ON THE MERITS

ROCKWELL INTERNATIONAL SYSTEMS, INC.,
v.
CITIBANK, N.A. and BANK TEJARAT,

United States Court of Appeals for the Second Circuit
719 F.2d 583
October 11, 1983, Decided

JUDGES: Friendly, Oakes, and Cardamone, Circuit Judges.

OAKES, Circuit Judge.

Citibank, N.A. (Citibank), and Bank Tejarat (Tejarat) appeal from an order granting a preliminary injunction issued by the United States District Court for the Southern District of New York, Vincent L. Broderick, Judge, on October 15, 1982, and from a second order, entered by Judge Broderick on March 1, 1983, denying appellants' motion to vacate the prior order. The October 15 order enjoined Tejarat from making, and Citibank from honoring, demands under two letters of credit issued by Citibank in favor of Tejarat to secure the performance of plaintiff Rockwell International Systems, Inc. (Rockwell), under a contract between Rockwell and the Ministry of War of the Imperial Government of Iran. The gist of Rockwell's case is that, as a result of the revolution in Iran and its aftermath, it was prevented by the new government in Iran from completing performance of the contract and that the subsequent calls by Iranian officials at Tejarat on the letters of credit were fraudulent. Judge Broderick denied the defendant-appellants' motion to vacate a temporary restraining order that had remained in effect by consent of the parties since May 5, 1980, and, after finding that Rockwell's showing satisfied the requirements of probable success on the merits and irreparable harm, granted the preliminary injunction. Tejarat and Citibank appeal; Rockwell cross-appeals that portion of Judge Broderick's order requiring it to indemnify Citibank against any damages resulting from the injunction. We affirm.

*　　*　　*

Background

In September of 1977 Rockwell entered into Contract 120 (the contract) with the Ministry of War of the Imperial Government of Iran. Under the contract Rockwell was to provide engineering and advisory services and material in connection with the establishment of a communications system in Iran. Article 7.1 of the contract required that Rockwell submit to the [Ministry of War] one or several Bank Guarantee[s] issued by one of the Iranian Bank[s] accepted by the [Ministry], which [sic] the total amount of them to be equal to 10% of the total amount of the Contract ... for the correct performance of the Contract....

Accordingly Tejarat's prerevolutionary predecessor, Iranians' Bank, issued two guarantees totalling $2,364,782 in favor of the Imperial Government to secure Rockwell's performance. These guarantees were in turn backed up by two letters of credit in favor of Iranians' Bank issued by Citibank at Rockwell's behest, thus establishing the four-corner arrangement customary in international transactions of this sort, involving what are commonly referred to as "standby letters of credit." See Getz, Enjoining the International Standby Letter of Credit: The Iranian Letter of Credit Cases, 21 Harv.Int'l L.J. 189, 198-200 (1980).

The events surrounding the Shah's fall and the seizure of the American Embassy in Iran need not be recounted here; suffice it to say that Rockwell, in a letter dated February 1, 1979, invoked the force majeure clause of Contract 120, demanded an extension of completion time and offered to "discuss th[e] matter ... by telephone ... or ... in Iran, as soon as circumstances permit." A meeting between Rockwell representatives and the Ministry of War, now called the Ministry of Defense, took place in Tehran on September 22, 1979, at which time Rockwell proposed that it be paid $3,159,400 for work to date and that the contract be terminated. This proposal was rejected, but neither Tejarat nor Citibank dispute Rockwell's contention that the Iranian representatives at the meeting "made it clear that they expected no further performance from [Rockwell] pending further negotiations, the termination of Contract 120, and the execution of new contracts." Although Rockwell arguably could have cancelled the contract, thus securing release of the letters of credit, it instead indicated its willingness to complete performance.

By November of 1979 relations between Iran and the United States had become hostile; in response to the embassy seizure, President Carter froze all Iranian assets on November 14, 1979. Diplomatic relations with Iran were severed on April 7, 1980, and the Iranian Assets Control Regulations, 31 C.F.R. §§ 535.101-535.904 (1982), were broadened so as to prohibit virtually all transactions between Iranian and American nationals. On April 25, 1980, Rockwell was informed by Citibank that it had, on March 31 and April 22, received Tejarat's demands for payments under the letters of credit.[8] Rockwell immediately filed suit, and on May 5, 1980, obtained a temporary restraining order preventing Citibank from honoring the demands.

Discussion

As a threshold matter we emphasize that we deal here only with the propriety of interim, i.e., preliminary, injunctive relief. Judge Broderick's order did not permanently enjoin Citibank from paying Tejarat's demands under the letters of credit and, except to the extent necessary to review the finding of probability of success on the merits, we do not address the merits of the issues involved in the contractual dispute or the continued validity of the letters of credit.

We reject at the outset Tejarat's argument that, by virtue of the January 19, 1981, "Hostage Agreement" establishing the Iran-United States Claim Tribunal (Tribunal), United States courts lack jurisdiction to grant preliminary injunctive relief. The Assets Control Regulations promulgated by the Executive Branch to implement the Tribunal Agreement prohibit only a "final judicial judgment or order (A) permanently enjoining, (B) terminating or nullifying, or (C) otherwise permanently disposing of any interest of Iran in any standby letter of credit...." 31 C.F.R. § 535.504(b)(3)(i) (1983). As the "supplementary information" accompanying this regulation makes clear, the purpose of the regulation "is to preserve the status quo by continuing to allow U.S. account parties to obtain preliminary injunctions or other temporary relief to prevent payment on standby letters of credit...." 47 Fed.Reg. 29,529 (1982). Although Iran is currently challenging the validity of this regulation before the Tribunal at least until such time as that body rules, precedent, as well as prudence, counsel deference to the Executive's view that preliminary injunctive relief is not inconsistent with the agreement establishing the Tribunal.

Having determined that the district court had the authority to grant the preliminary injunction, we next address whether it properly did so in this case. In this circuit a movant must make a "showing of (a) irreparable harm and (b) either (1) likelihood of success on the merits or (2) sufficiently serious questions going to the merits to make them a fair ground for litigation and a balance of hardships tipping decidedly" in its favor. We turn first to the question of irreparable harm.

1. IRREPARABLE HARM

Tejarat and Citibank argue that Rockwell has failed to show that in the absence of an injunction it would suffer irreparable harm because it could seek recovery either in a claim filed with the Tribunal or in a suit filed wherever Iran has assets subject to attachment. The defendants also argue that the plaintiff is not entitled to injunctive relief since "[a]ll that Rockwell has at stake is money," Citibank Br. at 18, and the availability of a remedy at law precludes a finding of irreparable injury. Although it is true that Rockwell, as the moving party, bears the burden of proving irreparable injury, we do not think it is necessary for Rockwell to show that without an injunction "rigor mortis [would] set in forthwith." We note, for example, that a remedy at law may be considered inadequate when the amount of damages would be difficult to prove, and it

---

8. The earlier demands were construed by Citibank as not conforming to the requirements of the letters of credit and were rejected.

would thus seem, a fortiori, that the same conclusion follows when the very availability of a forum is called into question. Our assessment of irreparable harm in the context of this action thus necessitates an inquiry into whether Rockwell does indeed enjoy the prospect of a real, rather than merely speculative or illusory, opportunity to press its claims elsewhere.

Judge Broderick's decision to grant the preliminary injunction was based largely on his finding that it was "highly probable that the Hague Tribunal will refuse to accept jurisdiction over plaintiff's claims." The letters of credit represent separate contractual undertakings that are, in legal contemplation, wholly distinct from whatever performance they ultimately secure. This is not merely an analytic nicety; the "independence" principle is an example of legal form following commercial function, and it is recognized in domestic as well as international law. Thus, it is far from clear that it has jurisdiction over Rockwell's claims against the defendants here, particularly those involving Citibank.

The availability of relief in other forums to which Rockwell might turn is even more problematic. Again, the forum selection clause in Rockwell's contract on its face compels resort to Iranian courts, and we note that it is possible, perhaps even probable, that other jurisdictions would reach a conclusion contrary to the Tribunal's, and decline to exercise jurisdiction. Neither Tejarat nor Citibank argues that the post-revolutionary Iranian judicial system is capable of affording an adequate remedy; courts that have passed on this contention have consistently rejected it.

We have little difficulty in distinguishing this case from our decision in KMW International v. Chase Manhattan Bank, N.A., 606 F.2d 10 (2d Cir.1979), a case in which we held preliminary injunctive relief inappropriate. In KMW the relief requested was essentially declaratory; no demands had been made on the letters of credit and any future damage was, at that time, "purely conjectural." Id. at 15. In the instant case, demands have, of course, been made, and the prospect of injury is immediate. It is also worth noting that, despite our holding in KMW that allegations regarding the then "unsettled situation in Iran" were insufficient to justify an injunction, we were willing to grant "a more limited form of relief," in the form of a notice requirement which would allow the plaintiff "to provide evidence of fraud or to take such other action" as might be appropriate in the event of a call. Id. at 16-17. Again, the posture of this case, arising as it does in the context of a wholesale series of calls on similar letters in other Iranian transactions,[9] leaves us with little doubt as to the certainty of injury and, therefore, the need for injunctive relief.

Finally, we see no merit in Tejarat's contention that Rockwell would suffer no injury because Citibank's payments under the letters would initially be made into a "blocked" account pursuant to current regulations. 31 C.F.R. § 535.508 (1982). These accounts are "blocked" in both directions, and their disposition is largely, if not entirely, a matter of Executive prerogative. Since the irreparability of

Rockwell's injury is measured, at least in part, by its ability to recoup payments made under the letters, we see little distinction between paying Tejarat directly and paying into blocked accounts. If we accept Tejarat's claim that Rockwell has little to lose if payments are made into such accounts we must at the same time conclude that Tejarat has little to gain and accordingly resolve doubt on this score in favor of preserving the status quo.

2. SUCCESS ON THE MERITS

The letters of credit issued here were by their very terms subject to the Uniform Customs and Practice for Documentary Credits (UCP). Although the UCP does not explicitly provide for a "fraud in the transaction" defense, New York law—the defendants have not argued that New York law is inapplicable or directed us to any Iranian law on this point—recognizes the availability of this defense under the UCP.

The "fraud in the transaction" defense marks the limit of the generally accepted principle that a letter of credit is independent of whatever obligation it secures. No bright line separates the rule from the exception, to be sure, but we agree with Rockwell that "fraud" embraces more than mere forgery of documents supporting a call. *Cf. United Bank Ltd. v. Cambridge Sporting Goods Corp.*, ("fraud in a required document" rejected in favor of "fraud in the transaction" by drafters of U.C.C. § 5-114(2)). The logic of the fraud exception necessarily entails looking beyond supporting documents, and this renders Tejarat's argument that the letters provide for unconditional payment unpersuasive, if not irrelevant. In this case, as in the leading case of *Sztejn v. J. Henry Schroder Banking Corp.*, we must look to the circumstances surrounding the transaction and the call to determine whether Tejarat's call amounted to an "outright fraudulent practice." *United Bank Ltd.*

In *Sztejn* and *United Bank Ltd.*, sellers called letters of credit after shipping goods—in the *Sztejn* case, garbage—that were clearly non-conforming, thus frustrating completion of the contract by non-performance. In the present case, the Iranian Ministry of Defense is in the position of a "buyer" and it has, for its own reasons, frustrated completion of the contract by suspending Rockwell's performance. We think that the essence of the fraud exception is that "the principle of the independence of [a] bank's obligation under the letter of credit should not be extended to protect" a party that behaves so as to prevent performance of the underlying obligation, [citing] *Sztejn*; the "fraud" inheres in first causing the default and then attempting to reap the

9. In a memorial filed with the Iran-United States Claim Tribunal on April 18, 1983, the United States noted that Iran had outstanding 230 claims based on stand-by letters of credit and similar undertakings issued by U.S. banks. . . . Of course, there may have been even more calls made than claims filed.

benefit of the guarantee. On this view of the fraud exception it is not necessary for Rockwell to demonstrate that either Tejarat or the Ministry of Defense acted deceitfully or with malicious intent. *Cf. SEC v. Capital Gains Research Bureau, Inc.*, 375 U.S. 180, 193, 84 S.Ct. 275, 283, 11 L.Ed.2d 237 (1963) (law of "fraud has not remained static .... It has varied ... with the nature of the relief sought, the relationship between the parties, and the merchandise in issue. It is not necessary in a suit for equitable or prophylactic relief to establish all the elements required in a suit for monetary damages.").

In deciding that Rockwell will probably be able to demonstrate that the call in this particular case was fraudulent we are necessarily influenced by the fact that this demand is not an isolated occurrence. While we may agree in principle with Tejarat's contention that the economic or political motivations of a letter of credit beneficiary are irrelevant, as a practical matter the fact that calls have been issued wholesale tends to support Rockwell's contention that these letters—issued to secure its "good performance"—were called for reasons entirely unrelated to that performance and were therefore fraudulent. Accordingly, we agree with Judge Broderick's conclusion that there is sufficient probability of success on the merits of the fraud claim to justify injunctive relief, although not necessarily because the guarantees were released under the contract when performance was suspended. Finally, we agree with Judge Broderick, for the reasons expressed below, that Tejarat was not a "holder in due course" of the letters and was therefore not entitled to avoid the fraud in the transaction defense. See UCC Section 5-114(2)(a).

3. ROCKWELL'S CROSS-APPEAL

Judge Broderick's order of March 1, 1983, requires Rockwell to indemnify "Citibank and its affiliates against any and all consequential damages Citibank and its affiliates may suffer, directly or indirectly, as a result of Citibank's compliance with this court's preliminary injunction...." Pursuant to the order, Citibank is required in any action or proceeding for payment under the letters either to "give Rockwell an opportunity to assume or participate in its defense or ... conduct its own defense with due diligence and reasonable prudence, so that [the] court's interlocutory judgment" with respect to fraud will be "adequately represented." Rockwell argues on its cross-appeal that, as a condition of indemnification, Citibank should be ordered to turn over to Rockwell its defense against claims of nonpayment made in the Tribunal or elsewhere. Rule 65(c) of the Federal Rules of Civil Procedure states that "[n]o restraining order or preliminary injunction shall issue except upon the giving of security by the applicant"; indemnification is, in short, a condition precedent to the grant of a preliminary injunction. The district court's order strikes us as eminently fair and we have no reason to believe that Citibank will shirk its obligation to present the fraud defense adequately, capably and with its best efforts.

Orders affirmed.

NOTES AND QUESTIONS

1. <u>Rockwell</u> is one of a series of business cases arising out of the political changes in Iran in the late 1970s. Many of these cases, including <u>Rockwell</u>, involve the so-called "stand-by" letter of credit. Before exploring the legal issues which are addressed in <u>Rockwell</u>, it is first useful to explore the mechanics and use of standby letters of credit.

    A. It is not unusual, in large scale construction projects or in the manufacture and installation of custom machinery or technological systems, for the parties to contract for a large downpaymnent at the beginning of the project, with progress payments along the way, and a significant final payment upon completion. In this way, the seller is assured that his basic costs are covered along the way; the buyer is assured of completion by the large payment which only has to be made at the end.

    B. In such a circumstance, it is the <u>buyer</u> who seeks protection the form of a guarantee. Typically, the buyer is seeking one of two types of protection: a guarantee that the downpayment will be returned if the job is not completed and/or a guarantee that, if the seller does not deliver, the buyer will receive a payment that will permit him to finish the job without additional cost. Domestically, as well as internationally, insurance companies have historically played the role of trusted guarantor, and the insurance guarantee is called a "surety bond" or "completion bond".

    C. Of course, the issuance of such guarantees is big business for the insurance industry - and the banks wanted to get in on the action. Banks, however, do not issue surety bonds, but they do issue third-party guarantees, in the form of letters of credit. Thus, the standby letter of credit is designed to take the place of a surety bond; how well it does so is a part of the lessons to be learned here. But in learning these lessons, we also learn about letters of credit generally, particularly the role of courts in "stopping payment".

2. The <u>Rockwell</u> decision addresses full-blown the requirements that must be fulfilled in order to obtain an injunction against payment of a letter of credit. To some extent, the question had been addressed in <u>Sztejn</u>, but, as we saw, the propriety of such injunctions was not passed upon by the New York Court of Appeals in <u>United Bank v. Cambridge Sporting Goods</u>. Nevertheless, the "fraud in the transaction" defense was established as law in <u>Sztejn</u> (albeit by a lower court). In 1960, the "defense" was codified in the United States with passage of the Uniform Commercial Code ("UCC"). In <u>Rockwell</u>, the court explains the two requirements for the issuance of injunctions: (1) proof that, absent an injunction, the plaintiff "irreparableharm" and (2) proof of a likelihood of "success on the merits." For purposes of explanation, we will here treat the second element before the first, because it is the one with which we have become most familiar.

3. The requirement of a probability of success "on the merits" in the context of these cases means a probability of being able to prove "fraud in the transaction". Judge Oakes, referring to <u>Sztejn</u>, thus begins his search for an "outright fraudulent practice". As Judge Oakes' decision explains, the term "fraud in the transaction" is broader than simply "forged documents"; it encompasses what Cardozo called "false documents", <u>i.e.</u> what we might call "a fraudulent presentation of genuine documents." But, as we asked before, how should we define "fraudulent presentation", or "outright fraudulent practice"?

A. Of course, fraud is a concept well-known to the common law; its elements typically include falsity; materiality; reliance; and a malicious or deceitful intent. In this regard, fraud is markedly different from breach of contract, which has no requirement of culpability. But exactly what is meant by "deceitful intent"?

1. The court notes, paranthetically that the law of fraud has not remained static; that it varies with the nature of the relief sought, the relationship between the parties, and the merchandise at issue; and that, when a suit seeks prophylactic relief, all the elements of fraud need not be proven with same the rigor as when the suit seeks a money judgment.

2. What does that all mean? Is it a blurring of the otherwise clear line between fraud and mere breach of contract? Is there a danger that, by viewing the definition of fraud expansively, the court is "lowering the bar" too much?

B. Notwithstanding the suggestion that the court has eased the standard for fraud in these cases, isn't the elasticity suggested by the court important to the underlying purpose: doing justice and acheiving the 'right' approach in a given case? After all, as <u>Rockwell</u> demonstrates, not every letter of credit/stop payment case is going to involve shipping rubbish in place of goods. As the facts of <u>Rockwell</u> shows, letters of credit have different uses - shouldn't the standard vary depending on the use? Or do you believe that consistency and predictability are more important?

C. In the end, the court in <u>Rockwell</u> makes no real attempt to define the term "outright fraudulent practice". Rather, the court takes a more inductive approach - it looks at what happened and then uses those observations to reach a conclusion that the demand for payment by Iran was fraudulent. Perhaps as was the case with "pornography" to Justice Potter Stewart, the Second Circuit appears confident that, even though it may not be able to define fraud, it knows it when it sees it. What facts, then, does the court marshall to support its conclusion that there was fraud? Put another way, what proof of fraud by Iran was present in the case? Identification of that proof will help in being able to understand the "fraud in the transaction" concept.

D. Of course, if one is to take this inductive approach, it is useful to see more examples, but the Second Circuit offered none in <u>Rockwell</u>. Fortunately for students of the subject, another case would soon come along - the <u>Semetex</u> case (which follows). In that case, the definition of fraud is examined, and that case serves a good example from which can discern a good definition of fraud.

4. Aside from the requirement of proof of fraud, in <u>Rockwell</u> the Second Circuit discusses the other requirement for an injunction - proof of irreparable harm. It is an old concept, going back to the development of early English jurisprudence, but it nevertheless plays an important role today.

A. The purpose of the irreparable harm requirement is to insure that the extraordinary relief called "injunction" will only be granted in cases where it is really necessary. The concept is that unless it can be shown that the plaintiff is about to suffer irreversible damage, courts should not place restrictions on freedom of action.

B. Here the action sought to be enjoined is the payment of money by the bank to the beneficiary of the letter of credit. If no injunction were allowed, the beneficiary would be paid (automatically and in all cases) by the bank. If the buyer wanted to recover that payment, he could sue on the underlying contract, and, if the court agrees with the buyer, the court can give judgment to the buyer for the money paid (as the House of Lords did in <u>The Julia</u>). That result should not be especially troubling, because, after all, that was the arrangement between the buyer and the seller in the first place (see <u>Biddell</u>).

C. But if, on the other hand, the party who procured the LC can show that such a judgment would be unobtainable, or, as a practical matter worthless, an injunction would be proper because it is the only thing that will prevent the harm from occuring. What facts did Rockwell point to as proof of irreparable harm? Do you think many buyers in ordinary LC transactions will be able point to similar facts in their situations, or do you think that, in ordinary commercial cases, proof of irreparable harm will be difficult to sustain? If your answer is that it is going to be more difficult, have we raised the bar to a height with which most sellers can live?

5. A final observation to be made in <u>Rockwell</u> is the role of Citibank in the case. At first, they sided with Rockwell, and tried to resist the demand for payment. Then they denied having done so, and switched sides, supporting the Iranian cause. Does that seem strange? Why are they siding with the outlaw Iran over their customer? What lesson does this teach about the point of view of banks issuing letters of credit?

A NOTE ON THE UNIFORM CUSTOMS AND PRACTICES
OF THE INTERNATIONAL CHAMBER OF COMMERCE

The International Chamber of Commerce ("ICC") is a private organization headquartered in Paris. One of its functions is that it promulgates a document known as the Uniform Customs and Practices ("UCP"). The UCP, as the court mentions in Rockwell, is not law. Rather, it is an internationally recognized and accepted statement expression of the meaning of standardized terms (such as CIF) and a statement of the general understanding of the obligations and incidents of international trade.

It is not unusual, indeed it was the case in both Rockwell and United Bank v. Cambridge Sporting Goods, that the contract between the parties (and the letter of credit as well) stated that it would be governed by the UCP. In this manner, the UCP is given the force of law as between the parties.

As the court noted in Rockwell, the Uniform Commercial Code ("UCC"), which is U.S. law, expressly states that, in cases of conflict, its provisions will give way to the provisions of the UCP if the parties so agree. The court also observed that the UCP is silent on whether "fraud in the transaction" is a defense to payment of a letter of credit, leaving doubt as to whether the court would apply the "fraud in the transaction" defense at all.[10]

The court's ruling was, however, that despite the fact that the UCP has no "fraud in the transaction" provision, under New York law at least, fraud in the transaction is a defense even in cases which are decided under the UCP.[11]

In 2000, New York (and the other states) adopted a modified and modernized series of statutes governing Letters of Credit. These new statutes replaced the previously-existing UCC Article 5 with a new Article 5. This new version made no important substantive changes in any of the subjects addressed in this Chapter. Nevertheless, the new statutory scheme:

---

10. A separate set of international trade "rules" is the United Nations Convention on the International Sale of Goods ("CISG"). The CISG is a treaty that has been ratified by many trading nations, including the United States. It creates rules for international sales contracts that supplant local law in transactions between nationals of countries that have signed the treaty. The focus of the CISG is not on letters of credit, however, and it does not materially change anything discussed in these two chapters. Rather it addresses issues arising from other aspects of the trade contract, particularly (a) formation (i.e. was a contract made) and (b) remedies for breach. As such, the provisions of the CISG (which derive from a combination of U.S., British and German commercial law) do not conflict with the UCP or the principles established here.

11. This particular issue, aside, there is minimal conflict between the UCP and the UCC, at least for a practical matter. One odd difference (which was recently eliminated) is that the UCC provides that all letters of credit shall be "revocable" unless they expressly state that they are "irrevocable". The UCP provides the opposite. The chaos this might seem to cause is, in practice, nonexistent: letters of credit are, by their nature, always intended to irrevocable, and they all expressly so provide.

1. Articulates (in (new) 5-103(d)) the "independence principle" more clearly than did (old) UCC 5-114(a);

2. Expressly states that an application for an injunction for fraud in the transaction must be accompanied by proof ("information"), not mere allegations, *and* requires that the fraud be "material" (new 5-109(b));

3. Banks are to apply the Rule of Strict Compliance (discussed infra) when examining documents for conformity with a Letter of Credit's requirement (new 5-108(a)); and

4. The time for the bank to honor or dishonor was extended from three (3) banking days to seven (7) calendar days.

There are other additions, including one that permits Letters of Credit that call for acceptance to provide that, following acceptance, no injunctions against payment may issue. The relevant portions of new Article 5 of the UCC are appended to this Chapter as Document 2.4

Relevant excerpts from the UCP are appended at Document 2.5.

THE BRITISH VIEW

The fraud-in-the-transaction doctrine, codified in the UCC and applied by U.S courts, albeit sparingly, has its roots in Cardozo's Maurice O'Meara defense. The UCP, as we saw in Rockwell, is silent on the question. What about Great Britain? They didn't have Cardozo - but do they have the fraud-in-the-transaction doctrine (or some form thereof)?

The answer is nicely articulated by by the Court of Appeal in *Hamzeh Malas & Sons v. Imex Industries Ltd*. The case involved the sale of reinforced steel rods from a British exporter to a Jordanian importer. According to the contract of sale, payment was to be by confirmed by Midland Bank Ltd., London. The contract of sale called for shipment (and payment) in two installments. The first installment was sent, and the drafts were honored by the bank upon presentment. When the goods arrived, however, buyer claimed that they were not of the contracted-for quality and that there were deviations from the contract specifications.

When the second installment was shipped, the buyer tried to prevent payment of the second draft by Midland Bank.

On December 9, 1957, one day before the letter of credit expired, buyer applied ex parte to the Court of Queens's Bench for an injunction to restrain seller from drawing on the letter of credit or receiving any money under it. The court granted an injunction to run until 2:30 p.m. on December 10, i.e. one half hour before expiration of the letter of credit. On the morning of December 10, the Jordanian buyer applied for an extension of the injunction until the dispute between the buyer and the seller could be adjudicated; the buyer pointed out that it was not seeking an order against the bank but only against the seller. The court refused to extend the injunction. At 12:30 p.m. buyer brought an appeal; at 2:45 p.m. the Court of Appeal gave judgment.

> JENKINS L.J: [I]t seems to be plain enough that the opening of a confirmed letter of credit constitutes a bargain between the banker and the vendor of the goods, which imposes upon the banker an absolute obligation to pay, irrespective of any dispute there may be between the parties as to whether the goods are up to contract or not. An elaborate commercial system has been built up on the footing that bankers' confirmed credits are of that character, and, in my judgment, it would be wrong for this court in the present case to interfere with that established practice.

> There is this to be remembered, too. A vendor of goods selling against a confirmed letter of credit is selling under the assurance that nothing will prevent him from receiving the price. That is of no mean advantage when goods manufactured in one country are being sold in another. It is, furthermore, to be observed that vendors are often reselling goods bought from third parties. When they are doing that, and when they are being paid by a confirmed letter of credit, their practice is – and I think it was followed by the defendants in this case –to finance the payments necessary to be made to their suppliers against the letter of credit. That system of financing these operations, as I see it, would break down completely if a dispute as between the vendor and the purchaser was to have the effect of "freezing," if I may use that expression, the sum in respect of which the letter of credit was opened.

> I agree with Mr. Gardiner that this is not a case where it can be said that the court has no jurisdiction to interfere. The court's jurisdiction to grant injunctions is wide, but, in my judgment, this is not a case in which the court ought, in the exercise of its discretion, to grant an injunction. Accordingly, I think this application should be refused.

> SELLERS L.J: I agree, but I would repeat what my Lord has said on jurisdiction. I would not like it to be taken that I accept, or that the court accepts, the submission if it was made, as I think it was, that the court has no jurisdiction. There may well be cases where the court would exercise jurisdiction as in a case where there is a fraudulent transaction.

PEARCE L.J. I agree.

Appeal dismissed.

V. Defining Fraud

As we have seen, by following the decision in <u>Rockwell</u>, the stage has been set for a full understanding of letters of credit. They serve as an important guarantee to the seller that he need not fear shipping in advance of payment, because a bank has "guaranteed" the payment against documents out of its own funds. Because the seller knows he can secure the appropriate documents, nothing can prevent the seller from being paid. This fact is of no small advantage in the world of international trade, where banks finance both imports and exports on a large scale every day.

Of course, because of the fallout from Cardozo's dissent in <u>Maurice O'Meara</u>, there is one thing that can prevent payment - an injunction from a court for fraud in the transaction. As we saw, banks that provide financing are protected as holders in due course, but sellers are not. Protection comes in the form of the high standards for issuance of an injunction - irreparable harm and a probability of success in proving fraud.

Injunctions aside, there remains the issue of whether a bank can, if it chooses, **elect, on grounds of fraud,** to not pay on a letter of credit even though the presented documents conform. From <u>Rockwell</u>, we learn that banks would rarely do so, because those banks which do serious international letter of credit business want to be seen standing by their credits, not backing their customer. Are there any cases in which banks might, notwithstanding this desire to appear neutral, choose to dishonor a conforming presentation and risk being sued by the beneficiary? If so, what can the bank claim? Can it claim fraud in the transaction? A review of UCC 5-114(2)(b) and the next case will answer that question.

Returning then to the general topic of fraud in the transaction, the only weakness we have identified so far is with the definition of fraud. We have, so far, taken a loose approach, but, if we are to be successful in understanding it and confining it to an appropriate set of circumstances, we need to better define it. Of course, that is the job that courts are constantly being called upon to perform, and new variations on facts are likely to keep arising so long as there are those bent on committing the offense.

One interesting example of such a case is <u>Semetex v. UBAF Arab American Bank</u>. Not only is it instructive on the meaning of fraud, it is instructive about several other topics, including shipment by air, the need to pay attention to details, and the availability of the fraud to defense to issuing and confirming banks. It will also bring us full circle to the cases we looked at Chapter 1.

SEMETEX CORPORATION and EATON CORPORATION,
v.
UBAF ARAB AMERICAN BANK,

United States District Court for
the Southern District of New York
853 F. Supp. 759
June 2, 1994

SAND, J.

Plaintiffs Semetex Corporation ("Semetex") and Eaton Corporation ("Eaton") bring this diversity action to compel payment on an international letter of credit issued by the Central Bank of Iraq and confirmed by Defendant UBAF Arab American Bank ("UBAF"). The controversy between the parties arises out of an extraordinary accident of timing — the fact that Iraq invaded Kuwait, and President Bush froze all Iraqi assets in the United States, at the very time that equipment manufactured by Eaton and procured by Semetex was en route from Austin, Texas to the purchaser in Baghdad in satisfaction of the contract underlying the letter of credit. As a result of the assets freeze, the equipment was diverted to a warehouse in Massachusetts (where it remains today), and UBAF refused to honor Plaintiffs' transport documents, which evidenced consignment of the equipment to an international carrier as the letter of credit required.

Semetex and Eaton brought this action only after applying twice for licenses from the Office of Foreign Assets Control ("OFAC"), the agency within the United States Department of the Treasury responsible for administering the Iraqi assets freeze. Plaintiffs' first attempt, an application with UBAF's consent for a license that would allow UBAF to pay Plaintiffs from its Iraqi assets, was unsuccessful. Plaintiffs' second attempt, for a narrower license allowing them to sue UBAF without OFAC's intervention, was successful, and in January 1993 Plaintiffs brought this action.

In April 1993, Plaintiffs' initial motion for summary judgment was denied. Following subsequent discovery, Plaintiffs moved again for summary judgment, and UBAF cross-moved. The cross-motions for summary judgment require us to consider the scope of the so-called "independence principle" governing documentary letters of credit, which provides that letters of credit impose obligations on participating parties independent of the contracts underlying them. In particular, the motions hinge on two issues: 1) whether Plaintiffs' recovery is barred by the Iraqi sanctions order and subsequent regulations; and 2) if not, whether UBAF has submitted evidence of fraud by Plaintiffs sufficient to excuse its obligation under the Letter of Credit. For the reasons set forth below, we answer "no" to both questions, and accordingly we grant Plaintiffs' motion for summary judgment and deny UBAF's cross-motion.

1. FACTUAL BACKGROUND

On a motion for summary judgment, we must view the facts in the light most favorable to the non-moving party, and resolve all ambiguities and draw all reasonable inferences against the moving party. In this case, both parties have cross-moved for summary judgment. Since we ultimately conclude that Plaintiffs' summary judgment motion prevails, we view Plaintiffs as the moving party for purposes of the analysis that follows, and accordingly resolve all factual ambiguities and draw all reasonable inferences against them. Drawing all reasonable inferences against Plaintiffs, the essential facts are as follows.

In 1988, Semetex entered into a written technology transfer agreement with the Al-Mansour Factory in Baghdad, Iraq ("Al-Mansour"), an enterprise owned and operated by the government of Iraq. In the contract, Semetex agreed to provide Al-Mansour with manufacturing equipment and technical services related to the upgrading of Al-Mansour's antiquated circuit-manufacturing facility. Among the required equipment was the item at issue in this dispute — an "ion implanter," a highly sensitive, custom-made piece of equipment used to mark circuitry pathways on microchips. Payment to Semetex was to be made through an irrevocable documentary letter of credit issued by an Iraqi bank and confirmed by a bank in the United States. The Central Bank of Iraq issued the letter of credit in February 1990 in the amount of $ 7,462,500 in favor of Semetex (the "Letter of Credit"). UBAF confirmed the Letter, which was fully collateralized by a cash deposit made by the Iraqi bank.

Semetex engaged Eaton to manufacture the ion implanter to Al-Mansour's specifications. In July 1990, with the ion implanter complete, Semetex executed an irrevocable Assignment of Proceeds directing UBAF to pay $ 720,000 of Semetex's first drawing on the Letter of Credit to Eaton as payment for the machine. At roughly the same time, through an agent, Semetex engaged a freight-forwarding company to ship the equipment from Eaton's factory in Austin, Texas to Baghdad. For reasons that the parties dispute, the shipment was scheduled in several stages — the initial leg was by United Van Lines from Austin to John F. Kennedy International Airport in New York, followed by a Lufthansa flight to Frankfurt and a connecting Iraqi Airways flight to Baghdad.

On August 1, with the truck carrying the ion implanter from Austin on its way to JFK, the freight forwarder hired by Semetex presented a set of transport documents to UBAF along with a drawing request for $ 964,640.81, representing Semetex's second attempt to obtain payment under the Letter of Credit for the ion implanter (it had tried and failed a few days earlier due to discrepancies in its documents). That night, while Semetex was awaiting payment on the Letter of Credit and while the truck carrying the ion implanter was approaching Baltimore, Iraq invaded Kuwait. Early on the morning of August 2, President Bush issued Executive Order No. 12722, blocking Iraqi assets in the United States.

The freeze order abruptly derailed the ion implanter transaction. Eaton called United Van Lines and asked that, in order to comply with the assets freeze, the shipment be diverted to Eaton's warehouse in Massachusetts, and United complied. UBAF then refused payment on the Letter of Credit. Plaintiffs subsequently applied to OFAC for a license that would allow payment to be made from Iraqi assets. Following OFAC's denial of their application, Plaintiffs applied for a narrower license allowing them to sue UBAF without OFAC's intervention for payment from the bank's unblocked (non-Iraqi) assets. OFAC granted Plaintiffs' application, and this litigation ensued.

Most of the material facts in this dispute concern the following topics: 1) the fairly elaborate shipping arrangements for the ion implanter, arranged through several intermediaries and then abruptly interrupted by the Iraq crisis; 2) the Letter of Credit, and Plaintiffs' unsuccessful efforts to draw on it; and 3) the Iraqi sanctions regulations and Plaintiffs' license applications. These are described in turn below, with all reasonable inferences drawn in favor of UBAF.

A. SHIPMENT OF THE ION IMPLANTER

Following completion of the ion implanter in June or July 1990 at Eaton's Austin factory, Eaton had the equipment picked up by Central Forwarding, an Austin moving company. Central Forwarding packaged the equipment for air transport and held it at its Austin facility pending shipping instructions from Semetex.

In order to facilitate the shipment of the ion implanter and other equipment ordered by Al-Mansour, Semetex engaged a logistics consultant, Michael Courtemanche. Courtemanche in turn engaged Alison Transport, Inc., a New York-based freight forwarder ("Alison"), to arrange shipment of the ion implanter. Robert Feldman of Alison contacted Iraqi Airways and informed a booking agent of the proposed shipment. Iraqi Airways at that time flew into only one airport in the United States, John F. Kennedy International Airport in New York ("JFK"). Additionally, the Iraqi Airways agent informed Feldman, the ion implanter was too large to be carried on the Iraqi Airlines flight from New York. Accordingly, the agent booked the equipment on a July 29 Lufthansa flight from JFK to Frankfurt, and from Frankfurt on a connecting Iraqi Airlines flight to Baghdad.

Feldman was unable to transport the equipment from Austin to New York by air because no air carrier servicing Austin at that time flew a plane large enough to transport the ion implanter. Feldman therefore arranged for the equipment to be transported by truck from Austin to JFK Airport. Feldman scheduled the equipment to be picked up at Central Forwarding in Austin on July 26 and delivered to Lufthansa at JFK in time for the July 29 flight. When a truck arrived at Central Forwarding on July 26, however, Central Forwarding personnel declared it unsatisfactory for transporting the sensitive equipment.

They informed Feldman that Central Forwarding was an agent for United Van Lines ("United"), and that United could supply an "air ride" truck which would provide a smoother ride that would be more appropriate for the job. Accordingly, Feldman arranged with Central Forwarding to have a United "air ride" truck pick up the equipment on July 31 for delivery to JFK. Feldman informed Iraqi Airways of the delay and rebooked the equipment on the Lufthansa flight scheduled to depart on August 2 for Frankfurt and to meet a connecting Iraqi Airways flight to Baghdad.

On July 31, United picked up the ion implanter at Central Forwarding in Austin and began the journey to JFK Airport. In the early morning hours of August 2, President Bush issued Executive Order 12722, freezing all Iraqi assets within the United States and prohibiting all shipments from the United States to Iraq. Upon learning of the Iraqi sanctions, Richard Landwehr of Eaton's Austin factory took steps to ensure that the shipment would not violate the Executive Order. After consulting with Eaton's headquarters in Cleveland, Landwehr contacted Central Forwarding to find out where on its route the equipment was and whether shipment to Iraq could be prevented. After consulting with United headquarters and requesting a written request from Eaton, United ordered its driver to deliver the shipment to Eaton's factory in Beverly, Massachusetts rather than to JFK Airport. The ion implanter never reached the Lufthansa terminal, where an Alison Transport employee was waiting with the transport documents to meet the shipment. Accordingly, neither the equipment nor the transport documents were ever consigned to the possession of Iraqi Airlines or its designated carrier, Lufthansa.

Shortly after the Iraqi sanctions order was issued, Semetex sent a telex to Al-Mansour informing it that delivery of the ion implanter had been prevented by the sanctions. Al-Mansour replied by telex instructing Semetex to continue to hold the equipment until the sanctions were resolved. On or about August 6, the ion implanter was delivered to Eaton's Beverly warehouse, where it has remained in storage ever since. Eaton reported the equipment to OFAC as blocked Iraqi property owned by Al-Mansour.

B. COMPLIANCE WITH THE LETTER OF CREDIT

The Letter of Credit, an irrevocable documentary letter of credit, required that drawing requests be accompanied by specific documents evidencing shipment of goods by the beneficiary, Semetex, to the account party, Al-Mansour. The Letter of Credit, as amended, required that, in order to obtain payment for goods under the Letter of Credit, Semetex must, among other requirements: (1) submit to UBAF (a) commercial invoices and a certificate of origin, attested and "legalized" (that is, officially stamped); and (b) an air waybill (a type of bill of lading for shipment by air, see N.Y. U.C.C. § 1-201(6) (McKinney 1993)) evidencing air shipment, freight prepaid, from the United States to Baghdad via Iraqi Airways or carriers authorized by Iraqi Airways; and (2) send a telex cable to Al-Mansour advising Al-Mansour of the flight number and date of arrival at the Baghdad airport. Notably, the Letter of Credit did not require an "on-board" bill of lading or other evidence that control of the ion implanter had passed to a designated carrier before payment could be made. Instead, payment was conditioned solely on Semetex's presentation of the air waybill and other documents specified by the Letter of Credit.[12] THIS CREDIT IS SUBJECT TO THE UNIFORM CUSTOMS AND PRACTICE FOR DOCUMENTARY CREDITS (1983 REVISION) INTERNATIONAL CHAMBER OF COMMERCE PUBLICATION NO 400 . . . .

The air waybill issued by Feldman of Alison Transport, covering the transport of the equipment from Austin to Baghdad, is at the center of the controversy between the parties. The source of the controversy, in part, is that the air waybill was created not by Iraqi Airways, the designated carrier, but by Alison Transport, Semetex's freight forwarder. A freight forwarder, a "travel agent for boxes," books space for freight shipments by its customers on carriers of commercial freight, much as a regular travel agent does with passengers. Alison was not a carrier or shipper of goods, but merely arranged transport by others. Alison was hired by, reported to, and was to be paid by Courtemanche, Semetex's logistics consultant. While Alison was not itself a carrier, though, it was authorized by Iraqi Airways to issue air waybills on its behalf, and Iraqi Airlines had issued blank air waybills to Alison Transport for this purpose.

By the time Alison presented the air waybill to UBAF, the original shipment schedule had been altered. Central Forwarding, Eaton's local freight company, had turned away the flatbed truck that arrived to pick up the ion implanter on July 26, and Feldman had scheduled a United Van Lines "air ride" truck to pick up the ion implanter on July 31 for delivery to JFK. Because of the five-day trucking delay, the original July 29 flight to Frankfurt had been rescheduled to August 2. When he prepared the air waybill, however, Feldman did not list the revised flight numbers and dates, but instead jotted down a curious amalgam. In the boxes marked "Flight/Date," he filled in "4220/31" and "232/02." "4220" apparently referred to Lufthansa flight 4220 from JFK to Frankfurt — the flight originally booked — and "232" apparently referred to the flight with which flight 4220 had been scheduled to connect, Iraqi Airways flight 232 from Frankfurt to Baghdad.

One would expect the numbers paired with these flight numbers — "31" and "02" — to refer to the dates of these flights, either before or after rescheduling, but they do not. July 31 was neither the date of the originally scheduled flight 4220 (scheduled for July 29) nor of the rescheduled flight from JFK (set for August 2); instead, it was the date on which the United Van Lines truck was scheduled to pick up the ion implanter in Austin. The second date — "02,"

---

12. The Letter of Credit (Defendant's Exhibit 1) is in the form of a telex cable from the Central Bank of Iraq to

apparently referring to August 2 — does not, as one would expect, refer to the date of the flight number with which it is paired, 232. Flight 232 was the originally scheduled flight from Frankfurt to Baghdad. Instead, August 2 was the date of the rescheduled flight from JFK to Frankfurt. To make matters even more unclear, Feldman listed as the "airport of departure" on the air waybill not JFK Airport but Robert Mueller Airport in Austin, which was never intended to be a port of departure for the shipment. On the line reserved for the signature of the issuing carrier or its agent, the air waybill purports to show a signature, dated July 24, 1990, on behalf of "Iraqi Airways, Robert Mueller Airport, Texas" — a signature which was apparently made by a representative of Alison Transport.[13]

When the air waybill, telex, and other shipping documents were presented to UBAF for payment on July 27, the bank, not surprisingly, found several internal inconsistencies and accordingly rejected the documents as not in conformity

---

13. In explanation, plaintiffs assert that by industry usage an air waybill, unlike the typical bill of lading, does not purport to evidence actual shipment dates and locations, but instead evidences merely that the seller has fully prepaid the shipment from point of origin to final destination. UBAF contests this. Given the summary judgment posture of the case, we follow UBAF's interpretation in our description of the facts. UBAF, dated February 5, 1990. It states in pertinent part (typographical errors reproduced as in original):

. . . WE ESTABLISH OUR IRREVOCABLE LETTER OF CREDIT NO 89/3/356 IN THEIR [Semetex's] FAVOUR FOR ACCOUNT OF AL MANSOUR FACTORY BAGHDAD UPTO THE AGGREGATE AMOUNT OGF USDOLLARS7462500/ . . . . AVAILABLE FOR IN USA VALID UNTIL 20.3.1991 AGAINST THEIR RECEIPT OR SIGHT DRAFT DRAWN ON US ACCOMPANIED BY DOCUMENTS SPECIFIED HERE-BELOW MARKEDWITH THIS CREDIT NUMBER

1. DOCUMENTS REQUIRED

A. BENEFICIARYS SIGNED COMMERCIAL INVOICES . . .

B. CERTIFICATE OF ORIGIN . . . .

C. AIRWAY [sic] BILL SHOWING PARCELS MADE OUT IN THE NAME OF OUR BANK MARKED WITH CLIENT'S NAME AND MARKED FREIGHT PREPAID PARCELS SHOULD BEAR BUYERS NAME AND LETTER OF CREDIT NUMBER.

2. EVIDENCING IN SEVERAL LOTS OF THE FOLLOWING GOODS: TECHNOLOGY TRANSFER AND SUPPLY OF SUPPLEMENTARY PROCESS EQUIPMENT AS CONTRACT SIGNED ON 21/12/1988

3. FROM USA TO C AND F BAGHDAD BY IRAQI AIRWAYS OR CARRIERS AUTHORIZED BY IRSQI [sic] AIRWAYS NOT LATER THAN 20/11/1989 [subsequently amended to March 20, 1991]

. . . .

10-TSPECIAL INSTRUCTION:

. . . .

C. ON DATE OF DESPATCH THE BENEFICIARIES SHOULD CABLE BUYERS ADVISING NAME OF AIR COMPANY FLIGHT NUMBER AND EXPECTED DATE OF ARRIVAL ALSO THEY SHOULD DIRECTLY AIR MAIL TO THE BUYERS COPIES OF THE DOCUMENTS FOR EACH SHIPMENT IN ADDITION TO THE DOCUMENTS REQUIRED UNDER THIS CREDIT.

with the terms of the Letter of Credit. The most significant of these discrepancies was that between the dates of shipment listed on the air waybill and those noted in the accompanying telex. While the air waybill listed flight dates of July 31 and August 2, the telex to Al-Mansour, dated July 24 and presented to UBAF for payment on July 27, stated that the ion implanter was to be dispatched on a July 26 Iraqi Airways flight which was scheduled to arrive in Baghdad on July 29 — a flight date three days earlier than the flight originally booked and seven days earlier than the August 2 flight eventually booked from JFK.

Before presenting the document package to UBAF a second time, Alison employees revised the shipping documents to fix the internal inconsistencies that the bank had noted. In particular, Alison changed the flight dates on the air waybill to conform to the flight dates represented in the telex — July 26 and 29 — which at that time were clearly no longer accurate (if indeed they ever were). Feldman then had the document package redelivered to UBAF, along with a sight draft for $ 964,640.48, repr esenting 80 percent of Semetex's charge to Al-Mansour for the ion implanter, of which $ 720,000 had been assigned as payment to Eaton. The bank received the documents on August 1. The parties dispute whether Courtemanche called the bank that afternoon and was informed by a UBAF employee that the documents complied with the Letter of Credit's terms and that UBAF would honor Plaintiffs' sight draft the following day.[14] The following day, of course, was too late. On August 2, UBAF telephoned Alison Transport and stated that, due to the issuance of Executive Order 12722, it would not make payment.

2. LETTERS OF CREDIT AND THE INDEPENDENCE PRINCIPLE

Under New York law, letters of credit are governed by N.Y. U.C.C. article 5. Article 5, however, provides that it is superseded by the Uniform Customs and Practice for Documentary Credits (the "UCP") promulgated by the International Chamber of Commerce, in cases where a letter of credit, by its terms or by agreement, course of dealing, or trade usage, is subject to the UCP. N.Y. U.C.C. § 5-102(4) (McKinney 1991). The UCP is not legislation or a

---

14. Courtemanche testified in his deposition that he called UBAF's Letter of Credit Department between 3 and 4 p.m. on August 1 to inquire about payment of the sight draft. He testified that he was told (by a man whose voice he recognized but whose name he did not obtain) that the documents complied with the terms of the Letter of Credit and had been accepted for payment by the bank, but that payment could not be made until the following day because it was too late in the day. UBAF, however, disputes the veracity of Courtemanche's testimony and offers in opposition an affidavit by the head of the payment section in its letter of credit department, declaring that no written record of any such communication exists in UBAF's files. Affidavit of Genaro Mesina, filed with the Court on March 22, 1993, P 15. Given the summary judgment posture of this case, we must conclude that UBAF has raised a triable issue and, for purposes of this motion, conclude that UBAF made no representations about the transport documents over the telephone.

treaty, but a compilation of internationally accepted commercial practices, which may be incorporated into the private law of a contract between parties. In this case, both the Letter of Credit and UBAF's confirmation Provide expressly that they are governed by the 1983 Revision of the UCP, ICC Pub. No. 400; thus, the UCP governs both of them.

The basic letter-of-credit mechanism involves three or, as in this case, four parties: (1) the customer (or "account party"), who opens an account with (2) the issuing bank, which authorizes (3) the confirming bank to make payment to (4) the beneficiary, upon the beneficiary's presentation of certain documents specified in the letter of credit. See UCP art. 2 (1983); In this case, the customer was Al-Mansour; the issuing bank was the Central Bank of Iraq; the confirming bank was UBAF; and the beneficiaries were intended to be Semetex and (under Semetex's assignment of proceeds) Eaton.

Employed frequently in international transactions, the letter of credit is a device whereby the customer and the beneficiary — who are parties to an underlying contract (generally buyer and seller respectively) but face each other over a distance — substitute the credit of the intermediate banks, one in the country of each party, for the buyer's credit. The device gives the seller (the beneficiary) immediate payment from a local bank upon shipment of the goods; merely by presenting to the confirming bank documents evidencing shipment of the ordered goods, the seller receives payment. The central principle of letter-of-credit transactions is the so-called "independence principle": letters of credit, "by their nature, are separate transactions from the sales or other contract(s) on which they may be based and banks are in no way concerned with or bound by such contract(s)." UCP art. 3.

As is commonly noted, the parties to a letter-of-credit transaction "deal in documents, and not in goods, services and/or other performances to which the documents may relate." UCP art. 4; Thus, the issuing or confirming bank must honor a proper demand even though the beneficiary has breached the underlying contract, even though the insolvency of the account party renders reimbursement impossible, and notwithstanding supervening illegality, impossibility, war or insurrection. This independence principle is universally viewed as essential to the proper functioning of letters of credit and to their particular value. The central purpose of the letter-of-credit mechanism would be defeated if courts felt free to examine the merits of underlying contract disputes in order to determine whether letters of credit should be paid. Id.

A. UBAF'S FRAUD CLAIM

Alternatively, UBAF invokes the fraud exception to the letter-of-credit independence principle. UBAF admits that the documents presented to it on August 1, 1990 complied on their face with the requirements of the Letter of Credit. It contends, however, that the documents were in compliance only because Plaintiffs misrepresented the flight information on the air waybill and forged the signature of an Iraqi Airways representative. Alison noted flight dates of July 26 and 29 on the air waybill when it made its second drawing attempt on August 1, UBAF contends, even though Alison and Plaintiffs knew that the ion implanter had only been picked up by truck in Austin on July 31 and that it was not scheduled to reach JFK Airport until August 2. UBAF contends that these discrepancies rise to the level of "outright fraudulent practice" that is required under New York law to supersede the independence principle.

Plaintiffs contest this assertion. They argue as well that UBAF, by stating and then repeatedly reconfirming that Plaintiffs' documents complied with the Letter of Credit's requirements, and by joining Plaintiffs in their initial license application, waived its right to assert a fraud defense. As described below, we conclude that triable issues of fact remain about whether UBAF waived its fraud defense with full knowledge of the material facts. We conclude, however, that UBAF has failed to present evidence of fraudulent intent motivating the discrepancies in Plaintiffs' documents. Since UBAF does not contest that Semetex's transport documents complied on their face with the Letter of Credit's terms, UBAF's failure to raise triable issues regarding fraud is dispositive.

2. "Outright Fraudulent Practice"

Fraud provides a well-established exception to the rule that banks must pay a beneficiary under a letter of credit when documents conforming on their face to the terms of the letter of credit are presented. See Rockwell Int'l Systems, Inc. v. Citibank, N.A; United Bank Ltd. v. Cambridge Sporting Goods Corp.; Sztejn v. J. Henry Schroder Banking Corp. The exception has been codified in New York U.C.C., which provides that an issuing bank may refuse to honor documents which "appear on their face to comply with the letter of credit terms" but for which "a required document . . . is forged or fraudulent or there is fraud in the transaction." N.Y. U.C.C. § 5-114(2) (McKinney 1991) (emphasis added). Although the UCP does not explicitly provide for a "fraud in the transaction" defense, New York law nevertheless recognizes the availability of this defense with regard to letters of credit governed by the UCP.

The fraud defense, however, is a narrow one. The defense is available only where intentional fraud is shown, not where the party alleges improper performance or breach of warranty. Id. It does not apply, for example, to situations in which performance of the underlying contract has been interrupted by "supervening illegality, impossibility, war or insurrection." Traditionally, it was restricted to situations in which the drafts presented under a letter of credit were forged or fraudulently procured, but the defense has gradually expanded. As the Second Circuit stated in Rockwell:

> The "fraud in the transaction" defense marks the limit of the generally accepted principle that a letter of credit is independent of whatever obligation it secures. No bright line separates the rule from the exception, to be sure, but . . .

> "fraud" embraces more than mere forgery of documents supporting a call. The logic of the fraud exception necessarily entails looking beyond supporting documents . . . . We must look to the circumstances surrounding the transaction and the call to determine whether [the] call amounted to an "outright fraudulent practice."

The courts have found such "outright fraudulent practice" only rarely. UBAF relies in particular on two cases within this circuit in which fraud has been found, Rockwell and Prutscher v. Fidelity Int'l Bank, 502 F. Supp. 535 (S.D.N.Y. 1980). Rockwell was one of the letter-of-credit cases to arise out of the Iranian hostage crisis and the resulting Iranian Assets Control Regulations, 31 C.F.R. part 535 (1993); see generally Getz, Enjoining the International Standby Letter of Credit: The Iranian Letter of Credit Cases, 21 Harv. Int'l L.J. 189 (1980). In these cases, United States and other western contractors had obtained the issuance of so-called "standby letters of credit" (equivalent to performance bonds) in favor of the pre-revolutionary government of Iran. These credits were issued to guarantee the contractors' performance under certain construction and supply contracts; if the contractors failed to complete performance under the contracts, the Iranian government could draw upon the credits at an Iranian bank by presenting documents evidencing the non-completion of the contracts.

After the fall of the Shah and the United States' imposition of sanctions on the new Iranian government, the western contracting parties invoked force majeure as a defense to their inability to continue to perform. In response, the Iranian beneficiaries attempted to draw on the standby letters of credit. In Rockwell, the Second Circuit upheld the district court's injunction against payment on the grounds of fraud. The Second Circuit found that the call by the Iranian Ministry of Defense on a standby letter of credit did in fact amount to an "outright fraudulent practice" because Iran "first caused the default and then attempted to reap the benefit." Id. at 589. The court found it significant that the call was one of scores of calls that were made by the Iranian government after its actions prevented performance of large numbers of international contracts. It concluded that that circumstance "tended to support Rockwell's contention that these letters — issued to secure its 'good performance' — were called for reasons entirely unrelated to that performance and were therefore fraudulent." Id.

UBAF relies as well on Prutscher, 502 F. Supp. 535, in which Judge Bonsal upheld the right of a confirming bank to refuse to honor a letter of credit on the ground of fraud. In that case, the bank confirmed a letter of credit issued by a Lebanese bank in favor of Prutscher, as seller of certain laboratory furniture. The letter of credit required that a full set of bills of lading be presented to the issuing bank before funds could be released, showing shipment of the furniture from Italy; partial shipments were prohibited, and an expiration date was set for shipment of the furniture. Prutscher presented the bank with a bill of lading that apparently represented that the furniture was exported in one timely shipment. However, on motion for summary judgment, uncontroverted evidence was presented which demonstrated that the furniture was in fact shipped in three partial shipments, one of which sailed from Italy after the expiration date. The court granted summary judgment in favor of the bank on the basis of the evidence that the bill of lading was fraudulent. It stated:

> A bank which has confirmed a letter of credit is not required to honor a draft presented thereunder if a bank receives information that a bill of lading required by the letter is forged or fraudulent and that the presenter is the original beneficiary or is otherwise chargeable with participation in the alleged fraud.

UBAF argues that Prutscher is "virtually on all fours" with the case before us. As in Prutscher, UBAF argues, the beneficiary (Semetex) presented a false air waybill to the confirming bank (UBAF) purporting to evidence shipment and export days earlier than in fact the shipment was scheduled. The air waybill was dated July 24 and signed by Iraqi Airways at Robert Mueller Airport in Austin, Texas, purporting to evidence consignment to that carrier on that date and a flight on July 26. In reality, by August 1, the ion implanter had not been delivered to the designated air carrier, Lufthansa. UBAF claims that Plaintiffs "never, in fact, complied with the most basic requirement of the Letter of Credit," that is, delivery of the ion implanter to the designated air carrier. Instead, UBAF claims, Plaintiffs "forged an airway [sic] bill allegedly signed by the air carrier in a fraudulent effort to obtain payment in advance of any right on their parts to be paid."

Although UBAF raises evidence of substantial discrepancies between the actual facts of the ion implanter's transport and the information on Semetex's transport documents, we conclude that UBAF has not presented evidence that rises to the level of "outright fraudulent practice" described in Rockwell and Prutscher. In particular, evidence of Plaintiffs' fraudulent intent is lacking.

UBAF has presented no evidence that, as in Rockwell, Plaintiffs "first caused the default and then attempted to reap the benefit of the guarantee." In contrast to Rockwell, where the beneficiary was the very Iranian government that caused the default, the beneficiaries in the case before us, Semetex and Eaton, defaulted on their obligations on the underlying contract because of an event over which they had absolutely no control — the Iraqi assets freeze.

UBAF likewise has presented no evidence that, as in Prutscher, 502 F.Supp. at 536, Plaintiffs either 1) failed to comply with an explicit term of the letter of credit or 2) did so with intent to defraud. Central to the holding in Prutscher was the fact that one of Prutscher's shipments sailed from Italy after the letter of credit's expiration date, and that Prutscher falsified a bill of lading in order to make it appear that the ship had sailed on time so that he could obtain payment under the letter of credit. Id. The materiality of the misrepresentations, in other words, suggested fraudulent intent. In the case before us, that is not the case. Unlike in Prutscher, UBAF has presented no evidence that Plaintiffs' alleged "forgery" of dates and a signature on the air waybill was material to the requirements of the Letter of Credit or was committed with intent to defraud.

There is no dispute that Eaton in fact manufactured an ion implanter to Al-Mansour's specifications, and there is likewise no dispute that, had it not been for the invasion of Kuwait and the subsequent Iraqi sanctions orders, the equipment would have reached its destination in Baghdad long before the Letter of Credit's revised expiration date of March 20, 1991. UBAF has presented no evidence of fraud in the five-day delay caused by the arrival of an inappropriate truck to pick up the equipment. Likewise, they have presented no evidence of fraudulent intent behind the seven-day discrepancy between the July 26 departure date represented on the air waybill and the actual planned flight date of August 2, and have presented no evidence that that discrepancy would have been material in any way in the absence of the unannounced invasion of Kuwait. Similarly, they have presented no evidence of fraudulent intent behind Plaintiffs' signing the air waybill as agents of Iraqi Airways and designating Robert Mueller Airport as the point of departure.

In this regard, it is significant that the Letter of Credit did not specify that shipment in the United States must begin at Robert Mueller Airport, or otherwise specify how the equipment was to be moved within the United States. We reject UBAF's contention that Plaintiffs' efforts to transport the ion implanter from Texas to New York "are totally irrelevant to the shipment required by the express terms of the Letter of Credit because "it is the air shipment from the United States to Iraq — by Iraqi Airways or another air carrier authorized by Iraqi Airways — that is significant under the letter of Credit — not the many myriad steps that may lead up to that event." Def.'s UBAF offers no authority in support of their assertion, and we have been able to find none. To the contrary, the UCP, which by the terms of the letter of credit governs this case, does not assign significance to the date of delivery to a designated air carrier unless the parties expressly incorporate such a term into their letter of credit. Instead, unless the parties stipulate otherwise in the letter of credit, the date of shipment under a letter of credit is deemed to be the date of issuance of the transport document (here, the air waybill) — that is, the date of issuance indicated on the air waybill.

In sum, none of the discrepancies on which UBAF focuses would have been material to Plaintiffs' ability to draw on the Letter of Credit if the parties' plans had not been unexpectedly dashed by the invasion of Kuwait and the subsequent freezing of Iraqi assets. Prutscher would be analogous to this case only if Semetex had had foreknowledge of the invasion of Kuwait and the resulting freeze of Iraqi assets, and so had conspired with Alison to falsify the dates on the air waybill in order to draw on the letter of credit funds before actually shipping the ion implanter. Of course, no such evidence was presented. Instead, the evidence that was submitted is closer to the facts in the New York case cited above, Fertico, 100 A.D.2d 165, 473 N.Y.S.2d 403, in which no fraud was found. We describe the case in some detail because its reasoning is applicable to the case before us.

As in this case, Fertico concerned certain discrepancies between the actual facts of shipment and the information provided on the bill of lading and confirming telex, discrepancies that the court determined did not rise to the level of fraud. The underlying contract in Fertico called for fertilizer to be shipped to the buyer in Antwerp. The contract did not specify an arrival date in Antwerp, but the buyer stated that time was of the essence. The letter of credit, which, as here, was subject to the UCP, specified shipment from "East or Gulf U.S. Port" to Antwerp and required an on-board ocean bill of lading "dated on-board not later than November 8, 1978" and a telex to the buyer "advising name of ship, sailing date, weight and Eta Antwerp, the same date as end of loading, and certified true." The seller booked the cargo on a ship and issued on-board bills of lading indicating loading on November 8 (the required date). The seller also sent the buyer a telex stating that the ship sailed on November 8 and was due in Antwerp on December 4. As it happened, the ship did not in fact leave port until three days later, November 11, and did not arrive in Antwerp until December 17, 13 days later than the telex represented and apparently too late for the buyer to be able to complete a planned resale. Id. at 406. The seller nevertheless presented the shipping documents to the confirming bank and was paid by the bank. The buyer sued, alleging that the telex contained "fraudulent misrepresentations."

The court rejected the buyer's claim. It concluded that the discrepancy between the date of the bill of lading and the date of sailing was immaterial, since under the UCP, the date of an onboard bill of lading is considered to be the date of shipment. Additionally, it concluded, the ship's late date of arrival was immaterial, since the letter of credit did not specify a delivery date. Other allegations of fraud by the buyer concerning details of the shipping arrangements (such as that the ship stopped to pick up additional cargo and then did not give priority in unloading to Fertico's cargo) were "matters totally extraneous to the text of the letter of credit and irrelevant to its interpretation." Id. at 407. Thus, the misrepresentations in Fertico, which, if anything, were more material than the evidence of misrepresentations in the case before us (given that the buyer in Fertico specified that the time of shipment was of the essence), were nevertheless found not to rise to the level of fraud. We conclude that UBAF likewise has raised no triable issue of fact with regard to its fraud defense.

UBAF raises an additional argument related to its fraud defense, which we also find to be without merit. UBAF asserts (Def.'s Reply Mem. at 6) that title and control over the ion implanter never changed hands since the shipment was never consigned to a carrier under the control of the buyer, such as Lufthansa (Iraqi Airways' designated carrier), but instead remained in the control and possession of United Van Lines, a carrier arguably acting as Plaintiffs' agent. If title did not pass, they contend, to require UBAF to honor a draw on the Letter of Credit would subject Al-Mansour to the type of risk that it expressly sought to eliminate when it specified that the ion implanter be placed in the custody of a designated carrier before the seller could draw on the Letter of Credit.

We agree that UBAF raises an issue of fact about whether title to the ion implanter ever passed from Semetex to Al-Mansour. However, this is not dispositive of the matter before us. Whether title and control of the equipment passed to Al-Mansour, and whether Al-Mansour successfully drafted a letter of credit that protected itself against the risks it sought to avoid, is not materially related to UBAF's duties under the Letter of Credit. Had Al-Mansour wished to assure that no draw could be made on the Letter of Credit until control of the ion implanter passed to a carrier of its choice or until air passage was under way, it could have required an "on board" bill of lading in the terms of the Letter of Credit (see UCP art. 27) or specified any other set of conditions that it desired. As for UBAF, its obligations under the Letter of Credit are fully collateralized by its Iraqi accounts, even if it cannot reach those accounts until the Iraqi sanctions are lifted.

The parties are thus left with the rights and obligations they bargained for: Semetex bargained for the right to be paid from UBAF's non-Iraqi assets, and UBAF attempted to protect itself against the risk of nonpayment by the Iraqi bank by fully collateralizing its obligation to Semetex. The parties having thus entered into the Letter of Credit arrangement, the material question regarding UBAF's liability is not whether control of the ion implanter had passed to Al-Mansour at the time that Plaintiffs attempted to draw on the Letter of Credit; rather, the question is whether UBAF has demonstrated either that the documents presented by Semetex failed to satisfy the Letter of Credit's terms, or that they were forged or fraudulent or there was fraud in the transaction. As set out above, UBAF admits that the documents satisfy the Letter of Credit's terms on their face, and it has failed to present evidence from which a reasonable factfinder could conclude that the fraud exception applies.

CONCLUSION

For the reasons set forth above, we conclude that Plaintiffs have demonstrated that they are entitled to judgment as a matter of law, and that UBAF has failed to present evidence in support of its two affirmative defenses sufficient to create a triable issue. Accordingly, we deny UBAF's cross-motion for summary judgment and grant Plaintiffs' motion, awarding judgment to Plaintiffs as a matter of law.

NOTES AND QUESTIONS

1. As promised, the <u>Semetex</u> case is nicely instructive on the meaning of fraud. The bank (which was being sued for wrongful dishonor) argued that the (agent of the) seller committed fraud by altering the shipping document to make them conform to the letter of credit's requirements even though the agent knew the information being provided about shipping dates was false. The court considered that argument, but it rejected it. On what basis did it do so? Which "elements" of fraud were missing?

    A. The first missing element is an "intention to deceive." On what basis did the court find that proof of such intent was lacking? Consider what the freight forwarder did. We have already said that his knowledge that he was entering false information was insufficient establish fraud. Why? What more is required?

    B. To answer that question, one must attempt to define the term "intention to deceive." What is meant by that term? Is it different from the concept of "malicious intent" that the <u>Rockwell</u> court said was not a necessary element of the "fraud in the transaction" defense? Or are the two cases sufficiently different to produce different legal rules?

    C. In considering the freight forwarder's expedient conduct, it is significant that the freight forwarder was not attempting to secure a payment that he was not entitled to. As the court observes, he could not have known, when he made the change, that world events would prevent the shipment of the merchandise. Compare that observation with the Second Circuit's conclusion in <u>Rockwell</u> that Iran was committing fraud. Are you closer to understanding where the dividing line is?

    D. Consider also the distinction drawn between the facts of <u>Semetex</u> and the facts of (and result in) <u>Prutscher v. Fidelity International Bank,</u> 502 F.Supp. 535 (S.D.N.Y. 1980). What underlay the distinction between <u>Prutscher</u> and <u>Semetex</u>? Being able to articulate the answer will make the definition of fraud even clearer.

    E. Toward the end of the opinion, the court also concludes that "none of the discrepencies on which UBAF focuses would have been material to Plaintiff's ability to draw on the Letter of Credit if the parties' plans had not been interrupted by the invasion of Kuwait. . . ." Why is the court referring to the concept of "materiality"? What role does it play in the determination of in <u>Semetex</u>?

2. Aside from the issue of "what is fraud", <u>Semetex</u> is procedurally very different from <u>Stzejn</u> and <u>Rockwell</u>. In those cases, the buyer, fearing he was about to be cheated, sought an injunction, <u>i.e.</u> an order from a court, directed to the bank, not to pay. In this case, no injunction was requested, probably because the Iraqis were in no position to appear in a U.S. court. What happened, then, that got this litigation started?

    A. The answer to the previous question is that UBAF dishonored the draft. Why did it do that? Is it because its customer (Iraq) asked it to? Or did it do it for some reason internal to the bank? If you say it was the bank's doing, why would the bank refuse to pay against a conforming presentation? After all, the LC was "fully collateralized" by Iraqi deposits at UBAF.

    B. When the bank refused to pay, Semetex (and Eaton) sued for wrongful dishonor. What defenses are available to UBAF?

        1. First, consider the defense: Semetex didn't perform all its obligations under the contract with the Iraqis, especially delivering conforming goods to the designated carrier (Iraqi Airlines). Will that defense work, or would it be violative of the independence principle?

        2. How about "fraud in the transaction" (assuming the bank could prove it)? Is that defense ever available to an issuing bank? Note, once again, that no judicial intervention was sought.

            a. When we looked at <u>Stzejn</u>, we observed that acceptance of the fraud in the transaction defense was palatable, in part, because judicial intervention was required. The presence of the judge as "policeman" assured some neutrality in the decision. How then can this court even consider letting the bank act of its own accord in situations like this? Is there a danger of run-away dishonoring of drafts by banks in LC situations, are there other checks and balances in place? If you think there are such checks and balances, what are they?

    C. The fraud discussion aside, note that there is no discussion in the case of "irreparable harm". Why is that? The answer is the same as the answer to the question about differences (between <u>Rockwell</u> and <u>Semetex</u>) in the definition of fraud.

3. Aside from enhancing our understanding of the meaning of fraud and the bank's ability to raise fraud in a wrongful dishonor case, <u>Semetex</u> is instructive on the business end of international sales and letters of credit.

A. The logistics of the shipment were not thought out when the contract of sale was made, leading to confusion at the crucial moment (confusion which the seller was able to "use" to its advantage). Additionally, the letter of credit called for an ordinary "airway bill" instead of an "on board air waybill". What is the difference? How would the buyer (and the bank) have been protected if the letter of credit had specificied the latter? What lesson does it teach about letters of credit and shipments by air?

B. Eaton, which manufactured the ion implanter, acted as Semetex's supplier. What security did it have that it would be paid by Semetex upon delivery to them of the machine? The answer is that Eaton was the "assignee" of a portion of the LC issued by UBAF in favor of Semetex. Why did Eaton and Semetex structure their transaction that way? Why didn't they use the back-to-back format described earlier? What are the practical differences between the two?

4. One can, of course, compare the situtation of the bank in <u>Semetex</u> with that of the seller in <u>The Julia</u>. The court in <u>Semetex</u> wrote:

> "We agree that UBAF raises an issue of fact about whether title to the ion implanter ever passed from Semetex to Al-Mansour [the buyer]. However, this is not dispositive of the issue before us. Whether title and control of the equipment passed to Al-Mansour, and whether Al-Mansour successfully drafted a letter of credit that protected itself against the risk it sought to avoid, is not materially related to UBAF's duties under the Letter of Credit.

In what way is this situation similar to (or different from) <u>The Julia</u>? Aren't both cases separating the time and terms of payment from the issue whether the seller has done what all it was obligated to do? Put another way, do you think that Iraq could win a "failure of consideration" case against Semetex, asserting that Semetex did not ship conforming goods and/or tender a document of title? Before saying no, consider <u>Tsakiroglou</u> again. You would also need to read the contract between them (its not quoted in the case). Of course, that event may never happen because even though Iraq didn't get the goods (or documents of title), Iraq hasn't paid the price to Semetex. Iraq's money is at OFAC; UBAF paid Semetex (after this case was affirmed on appeal).

5. Finally, consider the following article from Foreign Trade magazine. The author talks not only of problems created by the doctrine of strict compliance (many letter of credit presentations contain discrepencies and are rejected), he also argues that insisting on a letter of credit in every transaction can drive away business. We know what the lawyer would say - how do you react as a business person?

VI. BUSINESS, BANKING AND THE RULE OF STRICT COMPLIANCE

THE LETTER OF CREDIT:
THE PERFECT TOOL FOR RUNNING OFF BUSINESS
by: Richard B. Loth

REPRINTED FROM: March 1994 FOREIGN TRADE MAGAZINE

If millions of words have [already been] written on letters of credit, is there really a need for more commentary?

In a word, yes. One gets the impression the letter of credit is the only way to sell abroad, particularly for the newcomer or inexperienced exporter. The common view, shared by some export credit managers and reinforced by far too many foreign risk-averse bankers, is that this is the easy, no-hassle way of doing business with, and getting paid by, foreign buyers.

For example, an article last year extolled the virtues of L/C by stating "many consider the letters of credit the most valuable tool available in the credit manager's arsenal." The author then said, "Don't let customers dictate your credit terms," implying in rather warlike terms, exporters should stick to their "L/C guns!" This dogmatic, narrow view of selecting a method of payment for foreign sales may be called the "letter of credit syndrome."

Direct experience confirms that many exporters, particularly in the United States, tend to resort to the L/C alternative - an undeniably valuable payment mechanism- simply because they haven't done their homework on country and/or customer risk. It really is an easy way out when compared to the time and effort needed to qualify foreign customers for reasonable export credit terms. It can also hurt international sales and profits.

Unquestionably, the irrevocable letter of credit is a relatively problem-free method of payment for the exporter. The foreign buyer is also offered a high degree of protection for obtaining goods to its specifications. But L/C "syndromites" tend to overlook possible problem areas. Apart from the real possibility of limiting an exporter's market potential, the perception that L/C terms are risk-free for the exporter and resolve all credit issues connected with an export transaction is questionable.

Experienced intentional trade professionals are well aware a high percentage of L/Cs presented for payment contain discrepancies. To fully appreciate this, it is worthwhile noting the results of a Chase Bank study as reported by Joseph Nielson, vice president for trade risk services. Out of a 1,000 letters of credit processed by his bank, approximately 666 were discrepant. Of these, some 222 "could not be fixed." This means that two-thirds of so-called risk-free L/C transactions end up as collection items, dependent on the integrity of the foreign buyer for ultimate payment. Roughly one-third of them are not paid, at least not through the routine L/C process. The credit implications are obvious: Know your buyer and establish some acceptable level of evaluation of its creditworthiness even if you are selling on L/ C terms.

Qualifying a foreign buyer for trade credit is not easy. Through conventional sources, company information is often difficult to come by on a timely basis, can be somewhat lacking in detail and sometimes comes at a hefty cost. Commenting on this problematical situation, a credit manager, displaying a serious case of the "syndrome," once said; "International credit reports (unspecified) aren't any good. They usually don't tell you anything worthwhile and they're too expensive. We (credit managers) find it more cost-effective and quicker to simply ask for an L/C. It's easier than trying to get the information on the foreign buyer and it doesn't cost us anything," One can appreciate the credit manager's predicament, but the expedient solution is not necessarily the best solution for *your company* for *all* its international sales.

Unfortunately, many U.S. exporters, often encouraged by their commercial bankers, consider L/C terms as the only "safe" way to sell internationally. From a business development perspective, the dogmatic adherence to letters of credit, particularly sight, confirmed L/Cs, can certainly limit your sales prospects in certain markets, industry sectors, and/or with individual customers. Look at things from the foreign buyer's perspective:

- ➲ Competitor(s) have checked out the customer's creditworthiness and qualified it for more flexible and favorable credit terms than your L/C terms. Assuming price, quality and service are more or less comparable, who would you be more disposed to do business with?

- ➲ The customer is sophisticated in international trade matters, enjoys a good credit reputation and expects reasonable payment terms from foreign suppliers. Your L/C terms may be perceived as a judgment of the company as a lesser quality credit risk, thus complicating the process of building a solid business relationship.

- ➲ In many foreign markets, the red tape and time spent on opening a L/C are cumbersome and costly, e.g., for reasons of "reciprocity" and not credit risk, account parties (your customers) are sometimes required to make substantial prior deposits toward the payment of the letter of credit. These procedural factors are legitimate customer concerns.

⊃ Amounts outstanding under L/Cs use up a customer's local credit line used for general working capital purposes. In tight credit markets, this is not an attractive prospect. Also, the accompanying high cost of borrowing in these instances prompts buyers to seek financed-assisted supplier arrangements that generally provide more reasonable credit costs, which they are generally willing to absorb.

None of the above circumstances *per se* reflects adversely on the creditworthiness of a foreign buyer. To offer appropriate payment terms, the serious exporter needs to make a concerted effort to know its foreign customers and their respective country conditions that affect the extension of export credit. The important point to remember is that a letter of credit is one of many tools that needs to be employed intelligently. Blind faith in the capabilities of a L/C can lead to potential credit problems and also limit market penetration. Rational export credit terms will translate into healthy, long-term business relationships with your foreign buyers.

THE RULE OF "STRICT COMPLIANCE"

As the author of the article notes, many document presentations are discrepant. One reason is that, as was the case in the first presentations of documents in Rockwell and Semetex, the party presenting the documents does not take care to insure that they are conforming. There is no substitute for the parties' careful inspection of contracts, letters of credit and documents when engaged in a transaction of this type. But another reason for the spate of discrepancies is that banks are required to be real sticklers for the completeness and quality of a document presentation - a rule of law known as "strict compliance".

Strict compliance means that the documents presented must be in perfect and total conformity with the requirements of the letter of credit. The rule of strict compliance exists for the protection of all parties, and it is designed to remove from the bank all aspects of discretion. And while a buyer eager to obtain goods may be willing to waive certain immaterial discrepancies (rendering the doctrine an apparent bank formality), one can understand that, at times of stress, a buyer might just use a minor discrepancy as an excuse to avoid payment.

Still, disputes in this area do pop up, because banks have adopted many customs regarding letter of credit payment, such as allowing certain abbreviations to be used for standard things, e.g. "lbs" = pounds. Since banks, customarily, would ignore such discrepancies, are they entitled to take account of them when they wish to do so. The obvious answer is no, although it is not always so obvious what banks customarily do, and thus when they must pay (or not pay) when their are minor discrepancies.

The International Chamber of Commerce is constantly answering hypothetical questions about this topic, as guidance to parties. But the best guidance is the simplest to formulate and the hardest to accomplish: the party presenting documents should take the time to insure that the presentation conforms in every respect to the requirements of the letter of credit.

MULTIPLE CHOICE REVIEW QUESTIONS

1. A letter of credit is:

   a. a negotiable instrument
   b. a document of title
   c. a promise by a bank to honor a presentment
   d. issued by a confirming bank

2. A banker's acceptance:

   a. occurs when a bank issues a letter of credit
   b. occurs when a bank confirms a letter of credit
   c. occurs when a bank pays on a letter of credit
   d. is a kind of negotiable instrument

3. A bank that dishonors a presentment under a letter of credit:

   a. can be sued for wrongful dishonor if the documents conformed
   b. can defend the case by asserting fraud in the transaction
   c. will lose to a holder in due course of a negotiable instrument that was previously accepted by the bank
   d. all of the above

4. The "fraud in the transaction" doctrine:

   a. was created in *Maurice O'Meara*
   b. exists only in New York
   c. is part of the UCP
   d. applies in the rarest of circumstances

5. A court will issue an injunction:

   a. if there is proof of either irreparable harm or a likelihood of success
   b. if acceptance has not yet occurred
   c. if there is a danger of grave injustice
   d. none of the above

PROBLEM FOR ANALYSIS

PROBLEM 1

On May 1, 2006, Sigma (a US company) contracted to sell to Beta "a Hitachi 883 Magnetic Resonance Imaging System, C&F Oman, UAE, to be shipped by airfreight from JFK Airport on or before July 1, 2006, payment against 90-day time draft drawn on a letter of credit issued or confirmed by a reputable NY bank." The price of the MRI $775,000. The LC was to expire on July 5, 2006.

On May 5, Sigma received notice that a letter of credit had been opened by Beta at Chase Manhattan Bank. The Letter of Credit designated Sigma as beneficiary, and it required presentation to the bank of "an air waybill showing that the MRI had been delivered to the airline", together with an invoice, a time draft and a certificate of origin.

On June 27, Freddie, a freight forwarder and cargo handler working for Sigma, picked up the shipment in Easton, Pennsylvania, with instructions to truck it up to JFK. Freddie then arranged the transport with British Airways and prepared an air waybill covering the shipment. Freddie then appended that air waybill to the invoice, the draft and certificate of origin, and presented them in that form to Chase for payment.

Freddie then loaded the MRI on his truck and took the MRI to New York, where he delivered it to the airline.

The plane left New York that morning with the MRI on board. The plane never arrived in Oman, having crashed off the Canary Islands. While the cause of the crash was never finally determined, neither terrorism nor foul play is suspected.

{ed: insert on p.124, at end of Problem 1, instead of (A) and (B)}

(A)   Assume you work for Beta. Draft a letter, addressed to Chase, to try to persuade them not to honor the presentment.

(B)   Write a memo to your boss describing the situation and the prospects for getting the bank not to pay.

(C)   Assume that Chase honors the presentment, and that there was neither insurance nor liability on the part of the airline. Write another memo to your boss stating what actions, if any, can be taken by Beta to recover moneys from Chase and/or Sigma.

PROBLEM 2

SBC Corp. is a Tanzanian exporter of grain. On May 1, 2006, SBC made a contract with Buy-orama, a firm of grain importers located in Xandia (which is located on the Baltic coast between the former Yugoslavia and Albania). The contract provided that SBC would sell "1,000 tons of rye to Buy-orama, FOB East African port, July 2006 shipment via ocean steamer, to arrive at St. Swivensburg [the only ocean port in Xandia], before September 1, time being of the essence." The contract further provided that "in case of war, strike or epidemic, and in all cases of force majeur preventing performance, the obligations of the parties under this contract shall be terminated." Finally, the contract called for payment by letter of credit issued or confirmed at Citibank, New York.

The letter of credit was established at Citibank on June 1. It provided for payment against drafts drawn under the letter of credit. The letter of credit further provided that it would expire on August 2, 2006, and required presentation of a bill of lading showing "shipment of 1,000 tons of rye, FOB East African port, bound for St. Swivensburg, issued on or before July 31, 2006, to arrive before September 1, 2006."

In mid-July 2006, hostilities broke out in Xandia between former communists and the recently-elected government. The former communists, using their ties to the Xandian navy, commandeered several military ships and blockaded St. Swivensburg. Because of the unstable situation, at all times relevant hereto, there was no way to know how long the insurrection, or the blockade, would last.

On July 29, SBC delivered the grain to a steamship company at Mombasa in East Africa. The agent for the shipping company indicated that a ship was in port and that it was destined for St. Swivensburg. When querried about expected arrival dates, the ship's agent stated that he was unsure when the ship would arrive because of the blockade, but that, if the blockade was lifted soon, the ship would arrive before September 1. The voyage normally takes a week.

SBC's employee indicated that SBC required a ship that was then scheduled to arrive before September 1. The ship's agent said that he could make no such promises, nor could any other captain under the current circumstances. SBC shipped the goods nevertheless, and the ship's agent issued a bill of lading showing loading "of 1,000 tons rye, FOB Mombasa, bound for St. Swivensburg." The bill of lading was dated July 29, 2006. The bill at first said nothing about the expected date for arrival of the goods. SBC's employee, however, bribed the ship's agent to include on the bill a notation that the ship was "expected to arrive before September 1."

On August 1, SBC presented the bill of lading and appropriate draft to Citibank in New York. Citibank immediately informed Buy-orama of the presentation. Buy-orama told the Citibank representative that no shipments were coming into St. Swivensburg because of the blockade; that they didn't expect it to be lifted anytime soon (indeed, it was not broken until early October); that he had a contract to deliver the grain to a bread factory before September 15;

and that if Buy-orama was forced to pay on the letter of credit, and did not receive the grain until after September 1, the company would be forced to out of business.

1.   With the letter that Citibank will sad in response.

2.   If Buy-orama applies to a New York court for an order enjoining payment by Citibank, what result would you expect?

3.   Suppose that after the bill of lading had been procured, SBC prepared the requisite draft and endorsed it over to Merchant's Bank in exchange for payment of $95,000 in cash. How would you expect a court to rule if Merchant's Bank presented these documents to Citibank, and Buy-orama applied, at that point, for an injunction?

4.   If you were SBC, would you have acted the same way as the SBC employee did on July 29? What would you have done differently?

PROBLEM 3

You are a new employee at SellCo, a New York-based exporter.

Your first assignment involves a contract to sell 1,000 tons of Grade A Portland Cement CIF Genoa (Italy) for $200/ton to (buyer) Brunello, Ltda, of Rome, Italy.

In addition to the contract of sale to Brunello, the file contains:

a.   a Letter of Credit issued by JP Morgan/Chase (NY). The LC provides that JP Morgan/Chase will accept SellCo's 90-day time draft if presented along with bill(s) of lading showing shipment of 1,000 tons of Grade A Portland Cement with freight pre-paid to Genoa, Italy, together with a certificate of inspection from the Cement Institute certifying the quality of the shipment. The LC was to expire on October 31, 2007;

b.   an original Bill of Lading from Sealand Ocean Freight Inc. covering a shipment of 1,000 tons of Grade A Portland Cement, with freight pre-paid to Genoa, dated October 23, 2007, to the order of SellCo.

c.   a paid invoice from Sealand Ocean Freight, Inc. showing a freight charge of $100/ton to Genoa for 1,000 tons of cement, shipping point Port Newark, N.J.

d.   a marine insurance policy for the shipment, showing a paid premium of $1,000.

e.   a paid invoice from NJ Cementworks in Port Newark showing a delivery to Sealand Ocean Freight, Inc. of 1,000 tons of Grade A Portland Cement, for $50/ton FOB Port Newark, N.J.

f.   an original Certificate of Inspection from the Cement Institute certifying that the shipment is Grade A Portland Cement.

Question 1:   Your boss, Mr. F. Wilpon, asks you to prepare/create the remaining documents needed to make presentment to JP Morgan/Chase. Please prepare the needed documents _and_ prepare a list (for his secretary) of which documents from the file need to be given to Sellco's bank for presentment to JP Morgan/Chase. (Prepare/create the documents and the list only - no elaborate explanation is required; you do _not_ need to prepare the documents that are already in the file, just the ones that you'll need that aren't there).

Question 2:   FOR THE REMAINDER OF THIS PROBLEM: Assume that a conforming presentment is made to JP Morgan/Chase on Monday, October 29, 2007. How (and within what time frame) would you expect JP Morgan/Chase to act on the presentment?

Question 3:   Assume that on November 27, 2007, Brunello e-mails you and states that the cement arrived, and that it is not Grade A Cement, but instead is Grade C. Grade C, he tells you, is totally inappropriate for the work Brunello does, and they say that the problem may cost them ten million euros. The e-mail shows that Brunello is angry (or trying hard to look angry), using phrases such as "you deceived us" and "we will tell JP Morgan/Chase not to pay on the Letter of Credit." Prepare a memo to Mr. Wilpon (your boss) regarding the situation, telling him what to expect if Brunello tries to prevent payment by the bank, and offering a plan of action. (Note: you know nothing about the quality of the shipment, although the inspection certificate appears to be genuine)

SUBJECTS FOR RESEARCH AND FURTHER LEARNING

1.   What are the fees for various letter of credit services? Call several banks and make inquiry.

2.   What are the special features of stand-by letters of credit? What are the different uses for such credits? Are there any banks that specialize in that type of business? Are there any organizations that provide

information or standards for stand-by letters of credit? What benefits / pitfalls do stand-by credits in comparison to performance bonds?

3. What role does the ICC play in establishing customary practices in the banking/LC industry? How has the electronic revolution affected Letter of Credit and documentary sales practices? Research the UCP, and see what subjects it covers.

DOCUMENTS
SUPPLEMENT

Document 2.1

Sample Application and Agreement for Commercial Letter of Credit

Application and Agreement
for Commercial Letter of Credit

Letter of Credit Department Please issue an irrevocable Letter of Credit in favor of the Beneficiary substantially as shown below (the "Credit") and deliver the Credit by Teletransmission, if possible.	**Letter of Credit No.** *(For Bank Use Only)*	Date / /

1. Applicant (full name and address)

2. Beneficiary (full name and address)

3. Applicant Tax ID #

4. Individual(s) Authorized to Act on Applicant's Behalf:

5. Advising Bank
(Not Required, Bank will select correspondent)

6. Amount of Credit in U.S. dollars *(put in figures and words)*

7. Credit Expiry Date: Documents to be presented to the Negotiating or Paying Bank on or before:
(mm/dd/yyyy)   /   /
(Maximum credit Expiry Date is 90 days from date of issuance)

8. Available at sight draft drawn on Bank for _____% (100% applies when left blank) of the invoice value.
(Bank may at its option waive any draft requirement)

9. Shipping Terms (check one)   ☐ FCA   ☐ FOS   ☐ CFR   ☐ CIF   ☐ Other:

10. Latest Shipping Date: /   /

11. Documents Required:

☐ Commercial Invoice in _____ original(s) and _____ copies covering merchandise described briefly below:

_____   _____

_____

☐ Certificate of Origin in _____ Original(s) and _____ copies.
☐ Insurance Policy or Certificate for 110% of invoice value covering
    ☐ all risks   ☐ warehouse to warehouse   ☐ plus any other specific risks as follows: _____
OR   ☐ Insurance to be effected by Buyer (No Insurance document will be required in the LC)

☐ Packing List in _____ original(s) and _____ copies.

12. Transport Document (select the appropriate transport document, as applicable)
☐ Multimodal Transport Document   ☐ Marine/Ocean Bill of Lading (Seaport to Seaport only)   ☐ Air Transport Document

☐ Other Transport Document as follows:

| For Multimodal Transport Document or Marine/Ocean Bill of Lading:
    ☐ Consigned to the order of
    ☐ Consigned to the order of shipper, blank endorsed
    ☐ Consigned to Applicant (if non-negotiable) | For All Other Transport Documents:
    ☐ Consigned to Applicant
    ☐ Consigned to |

Marked Notify: (Applicant's name inserted if left blank)

13 a) Place of Taking In Charge/Dispatch From/Place of Receipt	**b)** Port of Loading/Airport of Departure	**c)** Port of Discharge/Airport of Destination	**d)** Place of Final Destination/For Transportation To/Place of Delivery

Days after date of Transport
14. Documents must be presented to the negotiating or paying bank no later than: _____ document
(On board validation applicable for ocean shipment) but within the validity of the Letter of Credit. (Will be 21 days if left blank) Partial   drawings are not allowed. All bank fees and charges other than those charged by Bank are for the account of the Beneficiary.

15. Tansshipment: ☐ Permitted   ☐ Not Permitted

16. The Applicant hereby authorizes Bank to debit its account number _____ prior to the issuance of the Credit for full amount of the Credit as stated above (the "Purchase Price") plus an administration fee of $350.00.
Completion and submission of this Application by Applicant does not obligate Bank to issue the requested Credit. The Applicant hereby acknowledges and agrees that the Application shall not be deemed to have been accepted by Bank nor shall it be binding on Bank or the Applicant until the requested Credit is issued by Bank. Applicant acknowledges that Applicant has read the attached Terms and Conditions for Commercial Letter of Credit and agrees to be bound.

NOTICE OF FINAL AGREEMENT. THIS WRITTEN AGREEMENT REPRESENTS THE FINAL AGREEMENT BETWEEN THE PARTIES AND MAY NOT BE CONTRADICTED BY EVIDENCE OF PRIOR, CONTEMPORANEOUS OR SUBSEQUENT ORAL AGREEMENTS OF THE PARTIES. THERE ARE NO UNWRITTEN ORAL AGREEMENTS BETWEEN THE PARTIES.

17. Applicant
Name of Company or Individual _____
By, Authorized By: (signature)
Title
Telephone   Fax

129

Document 2.2

Sample Letter of Credit

LETTER OF CREDIT ADVICE
05/01/06

OUR REFERENCE NO: EM700182
A360139

EXPIRY DATE: 07/30/06
EXPIRY PLACE: OUR COUNTERS

LETTER OF CREDIT AMOUNT: USD 290,117.35 MAXIMUM

BENEFICIARY:
[redacted]

ISSUING BANK:
[redacted]

APPLICANT:
[redacted]

CREDIT NO. OF ISSUING BANK:
IF-45000204105

DEAR BENEFICIARY:

WE HAVE BEEN INSTRUCTED BY THE ABOVE ISSUING BANK TO ADVISE YOU THAT THEY HAVE ESTABLISHED THEIR IRREVOCABLE DOCUMENTARY LETTER OF CREDIT IN YOUR FAVOR, AS BENEFICIARY.

WE HEREBY CONFIRM THIS LETTER OF CREDIT AND THEREBY UNDERTAKE TO HONOR ALL DEMANDS FOR PAYMENT MADE IN ACCORDANCE WITH THE TERMS THEREOF. HOWEVER, NOTWITHSTANDING THE FOREGOING, OUR CONFIRMATION IS CONTINGENT UPON ALL SUCH DRAWINGS BEING RESTRICTED TO THE COUNTERS OF [BANK]. IN THE EVENT THAT DOCUMENTS ARE NOT PRESENTED AT OUR SAID COUNTERS, OUR ENGAGEMENT AND CONFIRMATION HEREUNDER WILL BECOME NULL AND VOID.

WHEN PRESENTING DOCUMENTS UNDER THIS CREDIT PLEASE INCLUDE THE ORIGINAL LETTER OF CREDIT (UNLESS RETAINED BY US) AND AN ADDITIONAL COPY OF ALL REQUIRED DOCUMENTS STIPULATED IN THE CREDIT.

DOCUMENTS MUST CONFORM STRICTLY WITH THE TERMS OF THE ATTACHED LETTER OF CREDIT. IF YOU ARE UNABLE TO COMPLY WITH SAME, PLEASE COMMUNICATE DIRECTLY WITH THE APPLICANT IN ORDER TO HAVE THE ISSUING BANK AMEND THE RELEVANT CONDITIONS. THIS SHOULD ELIMINATE DIFFICULTIES AND DELAYS IN PAYMENT WHEN YOUR DOCUMENTS ARE PRESENTED FOR NEGOTIATION.

IN THE EVENT NON-CONFORMING DOCUMENTS ARE PRESENTED HEREUNDER, A DISCREPANCY FEE WILL BE LEVIED (IN ADDITION TO OUT-OF-POCKET EXPENSES) AND DEDUCTED FROM PAYMENT PROCEEDS.

ALTHOUGH THIS LETTER OF CREDIT BEARS OUR CONFIRMATION, IF DOCUMENTS PRESENTED FOR NEGOTIATION CONTAIN DISCREPANCIES MAKING IT NECESSARY FOR US TO EITHER CABLE FOR APPROVAL OR FORWARD DOCUMENTS ON A COLLECTION BASIS, PAYMENT WILL BE MADE ONLY UPON AUTHORIZATION FROM THE ISSUING BANK OR UPON RECEIPT OF FUNDS FROM THE ISSUING/REIMBURSING BANK. IN THE EVENT THAT ACCEPTANCE OF A TIME DRAFT IS INVOLVED, ACCEPTANCE/DISCOUNT WILL BE AVAILABLE ONLY UPON APPROVAL/ACCEPTANCE OF THE DISCREPANCIES BY THE ISSUING BANK/APPLICANT.

PAYMENT WILL BE EFFECTED THREE (3) BUSINESS DAYS AFTER THE DATE OF OUR REIMBURSEMENT CLAIM TO THE REIMBURSING/ISSUING BANK OR THE DATE OF OUR TELECOMMUNICATION TO THE ISSUING BANK ADVISING THEM OF A CREDIT CONFORMING DOCUMENT PRESENTATION. IN THE EVENT THE ISSUING/REIMBURSING BANK REQUIRED A PRE-ADVICE OF PAYMENT GREATER THAN 3 DAYS, THE NUMBER OF DAYS STIPULATED IN THE CREDIT WILL SUPERSEDE THE 3 DAYS PERIOD REFERRED TO ABOVE.

NOTE TO BENEFICIARY:
FOR THE PURPOSE OF EXPEDITING THE PAYMENT PROCESS, AND TO ENABLE US TO TRACE THIS ITEM SHOULD THE NEED ARISE, ALL DOCUMENTS PRESENTED TO US FOR EXAMINATION WILL BE FORWARDED TO THE ISSUING BANK VIA D.H.L., OR OTHER COURIER SERVICE, UNLESS WE ARE INSTRUCTED BY THE BENEFICIARY/FREIGHT FORWARDER TO THE CONTRARY. COURIER EXPENSES WILL BE DEDUCTED AT THE TIME OF PAYMENT.

WHEN PRESENTING DOCUMENTS, PLEASE INDICATE ON YOUR COVER LETTER OUR REFERENCE NUMBER, ISSUING BANK'S CREDIT NUMBER AND THE METHOD OF PAYMENT FROM THE CHOICES LISTED BELOW:

1.   WIRE TRANSFER (ABA NO. OF RECEIVING BANK AND ACCOUNT NUMBER)
2.   CREDIT TO ACCOUNT WITH [BANK].
NOTE: A PROCESSING FEE WILL BE DEDUCTED FROM THE PROCEEDS FOR OPTION (1) ABOVE.

FOR YOUR CONVENIENCE, ALL DOCUMENTS FOR NEGOTIATION MAY BE PRESENTED AT ANY OF OUR U.S. PROCESSING LOCATIONS LISTED BELOW:

        [ADDRESS OF BANK]

EXCEPT AS OTHERWISE EXPRESSLY STATED HEREIN, THIS LETTER OF CREDIT IS SUBJECT TO THE "UNIFORM CUSTOMS AND PRACTICE FOR DOCUMENTARY CREDITS (1993 REVISION), INTERNATIONAL CHAMBER OF COMMERCE PUBLICATION NO. 500".

* *

U.S. GOVERNMENT REGULATIONS REGARDING FOREIGN ASSET CONTROL REGULATIONS AND EXPORT DENIAL ORDERS:

                    EXPORT CREDITS

PLEASE NOTE: UNDER THE CUBAN ASSETS CONTROL REGULATIONS AND THE FOREIGN ASSETS CONTROL REGULATIONS, PERSONS SUBJECT TO THE JURISDICTION OF THE UNITED STATES ARE PROHIBITED FROM ENGAGING DIRECTLY OR INDIRECTLY WITH ANY NATIONALS OR SPECIALLY DESIGNATED NATIONALS OF:

        CUBA, IRAN, IRAQ, LIBYA, SUDAN, AND CERTAIN PROVINCES OF AFGHANISTAN UNDER THE CONTROL OF THE TALIBAN.

* *

UNDER THE FOREIGN ASSETS CONTROL REGULATIONS, WE ARE NOT PERMITTED TO DO CERTAIN TRANSACTIONS WITH ANY NATIONALS OR

SPECIALLY DESIGNATED NATIONALS OF:

SYRIA, BURMA (MYANMAR), NATIONAL UNION FOR THE TOTAL INDEPENDENCE OF ANGOLA (UNITA), NORTH KOREA, SIERRA LEONE, AND LIBERIA.

EXCEPT AS AUTHORIZED BY THE TREASURY DEPARTMENT'S OFFICE OF FOREIGN ASSETS CONTROL, BY MEANS OF A GENERAL LICENSE. PRESENTATION OF DOCUMENTS UNDER THIS CREDIT IMPLIES THAT THE EXPORTER CONFORMS IN EVER RESPECT WITH ALL EXISTING UNITED STATES GOVERNMENT REGULATIONS AND THAT YOU ARE NOT SUBJECT TO DENIAL ORDERS CURRENTLY AFFECTING EXPORT PRIVILEGES OF PRODUCTS UNDER THE ATTACHED CREDIT

FOR FURTHER INFORMATION, PLEASE CONTACT THE OFFICE OF FOREIGN ASSETS CONTROL (202) 622-2500

* *

THIS ORIGINAL LETTER OF CREDIT IS BEING HELD AT OUR COUNTERS PENDING PRESENTATION OF DOCUMENTS FOR EXAMINATION. HOWEVER, THE ORIGINAL LETTER OF CREDIT CAN BE RELEASED TO YOU UPON RECEIPT OF $100.00 ADVISING, $45.00 COURIER FEE AND $150.00 CONFIRMATION FEE.
KINDLY SEND US YOUR CHECK OR REMIT VIA FEDWIRE TRANSFER TO ABA 026005092 OR CHIPS 0509 ATTN: EXPORT LETTER OF CREDIT DEPARTMENT QUOTING OUR REFERENCE NUMBER.
PLEASE CONTACT ONE OF OUR CUSTOMER CARE UNITS REGARDING ANY INQUIRIES TO THIS LETTER OF CREDIT:

THIS IS A COMPUTER GENERATED ADVICE. NO BANK SIGNATURE IS REQUIRED.

FOR BANK USE ONLY:

27:    Sequence of Total
       1/1
40A: Form of Documentary Credit
       IRREVOCABLE
20:    Documentary Credit Number
       IF-45000204105
31C: Date of Issue
       060427
31D: Date and Place of Expiry
       060730 U.S.A.
50:    Applicant
       [redacted]

59:    Beneficiary
       [redacted]

32B   Currency Code, Amount
       USD290,117.35
39B   Maximum Credit Amount
       NOT EXCEEDING
43P: Partial Shipments
       NOT ALLOWED
43T: Transhipment
       NOT ALLOWED
44A: Loading on Board/Dispatch, Taking in Char
       ANY PORT OF U.S.A.
44B: For Transportation to . . .
       [redacted]

44C: Latest Date of Shipment
       060720
45A: Description of Goods and/or Services
       381 KGS. DIOCTYLSEBACATE Y
       1.000 KGS. ALUMINUM POWDER SPHERICAL MIL-A-23950, TYPE 1 FOB
46A: Documents Required

FULL SET CLEAN ON BOARD OCEAN BILLS OF LADING ISSUED TO THE ORDER OF [BUYER], INDICATING FREIGHT COLLECT.
ORIGINAL AND 5 COPIES COMMERCIAL INVOICE IN THE NAME OF [BUYER] AND 5 COPIES PACKING LIST.

47A: Additional Conditions
IF THE REQUIRED DOCUMENTS EVIDENCE ALTERATIONS, THESE MUST BE SIGNED AND STAMPED BY THE ISSUER OF THE RELATIVE DOCUMENT. A DISCREPANT DOCUMENT FEE OF USD 50.00 WILL BE DEDUCTED FROM THE PROCEEDS OF ANY DRAWING IF DOCUMENTS ARE PRESENTED WITH DISCREPANCY(IES)
ALL SHIPMENT DOCUMENTS MUST INDICATE L/C NUMBER AND O/C 126570-642/06
THE BENEFICIARY MUST SEND DIRECTLY TO FAMAE BY FAX NUMBER THE FOLLOWING DOCUMENTS:
L/C NUMBER
NUMBER AND DATE OF COMMERCIAL INVOICE
QUANTITY SHIPPING
FOB TOTAL VALUE
NUMBER AND DATE OF B/L
THE NAME OF SHIP
THE NAME OF NAVY COMPANY
THIS FAX MUST PRESENT IN NEGOTIATION TO THE BANK

71B: Charges
ALL BANKING CHARGES OUTSIDE CHILE
ARE FOR BENEFICIARY'S ACCOUNT.

48: Period of Presentation
10 DAYS AS FROM SHIPMENT DATE AND WITHIN THE VALIDITY OF THIS L/C

49: Confirmation Instructions
CONFIRM

78: Instructions to the Paying/Accepting/Neg
PAYMENT MUST BE MADE ONLY AGAINST PRESENTATION OF ALL THE REQUIRED DOCUMENTS AND STRICTLY IN ACCORDANCE WITH L/C TERMS. FOR YOUR PAYMENTS KINDLY DEBIT OUR ACCOUNT WITH YOURSELVES INDICATING OUR REFERENCE.
IMPORTANT: PLEASE ACKNOWLEDGE RECEIPT INDICATING YOUR REFERENCE NUMBER ASSIGNED TO THIS L/C.

END

Document 2.3.

<u>International Sales Draft</u>

_____ DATE _____

AT _____ OF THIS SOLE BILL OF EXCHANGE

PAY TO THE ORDER OF

_____

THE SUM OF

_____

FOR THE FULL INVOICE VALUE.

VALUE RECEIVED AND CHARGE THE SAME TO THE ACCOUNT

OF _____ UNDER

LETTER OF CREDIT NUMBER

_____

TO:

_____

AUTHORIZED SIGNATURE

Document 2.4

Uniform Commercial Code (NY) 2000

§ 5-103 Scope

(d) Rights and obligations of an issuer to a beneficiary . . . under a letter of credit are independent of the existence, performance, or nonperformance of a contract or arrangement out of which the letter of credit arises or which underlies it, including contracts or arrangements between the issuer and the applicant and between the applicant and the beneficiary.

§ 5-108. Issuer's Rights and Obligations

(a) Except as otherwise provided in Section 5-109, an issuer shall honor a presentation that, as determined by the standard practice referred to in subsection (e), appears on its face strictly to comply with the terms and conditions of the letter of credit. Except as otherwise provided in Section 5-113 and unless otherwise agreed with the applicant, an issuer shall dishonor a presentation that does not appear so to comply.

(b) An issuer has a reasonable time after presentation, but not beyond the end of the seventh business day of the issuer after the day of its receipt of documents:

    (1) to honor,

    (2) if the letter of credit provides for honor to be completed more than seven business days after presentation, to accept a draft or incur a deferred obligation, or

    (3) to give notice to the presenter of discrepancies in the presentation.

(c) Except as otherwise provided in subsection (d), an issuer is precluded from asserting as a basis for dishonor any discrepancy if timely notice is not given, or any discrepancy not stated in the notice if timely notice is given.

(d) Failure to give the notice specified in subsection (b) or to mention fraud, forgery, or expiration in the notice does not preclude the issuer from asserting as a basis for dishonor fraud or forgery as described in Section 5-109(a) or expiration of the letter of credit before presentation.

(e) An issuer shall observe standard practice of financial institutions that regularly issue letters of credit. Determination of the issuer's observance of the standard practice is a matter of interpretation for the court. The court shall offer the parties a reasonable opportunity to present evidence of the standard practice.

(f)   An issuer is not responsible for:

   (1)   the performance or nonperformance of the underlying contract, arrangement, or transaction, [or]

   (3)   observance or knowledge of the usage of a particular trade other than the standard practice referred to in subsection (e).

(h)   An issuer that has dishonored a presentation shall return the documents or hold them at the disposal of, and send advice to that effect to, the presenter.

(i)   An issuer that has honored a presentation as permitted or required by this article:

   (1)   is entitled to be reimbursed by the applicant in immediately available funds not later than the date of its payment of funds;

   (2)   takes the documents free of claims of the beneficiary or presenter;

   (5)   is discharged to the extent of its performance under the letter of credit unless the issuer honored a presentation in which a required signature of a beneficiary was forged.

§ 5-109. Fraud and forgery

(a)   If a presentation is made that appears on its face strictly to comply with the terms and conditions of the letter of credit, but a required document is forged or materially fraudulent, or honor of the presentation would facilitate a material fraud by the beneficiary on the issuer or applicant:

   (1)   The issuer shall honor the presentation, if honor is demanded by:

      (ii)   a confirm[ing bank] who has honored its confirmation in good faith, [or]

      (iii)   a holder in due course of a draft drawn under the letter of credit which was taken after acceptance by the issuer . . . .

   (2)   The issuer, acting in good faith, may honor or dishonor the presentation in any other case.

(b)   If an applicant claims that a required document is forged or materially fraudulent or that honor of the presentation would facilitate a material fraud by the beneficiary on the issuer or applicant, a court of competent jurisdiction may temporarily or permanently enjoin the issuer from honoring a presentation or grant similar relief against the issuer or other persons only if the court finds that:

(1) The relief is not prohibited under the law applicable to an accepted draft or deferred obligation incurred by the issuer;

(2) A beneficiary [or] issuer . . . who may be adversely affected is adequately protected against loss that it may suffer because the relief is granted;

(3) All of the conditions to entitle a person to the relief under the law of this state have been met; and

(4) On the basis of the information submitted to the court, the applicant is more likely than not to succeed under its claim of forgery or material fraud and the person demanding honor does not qualify for protection under paragraph (1) of the subsection (a) of this section.

Document 2.5

Uniform Customs and Practices (ICC)

(excerpts)

A. General Provisions and Definitions

Application of UCP

Article 1   The Uniform Customs and Practice for Documentary Credits, 1993 Revision, ICC Publication NN500, shall apply to all Documentary Credits (including to the extent to which they may be applicable, Standby Letter(s) of Credit) where they are incorporated into the text of the Credit. They are binding on all parties thereto, unless otherwise expressly stipulated in the Credit.

Meaning of Credit

Article 2   For the purposes of these Articles, the expressions "Documentary Credit(s) and "Standby Letter(s) of Credit" (hereinafter referred to as "Credits(s)"), mean any arrangement, however named or described, whereby a bank (the "Issuing Bank") acting at the request and on the instructions of a customer (the "Applicant") or on its own behalf,

  i.   is to make a payment to or to the order of a third party (the "Beneficiary"), or is to accept and pay bills of exchange (Draft(s)) drawn by the Beneficiary,

       or

  ii. Authorizes another bank to effect such payment, or to accept and pay such bills of exchange (Draft(s)),

       or

  iii. authorizes another bank to negotiate, against stipulated document(s), provided that the terms and conditions of the Credit are complied with.

       For the purposes of these Articles, branches of a bank in different countries are considered another bank.

Credits v. Contracts

Article 3   a.   Credits by their nature, are separate transactions from the sales or other contract(s) on which they may be based and banks are in no way concerned with or bound by such contract(s), even if any reference whatsoever to such contract(s) is included in the Credit. Consequently, the undertaking of a bank to pay, accept and pay Draft(s) or negotiate and/or to fulfill any other obligations under the Credit, is not subject to claims or defenses by the Applicant resulting from his relationships with the Issuing Bank or the Beneficiary.

b. A Beneficiary can in no case avail himself of the contractual relationships existing between the banks or between the Applicant and the Issuing Bank.

Documents v. Goods/Services/Performances

Article 4 a. Instructions for the issuance of a Credit, the Credit itself, instructions for an amendment thereto, and the amendment itself, must be complete and precise.

In order to guard against confusion and misunderstanding, banks should discourage any attempt:

   i.   to include excessive detail in the Credit or in any amendment thereto;

   ii.   To give instructions to issue, advise or confirm a Credit by reference to a Credit previously issued (similar Credit) where such previous Credit has been subject to accepted amendment(s), and/or unaccepted amendment(s).

b. All instructions for the issuance of a Credit and the Credit itself and, where applicable, all instructions for an amendment thereto and the amendment itself, must state precisely the document(s) against which payment, acceptance or negotiation is to be made.

B. Forms and Notification of Credits

Revocable v. Irrevocable Credits

Article 6 a. A credit may be either

   i.   revocable,

          or

   ii.   irrevocable.

143

b. The Credit, therefore, should clearly indicate whether it is revocable or irrevocable.

c. In the absence of such indication the Credit shall be deemed to be irrevocable.

Liability of Issuing and Confirming Banks

Article 9   a.   An irrevocable Credit constitutes a definite undertaking of the Issuing Bank, provided that the stipulated documents are presented to the Nominated Bank or to the Issuing Bank and that the terms and conditions of the Credit are complied with:

    i.   If the Credit provides for sight payment – to pay at sight;

    ii.   If the Credit provides for acceptance:

        a.   by the Issuing Bank – to accept Draft(s) drawn by the Beneficiary on the Issuing Bank and pay them at maturity,

            or

        b.   by another drawee bank – to accept and pay at maturity Draft(s) drawn by the Beneficiary on the Issuing Bank in the event the drawee bank stipulated in the Credit does not accept Draft(s) drawn on it, or to pay Draft(s) accepted but not paid by such drawee bank at maturity;

b.   A confirmation of an irrevocable Credit by another bank (the "Confirming Bank") upon the authorization or request of the Issuing Bank, constitutes a definite undertaking of the Confirming Bank, in addition to that of the Issuing Bank, provided that the stipulated documents are presented to the Confirming Bank or to any other Nominated Bank and that the terms and conditions of the Credit are complied with:

    i.   If the Credit provides for sight payment – to pay at sight;

    ii.   If the Credit provides for acceptance:

        a.   by the Confirming Bank – to accept Draft(s) drawn by the Beneficiary on the Confirming Bank and pay them at maturity,

            or

        b.   by another drawee bank – to accept and pay at maturity Draft(s) drawn by the Beneficiary on the Confirming Bank, in the event the drawee bank stipulated in the Credit does not accept Draft(s) drawn on it, or to pay Draft(s) accepted but not paid by such drawee bank at maturity;

Types of Credit

Article 10 a. All credits must clearly indicate whether they are available by sight payment, by deferred payment, by acceptance or be negotiation.

C. Liabilities and Responsibilities

Standard for Examination of Documents

Article 13 a. Banks must examine all documents stipulated in the Credit with reasonable care, to ascertain whether or not they appear, on their face, to be in compliance with the terms and conditions of the Credit. Compliance of the stipulated documents on their face with the terms and conditions of the Credit shall be determined by international standard banking practices as reflected in these Articles. Documents which appear on their face to be inconsistent with one another will be considered as not appearing on their face to be in compliance with the terms and conditions of the Credit.

Documents not stipulated in the Credit will not be examined by banks. If they receive such documents, they shall return them to the presenter or pass them on without responsibility.

b. The Issuing Bank, the Confirming Bank, if any, or a Nominated Bank acting on their behalf, shall each have a reasonable time, not to exceed seven banking days following the day of receipt of the documents, to examine the documents and determine whether to take up or refuse the documents and ot inform the party from which it received the documents accordingly.

Article 14 a. Upon receipt of the documents the Issuing Bank and/or Confirming Bank, if any, or a Nominated Bank acting on their behalf, must determine on the basis of the documents alone whether or not they appear on their face to be in compliance with the terms and conditions of the Credit. If the documents appear on their face not to be in compliance with the terms and conditions of the Credit, such banks may refuse to take up the documents.

b. If the Issuing Bank determines that the documents appear on their face not to be in compliance with the terms and conditions of the Credit, it may in its sole judgment approach the Applicant for a waiver of the discrepancy(ies). This does not, however, extend the period mentioned in sub-Article 13(b).

145

c. i. If the Issuing Bank and/or Confirming Bank, if any, or a Nominated Bank acting on their behalf, decides to refuse the documents, it must give notice to that effect by telecommunication or, if that is not possible, by other expeditious means, without delay but no later than the close of the seventh banking day following the day of receipt of the documents. Such notice shall be given to the bank from which it received the documents, or to the Beneficiary, if it received the documents directly from him.

d. ii. Such notice must state all discrepancies in respect of which the bank refuses the documents and must also state whether it is holding the documents at the disposal of, or is returning them to, the presenter.

CHAPTER 3

Jurisdiction to Adjudicate

THE ENFORCEABILITY OF
FOREIGN MONEY JUDGMENTS

> You have just been served with a Summons and Complaint from a Court in Kuala Lampur, Malaysia. You had recently sold goods to a Malaysian buyer, but the sale (and the delivery) were made in California. The buyer now claims the goods were defective. He seeks judgment against you for $1 million. You are citizen of New York with no assets outside the country. What should you do? Do you really have to go to Kuala Lampur to defend yourself? Or can you ignore these legal papers, confident that there is nothing the authorities down there can do to you?

The answer to the questions just posed depends on whether the court in Kuala Lampur had "jurisdiction to adjudicate" the claims made in the suit. If the court has such "jurisdiction", then the United States (and every other country, for that matter) will recognize the foreign court's action, _i.e._ whatever judgment that it renders. If, on the other hand, the Kuala Lampur court lacks "jurisdiction" over the defendant, that court does not, under customary international law,[1] have the power to make a binding adjudication of "the merits" of the foreign plaintiff's claims.

As the hypothetical asks, when such a jurisdictional question arises, an important decision must be made. Does the defendant have to go to Kuala Lampur to object to jurisdiction, or can he make the objection at home, where

---

1. Some countries, although not the U.S., continue to require "reciprocity" as an additional condition to recognition and enforcement of foreign money judgments.

the process of objecting will certainly be easier and cheaper, and where perhaps (perish the thought) the home-town judiciary will be more friendly?

The answer to that question is yes, the defendant can choose in which forum he wishes to make the jurisdictional objection. He can object to the Malaysian court's jurisdiction either there or here (but obviously not in both places, because you only get one opportunity to contest an issue). The defendant must be careful in making the choice, however, because the law visits serious consequences on one who chooses to stay home to make the jurisdictional objection if that party does not prevail on the issue.

The consequence is that, if the (home) court finds there was jurisdiction, the defendant will then be precluded from making any "merits" defense, such as claiming that the goods were not up to the contract, or that the statute of limitations has run, etc. That consequence is obviously a serious matter if the defendant thinks he can prove that he did no wrong is thus not liable. Certain other defenses may be available, such as a defense that the foreign country does not provide impartial tribunals or procedures compatible with due process,[2] or that the claim was based on a law repugnant to the public policy of this country. These other defenses are, however, difficult to establish in an ordinary commercial case, making the question of recognition turn mostly on the jurisdictional question.

Being able to make an intelligent assessment of jurisdictional issues is important for any businessperson in the situation described here. But the issue has other dimensions as well: a businessperson considering a sale, or a service contract, involving foreign trade might or should ask - if I do this deal, and something goes wrong, can I be sued over there? What about if I want to sue - can I do it here, or can I only sue in the foreign country? The answer to these questions may determine whether the transaction is too risky. The same problem might lead the same person to ask - to avoid these issues, can I make a binding agreement to have all disputes adjudicated in a neutral country? Or before a multinational tribunal? The answer to these questions are contained in this Chapter and the one which follows.

* * *

The best way to illustrate and explore the principles of jurisdiction to adjudicate is to walk through the process that will take place if the defendant ignores the Kuala Lampur summons. We can then explore the options available to defendant, and discuss the implications of each of these options. Then, we can begin a serious study of the subject known as jurisdiction to adjudicate.

If the defendant doesn't answer the Malaysian summons, the court in Kuala Lampur will render a default judgment against him. Perhaps they will hold

---

2. as well as lack of adequate notice and time to respond, or fraud on the tribunal.

a hearing to examine the plaintiff's evidence for sufficiency, perhaps they will simply accept whatever his papers say. The "judgment roll" in Kuala Lampur will reflect the fact and amount of the judgment, and the plaintiff (now a "judgment creditor") will have an official document evidencing the judgment. If the defendant has assets in Kuala Lampur, he best watch out, because they will be subject to "attachment" or "execution" by the authorities in that country.

If, on the other hand, the defendant has no assets in Kuala Lampur, the plaintiff will have to come to a court where the defendant has assets (we will presume that to be New York, but perhaps somewhere else if he has assets there) and ask that court to "recognize" the foreign judgment. As stated previously, the court in New York will recognize the foreign judgment if Kuala Lampur had jurisdiction, but it will not recognize the judgment if it finds that Kuala Lampur did not have jurisdiction. The consequence of losing was as-described - it visits sudden death on the defendant, who is not permitted to contest the "merits" of the dispute.

If that sounds straightforward enough, beware! There are additional complications. First, to create a level playing field and reduce forum shopping, the rule is that the court where recognition is sought (in the example, New York) will follow the summoning court's jurisdictional rules, at least as long as they do not exceed the bounds of reason. Second, as stated, the law only allows a defendant to make the jurisdictional objection in one place. Thus, the defendant <u>must</u> make a choice as described above. He may choose to make the jurisdictional objection in Kuala Lampur, so that if he loses on the jurisdictional point, he still has his "merits" defenses. But of course, going to Kuala Lampur to make the objection and defend the case will be inconvenient and expensive, and who knows what kind of "justice" a foreigner receives in that country. These problems notwithstanding, in many cases it will make sense to defend the action in the foreign court, especially when the merits defense is strong and/or the jurisdictional objection weak.[3]

The choice confronting the defendant in the example, and the consequences of making the wrong choice strike a delicate but useful balance. Every defendant essentially has the right to ignore a foreign proceeding knowing that he has the ability to make the jurisdictional objection at home when the "recognition and enforcement" is sought. But what he also gets when he

---

3. Note that if the court in Kuala Lampur rules that it has jurisdiction and then goes on to rule for Plaintiff, even though the plaintiff will still have to come to New York for recognition and enforcement, the defendant will not be able to resist recognition by New York. He will not be permitted to claim either that Kuala Lampur lacked jurisdiction, or that he should win on the merits, since both matters have been adjudicated. The foreign judgment will be conclusive and binding.

exercises his right to make the jurisdictional objection at home, cheaply and conveniently in front of a home-town judge, is that he gives up the right to defend the case on the merits if he is wrong on jurisdiction. In short, if the defendant decides to contest jurisdiction at home rather than abroad, he stakes everything on the jurisdictional point. By contrast, if he were to go to Kuala Lampur to defend himself there he is not staking everything on the jurisdictional point because if he loses on that issue he can still make a merits defense.

* * *

I. JURISDICTION TO ADJUDICATE

As demonstrated in the previous section, the enforce ability of foreign court judgments depends on whether the foreign court possessed "jurisdiction to adjudicate". What is this concept, and how does it operate? Is it uniform around the world, and are there any issues of "international law"?

HISTORICAL BACKGROUND

We begin with a small dose of legal history. Our study starts in 14th century England, although the concept is much older. If one were to travel back to England at that time he would see a legal system in its infancy. The legal system that was developing of course had two branches - criminal, i.e. offenses against the state, and civil, i.e. offenses against other citizens. Without getting into the details, we know that today these two branches of law have very different procedures. The criminal proceeding starts with an "arrest", for which the defendant must be physically present within the state.[4] Civil suits, by contrast, are commenced by "service of process", i.e. delivery of a Summons and Complaint to the defendant.[5]

Under modern law, in civil cases, the summons and complaint may be delivered to the defendant outside the territory of the court issuing them. But if you go back to England in the 14th or 15th Century, a civil lawsuit was started the same way as a criminal proceeding, i.e., with an "arrest." The authorities (in England, the "Sheriff") would make a "civil arrest" of the defendant, take him into custody, and bring him before the court for adjudication of the claim.

---

4. Thus, the concept of "extradition", as well as the abduction of Adolf Eichman in South America by Israel, and the military action against Manuel Noriega of Panama.

5 . The Summons serves the important purpose of providing notice of suit to the defendant. Restrictions on where it could be served, however, have led to the topics discussed in this chapter - the so-called "jurisdictional bases".

But, as is still the case in criminal matters, a sheriff's power to arrest a defendant stopped at the border, and since "jurisdiction to adjudicate" depended on "arrest", if the individual was outside the state, there was nothing the Sheriff could do. The court could not obtain jurisdiction over the absent defendant unless the defendant voluntarily came to appear before the court, or otherwise entered the territory and became subject to arrest.

The concept of jurisdiction to adjudicate was, for these reasons, dependent on the defendant's physical presence within the territory, and cases began with civil arrest. Toward the end of the 16th Century, however, the law began its development to its current state. First, England abolished civil arrest. In its place came the Summons, which is a piece of paper addressed by the Court to the Defendant. It might read:

> **Defendant:** You are hereby summoned to appear in Court at such and such a place, before such and such a time, to answer the allegations made in the attached Complaint, and if you fail to appear the Court will enter a Default Judgment against you.

While the Summons was designed to take the place of civil arrest, its advent did not change the basic power that the court had to assert its power, i.e. the jurisdiction, to adjudicate a given dispute. Just as the sheriff had no power to arrest people outside his territory, he had no power to serve the Summons outside his territory. Put differently, even after the advent of the Summons, the court's power "to summon" continued to stop at the border. This concept, known as "presence-based jurisdiction" continued pretty much intact and unaffected until the end of the 19th Century, when the law underwent another modification that expanded greatly the scope of a court's jurisdiction.

Before getting to the expansion, we should first cross the oceans, and take a look at the issue in the United States. While we never had civil arrest, we did have the historical restriction just described - that jurisdiction had to be based on the defendant's present in the territory at the time he was served with the Summons. In 1878, the United States Supreme Court upheld the restriction in Pennoyer v. Neff, 95 U.S. 714 (1878).

In Pennoyer, the Supreme Court did several things. First, it equated jurisdictional problems with a concept known as "due process of law", which is guaranteed to all by 5th and 14th Amendments to the United States Constitution. The "due process" concept has many meanings and application; here, it denotes the ideal that there are limits on the power of a state or nation to compel absent defendants to come to court and defend themselves or else suffer a Default Judgment. In equating jurisdiction to adjudicate with due process, the Supreme Court gave jurisdiction Constitutional dimensions.

The second thing that <u>Pennoyer</u> did was to expand the notion of presence-based jurisdiction to include domiciliaries of the forum, <u>i.e.</u> people who make their homes in the territory of the forum. While domicile is not equated directly with either citizenship or residence, the concepts are related. But rather than being based on such objective concepts, domicile is a subjective concept. Its definition is the place a person "subjectively treats as his home", and that is not necessarily where he or she actually resides at any given moment, or where he holds citizenship, although those facts are, in some cases, relevant to the determination.

The definition of domicile leads to several truisms. First, a person can have more than one residence but he can have only one domicile. A person can reside during the summer in New York and during the winter in Florida. Despite the existence of two residences, there can be only one domicile. Second, every person has a domicile. Even those who are "in transit" have a domicile, because the new domicile is not established until the person abandons the old one with an intent to make the new place "home".

Even though domicile is a subjective concept requiring an inquiry into intent, it is often judged by objective factors. Where does a person spend the majority of his time, or have a majority of his possessions? Where does the person have his passport? Where does he vote? Where does he have his driver's license? Where does his family reside? Does he have plans to leave the place where he currently lives, and return to a place he formerly lived? Etc. Of course, all of these are examples of objective criteria, but they bear on the subjective issue. No <u>one</u> is determinative of domicile, but they inform the ultimate determination which, as indicated, is a subjective one.

In <u>Pennoyer v. Neff</u>, the Supreme Court stated that domicile is the equivalence of presence, that one who is domiciled in New York, for example, is physically present there even if at the moment he happens to be somewhere else. The principle makes sense because jurisdiction deals with the power of the state to force a defendant to answer to its courts. To say that a domiciliary is required to answer in the courts of his home does not offend any notions of due process or fairness.

<u>Pennoyer</u> was thus the first case in this country to expand jurisdiction beyond its original limit - pure physical presence. But the third thing that the <u>Pennoyer</u> case said was quite limiting - that other than presence and domicile, there are no other constitutionally-permissible jurisdictional bases. That continuation of the rigid jurisdictional rules would pose a problem in the century to come.

CORPORATE PRESENCE

Before moving forward from <u>Pennoyer</u>, however, it is important to digress into a conceptual problem that is common in its appearance but elusive in its resolution. Nevertheless, the problem is one that must be tackled in the context of presence as a basis for jurisdiction.

When we talk about people, it is easy to decide (to know) where they are present - it is where their feet touch the ground. But there are a lot of business entities, particularly partnerships and corporations, that just don't have feet.

We start with partnerships. A partnership has no legal existence separate from its members. Put another way, a partnership isn't a "person" the law recognizes. It is a relationship, not a separate entity. Jurisdictionally, we thus say that a partnership is present wherever <u>any</u> of the partners (<u>i.e.</u> the owner) are present. So if four partners are operating a New Jersey partnership in New Jersey and the four are all in New Jersey today, then only a New Jersey can obtain jurisdiction today. If one of the partners comes to New York for a business dinner, however, the partnership is present in New York. Under those circumstances, a plaintiff could serve that partner in New York and get jurisdiction over the entire New Jersey partnership because the partnership is present wherever any partner is. The metaphor that "a partner carries the partnership around with him in his pocket" is thus apt. Wherever the partner goes, the partnership goes; it does not even matter whether the partner is on partnership business when he is served.

But the analysis is very different for corporations. The law treats a corporation as a legal entity, separate and distinct from its owners - the shareholders. Shareholders, officers, directors do not carry the corporation around with them in their pockets, and the corporation is not necessarily present where these individuals are, even if they are in the place "on business". Corporate presence is measured by a different standard. Corporate presence only exists whenever the corporate defendant is said to be "doing business" in the forum.[6]

What, however, is meant by the term "doing business"? In spite of the apparent fuzziness of the term, the definition of "doing business" comes from none other than Benjamin Nathan Cardozo, who in the famous case of <u>Tauza v. Susquehanna Coal Company</u>, offered the definition we continue to use to this day. Cardozo wrote that one is doing business in New York when a corporation is "here, not occasionally or casually, but with a fair measure of permanence and continuity." This definition, and the doing business concept, is now applied jurisdictionally to individuals as well as corporations.[7]

Cardozo's articulation of the doing business concept, has, over the years, been refined, although the classic formulation still serves as an important guidepost. Today we look to several objective indicia in making the

---

6 . Of course, a corporation is "domiciled" in its state of incorporation; we deal only with so-called "foreign corporations".

7. The <u>Pennoyer</u> restriction was avoided in these cases by requiring service of the summons at the Defendant's domicile (within the state), under the "fiction" that defendant would habitually check that place for correspondence, etc.

"presence" determination. The law asks questions such as - Does the Defendant have an office in the territory, because if the Defendant has an office there, it will be found to be doing business there, because the existence of the office meets the test of permanence and continuity. If the corporation doesn't have an office in the territory, but it has employees who are regularly stationed there, that too would meet the test of doing business. But as one moves down the scale of contact from those obvious situations to more instances where contact is more sporadic, things become more fuzzy, and the law starts to look at other factors, such as does the corporation have employees there at all, even if they are not here permanently or continuously. Another question asked is - Does the corporation have property in the territory of the forum? A bank account? Are they listed in the phone book there? Do they have a post office box there, etc.? None of these one factors would be determinative but, if enough of them exist such that it can be said, even metaphorically, that the defendant is "continuously here", corporate presence will be found.

One troubling situation is where the defendant has neither an office nor regular employees in the territory of the forum but who regularly <u>solicits</u> the business of citizens of the state. Can that type of conduct ever meet the "doing business" test? The traditional answer was "no"; that, under the so-called "solicitation rule", if all a corporation was doing was soliciting business from outside the state, the corporation could not be said to be "here" for purposes of jurisdiction. But some time around the early 1970s, most states abandoned the hard and fast solicitation rule and started to hold that solicitation combined with the presence of some other factors (<u>e.g.</u> having a post office box in the forum, or having an employee present on occasion) would be enough to meet the doing business test. Indeed, one case goes so far as to say that if you are regularly soliciting business here and deriving a substantial part of your revenues from the citizens of the state you are doing business there.

The change in the solicitation rule demonstrates, among other things, the increasing power of the state to summon non-domiciliaries who direct their conduct toward the forum. This broader phenomenon aside, however, the debate over whether solicitation amounts to doing business will arise with even greater frequency because of the advent of the Internet. There are cases already arising raising the issue of whether having a home page or web site accessible from the forum is enough to conclude that a state has jurisdiction over the owner of the site. Some of the cases say that having an Internet address accessible from the forum aimed at forum residents is more than a mere solicitation because a solicitation is a one-time thing. On the Internet, however, a web site is open and accessible 24 hours a day. The better reasoned cases, however, say that having an Internet address, by itself, does not expose the owner to the general jurisdiction of the forum. A harsher rule undoubtedly would discourage people from partaking of that new technology, out of fear that it would expose them to some sort of worldwide jurisdiction. Such a result should be avoided, at least for now.[8]

OTHER TRADITIONAL FORMS OF JURISDICTION - JURISDICTION IN REM

Presence-based jurisdiction, often termed "jurisdiction in personam" or personal jurisdiction, was undoubtedly the principal basis of jurisdiction available to aggrieved citizens - and it meant they often had to sue non-citizens in foreign courts. There was, however, another form of jurisdiction that existed, called "jurisdiction in rem",[9] that was also available to plaintiffs.

The explanation of jurisdiction in rem also leads us back to the 15th Century. Recall that at that time, jurisdiction in a civil case was obtained by civil arrest. The sheriff, however, had another option available to him if he was unable to find the Defendant within the territory. If the Defendant had **property** located within the territory, the sheriff could "arrest" (meaning seize or "attach") the property and obtain jurisdiction that way - in rem, over the thing. In practical terms, the sheriff would take custody of the property (if it was real estate or other immovable property he would affix a notice to it). Such notice (or seizure) was not only intended to advise the world that the property was the subject of a suit, but it also was deemed sufficient notice to the owner, since an owner is supposed to know what the status of his property (a convenient legal fiction, of course, since, in this manner, the law obviated the need to serve the summons outside its territory). The case would then proceed in rem.

Before addressing the details of jurisdiction in rem, how it works and what subspecies of jurisdiction in rem there are, there is a very important principle attendant on in rem jurisdiction. It is that in rem jurisdiction is a "limited" jurisdiction. The limit is that the jurisdiction a court obtained through an in rem seizure was limited to the value of the property seized. Unlike the case where a court obtained personal jurisdiction, an in rem judgment could not exceed the value of the property seized. (Actually, what happens is that, if the Plaintiff wins, the sheriff sells the seized asset and applies the proceeds to the Plaintiff's judgment. If the proceeds exceed the judgment, any surplus is given back to the Defendant. But if the proceeds of the sale are insufficient to satisfy the whole judgment (i.e. there is a deficit, the unsatisfied portion of the judgment is nullified.)

---

8 . That is not to say that jurisdiction can never be obtained over a foreign web site operator, only that the type of jurisdiction which obtains will not be based on the "doing business" concept. See discussion, infra, about "transacting business" as a jurisdictional basis.

9 . In English, jurisdiction over a "thing".

This principle limiting in rem jurisdiction means that a court acting in rem does not have power to give a judgment in excess of the value of the property it has seized. So to the extent that the Plaintiff had a claim in excess of the value of the property, he will have to go elsewhere if he wants to pursue the deficit. He can sue in personam somewhere else, or he can proceed in rem elsewhere based on the presence of the Defendant's property in the other forum. But the original in rem jurisdiction is limited to the value of the seized property.

There are various types of in rem proceedings. First, there are actions that we say proceed "strictly in rem". The best example of an action which proceeds strictly in rem is one in "admiralty", i.e. those involving maritime law, a form of international law or customary international law that is beyond the scope of this work. That disclaimer notwithstanding, actions in admiralty basically concern the legal relationships between the owner of an ocean-going ship and those who work on the ship (pilots, seamen), those who provide the ship with necessary services (longshoremen, stevedores, etc.), and those who might be injured through the operation of the ship (accident victims).

As one might imagine, the use of in rem jurisdiction for actions in admiralty began in the 15th century, when maritime commerce was really getting going. With the concomitant increase in maritime disputes, it was logical for a state to say that a ship's owner, who benefitted directly from the mobility of the vessel could not hide in his home port and escape the jurisdiction of fora where his ship might travel and make use of the services of the forum and its residents. It was thus perfectly logical to say that the owner was required to come and defend himself wherever his ship was. The ship could be kept in port (by the authorities) until the dispute was resolved; more often, the owner came to the forum, there was (still is) a brief proceeding to determine the value of the ship, a bond was posted by the owner, and the ship then was allowed to go on its way. If the owned failed to appear and post the bond, the ship remained in custody, and it could be sold to satisfy any unpaid judgment.

Another example of in rem proceedings is a mortgage foreclosure. A creditor wants to (a) decide that a loan is in default, (b) order that the property pledged as security be sold at auction, with the proceeds used to satisfy any judgment. The key is that the plaintiff seeks ownership, possession or adjudication of his rights in the "thing". He does not seeks a general money judgment. Actions to recover stolen goods, or to quiet title to disputed real estate, even divorce (to dissolve the thing, i.e. the marriage), are examples of in rem proceedings.

EXPANDING THE BASES OF JURISDICTION - JURISDICTION QUASI IN REM

In the United States, at a time when the restrictive approach of Pennoyer v. Neff was still the law of the land, a new species of jurisdiction was created -

jurisdiction quasi-in-rem. It was similar to traditional in rem jurisdiction because it was based on the presence of the defendant's property in the forum, but it is different because the property was unrelated to the underlying law suit, and the plaintiff was seeking a general money judgment to be satisfied out of the "thing" following a favorable judgment.

The leading case, indeed the one where the practice was sanctioned by the United Supreme Court, was Harris v. Balk. The facts (as well as the law) are somewhat convoluted, but they are understandable when viewed in historical context, i.e. the restriction on *in personam* jurisdiction over non-residents that was articulated in Pennoyer.

Harris was a citizen of Maryland. He was owed money by a fellow named Epstein, who was a citizen of Virginia. Epstein did not pay the money back. Since Epstein could not be lured into Maryland to receive service of process, he was not amenable to Maryland's jurisdiction, yet that was where Harris wanted to sue. The solution was found with another individual named Balk, who was also a citizen of Maryland. Balk, it seemed, owed an equal sum to Epstein. Using a little legal sleight of hand, Harris sued Epstein "through" Balk, by attaching the debt Balk owed to Epstein.[10]

Thus was born jurisdiction "quasi in rem", and it was quite useful. When suing banks, financial institutions, insurance companies and substantial commercial entities, the doctrine opened the door widely to a new way to obtain jurisdiction, because these entities often have assets in many jurisdictions. Additionally, they often are beneficiaries of a variety of intangible contractual obligations (including but limited to debts), obligations incurred by citizens of many different states. These businesses could, with the advent of quasi in rem jurisdiction, be sued almost anywhere - all one needed to do was find local assets or a local citizen or business that owed an obligation to the absent defendant, and Pennoyer became irrelevant.

Many years later, after the death of the Pennoyer doctrine, in 1977, the Supreme Court, in Schaffer v. Heitner, would all but retire quasi in rem jurisdiction. In that case, the Supreme Court ruled that any exercise of in rem jurisdiction, including jurisdiction quasi in rem, had to comport with due process, which in turn requires that there be a connection between the law suit and property being attached. Since in quasi in rem cases, by definition, the law suit is almost always unrelated to the property which supports jurisdiction, the constitutional test cannot be met.[11]

---

10. Since the intangible asset (the debt) was deemed to be property, and the property was deemed present in the place where the debtor was, Harris used the debt to get in rem jurisdiction (sort of) over Epstein.

11. By contrast, a mortgage foreclosure can still proceed in rem because the law suit is directly related to the property, so at least some in rem jurisdiction is preserved. So too, the Court chose not to disrupt strictly-in-rem actions under maritime law ships, because ocean-going ships are special things in international commerce.

EXPANDING CONCEPTS OF JURISDICTION - LONG-ARM JURISDICTION

The jurisdictional situation at the end of the 19th century was mired in the restriction of Pennoyer v. Neff, that jurisdiction had to be based on either presence (person or property) or domicile - nothing else would suffice. But, as we entered the 20th century, it became obvious that this restricted approach to jurisdiction would not work in the modern world. As the 20th century dawned, a new invention required a sea change in the law. It was the automobile. The increased mobility that attended the invention of the automobile virtually dictated the need for a new jurisdictional regime, and indeed it launched it. Yet it would still be nearly 40 years until the United States Supreme Court finally broke down and eliminated the rule of Pennoyer.[12] Before that, there was a slow slide toward a more expansive approach.

The principal event in that slide (the development of quasi in rem jurisdiction also occurred at that time) was the passage (and approval by the Supreme Court) of statutes in many states termed "non-resident motorist statutes". The purpose of these statutes was to expose motorists who were non-domiciliaries to the jurisdiction of states where they caused automobile accidents, thereby permitting victims of such accidents to sue the foreign driver at home. To achieve that result, the legislatures (and the courts) were forced to engage a bit of legal fiction - that the non-resident motorist, upon entry into the state, impliedly made the Secretary of State (or the Commissioner of Motor Vehicles) the driver's authorized agent for the service of legal process. Of course, no driver ever made such an express grant of authority, but the creation of the implication served the ends of justice, and it was approved as comporting with due process despite the rule of Pennoyer. The existence of the "agency" obviated the need to serve the summons outside the state.

Eventually, by 1940, with legal fiction heaped upon legal fiction, Pennoyer came crashing down. The watershed case was State of Washington v. International Shoe Company, and it exposed quite vividly the absurdity of the then-existing jurisdictional rules. The defendant, the International Shoe Company ("the Company"), was a huge company whose shoes were sold all over the country from its sole location in St. Louis, Missouri. The method of those sales, however, was dictated by the rules of jurisdiction. The Company had employees in every state, but the employees were not authorized to make contracts to sell shoes - they were only allowed to solicit orders. The salesman had catalogues, and they went door-to-door. If a customer liked the product, he or she was given an "order form" to send to the Company in St. Louis. The order form served as the offer, which the company accepted in St. Louis to make the contract of sale.

By restricting the employees only to soliciting orders,[13] the Company was assured that no court would say it was "doing business" in any state other

---

12. The British analogue fell much earlier - in 1910. See Order 11, reprinted at the end of this Chapter.

than Missouri. Not only did that prevent the Company from being sued by its customers anywhere but in Missouri, it had a greater effect - other states could not even sue the Company to collect sales taxes.

The State of Washington decided it had had enough. It sued the Company in Washington to recover the taxes. The state courts approved the exercise of jurisdiction over the Company, saying that it was fair to do so and thus due process was not offended. The case went up to the United States Supreme Court, which scrapped <u>Pennoyer</u> and, for the first time, approved a new species of jurisdiction - "long arm jurisdiction". The Court ruled that the "long arm" of the state could, consistent with due process, reach out beyond its borders to (metaphorically) "arrest" the non-resident Defendant and force him to come and defend himself or else suffer a default that would be recognized. For the first time, the Court approved an exercise of jurisdiction where the summons was served outside the state.

The key to the Court's ruling in <u>International Shoe</u> was a finding that service of process outside the state was not unreasonable if two things existed: (1) the defendant had sufficient contact with the state to meet an undefined "minimum", and (2) the defendant's contact with the state were related or connected to the claims being made in the law suit. If these two tests were met, the exercise of jurisdiction would not offend "traditional notions of fair play and substantial justice", and no constitutional challenge could be mounted against it.

In creating this new form of jurisdiction, it must be noted that the Court first lowered the quantum of contacts previously required of absent defendants - from "doing business", <u>i.e.</u> "permanence and continuity" - to a much lower threshold - the single and isolated business transaction involving the forum or its residents. To insure fairness, however, the Court created the second requirement - often called the "nexus" requirement - that the defendant's contact with the forum be related to the law suit. Since the State of Washington's claim that it was owed sales taxes arose directly from the Company's Washington activities, the Supreme Court approved the exercise of long-arm jurisdiction.

The creation of long arm jurisdiction was not only a boon for taxing states, it became important for consumers and plaintiffs as well. A Washington State consumer could now sue the manufacturer if a defect in the product (e.g. an errant nail) damaged his foot. The Company sold the shoe to him in Washington, and the claim arises out of the sale.[14] A supplier of products who did not get paid by a foreign customer might even be able to sue at home for non-payment and breach. All that was required was "minimum forum contact" and existence of the nexus.

---

13. To insure that the salesman could not even sell their samples, the Company went so far as to give each salesman only one shoe of each style.

14. Note, however, that if the shoe was bought while the consumer lived in California, the consumer could not gain long arm jurisdiction in Washington, even if the Company sold a lot of shoes in Washington, because of an inability to meet the nexus requirement.

The creation of the nexus requirement led to the creation of another term in the jurisdictional lexicon - "specific jurisdiction". The term connotes the principle that long arm jurisdiction is specific to claims arising out of the defendant's forum contact. In contrast to presence-based jurisdiction, termed "general jurisdiction", a long arm basis, with its lower level of required contact, cannot support jurisdiction for claims unrelated to the contacts.

When a court is confronted, of course, with the higher level of contact termed "doing business", the court has jurisdiction over **any dispute** involving the defendant. In such a case it doesn't matter what the lawsuit is about; there is no nexus requirement. If you were handed a Summons and Complaint in New York, are domiciled there or have an office there, you have to answer to New York Courts as to all matters, plain and simple. Such is the cost attendant on the privilege of being there, being domiciled there, or doing business there. But if you are there only occasionally or sporadically, and are served outside the territory, you might still be subject to their jurisdiction - not the general jurisdiction of Pennoyer but the specific jurisdiction of International Shoe, the jurisdiction that obtains when a plaintiff makes a claim **that arises out of** the defendant's forum contacts.

BASIC REQUIREMENTS FOR LONG ARM JURISDICTION - MINIMUM CONTACTS, FAIRNESS AND REASONABLENESS

The nexus requirement aside, the cases since International Shoe have addressed several questions: how much forum contact is necessary to meet the minimum contacts test, and what else, if anything, needs to be established? These questions are explored in the cases in this Chapter.

II. THE CONSTITUTIONAL "TEST"

WORLD-WIDE VOLKSWAGEN CORP. ET AL.
v.
WOODSON, DISTRICT JUDGE OF CREEK COUNTY, OKLAHOMA, ET AL.

Supreme Court of the United States
444 U.S. 286; 100 S. Ct. 559; 62 L. Ed.2d 490
Decided January 21, 1980,

MR. JUSTICE WHITE delivered the opinion of the Court.

The issue before us is whether, consistently with the Due Process Clause of the Fourteenth Amendment, an Oklahoma court may exercise in personam jurisdiction over a nonresident automobile retailer and its wholesale distributor in a products-liability action, when the defendants' only connection with Oklahoma is the fact that an automobile sold in New York to New York residents became involved in an accident in Oklahoma.

I

Respondents Harry and Kay Robinson purchased a new Audi automobile from petitioner Seaway Volkswagen, Inc. (Seaway), in Massena, N. Y., in 1976. The following year the Robinson family, who resided in New York, left that State for a new home in Arizona. As they passed through the State of Oklahoma, another car struck their Audi in the rear, causing a fire which severely burned Kay Robinson and her two children.

The Robinsons subsequently brought a products-liability action in the District Court for Creek County, Okla., claiming that their injuries resulted from defective design and placement of the Audi's gas tank and fuel system. They joined as defendants the automobile's manufacturer, Audi NSU Auto Union Aktiengesellschaft (Audi); its importer, Volkswagen of America, Inc. (Volkswagen); its regional distributor, petitioner World-Wide Volkswagen Corp. (World-Wide); and its retail dealer, petitioner Seaway. Seaway and World-Wide entered special appearances,[15] claiming that Oklahoma's exercise of jurisdiction over them would offend the limitations on the State's jurisdiction imposed by the Due Process Clause of the Fourteenth Amendment.

The facts presented to the District Court showed that World-Wide is incorporated and has its business office in New York. It distributes vehicles, parts, and accessories, under contract with Volkswagen, to retail dealers in New York, New Jersey, and Connecticut. Seaway, one of these retail dealers, is incorporated and has its place of business in New York. Insofar as the record reveals, Seaway and World-Wide are fully independent corporations whose relations with each other and with Volkswagen and Audi are contractual only. Respondents adduced no evidence that either World-Wide or Seaway does any business in Oklahoma, ships or sells any products to or in that State, has an agent to receive process there, or purchases advertisements in any media calculated to reach Oklahoma. In fact, as respondents' counsel conceded at oral argument, Tr. of Oral Arg. 32, there was no showing that any automobile sold by World-Wide or Seaway has ever entered Oklahoma with the single exception of the vehicle involved in the present case.

Despite the apparent paucity of contacts between petitioners and Oklahoma, the District Court rejected their constitutional claim and reaffirmed that ruling in denying petitioners' motion for reconsideration. Petitioners then sought a writ of prohibition in the Supreme Court of Oklahoma to restrain the District Judge, respondent Charles S. Woodson, from exercising in

---

15. Volkswagen also entered a special appearance in the District Court, but unlike World-Wide and Seaway did not seek review in the Supreme Court of Oklahoma and is not a petitioner here. Both Volkswagen and Audi remain as defendants in the litigation pending before the District Court in Oklahoma.

personam jurisdiction over them. They renewed their contention that, because they had no "minimal contacts," App. 32, with the State of Oklahoma, the actions of the District Judge were in violation of their rights under the Due Process Clause.

The Supreme Court of Oklahoma denied the writ, 585 P. 2d 351 (1978), holding that personal jurisdiction over petitioners was authorized by Oklahoma's "long-arm" statute, Okla. Stat., Tit. 12, § 1701.03 (a)(4)(1971).[16] Although the court noted that the proper approach was to test jurisdiction against both statutory and constitutional standards, its analysis did not distinguish these questions, probably because § 1701.03 (a)(4) has been interpreted as conferring jurisdiction to the limits permitted by the United States Constitution. The court's rationale was contained in the following paragraph,

> "In the case before us, the product being sold and distributed by the petitioners is by its very design and purpose so mobile that petitioners can foresee its possible use in Oklahoma. This is especially true of the distributor, who has the exclusive right to distribute such automobile in New York, New Jersey and Connecticut. The evidence presented below demonstrated that goods sold and distributed by the petitioners were used in the State of Oklahoma, and under the facts we believe it reasonable to infer, given the retail value of the automobile, that the petitioners derive substantial income from automobiles which from time to time are used in the State of Oklahoma. This being the case, we hold that under the facts presented, the trial court was justified in concluding that the petitioners derive substantial revenue from goods used or consumed in this State."

We granted certiorari to consider an important constitutional question with respect to state-court jurisdiction and to resolve a conflict between the Supreme Court of Oklahoma and the highest courts of at least four other States. We reverse.

---

16. This subsection provides:

"A court may exercise personal jurisdiction over a person, who acts directly or by an agent, as to a cause of action or claim for relief arising from the person's . . . causing tortuous injury in this state by an act or omission outside this state if he regularly does or solicits business or engages in any other persistent course of conduct, or derives substantial revenue from goods used or consumed or services rendered, in this state. . . ."

The State Supreme Court rejected jurisdiction based on @ 1701.03 (a)(3), which authorizes jurisdiction over any person "causing tortuous injury in this state by an act or omission in this state." Something in addition to the infliction of tortuous injury was required.

II

The Due Process Clause of the Fourteenth Amendment limits the power of a state court to render a valid personal judgment against a nonresident defendant. Kulko v. California Superior Court, 436 U.S. 84, 91 (1978). A judgment rendered in violation of due process is void in the rendering State and is not entitled to full faith and credit elsewhere. Pennoyer v. Neff, 95 U.S. 714, 732-733 (1878). Due process requires that the defendant be given adequate notice of the suit, Mullane v. Central Hanover Trust Co., 339 U.S. 306, 313-314 (1950), and be subject to the personal jurisdiction of the court, International Shoe Co. v. Washington, 326 U.S. 310 (1945). In the present case, it is not contended that notice was inadequate; the only question is whether these particular petitioners were subject to the jurisdiction of the Oklahoma courts.

As has long been settled, and as we reaffirm today, a state court may exercise personal jurisdiction over a nonresident defendant only so long as there exist "minimum contacts" between the defendant and the forum State. International Shoe Co. v. Washington, supra, at 316. The concept of minimum contacts, in turn, can be seen to perform two related, but distinguishable, functions. It protects the defendant against the burdens of litigating in a distant or inconvenient forum. And it acts to ensure that the States, through their courts, do not reach out beyond the limits imposed on them by their status as coequal sovereigns in a federal system.

The protection against inconvenient litigation is typically described in terms of "reasonableness" or "fairness." We have said that the defendant's contacts with the forum State must be such that maintenance of the suit "does not offend 'traditional notions of fair play and substantial justice.'" International Shoe Co. v. Washington, supra, at 316, quoting Milliken v. Meyer, 311 U.S. 457, 463 (1940). The relationship between the defendant and the forum must be such that it is "reasonable . . . to require the corporation to defend the particular suit which is brought there." 326 U.S., at 317. Implicit in this emphasis on reasonableness is the understanding that the burden on the defendant, while always a primary concern, will in an appropriate case be considered in light of other relevant factors, including the forum State's interest in adjudicating the dispute, see McGee v. International Life Ins. Co., 355 U.S. 220, 223 (1957); the plaintiff's interest in obtaining convenient and effective relief, see Kulko v. California Superior Court, supra, at 92, at least when that interest is not adequately protected by the plaintiff's power to choose the forum, cf. Shaffer v. Heitner, 433 U.S. 186, 211, n. 37 (1977); the interstate judicial system's interest in obtaining the most efficient resolution of controversies; and the shared interest of the several States in furthering fundamental substantive social policies, see Kulko v. California Superior Court, supra, at 93, 98.

The limits imposed on state jurisdiction by the Due Process Clause, in its role as a guarantor against inconvenient litigation, have been substantially relaxed over the years. As we noted in McGee v. International Life Ins. Co., supra, at 222-223, this trend is largely attributable to a fundamental transformation in the American economy:

> "Today many commercial transactions touch two or more States and may involve parties separated by the full continent. With this increasing nationalization of commerce has come a great increase in the amount of business conducted by mail across state lines. At the same time modern transportation and communication have made it much less burdensome for a party sued to defend himself in a State where he engages in economic activity."

The historical developments noted in McGee, of course, have only accelerated in the generation since that case was decided.

Nevertheless, we have never accepted the proposition that state lines are irrelevant for jurisdictional purposes, nor could we, and remain faithful to the principles of interstate federalism embodied in the Constitution. The economic interdependence of the States was foreseen and desired by the Framers. In the Commerce Clause, they provided that the Nation was to be a common market, a "free trade unit" in which the States are debarred from acting as separable economic entities. H. P. Hood & Sons, Inc. v. Du Mond, 336 U.S. 525, 538 (1949). But the Framers also intended that the States retain many essential attributes of sovereignty, including, in particular, the sovereign power to try causes in their courts. The sovereignty of each State, in turn, implied a limitation on the sovereignty of all of its sister States — a limitation express or implicit in both the original scheme of the Constitution and the Fourteenth Amendment.

Hence, even while abandoning the shibboleth that authority of every tribunal is necessarily restricted by the territorial limits of the State in which it is established," Pennoyer v. Neff, supra, at 720, we emphasized that the reasonableness of asserting jurisdiction over the defendant must be assessed "in the context of our federal system of government," International Shoe Co. v. Washington, 326 U.S., at 317, and stressed that the Due Process Clause ensures not only fairness, but also the "orderly administration of the laws," id., at 319. As we noted in Hanson v. Denckla, 357 U.S. 235, 250-251 (1958):

> "As technological progress has increased the flow of commerce between the States, the need for jurisdiction over nonresidents has undergone a similar increase. At the same time, progress in communications and transportation has made the defense of a suit in a foreign tribunal less burdensome. In response to these changes, the requirements for personal jurisdiction over

nonresidents have evolved from the rigid rule of Pennoyer v. Neff, 95 U.S. 714, to the flexible standard of International Shoe Co. v. Washington, 326 U.S. 310. But it is a mistake to assume that this trend heralds the eventual demise of all restrictions on the personal jurisdiction of state courts. [citation omitted.] Those restrictions are more than a guarantee of immunity from inconvenient or distant litigation. They are a consequence of territorial limitations on the power of the respective States."

Thus, the Due Process Clause "does not contemplate that a state may make binding a judgment in personam against an individual or corporate defendant with which the state has no contacts, ties, or relations." International Shoe Co. v. Washington, supra, at 319. Even if the defendant would suffer minimal or no inconvenience from being forced to litigate before the tribunals of another State; even if the forum State has a strong interest in applying its law to the controversy; even if the forum State is the most convenient location for litigation, the Due Process Clause, acting as an instrument of interstate federalism, may sometimes act to divest the State of its power to render a valid judgment. Hanson v. Denckla, supra, at 251, 254.

III

Applying these principles to the case at hand, we find in the record before us a total absence of those affiliating circumstances that are a necessary predicate to any exercise of state-court jurisdiction. Petitioners carry on no activity whatsoever in Oklahoma. They close no sales and perform no services there. They avail themselves of none of the privileges and benefits of Oklahoma law. They solicit no business there either through salespersons or through advertising reasonably calculated to reach the State. Nor does the record show that they regularly sell cars at wholesale or retail to Oklahoma customers or residents or that they indirectly, through others, serve or seek to serve the Oklahoma market. In short, respondents seek to base jurisdiction on one, isolated occurrence and whatever inferences can be drawn therefrom: the fortuitous circumstance that a single Audi automobile, sold in New York to New York residents, happened to suffer an accident while passing through Oklahoma.

It is argued, however, that because an automobile is mobile by its very design and purpose it was "foreseeable" that the Robinsons' Audi would cause injury in Oklahoma. Yet "foreseeability" alone has never been a sufficient benchmark for personal jurisdiction under the Due Process Clause.

If foreseeability were the criterion, a local California tire retailer could be forced to defend in Pennsylvania when a blowout occurs there [citation omitted]; a Wisconsin seller of a defective automobile jack could be haled before a distant court for damage caused in New Jersey, [citation omitted]; or a Florida soft-drink concessionaire could be summoned to Alaska to account for injuries happening there [citation omitted]. Every seller of chattels would in effect appoint the chattel his agent for service of process. His amenability to suit would travel with the chattel. We recently abandoned the outworn rule of Harris v. Balk, 198 U.S. 215 (1905), that the interest of a creditor in a debt could be extinguished or otherwise affected by any State having transitory jurisdiction over the debtor. Shaffer v. Heitner, 433 U.S. 186 (1977). Having interred the mechanical rule that a creditor's amenability to a quasi in rem action travels with his debtor, we are unwilling to endorse an analogous principle in the present case.

This is not to say, of course, that foreseeability is wholly irrelevant. But the foreseeability that is critical to due process analysis is not the mere likelihood that a product will find its way into the forum State. Rather, it is that the defendant's conduct and connection with the forum State are such that he should reasonably anticipate being haled into court there. See Kulko v. California Superior Court, supra, at 97-98; Shaffer v. Heitner, 433 U.S., at 216; and see id., at 217-219 (STEVENS, J., concurring in judgment). The Due Process Clause, by ensuring the "orderly administration of the laws," International Shoe Co. v. Washington, 326 U.S., at 319, gives a degree of predictability to the legal system that allows potential defendants to structure their primary conduct with some minimum assurance as to where that conduct will and will not render them liable to suit.

When a corporation "purposefully avails itself of the privilege of conducting activities within the forum State," Hanson v. Denckla, 357 U.S., at 253, it has clear notice that it is subject to suit there, and can act to alleviate the risk of burdensome litigation by procuring insurance, passing the expected costs on to customers, or, if the risks are too great, severing its connection with the State. Hence if the sale of a product of a manufacturer or distributor such as Audi or Volkswagen is not simply an isolated occurrence, but arises from the efforts of the manufacturer or distributor to serve, directly or indirectly, the market for its product in other States, it is not unreasonable to subject it to suit in one of those States if its allegedly defective merchandise has there been the source of injury to its owner or to others. The forum State does not exceed its powers under the Due Process Clause if it asserts personal jurisdiction over a corporation that delivers its products into the stream of commerce with the expectation that they will be purchased by consumers in the forum State.

But there is no such or similar basis for Oklahoma jurisdiction over World-Wide or Seaway in this case. Seaway's sales are made in Massena, N. Y. World-Wide's market, although substantially larger, is limited to dealers in New York, New Jersey, and Connecticut. There is no evidence of record that any automobiles distributed by World-Wide are sold to retail customers outside this tristate area. It is foreseeable that the purchasers of automobiles sold by World-Wide and Seaway may take them to Oklahoma. But the mere "unilateral activity of those who claim some relationship with a nonresident defendant cannot satisfy the requirement of contact with the forum State." Hanson v. Denckla, supra, at 253.

In a variant on the previous argument, it is contended that jurisdiction can be supported by the fact that petitioners earn substantial revenue from goods used in Oklahoma. The Oklahoma Supreme Court so found, 585 P. 2d, at 354-355, drawing the inference that because one automobile sold by petitioners had been used in Oklahoma, others might have been used there also. While this inference seems less than compelling on the facts of the instant case, we need not question the court's factual findings in order to reject its reasoning.

This argument seems to make the point that the purchase of automobiles in New York, from which the petitioners earn substantial revenue, would not occur but for the fact that the automobiles are capable of use in distant States like Oklahoma. Respondents observe that the very purpose of an automobile is to travel, and that travel of automobiles sold by petitioners is facilitated by an extensive chain of Volkswagen service centers throughout the country, including some in Oklahoma. However, financial benefits accruing to the defendant from a collateral relation to the forum State will not support jurisdiction if they do not stem from a constitutionally cognizable contact with that State. See Kulko v. California Superior Court, 436 U.S., at 94-95. In our view, whatever marginal revenues petitioners may receive by virtue of the fact that their products are capable of use in Oklahoma is far too attenuated a contact to justify that State's exercise of in personam jurisdiction over them.

Because we find that petitioners have no "contacts, ties, or relations" with the State of Oklahoma, International Shoe Co. v. Washington, supra, at 319, the judgment of the Supreme Court of Oklahoma is Reversed.

MR. JUSTICE BRENNAN, dissenting.

The Court holds that the Due Process Clause of the Fourteenth Amendment bars the States from asserting jurisdiction over the defendants in these two cases. In each case the Court so decides because it fails to find the "minimum contacts" that have been required since International Shoe Co. v. Washington, 326 U.S. 310, 316 (1945). Because I believe that the Court reads International Shoe and its progeny too narrowly, and because I believe that the standards enunciated by those cases may already be obsolete as constitutional boundaries, I dissent.

I

The Court's opinions focus tightly on the existence of contacts between the forum and the defendant. In so doing, they accord too little weight to the strength of the forum State's interest in the case and fail to explore whether there would be any actual inconvenience to the defendant. The essential inquiry in locating the constitutional limits on state-court jurisdiction over absent defendants is whether the particular exercise of jurisdiction offends "'traditional notions of fair play and substantial justice.'" International Shoe, supra, at 316, quoting Milliken v. Meyer, 311 U.S. 457, 463 (1940). The clear focus in International Shoe was on fairness and reasonableness. Kulko v. California Superior Court, 436 U.S. 84, 92 (1978). The Court specifically declined to establish a mechanical test based on the quantum of contacts between a State and the defendant:

> "Whether due process is satisfied must depend rather upon the quality and nature of the activity in relation to the fair and orderly administration of the laws which it was the purpose of the due process clause to insure. That clause does not contemplate that a state may make binding a judgment in personam against an individual or corporate defendant with which the state has no contacts, ties, or relations."

The existence of contacts, so long as there were some, was merely one way of giving content to the determination of fairness and reasonableness.

Surely International Shoe contemplated that the significance of the contacts necessary to support jurisdiction would diminish if some other consideration helped establish that jurisdiction would be fair and reasonable. The interests of the State and other parties in proceeding with the case in a particular forum are such considerations. McGee v. International Life Ins. Co., 355 U.S. 220, 223 (1957), for instance, accorded great importance to a State's "manifest interest in providing effective means of redress" for its citizens. See also Kulko v. California Superior Court, supra, at 92; Shaffer v. Heitner, 433 U.S. 186, 208 (1977); Mullane v. Central Hanover Trust Co., 339 U.S. 306, 313 (1950).

Another consideration is the actual burden a defendant must bear in defending the suit in the forum. McGee, supra. Because lesser burdens reduce the unfairness to the defendant, jurisdiction may be justified despite less significant contacts. The burden, of course, must be of constitutional dimension. Due process limits on jurisdiction do not protect a defendant from all inconvenience of travel, McGee, supra, at 224, and it would not be sensible to make the constitutional rule turn solely on the number of miles the defendant must travel to the courtroom. Instead, the constitutionally significant "burden" to be analyzed relates to the mobility of the defendant's defense. For instance, if having to travel to a foreign forum would hamper the defense because witnesses or evidence or the defendant himself were immobile, or if there were a disproportionately large number of witnesses or amount of evidence that would have to be transported at the defendant's expense, or if being away from home for the duration of the trial would work some special hardship on the defendant, then the Constitution would require special consideration for the defendant's interests.

That considerations other than contacts between the forum and the defendant are relevant necessarily means that the Constitution does not require that trial be held in the State which has the "best contacts" with the defendant. See Shaffer v. Heitner, supra, at 228 (BRENNAN, J., dissenting). The defendant has no constitutional entitlement to the best forum or, for that matter, to any particular forum. Under even the most restrictive view of International Shoe, several States could have jurisdiction over a particular cause of action. We need only determine whether the forum States in these cases satisfy the constitutional minimum.

* * *

B

In [this case] the interest of the forum State and its connection to the litigation is strong. The automobile accident underlying the litigation occurred in Oklahoma. The plaintiffs were hospitalized in Oklahoma when they brought suit. Essential witnesses and evidence were in Oklahoma. See Shaffer v. Heitner, 433 U.S., at 208. The State has a legitimate interest in enforcing its laws designed to keep its highway system safe, and the trial can proceed at least as efficiently in Oklahoma as anywhere else.

The petitioners are not unconnected with the forum. Although both sell automobiles within limited sales territories, each sold the automobile which in fact was driven to Oklahoma where it was involved in an accident. It may be true, as the Court suggests, that each sincerely intended to limit its commercial impact to the limited territory, and that each intended to accept the benefits and protection of the laws only of those States within the territory. But obviously these were unrealistic hopes that cannot be treated as an automatic constitutional shield.

An automobile simply is not a stationary item or one designed to be used in one place. An automobile is intended to be moved around. Someone in the business of selling large numbers of automobiles can hardly plead ignorance of their mobility or pretend that the automobiles stay put after they are sold. It is not merely that a dealer in automobiles foresees that they will move. Ante, at 295. The dealer actually intends that the purchasers will use the automobiles to travel to distant States where the dealer does not directly "do business." The sale of an automobile does purposefully inject the vehicle into the stream of interstate commerce so that it can travel to distant States.

Furthermore, an automobile seller derives substantial benefits from States other than its own. A large part of the value of automobiles is the extensive, nationwide network of highways. Significant portions of that network have been constructed by and are maintained by the individual States, including

Oklahoma. The States, through their highway programs, contribute in a very direct and important way to the value of petitioners' businesses. Additionally, a network of other related dealerships with their service departments operates throughout the country under the protection of the laws of the various States, including Oklahoma, and enhances the value of petitioners' businesses by facilitating their customers' traveling.

Thus, the Court errs in its conclusion, ante, at 299 (emphasis added), that "petitioners have no 'contacts, ties, or relations'" with Oklahoma. There obviously are contacts, and, given Oklahoma's connection to the litigation, the contacts are sufficiently significant to make it fair and reasonable for the petitioners to submit to Oklahoma's jurisdiction.

III

It may be that affirmance of the judgments in these cases would approach the outer limits of International Shoe's jurisdictional principle. But that principle, with its almost exclusive focus on the rights of defendants, may be outdated. As MR. JUSTICE MARSHALL wrote in Shaffer v. Heitner, 433 U.S., at 212: "'[Traditional] notions of fair play and substantial justice' can be as readily offended by the perpetuation of ancient forms that are no longer justified as by the adoption of new procedures. . . ."

International Shoe inherited its defendant focus from Pennoyer v. Neff, 95 U.S. 714 (1878), and represented the last major step this Court has taken in the long process of liberalizing the doctrine of personal jurisdiction. Though its flexible approach represented a major advance, the structure of our society has changed in many significant ways since International Shoe was decided in 1945. Mr. Justice Black, writing for the Court in McGee v. International Life Ins. Co., 355 U.S. 220, 222 (1957), recognized that "a trend is clearly discernible toward expanding the permissible scope of state jurisdiction over foreign corporations and other nonresidents." He explained the trend as follows:

> "In part this is attributable to the fundamental transformation of our national economy over the years. Today many commercial transactions touch two or more States and may involve parties separated by the full continent. With this increasing nationalization of commerce has come a great increase in the amount of business conducted by mail across state lines. At the same time modern transportation and communication have made it much less burdensome for a party sued to defend himself in a State where he engages in economic activity."

Id., at 222-223.

* * *

The conclusion I draw is that constitutional concepts of fairness no longer require the extreme concern for defendants that was once necessary. . . . Mr. Justice Black, dissenting in Hanson v. Denckla, 357 U.S., at 258-259, expressed similar concerns by suggesting that a State should have jurisdiction over a case growing out of a transaction significantly related to that State "unless litigation there would impose such a heavy and disproportionate burden on a nonresident defendant that it would offend what this Court has referred to as 'traditional notions of fair play and substantial justice.'" Assuming that a State gives a nonresident defendant adequate notice and opportunity to defend, I do not think the Due Process Clause is offended merely because the defendant has to board a plane to get to the site of the trial.

* * *

MR. JUSTICE MARSHALL, with whom MR. JUSTICE BLACKMUN joins, dissenting.

This is a difficult case, and reasonable minds may differ as to whether respondents have alleged a sufficient "relationship among the [defendants], the forum, and the litigation," Shaffer v. Heitner, 433 U.S. 186, 204 (1977), to satisfy the requirements of International Shoe. I am concerned, however, that the majority has reached its result by taking an unnecessarily narrow view of petitioners' forum-related conduct. The majority asserts that "respondents seek to base jurisdiction on one, isolated occurrence and whatever inferences can be drawn therefrom: the fortuitous circumstance that a single Audi automobile, sold in New York to New York residents, happened to suffer an accident while passing through Oklahoma." Ante, at 295. If that were the case, I would readily agree that the minimum contacts necessary to sustain jurisdiction are not present. But the basis for the assertion of jurisdiction is not the happenstance that an individual over whom petitioners had no control made a unilateral decision to take a chattel with him to a distant State. Rather, jurisdiction is premised on the deliberate and purposeful actions of the defendants themselves in choosing to become part of a nationwide, indeed a global, network for marketing and servicing automobiles.

Petitioners are sellers of a product whose utility derives from its mobility. The unique importance of the automobile in today's society, which is discussed in MR. JUSTICE BLACKMUN's dissenting opinion, post, at 318, needs no further elaboration. Petitioners know that their customers buy cars not only to make short trips, but also to travel long distances. In fact, the nationwide service network with which they are affiliated was designed to facilitate and encourage such travel. Seaway would be unlikely to sell many cars if authorized service were available only in Massena, N. Y. Moreover, local dealers normally derive a substantial portion of their revenues from their service operations and thereby obtain a further economic benefit from the opportunity to service cars which were sold in other States. It is apparent that petitioners have not attempted to minimize the chance that their activities will have effects in other States; on the contrary, they have chosen to do business in a way that increases that chance, because it is to their economic advantage to do so.

* * *

Of course, the Constitution forbids the exercise of jurisdiction if the defendant had no judicially cognizable contacts with the forum. But as the majority acknowledges, if such contacts are present the jurisdictional inquiry requires a balancing of various interests and policies. See ante, at 292; I believe such contacts are to be found here and that, considering all of the interests and policies at stake, requiring petitioners to defend this action in Oklahoma is not beyond the bounds of the Constitution. Accordingly, I dissent.

MR. JUSTICE BLACKMUN, dissenting.

I confess that I am somewhat puzzled why the plaintiffs in this litigation are so insistent that the regional distributor and the retail dealer, the petitioners here, who handled the ill-fated Audi automobile involved in this litigation, be named defendants. It would appear that the manufacturer and the importer, whose subjectability to Oklahoma jurisdiction is not challenged before this Court, ought not to be judgment-proof. It may, of course, ultimately amount to a contest between insurance companies that, once begun, is not easily brought to a termination. Having made this much of an observation, I pursue it no further.

For me, a critical factor in the disposition of the litigation is the nature of the instrumentality under consideration. It has been said that we are a nation on wheels. What we are concerned with here is the automobile and its peripatetic character. One need only examine our national network of interstate highways, or make an appearance on one of them, or observe the variety of license plates present not only on those highways but in any metropolitan area, to realize that any automobile is likely to wander far from its place of licensure or from its place of distribution and retail sale. Miles per gallon on the highway (as well as in the city) and mileage per tankful are familiar allegations in manufacturers' advertisements today. To expect that any new automobile will remain in the vicinity of its retail sale — like the 1914 electric car driven by the proverbial "little old lady" — is to blink at reality. The automobile is intended for distance as well as for transportation within a limited area.

It therefore seems to me not unreasonable — and certainly not unconstitutional and beyond the reach of the principles laid down in International Shoe Co. v. Washington, 326 U.S. 310 (1945), and its progeny — to uphold Oklahoma jurisdiction over this New York distributor and this New York dealer when the accident happened in Oklahoma. I see nothing more unfair for them than for the manufacturer and the importer. All are in the business of providing vehicles that spread out over the highways of our several States. It is not too much to anticipate at the time of distribution and at the time of retail sale that this Audi would be in Oklahoma. Moreover, in assessing "minimum contacts," foreseeable use in another State seems to me to be little different from foreseeable resale in another State. Yet the Court declares this distinction determinative. Ante, at 297-299.

MR. JUSTICE BRENNAN points out in his dissent, ante, at 307, that an automobile dealer derives substantial benefits from States other than its own. The same is true of the regional distributor. Oklahoma does its best to provide safe roads. Its police investigate accidents. It regulates driving within the State. It provides aid to the victim and thereby, it is hoped, lessens damages. Accident reports are prepared and made available. All this contributes to and enhances the business of those engaged professionally in the distribution and sale of automobiles. All this also may benefit defendants in the very lawsuits over which the State asserts jurisdiction.

My position need not now take me beyond the automobile and the professional who does business by way of distributing and retailing automobiles. Cases concerning other instrumentalities will be dealt with as they arise and in their own contexts.

I would affirm the judgment of the Supreme Court of Oklahoma. Because the Court reverses that judgment, it will now be about parsing every variant in the myriad of motor vehicle fact situations that present themselves. Some will justify jurisdiction and others will not. All will depend on the "contact" that the Court sees fit to perceive in the individual case.

NOTES AND QUESTIONS

1. Justice White's majority opinion begins with a reaffirmation of the minimum contacts test as providing the key to satisfying the demands of due process. He explains:

> The concept of minimum contacts . . . can be seen to perform two related, but distinguishable, functions. It protects the defendant against the burdens of litigating in a distant or inconvenient forum. And it acts to ensure that the States, through their courts, do not reach out beyond the limits imposed on them by their status as coequal sovereigns in a federal system.

Before beginning our attempt to define the level and type of forum contacts which will meet the minimum, ask a few basic questions:

A. Aside from the interests Justice White identified (the burden of the defendant and limitations on sovereignty), are there any other interests which need to be considered? What about, for example, the plaintiff's interest in having a convenient forum in which to sue?

  1. In <u>World-Wide</u>, the Robinsons were injured in Oklahoma, having left New York in their car to make a new home in the west. As far as we can tell, they had no intention of returning to New York. Now, in order to to vindicate their legal rights against the seller of the car, they will have to go back to New York.[17] Is that fair?

  2. In this regard, consider the comment of the Court in another earlier case, <u>Hanson v. Denckla</u>:

> As technological progress has increased the flow of commerce . . . the need for jurisdiction over nonresidents has undergone a similar increase. At the same time, progress in communications and transportation has made the defense of a suit in a foreign tribunal less burdensome. In response to these changes, the requirements for personal jurisdiction over nonresidents have evolved from the rigid rule of Pennoyer to the flexible standard of International Shoe.

> Is the a danger that the requirement of minimum contacts will somehow subvert the just-described goal?

  3. What about the interest of the forum itself? While the Court notes that a goal of the minimum contacts test is to limit the power of sovereigns, doesn't a sovereign have an interest in the outcome of litigation concerning an automobile which exploded on its street? How, if at all, is that interest accounted for in the majority's decision? And what about everyone's interest in creating an efficient adjudication, rather than having a situation where parts of a dispute are scattered between different fora because no one has jurisdiction over all the parties? Is that interest considered by the majority? By the dissenters?

B. Another question one might ask at the outset is: can a single standard, albeit a "flexible one" like "minimum contacts", ever achieve all that needs to be achieved to satisfy as complex a concept as due process

---

17. Or will they? See the comment made at the outset of Justice Blackmun's opinion.

of law? Can it even achieve the two, somewhat limited goals, that Justice White offers as performing? Could it be that the Court has created a new "shibboleth" to replace the old one?

C. The dissenters, particularly Justice Brennan, seem to ask many of these questions, and to disagree vehemently with the majority. That disagreement is not trivial, and it is not limited to a dispute about how one views the automobile. What, then, is the dispute about? What different philosophies are driving the division on the Court? That philosophical issue aside, however, do not ignore what the dissenters said in <u>World-Wide Volkswagen</u>, because it will influence the development of the law in the cases which follow.

2. Before looking at that next set of cases, however, we turn to the question we asked at the beginning of the <u>World-Wide</u> case - what kinds of contacts will suffice to meet the "minimum" required under <u>International Shoe</u>? Note that the Court does not directly answer that question (perhaps because it is too complex to answer). Rather, Justice White only deals with the converse, pointing, in support of the conclusion that the test has not been met, to all the contacts that are lacking:

> Petitioners carry on no activity whatsoever in Oklahoma. They close no sales and perform no services there. . . . They solicit no business there either through salespersons or through advertising reasonably calculated to reach the State. Nor does the record show that they regularly sell cars at wholesale or retail to Oklahoma customers or residents or that they indirectly, through others, serve or seek to serve the Oklahoma market.

A. Which of these "contacts", assuming such contact existed, would be enough to tip the balance against Seaway and in favor of jurisdiction? Would one even be enough, or would you need a combination? The Court simply doesn't say.

B. The Court does, however, reject the argument that the fact that it is foreseeable that the car might travel to Oklahoma and might cause injury there is not a contact sufficient to support jurisdiction. The foreseeability necessary to support a finding of due process, Justice White explains, is not "foreseeability of use", but rather it is the foreseeability that one might "reasonably anticipate being haled into court there". What does that mean? Should it be an important consideration? If so, why? Justice White says it has to do with permitting a business to make predictions about its jurisdictional exposure. How does that concern fit into your notions about the globalization of business today?

C. To explain why foreseeability of use or foreseeability of injury (by themselves) is insufficient to support a finding of "minimum contacts", Justice White invokes another legal construct - "purposeful availment".

1. If, Justice White opines, the defendant has "purposefully availed" itself of the benefits of the forum, it is not unfair to require that party to suffer the burden - being haled into court there. Justice White tells us that the standard is the key to san understanding of minimum contacts, because it focuses on the defendant's conduct, which in turn will define the instances in which the defendant will be required to defend a case away from home.

2. According to Justice White, purposeful availment is an appropriate key because it guarantees that the unilateral activity **of the plaintiff** (in this case moving the subject of the suit to Oklahoma) cannot, if that is all there is, expose the defendant to a foreign court's jurisdiction. By invoking the purposeful availment test, Justice White requires that some conscious activity of the **defendant** is required, and he gives as an example making an effort to serve, directly or indirectly, consumers in the forum state. Since there was no proof that either Seaway or World-Wide made such an effort (compare the activities of the German manufacturer, who was also sued but did not contest jurisdiction), they could not be held to account in the courts of Oklahoma.

3. In this manner, the majority seeks to achieve a jurisdictional test which assures that a business can predict where and when it might be exposed to a foreign court's jurisdiction. The goal is to permit the business to order its affairs in such a way that it can plan for such exposure, by, for example, factoring the risk into its pricing, or by purchasing insurance. Can that goal really be achieved? If it can be achieved, are there are any other competing goals that should be considered? If so, what are they, and how can they be reconciled?

3. Of course, Justice Brennan and his dissenting brethren disagree with Justice White's analysis. As suggested, they would take a larger view, looking not only at the burden on the defendant, but also at (a) the plaintiff's interest in having available a local forum for the adjudication of disputes; (b) interests of the forum itself in having a say as to the

outcome of a dispute which concerns them (in this case, that the cars which drive on their streets be safe); and (c) everyone's interest in producing an efficient resolution of the dispute. When these other interests are considered, they argue, the case for jurisdiction is much stronger.

A. The dissenters believe that (on these facts) these other goals outweigh the defendant's interest in avoiding the burden of defending in Oklahoma. They feel that the defendant's participation in interstate commercial activity, activity that is likely to produce consequences outside the defendant's home territory, is enough to satisfy due process concerns when that defendant is being called outside his home territory to account for that activity. Simply put, they don't agree that it is unfair to require the New York auto dealer to go to Oklahoma to defend itself. Why? Is it (a) because they are more concerned with the plaintiff's interests, or (b) because they don't care about the burden on the defendant? Or is it simply that they don't think it is all that much of a burden on the New York defendant to have to defend this case in Oklahoma?

B. The majority also discusses the interests of the plaintiffs and the forum, but they conclude that "[e]ven if the defendant would suffer minimal or no inconvenience from being forced to litigate before the tribunals of another State; even if the forum State has a strong interest in applying its law to the controversy; even if the forum State is the most convenient location for litigation, the Due Process Clause, acting as an instrument of interstate federalism, may sometimes act to divest the State of its power to render a valid judgment." Why? On what basis can they say that the interests of the defendant in this regard are always paramount?

C. If you are inclined to agree with the majority, what would you tell the Robinsons? And if you are inclined to agree with the dissenters, aren't you afraid of being haled unfairly into a foreign jurisdiction? Is there any way to find a middle ground? Put another way, would you expect Justice Brennan automatically to find jurisdiction when it comes to an international dispute? If you think that a middle ground can be achieved, where is it?

BURGER KING CORP.
v.
RUDZEWICZ

Supreme Court of the United States
471 U.S. 462; 105 S. Ct. 2174;
85 L. Ed. 2d 528; 53 U.S.L.W. 4541
Decided May 20, 1985

JUSTICE BRENNAN delivered the opinion of the Court.

The State of Florida's long-arm statute extends jurisdiction to "[any] person, whether or not a citizen or resident of this state," who, inter alia, "[breaches] a contract in this state by failing to perform acts required by the contract to be performed in this state," so long as the cause of action arises from the alleged contractual breach. Fla. Stat. § 48.193 (1)(g) (Supp. 1984). The United States District Court for the Southern District of Florida, sitting in diversity, relied on this provision in exercising personal jurisdiction over a Michigan resident who allegedly had breached a franchise agreement with a Florida corporation by failing to make required payments in Florida. The question presented is whether this exercise of long-arm jurisdiction offended "traditional. [conceptions] of fair play and substantial justice" embodied in the Due Process Clause of the Fourteenth Amendment. International Shoe Co. v. Washington, 326 U.S. 310, 320 (1945).

I
(A)

Burger King Corporation is a Florida corporation whose principal offices are in Miami. It is one of the world's largest restaurant organizations, with over 3,000 outlets in the 50 States, the Commonwealth of Puerto Rico, and 8 foreign nations. Burger King conducts approximately 80% of its business through a franchise operation that the company styles the "Burger King System" — "a comprehensive restaurant format and operating system for the sale of uniform and quality food products." App. 46. n1 Burger King licenses its franchisees to use its trademarks and service marks for a period of 20 years and leases standardized restaurant facilities to them for the same term. In addition, franchisees acquire a variety of proprietary information concerning the "standards, specifications, procedures and methods for operating a Burger King Restaurant." Id., at 52. They also receive market research and advertising assistance; ongoing training in restaurant management; and accounting, cost-control, and inventory-control guidance. By permitting franchisees to tap into Burger King's established national reputation and to benefit from proven procedures for dispensing standardized fare, this system enables them to go into the restaurant business with significantly lowered barriers to entry.

In exchange for these benefits, franchisees pay Burger King an initial $ 40,000 franchise fee and commit themselves to payment of monthly royalties, advertising and sales promotion fees, and rent computed in part from monthly gross sales. Franchisees also agree to submit to the national organization's exacting regulation of virtually every conceivable aspect of their operations. Burger King imposes these standards and undertakes its rigid regulation out of conviction that "[uniformity] of service, appearance, and quality of product is essential to the preservation of the Burger King image and the benefits accruing therefrom to both Franchisee and Franchisor." Id., at 31.

Burger King oversees its franchise system through a two-tiered administrative structure. The governing contracts provide that the franchise relationship is established in Miami and governed by Florida law, and call for payment of all required fees and forwarding of all relevant notices to the Miami headquarters. The Miami headquarters sets policy and works directly with its franchisees in attempting to resolve major problems. See nn. 7, 9, infra. Day-to-day monitoring of franchisees, however, is conducted through a network of 10 district offices which in turn report to the Miami headquarters.

The instant litigation grows out of Burger King's termination of one of its franchisees, and is aptly described by the franchisee as "a divorce proceeding among commercial partners." 5 Record 4. The appellee John Rudzewicz, a Michigan citizen and resident, is the senior partner in a Detroit accounting firm. In 1978, he was approached by Brian MacShara, the son of a business acquaintance, who suggested that they jointly apply to Burger King for a franchise in the Detroit area. MacShara proposed to serve as the manager of the restaurant if Rudzewicz would put up the investment capital; in exchange, the two would evenly share the profits. Believing that MacShara's idea offered attractive investment and tax-deferral opportunities, Rudzewicz agreed to the venture. 6 id., at 438-439, 444, 460.

Rudzewicz and MacShara jointly applied for a franchise to Burger King's Birmingham, Michigan, district office in the autumn of 1978. Their application was forwarded to Burger King's Miami headquarters, which entered into a preliminary agreement with them in February 1979. During the ensuing four months it was agreed that Rudzewicz and MacShara would assume operation of an existing facility in Drayton Plains, Michigan. MacShara attended the prescribed management courses in Miami during this period, see n. 2, supra, and the franchisees purchased $ 165,000 worth of restaurant equipment from Burger King's Davmor Industries division in Miami. Even before the final agreements were signed, however, the parties began to disagree over site-development fees, building design, computation of monthly rent, and whether the franchisees would be able to assign their liabilities to a corporation they had formed. During these disputes Rudzewicz and MacShara negotiated both with the Birmingham district office and with the Miami headquarters. With some misgivings, Rudzewicz and MacShara finally obtained limited concessions from the Miami headquarters, signed the final agreements, and commenced operations in June 1979. By signing the final agreements, Rudzewicz obligated himself personally to payments exceeding $ 1 million over the 20-year franchise relationship.

The Drayton Plains facility apparently enjoyed steady business during the summer of 1979, but patronage declined after a recession began later that year. Rudzewicz and MacShara soon fell far behind in their monthly payments to Miami. Headquarters sent notices of default, and an extended period of negotiations began among the franchisees, the Birmingham district office, and the Miami headquarters. After several Burger King officials in Miami had engaged in prolonged but ultimately unsuccessful negotiations with the franchisees by mail and by telephone, headquarters terminated the franchise and ordered Rudzewicz and MacShara to vacate the premises. They refused and continued to occupy and operate the facility as a Burger King restaurant.

(B)

Burger King commenced the instant action in the United States District Court for the Southern District of Florida in May 1981, invoking that court's diversity jurisdiction pursuant to 28 U. S. C. § 1332(a) and its original jurisdiction over federal trademark disputes pursuant to § 1338(a). Burger King alleged that Rudzewicz and MacShara had breached their franchise obligations "within [the jurisdiction of] this district court" by failing to make the required payments "at plaintiff's place of business in Miami, Dade County, Florida," para. 6, App. 121, and also charged that they were tortuously infringing its trademarks and service marks through their continued, unauthorized operation as a Burger King restaurant, paras. 35-53, App. 130-135. Burger King sought damages, injunctive relief, and costs and attorney's fees. Rudzewicz and MacShara entered special appearances and argued, inter alia, that because they were Michigan residents and because Burger King's claim did not "arise" within the Southern District of Florida, the District Court lacked personal jurisdiction over them. The District Court denied their motions after a hearing, holding that, pursuant to Florida's long-arm statute, "a non-resident Burger King franchisee is subject to the personal jurisdiction of this Court in actions arising out of its franchise agreements." Id., at 138. Rudzewicz and MacShara then filed an answer and a counterclaim seeking damages for alleged violations by Burger King of Michigan's Franchise Investment Law, Mich. Comp. Laws § 445.1501 et seq. (1979).

After a 3-day bench trial, the court again concluded that it had "jurisdiction over the subject matter and the parties to this cause." App. 159. Finding that Rudzewicz and MacShara had breached their franchise agreements with Burger King and had infringed Burger King's trademarks and service marks, the court entered judgment against them, jointly and severally, for $ 228,875 in contract damages. The court also ordered them "to immediately close Burger King Restaurant Number 775 from continued operation or to immediately give the keys and possession of said restaurant to Burger King Corporation," id., at 163, found that they had failed to prove any of the required elements of their counterclaim, and awarded costs and attorney's fees to Burger King.

Rudzewicz appealed to the Court of Appeals for the Eleventh Circuit. A divided panel of that Circuit reversed the judgment, concluding that the District Court could not properly exercise personal jurisdiction over Rudzewicz pursuant to Fla. Stat. § 48.193(1)(g) (Supp. 1984) because "the circumstances of the Drayton Plains franchise and the negotiations which led to it left Rudzewicz bereft of reasonable notice and financially unprepared for the prospect of franchise litigation in Florida." Burger King Corp. v. MacShara, 724 F.2d 1505, 1513 (1984). Accordingly, the panel majority concluded that "[jurisdiction] under these circumstances would offend the fundamental fairness which is the touchstone of due process." Ibid.

II
(A)

The Due Process Clause protects an individual's liberty interest in not being subject to the binding judgments of a forum with which he has established no meaningful "contacts, ties, or relations." International Shoe Co. v. Washington, 326 U.S., at 319. n13 By requiring that individuals have "fair warning that a particular activity may subject [them] to the jurisdiction of a foreign sovereign," Shaffer v. Heitner, 433 U.S. 186, 218 (1977) (STEVENS, J., concurring in judgment), the Due Process Clause "gives a degree of predictability to the legal system that allows potential defendants to structure their primary conduct with some minimum assurance as to where that conduct will and will not render them liable to suit," World-Wide Volkswagen Corp. v. Woodson, 444 U.S. 286, 297 (1980).

Where a forum seeks to assert specific jurisdiction over an out-of-state defendant who has not consented to suit there, this "fair warning" requirement is satisfied if the defendant has "purposefully directed" his activities at residents of the forum, Keeton v. Hustler Magazine, Inc., 465 U.S. 770, 774 (1984), and the litigation results from alleged injuries that "arise out of or relate to" those activities, Helicopteros Nacionales de Colombia, S.A. v. Hall, 466 U.S. 408, 414 (1984). Thus "[the] forum State does not exceed its powers under the Due Process Clause if it asserts personal jurisdiction over a corporation that delivers its products into the stream of commerce with the expectation that they will be purchased by consumers in the forum State" and those products subsequently injure forum consumers. World-Wide Volkswagen Corp. v. Woodson, supra, at 297-298. Similarly, a publisher who distributes magazines in a distant State may fairly be held accountable in that forum for damages resulting there from an allegedly defamatory story. Keeton v. Hustler Magazine, Inc., supra. And with respect to interstate contractual obligations, we have emphasized that parties who "reach out beyond one state and create continuing relationships and obligations with citizens of another state" are subject to regulation and sanctions in the other State for the consequences of their activities.

We have noted several reasons why a forum legitimately may exercise personal jurisdiction over a nonresident who "purposefully directs" his activities toward forum residents. A State generally has a "manifest interest" in providing its residents with a convenient forum for redressing injuries inflicted by out-of-state actors. Id., at 223; see also Keeton v. Hustler Magazine, Inc., supra, at 776. Moreover, where individuals "purposefully derive benefit" from their interstate activities, Kulko v. California Superior Court, 436 U.S. 84, 96 (1978), it may well be unfair to allow them to escape having to account in other States for consequences that arise proximately from such activities; the Due Process Clause may not readily be wielded as a territorial shield to avoid interstate obligations that have been voluntarily assumed. And because "modern transportation and communications have made it much less burdensome for a party sued to defend himself in a State where he engages in economic activity," it usually will not be unfair to subject him to the burdens of litigating in another forum for disputes relating to such activity.

Notwithstanding these considerations, the constitutional touchstone remains whether the defendant purposefully established "minimum contacts" in the forum State. International Shoe Co. v. Washington, supra, at 316. Although it has been argued that foreseeability of causing injury in another State should be sufficient to establish such contacts there when policy considerations so require, the Court has consistently held that this kind of foreseeability is not a "sufficient benchmark" for exercising personal jurisdiction. World-Wide Volkswagen Corp v. Woodson, 444 U.S., at 295. Instead, "the foreseeability that is critical to due process analysis . . . is that the defendant's conduct and connection with the forum State are such that he should reasonably anticipate being haled into court there." Id., at 297. In defining when it is that a potential defendant should "reasonably anticipate" out-of-state litigation, the Court frequently has drawn from the reasoning of Hanson v. Denckla, 357 U.S. 235, 253 (1958):

> "The unilateral activity of those who claim some relationship with a nonresident defendant cannot satisfy the requirement of contact with the forum State. The application of that rule will vary with the quality and nature of the defendant's activity, but it is essential in each case that there be some act by which the defendant purposefully avails itself of the privilege of conducting activities within the forum State, thus invoking the benefits and protections of its laws."

This "purposeful availment" requirement ensures that a defendant will not be haled into a jurisdiction solely as a result of "random," "fortuitous," or "attenuated" contacts, Keeton v. Hustler Magazine, Inc., 465 U.S., at 774; World-Wide Volkswagen Corp. v. Woodson, supra, at 299, or of the "unilateral activity of another party or a third person," Helicopteros Nacionales de Colombia, S.A. v. Hall, supra, at 417. Jurisdiction is proper, however, where the contacts proximately result from actions by the defendant himself that create a "substantial connection" with the forum State. McGee v. International Life Insurance Co., supra, at 223; see also Kulko v. California Superior Court, supra, at 94, n. 7. Thus where the defendant "deliberately" has engaged in significant activities within a State, Keeton v. Hustler Magazine, Inc., supra, at 781, or has created "continuing obligations" between himself and residents of the forum, Travelers Health Assn. v. Virginia, 339 U.S., at 648, he manifestly has availed himself of the privilege of conducting business there, and because his activities are shielded by "the benefits and protections" of the forum's laws it is presumptively not unreasonable to require him to submit to the burdens of litigation in that forum as well.

Jurisdiction in these circumstances may not be avoided merely because the defendant did not physically enter the forum State. Although territorial presence frequently will enhance a potential defendant's affiliation with a State and reinforce the reasonable foreseeability of suit there, it is an inescapable fact of modern commercial life that a substantial amount of business is transacted solely by mail and wire communications across state lines, thus obviating the need for physical presence within a State in which business is conducted. So long as a commercial actor's efforts are "purposefully directed" toward residents of another State, we have consistently rejected the notion that an absence of physical contacts can defeat personal jurisdiction there.

Once it has been decided that a defendant purposefully established minimum contacts within the forum State, these contacts may be considered in light of other factors to determine whether the assertion of personal jurisdiction would comport with "fair play and substantial justice." International Shoe Co. v. Washington, 326 U.S., at 320. Thus courts in "appropriate [cases]" may evaluate "the burden on the defendant," "the forum State's interest in adjudicating the dispute," "the plaintiff's interest in obtaining convenient and effective relief," "the interstate judicial system's interest in obtaining the most efficient resolution of controversies," and the "shared interest of the several States in furthering fundamental substantive social policies." World-Wide Volkswagen Corp. v. Woodson, 444 U.S., at 292. These considerations sometimes serve to establish the reasonableness of jurisdiction upon a lesser showing of minimum contacts than would otherwise be required. On the other hand, where a defendant who purposefully has directed his activities at forum residents seeks to defeat jurisdiction, he must present a compelling case that the presence of some other considerations would render jurisdiction unreasonable. Most such considerations usually may be accommodated through means short of finding jurisdiction unconstitutional. For example, the potential clash of the forum's law with the "fundamental substantive social policies" of another State may be accommodated through application of the forum's choice-of-law rules. Similarly, a defendant claiming substantial inconvenience may seek a change of venue. Nevertheless, minimum requirements inherent in the concept of "fair play and substantial justice" may defeat the reasonableness of jurisdiction even if the defendant has purposefully engaged in forum activities. World-Wide Volkswagen Corp. v. Woodson, supra, at 292; see also Restatement (Second) of Conflict of Laws §§ 36-37 (1971). As we previously have noted, jurisdictional rules may not be employed in such a way as to make litigation "so gravely difficult and inconvenient" that a party unfairly is at a "severe disadvantage" in comparison to his opponent. The Bremen v. Zapata Off-Shore Co., 407 U.S. 1, 18 (1972) (re forum-selection provisions).

B
(1)

Applying these principles to the case at hand, we believe there is substantial record evidence supporting the District Court's conclusion that the assertion of personal jurisdiction over Rudzewicz in Florida for the alleged breach of his franchise agreement did not offend due process. At the outset, we note a continued division among lower courts respecting whether and to what extent a contract can constitute a "contact" for purposes of due process analysis. If the question is whether an individual's contract with an out-of-state party alone can automatically establish sufficient minimum contacts in the other party's home forum, we believe the answer clearly is that it cannot. The Court long ago rejected the notion that personal jurisdiction might turn on "mechanical" tests, International Shoe Co. v. Washington, supra, at 319, or on "conceptualistic . . . theories of the place of contracting or of performance," Instead, we have emphasized the need for a "highly realistic" approach that recognizes that a "contract" is "ordinarily but an intermediate step serving to tie up prior business negotiations with future consequences which themselves are the real object of the business transaction." Id., at 316-317. It is these factors — prior negotiations and contemplated future consequences, along with the terms of the contract and the parties' actual course of dealing — that must be evaluated in determining whether the defendant purposefully established minimum contacts within the forum.

In this case, no physical ties to Florida can be attributed to Rudzewicz other than MacShara's brief training course in Miami. Rudzewicz did not maintain offices in Florida and, for all that appears from the record, has never even visited there. Yet this franchise dispute grew directly out of "a contract which had a substantial connection with that State." McGee v. International Life Insurance Co., 355 U.S., at 223 (emphasis added). Eschewing the option of operating an independent local enterprise, Rudzewicz deliberately "[reached] out beyond" Michigan and negotiated with a Florida corporation for the purchase of a long-term franchise and the manifold benefits that would derive from affiliation with a nationwide organization. Travelers Health Assn. v. Virginia, 339 U.S., at 647. Upon approval, he entered into a carefully structured 20-year relationship that envisioned continuing and wide-reaching contacts with Burger King in Florida. In light of Rudzewicz' voluntary acceptance of the long-term and exacting regulation of his business from Burger King's Miami headquarters, the "quality and nature" of his relationship to the company in Florida can in no sense be viewed as "random," "fortuitous," or "attenuated." Hanson v. Denckla, 357 U.S., at 253; Keeton v. Hustler Magazine, Inc., 465 U.S., at 774; World-Wide Volkswagen Corp. v. Woodson, 444 U.S., at 299. Rudzewicz' refusal to make the contractually required payments in Miami, and his continued use of Burger King's trademarks and confidential business information after his termination, caused foreseeable injuries to the corporation in Florida. For these reasons it was, at the very least, presumptively reasonable for Rudzewicz to be called to account there for such injuries.

The Court of Appeals concluded, however, that in light of the supervision emanating from Burger King's district office in Birmingham, Rudzewicz reasonably believed that "the Michigan office was for all intents and purposes the embodiment of Burger King" and that he therefore had no "reason to anticipate a Burger King suit outside of Michigan." 724 F.2d, at 1511. See also post, at 488-489 (STEVENS, J., dissenting). This reasoning overlooks substantial record evidence indicating that Rudzewicz most certainly knew that he was affiliating himself with an enterprise based primarily in Florida. The contract documents themselves emphasize that Burger King's operations are conducted and supervised from the Miami headquarters, that all relevant notices and payments must be sent there, and that the agreements were made in and enforced from Miami. Moreover, the parties' actual course of dealing repeatedly confirmed that decision making authority was vested in the Miami headquarters and that the district office served largely as an intermediate link between the headquarters and the franchisees. When problems arose over building design, site-development fees, rent computation, and the defaulted payments, Rudzewicz and MacShara learned that the Michigan office was powerless to resolve their disputes and could only channel their communications to Miami. Throughout these disputes, the Miami headquarters and the Michigan franchisees carried on a continuous course of direct communications by mail and by telephone, and it was the Miami headquarters that made the key negotiating decisions out of which the instant litigation arose.

Moreover, we believe the Court of Appeals gave insufficient weight to provisions in the various franchise documents providing that all disputes would be governed by Florida law. The franchise agreement, for example, stated:

"This Agreement shall become valid when executed and accepted by BKC at Miami, Florida; it shall be deemed made and entered into in the State of Florida and shall be governed and construed under and in accordance with the laws of the State of Florida. The choice of law designation does not require that all suits concerning this Agreement be filed in Florida." App. 72.

The Court of Appeals reasoned that choice-of-law provisions are irrelevant to the question of personal jurisdiction, relying on Hanson v. Denckla for the proposition that "the center of gravity for choice-of-law purposes does not necessarily confer the sovereign prerogative to assert jurisdiction." 724 F.2d, at 1511-1512, n. 10, citing 357 U.S., at 254. This reasoning misperceives the import of the quoted proposition. The Court in Hanson and subsequent cases has emphasized that choice-of-law analysis — which focuses on all elements of a transaction, and not simply on the defendant's conduct — is distinct from minimum-contacts jurisdictional analysis — which focuses at the threshold solely on the defendant's purposeful connection to the forum. Nothing in our cases, however, suggests that a choice-of-law provision should be ignored in considering whether a defendant has "purposefully invoked the benefits and protections of a State's laws" for jurisdictional purposes. Although such a provision standing alone would be insufficient to confer jurisdiction, we believe that, when combined with the 20-year interdependent relationship Rudzewicz established with Burger King's Miami headquarters, it reinforced his deliberate affiliation with the forum State and the reasonable foreseeability of possible litigation there. As Judge Johnson argued in his dissent below, Rudzewicz "purposefully availed himself of the benefits and protections of Florida's laws" by entering into contracts expressly providing that those laws would govern franchise disputes.

(2)

Nor has Rudzewicz pointed to other factors that can be said persuasively to outweigh the considerations discussed above and to establish the unconstitutionality of Florida's assertion of jurisdiction. We cannot conclude that Florida had no "legitimate interest in holding [Rudzewicz] answerable on a claim related to" the contacts he had established in that State. Moreover, although Rudzewicz has argued at some length that Michigan's Franchise Investment Law, Mich. Comp. Laws § 445.1501 et seq. (1979), governs many aspects of this franchise relationship, he has not demonstrated how Michigan's acknowledged interest might possibly render jurisdiction in Florida unconstitutional. Finally, the Court of Appeals' assertion that the Florida litigation "severely impaired [Rudzewicz'] ability to call Michigan witnesses who might be essential to his defense and counterclaim," 724 F.2d, at 1512-1513, is wholly without support in the record. And even to the extent that it is inconvenient for a party who has minimum contacts with a forum to litigate there, such considerations most frequently can be accommodated through a change of venue. Although the Court has suggested that inconvenience may at some point become so substantial as to achieve constitutional magnitude, McGee v. International Life Insurance Co., this is not such a case.

The Court of Appeals also concluded, however, that the parties' dealings involved "a characteristic disparity of bargaining power" and "elements of surprise," and that Rudzewicz "lacked fair notice" of the potential for litigation in Florida because the contractual provisions suggesting to the contrary were merely "boilerplate declarations in a lengthy printed contract." 724 F.2d, at 1511-1512. See also post, at 489-490 (STEVENS, J., dissenting). Rudzewicz presented many of these arguments to the District Court, contending that Burger King was guilty of misrepresentation, fraud, and duress; that it gave insufficient notice in its dealings with him; and that the contract was one of adhesion. See 4 Record 687-691. After a 3-day bench trial, the District Court found that Burger King had made no misrepresentations, that Rudzewicz and MacShara "were and are experienced and sophisticated businessmen," and that "at no time" did they "[act] under economic duress or disadvantage imposed by" Burger King. App. 157-158. See also 7 Record 648-649. Federal Rule of Civil Procedure 52(a) requires that "[findings] of fact shall not be set aside unless clearly erroneous," and neither Rudzewicz nor the Court of Appeals has pointed to record evidence that would support a "definite and firm conviction" that the District Court's findings are mistaken. To the contrary, Rudzewicz was represented by counsel throughout these complex transactions and, as Judge Johnson observed in dissent below, was himself an experienced accountant "who for five months conducted negotiations with Burger King over the terms of the franchise and lease agreements, and who obligated himself personally to contracts requiring over time payments that exceeded $ 1 million." 724 F.2d, at 1514. Rudzewicz was able to secure a modest reduction in rent and other concessions from Miami headquarters; moreover, to the extent that Burger King's terms were inflexible, Rudzewicz presumably decided that the advantages of affiliating with a national organization provided sufficient commercial benefits to offset the detriments.

* * *

The judgment of the Court of Appeals is accordingly reversed, and the case is remanded for further proceedings consistent with this opinion.

It is so ordered.

JUSTICE POWELL took no part in the consideration or decision of this case.

JUSTICE STEVENS, with whom JUSTICE WHITE joins, dissenting.

In my opinion there is a significant element of unfairness in requiring a franchisee to defend a case of this kind in the forum chosen by the franchiser. It is undisputed that appellee maintained no place of business in Florida, that he had no employees in that State, and that he was not licensed to do business there. Appellee did not prepare his French fries, shakes, and hamburgers in Michigan, and then deliver them into the stream of commerce "with the expectation that they [would] be purchased by consumers in" Florida. Ante, at 473. To the contrary, appellee did business only in Michigan, his business, property, and payroll taxes were payable in that State, and he sold all of his products there.

Throughout the business relationship, appellee's principal contacts with appellant were with its Michigan office. Notwithstanding its disclaimer, ante, at 478, the Court seems ultimately to rely on nothing more than standard boilerplate language contained in various documents, ante, at 481, to establish that appellee "'purposefully availed himself of the benefits and protections of Florida's laws.'" Ante, at 482. Such superficial analysis creates a potential for unfairness not only in negotiations between franchisers and their franchisees but, more significantly, in the resolution of the disputes that inevitably arise from time to time in such relationships.

Judge Vance's opinion for the Court of Appeals for the Eleventh Circuit adequately explains why I would affirm the judgment of that court. I particularly find the following more persuasive than what this Court has written today:

> Nothing in the course of negotiations gave Rudzewicz reason to anticipate a Burger King suit outside of Michigan. The only face-to-face or even oral contact Rudzewicz had with Burger King throughout months of protracted negotiations was with representatives of the Michigan office. Burger King had the Michigan office interview Rudzewicz and MacShara, appraise their application, discuss price terms, recommend the site which the defendants finally agreed to, and attend the final closing ceremony. There is no evidence that Rudzewicz ever negotiated with anyone in Miami or even sent mail there during negotiations. He maintained no staff in the state of Florida, and as far as the record reveals, he has never even visited the state.
>
> The contracts contemplated the startup of a local Michigan restaurant whose profits would derive solely from food sales made to customers in Drayton Plains. The sale, which involved the use of an intangible trademark in Michigan and occupancy of a Burger King facility there, required no performance in the state of Florida. Under the contract,

the local Michigan district office was responsible for providing all of the services due Rudzewicz, including advertising and management consultation. Supervision, moreover, emanated from that office alone. To Rudzewicz, the Michigan office was for all intents and purposes the embodiment of Burger King. He had reason to believe that his working relationship with Burger King began and ended in Michigan, not at the distant and anonymous Florida headquarters. . . .

Given that the office in Rudzewicz' home state conducted all of the negotiations and wholly supervised the contract, we believe that he had reason to assume that the state of the supervisory office would be the same state in which Burger King would file suit. Rudzewicz lacked fair notice that the distant corporate headquarters which insulated itself from direct dealings with him would later seek to assert jurisdiction over him in the courts of its own home state. . . .

Just as Rudzewicz lacked notice of the possibility of suit in Florida, he was financially unprepared to meet its added costs. The franchise relationship in particular is fraught with potential for financial surprise. The device of the franchise gives local retailers the access to national trademark recognition which enables them to compete with better-financed, more efficient chain stores. This national affiliation, however, does not alter the fact that the typical franchise store is a local concern serving at best a neighborhood or community. Neither the revenues of a local business nor the geographical range of its market prepares the average franchise owner for the cost of distant litigation. . . .

The particular distribution of bargaining power in the franchise relationship further impairs the franchisee's financial preparedness. In a franchise contract, 'the franchiser normally occupies [the] dominant role'. . .

We discern a characteristic disparity of bargaining power in the facts of this case. There is no indication that Rudzewicz had any latitude to negotiate a reduced rent or franchise fee in exchange for the added risk of suit in Florida. He signed a standard form contract whose terms were non-negotiable and which appeared in some respects to vary from the more favorable terms agreed to in earlier discussions. In fact, the final contract required a minimum monthly rent computed on a base far in excess of that discussed in oral negotiations. Burger King resisted price concessions, only to sue Rudzewicz far from home. In doing so, it severely impaired his ability to call Michigan witnesses who might be essential to his defense and counterclaim.

In sum, we hold that the circumstances of the Drayton Plains franchise and the negotiations which led to it left Rudzewicz bereft of reasonable notice and financially unprepared for the prospect of franchise litigation in Florida. Jurisdiction under these circumstances would offend the fundamental fairness which is the touchstone of due process."

724 F.2d 1505, 1511-1513 (1984) (footnotes omitted).

Accordingly, I respectfully dissent.

NOTES AND QUESTIONS

1. As was the case in <u>World-Wide Volkswagon,</u> <u>Burger King</u> concerned a defendant's claim that a particular exercise of long-arm jurisdiction was a violation of due process. Again, there was a dispute over whether the defendant's conduct met the "minimum contacts" test. And again, the defendant and the plaintiff were both U.S. citizens resident in different states. But there the similarities stop and the differences take over.

    a. <u>World-Wide</u> was a dispute between an injured consumer and a purveyor of goods alleged to be defective; <u>Burger King</u> is a contract dispute between business-people. How and why should that difference matter?

    b. In <u>World-Wide</u>, the plaintiff was not suing "at home", while in <u>Burger King</u>, the plaintiff brought suit in the courts of the state in which it had its main office. How does that factor fit into the "minimum contacts" analysis?

    c. In <u>World-Wide</u>, Justice Brennan authored the dissenting opinion; in <u>Burger King</u>, he writes for the majority. Has he changed his mind about what the law should be, or has he changed the law? If he changed his mind, why? If he changed the law, how has he changed it?

2. It is apparent almost from the outset of the opinion that change is in the wind. Read Justice Brennan's review of the Court's previous jurisdiction cases. Absent is any consideration of the burden on the defendant, the theme which lay beneath <u>World-Wide Volkswagen</u> (the potential for

burden on the defendant is relegated to the last sentence of the last paragraph of Part 2A of the opinion). Rather, the Court remarks that since "'modern transportation and communications have made it much less burdensome for a party sued to defend himself in a State where he engages in economic activity,' it usually will not be unfair to subject him to the burdens of litigating in another forum for disputes relating to such activity." That language was also cited in <u>World-Wide Volkswagen</u>, where it was offered as a rationale for the advent of long-arm jurisdiction. Here, it is being cited for much more - as a rationale for expanding the reach of long-arm jurisdiction and distancing the Court from the theme of <u>World-Wide</u>.

3.   Despite the obvious change in thrust, the Court's analysis in <u>Burger King</u> nevertheless begins with further refinement of the "purposeful availment" test that was set forth in <u>Hanson v. Denkla</u>, explaining that is designed to "ensure[] that a defendant will not be haled into a jurisdiction solely as a result of 'random,' 'fortuitous,' or 'attenuated' contacts," and we again warned to look to "the quality and nature" of the defendant's contacts with the forum. But, it is stated, where the defendant has a "substantial connection with forum" or where a defendant has "created 'continuing obligations' between himself and residents of the forum", it is "presumptively not unreasonable to require him to submit to the burdens of litigation in that forum as well." Are we getting any closer to defining minimum contacts? Are we getting closer to being able to decide this case? Put differently, would you say that the defendant's conduct meets this test by opening a Burger King restaurant?

   a.   The defendants in the case argued that they had no real physical contact with Florida. The Court responded that jurisdiction cannot be avoided because one did not enter the territory of the forum, although if it is present, it enhances the case for jurisdiction. So if physical contact is not required, what kind of contact is?

   b.   True to form, the Court prefers to answer a different question. It states that "[i]f the question is whether an individual's contract with an out-of-state party alone can automatically establish sufficient minimum contacts in the other party's home forum, we believe the answer clearly is that it cannot." Is that statement helpful? What category of cases can you now eliminate from the circle of cases in which there is sufficient contact?

   c.   Obviously, this case is not one of the ones to be excluded. The Court instructs us to look not just at the parties whereabouts at the time a contract was made, but rather to take the longer viewn, considering "prior negotiations and contemplated future consequences, along with the terms of the contract and the parties' actual course of dealing" in deciding whether there is **purposeful** availment. The Court thus finds that the franchisees "eschewed the option of operating an independent local enterprise" and "deliberately '[reached] out beyond' Michigan and negotiated with a Florida corporation for the purchase of a long-term franchise and the manifold benefits that would derive from affiliation with a nationwide organization." Do you see the distinction between the facts of this case and the facts of World-Wide Volkswagon? Are you able to develop an understanding of the kind of cases where there is purposeful availment?

III. THE INTERNATIONAL WRINKLE

ASAHI METAL INDUSTRY CO., LTD.
v.
SUPERIOR COURT OF CALIFORNIA, SOLANO COUNTY (CHENG SHIN RUBBER INDUSTRIAL CO., LTD., REAL PARTY IN INTEREST)

Supreme Court of the United States

480 U.S. 102; 107 S. Ct. 1026

February 24, 1987

JUSTICE O'CONNOR announced the judgment of the Court and delivered the unanimous opinion of the Court with respect to Part I, the opinion of the Court with respect to Part II-B, in which THE CHIEF JUSTICE, JUSTICE BRENNAN, JUSTICE WHITE, JUSTICE MARSHALL, JUSTICE BLACKMUN, JUSTICE POWELL, and JUSTICE STEVENS join, and an opinion with respect to Parts II-A and III, in which THE CHIEF JUSTICE, JUSTICE POWELL, and JUSTICE SCALIA join.

This case presents the question whether the mere awareness on the part of a foreign defendant that the components it manufactured, sold, and delivered outside the United States would reach the forum State in the stream of commerce constitutes "minimum contacts" between the defendant and the forum State such that the exercise of jurisdiction "does not offend 'traditional notions of fair play and substantial justice.'" International Shoe Co. v. Washington, 326 U.S. 310, 316 (1945)

I

On September 23, 1978, on Interstate Highway 80 in Solano County, California, Gary Zurcher lost control of his Honda motorcycle and collided with a tractor. Zurcher was severely injured, and his passenger and wife, Ruth Ann Moreno, was killed. In September 1979, Zurcher filed a product liability action in the Superior Court of the State of California in and for the County of Solano. Zurcher alleged that the 1978 accident was caused by a sudden loss of air and an explosion in the rear tire of the motorcycle, and alleged that the motorcycle tire, tube, and sealant were defective. Zurcher's complaint named, inter alia, Cheng Shin Rubber Industrial Co., Ltd. (Cheng Shin), the Taiwanese manufacturer of the tube. Cheng Shin in turn filed a cross-complaint seeking indemnification from its codefendants and from petitioner, Asahi Metal Industry Co., Ltd. (Asahi), the manufacturer of the tube's valve assembly. Zurcher's claims against Cheng Shin and the other defendants were eventually settled and dismissed, leaving only Cheng Shin's indemnity action against Asahi.

California's long-arm statute authorizes the exercise of jurisdiction "on any basis not inconsistent with the Constitution of this state or of the United States." Cal. Civ. Proc. Code Ann. § 410.10 (West 1973). Asahi moved to quash Cheng Shin's service of summons, arguing the State could not exert jurisdiction over it consistent with the Due Process Clause of the Fourteenth Amendment.

In relation to the motion, the following information was submitted by Asahi and Cheng Shin. Asahi is a Japanese corporation. It manufactures tire valve assemblies in Japan and sells the assemblies to Cheng Shin, and to several other tire manufacturers, for use as components in finished tire tubes. Asahi's sales to Cheng Shin took place in Taiwan. The shipments from Asahi to Cheng Shin were sent from Japan to Taiwan. Cheng Shin bought and incorporated into its tire tubes 150,000 Asahi valve assemblies in 1978; 500,000 in 1979; 500,000 in 1980; 100,000 in 1981; and 100,000 in 1982. Sales to Cheng Shin accounted for 1.24 percent of Asahi's income in 1981 and 0.44 percent in 1982. Cheng Shin alleged that approximately 20 percent of its sales in the United States are in California. Cheng Shin purchases valve assemblies from other suppliers as well, and sells finished tubes throughout the world.

In 1983 an attorney for Cheng Shin conducted an informal examination of the valve stems of the tire tubes sold in one cycle store in Solano County. The attorney declared that of the approximately 115 tire tubes in the store, 97 were purportedly manufactured in Japan or Taiwan, and of those 97, 21 valve stems were marked with the circled letter "A", apparently Asahi's trademark. Of the 21 Asahi valve stems, 12 were incorporated into Cheng Shin tire tubes. The store contained 41 other Cheng Shin tubes that incorporated the valve assemblies of other manufacturers. Declaration of Kenneth B. Shepard in Opposition to Motion to Quash Subpoena, App. to Brief for Respondent 5-6. An affidavit of a manager of Cheng Shin whose duties included the purchasing of component parts stated: "'In discussions with Asahi regarding the purchase of valve stem assemblies the fact that my Company sells tubes throughout the world and specifically the United States has been discussed. I am informed and believe that Asahi was fully aware that valve stem assemblies sold to my Company and to others would end up throughout the United States and in

California.'" 39 Cal. 3d 35, 48, n. 4, 702 P. 2d 543, 549-550, n. 4 (1985). An affidavit of the president of Asahi, on the other hand, declared that Asahi "'has never contemplated that its limited sales of tire valves to Cheng Shin in Taiwan would subject it to lawsuits in California.'" Ibid. The record does not include any contract between Cheng Shin and Asahi. Tr. of Oral Arg. 24.

Primarily on the basis of the above information, the Superior Court denied the motion to quash summons, stating: "Asahi obviously does business on an international scale. It is not unreasonable that they defend claims of defect in their product on an international scale."

The Court of Appeal of the State of California issued a peremptory writ of mandate commanding the Superior Court to quash service of summons. The court concluded that "it would be unreasonable to require Asahi to respond in California solely on the basis of ultimately realized foreseeability that the product into which its component was embodied would be sold all over the world including California."

The Supreme Court of the State of California reversed and discharged the writ issued by the Court of Appeal. The court observed: "Asahi has no offices, property or agents in California. It solicits no business in California and has made no direct sales [in California]." Id., at 48, 702 P. 2d, at 549. Moreover, "Asahi did not design or control the system of distribution that carried its valve assemblies into California." Id., at 49, 702 P. 2d, at 549. Nevertheless, the court found the exercise of jurisdiction over Asahi to be consistent with the Due Process Clause. It concluded that Asahi knew that some of the valve assemblies sold to Cheng Shin would be incorporated into tire tubes sold in California, and that Asahi benefitted indirectly from the sale in California of products incorporating its components. The court considered Asahi's intentional act of placing its components into the stream of commerce — that is, by delivering the components to Cheng Shin in Taiwan — coupled with Asahi's awareness that some of the components would eventually find their way into California, sufficient to form the basis for state court jurisdiction under the Due Process Clause.

We granted certiorari, and now reverse.

II

(A)

The Due Process Clause of the Fourteenth Amendment limits the power of a state court to exert personal jurisdiction over a nonresident defendant. "[The] constitutional touchstone" of the determination whether an exercise of personal jurisdiction comports with due process "remains whether the defendant purposefully established 'minimum contacts' in the forum State." Burger King Corp. v. Rudzewicz, 471 U.S. 462, 474 (1985), quoting International Shoe Co. v. Washington, 326 U.S., at 316. Most recently we have reaffirmed the oft-quoted reasoning of Hanson v. Denckla, 357 U.S. 235, 253 (1958), that minimum contacts must have a basis in "some act by which the defendant purposefully avails itself of the privilege of conducting activities within the forum State, thus invoking the benefits and protections of its laws." Burger King, 471 U.S., at 475. "Jurisdiction is proper . . . where the contacts proximately result from actions by the defendant himself that create a 'substantial connection' with the forum State." Ibid., quoting McGee v. International Life Insurance Co., 355 U.S. 220, 223 (1957)

Applying the principle that minimum contacts must be based on an act of the defendant, the Court in World-Wide Volkswagen Corp. v. Woodson, 444 U.S. 286 (1980), rejected the assertion that a consumer's unilateral act of bringing the defendant's product into the forum State was a sufficient constitutional basis for personal jurisdiction over the defendant. It had been argued in World-Wide Volkswagen that because an automobile retailer and its wholesale distributor sold a product mobile by design and purpose, they could foresee being haled into court in the distant States into which their customers might drive. The Court rejected this concept of foreseeability as an insufficient basis for jurisdiction under the Due Process Clause. Id., at 295-296. The Court disclaimed, however, the idea that "foreseeability is wholly irrelevant" to personal jurisdiction, concluding that "[the] forum State does not exceed its powers under the Due Process Clause if it asserts personal jurisdiction over a corporation that delivers its products into the stream of commerce with the expectation that they will be purchased by consumers in the forum State." Id., at 297-298 (citation omitted). The Court reasoned:

> "When a corporation 'purposefully avails itself of the privilege of conducting activities within the forum State,' Hanson v. Denckla, 357 U.S. [235,] 253 [(1958)], it has clear notice that it is subject to suit there, and can act to alleviate the risk of burdensome litigation by procuring insurance, passing the expected costs on to customers, or, if the risks are too great, severing its connection with the State. Hence if the sale of a product of a manufacturer or distributor . . . is not simply an isolated occurrence, but arises from the efforts of the manufacturer or distributor to serve, directly or indirectly, the market for its product in other States, it is not unreasonable to subject it to suit in one of those States if its allegedly defective merchandise has there been the source of injury to its owners or to others." Id., at 297.

In World-Wide Volkswagen itself, the state court sought to base jurisdiction not on any act of the defendant, but on the foreseeable unilateral actions of the consumer. Since World-Wide Volkswagen, lower courts have been confronted with cases in which the defendant acted by placing a product in the stream of commerce, and the stream eventually swept defendant's product into the forum State, but the defendant did nothing else to purposefully avail itself of the market in the forum State. Some courts have understood the Due Process Clause, as interpreted in World-Wide Volkswagen, to allow an exercise of personal jurisdiction to be based on no more than the defendant's act of placing the product in the stream of commerce. Other courts have understood the Due Process Clause and the above-quoted language in World-Wide Volkswagen to require the action of the defendant to be more purposefully directed at the forum State than the mere act of placing a product in the stream of commerce. The reasoning of the Supreme Court of California in the present case illustrates the former interpretation of World-Wide Volkswagen. The Supreme Court of California held that, because the stream of commerce eventually brought some valves Asahi sold Cheng Shin into California, Asahi's awareness that its valves would be sold in California was sufficient to permit California to exercise jurisdiction over Asahi consistent with the requirements of the Due Process Clause. The Supreme Court of California's position was consistent with those courts that have held that mere foreseeability or awareness was a constitutionally sufficient basis for personal jurisdiction if the defendant's product made its way into the forum State while still in the stream of commerce.

Other courts, however, have understood the Due Process Clause to require something more than that the defendant was aware of its product's entry into the forum State through the stream of commerce in order for the State to exert jurisdiction over the defendant. In the present case, for example, the State Court of Appeal did not read the Due Process Clause, as interpreted by World-Wide Volkswagen, to allow "mere foreseeability that the product will enter the forum state [to] be enough by itself to establish jurisdiction over the distributor and retailer." In Humble v. Toyota Motor Co., 727 F.2d 709 (CA8 1984), an injured car passenger brought suit against Arakawa Auto Body Company, a Japanese corporation that manufactured car seats for Toyota. Arakawa did no business in the United States; it had no office, affiliate, subsidiary, or agent in the United States; it manufactured its component parts outside the United States and delivered them to Toyota Motor Company in Japan. The Court of Appeals, adopting the reasoning of the District Court in that case, noted that although it "does not doubt that Arakawa could have foreseen that its product would find its way into the United States," it would be "manifestly unjust" to require Arakawa to defend itself in the United States. Id., at 710-711.

We now find this latter position to be consonant with the requirements of due process. The "substantial connection," Burger King, 471 U.S., at 475; McGee, 355 U.S., at 223, between the defendant and the forum State necessary for a finding of minimum contacts must come about by an action of the defendant purposefully directed toward the forum State. Burger King, supra, at 476; Keeton v. Hustler Magazine, Inc., 465 U.S. 770, 774 (1984). The placement of a product into the stream of commerce, without more, is not an act of the defendant purposefully directed toward the forum State. Additional conduct of the defendant may indicate an intent or purpose to serve the market in the forum State, for example, designing the product for the market in the forum State, advertising in the forum State, establishing channels for providing regular advice to customers in the forum State, or marketing the product through a distributor who has agreed to serve as the sales agent in the forum State. But a defendant's awareness that the stream of commerce may or will sweep the product into the forum State does not convert the mere act of placing the product into the stream into an act purposefully directed toward the forum State.

Assuming, arguendo, that respondents have established Asahi's awareness that some of the valves sold to Cheng Shin would be incorporated into tire tubes sold in California, respondents have not demonstrated any action by Asahi to purposefully avail itself of the California market. Asahi does not do business in California. It has no office, agents, employees, or property in California. It does not advertise or otherwise solicit business in California. It did not create, control, or employ the distribution system that brought its valves to California. Cf. Hicks v. Kawasaki Heavy Industries, 452 F.Supp. 130 (MD Pa. 1978). There is no evidence that Asahi designed its product in anticipation of sales in California. Cf. Rockwell International Corp. v. Costruzioni Aeronautiche Giovanni Agusta, 553 F.Supp. 328 (ED Pa. 1982). On the basis of these facts, the exertion of personal jurisdiction over Asahi by the Superior Court of California exceeds the limits of due process.

(B)

The strictures of the Due Process Clause forbid a state court from exercising personal jurisdiction over Asahi under circumstances that would offend "'traditional notions of fair play and substantial justice.'" International Shoe Co. v. Washington, 326 U.S., at 316.

We have previously explained that the determination of the reasonableness of the exercise of jurisdiction in each case will depend on an evaluation of several factors. A court must consider the burden on the defendant, the interests of the forum State, and the plaintiff's interest in obtaining relief. It must also weigh in its determination "the interstate judicial system's interest in obtaining the most efficient resolution of controversies; and the shared interest of the several States in furthering fundamental substantive social policies." World-Wide Volkswagen, 444. U.S., at 292 (citations omitted).

A consideration of these factors in the present case clearly reveals the unreasonableness of the assertion of jurisdiction over Asahi, even apart from the question of the placement of goods in the stream of commerce.

Certainly the burden on the defendant in this case is severe. Asahi has been commanded by the Supreme Court of California not only to traverse the distance between Asahi's headquarters in Japan and the Superior Court of California in and for the County of Solano, but also to submit its dispute with Cheng Shin to a foreign nation's judicial system. The unique burdens placed upon one who must defend oneself in a foreign legal system should have significant weight in assessing the reasonableness of stretching the long arm of personal jurisdiction over national borders.

When minimum contacts have been established, often the interests of the plaintiff and the forum in the exercise of jurisdiction will justify even the serious burdens placed on the alien defendant. In the present case, however, the interests of the plaintiff and the forum in California's assertion of jurisdiction over Asahi are slight. All that remains is a claim for indemnification asserted by Cheng Shin, a Tawainese corporation, against Asahi. The transaction on which the indemnification claim is based took place in Taiwan; Asahi's components were shipped from Japan to Taiwan. Cheng Shin has not demonstrated that it is more convenient for it to litigate its indemnification claim against Asahi in California rather than in Taiwan or Japan.

Because the plaintiff is not a California resident, California's legitimate interests in the dispute have considerably diminished. The Supreme Court of California argued that the State had an interest in "protecting its consumers by ensuring that foreign manufacturers comply with the state's safety standards." 39 Cal. 3d, at 49, 702 P. 2d, at 550. The State Supreme Court's definition of California's interest, however, was overly broad. The dispute between Cheng Shin and Asahi is primarily about indemnification rather than safety standards. Moreover, it is not at all clear at this point that California law should govern the question whether a Japanese corporation should indemnify a Taiwanese corporation on the basis of a sale made in Taiwan and a shipment of goods from Japan to Taiwan. The possibility of being haled into a California court as a result of an accident involving Asahi's components undoubtedly creates an additional deterrent to the manufacture of unsafe components; however, similar pressures will be placed on Asahi by the purchasers of its components as long as those who use Asahi components in their final products, and sell those products in California, are subject to the application of California tort law.

World-Wide Volkswagen also admonished courts to take into consideration the interests of the "several States," in addition to the forum State, in the efficient judicial resolution of the dispute and the advancement of substantive policies. In the present case, this advice calls for a court to consider the procedural and substantive policies of other nations whose interests are affected by the assertion of jurisdiction by the California court. The procedural and substantive interests of other nations in a state court's assertion of jurisdiction over an alien defendant will differ from case to case. In every case, however, those interests, as well as the Federal Government's interest in its foreign relations policies, will be best served by a careful inquiry into the reasonableness of the assertion of jurisdiction in the particular case, and an unwillingness to find the serious burdens on an alien defendant outweighed by minimal interests on the part of the plaintiff or the forum State. "Great care and reserve should be exercised when extending our notions of personal jurisdiction into the international field."

Considering the international context, the heavy burden on the alien defendant, and the slight interests of the plaintiff and the forum State, the exercise of personal jurisdiction by a California court over Asahi in this instance would be unreasonable and unfair.

III

Because the facts of this case do not establish minimum contacts such that the exercise of personal jurisdiction is consistent with fair play and substantial justice, the judgment of the Supreme Court of California is reversed, and the case is remanded for further proceedings not inconsistent with this opinion.

It is so ordered.

JUSTICE BRENNAN, with whom JUSTICE WHITE, JUSTICE MARSHALL, and JUSTICE BLACKMUN join, concurring in part and concurring in the judgment.

I do not agree with the interpretation in Part II-A of the stream-of-commerce theory, nor with the conclusion that Asahi did not "purposely avail itself of the California market." I do agree, however, with the Court's conclusion in Part II-B that the exercise of personal jurisdiction over Asahi in this case would not comport with "fair play and substantial justice," International Shoe Co. v. Washington, 326 U.S. 310, 320 (1945). This is one of those rare cases in which "minimum requirements inherent in the concept of 'fair play and substantial justice' . . . defeat the reasonableness of jurisdiction even [though] the defendant has purposefully engaged in forum activities." Burger King Corp. v. Rudzewicz, 471 U.S. 462, 477-478 (1985). I therefore join Parts I and II-B of the Court's opinion, and write separately to explain my disagreement with Part II-A.

Part II-A states that "a defendant's awareness that the stream of commerce may or will sweep the product into the forum State does not convert the mere act of placing the product into the stream into an act purposefully directed toward the forum State." Under this view, a plaintiff would be required to show "[additional] conduct" directed toward the forum before finding the exercise of jurisdiction over the defendant to be consistent with the Due Process Clause. Ibid. I see no need for such a showing, however. The stream of commerce refers not to unpredictable currents or eddies, but to the regular and anticipated flow of products from manufacture to distribution to retail sale. As long as a participant in this process is aware that the final product is being marketed in the forum State, the possibility of a lawsuit there cannot come as a surprise. Nor will the litigation present a burden for which there is no corresponding benefit. A defendant who has placed goods in the stream of commerce benefits economically from the retail sale of the final product in the forum State, and indirectly benefits from the State's laws that regulate and facilitate commercial activity. These benefits accrue regardless of whether that participant directly conducts business in the forum State, or engages in additional conduct directed toward that State. Accordingly, most courts and commentators have found that jurisdiction premised on the placement of a product into the stream of commerce is consistent with the Due Process Clause, and have not required a showing of additional conduct.

The endorsement in Part II-A of what appears to be the minority view among Federal Courts of Appeals represents a marked retreat from the analysis in World-Wide Volkswagen v. Woodson, 444 U.S. 286 (1980). In that case, "respondents [sought] to base jurisdiction on one, isolated occurrence and whatever inferences can be drawn therefrom: the fortuitous circumstance that a single Audi automobile, sold in New York to New York residents, happened to suffer an accident while passing through Oklahoma." Id., at 295. The Court held that the possibility of an accident in Oklahoma, while to some extent foreseeable in light of the inherent mobility of the automobile, was not enough to establish   minimum contacts between the forum State and the retailer or distributor. Id., at 295-296. The Court then carefully explained:

"[This] is not to say, of course, that foreseeability is wholly irrelevant. But the foreseeability that is critical to due process analysis is not the mere likelihood that a product will find its way into the forum State. Rather, it is that the defendant's conduct and connection with the forum State are such that he should reasonably anticipate being haled into Court there." Id., at 297.

The Court reasoned that when a corporation may reasonably anticipate litigation in a particular forum, it cannot claim that such litigation is unjust or unfair, because it "can act to alleviate the risk of burdensome litigation by procuring insurance, passing the expected costs on to consumers, or, if the risks are too great, severing its connection with the State." Ibid.

To illustrate the point, the Court contrasted the foreseeability of litigation in a State to which a consumer fortuitously transports a defendant's product (insufficient contacts) with the foreseeability of litigation in a State where the defendant's product was regularly sold (sufficient contacts). The Court stated:

> "Hence if the sale of a product of a manufacturer or distributor such as Audi or Volkswagen is not simply an isolated occurrence, but arises from the efforts of the manufacturer or distributor to serve, directly or indirectly, the market for its product in other States, it is not unreasonable to subject it to suit in one of those States if its allegedly defective merchandise has there been the source of injury to its owner or to others. The forum State does not exceed its powers under the Due Process Clause if it asserts personal jurisdiction over a corporation that delivers its products into the stream of commerce with the expectation that they will be purchased by consumers in the forum State." Id., at 297-298.

The Court in World-Wide Volkswagen thus took great care to distinguish "between a case involving goods which reach a distant State through a chain of distribution and a case involving goods which reach the same State because a consumer . . . took them there." Id., at 306-307 (BRENNAN, J., dissenting). The California Supreme Court took note of this distinction, and correctly concluded that our holding in World-Wide Volkswagen preserved the stream-of-commerce theory.

In this case, the facts found by the California Supreme Court support its finding of minimum contacts. The court found that "[although] Asahi did not design or control the system of distribution that carried its valve assemblies into California, Asahi was aware of the distribution system's operation, and it knew that it would benefit economically from the sale in California of products incorporating its components." Accordingly, I cannot join the determination in Part II-A that Asahi's regular and extensive sales of component parts to a manufacturer it knew was making regular sales of the final product in California is insufficient to establish minimum contacts with California.

JUSTICE STEVENS, with whom JUSTICE WHITE and JUSTICE BLACKMUN join, concurring in part and concurring in the judgment.

The judgment of the Supreme Court of California should be reversed for the reasons stated in Part II-B of the Court's opinion. While I join Parts I and II-B, I do not join Part II-A for two reasons. First, it is not necessary to the Court's decision. An examination of minimum contacts is not always necessary to determine whether a state court's assertion of personal jurisdiction is constitutional. See Burger King Corp. v. Rudzewicz, 471 U.S. 462, 476-478 (1985). Part II-B establishes, after considering the factors set forth in World-Wide Volkswagen Corp. v. Woodson, 444 U.S. 286, 292 (1980), that California's exercise of jurisdiction over Asahi in this case would be "unreasonable and unfair." This finding alone requires reversal; this case fits within the rule that "minimum requirements inherent in the concept of 'fair play and substantial justice' may defeat the reasonableness of jurisdiction even if the defendant has purposefully engaged in forum activities." Burger King, 471 U.S., at 477-478 (quoting International Shoe Co. v. Washington, 326 U.S. 310, 320 (1945)). Accordingly, I see no reason in this case for the plurality to articulate "purposeful direction" or any other test as the nexus between an act of a defendant and the forum State that is necessary to establish minimum contacts.

Second, even assuming that the test ought to be formulated here, Part II-A misapplies it to the facts of this case. The plurality seems to assume that an unwavering line can be drawn between "mere awareness" that a component will find its way into the forum State and "purposeful availment" of the forum's market. Over the course of its dealings with Cheng Shin, Asahi has arguably engaged in a higher quantum of conduct than "[the] placement of a product into the stream of commerce, without more. . . ." Ibid. Whether or not this conduct rises to the level of purposeful availment requires a constitutional determination that is affected by the volume, the value, and the hazardous character of the components. In most circumstances I would be inclined to conclude that a regular course of dealing that results in deliveries of over 100,000 units annually over a period of several years would constitute "purposeful availment" even though the item delivered to the forum State was a standard product marketed throughout the world.

NOTES AND QUESTIONS

1. Asahi is an important case for us because it, finally, addresses the jurisdictional equation when a foreign defendant is involved. The fact pattern, however, is a step from ordinary because of the procedural posture - the "plaintiff" (Cheng Shin) is a Taiwanese manufacturer who purchased component parts abroad (from Asahi) and then sold the finished product in California. A Californian was injured, and he sued everybody (i.e. the Taiwanese tire manufacturer and the Japanese valve-stem manufacturer). The manufacturer settled with the Californian, and, in this "tail end" of the case, the manufacturer seeks indemnification from the valve-stem manufacturer.

    A. In short, this case had, by the time it reached the United States Supreme Court, become a dispute between two foreign companies. Why is that fact relevant to the question of jurisdiction? It clearly has nothing to do with the burden on the defendant. What other interest is affected, and in what way?

B.   Because of the unusual posture, the decision should not be interpreted as insulating foreign businesses from the reach of U.S. courts. What effect, then, does <u>Asahi</u> have on more ordinary cases against foreign defendants? And what are those "ordinary" cases, anyway?

C.   In a partial answer to the last question, observe that in <u>Asahi</u>, the jurisdictional "contacts", if they existed, were indirect and not direct, since Asahi sells nothing directly in the United States. At the same time, however, Asahi could not claim that they didn't know that their products were being resold in New York.

  1.   As both this case and the <u>World-Wide Volkswagen</u> case point out, if the foreign seller is engaged in **direct** sales to United States residents, there is a much stronger case for jurisdiction (over claims arising out of those sales). Can there be a case where a direct foreign seller is outside the power of the U.S. courts?

  2.   At the same, it is clear that even an indirect seller might be subjected to jurisdiction if he otherwise takes overt steps aimed at forum consumers. What kind of overt steps would suffice to support a finding of "purposeful availment"?

2.   <u>Asahi</u> is an example of what happens when the Supreme Court fragments. All the justices agree that the exercise of jurisdiction over Asahi is unreasonable (Part IIB of Justice O'Connor's opinion). But they split badly on how to evaluate Asahi's U.S. contacts under the "purposeful availment" test

A.   Four justices, led by Justice O'Connor, argue that placing goods into the stream of commerce, even when combined with awareness that your product is being sold in the forum to forum consumers, is not sufficient to meet purposeful availment\minimum contacts.

  1.   To these Justices, one who places goods into the "stream of commerce", even with the knowledge "the stream of commerce may or will sweep the product into the forum State does not convert the mere act of placing the product into the stream into an act purposefully directed toward the forum State." Why is that so? What interest are they trying to protect? What interests are "harmed" by that analysis?

  2.   These four Justices would require that, in addition to knowledge of indirect sales, that the defendant have engaged in additional conduct directed at the forum. Why? What conduct, do you think, would satisfy the stricter, O'Connor interpretation of purposeful availment?

B.   Four other Justices, again led by Brennan (but, notably, this time including Justice White - author of <u>WWV</u>), would lower the bar. To them, the "stream of commerce refers not to unpredictable currents or eddies, but to the regular and anticipated flow of products from manufacture to distribution to retail sale. As long as a participant in this process is aware that the final product is being marketed in the forum State, the possibility of a lawsuit there cannot come as a surprise. Nor will the litigation present a burden for which there is no corresponding benefit. A defendant who has placed goods in the stream of commerce benefits economically from the retail sale of the final product in the forum State, and indirectly benefits from the State's laws that regulate and facilitate commercial activity. These benefits accrue regardless of whether that participant directly conducts business in the forum State, or engages in additional conduct directed toward that State.

1.   Do you accept this benefit-burden analysis? Is there a danger that business will, to avoid the jurisdictional exposure, choose not to sell, or not to sell internationally? Notice that, at least in this phase of the analysis, the fact that the defendant is foreign, as opposed to from a sister-state, is not considered. Nor is there any suggestion by Justice Brennan that we need to measure the volume of such sales (<u>i.e.</u> the benefit) in order to make the "purposeful availment" determination. Is that right?

C.   Justice Stevens (along with two of those who joined Justice Brennan's decision) conclude that a purposeful availment determination should take into account the volume and value of such sales, as well as "the hazardous character of the components".

1.   Is that a better formulation? Is it going to make lines harder to draw, or easier?

2.   Note also that Justice Stevens does not weigh in on the debate between Justice O'Connor and Justice Brennan on the precise purposeful availment formulation. He states that since all agree that jurisdiction is "unreasonable on balance" in this case, there is no need to reach the "purposeful availment" issue. Is that a sign that the jurisdictional test is moving away from "purposeful availment" as the "touchstone" of the jurisdictional test, replaced with a real analysis of benefits and burdens? If you agree, what does that observation say about jurisdiction over foreign nationals?

3. Take a careful look at the Court's conclusions about the reasonableness test. The Court says that the burden on Asahi is great because they are a foreign national. Can you create a list of "burdens" foreign defendants encounter when they are required to defend actions abroad. Is there a difference between some foreign defendants and others when it comes to the evaluation of burden? What other factors does the Court look to make a conclusion about reasonableness? How would these other considerations affect a contract case like <u>Burger King</u> (as opposed to product liability cases like <u>WWV</u> and <u>Asahi</u>) if the defendants in that case had been foreign nationals?

A NOTE ON LONG ARM JURISDICTIONAL STATUTES

While the jurisdiction of courts in the United States is limited by the due process clause of the Constitution, individual courts only have such jurisdiction as is granted to them by the legislature. Each state thus has a statute conferring jurisdiction on its courts.[18] Some state statutes, like California, simply provide that the courts there have jurisdiction "to the full extent permitted by the Constitution". But other states, like New York and Florida, attempt, in their jurisdictional statutes, to enumerate the instances where jurisdiction will lie. In these states, the court's jurisdiction to adjudicate is measured by both the statute and the Constitutional limit.

What follows are the relevant portions of New York's jurisdictional statute:

CPLR § 301. Jurisdiction over person, property or status

A court may exercise such jurisdiction over persons, property, or status as might have been exercised heretofore.

CPLR § 302. Personal jurisdiction by acts of non-domiciliaries

(a) **Acts which are the basis of jurisdiction.** As to a cause of action arising from any of the acts enumerated in this section, a court may exercise personal jurisdiction over any non-domiciliary, or his executor or administrator, who in person or through an agent:

　　1. transacts any business within the state or contracts anywhere to supply goods or services in the state; or

　　2. commits a tortuous act within the state, except as to a cause of action for defamation of character arising from the act; or

---

18. Note that the federal courts apply the jurisdictional rules of the state in which the courthouse is physically located. Thus a federal court in New York has the same power to summons as does the state court across the street. In this way, it should be observed, a plaintiff cannot obtain broader jurisdiction over an absent defendant simply by choosing to file the case in federal court. The federal court will apply the state's jurisdictional rules

3. commits a tortuous act without the state causing injury to person or property within the state, except as to a cause of action for defamation of character arising from the act, if he

    (i)   regularly does or solicits business, or engages in any other persistent course of conduct, or derives substantial revenue from goods used or consumed or services rendered, in the state, or

    (ii) expects or should reasonably expect the act to have consequences in the state and derives substantial revenue from interstate or international commerce; or

4. owns, uses or possess any real property situated within the state.

* * *

The Following is an excerpt from the **British** Long-Arm statute, first enacted in 1911:

ORDER 11

(R.S.C. 1965)
SERVICE OF PROCESS, ETC., OUT OF THE JURISDICTION

Principal cases in which service of writ out of jurisdiction is permissible (O. 11, r.1).

1. (1) Subject to Rule 3 and provided that the writ does not contain any such claim as is mentioned in Order 75, Rule 2 (1)(a), service of a writ, or notice of a writ, out of the jurisdiction is permissible with the leave of the Court in the following cases, that is to say—

    (a)   if the whole subject-matter of this action begun by the writ is land situate within the jurisdiction (with or without rents or profits) or the perpetuation of testimony relating to land so situate;

    (b)   if an act, deed, will, contract, obligation or liability affecting land situate within the jurisdiction is sought to be construed, rectified, set aside or enforced in the action begun by the writ;

    (c)   if the action begun by the writ relief is sought against a person domiciled or ordinarily resident within the jurisdiction;

    (d)   if the action begun by the writ is for the administration of the estate of a person who died domiciled within the jurisdiction or if the action begun by the writ is for any relief or remedy which might be obtained in any such action as aforesaid;

(e) if the action begun by the writ is for the execution, as to property situate within the jurisdiction, of the trusts of a written instrument, being trusts that ought to be executed according to English law and of which the person to be served with the writ is a trustee or if the action begun by the writ is for any relief or remedy which might be obtained in any such action as aforesaid;

(f) if the action begun by the writ is brought against a defendant not domiciled or ordinarily resident in Scotland to enforce, rescind, dissolve, annul or otherwise affect a contract, or to recover damages or obtain other relief in respect of the breach of a contract, being (in either case) a contract which

    (i) was made within the jurisdiction, or

    (ii) was made by or through an agent trading or residing within the jurisdiction on behalf of a principal trading or residing out of the jurisdiction, or

    (iii) is by its terms, or by implication, governed by English law;

(g) if the action begun by the writ is brought against a defendant not domiciled or ordinarily resident in Scotland or Northern Ireland, in respect of a breach committed within the jurisdiction of a contract made within or out of the jurisdiction, and irrespective of the fact, if such be the case, that the breach was preceded or accompanied by a breach committed out of the jurisdiction that rendered impossible the performance of so much of the contract as ought to have been performed within the jurisdiction;

(h) if the action begun by the writ is founded on a tort committed within the jurisdiction;

(i) if in the action begun by the writ an injunction is sought ordering the defendant to do or refrain from doing anything within the jurisdiction (whether or not damages are also claimed in respect of a failure to do or the doing of that thing);

(j) if the action begun by the writ being properly brought against a person duly served within the jurisdiction, a person out of the jurisdiction is a necessary or proper party thereto;

(k) if the action begun by the writ is either by a mortgagee of property situate within the jurisdiction (other than land) and seeks the sale of the property, the foreclosure of the mortgage or delivery by the mortgagor of possession of the property but not an order for payment of any moneys due under the mortgage or by a mortgagor of property so situate (other than land) and seeks redemption of the mortgage, reconveyance of the property or delivery by the mortgagee of possession of the property but not a personal judgment;

Service our of jurisdiction in certain actions of contract (O.11,r.2).

2. Where it appears to the Court that a contract contains a term to the effect that the High Court shall have jurisdiction to hear and determine any action in respect of the contract, the Court may, subject to rule 8, grant leave for service out of the jurisdiction of the writ, or notice of the writ, by which an action in respect of the contract is begun.

IV. JURISDICTION AND THE INTERNET

DATE: 20050916
COURT OF APPEAL FOR ONTARIO

B E T W E E N :	
CHEICKH BANGOURAPlaintiff (Respondent)	
- and -	
THE WASHINGTON POST, WILLIAM BRANIGIN, JAMES RUPERT, STEVEN BUCKLEY, UNITED NATIONS and FRED ECKHARDDefendants (Appellants)	
Heard: March 8, 2005	

On appeal from the order of Justice Romain W. M. Pitt of the Superior Court of Justice dated January 27, 2004 and reported at (2004), 235 D.L.R. (4th) 564.

ARMSTRONG J.A.:

BACKGROUND

[1]   The respondent, Cheickh Bangoura, sued the *Washington Post* and three
       of its reporters in respect of two newspaper articles, which he alleges are
       defamatory. When the articles were published in January 1997, Mr.
       Bangoura was employed by the United Nations in Nairobi, Kenya. The
       articles related to Mr. Bangoura's conduct in a prior posting with the
       United Nations in the Ivory Coast. At the time of publication of the
       articles, there were only seven subscribers to the *Washington Post* in
       Ontario. At that time, Mr. Bangoura was not an Ontario resident. When
       the action was commenced, more than six years after the publication of
       the articles, Mr. Bangoura was a resident of Ontario. The issue before us
       is whether the Ontario courts should assume jurisdiction in this case.

[2]   Counsel for the *Washington Post* and its reporters brought a motion to
       stay the action on the ground that there is no real and substantial
       connection between this action and Ontario or between the *Washington
       Post* and Ontario. They also submitted that Ontario is not the most
       convenient forum and that the service of the statement of claim *ex juris*
       should be set aside.

[3]   In dismissing the motion, Pitt J. of the Superior Court of Justice held
       that it was appropriate for the Ontario courts to assume jurisdiction,
       that Ontario was the most convenient forum and that the service *ex juris*
       of the statement of claim was proper. The *Washington Post* and its
       reporters now appeal the order of the motion judge.

THE FACTS

[4]   Mr. Bangoura was born and raised in Guinea. He was a student in
       Germany between 1978 and 1986. Between 1987 and 1993, he was
       employed by the United Nations in Austria. In September 1993, he was
       seconded to the United Nations Drug Control Program in the Ivory Coast
       as assistant regional director for West Africa, where he remained until
       December of 1994. He was then transferred to the United Nations Drug
       Control Program in Kenya under a contract that was to expire at the end
       of January 1997. In Kenya, Mr. Bangoura was assistant regional director
       of the UN Drug Control Program's regional office for Eastern and
       Southern Africa.

[5]   On Sunday, January 5, 1997, the *Washington Post* published an article
       under the headline, "Cloud of Scandal Follows UN Drug Control Official:
       Boutros-Ghali Ties Allegedly Gave Protection". The article refers specifically
       to Mr. Bangoura and alleges that his UN colleagues had accused him of

sexual harassment, financial improprieties and nepotism during his tenure in the Ivory Coast. The article suggests that he had eluded punishment in part by invoking close ties to Mr. Boutros-Ghali, the former UN secretary general, a close friend of Mr. Bangoura's father-in-law.

[6]   Mr. Bangoura was suspended from his position as assistant regional director of the UN Drug Control Program for Eastern and Southern Africa on January 9, 1997.

[7]   On Friday, January 10, 1997, the *Washington Post* published a second article under the headline, "UN Removes African from Drug Agency: Controversial Envoy's Misconduct Cited". The second article repeated the allegations that were contained in the earlier article.

[8]   In February 1997, Mr. Bangoura joined his wife and two children in Montreal, where they had moved in December 1996. Mr. Bangoura and his family lived in Montreal until June 2000, when they moved to Ontario in the Brampton area. This action was commenced in April 2003.

[9]   In addition to the *Washington Post,* the statement of claim named three reporters, William Branigin, James Rupert and Steven Buckley, as defendants. In 1997, William Branigin lived in Washington. He now lives in Reston, Virginia, adjacent to Washington. James Rupert was a foreign correspondent for the *Washington Post* in Abidjan, Ivory Coast. He now lives in the state of New York. Steven Buckley was a foreign correspondent for the *Washington Post* in Nairobi, Kenya. He now lives in Florida.

[10]   WP Company LLC carried on business as the *Washington Post.* It is a wholly owned subsidiary of The Washington Post Company, with its head office in the city of Washington in the District of Columbia. The circulation of the *Washington Post* on Sunday, January 5, 1997, was approximately 1,106,968. Over 95 per cent of the *Washington Post* newspapers were distributed in the District of Columbia area. Only 7 copies of the newspaper were delivered in Ontario. Approximately 781,704 copies of the *Washington Post* were distributed on Friday, January 10, 1997 – over 95 per cent in the District of Columbia area. Only 7 copies were delivered to subscribers in Ontario.

[11]   The two articles in issue were also published on the *Washington Post* Web site and were available free of charge for fourteen days following publication. Thereafter, the articles could be accessed through a paid archive. Only one person, counsel for Mr. Bangoura, has accessed the articles through the paid archive.

[12]   Summaries of the two articles, containing the gist of the allegations made against Mr. Bangoura, continue to be available free of charge through the Internet from the *Washington Post* archive.

[13] The *Washington Post* has a small office in Toronto for use by a reporter for news gathering purposes.

[14] The United Nations and an official of the UN Secretariat, Fred Eckhard, were also named as defendants in this action. However, Mr. Bangoura is no longer proceeding against the United Nations and Mr. Eckhard.

[15] The court had the benefit of submissions from counsel for the Media Coalition, which intervened in this appeal. The members of the Media Coalition publish newspapers, magazines and books worldwide and they broadcast radio and television programming in North America and elsewhere. They publish Internet Web sites that have been accessed by millions of viewers in more than two hundred countries. The members include national and international organizations in Canada, the United States of America, the United Kingdom and Europe. The members of the Media Coalition assist journalists and advocate for freedom of expression throughout the world.

THE ACTION

[16] In his statement of claim, Mr. Bangoura seeks the following relief against the *Washington Post*:

(i)   an order directing the *Washington Post* to cease the publication of the articles that had appeared on its web page since January 1997;

(ii)   an order directing the *Washington Post* to publish a retraction;

(iii) damages in the amount of $5 million for intentional interference with prospective economic advantage and inducing a breach of employment contract;

(iv)   damages in the amount of $1 million for intentional infliction of mental anguish;

(v)   damages in the amount of $1 million for negligence;

(vi)   damages in the amount of $1 million for refusing to post retractions and for unreasonable delay in removing defamatory messages posted on the *Washington Post* Web site;

(vii) punitive and exemplary damages in the amount of $2 million;

(viii) pre-judgment and post-judgment interest and costs on a substantial indemnity scale.

[17] Although Mr. Bangoura submits in his factum that the action is not a defamation action, there are numerous references throughout his statement of claim to defamation such as: "the tort of defamation", "publications of the defamation", "defamatory articles", "defamatory materials", "defamatory statements", "defamatory publication", "defamatory publications", "defamatory innuendos" and "the defamation". He also asserts in his statement of claim that, "The Plaintiff alleges that the said articles and website publications must be taken together as constituting a libel against the Plaintiff." It is perhaps worth noting that the motion judge approached the case as if it were a libel case. See para. 24 of his reasons.

[18] Counsel for Mr. Bangoura did not advise us why she takes the position that her client is not suing in defamation. It may be that she does so in an effort to avoid a potential problem concerning the notice and limitation provisions contained in ss. 5-6 of the *Libel and Slander Act*, R.S.O. 1990, c. L.12. However, that issue is not before us. In my view, whether this case is simply a libel case "dressed up" as something else does not change the analysis in respect of whether the Ontario courts should assume jurisdiction.

ANALYSIS OF THE MOTION JUDGE'S REASONS

[19] The motion judge began his analysis of the jurisdictional issue by considering the eight factors articulated by Sharpe J.A. in *Muscutt v. Courcelles* (2002), 60 O.R. (3d) 20 (C.A.). In that case, the court considered the real and substantial connection test developed by the Supreme Court of Canada in *Morguard Investments Ltd. v. De Savoye*, [1990] 3 S.C.R. 1077. Sharpe J.A. observed at para. 75 that "it is not possible to reduce the real and substantial connection test to a fixed formula." However, he found it useful to identify the factors which appear to have been considered by the Supreme Court of Canada and other courts in addressing the question of whether a court should assume jurisdiction in a case involving an out-of-province defendant on the basis of damage sustained in Ontario, as a result of a tort committed outside the province. Sharpe J.A. was careful to note at para. 76 that "no factor is determinative". The factors considered in *Muscutt* are the following:

(i)   the connection between the forum and the plaintiff's claim;

(ii)   the connection between the forum and the defendant;

(iii) unfairness to the defendant in assuming jurisdiction;

(iv)   unfairness to the plaintiff in not assuming jurisdiction;

(v)   the involvement of other parties to the suit;

(vi) the court's willingness to recognize and enforce an extra-provincial judgment rendered on the same juris-dictional basis;

(vii) whether the case is interprovincial or international in nature; and

(viii) comity and the standards of jurisdiction, recognition and enforcement prevailing elsewhere.

[20] *Muscutt* and *Morguard* were both interprovincial cases. However, *Muscutt* was argued together with four other appeals, all of which involved defendants in foreign jurisdictions. [1] The recent judgment of the Supreme Court of Canada in *Beals v. Saldanha*, [2003] 3 S.C.R. 416, has made it clear that the real and substantial connection test applies to international cases.

The motion judge's application of the *Muscutt* factors

(i)   The connection between the forum and the plaintiff's claim

[21] The motion judge acknowledged that Mr. Bangoura had resided in Ontario for a relatively short period and that when the articles were originally published, he did not reside in Ontario. However, he concluded at para. 22(1) that Mr. Bangoura was "an international public servant, who has found a home and work in Ontario where the damages to his reputation would have the greatest impact."

[22] The connection between Ontario and Mr. Bangoura's claim is minimal at best. In fact, there was no connection with Ontario until more than three years after the publication of the articles in question. In *Muscutt*, Sharpe J.A. raised this very issue at para. 79 of his reasons:

On the other hand, if the plaintiff lacks a significant connection with the forum, the case for assuming jurisdiction on the basis of damage sustained within the jurisdiction is weaker. If the connection is tenuous, courts should be wary of assuming jurisdiction. Mere residence in the jurisdiction does not constitute a sufficient basis for assuming jurisdiction. See V. Black, "Territorial Jurisdiction Based on the Plaintiff's Residence: *Dennis v. Salvation Army Grace General Hospital Board*" (1997), 14 C.P.C. (4th) 207 at p. 232, 156 N.S.R. (2d) 372 (C.A.), where the author writes:

Permitting a plaintiff to assume a new residence and sue a defendant there in respect of events that occurred elsewhere seems to be harsh to defendants, and this is particularly so when those events comprise a completed tort.

Even if the connection is significant, however, the case for assuming jurisdiction is proportional to the degree of damage sustained within the jurisdiction. It is difficult to justify assuming jurisdiction against an out-of-province defendant unless the plaintiff has suffered significant damage within the jurisdiction.

[23] In an affidavit filed by Mr. Bangoura, he deposed:

As a result of the continued action of the Washington Post, I have sustained damages in Ontario and elsewhere in that my opportunities for economic advancement in my profession have been adversely affected.

No details are provided. The distribution of the articles was minimal. Only Mr. Bangoura's lawyer accessed the two articles on the *Washington Post* Internet database. Whatever damages were suffered by Mr. Bangoura's losing his job with the UN, more than three years before he took up residence in Ontario, are not damages suffered in Ontario. In my view, there is no evidence that Mr. Bangoura has suffered significant damages within Ontario.

(ii)   The connection between the forum and the defendant

[24] The motion judge concluded that the defendants had no connection to Ontario, but observed at para. 22(2) that the *Washington Post* is a major newspaper which is "often spoken of in the same breath as the *New York Times* and the *London Telegraph*." He concluded that "the defendants should have reasonably foreseen that the story would follow the plaintiff wherever he resided."

[25] I agree with the submissions of counsel for the appellants that there is no significant connection between the *Washington Post* defendants and Ontario. I cannot agree with the motion judge when he concluded that the appellants "should have reasonably foreseen that the story would follow the plaintiff wherever he resided." It was not reasonably foreseeable in January 1997 that Mr. Bangoura would end up as a resident of Ontario three years later. To hold otherwise would mean that a defendant could be sued almost anywhere in the world based upon where a plaintiff may decide to establish his or her residence long after the publication of the defamation.

(iii) Any unfairness to the defendant in assuming jurisdiction

[26] In respect of this factor, the motion judge said at para. 22(3):

While the personal defendants have no connection to Ontario, the *Post* is a newspaper with an international profile, and its writers influence viewpoints throughout the English-speaking world. I would be surprised if it were not insured for damages for libel or defamation anywhere in the world, and if it is not, then it should be.

[27] There is no evidence in the record in respect of the *Washington Post's* insurance coverage.

(iv) Any unfairness to the plaintiff in not assuming jurisdiction

[28] In his reasons, the motion judge stated at para. 22(4):

> The plaintiff has no connection with any of the jurisdictions in which the defendants reside. Since Washington is the residence of only one of the defendants, the plaintiff could be faced with the same objections from the personal defendants if the action were commenced in Washington, where the [plaintiff] has no reputation to defend. What is more, there is a clear juridical advantage to the plaintiff in Ontario implicitly acknowledged by the *Post*. The delay argument advanced by the *Post* in terms of a potential statutory impediment is neutral on this issue.

[29] Although unfairness to the plaintiff in not assuming jurisdiction might often be a powerful factor within a *Muscutt* analysis, it must be remembered that the plaintiff had no connection with Ontario until more than three years after the publication of the articles in question. While in *Muscutt*, Sharpe J.A. found at para. 88 that "the principles of order and fairness should be considered in relation to the plaintiff as well as the defendant", he followed by adverting to *Morguard, supra,* at p. 1108, in which La Forest J. held that this factor comes into play only where there is otherwise a real and substantial connection with the action. If the plaintiff's evidence does not support such a connection elsewhere within the *Muscutt* analysis, it becomes increasingly difficult to accord weight to this factor.

(v) The involvement of other parties in the suit

[30] The motion judge stated at para. 22(5) that "the involvement of other defendants residing respectively in New York and Florida is a factor, in my view, in favour of the plaintiff's choice of forum."

[31] In my view, the fact that two of the personal defendants now live in New York and Florida does not favour Ontario. This factor relates more to a *forum conveniens* argument than to the assumption of jurisdiction. In any event, the main defendant, the *Washington Post*, is located in Washington, D.C., and the remaining personal defendant, William Branigin, resides in nearby Virginia.

(vi) The court's willingness to recognize and enforce an extra-provincial judgment rendered on the same jurisdictional basis

[32] The motion judge observed at para. 22(6) that:

I can see no reason why Ontario would be unwilling to enforce a judgment of a foreign court against an Ontario newspaper with a worldwide reputation, even if the damages were limited to the foreign jurisdiction, especially where, as here, the plaintiff is an international public servant. Such a newspaper should reasonably contemplate the likelihood of such damage occurring.

[33] Sharpe J.A. in *Leufkens* cautioned that if an Ontario court assumes jurisdiction against a foreign defendant, it would require Ontario courts to enforce foreign judgments pronounced on the same jurisdictional basis against Ontario defendants. Although *Leufkens* involved a lawsuit by an Ontario plaintiff against a Swiss travel company for injuries suffered in Costa Rica, the principle raised by Sharpe J.A. at para. 33 of his judgment is apt:

When assessing the real and substantial connection test and the principles of order and fairness, it is important to consider the interests of potential Ontario defendants as well as those of Ontario plaintiffs. In light of *Morguard* and *Hunt* [*Hunt v. T & N plc*, [1993] 4 S.C.R. 289], finding that the real and substantial connection test has been met would require Ontario courts to enforce foreign judgments rendered on the same jurisdictional basis against Ontario defendants who offer tourism services to visitors of this province. In my view, we should not adopt such a rule, since it would impose an unreasonable burden on providers of tourism services in Ontario. To take the example mentioned during oral argument, it would seem harsh to require an Algonquin Park canoe rental operator to litigate the claim of an injured Japanese tourist in Tokyo. Although negligent operators should certainly be held to account for their negligence, if they confine their activities to Ontario, they are entitled to expect that claims will be litigated in the courts of this province.

[34] Admittedly, while the facts in *Leufkens* are more "confined" than they could ever be in litigation involving articles published on the Internet, it must be remembered that on the evidence presented before the motion judge, the articles did not reach significantly into Ontario. As I have mentioned, Mr. Bangoura's lawyer was the only person in Ontario to access the two articles on the *Washington Post* Internet database. While other articles published on the Internet may proliferate well beyond their original target audiences into other jurisdictions, the fact scenario before me falls far closer to the situation described in *Leufkens*. If the cautionary warning of Sharpe J.A. is not taken into account, it could lead to Ontario publishers and broadcasters being sued anywhere in the world with the prospect that the Ontario courts would be obliged to enforce foreign judgments obtained against them.

(vii) Whether the case is interprovincial or international in nature

[35] The motion judge agreed that since the case is international in nature, rather than interprovincial, it is more difficult to justify the assumption of jurisdiction.

(viii) Comity and the standards of jurisdiction, recognition and enforcement prevailing elsewhere

[36] In considering this factor, the motion judge referred to *New York Times Co. v. Sullivan*, 376 U.S. 254 (1964), a judgment of the United States Supreme Court, and *Hill v. Church of Scientology*, [1995] 2 S.C.R. 1130, a judgment of the Supreme Court of Canada. In *New York Times v. Sullivan*, the United States Supreme Court held that public officials could only succeed in a defamation claim where they could establish that the defamatory statement was made "with knowledge that it was false or with reckless disregard of whether it was false or not." See *New York Times v. Sullivan* at p. 280.

[37] In *Hill v. Scientology*, the Supreme Court of Canada refused to adopt the so-called actual malice rule in *New York Times v. Sullivan*. Counsel for the *Washington Post* had filed on the return of the motion a legal opinion from Lee Levine, a defamation lawyer in Washington, D.C., who stated:

> In the circumstances you posit – i.e., a foreign libel judgment that could not be rendered in the first instance by a court bound by *New York Times Co. v. Sullivan* and its progeny – it is my opinion that a District of Columbia court would deem such a judgment to be repugnant to the public policy of the District and of the United States and would therefore decline to recognize or enforce it.

> Courts in the District of Columbia and in other American jurisdictions have uniformly held that libel judgments rendered in foreign courts where the law does not comport with the principle set forth in *New York Times Co. v. Sullivan* and its progeny are repugnant to the public policy of those jurisdictions and must therefore be denied recognition.

[38] The motion judge concluded at para. 23:

> Frankly, I see the unwillingness of an American court to enforce a Canadian libel judgment as an unfortunate expression of lack of comity. This should not be allowed to have an impact on Canadian values. The Washington Post defendants' home jurisdiction's unwillingness to enforce such an order is not determinative of whether the court should assume jurisdiction. See *Wilson v. Servier Canada Inc.* (2000), 50 O.R. (3d) 219 (Ont. Sup. Ct.)...

217

[39] The motion judge's conclusion does not take into account that the rule in *New York Times v. Sullivan* is rooted in the guarantees of freedom of speech and of the press under the First Amendment of the U.S. Constitution. In any event, the reality is that American courts will not enforce foreign libel judgments that are based on the application of legal principles that are contrary to the actual malice rule. Although the Supreme Court of Canada has rejected the rule for perfectly valid reasons, it is, in my view, not correct to say that the American courts' unwillingness to enforce a Canadian libel judgment is "an unfortunate expression of lack of comity". Canada and the U.S. have simply taken different approaches to a complex area of the law, based upon different policy considerations related to freedom of speech and the protection of individual reputations.

[40] The Supreme Court of Canada has recognized that Canadian courts may refuse to enforce a judgment of a foreign court which is deemed to be contrary to the Canadian concept of justice. In *Beals v. Saldanha, supra*, Major J., writing for the majority, said at para. 71:

The third and final defence is that of public policy. This defence prevents the enforcement of a foreign judgment which is contrary to the Canadian concept of justice. The public policy defence turns on whether the foreign law is contrary to our view of basic morality. As stated in Castel and Walker, *supra*, at p. 14-28:

...the traditional public policy defence appears to be directed at the concept of repugnant laws and not repugnant facts.

Given the centrality of freedom of speech to the United States Constitution, it could be argued that an American court's refusal to recognize a Canadian judgment based on principles divergent from *New York Times v. Sullivan* would fall into the category of repugnant law rather than repugnant fact.

[41] The motion judge supported his decision by relying upon the judgment of the High Court of Australia in *Dow Jones & Co. Inc. v. Gutnick* (2002), 210 C.L.R. 575 (H.C.A.).

[42] *Dow Jones v. Gutnick* involved an article published in both *Barron's* magazine and *Barron's Online*. Mr. Gutnick was an Australian businessman who resided in the State of Victoria. He commenced his action in Victoria. Dow Jones was served with the originating process outside Australia. The issue in the case was *forum non conveniens*. The court held that Victoria was the appropriate forum.

218

[43] In respect of *Dow Jones v. Gutnick*, the motion judge quoted at para. 22(8) of his reasons from a number of paragraphs of the factum filed by counsel for Mr. Bangoura that he said put "the whole issue in a proper perspective". The motion judge was presumably of the view that counsel's analysis of the *Dow Jones v. Gutnick* case supported his view that Ontario should assume jurisdiction.

[44] Gutnick was a well-known businessman who resided in Victoria at the time of the impugned publication. There was evidence that *Barron's* had some 1,700 Internet subscribers in Australia. Gutnick undertook that he would sue only in Victoria and only in respect of damages to his reputation in that state.

[45] I do not find the Australian case to be helpful in determining the issue before this court.

CONCLUSION

[46] As a result of the above analysis, I conclude that the motion judge erred in his application of the *Muscutt* factors. This leads me to conclude further that there is simply no real and substantial connection between this action and Ontario and that it is not appropriate for the courts of Ontario to assume jurisdiction.

SUBMISSIONS ON BEHALF OF THE MEDIA COALITION

[47] Counsel for the Media Coalition adopted the submissions of counsel for the *Washington Post* in his analysis of the real and substantial connection test and the application of the *Muscutt* factors. In addition, counsel for the Media Coalition offered alternative approaches to the issue of jurisdiction, which he submitted are consistent with the real and substantial connection test and capable of incorporation into the proper application of the *Muscutt* factors.

[48] The alternative approaches relate to publication on the Internet, which is a matter of considerable concern, given the Internet's worldwide, multi-jurisdictional reach. The approaches suggested by the Media Coalition include:

(i)   The Targeting Approach – under this approach, a court would take jurisdiction where the publication is targeted at the particular forum of the court.

(ii) The Active/Passive Approach – under this approach, a foreign defendant who actively sends electronic publications to a particular forum would be subject to the jurisdiction of that forum's courts. A defendant who simply posts to a passive Web site would not be subject to such jurisdiction.

(iii) The Country of Origin Approach – under this approach, jurisdiction is taken where the publication originated. The theory of this approach is that it is in the country of origin where the publisher has the last opportunity to control the content of the publication.

(iv) Foreseeability and Totality of Circumstances – this approach is similar to the approach taken by the court in *Muscutt* and its companion cases.

[49] The submissions made on behalf of the Media Coalition were helpful and interesting. However, I do not find it necessary to adopt any of the particular approaches that are proposed by the Coalition. It is not necessary to do so in order to decide this case. It may be that in some future case involving Internet publication, this court will find it useful to consider and apply one or more of the proposed approaches. However, that is for another day.

SERVICE *EX JURIS* AND *FORUM NON CONVENIENS*

[50] In view of my conclusion that it is not appropriate for the Ontario courts to assume jurisdiction in this case, I find it unnecessary to deal with the issues of service *ex juris* and *forum non conveniens*.

DISPOSITION

[51] For the reasons discussed above, I would allow the appeal, set aside the order of the motion judge and grant an order staying the action.

COSTS

[52] Counsel for the appellants shall have their costs of the appeal on a partial indemnity basis fixed in the amount of $7,500 including disbursements and Goods and Services Tax. The appellants are also entitled to their costs on a partial indemnity scale before the motion judge. If the parties cannot agree on the quantum of the costs before the motion judge, then the appellants should make brief written submissions (not to exceed five pages double-spaced) within ten days of the release of this judgment. The respondent shall file a brief written response (not to exceed five pages double-spaced) within ten days of receiving the appellants' costs submission. If so advised, counsel for the appellants may file a reply (not to exceed three pages double-spaced) within five days of the receipt of the respondent's response.

RELEASED:

"SEP 16 2005" "Robert P. Armstrong J.A."

"RRM" "I agree Roy McMurtry C.J.O."

"I agree S. E. Lang J.A."

* * *

The Internet has spawned a series of "defamation" cases (like Bangoura) affecting the publishing industry; but internet businesses are more likely to encounter jurisdictional issues in the context of trademark law. The following is a recent case.

PEBBLE BEACH COMPANY
v.
MICHAEL CADDY

United States Court of Appeals, Ninth Circuit
453 F.3d 1151
July 12, 2006.

Before: SCHROEDER, Chief Judge, TROTT and KLEINFELD, Circuit Judges.

TROTT, Circuit Judge:

Pebble Beach Company ("Pebble Beach"), a golf course resort in California, appeals the dismissal for lack of jurisdiction of its complaint against Michael Caddy ("Caddy"), a small-business owner located in southern England. In addition, Pebble Beach seeks review of an order denying its request for an opportunity to conduct jurisdictional discovery. Because Caddy did not expressly aim his conduct at California or the United States, we hold that the district court determined correctly that it lacked personal jurisdiction. Given the nature of the claims and the facts of this case, we conclude also that the district court properly exercised its discretion by denying Pebble Beach's motion to conduct additional jurisdictional discovery. Thus, we affirm.

Pebble Beach is a well-known golf course and resort located in Monterey County, California. The golf resort has used "Pebble Beach" as its trade name for 50 years. Pebble Beach contends that the trade name has acquired secondary meaning in the United States and the United Kingdom. Pebble Beach operates a website located at *www.pebblebeach.com.*

Caddy, a dual citizen of the United States and the United Kingdom occupies and runs a three-room bed and breakfast, restaurant, and bar located in southern England. Caddy's business operation is located on a cliff overlooking the pebbly beaches of England's south shore, in a town called Barton-on-Sea. The name of Caddy's operation is "Pebble Beach," which, given its location, is no surprise. Caddy advertises his services, which do not include a golf course, at his website, *www.pebblebeach-uk.com.* Caddy's website includes general information about the accommodations he provides, including lodging rates in pounds sterling, a menu, and a wine list. The website is not interactive.

Visitors to the website who have questions *1154 about Caddy's services may fill out an on-line inquiry form. However, the website does not have a reservation system, nor does it allow potential guests to book rooms or pay for services on-line.

Except for a brief time when Caddy worked at a restaurant in Carmel, California, his domicile has been in the United Kingdom.

On October 8, 2003, Pebble Beach sued Caddy under the Lanham Act and the California Business and Professions Code for intentional infringement and dilution of its "Pebble Beach" mark. Caddy moved to dismiss the complaint for lack of personal jurisdiction and insufficiency of service of process. On March 1, 2004, the district court granted Caddy's motion on personal jurisdiction grounds, without addressing the insufficiency of service of process issue. The district court denied also Pebble Beach's request for additional discovery. Pebble Beach timely appealed to the Ninth Circuit.

II
A. Personal Jurisdiction

The arguments are straight forward. Caddy contends that the district court may not assert personal jurisdiction over him, and, consequently, that the complaint against him was properly dismissed. Pebble Beach argues in return that Caddy is subject to specific personal jurisdiction in California, or, alternatively, in any forum in the United States, because he has expressly aimed tortious conduct at California and the United States.[19] Pebble Beach asserts that it may look to the entire United States as a litigation forum pursuant to Federal Rule of Civil Procedure 4(k)(2) if Caddy's contacts with California are insufficient to warrant jurisdiction. As explained more thoroughly below, Rule 4(k)(2) may, in limited circumstances, be a basis for establishing jurisdiction where "the United States serves as the relevant forum for a minimum contacts analysis." *Glencore Grain Rotterdam B.V. v. Shivnath Rai Harnarain Co.*, 284 F.3d 1114, 1126 (9th Cir.2002).

When a defendant moves to dismiss for lack of personal jurisdiction, the plaintiff bears the burden of demonstrating that the court has jurisdiction over the defendant. [citation omitted]. However, this demonstration requires that the plaintiff "make only a prima facie showing of jurisdictional facts to withstand the motion to dismiss. [citation omitted]. Moreover, for the purpose

---

19. Caddy's contacts with California or the United States are not continuous or substantial enough to establish general jurisdiction. See Glencore Grain Rotterdam B.V. v. Shivnath Rai Harnarain Co., 284 F.3d 1114, 1125 (9th Cir.2002) Thus, we consider only the question of whether Caddy's contacts are sufficient to establish specific jurisdiction.

of this demonstration, the court resolves all disputed facts in favor of the plaintiff, here, Pebble Beach. *Id.*

The general rule is that personal jurisdiction over a defendant is proper if it is permitted by a long-arm statute and if the exercise of that jurisdiction does not violate federal due process. [citation omitted]. Here, both the California long-arm statute and Rule 4(k)(2)-what is often referred to as the federal long-arm statute-require compliance with due process requirements. [citation omitted]. Consequently, under both arguments presented by Pebble Beach, resolution turns on due process.

For due process to be satisfied, a defendant, if not present in the forum, must have "minimum contacts" with the forum state such that the assertion of jurisdiction "does not offend traditional notions of fair play and substantial justice." *Int'l Shoe Co. v. Washington*, 326 U.S. 310, 315, 66 S.Ct. 154, 90 L.Ed. 95 (1945).

In this circuit, we employ the following three-part test to analyze whether a party's "minimum contacts" meet the Supreme Court's directive. This "minimum contacts" test is satisfied when,

> (1) the defendant has performed some act or consummated some transaction within the forum or otherwise purposefully availed himself of the privileges of conducting activities in the forum,

> (2) the claim arises out of or results from the defendant's forum-related activities, and

> (3) the exercise of jurisdiction is reasonable.

[citation omitted]. "If any of the three requirements is not satisfied, jurisdiction in the forum would deprive the defendant of due process of law." [citation omitted]. The plaintiff bears the burden of satisfying the first two prongs of the "minimum contacts" test. [citation omitted]. Here, Pebble Beach's arguments fail under the first prong. Accordingly, we need not address whether the claim arose out of or resulted from Caddy's forum-related activities or whether an exercise of jurisdiction is reasonable per the factors outlined by the Supreme Court in *Burger King Corp. v. Rudzewicz*, 471 U.S. 462, 476-77, 105 S.Ct. 2174, 85 L.Ed.2d 528 (1985).

Under the first prong of the "minimum contacts" test, Pebble Beach has the burden of establishing that Caddy "has performed some act or consummated some transaction within the forum or otherwise purposefully availed himself of the privileges of conducting activities in the forum." [citation omitted]. We have refined this to mean whether Caddy has either (1) "purposefully availed" himself of the privilege of conducting activities in the forum, or (2) "purposefully directed" his activities toward the forum. [citation omitted]. Although we sometimes use the phrase "purposeful availment" to include both purposeful availment and direction, "availment and direction are, in fact, two distinct concepts." *Id.*

Thus, in order to satisfy the first prong of the "minimum contacts" test, Pebble Beach must establish either that Caddy (1) purposefully availed himself of the privilege of conducting activities in California, or the United States as a whole, or (2) that he purposefully directed its activities toward one of those two forums. *Id.*

1. Purposeful Availment

Pebble Beach fails to identify any conduct by Caddy that took place in California or in the United States that adequately supports the availment concept. Evidence of availment is typically action taking place in the forum that invokes the benefits and protections of the laws in the forum. *Id.* at 803. Evidence of direction generally consists of action taking place outside the forum that is directed at the forum. *Id.* (suggesting evidence of purposeful direction includes activities such as distribution and advertising). All of Caddy's action identified by Pebble Beach is action taking place outside the forum. Thus, if anything, it is the type of evidence that supports a purposeful direction analysis. Accordingly, we reject Pebble Beach's assertion that Caddy has availed himself of the jurisdiction of the district court under both concepts and proceed only to determine whether Caddy has purposefully directed his action toward one of two applicable forums.

2. Purposeful Direction: California

In *Calder v. Jones,* the Supreme Court held that a foreign act that is both aimed at and has effect in the forum satisfies the first prong of the specific jurisdiction analysis. 465 U.S. 783, 104 S.Ct. 1482, 79 L.Ed.2d 804 (1984). We have commonly referred to this holding as the "*Calder* effects test." *See, e.g., Bancroft,* 223 F.3d at 1087. To satisfy this test the defendant "must have (1) committed an intentional act, which was (2) expressly aimed at the forum state, and (3) caused harm, the brunt of which is suffered and which the defendant knows is likely to be suffered in the forum state." *Id.* at 1088 (citing *Panavision Int'l v. Toeppen,* 141 F.3d 1316, 1321 (9th Cir.1998)). However, referring to the *Calder* test as an "effects" test can be misleading. For this reason, we have warned courts not to focus too narrowly on the test's third prong-the effects prong-holding that "something more" is needed in addition to a mere foreseeable effect. *Bancroft,* 223 F.3d at 1087. Specifically we have stated,

> Subsequent cases have struggled somewhat with *Calder's* import, recognizing that the case cannot stand for the broad proposition that a foreign act with foreseeable effects in the forum state will always give rise to specific jurisdiction. We have said that there must be "something more".... We now

conclude that "something more" is what the Supreme Court described as "express aiming" at the forum state.

Id. Thus, the determinative question here is whether Caddy's actions were "something more"-precisely, whether his conduct was expressly aimed at California or alternatively the United States.

We conclude that Caddy's actions were not expressly aimed at California. The only acts identified by Pebble Beach as being directed at California are the website and the use of the name "Pebble Beach" in the domain name. These acts were not aimed at California and, regardless of foreseeable effect, are insufficient to establish jurisdiction.

In support of its contention that Caddy has expressly aimed conduct at California, Pebble Beach identifies a list of cases where we have found that a defendant's actions have been expressly aimed at the forum state sufficient to establish jurisdiction over the defendant. Pebble Beach asserts that these cases show that Caddy's website and domain name, coupled by his knowledge of the golf resort as a result of his working in California, are sufficient to satisfy the express aiming standard that it is required to meet. We disagree. If anything, these cases establish that "something more"-the express aiming requirement-has not been met by Pebble Beach.

In *Panavision,* the defendant, a cybersquatter, registered the plaintiff's trademark as part of a domain name. 141 F.3d at 1318-19. The use of the domain name by the defendant prevented the plaintiff from registering its own domain name and was part of a plan to obtain money from the plaintiff in exchange for the rights to the domain name. *Id.* The court found personal jurisdiction, not merely because of the domain name use, but because the plan was expressly aimed at the plaintiff:

> [The Defendant] did considerably more than simply register Panavision's trademarks as his domain names on the Internet. He registered those names as part of a scheme to obtain money from Panavision. Pursuant to that scheme, he demanded $13,000 from Panavision to release the domain names to it. His acts were aimed at Panavision in California, and caused it to suffer injury there.

Id. at 1318.

Here, Caddy has hatched no such plan directed at Pebble Beach. He is not a cybersquatter trying to obtain money from Pebble Beach.His operation is legitimate and his website relates directly to that end.

In *Metropolitan Life Insurance Co. v. Neaves,* similar to *Panavision,* the defendant's alleged plan to defraud the insurance company involved direct

225

interaction with the forum state. 912 F.2d 1062 (1990). We held that the action at issue satisfied *Calder's* "effects test" because the defendant sent a letter to the forum state addressed to the plaintiff, thereby defrauding a forum state entity. *Id.* at 1065.

In *Bancroft & Masters, Inc. v. Augusta National Inc.*, a dispute over the domain name *www.masters.org* was triggered by a letter sent by Augusta that required Bancroft & Masters, a computer corporation in California, to sue or lose the domain name. 223 F.3d 1082 (9th Cir.2000). We stated that the "expressly aiming" standard was satisfied when "individualized targeting was present." *Id.* at 1088. We reasoned that specific jurisdiction was proper and that the expressly aiming requirement was satisfied because the letter sent by Augusta constituted "individualized targeting." *Id.*

The defendant in both *Bancroft* and *Metropolitan Life* did "something more" than commit a "foreign act with foreseeable effects in the forum state." *Id.* at 1087. In both cases this "individualized targeting" was correspondence that was a clear attempt to force the plaintiff to act. Here, Caddy engaged in no "individualized targeting." There is no letter written by Caddy forcing Pebble Beach to act. The only substantial action is a domain name and non-interactive informative web site along with the extraneous fact that Caddy had worked, at some point in his past, in California. This does not constitute "individualized targeting." Indeed, to hold otherwise would be contrary to what we have suggested in earlier case law.

In *Rio Properties, Inc. v. Rio Int'l Interlink*, 284 F.3d 1007, 1020 (9th Cir.2000), we cited *Cybersell, Inc. v. Cybersell, Inc.*, 130 F.3d 414, 418-20 (9th Cir.1997), for the proposition that when a "website advertiser [does] nothing other than register a domain name and post an essentially passive website" and nothing else is done "to encourage residents of the forum state," there is no personal jurisdiction. Similarly, in *Panavision* we stated, "We agree that simply registering someone else's trademark as a domain name and posting a web site on the Internet is not sufficient to subject a party domiciled in one state to jurisdiction in another." 141 F.3d at 1322. Why? Because "the objectionable webpage simply was not aimed intentionally at the [forum state] knowing that harm was likely to be caused there," and "[u]nder the effects doctrine, 'something more' was required to indicate that the defendant purposefully directed its activity in a substantial way to the forum state." [citation omitted]. [20]

These cases establish two salient points. First, there can be no doubt that we still require "something more" than just a foreseeable effect to conclude that

---

20. In Rio Properties it was shown that the defendant did more than put up a passive website. Id. at 1021. Indeed, the defendant was actively competing with the plaintiff by targeting Nevada consumers with radio and print media. Id. Accordingly, in Rio Properties there was no doubt that action was expressly directed at Nevada and that jurisdiction was proper.

personal jurisdiction is proper. *Bancroft*, 223 F.3d at 1087. Second, an internet domain name and passive website alone are not "something more," and, therefore, alone are not enough to subject a party to jurisdiction. *Rio Properties*, 284 F.3d at 1020; *Panavision*, 141 F.3d at 1322.

In contrast to those cases where jurisdiction was proper because "something more" existed, the circumstances here are more analogous to *Schwarzenegger v. Fred Martin Motor Co.* 374 F.3d 797 (9th Cir.2004). In *Schwarzenegger*, we determined that personal jurisdiction based solely on a non-interactive print advertisement would be improper. *Id.* at 807. In *Schwarzenegger*, the former movie star and current California governor, brought an action in California alleging that an Ohio car dealership used impermissibly his "Terminator" image in a newspaper advertisement in Akron, Ohio. *Id.* at 800. The federal district court in California dismissed the complaint for lack of personal jurisdiction. *Id.* Applying the *Calder* "effects test," we affirmed, concluding that even though the advertisement might lead to eventual harm in California this "foreseeable effect" was not enough because the advertisement was expressly aimed at Ohio rather than California. *Id.* at 807. We concluded that, without "something more" than possible effect, there was simply no individualized targeting of California, or the type of wrongful conduct, that could be construed as being directed at the forum state. *Id.* We held that Schwarzenegger had not established jurisdiction over the car dealership.

Pebble Beach, like Schwarzenegger, relies almost exclusively on the possible foreseeable effects. Like Schwarzenegger, Pebble Beach's arguments depend on the possible effects of a non-interactive advertisement-here, Caddy's passive website. Notably absent in both circumstances is action that can be construed as being expressly aimed at California. The fact that Caddy once lived in California and therefore has knowledge of the Pebble Beach golf resort goes to the foreseeable effect prong of the "effects test" and is not an independent act that can be interpreted as being expressly aimed at California. Consistent with the dicta of *Cybersell, Panavision,* and *Rio Properties,* we reject also any contention that a passive website constitutes expressed aiming. Thus, today, we extend the holding of *Schwarzenegger* to the situations described in *Panavision* and *Rio Properties,* where the sole basis for asserting jurisdiction is a non-interactive passive website. As with the print advertisement in Schwarzenegger, the fact that Caddy's website is not directed at California is controlling.

3. Purposeful Direction: United States

Even if Pebble Beach is unable to show purposeful direction as to California, Pebble Beach can still establish jurisdiction if Caddy purposefully directed his action at the United States. This ability to look to the aggregate contacts of a defendant with the United States as a whole instead of a particular state forum is a product of Rule 4(k)(2). Thus, Rule 4(k)(2) is commonly referred to as the federal long-arm statute. *Id.*[21]

The exercise of Rule 4(k)(2) as a federal long-arm statute requires the plaintiff to prove three factors. *Id.* First, the claim against the defendant must arise under federal law. *Id.* Second, the defendant must not be subject to the personal jurisdiction of any state court of general jurisdiction. Third, the federal court's exercise of personal jurisdiction must comport with due process. *Id.* Here, the first factor is satisfied because Pebble Beach's claims arises under the Lanham Act. And, as established above, the second factor is satisfied as Caddy is not subject to personal jurisdiction of California, or any state court.

That leaves the third factor-due process. The due process analysis is identical to the one discussed above when the forum was California, except here the relevant forum is the entire United States. And, as with the foregoing analysis, our resolution here depends on whether Caddy's actions were purposefully directed at the United States. Pebble Beach contends that the "purposeful direction" requirement is satisfied under the *Calder* "effects test" because Caddy's operation is expressly aimed at the United States. Pebble Beach makes four arguments.

First, Pebble Beach claims that because Caddy selected a ".com" domain name it shows that the United States was his "primary" market and that he is directly advertising his services to the United States. Second, Pebble Beach asserts that his selection of the name "Pebble Beach" shows the United States is his primary target because "Pebble Beach" is a famous United States trademark. Third, Pebble Beach asserts that Caddy's intent to advertise to the United States is bolstered by the fact that Caddy's facilities are located in a resort town that caters to foreigners, particularly Americans. Finally, Pebble Beach asserts that a majority of Caddy's business in the past has been with Americans.

As before, Pebble Beach's arguments focus too much on the effects prong and not enough on the "something more" requirement. First, following the rationale articulated in *Cybersell, Rio Properties,* and *Panavision,* we conclude that the selection of a particular domain name is insufficient by itself to confer jurisdiction over a non-resident defendant, even under Rule 4(k)(2), where the forum is the United States. The fact that the name "Pebble Beach" is a famous mark known world-wide is of little practical consequence when

---

21. Rule 4(k)(2) provides in whole:

If the exercise of jurisdiction is consistent with the Constitution and laws of the United States, serving a summons or filing a waiver of service is also effective, with respect to claims arising under federal law, to establish personal jurisdiction over the person of any defendant who is not subject to the jurisdiction of the courts of general jurisdiction of any state.

deciding whether action is directed at a particular forum via the world wide web. Also of minimal importance is Caddy's selection of a ".com" domain name instead of a more specific United Kingdom or European Union domain. To suggest that ".com" is an indicator of express aiming at the United States is even weaker than the counter assertion that having "U.K." in the domain name, which is the case here, is indicative that Caddy was only targeting his services to the United Kingdom. Neither provides much more than a slight indication of where a website may be located and does not establish to whom the website is directed. Accordingly, we reject these arguments.

This leaves Pebble Beach's arguments that because Caddy's business is located in an area frequented by Americans, and because he occasionally services Americans, jurisdiction is proper. These arguments fail for the same reasons; they go to effects rather than express aiming. Pebble Beach's arguments do have intuitive appeal-they suggest a real effect on Americans. However, as reiterated throughout this opinion, showing "effect" satisfies only the third prong of the *Calder* test-it is not the "something more" that is required. In *Bancroft*, we stated that foreseeable effects alone are not sufficient to exercise jurisdiction, that "something more" is required and that " 'something more' is what the Supreme Court described as 'express aiming' at the forum state." 223 F.3d at 1087 (internal citations omitted). The "something more" additional requirement is important simply because the effects cited may not have been caused by the defendant's actions of which the plaintiff complains. Here, although Caddy may serve vacationing Americans, there is not a scintilla of evidence indicating that this patronage is related to either Caddy's choice of a domain name or the posting of a passive website. Accordingly, we find no action on the part of Caddy expressly directed at the United States and conclude that an exercise of personal jurisdiction over Caddy would offend due process.

B. Jurisdictional Discovery

The district court properly exercised its discretion by refusing to grant a continuance to allow Pebble Beach to conduct additional jurisdictional discovery. "[W]here a plaintiff's claim of personal jurisdiction appears to be both attenuated and based on bare allegations in the face of specific denials made by the defendants, the Court need not permit even limited discovery...." [citation omitted] Here, we have rejected Pebble Beach's assertion of personal jurisdiction based on Caddy's chosen domain name and website. As a matter of law, we have concluded that a passive website and domain name are an insufficient basis for asserting personal jurisdiction. Caddy's website is passive, and, therefore, additional discovery on this issue would not be helpful. Furthermore, the record was sufficiently developed for the district court to rule on all remaining issues pertaining to jurisdiction. As a result, there was no need for the district court to grant additional time for discovery.

229

III

Caddy did not expressly aim his conduct at California or the United States and therefore is not subject to the personal jurisdiction of the district court. A passive website and domain name alone do not satisfy the *Calder* effects test and there is no other action expressly aimed at California or the United States that would justify personal jurisdiction. Also, the district court exercised properly its discretion by denying additional jurisdictional discovery.

V. RECOGNITION OF FOREIGN MONEY JUDGMENTS

Affirmed

The United States Constitution provides that the judgments of "sister-states", i.e. the other states of the United States are entitled to "full faith and credit", meaning that the courts of state 1 **must** recognize the (valid) judgments of state 2. "Validity" in this context is tested solely by whether state 1 had jurisdiction. No other inquiry whatsoever is permitted. Indeed, where state 1's judgment was not a product of default (meaning defendant appeared in the action in state 1), there is a simplified "registration" procedure which does even involve bringing a "recognition action" in state 2.

As to foreign money judgments, the rule is different. Recognition is not mandatory, but rather is permissive. The following is the New York statutory rule:

S 5304. Grounds for Non-recognition

(a) No recognition. A foreign country judgment is not conclusive if:

   1. the judgment was rendered under a system which does not provide impartial tribunals or procedures compatible with the requirements of due process of law;

   2. the foreign court did not have personal jurisdiction over the defendant.

(b) Other grounds for non-recognition. A foreign country judgment need not be recognized if:

   1. the foreign court did not have jurisdiction over the subject matter;

   2. the defendant in the proceedings in the foreign court did not receive notice of the proceedings in sufficient time to enable him to defend;

   3. the judgment was obtained by fraud;

4. the cause of action on which the judgment is based on a law that is repugnant to the public policy of this state;

5. the judgment conflicts with another final and conclusive judgment;

6. the proceeding in the foreign court was contrary to an agreement between the parties under which the dispute in question was to be settled otherwise than by proceedings in that court; or

7. in the case of jurisdiction based only on personal service, the foreign court was a seriously inconvenient forum for the trial of the action.

* * *

Briefly summarized, the statute provides that New York will not recognize a foreign money judgment if that judgment:

(A) Came from a forum who courts are not fair and impartial;

(B) was a default judgment from a court that lacked jurisdiction (non-default judgments cannot be attacked this way, see discussion, supra); or

(C) the judgment is "based on a law that is repugnant to the public policy of this state".

Each of these issues is addressed in the case that follows.

SUNG HWAN CO., LTD.
v.
RITE AID CORPORATION

NY Court of Appeals
June 6, 2006

CIPARICK, J.:

Plaintiff seeks enforcement of a foreign money judgment under CPLR article 53 — Recognition of Foreign Country Money Judgments — that was entered by the District Court of Seoul, Republic of Korea. Defendant argues that the Korean court was without jurisdiction, as the judgment was based on a cause of action that, although cast in terms of tort, would be considered a breach of contract claim in New York and would therefore not qualify as a basis for CPLR 302 long-arm jurisdiction. The fact that a foreign country's substantive law differs from New York law, plaintiff counters, is not a sufficient basis for the non- recognition of its judgments, and the principles of comity warrant mutual respect of such judgments if jurisdiction is otherwise proper. We agree with plaintiff that defendant failed to demonstrate that the Korean court's exercise of jurisdiction is not entitled to comity. We therefore reinstate the complaint.

In 1995, Sangshin Trading Co., a Korean exporter/importer of dairy products, entered into a sales agreement in California to purchase large quantities of ice cream from Thrifty Payless, Inc., an ice cream manufacturer. The contract provided that Sangshin would accept delivery of the ice cream in California and that it would be resold only in Korea. The contract had an initial term of one year and automatically renewed itself annually with an opportunity for Sangshin to obtain exclusive agency status if more than 32,000 gallons of ice cream were purchased in the first year.

Plaintiff, Sung Hwan Co., is a Korean Company that operates a chain of Thrifty brand ice cream stores throughout Korea. Sung Hwan contracted with Sangshin for the purchase of Thrifty ice cream for sale in its 340 stores. Upon Sung Hwan's entering into the market, gross sales of Thrifty ice cream in Korea grew from approximately $50,000 in 1995 to over $7,000,000 in 1996. However, sales rapidly declined in late 1997 after a highly publicized discovery by the Korean government of listeria monocytogenes in Thrifty brand ice cream. Initially, the Korean government announced that it had found excessive levels of listeria in two flavors of Thrifty ice cream. However, upon additional testing, the Korean Food and Drug Administration found listeria in six flavors of Thrifty ice cream. As a result, the Korean government sent Sung Hwan notice recalling the six flavors and halting sales of all Thrifty ice cream pending further testing.

After suffering a sudden drop in business, Sung Hwan sent several letters to Thrifty seeking assistance in handling the ramifications of the listeria problem but allegedly received no response. In December 1997, Sung Hwan again sent Thrifty a letter but this time detailed its claims for compensation for loss of business as well as for losses related to the non- marketable ice cream stock left in its warehouses. Rite Aid, which had purchased Thrifty Payless Inc. in 1997, responded by having its General Counsel meet with Sung Hwan's attorneys in San Francisco in March 1998 for settlement negotiations. Rite Aid requested Korean testing details, which plaintiff provided, but no reply or offer of settlement was forthcoming.

Sung Hwan ultimately filed a complaint against Rite Aid in Seoul District Court seeking, among other things, "Liability for Damages Based Upon Torts." The complaint and a translated version were served on Rite Aid at its corporate headquarters in Harrisburg, Pennsylvania. However, Rite Aid failed to respond and on February 9, 2001, a default judgment was entered in Korea on the tort claim against Rite Aid for 5.5 billion Korean Won (approximately $5,000,000).

Upon entry of the judgment, Sung Hwan sought enforcement in New York under CPLR article 53. In June 2001, Sung Hwan moved for summary judgment in lieu of complaint. The court denied the motion, finding unresolved issues of fact regarding the relationship between Thrifty and Rite Aid, and ordered the filing of a formal complaint. After the filing of a complaint, answer and amended complaint, Rite Aid moved for dismissal pursuant to CPLR 3211 (a)(1) and (7) and CPLR 5304 (a)(2). Supreme Court granted Rite Aid's motion and dismissed the complaint, foreclosing entry of a New York judgment based on the Korean judgment. The Appellate Division affirmed, stating that there was no cognizable basis for asserting personal jurisdiction over Rite Aid. We granted leave and now reverse.

"New York has traditionally been a generous forum in which to enforce judgments for money damages rendered by foreign courts" [citation omitted] Historically, New York courts have accorded "recognition to the judgments rendered in a foreign country under the doctrine of comity . . . [a]bsent some showing of fraud in the procurement of the foreign country judgment or that recognition of the judgment would do violence to some strong public policy of this State" [citation omitted] The public policy inquiry rarely results in refusal to enforce a judgment unless it is "inherently vicious, wicked or immoral, and shocking to the prevailing sense." [citation omitted]

In accordance with this rationale, CPLR article 53, the Uniform Foreign Money-Judgments Recognition Act, was enacted in 1970 to "promote the efficient enforcement of New York judgments abroad by assuring foreign jurisdictions that their judgments would receive streamlined enforcement here" [citation omitted] CPLR 5302 states that the "article applies to any foreign judgment which is final, conclusive and enforceable where rendered." CPLR 5303 declares that such judgments are enforceable except as provided in CPLR 5304 . As relevant here, CPLR 5304 (a)(1) articulates our common law jurisprudence that a foreign judgment is not conclusive if it "was rendered under a system which does not provide impartial tribunals or procedures compatible with the requirements of due process of law," and CPLR 5304 (a)(2) states that a foreign judgment will not be recognized if the foreign court did not have personal jurisdiction over the judgment debtor. CPLR 5305 , entitled "Personal Jurisdiction," in turn, enumerates six bases for jurisdiction as well as a catch-all phrase providing that "[t]he courts of this state may recognize other bases of jurisdiction" (CPLR 5305 [b]).

Thus, the inquiry turns on whether exercise of jurisdiction by the foreign court comports with New York's concept of personal jurisdiction, and if so, whether that foreign jurisdiction shares our notions of procedure and due process of law. If the above criteria are met, and enforcement of the foreign judgment is not otherwise repugnant to our notion of fairness, the foreign judgment should be enforced in New York under well-settled comity principles without microscopic analysis of the underlying proceeding.

When addressing article 53, absent a finding of personal jurisdiction under CPLR 5305 (a), our courts have typically looked to the framework of CPLR 302 , New York's long- arm statute, using it as a parallel to assess the propriety of the foreign court's exercise of jurisdiction over a judgment debtor (see CPLR 5305 [b]; [citations omitted]). Under CPLR 5305 (b) courts have recognized the validity of a foreign judgment using any of the jurisdictional bases New York recognizes. One such basis is CPLR 302 (a), which states:

> "a court may exercise personal jurisdiction over any non-domiciliary, . . . , who in person or through an agent: . . . (3) commits a tortious act without the state causing injury to person or property within the state . . . if he (i) regularly does or solicits business, or engages in any other persistent course of conduct, or derives substantial revenue from goods used or consumed or services rendered, in the state, or (ii) expects or should reasonably expect the act to have consequences in the state and derives substantial revenue from interstate or international commerce."

In LaMarca v Pak-Mor Manufacturing Co., [citation omitted] we identified five elements for predicating jurisdiction under CPLR 302 (a)(3)(ii):

> "First, that defendant committed a tortious act outside the State; second, that the cause of action arises from that act; third, that the act caused injury to a person or property within the State; fourth, that defendant expected or should reasonably have expected the act to have consequences in the State; and fifth, that defendant derived substantial revenue from interstate or international commerce."

Thus, in New York, jurisdiction can be premised on commission of a tortious act "out of the state" causing injury "within the state," and the specific inquiry here is whether Korea's exercise of jurisdiction over Rite Aid was consistent with New York law. For purposes of this inquiry, Korea is "the state" referenced in CPLR 302 (a)(3) and the issue turns on whether Sung Hwan sufficiently alleged that Rite Aid committed "a tortious act" outside Korea, causing injury within Korea.

Rite Aid here contests only the first element, that a tortious act occurred. Specifically, Rite Aid argues that Sung Hwan's claim is nothing more than an allegation of breach of contract under the guise of a tort since New York does not award economic damages for a tort cause of action, and accordingly falls outside the scope of CPLR 302(3).

Sung Hwan, on the other hand, argues that Rite Aid's ice cream was defective and that Rite Aid negligently breached its duty of care to properly test the products for contaminants before placing its product — manufactured in California — into the stream of commerce, ultimately causing loss of inventory and business in Korea. The Korean court ruled in favor of Sung Hwan and found that the conduct was tortious under Korean Law in that "[d]efendant, as a manufacturer of ice cream, has a duty of care to test and examine whether the subject ice cream includes Listeria or any other bacteria causing of food poisoning or harmful to the health, [defendant] was negligent in failing to exercise such duty by selling the goods containing Listeria to the plaintiff, and thus such negligence caused damages . . ."

Rite Aid erroneously focuses on the remedy sought — damages for economic loss — in arguing that no tortious act occurred since New York does not allow recovery for economic loss based on negligence. This argument is contrary to our case law and would undermine the principles of comity by supplanting New York substantive law in place of that of the foreign jurisdiction. As stated in Sybron Corp. v Wetzel, 46 NY2d 197, 205 [1978]), "[CPLR 302], drafted by sophisticated experts, does not limit the kinds of tortious acts covered to personal injury, property damage, or other noncommercial torts. Under such circumstances the statute should be read with the breadth it easily carries, and the unqualified legislative enactment respected." In Sybron, this Court held that a tortious act committed out-of-state that was likely to cause injury through loss of business in-state was sufficient to satisfy personal jurisdiction regardless of whether damages were ascertainable or likely recoverable (id. at 204-205). This is directly analogous to Sung Hwan's claims here.

Furthermore, as conceded by the parties, had plaintiff been an individual who brought suit for personal injury resulting from listeria poisoning, jurisdiction would plainly exist. We see no reason why jurisdiction should be denied merely because a plaintiff is relying on a theory of economic loss resulting from a tortious act rather than seeking compensation for personal injury resulting from that same tortious act.

For purposes of establishing long-arm jurisdiction, a tort should be broadly defined to encompass one that causes economic injury. Certainly such recovery, although not recognized in New York, is neither repugnant to our public policy nor offensive to our notions of fairness. The argument that New York generally fails to recognize economic loss as a basis for damages in proceedings based on tort is immaterial (cf. Loucks v Standard Oil Co., 224 NY 99, 110-111 [1918] ["If a foreign statute gives the right, the mere fact that we do not give a like right is no reason for refusing to help the plaintiff in getting what belongs to him. We are not so provincial as to say that every solution of a problem is wrong because we deal with it otherwise at home"]). To hold otherwise would undermine the fundamental principles of comity by interfering with the acts of a foreign jurisdiction's legislature or judicial body (see Hilton v Guyot, 159 US 113, 163-164 [1895]). Here, although Korean law appears more expansive than New York law in imposing liability for economic loss under a tort theory, we see no reason to foreclose the use of CPLR 302 3) as a basis for Korea's exercise of personal jurisdiction over Rite Aid merely because of this difference in the substantive tort law of the two jurisdictions.

Thus, we conclude that the lower courts erred in granting Rite Aid's motion to dismiss the complaint for lack of personal jurisdiction. We need not reach the parties' remaining arguments.

Accordingly, the order of the Appellate Division should be reversed, with costs, defendant's motion to dismiss the complaint denied and the matter remitted to Supreme Court for further proceedings.

Order reversed, with costs, and defendant's motion to dismiss the complaint denied. Opinion by Judge Ciparick. Chief Judge Kaye and Judges G.B. Smith, Rosenblatt, Graffeo, Read and R.S. Smith concur.

* * *

As the *Rite Aid* case demonstrates, most foreign country's "commercial" courts satisfy the fairness/impartiality test (even if their domestic "political" courts do not), and even where foreign laws are different, most foreign laws are not "repugnant" to New York. But a foreign law that, e.g., is discriminatory based on ethnicity, would obviously be repugnant. But what of a foreign judgment based upon foreign defamation law that does not take appropriate account of US 1st Amendment privileges. For an unusual but fascinating example of a case where that issue arose, see *Yahoo!, Inc. v. La Ligue Contre Le Racisme et L'Antisemitisme*, 169 F.Supp.2d 1181 (N.D.Cal. 2001) (NO. C-00-21275 JF), reversed and eventually dismissed on other grounds, 433 F.3d 1199 (9th Cir. 2006)

It is, of course, dangerous to default in a foreign forum, as the WSJ knew when it appeared in the Canadian court in *Bangoura* and (before that) in Australia in *Gutnick v. Dow Jones*. The WSJ's international presence is too great to risk a foreign judgment. Thus, the Journal tried a more aggressive approach to the problem in a different dispute – this time in a humorous tale involving Harrod's of London. As the following article explains, the WSJ did not succeed in an attempted pre-emptive strike in a New York federal court, but it eventually prevailed in the English court.

BRITISH COURT THROWS OUT LIBEL SUIT AGAINST DOW JONES CO.

Feb. 19, 2004 — A jury in London's High Court yesterday dismissed a libel lawsuit against Dow Jones Co., owner of The Wall Street Journal, rejecting a claim that British department store Harrods was harmed by a 2002 article that jokingly compared the company to Enron.

The newspaper asserted in court filings that the article was meant as a "tongue-in-cheek" humor story. In addition to throwing out the suit, the court ordered Harrods to pay a portion of Dow Jones's legal bills within 14 days.

"It was unfortunate that an article published in the U.S. and seen by millions there, but only 22, at most, in England, was hauled into the English legal system to be defended at a cost of tens of thousands of pounds," said Brigitte Trafford, vice president of communications at Dow Jones.

"It seems ridiculous that Harrods, that could not sue in the U.S., took the time of an English court and jury on an article with the most tenuous connection imaginable to England and with absolutely no evidence of any actual loss," Trafford added.

The case began as an April Fool's joke. On March 31, 2002, Harrods issued a mock press release announcing plans to "float" the company. The notice mentioned "a first-come-first-served share option offer." A later press release described the plans of Harrods owner Mohammed Al-Fayed to "float" the company by mooring a boat version of the store on the Thames River in London.

Editors at the Journal read the first press release as a genuine announcement that Harrods planned to "float shares" — make a public offering of stock shares — and published a story about it on April 1. After learning it had been duped, the Journal printed a correction and an article titled "The Enron of Britian?" The article acknowledged that the newspaper's editors were fooled, and questioned the propriety of issuing false press releases.

According to a Feb. 18 article in the Journal, Al-Fayed said he was "surprised and disappointed" by the court's decision to dismiss his libel claim. He added that the comparison of Harrods to the scandal-ridden Enron, which declared bankruptcy in December 2001, was "extremely damaging" to the company's interests.

Harrods was ordered to pay approximately $60,000 worth of Dow Jones's legal fees.

In May 2002, Dow Jones attempted to halt the lawsuit before it could begin in Britain, asking a federal district court in New York to issue a declaratory judgment under the Declaratory Judgments Act. The act allows courts to declare the legal rights of the party seeking the declaration, provided an actual controversy exists.

The court declined in October 2002 to issue a judgment, finding that no actual controversy existed and questioned the effect such a judgment would have in the United Kingdom. In October 2003, the U.S. Court of Appeals in New York City (2nd Cir.) upheld the district court ruling.

For an interesting analysis of these internet defamation cases, see Wolf, A Comment on Private Harms in the Cyber-World, 2005 Washington and Lee Law Review, viewable at

http://www.findarticles.com/p/articles/mi_qa3655/is_200501/ai_n13639198/pg_1

VI. THE DOCTRINE OF FORUM NON CONVENIENS

Even though a court may have jurisdiction over the parties to a controversy, there still exists the inherent power of the court to decline its facilities to the litigants for reasons of policy. Since it would be unjust to allow a plaintiff to severely burden a defendant (even one technically subject to the court's jurisdiction) by commencing suit in a seriously inconvenient forum, the doctrine of "forum non conveniens" exists. The doctrine is invoked by courts only rarely, and only in cases of (a) serious inconvenience and (b) where another, more convenient forum is available. The following case discusses the applicability of the doctrine in the federal courts in United States.

GULF OIL CORP.
v.
GILBERT

United States Court of Appeals, Ninth Circuit

330 U.S. 501; 67 S. Ct. 839; 91 L. Ed. 1055
March 10, 1947, Decided

MR. JUSTICE JACKSON delivered the opinion of the Court.

The questions are whether the United States District Court has inherent power to dismiss a suit pursuant to the doctrine of forum non conveniens and, if so, whether that power was abused in this case.

The respondent-plaintiff brought this action in the Southern District of New York, but resides at Lynchburg, Virginia, where he operated a public warehouse. He alleges that the petitioner-defendant, in violation of the ordinances of Lynchburg, so carelessly handled a delivery of gasoline to his warehouse tanks and pumps as to cause an explosion and fire which consumed the warehouse building to his damage of $ 41,889.10, destroyed merchandise and fixtures to his damage of $ 3,602.40, caused injury to his business and profits of $ 20,038.27, and burned the property of customers in his custody under warehousing agreements to the extent of $ 300,000. He asks judgment of $ 365,529.77 with costs and disbursements, and interest from the date of the fire. The action clearly is one in tort.

The petitioner-defendant is a corporation organized under the laws of Pennsylvania, qualified to do business in both Virginia and New York, and it has designated officials of each state as agents to receive service of process. When sued in New York, the defendant, invoking the doctrine of forum non conveniens, claimed that the appropriate place for trial is Virginia, where the plaintiff lives and defendant does business, where all events in litigation took place, where most of the witnesses reside, and where both state and federal courts are available to plaintiff and are able to obtain jurisdiction of the defendant.

The case, on its merits, involves no federal question and was brought in the United States District Court solely because of diversity in citizenship of the parties. The District Court considered that the law of New York as to forum non conveniens applied and that it required the case to be left to Virginia courts. It therefore dismissed.

The Circuit Court of Appeals disagreed as to the applicability of New York law, took a restrictive view of the application of the entire doctrine in federal courts and, one judge dissenting, reversed. The case is here on certiorari.

I

This Court, in one form of words or another, has repeatedly recognized the existence of the power to decline jurisdiction in exceptional circumstances. As formulated by Mr. Justice Brandeis, the rule is:

> Obviously, the proposition that a court having jurisdiction must exercise it, is not universally true; else the admiralty court could never decline jurisdiction on the ground that the litigation is between foreigners. Nor is it true of courts administering other systems of our law. Courts of equity and of law also occasionally decline, in the interest of justice, to exercise jurisdiction, where the suit is between aliens or non-residents or where for kindred reasons the litigation can more appropriately be conducted in a foreign tribunal. Canada Malting Co., Ltd., v. Paterson Steamships, Ltd., 285 U.S. 413, 422-23.

We later expressly said that a state court "may in appropriate cases apply the doctrine of forum non conveniens." Broderick v. Rosner, 294 U.S. 629, 643; Williams v. North Carolina, 317 U.S. 287, 294, n. 5. Even where federal rights binding on state courts under the Constitution are sought to be adjudged, this Court has sustained state courts in a refusal to entertain a litigation between a nonresident and a foreign corporation or between two foreign corporations.

239

Douglas v. New York, N. H. & H. R. R., 279 U.S. 377; Anglo-American Provision Co. v. Davis Provision Co. No. 1, 191 U.S. 373. It has held the use of an inappropriate forum in one case an unconstitutional burden on interstate commerce. Davis v. Farmers Co-operative Equity Co., 262 U.S. 312. On substantially forum non conveniens grounds we have required federal courts to relinquish decision of cases within their jurisdiction where the court would have to participate in the administrative policy of a state. Railroad Commission v. Rowan & Nichols Oil Co., 311 U.S. 570; Burford v. Sun Oil Co., 319 U.S. 315; but cf. Meredith v. Winter Haven, 320 U.S. 228. And most recently we decided Williams v. Green Bay & Western R. R. Co., 326 U.S. 549, in which the Court, without questioning the validity of the doctrine, held it had been applied in that case without justification.

In all cases in which the doctrine of forum non conveniens comes into play, it presupposes at least two forums in which the defendant is amenable to process; the doctrine furnishes criteria for choice between them.

II

The principle of forum non conveniens is simply that a court may resist imposition upon its jurisdiction even when jurisdiction is authorized by the letter of a general venue statute. These [venue] statutes are drawn with a necessary generality and usually give a plaintiff a choice of courts, so that he may be quite sure of some place in which to pursue his remedy. But the open door may admit those who seek not simply justice but perhaps justice blended with some harassment. A plaintiff sometimes is under temptation to resort to a strategy of forcing the trial at a most inconvenient place for an adversary, even at some inconvenience to himself. Many of the states have met misuse of venue by investing courts with a discretion to change the place of trial on various grounds, such as the convenience of witnesses and the ends of justice. The federal law contains no such express criteria to guide the district court in exercising its power. But the problem is a very old one affecting the administration of the courts as well as the rights of litigants, and both in England and in this country the common law worked out techniques and criteria for dealing with it.

Wisely, it has not been attempted to catalogue the circumstances which will justify or require either grant or denial of remedy. The doctrine leaves much to the discretion of the court to which plaintiff resorts, and experience has not shown a judicial tendency to renounce one's own jurisdiction so strong as to result in many abuses.

If the combination and weight of factors requisite to given results are difficult to forecast or state, those to be considered are not difficult to name. An interest to be considered, and the one likely to be most pressed, is the private interest of the litigant. Important considerations are the relative ease of access to sources of proof; availability of compulsory process for attendance of unwilling, and the cost of obtaining attendance of willing, witnesses; possibility of view of premises, if view would be appropriate to the action; and all other practical problems that make trial of a case easy, expeditious and inexpensive. There may also be questions as to the enforcibility of a judgment if one is obtained. The court will weigh relative advantages and obstacles to fair trial. It is often said that the plaintiff may not, by choice of an inconvenient forum, "vex," "harass," or "oppress" the defendant by inflicting upon him expense or trouble not necessary to his own right to pursue his remedy. But unless the balance is strongly in favor of the defendant, the plaintiff's choice of forum should rarely be disturbed.

Factors of public interest also have place in applying the doctrine. Administrative difficulties follow for courts when litigation is piled up in congested centers instead of being handled at its origin. Jury duty is a burden that ought not to be imposed upon the people of a community which has no relation to the litigation. In cases which touch the affairs of many persons, there is reason for holding the trial in their view and reach rather than in remote parts of the country where they can learn of it by report only. There is a local interest in having localized controversies decided at home. There is an appropriateness, too, in having the trial of a diversity case in a forum that is at home with the state law that must govern the case, rather than having a court in some other forum untangle problems in conflict of laws, and in law foreign to itself. The law of New York as to the discretion of a court to apply the doctrine of forum non conveniens, and as to the standards that guide discretion is, so far as here involved, the same as the federal rule. Murnan v. Wabash R. Co., 246 N. Y. 244, 158 N. E. 508; Wedemann v. United States Trust Co., 258 N. Y. 315, 179 N. E. 712; see Gregonis v. Philadelphia and Reading Co., 235 N. Y. 152, 139 N. E. 223. It would not be profitable, therefore, to pursue inquiry as to the source from which our rule must flow.

III

Turning to the question whether this is one of those rather rare cases where the doctrine should be applied, we look first to the interests of the litigants. The plaintiff himself is not a resident of New York, nor did any event connected with the case take place there, nor does any witness, with the possible exception of experts, live there. No one connected with that side of the case save counsel for the plaintiff resides there, and he has candidly told us that he was retained by insurance companies interested presumably because of subrogation. His affidavits and argument are devoted to controverting claims as to defendant's inconvenience rather than to showing that the present forum serves any convenience of his own, with one exception. The only justification for trial in New York advanced here is one rejected by the district court and is set forth in the brief as follows:

This Court can readily realize that an action of this type, involving as it does a claim for damages in an amount close to $ 400,000, is one which may stagger the imagination of a local jury which is surely unaccustomed to dealing with amounts of such a nature. Furthermore, removed from Lynchburg, the respondent will have an opportunity to try this case free from local influences and preconceived notions which may make it difficult to procure a jury which has no previous knowledge of any of the facts herein.

This unproven premise that jurors of New York live on terms of intimacy with $ 400,000 transactions is not an assumption we easily make. Nor can we assume that a jury from Lynchburg and vicinity would be "staggered" by contemplating the value of a warehouse building that stood in their region, or of merchandise and fixtures such as were used there, nor are they likely to be staggered by the value of chattels which the people of that neighborhood put in storage. It is a strange argument on behalf of a Virginia plaintiff that the community which gave him patronage to make his business valuable is not capable of furnishing jurors who know the value of the goods they store, the building they are stored in, or the business their patronage creates. And there is no specification of any local influence, other than accurate knowledge of local conditions, that would make a fair trial improbable. The net of this is that we cannot say the District Court was bound to entertain a provincial fear of the provincialism of a Virginia jury. That leaves the Virginia plaintiff without even a suggested reason for transporting this suit to New York.

Defendant points out that not only the plaintiff, but every person who participated in the acts charged to be negligent, resides in or near Lynchburg. It also claims a need to interplead an alleged independent contractor which made the delivery of the gasoline and which is a Virginia corporation domiciled in Lynchburg, that it cannot interplead in New York. There also are approximately 350 persons residing in and around Lynchburg who stored with plaintiff the goods for the damage to which he seeks to recover. The extent to which they have left the community since the fire and the number of them who will actually be needed is in dispute. The complaint alleges that defendant's conduct violated Lynchburg ordinances. Conditions are said to require proof by firemen and by many others. The learned and experienced trial judge was not unaware that litigants generally manage to try their cases with fewer witnesses than they predict in such motions as this. But he was justified in concluding that this trial is likely to be long and to involve calling many witnesses, and that Lynchburg, some 400 miles from New York, is the source of all proofs for either side, with possible exception of experts. Certainly to fix the place of trial at a point where litigants cannot compel personal attendance and may be forced to try their cases on deposition, is to create a condition not satisfactory to court, jury or most litigants. Nor is it necessarily cured by the statement of plaintiff's counsel that he will see to getting many of the witnesses to the trial and that some of them "would be delighted to come to New York to testify." There may be circumstances where such a proposal should be given weight. In others, the offer may not turn out to be as generous as defendant or court might suppose it to be. Such matters are for the District Court to decide in exercise of a sound discretion.

The court likewise could well have concluded that the task of the trial court would be simplified by trial in Virginia. . . . The course of adjudication in New York federal court might be beset with conflict of laws problems all avoided if the case is litigated in Virginia where it arose.

We are convinced that the District Court did not exceed its powers or the bounds of its discretion in dismissing plaintiff's complaint and remitting him to the courts of his own community. The Circuit Court of Appeals took too restrictive a view of the doctrine as approved by this Court. Its judgment is Reversed.

MR. JUSTICE BLACK, dissenting.

The defendant corporation is organized under the laws of Pennsylvania, but is qualified to do business and maintains an office in New York. Plaintiff is an individual residing and doing business in Virginia. The accident in which plaintiff alleges to have been damaged occurred in Lynchburg, Virginia. Plaintiff brought this action in the Federal District Court in New York. . . . The Court does not suggest that the federal district court in New York lacks jurisdiction under this statute or that the venue was improper in this case. [citation omitted] But it holds that a district court may abdicate its jurisdiction when a defendant shows to the satisfaction of a district court that it would be more convenient and less vexatious for the defendant if the trial were held in another jurisdiction. Neither the venue statute nor the statute which has governed jurisdiction since 1789 contains any indication or implication that a federal district court, once satisfied that jurisdiction and venue requirements have been met, may decline to exercise its jurisdiction. Except in relation to the exercise of the extraordinary admiralty and equity powers of district courts, this Court has never before held contrary to the general principle that "the courts of the United States are bound to proceed to judgment, and to afford redress to suitors before them, in every case to which their jurisdiction extends. They cannot abdicate their authority or duty in any case in favor of another jurisdiction." [citations omitted] Never until today has this Court held, in actions for money damages for violations of common law or statutory rights, that a district court can abdicate its statutory duty to exercise its jurisdiction for the alleged convenience of the defendant to a lawsuit. . . .

No such discretionary authority to decline to decide a case, however, has, before today, been vested in federal courts in actions for money judgments deriving from statutes or the common law. To engraft the doctrine of forum non conveniens upon the statutes fixing jurisdiction and proper venue in the district courts in such actions, seems to me to be far more than the mere filling in of the interstices of those statutes.

It may be that a statute should be passed authorizing the federal district courts to decline to try so-called common law cases according to the convenience of the parties. But whether there should be such a statute, and determination of its scope and the safeguards which should surround it, are, in my judgment, questions of policy which Congress should decide. There are strong arguments presented by the Court in its opinion why federal courts exercising their common law jurisdiction should have the discretionary powers which equity courts have always possessed in dispensing equitable relief. I think equally strong arguments could be advanced to show that they should not. . . . But in any event, Congress has not yet [spoken]; and I do not think that this Court should, 150 years after the passage of the Judiciary Act, fill in what it thinks is a deficiency in the deliberate policy which Congress adopted. Whether the doctrine of forum non conveniens is good or bad, I should wait for Congress to adopt it.

MR. JUSTICE RUTLEDGE joins in this opinion.

MULTIPLE CHOICE REVIEW QUESTIONS

1. Before the industrial revolution, a sovereign's jurisdiction to adjudicate:

    a. was limited to the sovereign's territory;

    b. was governed by the rules of long-arm jurisdiction

    c. was always based on jurisdiction "in rem"

    d. Required the voluntary appearance of the defendant

2. In World-Wide Volkswagen, the Supreme Court held that:

    a. Seaway had not "purposefully availed" itself of the benefits of Oklahoma

    b. Seaway would have been subject to jurisdiction in Oklahoma if Mrs. Robinson had started the case in federal rather than state court

    c. It was reasonable to assert jurisdiction over World-Wide Volkswagen

    d. It was reasonable to assert jurisdiction over Volkswagenwerk A.G.

3. In Burger King, Justice Brennan:

    a. relied exclusively on the purposeful availment standard

    b. held that the "Choice of Law" clause in the contract was conclusive as to the issue of jurisdiction

    c. looked broadly at the reasonableness of jurisdiction by considering, inter alia, criteria such as the interest of the plaintiff, the interest of the forum state

    d. was most concerned with the burden on a foreign defendant

4. One nation will generally recognize a foreign default judgment so long as:

    a. the nation that rendered the judgment had jurisdiction over the defendant

    b. the nation that rendered the judgment has tribunals that are fair and impartial

    c. the nation that rendered the judgment has laws that are not repugnant to those of the forum

    d. all of the above

5. A web site's owner is:

    a. subject to jurisdiction only in the place where its servers are located

    b. subject to jurisdiction in every place where its web site can foreseeably be viewed

    c. subject to jurisdiction in every place where it targets consumers

    d. none of the above

PROBLEMS FOR ANALYSIS

PROBLEM 1

Navitas is a Japanese Company which has no offices, employees or assets in the United States. Navitas is not licensed to transact business in New York, nor has it ever directly transacted business with a citizen of New York. Navitas has never provided any service in New York, nor has it ever made a contract in New York.

Navitas manufactures business equipment for sale around the world. In 1977, Navitas entered into an agreement with Kurz, a Pennsylvania corporation, giving Kurz the exclusive right to sell Navitas equipment throughout the United States and Europe. Thereafter, Navitas provided Kurz not only with machines for resale, but also with know-how sufficient to allow Kurz to service the machines and function effectively.

In 1989, Kurz sold a Navitas hot stamp press to Forbes Products Corp, a New York corporation, and Kurz shipped the machine to Forbes' plant in upstate New York. In 1996, an employee named Lillian Kernan was operating the machine at the Forbes plant, when she was severely injured by the machine.

Ms. Kernan brought suit against Kurz and Navitas in the federal court for the Western District of New York. Navitas moved to dismiss for lack of personal jurisdiction. How should a court rule?

See Kernan v. Kurz-Hastings, Inc., 175 F.3d 236 (2d cir 1999).

PROBLEM 2

Since 1990, Electronic Broking Services, a British company, has provided goods and services and computer software, to the banking and financial services industry (including U.S. firms) under the name and trademark "Electronic Broking Services, Ltd." Electronic Broking Services owns the US and British trademarks "EBS" in connection with banking services, electronic banking and data processing services for foreign exchange and brokerage services.

"e-Business Solutions," a separate company, is Egyptian. e-Business Solutions is based in Cairo and owns the Egyptian trademark "eBS". "eBS" is also the owner of the internet domain name "ebs.com", which it uses as its website. In order to obtain the web site, eBS was required to mail an application form and a check to VeriSign (a U.S. company) at a post office in Virginia.

Through the "ebs.com" website, the Egyptian firm offers a number of software products and services for banking and financial entities, including programs that deliver electronic banking services and Internet-based solutions for stock brokers and foreign exchange brokers. eBS (Egypt) conducts some business with entities in other countries in Africa, but eBS is not seeking business opportunities outside of Africa. eBS recently did, however, enter into a marketing joint venture with a U.S. firm located in Maryland; the joint venture involved exploring customer prospects in South Africa and Zimbabwe. Other than the business activities described here, Electronic Broking will be unable to allege any other contacts between eBS and the U.S.

On November 6, 2005, Electronic Broking sent a written demand to eBS requesting that it cease and desist all use of the "ebs.com" domain name by February 1, 2006. When E-Business Solutions failed to abandon its use of the domain name, Electronic Broking brought suit in Maryland federal court against eBS for trademark infringement under U.S. law. E-Business Solutions moved to dismiss for lack of jurisdiction. What result do you expect? Why?

See Electronic Broking Services, Ltd. v. E-Business Solutions & Services285 F.Supp.2d 686 (D.Md.,2003)

IDEAS FOR RESEARCH AND FURTHER LEARNING

1   Conduct research into the negotiations conducted at the Hague to try to create a multi-lateral treaty on the enforcement of foreign money judgments? What is the status of the negotiations? What are the issues? What are the prospects?

2.   What are the jurisdictional rules in civil law countries, such as France, Germany, Mexico and Japan? What countries present the largest obstacles to recognition?

3.   Jurisdiction "In Rem" remains important in Maritime Law (a/k/a "Actions in Admiralty"). What sorts of cases are covered by this subject? How does in rem jurisdiction work in this arena? What legal/strategic issues can arise in such cases?

4.   Internet jurisdiction cases are increasing. Find some recent controversies, and see how they were resolved. Have there been any important or subtle recent changes or trends in the law?

CHAPTER 4

Choice of Forum and International Arbitration

I. CHOICE OF A JUDICIAL FORUM

THE BREMEN ET AL.
V.
ZAPATA OFF-SHORE CO.

Supreme Court of the United States
407 U.S. 1; 92 S. Ct. 1907; 32 L. Ed. 2d 513
Decided June 12, 1972

MR. CHIEF JUSTICE BURGER delivered the opinion of the Court.

We granted certiorari to review a judgment of the United States Court of Appeals for the Fifth Circuit declining to enforce a forum-selection clause governing disputes arising under an international towage contract between petitioners and respondent. The circuits have differed in their approach to such clauses. For the reasons stated hereafter, we vacate the judgment of the Court of Appeals.

In November 1967, respondent Zapata, a Houston-based American corporation, contracted with petitioner Unterweser, a German corporation, to tow Zapata's ocean-going, self-elevating drilling rig Chaparral from Louisiana to a point off Ravenna, Italy, in the Adriatic Sea, where Zapata had agreed to drill certain wells.

Zapata had solicited bids for the towage, and several companies including Unterweser had responded. Unterweser was the low bidder and Zapata requested it to submit a contract, which it did. The contract submitted by Unterweser contained the following provision, which is at issue in this case:

> "Any dispute arising must be treated before the London Court of Justice."

In addition the contract contained two clauses purporting to exculpate Unterweser from liability for damages to the towed barge.[1]

> "2(b) Damages suffered by the towed object are in any case for account of its Owners."

After reviewing the contract and making several changes, but without any alteration in the forum-selection or exculpatory clauses, a Zapata vice president executed the contract and forwarded it to Unterweser in Germany, where Unterweser accepted the changes, and the contract became effective.

On January 5, 1968, Unterweser's deep sea tug Bremen departed Venice, Louisiana, with the Chaparral in tow bound for Italy. On January 9, while the flotilla was in international waters in the middle of the Gulf of Mexico, a severe storm arose. The sharp roll of the Chaparral in Gulf waters caused its elevator legs, which had been raised for the voyage, to break off and fall into the sea, seriously damaging the Chaparral. In this emergency situation Zapata instructed the Bremen to tow its damaged rig to Tampa, Florida, the nearest port of refuge.

On January 12, Zapata, ignoring its contract promise to litigate "any dispute arising" in the English courts, commenced a suit in admiralty in the United States District Court at Tampa, seeking $3,500,000 damages against Unterweser in personam and the Bremen in rem, alleging negligent towage and breach of contract.[2] Unterweser responded by invoking the forum clause of the towage contract, and moved to dismiss for lack of jurisdiction or on forum non conveniens grounds, or in the alternative to stay the action pending submission of the dispute to the "London Court of Justice." Shortly thereafter, in February, before the District Court had ruled on its motion to stay or dismiss the United States action, Unterweser commenced an action against Zapata seeking damages for breach of the towage contract in the High Court of Justice in London, as the contract provided. Zapata appeared in that court to contest

---

1 The General Towage Conditions of the contract included the following:

> "1. . . . [Unterweser and its] masters and crews are not responsible for defaults and/or errors in the navigation of the tow. . . .

2 The Bremen was arrested by a United States marshal acting pursuant to Zapata's complaint immediately upon her arrival in Tampa. The tug was subsequently released when Unterweser furnished security in the amount of $ 3,500,000.

jurisdiction, but its challenge was rejected, the English courts holding that the contractual forum provision conferred jurisdiction.[3] "I approach the matter, therefore, in this way, that the Court has a discretion, but it is a discretion which, in the ordinary way and in the absence of strong reason to the contrary, will be exercised in favour of holding parties to their bargain. The question is whether sufficient circumstances have been shown to exist in this case to make it desirable, on the grounds of balance of convenience, that proceedings should not take place in this country . . . ."

In the meantime, Unterweser was faced with a dilemma in the pending action in the United States court at Tampa. The six-month period for filing action to limit its liability to Zapata and other potential claimants was about to expire, but the United States District Court in Tampa had not yet ruled on Unterweser's motion to dismiss or stay Zapata's action. On July 2, 1968, confronted with difficult alternatives, Unterweser filed an action to limit its liability in the District Court in Tampa. That court entered the customary injunction against proceedings outside the limitation court, and Zapata refilled its initial claim in the limitation action.

It was only at this juncture, on July 29, after the six-month period for filing the limitation action had run, that the District Court denied Unterweser's January motion to dismiss or stay Zapata's initial action. In denying the motion, that court relied on the prior decision of the Court of Appeals in Carbon Black Export, Inc. v. The Monrosa, 254 F.2d 297 (CA5 1958), cert. dismissed, 359 U.S. 180 (1959). In that case the Court of Appeals had held a forum-selection clause unenforceable, reiterating the traditional view of many American courts that "agreements in advance of controversy whose object is to oust the jurisdiction of the courts are contrary to public policy and will not be enforced." 254 F.2d, at 300-301. Apparently concluding that it was bound by the *Carbon Black* case, the District Court gave the forum-selection clause little, if any, weight. Instead, the court treated the motion to dismiss under normal forum

---

3 Zapata appeared specially and moved to set aside service of process outside the country. Justice Karminski of the High Court of Justice denied the motion on the ground the contractual choice-of-forum provision conferred jurisdiction and would be enforced, absent a factual showing it would not be "fair and right" to do so. He did not believe Zapata had made such a showing, and held that it should be required to "stick to [its] bargain." App. 206, 211, 213. The Court of Appeal dismissed an appeal on the ground that Justice Karminski had properly applied the English rule. Lord Justice Willmer stated that rule as follows:

> "The law on the subject, I think, is not open to doubt . . . . It is always open to parties to stipulate . . . . that a particular Court shall have jurisdiction over any dispute arising out of their contract. Here the parties chose to stipulate that disputes were to be referred to the 'London Court,' which I take as meaning the High Court in this country. Prima facie it is the policy of the Court to hold parties to the bargain into which they have entered.

> . . . But that is not an inflexible rule, as was shown, for instance, by the case of The Fehmarn, [1957] 1 Lloyd's Rep. 511; (C. A.) [1957] 2 Lloyd's Rep. 551 . . . ."

non conveniens doctrine applicable in the absence of such a clause, citing
Gulf Oil Corp. v. Gilbert, plaintiff's choice of forum should rarely be disturbed."
Id., at 508. The District Court concluded:

> "The balance of conveniences here is not strongly in favor of
> [Unterweser] and [Zapata's] choice of forum should not be
> disturbed."

Thereafter, on January 21, 1969, the District Court denied another motion by
Unterweser to stay the limitation action pending determination of the
controversy in the High Court of Justice in London and granted Zapata's motion
to restrain Unterweser from litigating further in the London court. The District
Judge ruled that, having taken jurisdiction in the limitation proceeding, he
had jurisdiction to determine all matters relating to the controversy. He ruled
that Unterweser should be required to "do equity" by refraining from also
litigating the controversy in the London court, not only for the reasons he had
previously stated for denying Unterweser's first motion to stay Zapata's action,
but also because Unterweser had invoked the United States court's jurisdiction
to obtain the benefit of the Limitation Act.

On appeal, a divided panel of the Court of Appeals affirmed, and on
rehearing en banc the panel opinion was adopted, with six of the 14 en
banc judges dissenting. As had the District Court, the majority rested on
the *Carbon Black* decision, concluding that "'at the very least'" that case
stood for the proposition that a forum-selection clause "'will not be enforced
unless the selected state would provide a more convenient forum than the
state in which suit is brought.'" From that premise the Court of Appeals
proceeded to conclude that, apart from the forum-selection clause, the
District Court did not abuse its discretion in refusing to decline jurisdiction
on the basis of forum non conveniens. It noted that (1) the flotilla never
"escaped the Fifth Circuit's *mare nostrum*, and the casualty occurred in
close proximity to the district court"; (2) a considerable number of potential
witnesses, including Zapata crewmen, resided in the Gulf Coast area; (3)
preparation for the voyage and inspection and repair work had been
performed in the Gulf area; (4) the testimony of the Bremen crew was
available by way of deposition; (5) England had no interest in or contact
with the controversy other than the forum-selection clause. The Court of
Appeals majority further noted that Zapata was a United States citizen
and "the discretion of the district court to remand the case to a foreign
forum was consequently limited" — especially since it appeared likely that
the English courts would enforce the exculpatory clauses.[4] In addition, it

---

4 The record contains an undisputed affidavit of a British solicitor stating an opinion that the exculpatory clauses
of the contract would be held "prima facie valid and enforceable" against Zapata in any action maintained in
England in which Zapata alleged that defaults or errors in Unterweser's tow caused the casualty and damage
to the Chaparral.

is not disputed that while the limitation fund in the District Court in Tampa amounts to $ 1,390,000, the limitation fund in England would be only slightly in excess of $80,000 under English law. In the Court of Appeals' view, enforcement of such clauses would be contrary to public policy in American courts under Bisso v. Inland Waterways Corp., 349 U.S. 85 (1955), and Dixilyn Drilling Corp. v. Crescent Towing & Salvage Co., 372 U.S. 697 (1963). Therefore, "the district court was entitled to consider that remanding Zapata to a foreign forum, with no practical contact with the controversy, could raise a bar to recovery by a United States citizen which its own convenient courts would not countenance."

We hold, with the six dissenting members of the Court of Appeals, that far too little weight and effect were given to the forum clause in resolving this controversy. For at least two decades we have witnessed an expansion of overseas commercial activities by business enterprises based in the United States. The barrier of distance that once tended to confine a business concern to a modest territory no longer does so. Here we see an American company with special expertise contracting with a foreign company to tow a complex machine thousands of miles across seas and oceans. The expansion of American business and industry will hardly be encouraged if, notwithstanding solemn contracts, we insist on a parochial concept that all disputes must be resolved under our laws and in our courts. Absent a contract forum, the considerations relied on by the Court of Appeals would be persuasive reasons for holding an American forum convenient in the traditional sense, but in an era of expanding world trade and commerce, the absolute aspects of the doctrine of the Carbon Black case have little place and would be a heavy hand indeed on the future development of international commercial dealings by Americans. We cannot have trade and commerce in world markets and international waters exclusively on our terms, governed by our laws, and resolved in our courts.

Forum-selection clauses have historically not been favored by American courts. Many courts, federal and state, have declined to enforce such clauses on the ground that they were "contrary to public policy," or that their effect was to "oust the jurisdiction" of the court. Although this view apparently still has considerable acceptance, other courts are tending to adopt a more hospitable attitude toward forum-selection clauses. This view, advanced in the well-reasoned dissenting opinion in the instant case, is that such clauses are prima facie valid and should be enforced unless enforcement is shown by the resisting party to be "unreasonable" under the circumstances. We believe this is the correct doctrine to be followed by federal district courts sitting in admiralty. It is merely the other side of the proposition recognized by this Court in National Equipment Rental, Ltd. v. Szukhent, 375 U.S. 311 (1964), holding that in federal courts a party may validly consent to be sued in a jurisdiction where he cannot be found for service of process through contractual designation of an "agent" for receipt of process in that jurisdiction. In so holding, the Court stated:

> "It is settled . . . that parties to a contract may agree in advance to submit to the jurisdiction of a given court, to permit notice to be served by the opposing party, or even to waive notice altogether." Id., at 315-316.

This approach is substantially that followed in other common-law countries including England. It is the view advanced by noted scholars and that adopted by the Restatement of the Conflict of Laws. It accords with ancient concepts of freedom of contract and reflects an appreciation of the expanding horizons of American contractors who seek business in all parts of the world. Not surprisingly, foreign businessmen prefer, as do we, to have disputes resolved in their own courts, but if that choice is not available, then in a neutral forum with expertise in the subject matter. Plainly, the courts of England meet the standards of neutrality and long experience in admiralty litigation. The choice of that forum was made in an arm's-length negotiation by experienced and sophisticated businessmen, and absent some compelling and countervailing reason it should be honored by the parties and enforced by the courts.

The argument that such clauses are improper because they tend to "oust" a court of jurisdiction is hardly more than a vestigial legal fiction. It appears to rest at core on historical judicial resistance to any attempt to reduce the power and business of a particular court and has little place in an era when all courts are overloaded and when businesses once essentially local now operate in world markets. It reflects something of a provincial attitude regarding the fairness of other tribunals. No one seriously contends in this case that the forum-selection clause "ousted" the District Court of jurisdiction over Zapata's action. The threshold question is whether that court should have exercised its jurisdiction to do more than give effect to the legitimate expectations of the parties, manifested in their freely negotiated agreement, by specifically enforcing the forum clause.

There are compelling reasons why a freely negotiated private international agreement, unaffected by fraud, undue influence, or overweening bargaining power, should be enforced. "Zapata has neither presented evidence of nor alleged fraud or undue bargaining power in the agreement. Unterweser was only one of several companies bidding on the project. No evidence contradicts its Managing Director's affidavit that it specified English courts 'in an effort to meet Zapata Off-Shore Company half way.' Zapata's Vice President has declared by affidavit that no specific negotiations concerning the forum clause took place. But this was not simply a form contract with boilerplate language that Zapata had no power to alter. The towing of an oil rig across the Atlantic was a new business. Zapata did make alterations to the contract submitted by Unterweser. The forum clause could hardly be ignored. It is the final sentence of the agreement, immediately preceding the date and the parties' signatures. . . ." such as that involved here, should be given full effect. In this case, for example, we are concerned with a far from routine transaction between companies of two different nations contemplating the tow of an extremely costly piece of equipment from Louisiana across the Gulf of Mexico and the Atlantic Ocean, through the Mediterranean Sea to its final destination in the Adriatic Sea. In the course of its voyage, it was to traverse the waters of many jurisdictions. The Chaparral could have been damaged at any point along the route, and there were countless possible ports of refuge. That the accident occurred in the Gulf of Mexico and the barge was towed to Tampa in an emergency were mere fortuities. It cannot be doubted for a moment that the parties sought to provide for a neutral forum for the resolution of any disputes arising during the tow. Manifestly much uncertainty and possibly great inconvenience to both parties could arise if a suit could be maintained in any jurisdiction in which an accident might occur or if jurisdiction were left to any place where the Bremen or Unterweser might happen to be found.[5] The elimination of all such uncertainties by agreeing in advance on a forum acceptable to both parties is an indispensable element in international trade, commerce, and contracting. There is strong evidence that the forum clause was a vital part of the agreement,[6] and it would be unrealistic to think that the parties did not conduct their negotiations, including fixing the monetary terms, with the consequences of the forum clause figuring prominently in their calculations. Under these circumstances, as Justice Karminski reasoned in sustaining jurisdiction over Zapata in the High Court of Justice, "the force of an agreement for litigation in this country, freely entered into between two competent parties, seems to me to be very powerful."

Thus, in the light of present-day commercial realities and expanding international trade we conclude that the forum clause should control absent a strong showing that it should be set aside. Although their opinions are not altogether explicit, it seems reasonably clear that the District Court and the Court of Appeals placed the burden on Unterweser to show that London would be a more convenient forum than Tampa, although the contract expressly resolved that issue. The correct approach would have been to enforce the forum clause specifically unless Zapata could clearly show that enforcement would be unreasonable and unjust, or that the clause was invalid for such reasons as fraud or overreaching. Accordingly, the case must be remanded for reconsideration.

---

5 At the very least, the clause was an effort to eliminate all uncertainty as to the nature, location, and outlook of the forum in which these companies of differing nationalities might find themselves. Moreover, while the contract here did not specifically provide that the substantive law of England should be applied, it is the general rule in English courts that the parties are assumed, absent contrary indication, to have designated the forum with the view that it should apply its own law. [citations omitted] It is therefore reasonable to conclude that the forum clause was also an effort to obtain certainty as to the applicable substantive law.

6 Zapata has denied specifically discussing the forum clause with Unterweser, but, as Judge Wisdom pointed out, Zapata made numerous changes in the contract without altering the forum clause, which could hardly have escaped its attention. Zapata is clearly not unsophisticated in such matters. The contract of its wholly owned subsidiary with an Italian corporation covering the contemplated drilling operations in the Adriatic Sea provided that all disputes were to be settled by arbitration in London under English law, and contained broad exculpatory clauses.

We note, however, that there is nothing in the record presently before us that would support a refusal to enforce the forum clause. The Court of Appeals suggested that enforcement would be contrary to the public policy of the forum under Bisso v. Inland Waterways Corp., 349 U.S. 85 (1955), because of the prospect that the English courts would enforce the clauses of the towage contract purporting to exculpate Unterweser from liability for damages to the Chaparral. A contractual choice-of-forum clause should be held unenforceable if enforcement would contravene a strong public policy of the forum in which suit is brought, whether declared by statute or by judicial decision. It is clear, however, that whatever the proper scope of the policy expressed in Bisso, it does not reach this case. Bisso rested on considerations with respect to the towage business strictly in American waters, and those considerations are not controlling in an international commercial agreement. Speaking for the dissenting judges in the Court of Appeals, Judge Wisdom pointed out:

> "We should be careful not to over-emphasize the strength of the [Bisso] policy. . . . Two concerns underlie the rejection of exculpatory agreements: that they may be produced by overweening bargaining power; and that they do not sufficiently discourage negligence. . . . Here the conduct in question is that of a foreign party occurring in international waters outside our jurisdiction.

The evidence disputes any notion of overreaching in the contractual agreement. And for all we know, the uncertainties and dangers in the new field of transoceanic towage of oil rigs were so great that the tower was unwilling to take financial responsibility for the risks, and the parties thus allocated responsibility for the voyage to the tow. It is equally possible that the contract price took this factor into account. I conclude that we should not invalidate the forum selection clause here unless we are firmly convinced that we would thereby significantly encourage negligent conduct within the boundaries of the United States." 428 F.2d, at 907-908.

Courts have also suggested that a forum clause, even though it is freely bargained for and contravenes no important public policy of the forum, may nevertheless be "unreasonable" and unenforceable if the chosen forum is seriously inconvenient for the trial of the action. Of course, where it can be said with reasonable assurance that at the time they entered the contract, the parties to a freely negotiated private international commercial agreement contemplated the claimed inconvenience, it is difficult to see why any such claim of inconvenience should be heard to render the forum clause unenforceable. We are not here dealing with an agreement between two Americans to resolve their essentially local disputes in a remote alien forum. In such a case, the serious inconvenience of the contractual forum to one or both of the parties might carry greater weight in determining the reasonableness of the forum clause. The remoteness of the forum might suggest that the agreement was an adhesive one, or that the parties did not have the particular controversy in mind when they made their agreement; yet even there the party claiming should bear a heavy burden of proof. Similarly, selection of a remote forum to apply differing foreign law to an essentially American controversy might contravene an important public policy of the forum. For example, so long as Bisso governs American courts with respect to the towage business in American waters, it would quite arguably be improper to permit an American tower to avoid that policy by providing a foreign forum for resolution of his disputes with an American towee.

This case, however, involves a freely negotiated international commercial transaction between a German and an American corporation for towage of a vessel from the Gulf of Mexico to the Adriatic Sea. As noted, selection of a London forum was clearly a reasonable effort to bring vital certainty to this international transaction and to provide a neutral forum experienced and capable in the resolution of admiralty litigation. Whatever "inconvenience" Zapata would suffer by being forced to litigate in the contractual forum as it agreed to do was clearly foreseeable at the time of contracting. In such circumstances it should be incumbent on the party seeking to escape his contract to show that trial in the contractual forum will be so gravely difficult and inconvenient that he will for all practical purposes be deprived of his day in court. Absent that, there is no basis for concluding that it would be unfair, unjust, or unreasonable to hold that party to his bargain.

In the course of its ruling on Unterweser's second motion to stay the proceedings in Tampa, the District Court did make a conclusory finding that the balance of convenience was "strongly" in favor of litigation in Tampa. However, as previously noted, in making that finding the court erroneously placed the burden of proof on Unterweser to show that the balance of convenience was strongly in its favor. Moreover, the finding falls far short of a conclusion that Zapata would be effectively deprived of its day in court should it be forced to litigate in London. Indeed, it cannot even be assumed that it would be placed to the expense of transporting its witnesses to London. It is not unusual for important issues in international admiralty cases to be dealt with by deposition. Both the District Court and the Court of Appeals majority appeared satisfied that Unterweser could receive a fair hearing in Tampa by using deposition testimony of its witnesses from distant places, and there is no reason to conclude that Zapata could not use deposition testimony to equal advantage if forced to litigate in London as it bound itself to do. Nevertheless, to allow Zapata opportunity to carry its heavy burden of showing not only that the balance of convenience is strongly in favor of trial in Tampa (that is, that it will be far more inconvenient for Zapata to litigate in London than it will be for Unterweser to litigate in Tampa), but also that a London trial will be so manifestly and gravely inconvenient to Zapata that it will be effectively deprived of a meaningful day in court, we remand for further proceedings.

The judgment of the Court of Appeals is vacated and the case is remanded for further proceedings consistent with this opinion.

Vacated and remanded.

MR. JUSTICE DOUGLAS, dissenting.

. . . Respondent is a citizen of this country. Moreover, if it were remitted to the English court, its substantive rights would be adversely affected. Exculpatory provisions in the towage control provide (1) that petitioners, the masters and the crews "are not responsible for defaults and/or errors in the navigation of the tow" and (2) that "damages suffered by the towed object are in any case for account of its Owners."

Under our decision in Dixilyn Drilling Corp v. Crescent Towing & Salvage Co., 372 U.S. 697, 698, "a contract which exempts the tower from liability for its own negligence" is not enforceable, though there is evidence in the present record that it is enforceable in England. That policy was first announced in Bisso v. Inland Waterways Corp., 349 U.S. 85. Although the casualty occurred on the high seas, the *Bisso* doctrine is nonetheless applicable.

Moreover, the casualty occurred close to the District Court, a number of potential witnesses, including respondent's crewmen, reside in that area, and the inspection and repair work were done there. The testimony of the tower's crewmen, residing in Germany, is already available by way of depositions taken in the proceedings.

All in all, the District Court judge exercised his discretion wisely in enjoining petitioners from pursuing the litigation in England.

It is argued, however, that one of the rationales of the *Bisso* doctrine, "to protect those in need of goods or services from being overreached by others who have power to drive hard bargains" does not apply here because these parties may have been of equal bargaining stature. Yet we have often adopted prophylactic rules rather than attempt to sort the core cases from the marginal ones. In any event, the other objective of the Bisso doctrine, to "discourage negligence by making wrongdoers pay damages" (ibid.) applies here and in every case regardless of the relative bargaining strengths of the parties.

I would affirm the judgment below.

NOTES AND QUESTIONS

A. This case provides a brief introduction to and example of the complexity of what is known as "Cases in Admiralty" and the subject of maritime law. Even though this area of law is very old and fairly uniform throughout the world, there are differences from one nation to another.

1. Note (a) the use of *in rem* jurisdiction through the "arrest" of the ship; (b) the so-called "limitation action"; (c) the injunction against actions outside the "limitations court"; and (d) terms such as *mare nostrum* and navigable waterways.

2. While these "maritime law" issues are not directly relevant to the Supreme Court's decision, note Chief Justice Burger's observation that the size of the "limitations action" in the U.S. is 1500% of what it would be in London. Even aside from the substantive issue about the validity (under US law) of "exculpatory clauses" that bothers Justice Douglas, the difference in the size of the action is enough to explain all the preliminary skirmishing over forum.

B. After studying the travails of forum-battles in Chapter 3, doesn't a "choice of forum" agreement seem wise? In which of the Chapter 3 cases did we encounter a situation where use of a choice-of-forum clause would have obviated a lot of expensive litigation over forum? In which cases would such an approach not have been available?

1. Note that Zapata, having made just such an agreement, now wants to avoid it. Why? What arguments do they make?

2. Note also that such agreements are common. As the Supreme Court observes in a footnote:

> Zapata has denied specifically discussing the forum clause with Unterweser, but, as Judge Wisdom pointed out, Zapata made numerous changes in the contract without altering the forum clause, which could hardly have escaped its attention. Zapata is clearly not unsophisticated in such matters. The contract of its wholly owned subsidiary with an Italian corporation covering the contemplated drilling operations in the Adriatic Sea provided that all disputes were to be settled by arbitration in London under English law, and contained broad exculpatory clauses.

C. The district court's ruling (as well as that of the Court of Appeals - both in its usual 3-person profile <u>and</u> sitting "en banc") relied on the *Carbon Black* precedent. Under that case, forum selection clauses directing U.S. litigants to foreign forums were disfavored because they were deemed to "oust" the U.S. court of their "jurisdiction." As can be seen in the dissent, Justice William O. Douglas (long a liberal icon on the Court) is the only one of the Justices to hold fast to that view (or some version of it).

1. But Chief Justice Burger and his colleagues have a different view:

    > For at least two decades we have witnessed an expansion of overseas commercial activities by business enterprises based in the United States. The barrier of distance that once tended to confine a business concern to a modest territory no longer does so. Here we see an American company with special expertise contracting with a foreign company to tow a complex machine thousands of miles across seas and oceans. The expansion of American business and industry will hardly be encouraged if, notwithstanding solemn contracts, we insist on a parochial concept that all disputes must be resolved under our laws and in our courts.

    Do you agree? If sent to England, the English views of this case will undoubtedly prevail, probably to the prejudice of U.S. interests. Why should a U.S. court act that way? Do the Brits have any care about the safety of our waterways? Does the Supreme Court?

2. To the British court, it's a simple matter of contract. The London Court stated simply that Zapata should be required to "stick to [its] bargain." Is that all there is to it? Why was the U.S. view so different for so long?

3. Chief Justice Burger states that "[t]here are compelling reasons why a freely negotiated private international agreement, unaffected by fraud, undue influence, or overweening bargaining power, should be enforced." We've learned about fraud, but what does he mean by "undue influence or overweening bargaining power"? Zapata was a big corporation, with experienced businesspeople in charge with access to lawyers. Do you think the Court would have ruled the same way if an inexperienced consumer was involved? How about a 2-person trading company? And what if the contractual choice is a remote, obscure forum, like Roadtown in the British Virgin Islands?

4. The Supreme Court looks at this matter not only in terms of "contract" and broad policies, but also in terms of the specifics involved:

    > we are concerned with a far from routine transaction between companies of two different nations contemplating the tow of an extremely costly piece of equipment from Louisiana across the Gulf of Mexico and the Atlantic Ocean, through the Mediterranean Sea to its final destination in the Adriatic Sea. In the course of its voyage, it was to traverse the waters of

many jurisdictions. The Chaparral could have been damaged at any point along the route, and there were countless possible ports of refuge. That the accident occurred in the Gulf of Mexico and the barge was towed to Tampa in an emergency were mere fortuities. It cannot be doubted for a moment that the parties sought to provide for a neutral forum for the resolution of any disputes arising during the tow. Manifestly much uncertainty and possibly great inconvenience to both parties could arise if a suit could be maintained in any jurisdiction in which an accident might occur or if jurisdiction were left to any place where the Bremen or Unterweser might happen to be found. The elimination of all such uncertainties by agreeing in advance on a forum acceptable to both parties is an indispensable element in international trade, commerce, and contracting.

Is such an "economic" view of the "bargain" justified? Is Britain really chosen as a "neutral" forum, or was it chosen (by Unterweser) because its law was friendly to the (substantive) terms of the towing contract?

5. In addition to his concerns about the policies underlying *Bisso*, Justice Douglas is also concerned about practical considerations:

> Moreover, the casualty occurred close to the District Court, a number of potential witnesses, including respondent's crewmen, reside in that area, and the inspection and repair work were done there. . . .

> All in all, the District Court judge exercised his discretion wisely in enjoining petitioners from pursuing the litigation in England.

How does Chief Justice Burger respond?

D. It ought not to be surprising that, historically, England has been a preferred choice of "neutral" forum for international business. Note, for example, that in *The Julia* and *Tsakiroglou*, the parties had selected London, even though none was British. But what, aside from travel, are the practical effects of choosing a third country's forum for the resolution of disputes? Language, culture and law and legal procedure are all sure to play a part.

1. The British, like much of the world, apply a system known as "taxation of costs"; unlike the so-called "American Rule", the loser can be compelled by the court to pay the winner's attorneys fees. Also, in England, there is no right to a jury trial in commercial cases; and the lawyers wear wigs.

2. Suppose instead of England, the parties had chosen the Commercial Court in Paris, France. In a Continental, Civil Law country, the legal process and the law itself is very, very different. Suppose you are dealing with a Belgian company. Would you ever agree to such a forum? If they rejected the US and England, what other alternatives are open?

E. Before leaving this subject, note the references to the English court's consideration of the "fairness" issue. Are there any situations where you think an English court might exercise the discretion to not enforce the forum selection clause in a contract? Before answering, consider the next case. Be sure to read the separate concurring opinion of Lord Geoffrey Lane. It has a surprising twist.

CARVALHO
v.
HULL, BLYTH (ANGOLA) LTD.

United Kingdom Court of Appeal
(1979) 1 W.R.L. 1228

On April 29, 1977, the plaintiff, Joaquim Carvalho, resident in Portugal, issued a specially indorsed writ in the High Court in London claiming against Hull, Blyth (Angola) Ltd., a company registered in England, but carrying on business in independent Angola, the balance of moneys (20,000,000 escudos) due under a contract made between the parties on December 5, 1973, in Luanda, Angola, then a province of metropolitan Portugal. By his statement of claim endorsed on the writ the plaintiff claims inter alia, that by the contract be had sold an his shares in a group of Angolan companies to the defendants who were the majority shareholders in each company for a total consideration of escudos 76,000,000, and that the first three instalments of the price (escudos 56,000,000) had been paid in accordance with the term of the contract, under which the money of account was in the currency of Portugal, but that the fourth instalment now claimed had not been paid when it was due in January 1976; and he claimed as a liquidated demand the sum of escudos 20,000,000 or the sterling equivalent and statutory interest thereon. It was certified that the sterling equivalent the day before the writ was issued amounted to 301,431 pounds sterling.

On July 22, 1977, a summons was issued on behalf of the defendants asking that the writ be set aside on the ground that the High Court had no jurisdiction in the matter, or alternatively that the proceedings be stayed on the ground that the parties had agreed to submit the dispute to the exclusive jurisdiction of the courts of Angola. Clause 14 of the contract on which the plaintiffs claim was based, provided (as translated in the documents included in the defendants' affidavit evidence):

> "In the case of litigation arising, the District Court of Angola be considered the sole competent court to adjudicate to the exclusion of all others"

BROWNE LJ. This is an appeal by the defendants from a decision of Donaldson J. given on February 19, 1979, when he refused the defendants' application to stay the plaintiffs action, but gave leave to appeal.

The plaintiff formerly lived in Angola, but left in August 1975 and now lives in Portugal. The defendants are an English registered company, so there is no doubt that the English courts have jurisdiction, but we are told that the defendants have no assets here. They have carried on still carry on business entirely in Angola. They have carried on busiess there for 100 years. Their present business is that of ships' agents, and they also carry on business as motor traders through subsidiary companies.

Until 1951 Angola was a colony of Portugal. In 1951 it became a province of PortugaL In January 1975, after a coup d'etat in Portugal in 1974 the new Portuguese government announced that Angola would become independent in November 1975. In 1975 civil war broke out in Angola, but on November 11 Angola did become independent and, in due course, a new constitution was promulgated to which I will refer in a moment. A party or group known as M.P.L.A assumed power-that being the Popular Movement for the Liberation of Angola-and Dr. Neto became President. Since then Angola has been recognised by her Majesty's Government, among a number of other states, and ambassadors have been exchanged between Angola and this country.

> The plaintiff . . . left Angola in August 1975. There was before Donaldson J. an affidavit by Mr. Englefield, the plaintiffs solicitor, in these terms:
>
> I have the carriage of this action on behalf of the plaintiff and have spoken to him on a number of occasions both in this country and in Portugal. The plaintiff has informed me that in August 1975 he was forced to leave Angola with his family and received threats against his life and the lives of family. The plaintiff left behind in Angola his house, furniture, balance in his bank account and four farms belonging to him. The plaintiffs property and farms have now been taken over by officers of the Marxists's government. The plaintiff is unwilling to return to Angola and believes that if he does so he will be liquidated.
>
> [The court discussed certain provisions of the Angolan Constitution which provides, inter alia, for an independent judiciary and protection of the interests of foreign citizens]

In *The Eleftheria* [1970], the court said:

> The principles established by the authorities can, I think. be summarised as follows: (1) Where plaintiffs sue in England in breach of an agreement to refer disputes to a foreign court, and the defendants apply for a stay, the English court, assuming the claim to be otherwise within its jurisdiction, is not bound to grant a stay but has a discretion whether to do so or not. (2) The discretion should be exercised by granting a stay unless strong cause for not doing so is shown. (3) The burden of proving such strong cause is on the plaintiffs. (4) In exercising its discretion the court should take into account all the circumstances of the particular case. (5) In particular, but without prejudice to (4), the following matters, where they arise, may properly be regarded: (a) In what country the evidence on the issues of fact is situated, or more readily available, and the effect of that on the relative convenience and expense of trial as between the English and foreign courts. (b) Whether the law of the foreign court applies and, if so, whether it differs from English law in any material respects. (c) With what country either party is connected, and how closely. (d) Whether the defendants genuinely desire trial in the foreign country, or are only seeking procedural advantages. (e) Whether the plaintiffs would be prejudiced by having to sue in the foreign court because they would: (i) be deprived of security for their claim; (ii) be unable to enforce any judgment obtained; (iii) be faced with a time-bar not applicable in England; or (iv) for political, racial, religious or other reasons be unuely to get a fair trial"

It is clear from the affidavits filed on behalf of the plaintiff, and is not disputed by the defendants, that, when the contract was made in December 1973, Angola was a province of Portugal. The law was Portuguese law and the legal system then in force was Portuguese and substantively Portuguese. The judicial organisation of Portuguese Angola was part of the judicial system of Portuguese Europe and was in every respect identical with it. The qualification of judges was the same as in Portugal. Angola then had no separate legal system and there was no such thing as Angolan law except, perhaps, in some native customary courts. Now Angola is an independent sovereign state with a new constitution. It is true that it seems, from the affidavits filed on behalf of the defendants, that in general Portuguese law is still applied and that the previous structure of the courts still exists, except for the abolition of the right of appeal to the Supreme Court in Lisbon. But it seems to me plain from the Constitution that this situation can be changed at any moment. . . .

It is also clear from the defendants' evidence that the system for the appointment of judges has completely changed. According to the evidence filed on behalf of the defendants, the District Court of Luanda still exists under the same name but, in my judgment, the judge was right in holding that it is a different court from the court in contemplation when the contract was made. It was then a Portuguese court in all the respects to which I have already referred. It is now an Angolan court operating within the framework of the Angolan constitution and legal system and applying Angolan law.

One can perhaps test it in this way. If the parties had known in December 1973 what the situation would be in Angola now, would they have agreed to include clause 14 in the contract? I think it is impossible to say that the answer must be " Yes." There is a complete conflict in the affidavit evidence about the present situation as to the administration of justice in Angola. This court cannot resolve this conflict but, in mv view, it is unnecessary to do so to arrive at the conclusion that the preseit District Court of Luanda is a different court from that contemplated by the contract. If my conclusion on the construction point is right, it is unnecessary to decade the discretion point. . . .

GEOFFREY LANE L.J.

I agree.

I wish to add only this. One of the matters which the judge did mention was the fact that the plaintiff was reluctant to return to Angola and, indeed, has declared his intention of not returning to Angola on the basis that he feared for his life if he were to go back there. On all the evidence, it seems to me that, plainly, the plaintiff was the sort of person who would be anathema to the present government in Angola. That can scarcely be disputed, and it seems to me there was a ground for the plaintiff's fear. However, that is not a matter on which I would desire to base my decision.

Appeal dismissed with costs.

II.   CHOICE OF A PRIVATE FORUM: INTERNATIONAL ARBITRATION

While certain courts, like the High Court of Justice in London, are considered dispassionate and neutral forums for dispute resolution, they are not "international" tribunals. And although some international tribunals, like the International Court of Justice in the Hague and the World Trade Organization ("WTO"), exist for the resolution of international disputes, these "courts" are only for government v. government disputes; there are no "international" courts for the adjudication of commercial disputes. Businesses wanting to make a contractual choice of a judicial forum are thus limited to the national courts of the various governments around the world.

But there is another "choice" available to contracting parties - one that can indeed be truly "international". It is "international arbitration", and its use is typically invoked through a pre-dispute arbitration clause in a business contract. Before exploring such agreements, especially their validity and enforceability in international dispute resolution, one must first learn the basics of the arbitration process.

A. AN ARBITRATION PRIMER

"Litigation" is dispute resolution administered by a government, taking place in a "court", where the judges and clerks are all public officials. In court, the rules that apply are created by the legislature and by the courts themselves. When one undertakes litigation, one must follow carefully the court's rules and procedures, and one can usually expect a lengthy and expensive process, ending with the potential for at least one appeal.

Arbitration is private dispute resolution. It is neither administered nor sponsored by any government or court. The parties' agreement creates the ground-rules for the arbitration, and it is the parties who must "hire" and pay the arbitrator[s]. Typically, international arbitration is administered through an arbitration organization, such as the International Chamber of Commerce (ICC) or the American Arbitration Association (AAA). These organizations have pre-set rules, lists of potential arbitrators, and administrators to handle the paperwork.[1]

Even though the arbitration "system" is private, courts do sometimes become involved in disputes about arbitration. As we will see, courts routinely enforce agreements to arbitrate in the event one of the parties decides to ignore the arbitration agreement and bring a suit in a court; and courts regularly enforce the results of arbitration proceedings by converting "arbitration awards" to judicial judgments by a process known as "confirmation". But aside from these pre- and post-arbitration proceedings, courts almost never interfere with or become involved in an on-going arbitration proceeding.

Arbitration is the product of a contract. Faced with the dispute-resolution-dilemmas exposed in Chapter 3 and the first part of this Chapter, an increasing number of disputes are being resolved through arbitration. International businesses are willing to commit to arbitration as a way to reduce both the uncertainty of where disputes will be resolved and the cost of dispute resolution. A party desiring arbitration will thus, as it proposes and negotiates contracts, seek inclusion of an "arbitration clause" when it makes agreements to buy, sell, perform services, etc.

When agreeing to arbitrate, the parties must make their commitment in writing[2]. The agreement will provide that, if and when there is a dispute, the parties will

---

1 Engaging such an organization is common, but not required. The parties to a contract can agree to a set of rules (like the UN's UNCITRAL rules) and self-administer, a process sometimes called *ad hoc* arbitration.

2 While the law requires that arbitration agreements be in writing, there is no requirement that the agreement be "signed."

forego the opportunity to seek a judicial (court) resolution, and instead resort exclusively to a private[3] arbitration forum. A typical arbitration clause will thus (a) define the scope of the dispute committed to arbitration; and (b) designate the administering agency and/or the rules to be followed, *e.g.*:

> All disputes arising out of or concerning this agreement shall be settled by arbitration under the rules, then in effect, of the International Chamber of Commerce.[4]

Then, if a dispute arises, the injured party, instead of serving a Summons and Complaint on the other side, will make a "Demand for Arbitration".

After one or more rounds of paper submissions (at least a "Statement of Claim" and an "Answer"), the parties (called "Claimant" and "Respondent") will proceed to select arbitrators. The typical international model for arbitrator selection is "party appointment". Under this system, each party selects one arbitrator, and the two "party-appointed arbitrators" then select the "Chair" (in Britain, called the "Umpire"):

INTERNATIONAL CHAMBER OF COMMERCE

Rules of Arbitration

Article 8: Number of Arbitrators

1.   The disputes shall be decided by a sole arbitrator or by three arbitrators.

2.   Where the parties have not agreed upon the number of arbitrators, the [ICC] Court [of Arbitration] shall appoint a sole arbitrator, save where it appears to the Court that the dispute is such as to warrant the appointment of three arbitrators. [In cases requiring three (3) arbitrators], the Claimant shall nominate an arbitrator within a period of 15 days from the receipt of the notification of the decision of the Court, and the Respondent shall nominate an arbitrator within a period of 15 days from the receipt of the notification of the nomination made by the Claimant.

---

3 "Private" does not mean "secret", although arbitration hearings, unlike court proceedings, are not open to the public. Certainly, some businesses seek arbitration because they do not want their disputes heard in public.

4 This clause is referred to as a "plenary" arbitration agreement because it covers "all controversies"; note however, that even this broad clause is limited by reference to disputes "arising out of or concerning this agreement". Parties to a contract can, of course, choose to limit the scope of the commitment to arbitration, as well as to add whatever additional conditions or features they can agree to. What issues might arise, *e.g.*, in a dispute between a US company and a foreign company? The language of the proceedings is one such issue. Which country's substantive law is to be applied is another. What other issues might you want to discuss, *e.g.* with a Japanese company you are about to do business with?

4. Where the dispute is to be referred to three arbitrators, each party shall nominate in the Request and the Answer, respectively, one Arbitrator for confirmation. If a party fails to nominate an arbitrator, the appointment shall be made by the Court. The third arbitrator, who will act as chairman of the Arbitral Tribunal, shall be appointed by the Court, unless the parties have agreed upon another procedure for such appointment, in which case the nomination will be subject to confirmation pursuant to Article 9. Should such procedure not result in a nomination within the time limit fixed by the parties or the Court, the third arbitrator shall be appointed by the Court.

* * *

While each arbitrator is typically expected to act "as a neutral",[5] the party-appointment method of arbitrator selection[6] allows each side to pick a trustworthy (and perhaps sympathetic) arbitrator from its home country. The expectation (though not a requirement) is that those two party-appointed arbitrators will then choose a Chair from a third country. In that way, a truly international, multi-cultural tribunal is created - something that is impossible in any national court.

Arbitrators often are, but need not be, lawyers; businesspeople, retired judges, professors and other professionals are commonly seen serving as arbitrators. The parties must pay the arbitrators' fees, and these can be substantial. Nevertheless, arbitration, with its streamlined procedures, ought, after everything, to be less expensive than court (although sometimes in over-lawyered or complex disputes these benefits are not realized). In arbitration, there is virtually no "motion practice" (thus no procedural "Motions to Dismiss" or "Motions for Summary Judgment"), and the "discovery" process is much less extensive than in court (no depositions, limited pre-hearing exchange of documents).

An arbitration "hearing" (the word "trial" is not used) will then take place before the arbitrators. An arbitration hearing is less formal than a trial; *e.g.* a conference room table is used instead of the usual courtroom set-up, and the lawyers conduct the proceedings while seated. Still there will be a presentation of evidence and examination of witnesses.

---

5 Arbitration must be distinguished from "mediation". Mediation is a conciliation-seeking process where the parties are encouraged to negotiate a final resolution to their dispute. Like an arbitrator, a mediator acts as a neutral, but a mediator has no power to impose a resolution; a mediator can only facilitate settlement. Both arbitration and mediation fall under the heading "Alternative Dispute Resolution" ("ADR").

6 In a domestic (US) arbitration, the most-often-used method of arbitrator selection is "list selection", where the sponsoring organization proposes a list of potential arbitrators, and the parties engage in a blind process known as "strike and rank". In labor arbitrations, which are yet another species of arbitration, the contract itself is likely to name the arbitrator.

When making their decision, arbitrators are not required to follow the strict law the way courts are expected to, and their decisions cannot be reversed for "error". The arbitrators' decision, called an "award", may or may not have "reasons" accompanying it, depending on the rules chosen and/or the inclination of the arbitrators.

A party dissatisfied by an arbitration award has few options short of compliance. A motion to "vacate" the award can be made to a court, but, in the absence of proof of corruption or fraud, courts routinely and summarily "confirm" arbitration awards. Once confirmed, the award becomes a judgment of the court, and it can be enforced in the manner provided for judgments.

Additional information about the leading arbitration service providers can be found at:

www.iccwbo.org (Int'l Chamber of Commerce)

www.adr.org (American Arbitration Association)

www.jamsadr.com (Judicial Arbitration and Mediation Service)

www.cpradr.org (CPR Institute)

www.nasd.com (National Association of Securities Dealers)

B.   THE "NEW YORK CONVENTION"

In 1958, under the auspices of the U.N., an international treaty was created called the "New York Convention on the Recognition and Enforcement of Foreign Arbitral Awards". The U.S. was an original signatory; there are now 142 nations that have signed.

The treaty calls for the universal enforcement of arbitration agreements (subject to exceptions), and for the universal recognition and enforcement of arbitration awards (subject to exceptions).

THE NEW YORK CONVENTION
ON THE RECOGNITION AND ENFORCEMENT
OF FOREIGN ARBITRAL AWARDS

Article I

1.   This Convention shall apply to the recognition and enforcement of arbitral awards made in the territory of a State other than the State where the recognition and enforcement of such awards are sought, and arising

out of differences between persons, whether physical or legal. It shall also apply to arbitral awards not considered as domestic awards in the State where their recognition and enforcement are sought.

2. The term "arbitral awards" shall include not only awards made by arbitrators appointed for each case but also those made by permanent arbitral bodies to which the parties have submitted.

3. When signing, ratifying or acceding to this Convention, or notifying extension under article X hereof, any State may on the basis of reciprocity declare that it will apply the Convention to the recognition and enforcement of awards made only in the territory of another Contracting State. It may also declare that it will apply the Convention only to differences arising out of legal relationships, whether contractual or not, which are considered as commercial under the national law of the State making such declaration.

Article II

1. Each Contracting State shall recognize an agreement in writing under which the parties undertake to submit to arbitration all or any differences which have arisen or which may arise between them in respect of a defined legal relationship, whether contractual or not, concerning a subject matter capable of settlement by arbitration.

2. The term "agreement in writing" shall include an arbitral clause in a contract or an arbitration agreement, signed by the parties or contained in an exchange of letters or telegrams.

3. The court of a Contracting State, when seized of an action in a matter in respect of which the parties have made an agreement within the meaning of this article, at the request of one of the parties, refer the parties to arbitration, unless it finds that the said agreement is null and void, inoperative or incapable of being performed.

Article III

Each Contracting State shall recognize arbitral awards as binding and enforce them in accordance with the rules of procedure of the territory where the award is relied upon, under the conditions laid down in the following articles. There shall not be imposed substantially more onerous conditions or higher fees or charges on the recognition or enforcement of arbitral awards to which this Convention applies than are imposed on the recognition or enforcement of domestic arbitral awards.

Article IV

1. To obtain the recognition and enforcement mentioned in the preceding article, the party applying for recognition and enforcement shall, at the time of the application, supply:

    (a) The duly authenticated original award or a duly certified copy thereof;

    (b) The original agreement referred to in article II or a duly certified copy thereof.

2. If the said award or agreement is not made in an official language of the country in which the award is relied upon, the party applying for recognition and enforcement of the award shall produce a translation of these documents into such language. The translation shall be certified by an official or sworn translator or by a diplomatic or consular agent.

Article V

1   Recognition and enforcement of the award may be refused, at the request of the party against whom it is invoked, only if that party furnishes to the competent authority where the recognition and enforcement is sought, proof that:

    (a) The parties to the agreement referred to in article II were, under the law applicable to them, under some incapacity, or the said agreement is not valid under the law to which the parties have subjected it or, failing any indication thereon, under the law of the country where the award was made; or

    (b) The party against whom the award is invoked was not given proper notice of the appointment of the arbitrator or of the arbitration proceedings or was otherwise unable to present his case; or

    (c) The award deals with a difference not contemplated by or not falling within the terms of the submission to arbitration, or it contains decisions on matters beyond the scope of the submission to arbitration, provided that, if the decisions on matters submitted to arbitration can be separated from those not so submitted, that part of the award which contains decisions on matters submitted to arbitration may be recognized and enforced; or

    (d) The composition of the arbitral authority or the arbitral procedure was not in accordance with the agreement of the parties, or, failing such agreement, was not in accordance with the law of the country where the arbitration took place; or

(e)   The award has not yet become binding on the parties, or has been set aside or suspended by a competent authority of the country in which, or under the law of which, that award was made.

2.   Recognition and enforcement of an arbitral award may also be refused if the competent authority in the country where recognition and enforcement is sought finds that:

(a)   The subject matter of the difference is not capable of settlement by arbitration under the law of that country; or

(b)   The recognition or enforcement of the award would be contrary to the public policy of that country.

Article VI

If an application for the setting aside or suspension of the award has been made to a competent authority referred to in article V (1) (e), the authority before which the award is sought to be relied upon may, if it considers it proper, adjourn the decision on the enforcement of the award and may also, on the application of the party claiming enforcement of the award, order the other party to give suitable security.

*   *   *

Additional information about the treaty, including a list of signatory countries, can be found at http://www.uncitral.org/uncitral/en/uncitral_texts/arbitration/NYConvention.html

C. THE NEW YORK CONVENTION AND THE U.S.

The Federal Arbitration Act (US) incorporates the provisions of the Convention. Note, however, that in Article II(1), the treaty reserves from enforcement agreements to arbitrate matters "concerning a subject matter not capable of settlement by arbitration." Those words were important to the US in 1958, because it was a time when arbitration, like judicial forum selection, was disfavored as to some types of cases (principally cases involving either antitrust or securities law).

In the wake of *The Bremen*, however, the United States revisited the "arbitrability" issue. Here is the result.

MITSUBISHI MOTORS CORP.
v.
SOLER CHRYSLER-PLYMOUTH, INC.

United States Court of Appeals, Ninth Circuit

473 U.S. 614; 105 S. Ct. 3346; 87 L.Ed. 2d 444

July 2, 1985, Decided

JUSTICE BLACKMUN delivered the opinion of the Court.

The principal question presented by these cases is the arbitrability, pursuant to the Federal Arbitration Act, 9 U. S. C. Sec. 1 et seq., and the Convention on the Recognition and Enforcement of Foreign Arbitral Awards (Convention), [1970] 21 U.S.T. 2517, T.I.A.S. No. 6997, of claims arising under the Sherman Act, 15 U. S. C. Sec 1 et seq., and encompassed within a valid arbitration clause in an agreement embodying an international commercial transaction.

I

Petitioner-cross-respondent Mitsubishi Motors Corporation (Mitsubishi) is a Japanese corporation which manufactures automobiles and has its principal place of business in Tokyo, Japan. Mitsubishi is the product of a joint venture between, on the one hand, Chrysler International, S.A. (CISA), a Swiss corporation registered in Geneva and wholly owned by Chrysler Corporation, and, on the other, Mitsubishi Heavy Industries, Inc., a Japanese corporation. The aim of the joint venture was the distribution through Chrysler dealers outside the continental United States of vehicles manufactured by Mitsubishi and bearing Chrysler and Mitsubishi trademarks. Respondent-cross-petitioner Soler Chrysler-Plymouth, Inc. (Soler), is a Puerto Rico corporation with its principal place of business in Pueblo Viejo, Guaynabo, Puerto Rico.

On October 31, 1979, Soler entered into a Distributor Agreement with CISA which provided for the sale by Soler of Mitsubishi-manufactured vehicles within a designated area, including metropolitan San Juan. App. 18. On the same date, CISA, Soler, and Mitsubishi entered into a Sales Procedure Agreement (Sales Agreement) which, referring to the Distributor Agreement, provided for the direct sale of Mitsubishi products to Soler and governed the terms and conditions of such sales. Id., at 42. Paragraph VI of the Sales Agreement, labeled "Arbitration of Certain Matters," provides:

> "All disputes, controversies or differences which may arise between [Mitsubishi] and [Soler] out of or in relation to Articles I-B through V of this Agreement or for the breach thereof, shall be finally settled by arbitration in Japan in accordance with the rules and regulations of the Japan Commercial Arbitration Association." Id., at 52-53.

Initially, Soler did a brisk business in Mitsubishi-manufactured vehicles. As a result of its strong performance, its minimum sales volume, specified by Mitsubishi and CISA, and agreed to by Soler, for the 1981 model year was substantially increased. Id., at 179. In early 1981, however, the new-car market slackened. Soler ran into serious difficulties in meeting the expected sales volume, and by the spring of 1981 it felt itself compelled to request that Mitsubishi delay or cancel shipment of several orders. About the same time, Soler attempted to arrange for the transshipment of a quantity of its vehicles for sale in the continental United States and Latin America. Mitsubishi and CISA, however, refused permission for any such diversion, citing a variety of reasons, and no vehicles were transshipped. Attempts to work out these difficulties failed. Mitsubishi eventually withheld shipment of 966 vehicles, apparently representing orders placed for May, June, and July 1981 production, responsibility for which Soler disclaimed in February 1982.

The following month, Mitsubishi brought an action against Soler in the United States District Court for the District of Puerto Rico under the Federal Arbitration Act and the Convention. Mitsubishi sought an order, pursuant to 9 U. S. C. @@ 4 and 201, to compel arbitration in accord with para. VI of the Sales Agreement. Shortly after filing the complaint, Mitsubishi filed a request for arbitration before the Japan Commercial Arbitration Association.

Soler denied the allegations and counterclaimed against both Mitsubishi and CISA. It alleged numerous breaches by Mitsubishi of the Sales Agreement, raised a pair of defamation claims, and asserted causes of action under the Sherman Act, 15 U. S. C. @ 1 et seq.; the federal Automobile Dealers' Day in Court Act, 70 Stat. 1125, 15 U. S. C. @ 1221 et seq.; the Puerto Rico competition statute, P.R. Laws Ann., Tit. 10, @ 257 et seq. (1976); and the Puerto Rico Dealers' Contracts Act, P.R. Laws Ann., Tit. 10, @ 278 et seq. (1976 and Supp. 1983). In the counterclaim premised on the Sherman Act, Soler alleged that Mitsubishi and CISA had conspired to divide markets in restraint of trade. To effectuate the plan, according to Soler, Mitsubishi had refused to permit Soler to resell to buyers in North, Central, or South America vehicles it had obligated itself to purchase from Mitsubishi; had refused to ship ordered vehicles or the parts, such as heaters and defoggers, that would be necessary to permit Soler to make its vehicles suitable for resale outside Puerto Rico; and had coercively attempted to replace Soler and its other Puerto Rico distributors with a wholly owned subsidiary which would serve as the exclusive Mitsubishi distributor in Puerto Rico.

After a hearing, the District Court ordered Mitsubishi and Soler to arbitrate each of the issues raised in the complaint and in all the counterclaims save two and a portion of a third. n7 With regard to the federal antitrust issues, it recognized that the Courts of Appeals, following American Safety Equipment Corp. v. J. P. Maguire & Co., 391 F.2d 821 (CA2 1968), uniformly had held that the rights conferred by the antitrust laws were "'of a character inappropriate for enforcement by arbitration.'" App. to Pet. for Cert. in No. 83-1569, p. B9, quoting Wilko v. Swan, 201 F.2d 439, 444 (CA2 1953), rev'd, 346 U.S. 427 (1953). The District Court held, however, that the international character of the Mitsubishi-Soler undertaking required enforcement of the agreement to arbitrate even as to the antitrust claims. It relied on Scherk v. Alberto-Culver Co., 417 U.S. 506, 515-520 (1974), in which this Court ordered arbitration, pursuant to a provision embodied in an international agreement, of a claim arising under the Securities Exchange Act of 1934 notwithstanding its assumption, arguendo, that Wilko, supra, which held nonarbitrable claims arising under the Securities Act of 1933, also would bar arbitration of a 1934 Act claim arising in a domestic context.

The United States Court of Appeals for the First Circuit affirmed in part and reversed in part. 723 F.2d 155 (1983). It first rejected Soler's argument that Puerto Rico law precluded enforcement of an agreement obligating a local dealer to arbitrate controversies outside Puerto Rico. It also rejected Soler's suggestion that it could not have intended to arbitrate statutory claims not mentioned in the arbitration agreement. Assessing arbitrability "on an allegation-by-allegation basis," id., at 159, the court then read the arbitration clause to encompass virtually all the claims arising under the various statutes, including all those arising under the Sherman Act.

Finally, after endorsing the doctrine of American Safety, precluding arbitration of antitrust claims, the Court of Appeals concluded that neither this Court's decision in Scherk nor the Convention required abandonment of that doctrine in the face of an international transaction. 723 F.2d, at 164-168. Accordingly, it reversed the judgment of the District Court insofar as it had ordered submission of "Soler's antitrust claims" to arbitration. n10 Affirming the remainder of the judgment, n11 the court directed the District Court to consider in the first instance how the parallel judicial and arbitral proceedings should go forward.

We granted certiorari primarily to consider whether an American court should enforce an agreement to resolve antitrust claims by arbitration when that agreement arises from an international transaction.

* * *

III

We [] turn to consider whether Soler's antitrust claims are nonarbitrable even though it has agreed to arbitrate them. In holding that they are not, the Court of Appeals followed the decision of the Second Circuit in American Safety Equipment Corp. v. J. P. Maguire & Co., 391 F.2d 821 (1968). Notwithstanding the absence of any explicit support for such an exception in either the Sherman Act or the Federal Arbitration Act, the Second Circuit there reasoned that "the pervasive public interest in enforcement of the antitrust laws, and the nature of the claims that arise in such cases, combine to make . . . antitrust claims . . . inappropriate for arbitration." Id., at 827-828. We find it unnecessary to assess the legitimacy of the *American Safety* doctrine as applied to agreements to arbitrate arising from domestic transactions. As in Scherk v. Alberto-Culver Co., 417 U.S. 506 (1974), we conclude that concerns of international comity, respect for the capacities of foreign and transnational tribunals, and sensitivity to the need of the international commercial system for predictability in the resolution of disputes require that we enforce the parties' agreement, even assuming that a contrary result would be forthcoming in a domestic context.

Even before *Scherk*, this Court had recognized the utility of forum-selection clauses in international transactions. In *The Bremen*, supra, an American oil company, seeking to evade a contractual choice of an English forum and, by implication, English law, filed a suit in admiralty in a United States District Court against the German corporation which had contracted to tow its rig to a location in the Adriatic Sea. Notwithstanding the possibility that the English court would enforce provisions in the towage contract exculpating the German party which an American court would refuse to enforce, this Court gave effect to the choice-of-forum clause. It observed:

> "The expansion of American business and industry will hardly be encouraged if, notwithstanding solemn contracts, we insist on a parochial concept that all disputes must be resolved under our laws and in our courts. . . . We cannot have trade and commerce in world markets and international waters exclusively on our terms, governed by our laws, and resolved in our courts."

Recognizing that "agreeing in advance on a forum acceptable to both parties is an indispensable element in international trade, commerce, and contracting," id., at 13-14, the decision in *The Bremen* clearly eschewed a provincial solicitude for the jurisdiction of domestic forums.

Identical considerations governed the Court's decision in *Scherk*, which categorized "[an] agreement to arbitrate before a specified tribunal [as], in effect, a specialized kind of forum-selection clause that posits not only the situs of suit but also the procedure to be used in resolving the dispute." 417 U.S., at 519. In *Scherk*, the American company Alberto-Culver purchased several interrelated business enterprises, organized under the laws of Germany and Liechtenstein, as well as the rights held by those enterprises in certain trademarks, from a German citizen who at the time of trial resided in Switzerland. Although the contract of sale contained a clause providing for arbitration before the International Chamber of Commerce in Paris of "any controversy or claim [arising] out of this agreement or the breach thereof," Alberto-Culver subsequently brought suit against Scherk in a Federal District

Court in Illinois, alleging that Scherk had violated section 10(b) of the Securities Exchange Act of 1934 by fraudulently misrepresenting the status of the trademarks as unencumbered. The District Court denied a motion to stay the proceedings before it and enjoined the parties from going forward before the arbitral tribunal in Paris. The Court of Appeals for the Seventh Circuit affirmed, relying on this Court's holding in Wilko v. Swan, 346 U.S. 427 (1953), that agreements to arbitrate disputes arising under the Securities Act of 1933 are nonarbitrable. This Court reversed, enforcing the arbitration agreement even while assuming for purposes of the decision that the controversy would be nonarbitrable under the holding of *Wilko* had it arisen out of a domestic transaction. Again, the Court emphasized:

> "A contractual provision specifying in advance the forum in which disputes shall be litigated and the law to be applied is . . . an almost indispensable precondition to achievement of the orderliness and predictability essential to any international business transaction. . . .

> "A parochial refusal by the courts of one country to enforce an international arbitration agreement would not only frustrate these purposes, but would invite unseemly and mutually destructive jockeying by the parties to secure tactical litigation advantages. . . . [It would] damage the fabric of international commerce and trade, and imperil the willingness and ability of businessmen to enter into international commercial agreements." 417 U.S., at 516-517.

Accordingly, the Court held Alberto-Culver to its bargain, sending it to the international arbitral tribunal before which it had agreed to seek its remedies.

The Bremen and *Scherk* establish a strong presumption in favor of enforcement of freely negotiated contractual choice-of-forum provisions. Here, as in *Scherk*, that presumption is reinforced by the emphatic federal policy in favor of arbitral dispute resolution. And at least since this Nation's accession in 1970 to the Convention, see [1970] 21 U.S.T. 2517, T.I.A.S. 6997, and the implementation of the Convention in the same year by amendment of the Federal Arbitration Act, that federal policy applies with special force in the field of international commerce. Thus, we must weigh the concerns of American Safety against a strong belief in the efficacy of arbitral procedures for the resolution of international commercial disputes and an equal commitment to the enforcement of freely negotiated choice-of-forum clauses. . . .

. . . .[We turn to] the core of the *American Safety* doctrine — the fundamental importance to American democratic capitalism of the regime of the antitrust laws. Without doubt, the private cause of action plays a central role in enforcing this regime. As the Court of Appeals pointed out:

"'A claim under the antitrust laws is not merely a private matter. The Sherman Act is designed to promote the national interest in a competitive economy; thus, the plaintiff asserting his rights under the Act has been likened to a private attorney-general who protects the public's interest.'"

The treble-damages provision wielded by the private litigant is a chief tool in the antitrust enforcement scheme, posing a crucial deterrent to potential violators.

The importance of the private damages remedy, however, does not compel the conclusion that it may not be sought outside an American court. Notwithstanding its important incidental policing function, the treble-damages cause of action conferred on private parties by @ 4 of the Clayton Act, 15 U. S. C. §15, and pursued by Soler here by way of its third counterclaim, seeks primarily to enable an injured competitor to gain compensation for that injury.

*   *   *

There is no reason to assume at the outset of the dispute that international arbitration will not provide an adequate mechanism. To be sure, the international arbitral tribunal owes no prior allegiance to the legal norms of particular states; hence, it has no direct obligation to vindicate their statutory dictates. The tribunal, however, is bound to effectuate the intentions of the parties. Where the parties have agreed that the arbitral body is to decide a defined set of claims which includes, as in these cases, those arising from the application of American antitrust law, the tribunal therefore should be bound to decide that dispute in accord with the national law giving rise to the claim. Cf. Wilko v. Swan, 346 U.S., at 433-434. And so long as the prospective litigant effectively may vindicate its statutory cause of action in the arbitral forum, the statute will continue to serve both its remedial and deterrent function.

Having permitted the arbitration to go forward, the national courts of the United States will have the opportunity at the award-enforcement stage to ensure that the legitimate interest in the enforcement of the antitrust laws has been addressed. The Convention reserves to each signatory country the right to refuse enforcement of an award where the "recognition or enforcement of the award would be contrary to the public policy of that country." Art. V(2)(b), 21 U.S.T., at 2520; see Scherk, 417 U.S., at 519, n. 14. While the efficacy of the arbitral process requires that substantive review at the award-enforcement stage remain minimal, it would not require intrusive inquiry to ascertain that the tribunal took cognizance of the antitrust claims and actually decided them.

As international trade, has expanded in recent decades, so too has the use of, international arbitration to resolve disputes arising in the course of that trade. The controversies that international arbitral institutions are called upon to resolve have increased in diversity as well as in complexity. Yet the potential of these tribunals for efficient disposition of legal disagreements arising from commercial relations has not yet been tested. If they are to take a central place in the international legal order, national courts will need to "shake off the old judicial hostility to arbitration," Kulukundis Shipping Co. v. Amtorg Trading Corp., 126 F.2d 978, 985 (CA2 1942), and also their customary and understandable unwillingness to cede jurisdiction of a claim arising under domestic law to a foreign or transnational tribunal. To this extent, at least, it will be necessary for national courts to subordinate domestic notions of arbitrability to the international policy favoring commercial arbitration.[13]

In acceding to the Convention the Senate restricted its applicability to commercial matters, in accord with Art. I(3). Yet in implementing the Convention by amendment to the Federal Arbitration Act, Congress did not specify any matters it intended to exclude from its scope. . . . The utility of the Convention in promoting the process of international commercial arbitration depends upon the willingness of national courts to let go of matters they normally would think of as their own. Doubtless, Congress may specify categories of claims it wishes to reserve for decision by our own courts without contravening this Nation's obligations under the Convention. But we decline to subvert the spirit of the United States' accession to the Convention by recognizing subject-matter exceptions where Congress has not expressly directed the courts to do so.

Accordingly, we "require this representative of the American business community to honor its bargain," by holding this agreement to arbitrate "[enforceable] . . . in accord with the explicit provisions of the Arbitration Act."

The judgment of the Court of Appeals is affirmed in part and reversed in part, and the cases are remanded for further proceedings consistent with this opinion.

It is so ordered.

JUSTICE POWELL took no part in the decision of these cases.

JUSTICE STEVENS, with whom JUSTICE BRENNAN joins, and with whom JUSTICE MARSHALL joins, dissenting.

. . .

This Court's holding rests almost exclusively on the federal policy favoring arbitration of commercial disputes and vague notions of international comity arising from the fact that the automobiles involved here were manufactured

---

13 We do not quarrel with the Court of Appeals' conclusion that Art. II(1) of the Convention, which requires the recognition of agreements to arbitrate that involve "subject matter capable of settlement by arbitration," contemplates exceptions to arbitrability grounded in domestic law. And it appears that before acceding to the Convention the Senate was advised by a State Department memorandum that the Convention provided for such exceptions.

in Japan. Because I am convinced that the Court of Appeals' construction of the arbitration clause is erroneous, and because I strongly disagree with this Court's interpretation of the relevant federal statutes, I respectfully dissent.

* * *

Section 2 of the Federal Arbitration Act . . . reads as follows:

> "A written provision in . . . a contract evidencing a transaction involving commerce to settle by arbitration a controversy thereafter arising out of such contract . . . or the refusal to perform the whole or any part thereof, . . . shall be valid, irrevocable, and enforceable, save upon such grounds as exist at law or in equity for the revocation of any contract."

The plain language of this statute encompasses Soler's claims that arise out of its contract with Mitsubishi, but does not encompass a claim arising under federal law, or indeed one that arises under its distributor agreement with Chrysler. Nothing in the text of the 1925 Act, nor its legislative history, suggests that Congress intended to authorize the arbitration of any statutory claims.

On several occasions we have drawn a distinction between statutory rights and contractual rights and refused to hold that an arbitration barred the assertion of a statutory right. Thus, in Alexander v. Gardner-Denver Co., 415 U.S. 36 (1974), we held that the arbitration of a claim of employment discrimination would not bar an employee's statutory right to damages under Title VII of the Civil Rights Act of 1964, 42 U. S. C. sections 2000e — 2000e-17, notwithstanding the strong federal policy favoring the arbitration of labor disputes. In that case the Court explained at some length why it would be unreasonable to assume that Congress intended to give arbitrators the final authority to implement the federal statutory policy:

> "[We] have long recognized that 'the choice of forums inevitably affects the scope of the substantive right to be vindicated.' U.S. Bulk Carriers v.Arguelles, 400 U.S. 351, 359-360 (1971)(Harlan, J., concurring). Respondent's deferral rule is necessarily premised on the assumption that arbitral processes are commensurate with judicial processes and that Congress impliedly intended federal courts to defer to arbitral decisions on Title VII issues. We deem this supposition unlikely.

> "Arbitral procedures, while well suited to the resolution of contractual disputes, make arbitration a comparatively inappropriate forum for the final resolution of rights created by Title VII. This conclusion rests first on the special role of the arbitrator, whose task is to effectuate the intent of the parties

rather than the requirements of enacted legislation. . . . But other facts may still render arbitral processes comparatively inferior to judicial processes in the protection of Title VII rights. Among these is the fact that the specialized competence of arbitrators pertains primarily to the law of the shop, not the law of the land. Parties usually choose an arbitrator because they trust his knowledge and judgment concerning the demands and norms of industrial relations. On the other hand, the resolution of statutory or constitutional issues is a primary responsibility of courts, and judicial construction has proved especially necessary with respect to Title VII, whose broad language frequently can be given meaning only by reference to public law concepts."

In addition, the Court noted that the informal procedures which make arbitration so desirable in the context of contractual disputes are inadequate to develop a record for appellate review of statutory questions.[14] Such review is essential on matters of statutory interpretation in order to assure consistent application of important public rights.

In Barrentine v. Arkansas-Best Freight System, Inc., 450 U.S. 728 (1981), we reached a similar conclusion with respect to the arbitrability of an employee's claim based on the Fair Labor Standards Act. We again noted that an arbitrator, unlike a federal judge, has no institutional obligation to enforce federal legislative policy:

> Because the arbitrator is required to effectuate the intent of the parties, rather than to enforce the statute, he may issue a ruling that is inimical to the public policies underlying the FLSA, thus depriving an employee of protected statutory rights.

Finally, not only are arbitral procedures less protective of individual statutory rights than are judicial procedures, but arbitrators very often are powerless to grant the aggrieved employees as broad a range of relief. Under the FLSA, courts can award actual and liquidated damages, reasonable attorney's fees, and costs. An arbitrator, by contrast, can award only that compensation authorized by the wage provision of the collective-bargaining agreement. . . . It is most unlikely that he will be authorized to award liquidated damages, costs, or attorney's fees.

---

14 Moreover, the factfinding process in arbitration usually is not equivalent to judicial factfinding. The record of the arbitration proceedings is not as complete; the usual rules of evidence do not apply; and rights and procedures common to civil trials, such as discovery, compulsory process, cross-examination, and testimony under oath, are often severely limited or unavailable. And as this Court has recognized, '[arbitrators] have no obligation to the court to give their reasons for an award.' Indeed, it is the informality of arbitral procedure that enables it to function as an efficient, inexpensive, and expeditious means for dispute resolution. This same characteristic, however, makes arbitration a less appropriate forum for final resolution of Title VII issues than the federal courts.

The Court has applied the same logic in holding that federal claims asserted under the Ku Klux Act of 1871, and claims arising under sec. 12(2) of the Securities Act of 1933, may not be finally resolved by an arbitrator.

The Court's opinions in *Alexander*, *Barrentine*, *McDonald*, and *Wilko* all explain why it makes good sense to draw a distinction between statutory claims and contract claims. In view of the Court's repeated recognition of the distinction between federal statutory rights and contractual rights, together with the undisputed historical fact that arbitration has functioned almost entirely in either the area of labor disputes or in "ordinary disputes between merchants as to questions of fact," it is reasonable to assume that most lawyers and executives would not expect the language in the standard arbitration clause to cover federal statutory claims. Thus, in my opinion, both a fair respect for the importance of the interests that Congress has identified as worthy of federal statutory protection, and a fair appraisal of the most likely understanding of the parties who sign agreements containing standard arbitration clauses, support a presumption that such clauses do not apply to federal statutory claims.

III

The Court has repeatedly held that a decision by Congress to create a special statutory remedy renders a private agreement to arbitrate a federal statutory claim unenforceable. Thus, as I have already noted, the express statutory remedy provided in the Ku Klux Act of 1871, the express statutory remedy in the Securities Act of 1933, the express statutory remedy in the Fair Labor Standards Act, and the express statutory remedy in Title VII of the Civil Rights Act of 1964, each provided the Court with convincing evidence that Congress did not intend the protections afforded by the statute to be administered by a private arbitrator. The reasons that motivated those decisions apply with special force to the federal policy that is protected by the antitrust laws.

To make this point it is appropriate to recall some of our past appraisals of the importance of this federal policy and then to identify some of the specific remedies Congress has designed to implement it. It was Chief Justice Hughes who characterized the Sherman Antitrust Act as "a charter of freedom" that may fairly be compared to a constitutional provision. In United States v. Philadelphia National Bank, 374 U.S. 321, 371 (1963), the Court referred to the extraordinary "magnitude" of the value choices made by Congress in enacting the Sherman Act. More recently, the Court described the weighty public interests underlying the basic philosophy of the statute:

> "Antitrust laws in general, and the Sherman Act in particular, are the Magna Carta of free enterprise. They are as important to the preservation of economic freedom and our free-enterprise system as the Bill of Rights is to the protection of our fundamental personal freedoms. . . ." United States v. Topco Associates, Inc., 405 U.S. 596, 610 (1972).

The Sherman and Clayton Acts reflect Congress' appraisal of the value of economic freedom; they guarantee the vitality of the entrepreneurial spirit. Questions arising under these Acts are among the most important in public law.

The unique public interest in the enforcement of the antitrust laws is repeatedly reflected in the special remedial scheme enacted by Congress. Since its enactment in 1890, the Sherman Act has provided for public enforcement through criminal as well as civil sanctions. The pre-eminent federal interest in effective enforcement once justified a provision for special three-judge district courts to hear antitrust claims on an expedited basis, as well as for direct appeal to this Court bypassing the courts of appeals.

.   .   .

The provision for mandatory treble damages — unique in federal law when the statute was enacted — provides a special incentive to the private enforcement of the statute, as well as an especially powerful deterrent to violators. What we have described as "the public interest in vigilant enforcement of the antitrust laws through the instrumentality of the private treble-damage action," is buttressed by the statutory mandate that the injured party also recover costs, "including a reasonable attorney's fee." The interest in wide and effective enforcement has thus, for almost a century, been vindicated by enlisting the assistance of "private Attorneys General"; we have always attached special importance to their role because "[every] violation of the antitrust laws is a blow to the free-enterprise system envisaged by Congress."

.   .   .

In view of the history of antitrust enforcement in the United States, it is not surprising that all of the federal courts that have considered the question have uniformly and unhesitatingly concluded that agreements to arbitrate federal antitrust issues are not enforceable. In a landmark opinion for the Court of Appeals for the Second Circuit, Judge Feinberg wrote:

> "A claim under the antitrust laws is not merely a private matter. The Sherman Act is designed to promote the national interest in a competitive economy; thus, the plaintiff asserting his rights under the Act has been likened to a private attorney-general who protects the public's interest. . . . Antitrust violations can affect hundreds of thousands — perhaps millions — of people and inflict staggering economic damage...." American Safety Equipment Corp. v. J.P. Maguire & Co. [citation omitted]

This view has been followed in later cases from that Circuit and by the First, Fifth, Seventh, Eighth, and Ninth Circuits. It is clearly a correct statement of the law.

This Court would be well advised to endorse the collective wisdom of the distinguished judges of the Courts of Appeals who have unanimously concluded that the statutory remedies fashioned by Congress for the enforcement of the antitrust laws render an agreement to arbitrate antitrust disputes unenforceable. Arbitration awards are only reviewable for manifest disregard of the law, and the rudimentary procedures which make arbitration so desirable in the context of a private dispute often mean that the record is so inadequate that the arbitrator's decision is virtually unreviewable. Despotic decisionmaking of this kind is fine for parties who are willing to agree in advance to settle for a best approximation of the correct result in order to resolve quickly and inexpensively any contractual dispute that may arise in an ongoing commercial relationship. Such informality, however, is simply unacceptable when every error may have devastating consequences for important businesses in our national economy and may undermine their ability to compete in world markets. Instead of "muffling a grievance in the cloakroom of arbitration," the public interest in free competitive markets would be better served by having the issues resolved "in the light of impartial public court adjudication."

IV

The Court assumes for the purposes of its decision that the antitrust issues would not be arbitrable if this were a purely domestic dispute, ante, at 629, but holds that the international character of the controversy makes it arbitrable. The holding rests on vague concerns for the international implications of its decision and a misguided application of Scherk v. Alberto-Culver Co., 417 U.S. 506 (1974).

International Obligations of the United States

Before relying on its own notions of what international comity requires, it is surprising that the Court does not determine the specific commitments that the United States has made to enforce private agreements to arbitrate disputes arising under public law. As the Court acknowledges, the only treaty relevant here is the Convention on the Recognition and Enforcement of Foreign Arbitral Awards. [1970] 21 U.S.T. 2517, T.I.A.S. No. 6997. The Convention was adopted in 1958 at a multilateral conference sponsored by the United Nations. This Nation did not sign the proposed convention at that time; displaying its characteristic caution before entering into international compacts, the United States did not accede to it until 12 years later.

. . .

Article II(3) of the Convention provides that the court of a Contracting State, "when seized of an action in a matter in respect of which the parties have made an agreement within the meaning of this article, shall, at the request of one of the parties, refer the parties to arbitration." This obligation does not arise, however, (i) if the agreement "is null and void, inoperative or incapable of being performed," Art. II(3), or (ii) if the dispute does not concern "a subject matter capable of settlement by arbitration," Art. II(1). The former qualification principally applies to matters of fraud, mistake, and duress in the inducement, or problems of procedural fairness and feasibility. [citation omitted] The latter clause plainly suggests the possibility that some subject matters are not capable of arbitration under the domestic laws of the signatory nations, and that agreements to arbitrate such disputes need not be enforced.

This construction is confirmed by the provisions of the Convention which provide for the enforcement of international arbitration awards. Article III provides that each "Contracting State shall recognize arbitral awards as binding and enforce them." However, if an arbitration award is "contrary to the public policy of [a] country" called upon to enforce it, or if it concerns a subject matter which is "not capable of settlement by arbitration under the law of that country," the Convention does not require that it be enforced. Arts. V(2)(a) and (b). Thus, reading Articles II and V together, the Convention provides that agreements to arbitrate disputes which are nonarbitrable under domestic law need not be honored, nor awards rendered under them enforced.

This construction is also supported by the legislative history of the Senate's advice and consent to the Convention. In presenting the Convention for the Senate's consideration the President offered the following interpretation of Article II(1):

> "The requirement that the agreement apply to a matter capable of settlement by arbitration is necessary in order to take proper account of laws in force in many countries which prohibit the submission of certain questions to arbitration. In some States of the United States, for example, disputes affecting the title to real property are not arbitrable."

The Senate's consent to the Convention presumably was made in light of this interpretation, and thus it is to be afforded considerable weight.

International Comity

It is clear then that the international obligations of the United States permit us to honor Congress' commitment to the exclusive resolution of antitrust disputes in the federal courts. The Court today refuses to do so, offering only vague concerns for comity among nations. The courts of other nations, on the other hand, have applied the exception provided in the Convention, and refused to enforce agreements to arbitrate specific subject matters of concern to them.[15]

---

15 For example, the Cour de Cassation in Belgium has held that disputes arising under a Belgian statute limiting the unilateral termination of exclusive distributorships are not arbitrable under the Convention in that country, and the Corte di Cassazione in Italy has held that labor disputes are not arbitrable under the Convention in that country.

It may be that the subject-matter exception to the Convention ought to be reserved — as a matter of domestic law — for matters of the greatest public interest which involve concerns that are shared by other nations. The Sherman Act's commitment to free competitive markets is among our most important civil policies. This commitment, shared by other nations which are signatory to the Convention, is hardly the sort of parochial concern that we should decline to enforce in the interest of international comity.

*   *   *

V

The Court's repeated incantation of the high ideals of "international arbitration" creates the impression that this case involves the fate of an institution designed to implement a formula for world peace. But just as it is improper to subordinate the public interest in enforcement of antitrust policy to the private interest in resolving commercial disputes, so is it equally unwise to allow a vision of world unity to distort the importance of the selection of the proper forum for resolving this dispute. Like any other mechanism for resolving controversies, international arbitration will only succeed if it is realistically limited to tasks it is capable of performing well — the prompt and inexpensive resolution of essentially contractual disputes between commercial partners. As for matters involving the political passions and the fundamental interests of nations, even the multilateral convention adopted under the auspices of the United Nations recognizes that private international arbitration is incapable of achieving satisfactory results.

In my opinion, the elected representatives of the American people would not have us dispatch an American citizen to a foreign land in search of an uncertain remedy for the violation of a public right that is protected by the Sherman Act. This is especially so when there has been no genuine bargaining over the terms of the submission, and the arbitration remedy provided has not even the most elementary guarantees of fair process. Consideration of a fully developed record by a jury, instructed in the law by a federal judge, and subject to appellate review, is a surer guide to the competitive character of a commercial practice than the practically unreviewable judgment of a private arbitrator.

Unlike the Congress that enacted the Sherman Act in 1890, the Court today does not seem to appreciate the value of economic freedom. I respectfully dissent.

NOTES AND QUESTIONS

A. As Justice Stevens explains in his dissent, arbitrators are not required to follow the law or give strict regard the public's interest in business regulation.

    1.   To say arbitrators are not required to do follow the law is not to say that they won't. But arbitration is private, and business is less likely to rule against the interests of business. Isn't Justice Stevens' concern valid? Or is he just being parochial?

    2.   The New York Court of Appeals, in *Silverman v. Benmor Coats*, wrote:

> [A]bsent provision in the arbitration clause itself, an arbitrator is not bound by principles of substantive law or by rules of evidence. He may do justice as he sees it, applying his own sense of law and equity to the facts as he finds them to be and making an award reflecting the spirit rather than the letter of the agreement, even though the award exceeds the remedy requested by the parties His award will not be vacated even though the court concludes that his interpretation of the agreement misconstrues or disregards its plain meaning or misapplies substantive rules of law, unless it is violative of a strong public policy, or is totally irrational, or exceeds a specifically enumerated limitation on his power.

> This (judicial) approach to arbitration awards is designed, inter alia, to provide the arbitrators with flexibility while at the same time promoting finality. What concerns are raised by this "loose" approach to dispute resolution and review of arbitration awards.[7]

    3.   Note also Justice Stevens' expression of concern about the fairness of the bargaining process that led to the arbitration agreement. Is this case just like *The Bremen*, or do you have doubts about the way the agreement was reached? Remember, too Justice Stevens' dissent in *Burger King*.

B. A novel use of international arbitration exists for international internet domain name disputes. Whenever a domain name is registered anywhere in the world, the registrant is required to submit, upon the demand of any owner of a trademark that is similar to the domain name, to arbitration over the registrant's right to use that domain name on the internet. These Uniform Dispute Resolution Procedures ("UDRP") create a single, expeditious, international standard for domain name disputes.[16]

---

7 The trademark owner, unlike the domain name registrant, is not required to submit to the UDRP procedures, and can instead go to a court of competent jurisdiction to enforce its trademark rights.

The procedures can be found at http://www.icann.org/udrp/. The domain name registrars, such as Verisign (".com") have designated certain arbitration providers, such as the WTO, to administer the arbitrations. More information about the standards, and the results of these arbitrations, can found at Harvard's Berkman Center. See http://cyber.law.harvard.edu/udrp/library.html

C.   International dispute resolution is always a dicey subject. As one goes from nation-to-nation, and even more so from continent-to-continent, differences in laws and procedures grow exponentially. Cultural differences, business and legal, can also create a divide. While arbitration may be better able to tailor itself to the parties and their dispute, remember that dispute resolution is never painless, never simple, never smooth and never cheap. As each of these chapters has shown, it is important to make good contracts with businesses of good reputation. That is not itself an easy assignment, but the lessons of cases like *Biddell, the Julia, Rockwell, Semetex, Burger King* and *The Bremen*, if learned and remembered, will make for better business and fewer disputes.

Jurisdiction to Prescribe: The Public Law Taboo

INTRODUCTION

In the last two chapters, we considered the question of jurisdiction to adjudicate - "where" disputes will be resolved. The subject to which we now turn also bears the title "jurisdiction", but it is a subject completely separate from the one we just completed. In this chapter (and the next), we explore not "which legal tribunal has power to make a binding adjudication" - rather, we deal with the question "what country's laws govern the controversy?"

While one might expect that a national court would always apply its own law, the fact is that courts do not always do so. Rather, in appropriate cases, courts will choose the laws of other states or nations when deciding cases that have some interstate or international context. The question we will be considering is the way courts go about deciding whether, when, and how they will "choose" another country's law.

Suppose, for example, that a citizen of Patria and a citizen of Xandia make a contract to engage in a joint venture in Tertia. If there is a dispute, will the court apply Patrian law, Xandian law, Tertian law, or some amalgam of all three? It is not a question easily answered. And since more than one court is likely to have jurisdiction to adjudicate, another question must be posed: will it matter what court resolves the dispute? The answer, in some cases, is "yes".

In law school, the subject we are about to study is sometimes referred to as "Conflict of Laws". That term is not quite descriptive of the subject, because Patrian and Xandia might be the same, or there might be small discrepancies. Perhaps Xandian law is permissive on a given subject, but Patrian law creates a prohibition. Even if there may be no direct "conflict of laws", there will still be a need to address the "choice of law" question. For this reason, this text will, where possible, eschew the term "conflict of laws", expect where there is an actual conflict. The term "choice of law" is far more descriptive of the problem and the process.

In the international arena, the subject being studied is often referred to by a different name - "jurisdiction to prescribe" or "legislative jurisdiction".[1] These terms posit the problem as one of a limit on sovereign power, much like "jurisdiction to adjudicate" limits judicial power. We will see, however, that even this nomenclature has become controversial. In <u>California v. Hartford Fire Insurance</u> (toward the end of the next chapter), we will see a colloquy between two Justices of the United States Supreme Court about whether the term "jurisdiction" is appropriate to describe the jurisprudential issues surrounding this area. We will not now get involved in that "controversy" (if it is one), although it is a question to consider as we work our way through the cases.

Another question to consider is whether the rules in this area (if there are rules) can be classified as part of "international law." Of course, that very question raises an even more fundamental one - what is meant by the term "international law"? While we are not prepared even to try to answer that question, it nevertheless lurks in the background, and we will, eventually, consider it.

The cases we will explore will again involve important international incidents, only here, the incidents are the cases themselves. In a world where international trade is commonplace, and legal regulation of business exists in every country, it is inevitable that different sovereigns with different policies will occasionally clash over the right to regulate various types of business conduct.

It should surprise no one that the United States has been a participant in a number of these clashes, as has Great Britain. The lessons to be learned are, however, more universal, and the stream of cases, to some extent, has been affected by the ebbs and flows of international business. Before turning to those cases, however, we first consider the historical antecdents and dimensions of a legal principle known as "the revenue rule".

CONTRACTUAL CHOICE OF LAW

As one would expect, the process of determining jurisdiction to prescribe is not only difficult, it is subject to considerable vagaries. In addition, the subject itself comes with some political and diplomatic baggage, and any particular

---

1. In Eurpoe, the subject is sometimes referred to as "private international law"; unfortunately, that term is not particularly useful in understanding either the parameters of the problem or the solution.

case may well raise sensitive political and/or diplomatic issues. Under those circumstances, it is of course advisable that the parties to an international contract make a contractual choice of law in the same way they were advised in the last chapter to consider a contractual choice of forum.

Such agreement, if it can be reached, will obviate the need to later spend money litigating the "choice of law" issue, because a court can be expected to honor a choice of law clause. But not every litigation arises out of a contract gone awry: sometimes litigation is commenced in which one person or business claims that another's conduct is causing injury to person, property or reputation. Such international disputes might involve a claim (in our earlier hypothetical) that a citizen of Patria is violating Xandian law, and injuring a citizen of that state. Perhaps the law concerns competition policy (a/k/a antitrust law), or perhaps it concerns some other regulatory law, like labor law or environmental law. In such a case, it is unlikely that there was an agreement between the parties, so the choice of law analysis will have to proceed without the benefit of agreement. For this reason (and also sometimes the parties do not, or cannot agree as to choice of law), we spend a considerable number of words addressing this topic.

I. THE ADVENT OF "THE REVENUE RULE"

Our exploration of the important cases on jurisdiction to prescribe takes us back to 18th century England, and the famous international smuggling case Holman v. Johnson. The case has become famous because of its profound effect on international law. But it became famous not just because it is an articulate, wonderful solution to a complex legal question, but also because it was decided by Lord Mansfield, one of England's greatest jurists.

HOLMAN
v.
JOHNSON

1 Cowp. 341

King's Bench (1775)

SUMMARY: Assumpsit for goods sold and delivered: Plea *non assumpsit* and verdict for the plaintiff. Upon a rule to show cause why a new trial should not be granted, Lord Mansfield reported the case, which was shortly this: The plaintiff who was resident at, and inhabitant of, Dunkirk, together with his partner, a native of that place, sold and delivered a quantity of tea, for the price of which the action was brought, to the order of the defendant, knowing it was intended to be smuggled by him into England: they had, however, no concern in the smuggling scheme itself, but merely sold this tea to him, as they would have done to any other person in the common and ordinary course of their trade.

Mr. *Mansfield* [attorney for the defendant buyer], in support of the rule, insisted, that the contract for the sale of this tea being founded upon an intention to make an illicit use of it, which intention and purpose was with the privity and knowledge of the plaintiff, he was not entitled to the assistance of the laws of this country to recover the value of it.

Mr. *Dunning*, Mr. *Davenport* and Mr. *Buller*, contra, for the plaintiff, contended, the contract being complete by the delivery of the goods at Dunkirk, where the plaintiff might lawfully sell, and the defendant lawfully buy, it could neither directly nor indirectly be said to be done in violation of the laws of this country; consequently it was a good and valid contract, and the plaintiff entitled to recover. It was of no moment or concern to the plaintiff what the defendant meant to do with the tea, nor had he any interest in the event. If he had, or if the contract had been that the plaintiff should deliver the tea in England, it would have been a different question; but there was no such undertaking on his part.

Opinion of the Court: Lord Mansfield - There can be no doubt, but that every action tried here must be tried by the law of England; but the law of England says, that in a variety of circumstances, with regard to contracts legally made abroad, the laws of the country where the cause of action arose shall govern.- There are a great many cases which every country says shall be determined by the laws of the foreign countries where they arise. But I do not see how the principles on which that doctrine obtains are applicable to the present case. For no country ever takes notice of the revenue laws of another.

The objection, that a contract is immoral or illegal as between plaintiff and defendant, sounds at all times very ill in the mouth of the defendant. It is not for his sake, however, that the objection is ever allowed; but it is founded in general principles of policy, which the defendant has the advantage of, contrary to the real justice, as between him and the plaintiff, by accident, if I may so say. The principle of public policy is this: No court will lend its aid to a man who has found his cause of action upon an immoral or an illegal act. If, from the plaintiff's own stating or otherwise, the cause of action, appears to arise *ex turpi causa* [out of an immoral or illegal consideration], or the transgression of a positive law of this country, there court says he has no right to be assisted. It is upon that ground the court goes; not for the sake of the defendant, but because they will not lend their aid to such a plaintiff. So if the plaintiff and the defendant were to change sides, and the defendant was to bring his action against the plaintiff, the latter would then have the advantage of it; for where both are equally in fault. . . .

The question therefore is, whether, in this case, the plaintiff's demand is founded upon the ground of any immoral act or contract, or upon the ground of his being guilty of any thing which is prohibited by a positive law of this country. - An immoral contract it certainly is not; for the revenue laws themselves, as well as the offenses against them, are all *politici juris*. What then is, the contract of the plaintiff? It is this: being a resident and inhabitant of Dunkirk, together with his partner, who was born there, he sells a quantity of tea to the defendant, and delivers it at Dunkirk to the defendant's order, to be paid for in ready money there, or by bills drawn personally upon him in England. This is an action brought merely for goods sold and delivered at Dunkirk. Where then, or in what respect is the plaintiff guilty of any crime? Is there any law of England transgressed by a person making a complete sale of a parcel of goods at Dunkirk, and giving credit for them? The contract is complete, and nothing is left to be done. The seller, indeed, knows what the buyer is going to do with the goods, but has the no concern in the transaction itself. It is not a bargain to be paid in case the vendee should succeed in landing the goods; but the interest of the vendor is totally at an end, and his contract complete by the delivery of the goods at Dunkirk.

To what a dangerous extent would this go if it were to be held a crime. If contraband clothes are bought in France, and brought home hither; or if glass bought abroad, which ought to pay a great duty, is run into England; shall the French taylor or the glass manufacturer stand to the risk of loss attending their being run into England? Clearly not. Debts follow the person, and may be recovered in England, let the contract of debt be made where it will; and the law allows an action for the sake of expediting the remedy. Therefore, I am clearly of the opinion, that the vendors of these goods are not guilty of any offence, nor have they transgressed against the provisions of any act of parliament.

I am very glad the old books have been looked into. The doctrine Huberus lays down, is founded in goods sense, and upon general principles of justice. I entirely agree with him. He puts the general case in question; thus; [latin omitted] Translated, it might be rendered thus: In England, tea, which has not been paid duty, is prohibited; and if sold there the contract is null and void. But if sold and delivered at a place where it is not prohibited, as at Dunkirk, and action is brought for the price of it in England, the buyer shall be condemned to pay the price; because the original contract was good and valid. - He goes on thus: "Verum si merces venditae in altero loco, ubi prohibita "sunt essent tradende, jam non fieret condemnatio, quia repugra" ret hoc juri et commodo republicae quae merces prohibit" Apply this in the same manner.- But if the goods sold were to be delivered in England, where they are prohibited; the contract is void, and the buyer shall not be liable in an action for the price, because it would be an inconvenience and prejudice to the state if such an action could be maintained.

The gist of the whole turns upon this, that the conclusive delivery was at Dunkirk. If the defendant had bespoke the tea at Dunkirk to be sent to England at a certain price ; and the plaintiff had undertaken to send it into England, or had any concern in running it into England, he would have been an offender against the laws of this country. But upon the facts of this case, from the first to the last, he clearly has offended against no law of England. Therefore, let the rule for a new trial be discharged.

The three other judges concurred.

NOTES AND QUESTIONS

1. Lord Mansfield's decision is famous not only for the way it addresses the choice of law issue, but also for the way it explains English law as it applies to illegal contracts. On that score, Lord Mansfield explains that such contracts are void, meaning that neither side can enforce them. The defendant in the case was the English buyer whose conduct violated the law of his own country. This buyer was trying to raise his own illegality as a defense to the claim he had not paid the price. In explaining why the buyer could make such a bold defense, Mansfield invokes his famous dicta that "the objection, sounds at all times very ill in the mouth of the defendant." But, the great judge explains:

    > it is not for his sake, however, that the objection . . . is ever allowed; but it is founded in general principles of policy, which the defendant has the advantage of, contrary to the real justice, as between him and the plaintiff, by accident, if I may so say. The principle of public policy is this: No court will lend its aid to a man who has found his cause of action upon an immoral or an illegal act.

    While this discussion is interesting and an important expression of law and policy, it is not the basis for Mansfield's decision. It does, however, underscore the startling decision he reaches - that the English court declines to follow the English law which makes the smuggling of tea illegal.

2. For us (at least), the most important part of Holman v. Johnson is found in the first paragraph of Mansfield's opinion. It should be analyzed sentence by sentence.

    A. **"There can be no doubt, but that every action tried here must be tried by the law of England."** With this phrase, Mansfield begins the choice of law analysis. He is an English judge empowered by an English sovereign - he must begin with English law. The British call this principle *lex loci fori*, the "law of the forum".

    B. **"but the law of England says, that in a variety of circumstances, with regard to contracts legally made abroad, the laws of the country where the cause of action arose shall govern."** English law, Mansfield explains, has a choice of law rule, which is invoked "in a variety of circumstances." The rule is fairly simple - the question of the legality of the contract is governed by the law of the place where the contract was made (*lex loci contractus*), and, if there is a claim of breach, the law of the place "where the cause of action arose", i.e. the place of the wrong (*lex loci delictus*) shall govern. These English "choice of law" rules continue to be used today by British courts. In the United States, however, the issue is more likely to be resolved by a method known as "governmental interest analysis". See Note, Choice of Law Issues in Private Law Cases infra.

C. **"There are a great many cases which every country says shall be determined by the laws of the foreign countries where they arise."** Mansfield explains that every country (including, presumably, France) has a choice of law rule. Is Mansfield invoking international law? Or is he about to say something about it, or at least affect its development?

D. **"But I do not see how the principles on which that doctrine obtains are applicable to the present case. For no country ever takes notice of the revenue laws of another."** Regardless of the existence of choice of law rules, Mansfield concludes, they do not apply here because the law at issue is a "revenue law".

1. Why does Mansfield articulate a different choice of law approach when it comes to revenue laws? What is it about "revenue laws" that make them different from other laws? Why should we single out such laws for different treatment, i.e. a lower level of recognition?

2. Later on in the case, Lord Mansfield tells us that revenue laws, like penal (i.e. criminal) law, are "*politici juris*" - laws that express a political, or public, policy. He refers to (extends?) a rule that has long-existed, that enforcement of criminal law is for the country where the crime occurred.[2] Was it right to treat revenue laws like penal laws? If you say yes (after all, Lord Mansfield did), to what other kinds of laws would the revenue rule apply?

3. When Mansfield refers to "no country" noticing the revenue laws of another, to what country is he referring? If you answer "France", how did Mansfield get to French law? And how does Mansfield know that the French would, once he got to their law, refuse the reference back to English law? Is the principle he is articulating international custom? Is it international law? Or is it just a prediction about what France would do?

---

2. Thus, the concept of "extradition" developed, where the country where the crime occurred "requests" that a country where the alleged criminal is to send the defendant back for trial.

3.   The balance of the decision demonstrates how the choice-of-law mechanism functions.

   A.   Mansfield first observes that the contract to run tea into England is not immoral. Why is that important? Is it because France would then consider the contract void? Or is it because a court of England will not "lend its aid" to one who founds his cause upon an immoral (as opposed to a merely illegal) act? Can it be both?

   B.   Mansfield then compares this case to another - a contract where the seller's right to be paid is conditioned on the successful smuggling. In such a case, Mansfield says, the seller cannot recover the price. Why is that case different from the instant one?

      1.   The answer, we are told, lies in the fact that in this case, the contract was complete at Dunkirk. That observation is important to the English choice-of-law rule that "with regard to contracts legally made abroad, the laws of the country where the cause of action arose shall govern." Isn't Mansfield saying that the contract was "legally made" in France, and that that is where "the cause of action arose"? Then, by invoking the "revenue rule", Mansfield is able to ignore his own country's laws and permit enforcement of the contract.

      2.   Mansfield also refers to the case of a contract to resell goods smuggled into England, saying that such a contract is void. So too a contract to deliver smuggled goods into England. Why are those contracts void? Can you perform the choice of law analysis?

4.   Mansfield's "revenue rule", that one country never takes notice of the revenue laws of another, quickly became ingrained in English law, if not "international law" (whatever that term might mean). While Mansfield offers little explanation about the reasons for the rule (can you think of any?), the rule came to be understood to cover not just tax laws and criminal laws, but also all laws that are *politici juris*, so-called "public laws". Thus, as Mansfield demonstrates, while choice of law rules have existed for centuries, historically, when it came to these "public laws", it seems that no reference would be made, that no recognition would be granted. Do you think that approach makes sense for modern times? If so, why? If not, what would you suggest instead?

II. MODERN ANALOGS OF THE REVENUE RULE

GOVERNMENT OF INDIA
v.
TAYLOR

House of Lords

(1955) A.C. 49

The facts, stated by Viscount Simmonds, were as follows:

The respondents to this appeal were the liquidators in the voluntary winding up of an English company, the Delhi Electric Supply & Traction Co. Ld., which was in the year 1906 incorporated for the purpose of operating an electricity supply undertaking and tramway undertakings under a license and order granted by the Municipality of Delhi. The appellant was the Government of India, a sovereign independent republic which acknowledged Her Majesty as head of the British Commonwealth. The question for decision was whether Vaisey J. and the Court of Appeal were right in rejecting the appellant's claim to prove in the liquidation of the company in respect of an amount of income tax due from the company to the appellant under Indian income tax law.

The company having carried on its undertaking in India until the year 1947, in that year sold the whole of them to the Government of India as from March 2, 1947, for the sum of Rs.82.11,580. The greater part of that sum was paid to the company in India on March 1,1947, and was remitted to England a few days later. The balance was paid to the company in India in September 1948, and remitted to England shortly afterwards.

On April 19, 1947, the Indian Income Tax and Excess Profits Tax (Amendment) Act, 1947, was passed, and by section 6 thereof section 12B was inserted in the Indian Income Tax Act 1922. The opening words of section 12B were as follows:" The tax "shall be payable by an assessee under the head 'Capital gains' in respect of any profits or gains arising from the sale, exchange, or transfer of a capital asset effected after March 31, 1940; and such profits and gains shall be deemed to be income of the previous year in which the sale, exchange or transfer took place." This amendment was deemed by section 1(2) of the Act of 1947 to have come into force on March 1947.

On May 25, 1949, the company went into voluntary liquidation by special resolution and the respondent Taylor and one Lovering were appointed joint liquidators. They had previously as directors of the company made a statutory declaration as to the solvency of the company and later in their statement as to the position of the liquidation of the company they referred to the liability for special taxation in India. They also in March, 1951, inserted a notice in the Gazette of India calling upon all creditors to prove their debts or claims and acceded to a request by the Commissioner of Income Tax at Delhi to stay the liquidation proceedings to enable his Department to prove their claim.

On October 24, 1951, the Commissioner of Income Tax served a demand notice under section 29 of the Indian Income Tax Act, 1922, for the year 1948-49 calling on the company to pay Rs. 16.54,945.11.0 of tax, which consisted mainly of a sum of Rs. 15.62.817.3.0 representing tax on the surplus on the sale of the company's undertakings. Various steps were taken in India, appeals against the assessment, payment of a sum on account out of assets which were still in India, re-assessment of the amounts claimed to be due under the head "capital gains" and further demands which culminated in a claim upon the surviving liquidators Taylor in February 1953 (Lovering having in the meantime died), for sums of Rs.15.62.S17.3.0 and Rs.13.001.10.0. The quantum of those assessments was still a matter of appeal in India, but that there was some liability in India in respect of tax for capital gains was beyond doubt, and there appeared to be also as ascertained liability in respect of ordinary income tax which was not under appeal.

It was in those circumstances that the respondent Taylor in April and May 1953, rejected the appellant's claim stating that no part of the company's assets (all of which were then in England) could properly be applied in payment of any claim for taxes by a foreign Government. Thereupon the appellant applied to the High Court in England for an order reversing the rejection of its claim and on July 30, 1953 (the respondent Hume having in the meantime been appointed joint liquidator with the respondent Taylor), Vaisey J. made an order refusing the appellant's application. From that order the appellant appealed to the Court of Appeal (Evershed M.R. Jenkins and Morris L.JJ) and that court unanimously dismissed the appeal.

VISCOUNT SIMONDS

My Lords, I will admit that I was greatly surprised to hear it suggested that the courts of this country would and should entertain a suit by a foreign state to recover a tax. For at any time since I have had any acquaintance with the law I should have said as Rowlatt J. said in the King of the Hellence v. Brostron. "It is perfectly elementary that a foreign government cannot come here - nor will the courts of other countries allow our Government to go there - and sue a person found in that jurisdiction for taxes levied and which he is declared to be liable to in the country to which he belongs." . . .

My Lords, the history and origin of the rule, if it be a rule, are not easy to ascertain and there is on the whole remarkably little authority upon the subject. I am inclined to agree with the Court of Appeal that the early cases of Attorney General v. Lutwydge and Boucher v. Lawson, to which some reference was made, do not give much help. It is otherwise when we advance a few years to the age of Lord Mansfield C.J. That great judge in a series of cases repeated the formula "For no country ever takes notice of the revenue laws of another." Where Lord Mansfield led Lord Kenyon, C.J., followed, though he was not a judge who followed blindly. . . . Here my Lords, is a formidable array of authority.

The matter is carried one step further by the fact that the rule appears to have been recognized by Parliament. For I see no other reason for the exclusion from the advantages of the Foreign Judgements (Reciprocal Enforcement) Act, 1933, of a judgment for "a sum payable in respect of taxes or other charges of a like nature or in respect of a fine or other penalty" (section 1(2)(b)), except that it was regarded as axiomatic that the courts of one country do not have regard to the revenue laws of another and therefore will not allow judgments for foreign taxes to be enforced.

It may well be asked, then, upon what grounds this appeal is founded. I think that counsel relied upon two main grounds, first that Lord Mansfield's proposition, which I have more than once quoted, extended to revenue law a doctrine properly applicable only to penal law and (I think it must be faced) that Lord Mansfield was wrong in so extending it and everyone who has since followed him was wrong; and secondly that, whatever may have been the rule in the past, there ought to be and is a trend towards a mitigation of the rule, particularly as between States which are united by the bonds of federal union or by such looser ties as bind the British Commonwealth of nations.

My Lords, these seem to me frail weapons with which to attack a strong fortress. . . .

I would dismiss this appeal with costs.

LORD KEITH OF AVONHOLM

One explanation of the rule . . . may be thought to be that enforcement of a claim for taxes is but an extension of the sovereign power which imposed the taxes, and that an assertion of sovereign authority by one State within the territory of another, as distinct from a patrimonial claim by a foreign sovereign, is (treaty or convention apart) contrary to all concepts of independent sovereignties. Another explanation has been given by an eminent American judge, Judge Learned Hand, in the case of Moore v. Mitchell, in a passage quoted also by Kingsmill Moore J in the case of Peter Buchanan Ld. as follows:

"While the origin of the exception in the case of penal liabilities does not appear in the books, a sound basis for it exists, in my judgment, which includes liabilities for taxes as well. Even in the case of ordinary municipal liabilities, a court will not recognize those arising in a foreign State, if they run counter to the 'settled public policy' of its own. Thus a scrutiny of the liability is necessarily always in reserve, and possibility that it will be found not to accord with the policy of the domestic State. This is not a troublesome or delicate inquiry when the question arises between private persons, but it takes on quite another face when it concerns the relations between the foreign State and its own citizens or even those who may be temporarily within its borders. To pass upon the provisions for the public order of another State is, or at any rate should be, beyond the powers of the court; it involves the relations between the States themselves, with which courts are incompetent to deal, and which are intrusted to other authorities. It may commit the domestic State to a position which would seriously embarrass its neighbour. Revenue laws fall within the same reasoning; they effect a State in matters as vital to its existence as its criminal laws. No court ought to undertake an inquiry which it cannot prosecute without determining whether those laws are consonant with its own notions of what is proper."

On either of the explanations which I have just stated I find a solid basis of principle for a rule which has long been recognized and which has been applied by a consistent train of decisions. It may be possible to find reasons for modifying the rule as between States of a federal union. But that consideration, in my opinion, has no relevance to this case.

I agree the appeal should be dismissed.

LORD SOMERVELL OF HARROW

The first issue in the present appeal is whether a foreign State can use the courts of this country for the collection of its taxes. The statement by Lord Mansfield in Holman v. Johnson: "For no country ever takes notice of the revenue 'laws of another,' may include the present issue but goes beyond it and is, I think, directed to a different problem. The plaintiff claimed the price of tea delivered in Dunkirk. The defendant intended as the plaintiff knew, to smuggle the tea into England. Lord Mansfield uses the words cited in considering lex loci contractus. He is stating that the courts there would be in no circumstances have regard to any illegality arising under the revenue laws of this or any other country. He then proceeds to consider the alleged illegality under our laws. The question whether today our courts would as between the parties enforce a contract to break the revenue laws of another country has little if any relevance to the issue which we have to decide. In Ralli Brothers v. Compania Naviera Sota y Aznar Scrutton L.J., in a passage cited by the Master of the Rolls, reserved that the issue for consideration should it arise. What I desire to make clear is that I am not dealing with that issue.

There is no decision binding on your Lordships' House and the matter therefore falls to be considered in principle. If one State could collect its taxes through the courts of another, it would have arisen through what is described, vaguely perhaps, as comity or the general practice of nations inter se. The appellant was therefore in a difficulty from the outset in that after considerable research no case of any country could be found in which taxes due to State A had been enforced in the courts of State B. Apart from the comparatively recent English, Scotch, and Irish cases there is no authority. There are, however, many propositions for which no express authority can be found because they have been regarded as self evident to all concerned. There must have been many potential defendants.

Tax gathering is an administrative act, though in settling the quantum as well as in the final act of collection judicial process may be involved. Our courts will apply foreign law if it is the proper law of a contract, the subject of a suit. Tax gathering is not a matter of contract but of authority and administration as between the State and those within its jurisdiction. If one considers the initial stages of the process, which may, as the records of your Lordships' House show, be intricate and prolonged it would be remarkable comity if State B allowed the time of its courts to be expended in assisting in this regard the tax gatherers of State A. Once a judgment has been obtained and it is a question only of its enforcement the factor of time and expense will normally have disappeared. The principle remains. The claim is one for a tax.

The appellant is asking the English courts to do what the courts of no other country have done. In some fields this might commend the argument but here, for the reason which I stated at the outset, it is fatal.

Appeal dismissed.

NOTES AND QUESTIONS

1. Government of India v. Taylor arises in a context that is obviously different from Holman v. Johnson. The older case concerned a suit by an aggrieved seller against a buyer who had not paid the price, claiming the contract violated a law concerning import duties. In Taylor, the case concerned a suit by a foreign government to collect income taxes. Should these contextual differences render Holman v. Johnson inapplicable in Taylor? If so, what rule would you apply?

2   Viscount Simonds offers one, very British answer: he was "greatly surprised to hear it suggested that the courts of this country would and should entertain a suit by a foreign state to recover a tax." The reason - Lord Mansfield, and Holman v. Johnson.

    A.   While Viscount Simonds concedes that "there is on the whole remarkably little authority upon the subject", there is Mansfield, and Lord Kenyon (another famous English judge, who, we are told "did not follow blindly"). And there is a piece of English legislation called the Foreign Judgements (Reciprocal Enforcement) Act, 1933, which seems to apply Mansfield's revenue rule in the context before the House in Taylor.

    B.   Despite his "surprise", Viscount Simonds considers the argument made to the Law Lords by the Indian Government:

         1.   First, "that Lord Mansfield's proposition, extended to revenue law a doctrine properly applicable only to penal law and (I think it must be faced) that Lord Mansfield was wrong in so extending it and everyone who has since followed him was wrong;"

2. Second, "that, whatever may have been the rule in the past, there ought to be and is a trend towards a mitigation of the rule, particularly as between States which are united by the bonds of federal union or by such looser ties as bind the British Commonwealth of nations."

These seem decent arguments, but they are summarily rejected: "My Lords, these seem to me frail weapons with which to attack a strong fortress," he says.

3. Lord Somervell also looks to the precedent, but, interestingly, he seems to doubt that <u>Holman v. Johnson</u> is the appropriate case. He even goes on to question whether that case would have been decided the same way today. He thus states that "the matter therefore falls to be considered in principle."

   A. What principle does he apply? He states that he can find no precedent establishing the right of State A to collect its taxes in the courts of State B. "There are, however, many propositions for which no express authority can be found because they have been regarded as self evident to all concerned," but, here that fact does not commend itself. He explains: "There must have been many potential defendants."

   B. What other "principles", other than the lack of precedent, does Lord Somervell offer in support of his decision? Tax gathering is a complex administrative act, it was argued, and one country ought not to commit its resources to collect taxes for another. The argument has a certain appeal, but Lord Sommervell is quick to point out that when the claim is based on an existing tax judgment, "the factor of time and expense will normally have disappeared. The principle remains," we are told. "The claim is one for a tax." OK. So, what's the principle, M'Lord?

4. Lord Keith, it seems, does best on the subject of principle, but, to explain it, he quotes a famous American judge, Learned Hand (whom we shall meet later, and with whom the British are generally not enamored). What principle is Hand applying?

   A. Hand is concerned that, in deciding whether to apply a particular foreign penal or revenue law, courts risk insulting the foreign state, and that it is best, therefore, to stay out of the business altogether. Do you agree? Do you think the judiciary is abdicating its responsibility to assist friendly foreign states collect perfectly reasonable taxes from those who would otherwise abscond? Or is Hand pointing the way to a different solution?

B.   Before considering the solution suggested in the previous paragraph, note that Hand states that the delicate inquiry he would have courts avoid "is not a[s] troublesome . . . when the question arises between private persons." What does that mean?

5.   Needless to say, the nations of the world could not leave the tax situation the way it appears after <u>Taylor</u>. Thus, as Hand suggested, the political branches of governments, in the exercise of foreign policy, have created a series of bilateral tax treaties, providing for the reciprocal enforcement of taxes and tax judgments. The U.S. is signatory to over 100 of these treaties. By going the treaty route, the judiciary is able to avoid the sensitive task of deciding which foreign countries and which foreign taxes are consistent with forum policy, and which are not. As Hand suggests, these issues are best left to the diplomats and the legislatures.

6.   The particular issue in <u>Government of India v. Taylor</u> having been settled, three years later the House of Lords would be called upon to revisit <u>Holman v. Johnson</u> itself, this time in a case with striking similarities to it. The outcome, remarkably, is not what you might expect.

REGAZZONI
v.
K.C. SETHIA (1944) LTD.

House of Lords
1958 A.C. 301

The facts as stated by Viscount Simonds were as follows:

The appellant, who resided in Switzerland, brought the action out of which this appeal arose against the respondents claiming damages for breach of contract. He alleged that the respondents had agreed to sell and deliver to him September/ October 1948. c.i.f. Genoa 500,000 jute bags of the quality and standard known in the trade as new B twills and that they had wrongfully repudiated the agreement. The respondents defended the action on numerous grounds with only one which the House of Lords were now concerned, namely, that "the said contract, if any, was to the (appellant's) knowledge an illegal contract and/or was void and unenforceable in that it had for its purpose an object which was illegal and or contrary to public policy, namely, the taking and shipment of jute goods from India where the ultimate destination was the Union of South Africa in breach of a certain Act of the Indian Parliament and Regulations made thereunder.

The Act in question was the Sea Customs Act, 1878, which (as modified up to December 1,1950) provided by section 19 that the Central Government might "from time to time by notification in the (Official Gazzette) prohibit or restrict the bringing or taking by sea or by land goods of any specified description into or out of (the State across any custom frontier as defined by the Central Government)" and by section 134 that the Central Government might from time to time by similar notification "prohibit at any specified port or at all ports, the transhipment of any specified class of goods, generally or, when destined for any specified ports." By section 138 of the Act provision was made for security for the due shipment, export and landing of the goods and by section 167 for the punishment of offenses. The prescribed penalties were severe. It was provided that if any goods, the importation or exportation of which was prohibited or restricted by or under the Act, should be imported into or exported from India contrary to such prohibition or restriction, or if any attempt should be made so to import or export any such goods, the goods themselves should be liable to confiscation, and any person concerned in any such offence should be liable to a penalty not exceeding three times the value of the goods or not exceeding 1000 rupees.

In exercise of the powers conferred by this Act on July 17, 1946, the Central Government of India duly made an order prohibiting the taking "by sea or land out of British India of goods from whatever place arriving which are destined for any port or place in the Union of South Africa or in respect of which the Chief Customs Officer is satisfied that the goods although destined for a port or place outside the Union of South Africa are intended to be taken to the Union of South Africa."

VISCOUNT SIMONDS stated the claim and the defense and the Indian legislation and continued:

My Lords, I do not think it necessary to state at length the facts of the case. They have been found by Sellers J. and his findings were accepted by the Court of Appeal. No other conclusion was, in my opinion, possible than that (in the words of the learned judge) "both parties . . . contemplated and intended that the contract goods would be shipped from India and be made available in Genoa so that the plaintiff might make a resale or fulfil a bargain of resale to the South African buying agency". Nor is to be doubted that both parties were well aware of the restrictions imposed by the order of July 17, 1946. A strenuous attempt was made to persuade your Lordships that the contract did not infringe Indian law and this was vouched by a Mr. Nissim, whose qualification to give expert evidence was not challenged. But I must say, with all respect to him, that I find his testimony confused and unconvincing. It may well be that an Indian shipper would not be subject to any penalty if he could prove that he was unaware that of the ultimate destination of the goods. But it is not possible for parties whose common intention it is to procure the shipment of goods from India directly or indirectly to the Union of South Africa to plead the innocence of the transaction on the ground that the Indian shipper may be deceived or even that Custom Chief Officer may be satisfied (contrary to the fact) that the ultimate destination is not the Union of the

South Africa. On the contrary, it must be assumed that the Chief Customs Officer would not be so satisfied: if so, the shipment inevitably falls within the prohibition and could only be carried out in violation of Indian law.

The question then arises - and it is, as I say, the only question for your Lordship's consideration - whether the respondents were justified in repudiating the contract. They claim to be justified on the ground that I have already stated. Their broad proposition is that whether or not the proper law of the contract is English law, an English court will not enforce a contract, or award damages for its breach, if its performance will involve the doing of an act in a foreign and friendly State which violates the law of that State. For this they cite the authority of the well-known case of Foster v. Driscoll and much of the debate in this House has been whether that case was rightfully decided, and if so, whether it is distinguishable from the present case. The appellant contends that it was not rightly decided and further invokes a familiar principle which he states in these wide but questionable terms, "An English court will not have regard to a foreign law of a penal, revenue or political character" and claims that the Indian law here in question is of such a character.

My Lords, in the consideration of this matter I deem it of the utmost importance to bear in mind that we are not here concerned with a suit by a foreign State to enforce its law. The recent case in this House of *Government of India v. Taylor* shows beyond all doubt that an English court will not enforce the penal or revenue laws of another country at the suit of that country. That proposition was there exhaustively examined and nothing remains to be said about it except that there is still a question how far, if at all, the doctrine extends to laws which are described as having a "political" or "public" character. It is clear at least, as Denning L.J. said in this case, that "these courts do not sit to collect taxes for another country or to inflict punishment for it." But, as I say, we are not concerned with such a case, but with a very different question viz., whether in a suit between private persons the courts will enforce a contract which involves the doing in a foreign country of an act which is illegal by, and violates, the law of that country. When I say "foreign country" I mean a foreign and friendly country and will not repeat the phrase. In the statement of the question I call particular attention to the words "the doing in a foreign country" for it may well be that different considerations will arise and a different

conclusion will be reached if the law of the contract is English and the contract can be wholly performed in England, or at least in some other country than whose law makes the act illegal.

There are points at which the two questions appear to touch each other and sometimes the one proposition has been treated as an exception on the other. But there is, I think, a fundamental difference. It can hardly be regarded as a matter of comity that the courts of this country will not entertain a suit by a foreign State to enforce its revenue laws. It is, on the other hand, nothing else than comity which has influenced our courts to refuse as a matter of public policy to enforce, or to award damages for breach of a contract, which involves the violation of foreign law on foreign soil, and it is the limits of this principle that we have to examine. If the principle is, as I think it clearly is, based on public policy, your Lordships will not hesitate, while disclaiming any intention to create any new head of public policy, to apply an old principle to new circumstances.

Just as public policy avoids contracts which offend against our own law, so it will avoid at least some contracts which violate the laws of a foreign State, and it will do so because public policy demands that deference to international comity. The question is what contracts? . . . The principle being based on public policy, exceptions to it must be similarly based. It would, therefore, not be surprising if a contract, in one age, falls within the proposition, in another, without it. This observation has particular relevance to the first case that I shall cite. In <u>Boucher v Lawson</u>, the trade of exporting gold from Portugal being prohibited by the law of that country. Lord Hardwicke, then Lord Chief Justice, nevertheless upheld a contract which involved the violation of that law, observing that "if it should be laid down that because goods are prohibited to be exported by the laws of any foreign country from whence they are brought, therefore the parties should have no remedy or action here, it would cut off all benefits of such trade from this kingdom which would be of very bad consequences to the principal and most beneficial branches of our trade, nor does it ever seem to have been admitted." I must admit to some doubt whether, if this case had come before the court two hundred years later, so robust an assertion in favour of national interest to the prejudice of international comity would have been made. But, at any rate, in what might be regarded as purely revenue laws the same idea persisted.

It does not follow from the fact that today the court will not enforce a revenue law at the suit of a foreign State that today it will enforce a contract which requires the doing of an act in a foreign country which violates the revenue laws of that country. The two things are not complementary or co-extensive. This may be seen if for the revenue law penal law is substituted. For an English court will not enforce a penal law at the suit of a foreign State, yet it would be surprizing if it would enforce a contract which required the commission of a crime in that State. It is sufficient, however for the purpose of the present appeal to say that, whether or not an exception must still be made in regard to the breach of a revenue law in deference to old authority, there is no ground for making an exception in regard to any other law. I should myself have said-and this is, I think, the only point upon which I do not agree with the Court of Appeal-that the present case was precisely covered by the decision in Ralli Brothers. For when the fact is found that the very thing which the parties intended to do was to export the jute bags from India in order that they might go via Genoa to the Union of South Africa, it appears to me irrelevant that upon the face of the documents that the wrongful intention was not disclosed. But, whether this is so or not, it is clearly covered by Foster v Driscoll, a decision the correctness of which is not to be doubted.

306

The appeal should, in my opinion be dismissed with costs.

LORD REID

To my mind, the question whether this contract is enforceable by English courts is not, properly speaking, a question of international law. The real question is one of public policy in English law: but in considering this question we must have in mind the background of international law and international relationships often referred to as the comity of nations. This is not a case of a contract being made in good faith but one party thereafter finding that he cannot perform his part of the contract without committing a breach of foreign law in the territory of the foreign country. If this contract is held unenforceable, it should, in my opinion, be because from the beginning the contract was tainted so that the courts of this country will not assist either party to enforce it.

I do not wish to express any opinion about a case where parties agree to deal with goods which they both know have already been smuggled out of a foreign country, or about a case where the seller knows that the buyer intends to use the goods for an illegal purpose or to smuggle them into a foreign country. Such cases may raise difficult questions. The crucial fact in this case appears to me to be that both parties knew that the contract could not be performed without the respondents procuring a breach of the law in India within the territory of that country.

On that question I do not get much assistance from the older cases. Most of them do not deal with that point and further, it must, I think, be borne in mind that they date from a time when international relationships were somewhat different and when theories of political economy now outmoded were generally accepted. Many dealt with revenue laws or penal laws which have always been regarded as being in a special position and I do not wish on this occasion to say more than that probably some reexamination of some of these cases may in future be necessary. The Indian law prohibiting exports to South Africa does not appear to me to be a revenue or penal law any more than was the law of exchange control considered by this House in Kahler v Midland Bank Ltd.

Further, this case does not, in my view involve the enforcement of Indian law in England. In fact, no breach of Indian law in the execution of this contract was ever committed or attempted because the contract came to an end by its repudiation by the respondents within a few days after it was made.

Finally, it was argued that, even if there be a general rule that our courts will take notice of foreign laws so that agreements to break them are unenforceable, that rule must be subject to exceptions and this Indian law is one of which we ought not to take notice. It may be that there are exceptions. I can imagine a foreign law involving persecution of such a character that we would regard an agreement to break it as meritorious. But this Indian law is very far removed anything of that kind. It was argued that this prohibition of exports to South

Africa was a hostile act against a Commonwealth country with which we have close relations, that such a prohibition is contrary to international usage, and that we cannot recognize it without taking sides in the dispute between India and South Africa.

My Lords, it is quite impossible for a court in this country to set itself up as a judge of the rights and wrongs of a controversy between two friendly countries, we cannot judge the motives or the justifications of governments of other countries in these matters and, if we tried to do so, the consequences might seriously prejudice international relations. By recognizing this Indian law so that an agreement which involves a breach of that law within Indian territory is unenforceable we express no opinion whatever either favourable or adverse, as to the policy which caused its enactment. In my judgment this appeal should be dismissed.

LORD COHEN. My Lords, I concur.

LORD KEITH OF AVONHOLM.

My Lords, on the only question of fact in this case I agree that the contracting parties knew that the contract could only be carried out, and intended that it should be carried out in circumstances which, if all the facts were known to the Indian shipper, would be a violation of Indian law.

It is accepted that the proper law of the contract is English law, and the only other question is whether the contract is one which the English courts will enforce. I am clear that it is not.

In the present case I see no escape from the view that to recognize the contract between the appellant and the respondent as an enforceable contract would give a just cause for complaint by the Government of India and should be regarded as contrary to conceptions of international comity. On grounds of public policy, therefore, this is a contract which our courts ought not to recognize. It is said that the Indian legislation is discriminatory legislation against a country which is a member of the Commonwealth and with which this country is on friendly terms. But that, in my opinion, is irrelevant. The English courts cannot be called on to adjudicate upon political issues between India and South Africa. The Indian law is not a law repugnant to English conceptions of what may be regarded as within the ordinary field of legislation or administrative order even in this country. It is the illegality under the foreign law that is to be considered and not the effect of the foreign law on another country.

I would dismiss the appeal.

LORD SOMERVELL OF HARROW.

It seems to me impossible to suggest that our courts would enforce an agreement to commit in country A a crime such as murder, arson or burglary. Is there any justification for drawing a line between what are evils generally and acts prohibited by the foreign State, no doubt because they are regarded as local evils?

The statements in the old cases support the view that it is the illegality under the foreign law which is the test and one does not have to distinguish or attempt to distinguish between what is "wrong" from what is prohibited.

Your Lordships were invited to make an exception to the principle on the grounds that the law in question was directed against the Union of South Africa arising out of a dispute between the two States. I do not think this would justify taking the case out of the rule.

The statement that in this field one country takes no notice of the revenue laws of another seems to have been based on the principle that smuggling and freedom "gang together"......

...It was submitted that the prohibition in the present case of export to a particular destination was a revenue law, and one can imagine such a prohibition being a revenue law. On the evidence in the present case it would seem not to fall within the ordinary meaning of the phrase, but in any event I myself think that the courts of this country should not today enforce a contract to smuggle goods into or out of a foreign and friendly State.

There may, of course, be laws the enforcement of which would be against "morals". In such a case an exception might be made to the general principle. The point can be dealt with if it arises.

I would dismiss the appeal.

Appeal dismissed.

NOTES AND QUESTIONS

1. Like Holman v. Johnson, Regazzoni is an international smuggling case, this time involving a politically-motivated trade embargo, rather than a tax.

    A. Note first that when the issue comes up whether to characterize the Indian law as a tax, at least two of the Lords doubt that the Indian law fits the bill. Should that matter, or should we reject the "characterization" approach altogether and "consider the matter in principle", as we were advised in Taylor? What do the Law Lords do?

B.   There are, of course, other distinctions which can be drawn with <u>Holman v. Johnson</u>. For example, <u>Reggazoni</u> involves "smuggling out", while <u>Holman v. Johnson</u> involved "smuggling in". Does that matter? Also, <u>Reggazoni</u> involved a law of a nation that was a member of the British Commonwealth. Does that matter? Should it?

C.   Note also that the cast of judges is essentially the same as it was <u>Taylor</u>. Both cases obviously involve the "revenue rule". Why are they being treated differently? And are the judges being consistent with the statements they made in <u>Taylor</u>?

2.   Viscount Simonds is consistent, at least in one regard. He unequivocally stands by <u>Taylor</u>, pronouncing it correct and immutable. Fair enough. But he then opines that that case dealt with a completely different proposition than the instant one. By doing so, he avoids application of the revenue rule, explaining that it has been supplanted by a new principle, which he refers to as "comity". What does that term mean in this context? Where did it come from? Did it figure in the <u>Taylor</u> case?

A.   Comity, Viscount Simonds explains, is based on public policy. Whose policy? Note that Lord Reid states that whatever the rule, it is not a rule of international law. What does he mean by that? And what policy is he talking about, anyway? Is the policy a desire to satisfy an important foreign power? Is it a hope for reciprocal treatment? Is it a desire to promote the rule of law? Is it all of these things? Is it something else? And why is it important?

B.   If a court is going to recognize concerns such as those listed in the last paragraph, how will it do so? And why was that policy not applied in <u>Holman v. Johnson</u>? Viscount Simonds explains:

> The principle being based on public policy, exceptions to it must be similarly based. It would, therefore, not be surprising if a contract, in one age, falls within the proposition, in another, without it.

C.   Is Viscount Simonds merely trying to appease the gods of precedent? Or do you agree that times have changed since the 18th century? If you say things have changed, which changes (exactly) are causing the House of Lords to retreat from <u>Holman v. Johnson</u>? On this point, Lord Reid's explanation is quite good:

> Most of [the older cases] date from a time when international relationships were somewhat different and when theories of political economy now outmoded were generally accepted.

Can you elaborate? Is it because of the Commonwealth? Because England has lost her power, and is trying to use the case to regain it?

D. Consider Lord Somervell's explanation:

The statement that in this field one country takes no notice of the revenue laws of another seems to have been based on the principle that smuggling and freedom "gang together"...

What does he mean by that? As Viscount Simonds observes, one of the early cases (<u>Boucher v. Lawson</u>) involved a contract to smuggle gold out of Portugal at a time when that country prohibited the removal of any gold from the country. The British court applied the revenue rule and enforced the contract despite the illegality. Consider the importance of gold in the 18th century, and the motivations of the Portuguese and British governments regarding the prohibition of export. Does that help you to understand the comment that, years ago, "smuggling and freedom gang together"? Maybe they just don't anymore. If that is so, what more modern principle is being applied in this case?

3. Another policy discussed in several of the opinions is a desire to not compel a citizen of a friendly foreign state to commit an act in his home country that would be illegal.

A. Do you find this argument persuasive? Is Plaintiff really requesting an order that will require Defendant to act in an illegal fashion. The answer is "no", Plaintiff seeks money damages (for breach), not an order of "specific performance". So why is the Court concerned with the issue of foreign compulsion?

B. And what ever happened to the policy, under English law, that if a contract is illegal, the court should not let either party enforce it, so that the court cannot be accused of becoming a party to the illegality? Note that Lord Reid states that by recognizing the Indian law, the Court is not "taking sides" in the dispute between India and South Africa. How can he say that? Obviously, the South Africans would not agree. Can you articulate more fully the argument Lord Reid makes on this point?

4. Lord Keith and Lord Somervell also delve into the policy issue, the former stating that "to recognize the contract . . . as enforceable . . . would give a just cause for complaint by the Government of India"; the latter stating "I myself think that the courts of this country should not today enforce a contract to smuggle goods into or out of a foreign and friendly State." Both rely on the newly-minted concept of comity.

A. Are there any limits to the recognition comity requires? Should there be? If so, what are they?

B. Both Lord Keith and Lord Somervell try to answer the question. Lord Keith notes that the Indian law is not "repugnant"; Lord Somervell states that

> [t]here may, of course, be laws the enforcement of which would be against "morals". In such a case an exception might be made to the general principle. The point can be dealt with if it arises.

Can you think of an example?

A NOTE ON CHOICE OF LAW IN "PRIVATE LAW" CASES

As Lord Mansfield indicated in <u>Holman v. Johnson</u>, every nation has a choice of law rule to be applied "in a great many cases". The English rules alluded to in that case, *lex loci fori*, *lex loci contractus*, and *lex loci delictus* are still applied in England. In the United States, however, they have increasingly been replaced with a less rigid, more open-ended approach known as "governmental interest analysis". In "governmental interest analysis", a court considers which state or nation has the greatest interest in setting the rules and policies that will govern the relationship between the parties, and the court then "chooses" that state or country's law.

The British approach seems easy to apply and more likely than the American approach to produce a predictable outcome. One might ask the British, nevertheless: where is a contract made when it is mad over the wires, or, better yet, over the internet? Where does a cause of action arise if the effects of one's conduct are felt across borders? Before you laugh at these questions, remember - the British are stubborn, and they take their legal tradition very seriously.

The simplest example of "governmental interest analysis" is in the field of auto accidents (where, interestingly, it first developed). Suppose a citizen of New York gives a ride to a citizen of New Jersey, and there is an accident in New Jersey. The New Jersey passenger is injured, and he blames the New York driver who gave him the ride, suing in New York for "negligence". Under New Jersey law, however, a guest in a vehicle cannot, by statute, sue his host for negligence. New York law is silent on the issue.

The first thing a court in New York would do is state that, like Mansfield, it begins the analysis by looking to the whole of New York including New York's choice of law rule. The New York court would then consider the policy behind the New Jersey law (to discourage suits against "hosts" and thus encouraging people to car pool), and New York would likely recognize the New Jersey law, because, although New York law is silent, New Jersey's policies are more important here than New York's, especially since the accident occurred in Jersey and because the plaintiff appears to be forum shopping.

A slight change in the facts yields a different result. If the accident happened in New York, and the passenger was hospitalized in New York, a New York court would apply New York law, because now New York has the predominant interest.

Now, suppose instead of an auto accident the case involved a loan. New York has law that prohibits "usury", which New York defines as charging more than 16% interest per annum. Suppose New Jersey has no usury statute. Would a New York court enforce a loan that required payment of 30% interest per annum? The answer is "no". That would be true regardless of which party was the lender and which the borrower, and regardless of where the loan was made. Why is that? Why would New York be prepared to recognize the New Jersey guest-host law, but not New Jersey law on loans?[3]

Regardless of what choice of law approach is taken for "private law" issues, i.e. those issues which involve laws which are not *politici juris*, there seems to be historical and practical reluctance to apply those rules in the public law arena. Why that is the case is not entirely clear, since every state taxes and punishes. And it is (to some extent) folly to believe that laws involving contracts and torts are not affected by public policies and political purposes.[4] Nevertheless, courts continue to be involved in the difficult task of characterizing foreign law, and, if it is found to be in the forbidden category, to look askance at it and at least muse about the historical hesitance to enforce it. Why that is so it is difficult to say, except to observe that we in the U.S. had Cardozo, and the British had Lord Mansfield.

---

3. In the area of contract law, most states in the U.S. apply a variation on interest analysis known as the "center of gravity" test, looking at a variety of factors to determine where the contract's "center of gravity" is. By undertaking this analysis, courts in the U.S. have crafted a much more flexible and pragmatic approach than the English courts, who have retained the more mechanistic (and perhaps more predictable) approach.

4. For instance, the law of Patria might favor the buyer in a contract case, or, the lineal decendants in an estate case. Still, a foreign court that hears the dispute will not hesitate (generally) to consider and perhaps recognize the contract and/or inheritance law of Patria, if it is "appropriate" to do so (e.g. when the contract was made there, or where the decedent died a resident of that country). Obviously, both these areas of law have some policy overtones, yet choice of law rules have been applied to them for hundreds of years without any hesitation, and without any reference to the public law taboo.

III. MODERN SMUGGLING AND THE REVENUE RULE IN THE UNITED STATES

BANCO DO BRASIL, S. A.
v.
A. C. ISRAEL COMMODITY CO., INC.

Court of Appeals of New York

12 N.Y.2d 371; 190 N.E.2d 235; 239 N.Y.S.2d 872

April 4, 1963, Decided

JUDGE BURKE delivered the opinion of the Court

The action upon which the attachment here challenged is based is brought by appellant as an instrumentality of the Government of Brazil to recover damages for a conspiracy to defraud the Government of Brazil of American dollars by illegally circumventing the foreign exchange regulations of Brazil.

Defendant-respondent, Israel Commodity, a Delaware corporation having its principal place of business in New York, is an importer of Brazilian coffee. The gist of plaintiff's complaint is that Israel conspired with a Brazilian exporter of coffee to pay the exporter American dollars which the exporter could sell in the Brazilian free market for 220 Brazilian cruzeiros each instead of complying with Brazil's foreign exchange regulations which in effect required a forced sale of the dollars paid to the exporter to the Government of Brazil for only 90 cruzeiros. Through this conspiracy, the Brazilian exporter profited by the difference between the amount (in cruzeiros) it would have received for the dollars from the Government of Brazil and the amount it received in the open market in violation of Brazilian law, Israel profited by being able to pay less dollars for the coffee (because the dollars were worth so much more to the seller), and the plaintiff suffered a loss measured by the difference in amount it would have to pay for the same number of dollars in the open market and what it could have paid for them through the "forced sale" had its foreign exchange regulations been obeyed. The evasion was allegedly accomplished through the exporter's forgery of the documents evidencing receipt of the dollars by plaintiff Banco Do Brasil, S. A., and without which the coffee could not have left Brazil.

Plaintiff argues that respondent's participation in the violation of Brazilian exchange control laws affords a ground of recovery because of article VIII (§ 2, subd. [b]) of the Bretton Woods Agreement, a multilateral treaty to which both this country and Brazil are signatories. The section provides:

"Exchange contracts which involve the currency of any member and which are contrary to the exchange control regulations of that member maintained or imposed consistently with this Agreement shall be unenforceable in the territories of any member." (60 U.S. Stat. 1411.)

It is far from clear whether this sale of coffee is covered by subdivision (b) of section 2. The section deals with "exchange contracts" which "involve" the "currency" of any member of the International Monetary Fund, "and * * * are contrary to the exchange control regulations of that member maintained or imposed consistently with" the agreement. Subdivision (b) of section 2 has been construed as reaching only "transactions which have as their immediate object 'exchange,' that is, international media of payment" (Nussbaum, Exchange Control and the International Monetary Fund, 59 Yale L. J. 421, 426), or a contract where the consideration is payable in the currency of the country whose exchange controls are violated (Mann, The Exchange Control Act, 1947, 10 Mod. L. Rev. 411, 418). More recently, however, it has been suggested that it applies to "contracts which in any way affect a country's exchange resources" (Mann, The Private International Law of Exchange Control Under the International Monetary Fund Agreement, 2 International and Comp. L. Q. 97, 102; Gold and Lachman, The Articles of Agreement of the International Monetary Fund and the Exchange Control Regulations of Member States, Journal du Droit International, Paris (July-Sept., 1962). A similar view has been advanced to explain the further textual difficulty existing with respect to whether a sale of coffee in New York for American dollars "involves the currency" of Brazil, the member whose exchange controls were allegedly violated. Again it is suggested that adverse effect on the exchange resources of a member ipso facto "involves" the "currency" of that member (Gold and Lachman, op. cit.). We are inclined to view an interpretation of subdivision (b) of section 2 that sweeps in all contracts affecting any members' exchange resources as doing considerable violence to the text of the section. It says "involve the currency" of the country whose exchange controls are violated; not "involve the exchange resources".

While noting these doubts, we nevertheless prefer to rest this decision on other and clearer grounds. The sanction provided in subdivision (b) of section 2 is that contracts covered thereby are to be "unenforceable" in the territory of any member. The clear import of this provision is to insure the avoidance of the affront inherent in any attempt by the courts of one member to render a judgment that would put the losing party in the position of either complying with the judgment and violating the exchange controls of another member or complying with such controls and refusing obedience to the judgment. A further reasonable inference to be drawn from the provision is that the courts of no member should award any recovery for breach of an agreement in violation of the exchange controls of another member. Indeed, the International Monetary Fund itself, in an official interpretation of subdivision (b) of section 2 issued by the Fund's Executive Directors, construes the section as meaning that "the obligations of such contracts will not be implemented by the judicial or administrative authorities of member countries, for example, by decreeing performance of the contracts or by awarding damages for their nonperformance". (International Monetary Fund Ann. Rep. 82-83 [1949], 14 Fed. Reg. 5208, 5209 [1949].) An obligation to withhold judicial assistance to secure the benefits of such contracts does not imply an obligation to impose tort penalties on those who have fully executed them.

From the viewpoint of the individuals involved, it must be remembered that the Bretton Woods Agreement relates to international law. It imposes obligations among and between States, not individuals. The fact that by virtue of the agreement New York must not "enforce" a contract between individuals which is contrary to the exchange controls of any member, imposes no obligation (under the law of the transaction — New York law[5]) on such individuals not to enter into such contracts. While it does mean that they so agree at their peril inasmuch as they may not look to our courts for enforcement, this again is far from implying that one who so agrees commits a tort in New York for which he must respond in damages. It is significant that a proposal to make such an agreement an "offense" was defeated at Bretton Woods. (1 Proceedings and Documents of the United Nations Monetary and Financial Conference 334, 341, 502, 543, 546 — referred to in Nussbaum, Exchange Control and the International Monetary Fund, 59 Yale L. J. 421, 426, 429, supra.)

Lastly, and inseparable from the foregoing, there is a remedial consideration which bars recovery in this case. Plaintiff is an instrumentality of the Government of Brazil and is seeking, by use of an action for conspiracy to defraud, to enforce what is clearly a revenue law. Whatever may be the effect of the Bretton Woods Agreement in an action on "A contract made in a foreign country between citizens thereof and intended by them to be there performed" (see Perutz v. Bohemian Discount Bank in Liquidation, 304 N. Y. 533, 537), it is well established since the day of Lord Mansfield (Holman v. Johnson, 1 Cowp. 341, 98 E. R. 1120 [1775]) that one State does not enforce the revenue laws of another. (Government of India v. Taylor, 1 All E. R. 292 [1955]; City of Philadelphia v. Cohen, 11 N Y 2d 401; 1 Oppenheim, International Law, § 144b [Lauterpacht ed., 1947].) Nothing in the Bretton Woods Agreement is to the contrary. In fact its use of the unenforcibility device for effectuation of its purposes impliedly concedes the unavailability of the more direct method of enforcement at the suit of the aggrieved government. By the second sentence of subdivision (b) of section 2, further measures to make exchange controls more effective may be agreed upon by the member States. This is a matter for the Federal Government which not only has not entered into such further accords but has not even enacted the enabling provision into law (U. S. Code, tit. 22, § 286h).

---

5. All of respondent's acts allegedly in furtherance of the conspiracy took place in New York where it regularly did business.

Therefore, the order should be affirmed and the certified questions answered no and yes respectively.

Chief Judge Desmond (dissenting):

The order should be reversed and the warrant of attachment reinstated since the complaint alleges a cause of action within the jurisdiction of the New York State courts.

If there had never been a Bretton Woods Agreement and if this were a suit to enforce in this State the revenue laws of Brazil it would have to be dismissed under the ancient rule most recently restated in City of Philadelphia v. Cohen (11 N Y 2d 401). But Cohen and its predecessor cases express a public policy which lacks applicability here because of the adherence of the United States to the Bretton Woods Agreement. As we noted in Perutz v. Bohemian Discount Bank in Liquidation (304 N. Y. 533, 537), the membership of our Federal Government in the International Monetary Fund and other Bretton Woods enterprises makes it impossible to say that the currency control laws of other member States are offensive to our public policy. Furthermore, the argument from City of Philadelphia v. Cohen (supra) and similar decisions assumes erroneously that this is a suit to collect internal taxes assessed by the Brazilian Government. In truth, it is not even an effort to enforce Brazil's currency regulations. This complaint and other papers charge a tortious fraud and conspiracy to deprive plaintiff, an instrumentality of the Brazilian Government, of the dollar proceeds of coffee exports to which proceeds the bank and its government were entitled. This fraud, it is alleged, was accomplished by inserting in coffee shipping permits references to nonexistent exchange contracts and to nonexistent assignments to plaintiff of the foreign exchange proceeds of the coffee exports and by forging the signatures of banking officials and Brazilian officials, all with the purpose of making it appear that there had been compliance with the Brazilian statutes or regulations. The alleged scheme and effect of the conspiracy as charged was to obtain for defendant-respondent coffee in New York at a reduced price, to enable the Brazilian defendants to get more "cruzeiros" per dollar in violation of law and to deprive Brazil of the cruzeiros which it would have received from these coffee sales had the fraud not been committed. According to the complaint and affidavits defendant Israel not only knew of and intended to benefit by the perpetration of this fraud but participated in it in New York by making its purchase agreements here and by here receiving the shipping documents and making payments. The Israel corporation is alleged to have been one of the consignees of some 36,000 bags of coffee exported from Brazil to New York in 1961 without compliance with the Brazilian law and thus to have fraudulently and conspiratorially caused to Brazil damage of nearly $ 2,000,000. Refusal to entertain this suit does violence to our national policy of co-operation with other Bretton Woods signatories and is not required by anything in our own State policy.

BANCO FRANCES E BRASILEIRO S. A.
V.
JOHN DOE NO.1

Court of Appeals of New York

36 N.Y.2d 592; 331 N.E.2d 502; 370 N.Y.S.2d 534

May 8, 1975

JASEN, J.

The principal question before us is whether a private foreign bank may avail itself of the New York courts in an action for damages for tortious fraud and deceit and for rescission of currency exchange contracts arising from alleged violations of foreign currency exchange regulations.

Plaintiff, a private Brazilian bank, brings this action for fraud and deceit, and conspiracy to defraud and deceive, against 20 "John Doe" defendants whose identities are unknown to it. The gravamen of plaintiff's complaint is that these defendants over a period of approximately six weeks participated, in violation of Brazilian currency regulations, in the submission of false applications to Banco-Brasileiro of Brazil, which the plaintiff relied upon, resulting in the improper exchange by the bank of Brazilian cruzeiros into travelers checks in United States dollars totaling $ 1,024,000. A large amount of the fraudulently obtained travelers checks were deposited by defendant "John Doe No. 1" in an account having a code name of "Alberta" at Bankers Trust Company, New York. Other of such travelers checks were deposited by defendant "John Doe No. 2" in an account having the code name of "Samso" at Manfra Tordella & Brookes, Inc., New York. An order of attachment was granted at Special Term against the property of defendants John Doe No. 1 and John Doe No. 2 held by Bankers Trust and Manfra Tordella & Brookes, Inc. Service of summons by publication was authorized by Special Term.

Subsequent to the granting of the order of attachment and the service of the summons by publication, motions were made by the plaintiff for disclosure from Bankers Trust Co. and Manfra Tordella & Brookes of the true names and addresses of John Doe Nos. 1 and 2 and to direct the attorney for defendant John Doe No. 1 to disclose the true name(s) and address(es) of defendant(s) and the basis of the attorney's authority to act, or, in the alternative, to vacate his appearance in the action. The defendant John Doe No. 1, by way of order to show cause, moved to vacate the order of attachment, to dismiss plaintiff's complaint and to intervene in the motion of plaintiff for disclosure from Bankers Trust Co. so as to defend against the disclosure.

Special Term, inter alia, denied the motion to vacate the order of attachment and to dismiss the complaint except as to the third cause of action for damages which

was dismissed for failure to plead actual damages. Motions for ancillary relief —
for discovery and inspection and for disclosure from the attorney for defendant
"John Doe No. 1" of the name and address of his client — were granted.

On cross appeals, the Appellate Division, by a unanimous court (44 AD2d
353), relying on Banco do Brasil v Israel Commodity Co. (12 NY 2d 371, cert
den 376 U.S. 906), modified by granting defendants' motion to dismiss the
complaint and denying all applications for ancillary relief on the ground that
the New York courts were not open to an action arising from a tortious violation
of foreign currency regulations.

Plaintiff bank appeals as of right to this court. (CPLR 5601, subd [a].) We are
unable to assent to the decision of the Appellate Division and, accordingly,
modify the order appealed from by reinstating the order of attachment and
the first two causes of action, with leave to plaintiff, if so advised, to apply to
Special Term for permission to serve a supplemental pleading alleging special
damages in its third cause of action for damages, and by granting the ancillary
relief requested to the extent hereafter specified.

It is an old chestnut in conflict of laws that one State does not enforce the
revenue laws of another. By way of rationale, an analogy is drawn to foreign
penal laws, extrastate enforcement of which is denied (see The Antelope, 10
Wheat [23 U.S.] 66, 123) to deny recognition to foreign tax assessments,
judicially expanded also to include foreign currency exchange regulations.
The analogy, reformulated in the Restatement (Restatement, Conflict of Laws,
§§ 610, 611), but interestingly withdrawn in the Restatement Second (§ 89),
traces from Lord Mansfield's now famous dictum in an international smuggling
case that "no country ever takes notice of the revenue laws of another."
(Holman v Johnson, 1 Cowp 341, 343.) But the modern analog of the revenue
law rule is justifiable neither precedentially nor analytically.

Holman v Johnson was an action for goods had and received. The plaintiffs,
Frenchmen, sold and delivered tea to the defendant in France. The tea was then
smuggled into England by the defendant in violation of the revenue laws. In an
action for the price, Lord Mansfield's holding was simply to the effect that a
French court would not invalidate a sale of tea by a Frenchman in France made
in violation of an English prohibition. The decision was concerned largely with
the impact of foreign revenue laws on international commerce, but the quoted
dictum became the basis in this country for denying foreign tax authorities the
right to collect taxes assessed by them. But certainly that case and earlier (e.g.,
Boucher v Lawson, 95 Eng Rep 53) and later (e.g., Planche v Fletcher, 1 Dougl
250) dicta in other cases denying extraterritorial effect to forum defenses, should
not have been relied upon to deny forum effect to foreign claims.

Nor is the rule analytically justifiable. Indeed, much doubt has been expressed
that the reasons advanced for the rule, if ever valid, remain so. (E.g., Leflar,

Extrastate Enforcement of Penal and Governmental Claims, 46 Harv L Rev 193.) But inroads have been made. In interstate cases, for example, where the rule made least sense, administrative tax assessments are increasingly equated with tax judgments (Milwaukee County v White Co., 296 U.S. 268) and on that basis generally afforded full faith and credit. (State of Oklahoma ex rel. Oklahoma Tax Comm. v Neely, 225 Ark 230; Ehrenzweig, Conflict of Laws, § 49; but see City of Philadelphia v Cohen, 11 NY 2d 401.) Some do consider that, in light of the economic interdependence of all nations, the courts should be receptive even to extranational tax and revenue claims as well, especially where there is a treaty involved, but also without such constraint. (Scoles, Interstate and International Distinctions in Conflict of Laws in the United States, 54 Cal L Rev 1599, 1607-1608.) Indeed, there may be strong policy reasons for specially favoring a foreign revenue regulation, using that term in its broadest sense, especially one involving currency exchange or control.

In the international sphere, cases involving foreign currency exchange regulations represent perhaps the most important aspect of the revenue law rule. This assumes, of course, that a currency exchange regulation, normally not designed for revenue purposes as such, but rather, to prevent the loss of foreign currency which in turn increases the country's foreign exchange reserves, is properly characterizable as a revenue law. (Contra, Kahler v Midland Bank [1950], A C 24; Dicey, Conflict of Laws [7th ed], p 920.) At any rate, it is for the forum to characterize such a regulation and in this State the question would appear to have been resolved for the present at least by Banco do Brasil v Israel Commodity Co. (12 NY 2d 371, 377, cert den 376 U.S. 906, supra).

But even assuming the continuing validity of the revenue law rule and the correctness of the characterization of a currency exchange regulation thereunder, United States membership in the International Monetary Fund (IMF) makes inappropriate the refusal to entertain the instant claim. The view that nothing in article VIII (§ 2, subd [b]) of the Bretton Woods Agreements Act (60 U.S. Stat 1401, 1411) requires an American court to provide a forum for a private tort remedy, while correct in a literal sense (see Banco do Brasil v Israel Commodity Co., supra, p 376), does not represent the only perspective. Nothing in the agreement prevents an IMF member from aiding, directly or indirectly, a fellow member in making its exchange regulations effective. And United States membership in the IMF makes it impossible to conclude that the currency control laws of other member States are offensive to this State's public policy so as to preclude suit in tort by a private party.

Indeed, conduct reasonably necessary to protect the foreign exchange resources of a country does not offend against international law. (Restatement, 2d, Foreign Relations Law of the United States, § 198, comment b.) Moreover, where a true governmental interest of a friendly nation is involved — and foreign currency reserves are of vital importance to a country plagued by balance of payments difficulties — the national policy of co-operation with Bretton Woods signatories is furthered by providing a State forum for suit.

The Banco do Brasil case relied upon by the Appellate Division is quite distinguishable. There the Government of Brazil, through Banco do Brasil, a government bank, sought redress for violations of its currency exchange regulations incident to a fraudulent coffee export transaction. Here, the plaintiff is a private bank seeking rescission of the fraudulent currency exchange transactions and damages. And no case has come to our attention where a private tort remedy arising from foreign currency regulations has been denied by the forum as an application of the revenue law rule and we decline so to extend the Banco do Brasil rationale. Thus, in the instant case we find no basis for reliance upon the revenue law rule to deny a forum for suit. Moreover, where the parties are private, the "jealous sovereign" rationale is inapposite (cf. Loucks v Standard Oil Co., 224 NY 99, 102-103 [Cardozo, J.]) even as it might seem inapposite in the Banco do Brasil situation where the sovereign itself, or its instrumentality, asks redress and damages in a foreign forum for violation of the sovereign's currency laws. (But cf. Moore v Mitchell, 30 F2d 600, 603 [L. Hand, J., concurring].)

Perutz v Bohemian Discount Bank in Liquidation (304 NY 533) is consistent with an expansive application of the IMF agreement to which we here ascribe (cf. Kolovrat v Oregon, 366 U.S. 187, 196-198), although there it is true defensive use of foreign currency exchange regulation was made and upheld by this court. But interestingly, in Perutz, in contrast to the instant case, political relations at the time were not conducive to comity which nevertheless was extended.

Finally, subsequent to the commencement of this action, a penalty was levied by the Central Bank of Brazil, and paid by the plaintiff, on account of the alleged fraudulent currency exchange transactions. Therefore, our decision today is without prejudice to a proper application by plaintiff to Special Term to allege by supplemental pleading such sum as an element of special damages on the third cause of action. (CPLR 3025, subd [b]; cf. Morrison v National Broadcasting Co., 19 NY 2d 453.)

Accordingly, the order of the Appellate Division should be modified in accordance with the views here expressed and the action remitted to the Supreme Court, New York County.

WACHTLER, J. (dissenting).

We are asked to determine when claims between private parties which spring from jural relationships created by the laws of a foreign country, here Brazil, may be enforced in our courts. The issue turns on the essential nature of the rights and obligations sought to be enforced as the forum court characterizes them. As stated by the United States Supreme Court: "The test is not by what name the statute is called by the legislature or the courts of the State in which it was passed, but whether it appears to the tribunal which is called upon to enforce it to be, in its essential character and effect, a punishment of an offense against the public, or a grant of a civil right to a private person." (Huntington v Attrill, 146 U.S. 657, 683; also City of Philadelphia v Cohen, 11 NY 2d 401, 406; State of Maryland v Turner, 75 Misc 9, 11.)

I believe that the relief sought here, albeit indirectly through plaintiff bank, is an aspect of the Brazilian government's sovereign management of the economy of its own country. This is not a matter involving the resolution of private rights only as those rights are defined under the laws of a foreign State. Were that so our courts would not withhold judicial sanction even if the definition of such private rights were somewhat different from our own, "unless some sound reason of public policy makes it unwise for us to lend our aid" (Loucks v Standard Oil Co., 224 NY 99, 110).

There is no allegation in this complaint that defendants intended to or succeeded in defrauding plaintiff of foreign currency exchange in the private rights sense. On the contrary, from all that appears, defendants obtained no more United States dollars in consequence of their alleged fraud than they would have been entitled to receive at the then currently effective exchange rate for the Brazilian cruzeiros which they exchanged with plaintiff bank. The gravamen rather is that the fraud and deceit practiced by the defendants induced plaintiff bank to violate Brazilian currency exchange regulations, thereby exposing that bank to consequent penalties which would be imposed by the Brazilian Government.

It has long been recognized that the courts of one jurisdiction will not enforce the tax laws, penal laws, or statutory penalties and forfeitures of another jurisdiction. "The rule that the courts of no country execute the penal laws of another applies not only to prosecutions and sentences for crimes and misdemeanors, but to all suits in favor of the State for the recovery of pecuniary penalties for any violation of statutes for the protection of its revenue, or other municipal laws". (Wisconsin v Pelican Ins. Co., 127 U.S. 265, 290; also The Antelope, 10 Wheat [23 U.S.] 66, 122-123, Huntington v Attrill, supra; Holman v Johnson, 1 Cowp 341; Banco do Brasil v Israel Commodity Co., 12 NY 2d 371, 377, cert den 376 U.S. 906; City of Philadelphia v Cohen, supra; James & Co. v Second Russian Ins. Co., 239 NY 248, 257.) Under the principle of territorial supremacy, fundamental to the community of nations, courts refuse to enforce any claim which in their view is a manifestation of a foreign State's sovereign authority (Dicey & Morris, Conflict of Laws [8th ed], p 160; cf. Judge Learned Hand's concurring opinion in Moore v Mitchell, 30 F 2d 600). The proper question is whether in the particular instance the claim sought to be enforced is a manifestation of such sovereign authority.

In previous cases our court held that governmental foreign exchange regulation may present an aspect of the exercise of sovereign power by a foreign State to implement its national fiscal policy. Thus, in Banco do Brasil v Israel Commodity Co. (supra), we decided that our courts were not open to enforce a Brazilian foreign currency exchange regulation. Although the regulation in that case was characterized as a revenue measure, the essence of the matter was that we declined to enforce what we considered to be an exercise of Brazil's sovereign power. Whether a regulation denominated "currency exchange regulation" has or does not have a revenue-producing effect, it must be presumed to have been adopted to accomplish fiscal regulation and ultimate economic objectives significantly similar to, if not identical with, the objectives which underlie what would be characterized as revenue measures — namely, governmental management of its economy by a foreign country.

Accordingly, the result is not determined by the threshold appearance of the particular law sought to be enforced or whether such law be denominated by the foreign government as a penal law or a revenue law or otherwise. The bottom line is that the courts of one country will not enforce the laws adopted by another country in the exercise of its sovereign capacity for the purpose of fiscal regulation and management.

Although our earlier decisions in Perutz v Bohemian Discount Bank in Liquidation (304 NY 533), and Industrial Export & Import Corp. v Hongkong & Shanghai Banking Corp. (302 NY 342), may appear to be to the contrary, a studied analysis dispels this apparent inconsistency. These cases merely refine the traditional conflict-of-laws rule by holding that the provisions of any international agreement to which the United States is a party supplement, and to that extent, supersede the traditional rule. For instance, the Bretton Woods Agreement Act (US Code, tit 22, § 286), authorizes United States membership in the International Monetary Fund (60 U.S. Stat 1401; 2 US Treaty Developments, Dec. 27, 1945, T.I.A.S. 1501). Another example of such a treaty is article VIII (§ 2, subd [b]) of the International Monetary Fund Agreement (60 U S Stat 1411) making exchange contracts which are contrary to the exchange control regulations of a member (Brazil is a member) unenforceable in the territory of another member (United States). . . . Thus, by treaty provision what would otherwise have been the applicable rule of judicial nonrecognition of sovereign acts of a foreign State may be modified in the area of currency exchange control to require courts in the member States (including courts in the United States) to recognize foreign currency regulation as a defense.

Nothing in the Bretton Woods Agreement Act or in any other agreement between the United States and Brazil of which we are aware, however, mandates a complete abrogation of the normal conflicts rule or requires our courts Affirmatively to enforce foreign currency regulation, as we are invited to do in the present case. This distinction was expressly recognized and held to be dispositive in Banco do Brasil (supra), in which we said (p 376): "An obligation to withhold judicial assistance to secure the benefits of such contracts [i.e., those violative of the foreign currency control regulation] does not imply an obligation to impose tort penalties on those who have fully executed them." (See Dicey & Morris, Conflict of Laws [8th ed], op. cit., p 161, n 19; pp898-900.)

. . .

I recognize that this case is not an instance of recourse sought by a foreign country in our courts for the direct enforcement of its foreign currency exchange regulations, as would be the case were the Brazilian Government seeking here to recover penalties from either Banco-Brasileiro or from the defendants. The rights of private parties will be significantly affected; it is alleged that plaintiff bank has suffered and will suffer detriment in its private capacity in consequence of the fraud and deceit of defendants. The resolution of the issue posed by the motion to dismiss does not depend on the incidental, inescapable fact that private rights have already been, and would be affected by the judicial relief sought. Rather, the determinative factor is that the primary objective and the ultimate practical effect of the relief sought would be the enforcement of the currency regulation system of a foreign country. Our courts are not open for the accomplishment of that end, and that it may be sought through private intermediaries does not change the result. It matters not whether enforcement is sought directly or indirectly (Dicey & Morris, Conflict of Laws [8th ed], op. cit., pp. 160-161).

I consider the plaintiff's complaint as an attempt to utilize the judicial machinery of our courts to enforce the exercise of the sovereign power by the Government of Brazil. I believe that our courts, under traditional and established principle, are not available for this purpose.

The majority, however, argues that the time may have come for a change in what historically has been the applicable rule. I recognize that strong arguments can be mounted for a change in view of the increased frequency and importance of international commerce and the significantly different perspective in today's world in which one nation views another nation and its interests. In my opinion, however, the responsibility for any change lies with our Federal Government rather than with the highest court of any single State. Change, if at all, in my view, would better come at the hands of the State Department and the Congress, through the negotiation of international agreement or otherwise in the discharge of the constitutional responsibility of the Federal Government "to regulate commerce with foreign nations" (cf. Bretton Woods Agreement Act). A fitting sense of judicial restraint would dictate that the courts of no single State should enunciate a change, however large that State's relative proportion of foreign commerce may be, particularly since the authoritative effect thereof would necessarily be confined to the borders of that State.

Accordingly, I believe the order of the Appellate Division should be affirmed.

NOTES AND QUESTIONS

1. These two cases, in many ways, mirror <u>Government of India v. Taylor</u> and <u>Reggazoni v. Sethia</u>. The first can be categorized as an attempt by a foreign state to collect a tax; the latter, a private suit for damages arising out of a smuggling scheme.

    A. Was it correct to characterize the Brazilian currency control law as a tax or revenue law? Note that in the first case, the Court of Appeals does so (although the result was not pre-ordained), and in the second, the Court questions the characterization, but concludes that, "in this State the question would appear to have been resolved for the present at least by <u>Banco do Brasil v Israel</u>." Recall that the British, apparently, drew the opposite conclusion in <u>Kahler v. Midland Bank</u> (mentioned by Lord Reid in <u>Reggazoni</u>).

    B. In the second case, the private bank's motivation to sue in New York was that the Central Bank had threatened legal action (a fine) because the bank had been duped. Has Brazil found a clever way to circumvent the earlier case? Certainly that is what Judge Wachtler believes. Who is right?

    C. And, as was the case in the English cases with respect to membership in the Commonwealth, the fact that both nations involved are signatories to the Bretton Woods agreement augurs in favor of recognition of the foreign law. It also vitiates any suggestion that the Brazilian law is "repugnant" "or immoral". Notwithstanding the lack of discussion of such limits on comity, do you think the U.S. courts would apply those comity limits?

2. In rejecting the revenue rule in the second case, the New York Court of Appeals is blunt in its statement:

    > [T]he modern analog of the revenue law rule is justifiable neither precedentially nor analytically.

    Why is that so? Compare Judge Jasen's rationale with that of the Law Lords in <u>Reggazoni</u>. Which is more persuasive? Which court, do you think, is more likely to adopt, in broad terms, the "comity" approach? The answer may suprise you.

3. On the business side, these two New York cases demonstrate that today smuggling is more likely to involve foreign currencies than goods. This phenomenon exists, in large part, because nations today are more likely to place restrictions on currency transfers than goods transactions.

A.   In <u>Banco do Brasil v. Israel</u> a Brazilian citizen is smuggling U.S. dollars into Brazil (presumably for sale on the black market), rather than declare these dollars to his government, whose laws would have forced him to turn in those dollars to the government at a lower exchange rate. Why is the U.S. company being implicated? How were they involved? How did they prosper from the fraudulent scheme?

B.   In <u>Banco Frances e Brasileiro v. John Doe</u>, a Brazilian citizen is trying to smuggle his wealth out of Brazil. He approached a private bank, and induced them to give him scarce foreign exchange (dollars). If he revealed his true purpose (retirement in Miami?), they would obviously have turned him down. So what did he tell them? Why was it fraud? In what way was the Brazilian currency law involved?

PASQUANTINO
v.
UNITED STATES

Argued Nov. 9, 2004.
Decided April 26, 2005.

Justice THOMAS delivered the opinion of the Court.

At common law, the revenue rule generally barred courts from enforcing the tax laws of foreign sovereigns. The question presented in this case is whether a plot to defraud a foreign government of tax revenue violates the federal wire fraud statute, 18 U.S.C. § 1343 (2000 ed., Supp. II). Because the plain terms of § 1343 criminalize such a scheme, and because this construction of the wire fraud statute does not derogate from the common-law revenue rule, we hold that it does.

I

Petitioners Carl J. Pasquantino, David B. Pasquantino, and Arthur Hilts were indicted for and convicted of federal wire fraud for carrying out a scheme to smuggle large quantities of liquor into Canada from the United States. According to the evidence presented at trial, the Pasquantinos, while in New York, ordered liquor over the telephone from discount package stores in Maryland. See 336 F.3d 321, 325 (C.A.4 2003) (en banc). They employed Hilts and others to drive the liquor over the Canadian border, without paying the required excise taxes. *Ibid.* The drivers avoided paying taxes by hiding the liquor in their vehicles and failing to declare the goods to Canadian customs officials. *Id.,* at 333. During the time of petitioners' smuggling operation, between 1996 and 2000, Canada heavily taxed the importation of alcoholic beverages. Uncontested evidence at trial showed that Canadian taxes then due on alcohol purchased in the United States and transported to Canada were approximately double the liquor's purchase price.

Before trial, petitioners moved to dismiss the indictment on the ground that it stated no wire fraud offense. The wire fraud statute prohibits the use of interstate wires to effect "any scheme or artifice to defraud, or for obtaining money or property by means of false or fraudulent pretenses, representations, or promises." 18 U.S.C. § 1343 (2000 ed., Supp. II). Petitioners contended that the Government lacked a sufficient interest in enforcing the revenue laws of Canada, and therefore that they had not committed wire fraud. The District Court denied the motion, and the case went to trial. The jury convicted petitioners of wire fraud.

Petitioners appealed their convictions to the United States Court of Appeals for the Fourth Circuit, again urging that the indictment failed to state a wire fraud offense. They argued that their prosecution contravened the common-law revenue rule, because it required the court to take cognizance of the revenue laws of Canada. Over Judge Hamilton's dissent, the panel agreed and reversed the convictions. 305 F.3d 291, 295 (C.A.4 2002). Petitioners also argued that Canada's right to collect taxes from them was not "money or property" within the meaning of the wire fraud statute, but the panel unanimously rejected that argument. Id., at 294-295; id., at 299 (Hamilton, J., dissenting).

The Court of Appeals granted rehearing en banc, vacated the panel's decision, and affirmed petitioners' convictions. It concluded that the common-law revenue rule, rather than barring any recognition of foreign revenue law, simply allowed courts to refuse to enforce the tax judgments of foreign nations, and therefore did not preclude the Government from prosecuting petitioners. The Court of Appeals held as well that Canada's right to receive tax revenue was "money or property" within the meaning of the wire fraud statute.

We granted certiorari to resolve a conflict in the Courts of Appeals over whether a scheme to defraud a foreign government of tax revenue violates the wire fraud statute. Compare *United States v. Boots*, 80 F.3d 580, 587 (C.A.1 1996) (holding that a scheme to defraud a foreign nation of tax revenue does not violate the wire fraud statute), with *United States v. Trapilo*, 130 F.3d 547, 552-553 (C.A.2 1997) (holding that a scheme to defraud a foreign nation of tax revenue violates the wire fraud statute). We agree with the Court of Appeals that it does and therefore affirm the judgment below.

II

We first consider whether petitioners' conduct falls within the literal terms of the wire fraud statute. The statute prohibits using interstate wires to effect "any scheme or artifice to defraud, or for obtaining money or property by means of false or fraudulent pretenses, representations, or promises." 18 U.S.C. § 1343 . Two elements of this crime, and the only two that petitioners dispute here, are that the defendant engage in a "scheme or artifice to defraud," *ibid.*, and that the "object of the fraud ... be '[money or] property' in the victim's hands," [citation omitted] Petitioners' smuggling operation satisfies both elements.

Taking the latter element first, Canada's right to uncollected excise taxes on the liquor petitioners imported into Canada is "property" in its hands. This right is an entitlement to collect money from petitioners, the possession of which is "something of value" to the Government of Canada. [citation omitted] Valuable entitlements like these are "property" as that term ordinarily is employed. ("When interpreting a statute, we must give words their ordinary or natural meaning" (internal quotation marks omitted)); Black's Law Dictionary 1382 (4th ed.1951) (defining "property" as "extend[ing] to every species of valuable right and interest"). Had petitioners complied with this legal obligation, they would have paid money to Canada. Petitioners' tax evasion deprived Canada of that money, inflicting an economic injury no less than had they embezzled funds from the Canadian treasury. The object of petitioners' scheme was to deprive Canada of money legally due, and their scheme thereby had as its object the deprivation of Canada's "property."

The common law of fraud confirms this characterization of Canada's right to excise taxes. The right to be paid money has long been thought to be a species of property. See 3 W. Blackstone, Commentaries on the Laws of England 153-155 (1768) (classifying a right to sue on a debt as personal property); 2 J. Kent, Commentaries on American Law (same). Consistent with that understanding, fraud at common law included a scheme to deprive a victim of his entitlement to money. For instance, a debtor who concealed his assets when settling debts with his creditors thereby committed common-law fraud. 1 J. Story, Equity Jurisprudence § 378 (I. Redfield 10th rev. ed. 1870); *Chesterfield v. Janssen*, 28 Eng. Rep. 82, 2 Ves. Sen. 125 (ch. 1750); 1 S. Rapalje & R. Lawrence, A Dictionary of American and English Law 546 (1883). That made sense given the economic equivalence between money in hand and money legally due. The fact that the victim of the fraud happens to be the government, rather than a private party, does not lessen the injury.

.   .   .

Turning to the second element at issue here, petitioners' plot was a "scheme or artifice to defraud" Canada of its valuable entitlement to tax revenue. The evidence showed that petitioners routinely concealed imported liquor from Canadian officials and failed to declare those goods on customs forms. By this conduct, they represented to Canadian customs officials that their drivers had no goods to declare. This, then, was a scheme "designed to defraud by representations," [citation omitted] and therefore a "scheme or artifice to defraud" Canada of taxes due on the smuggled goods. . . .

III

We next consider petitioners' revenue rule argument. Petitioners argue that, to avoid reading § 1343 to derogate from the common-law revenue rule, we should construe the otherwise-applicable language of the wire fraud statute to except frauds directed at evading foreign taxes. Their argument relies on the canon of construction that "[s]tatutes which invade the common law ... are to be read with a presumption favoring the retention of long-established and familiar principles, except when a statutory purpose to the contrary is evident." This presumption is, however, no bar to a construction that conflicts with a common-law rule if the statute " 'speak[s] directly' to the question addressed by the common law."

Whether the wire fraud statute derogates from the common-law revenue rule depends, in turn, on whether reading § 1343 to reach this prosecution conflicts with a well-established revenue rule principle. We clarified this constraint on the application of the nonderogation canon in *United States v. Craft*, 535 U.S. 274, 122 S.Ct. 1414, 152 L.Ed.2d 437 (2002). The issue in *Craft* was whether the property interest of a tenant by the entirety was exempt from a federal tax lien. We construed the federal tax lien statute to reach such a property interest, despite the tension between that construction and the common-law rule that entireties property enjoys immunity from liens, because this "common-law rule was not so well established with respect to the application of a federal tax lien that we must assume that Congress considered the impact of its enactment on the question now before us." So too here, before we may conclude that Congress intended to exempt the present prosecution from the broad reach of the wire fraud statute, we must find that the common-law revenue rule clearly barred such a prosecution. We examine the state of the common law as of 1952, the year Congress enacted the wire fraud statute.

The wire fraud statute derogates from no well-established revenue rule principle. We are aware of no common-law revenue rule case decided as of 1952 that held or clearly implied that the revenue rule barred the United States from prosecuting a fraudulent scheme to evade foreign taxes. The traditional rationales for the revenue rule, moreover, do not plainly suggest that it swept so broadly. We consider these two points in turn.

A

We first consider common-law revenue rule jurisprudence as it existed in 1952, the year Congress enacted § 1343. Since the late 19th and early 20th century, courts have treated the common-law revenue rule as a corollary of the rule that, as Chief Justice Marshall put it, "[t]he Courts of no country execute the penal laws of another." *The Antelope*, 10 Wheat. 66, 123, 6 L.Ed. 268 (1825). The rule against the enforcement of foreign penal statutes, in turn, tracked the common-law principle that crimes could only be prosecuted in the country in which they were committed. See, *e.g.,* J. Story, Commentaries on the Conflict of Laws § 620, p. 840 (M. Bigelow ed. 8th ed. 1883). The basis for inferring the revenue rule from the rule against foreign penal enforcement was an analogy between foreign revenue laws and penal laws. See *Wisconsin v. Pelican Ins. Co.,* 127 U.S. 265, 290, 8 S.Ct. 1370, 32 L.Ed. 239 (1888); Leflar, Extrastate Enforcement of Penal and Governmental Claims, 46 Harv. L.Rev. 193, 219 (1932) (hereinafter Leflar).

Courts first drew that inference in a line of cases prohibiting the enforcement of tax liabilities of one sovereign in the courts of another sovereign, such as a suit to enforce a tax judgment. The revenue rule's grounding in these cases shows that, at its core, it prohibited the collection of tax obligations of foreign nations. Unsurprisingly, then, the revenue rule is often stated as prohibiting the collection of foreign tax claims. See Brief for Petitioners 16 (noting that "[t]he most straightforward application of the revenue rule arises when a foreign sovereign attempts to sue directly in its own right to enforce a tax judgment in the courts of another nation").

The present prosecution is unlike these classic examples of actions traditionally barred by the revenue rule. It is not a suit that recovers a foreign tax liability, like a suit to enforce a judgment. This is a criminal prosecution brought by the United States in its sovereign capacity to punish domestic criminal conduct. Petitioners nevertheless argue that common-law revenue rule jurisprudence as of 1952 prohibited such prosecutions. Revenue rule cases, however, do not establish that proposition, much less clearly so.

1

Petitioners first analogize the present action to several cases that have applied the revenue rule to bar indirect enforcement of foreign revenue laws, in contrast to the direct collection of a tax obligation. They cite, for example, a decision of an Irish trial court holding that a private liquidator could not recover assets unlawfully distributed and moved to Ireland by a corporate director, because the recovery would go to satisfy the company's Scottish tax obligations. The court found that "the sole object of the liquidation proceedings in Scotland was to collect a revenue debt," because if the liquidator won, "every penny recovered after paying certain costs ... could be claimed by the Scottish Revenue." According to the *Buchanan* court, "[i]n every case the substance of the claim must be scrutinized, and if it then appears that it is really a suit brought for the purpose of collecting the debts of a foreign revenue it must be rejected." [citations omitted]

Buchanan and the other cases on which petitioners rely cannot bear the weight petitioners place on them. Many of them were decided after 1952, too late for the Congress that passed the wire fraud statute to have relied on them. Others come from foreign courts. Drawing sure inferences regarding Congress' intent from such foreign citations is perilous, as several of petitioners' cases illustrate.[6]

More important, none of these cases clearly establishes that the revenue rule barred this prosecution. None involved a domestic sovereign acting pursuant to authority conferred by a criminal statute. The difference is significant. An action by a domestic sovereign enforces the sovereign's own penal law. A prohibition on the enforcement of *foreign* penal law does not plainly prevent the Government from enforcing a *domestic* criminal law. Such an extension, to our knowledge, is unprecedented in the long history of either the revenue rule or the rule against enforcement of penal laws.

Moreover, none of petitioners' cases (with the arguable exception of *Banco Do Brasil, S.A. v. A.C. Israel Commodity Co.,*[citation omitted]) barred an action that had as its primary object the deterrence and punishment of fraudulent conduct-a substantial domestic regulatory interest entirely independent of foreign tax enforcement. The main object of the action in each of those cases was the collection of money that would pay foreign tax claims. The absence of such an object in this action means that the link between this prosecution and foreign tax collection is incidental and attenuated at best, making it not plainly one in which "the whole object of the suit is to collect tax for a foreign revenue." [citation omitted] Even those courts that as of 1952 had extended the revenue rule beyond its core prohibition had not faced a case closely analogous to this one-and thus we cannot say with any reasonable certainty whether Congress in 1952 would have considered this prosecution within the revenue rule.

Petitioners answer that the recovery of taxes is indeed the object of this suit, because restitution of the lost tax revenue to Canada is required under the Mandatory Victims Restitution Act of 1996, 18 U.S.C. §§ 3663A-3664. We do not think it matters whether the provision of restitution is mandatory in this prosecution. Regardless, the wire fraud statute advances the Federal Government's independent interest in punishing fraudulent domestic criminal conduct, a significant feature absent from all of petitioners' revenue rule cases. The purpose of awarding restitution in this action is not to collect a foreign tax, but to mete out appropriate criminal punishment for that conduct.

---

6. For example, in *Government of India v. Taylor,* 1955 A.C. 491 (H.L.), on which petitioners rely heavily, the court's application of the revenue rule rested in part on a ground peculiar to English law, namely, that an Act of Parliament had excluded tax judgments from a statute that provided for the enforcement of foreign judgments. That Act thus demonstrated that the revenue rule "appear[ed] to have been recognized by Parliament." *Id.,* at 506. For example, in *Government of India v. Taylor,* 1955 A.C. 491 (H.L.), on which petitioners rely heavily, the court's application of the revenue rule rested in part on a ground peculiar to English law, namely, that an Act of Parliament had excluded tax judgments from a statute that provided for the enforcement of foreign judgments. That Act thus demonstrated that the revenue rule "appear[ed] to have been recognized by Parliament." *Id.,* at 506; . . . In addition, as we explain below, features peculiar to the American system of separation of powers cast doubt on the notion that the revenue rule bars this prosecution.

In any event, any conflict between mandatory restitution and the revenue rule would not change our holding today. If awarding restitution to foreign sovereigns were contrary to the revenue rule, the proper resolution would be to construe the Mandatory Victims Restitution Act not to allow such awards, rather than to assume that the later enacted restitution statute impliedly repealed § 1343 as applied to frauds against foreign sovereigns.

2

We are no more persuaded by a second line of cases on which petitioners rely. Petitioners analogize the present case to early English common-law cases from which the revenue rule originally derived. Those early cases involved contract law, and they held that contracts executed with the purpose of evading the revenue laws of other nations were enforceable, notwithstanding the rule against enforcing contracts with illegal purposes. See *Boucher v. Lawson,* Cas. T. Hard. 85, 89-90, 95 Eng. Rep. 53, 55-56 (K.B.1734); *Planche v. Fletcher,* 1 Dougl. 251, 99 Eng. Rep. 164 (K.B.1779). Petitioners argue that these cases demonstrate that "indirect" enforcement of revenue laws is at the very core of the common-law revenue rule, rather than at its margins.

The argument is unavailing. By the mid-20th century, the revenue rule had developed into a doctrine very different from its original form. Early revenue rule cases were driven by the interest in lessening the commercial disruption caused by the high tariffs of the day. As Lord Hardwicke explained, if contracts that aimed at circumventing foreign revenue laws were unenforceable, "it would cut off all benefit of such trade from this kingdom, which would be of very bad consequence to the principal and most beneficial branches of our trade." *Boucher, supra,* at 89, 95 Eng. Rep., at 56. By the 20th century, however, that rationale for the revenue rule had been supplanted. By then, as we have explained, courts had begun to apply the revenue rule to tax obligations on the strength of the analogy between a country's revenue laws and its penal ones, superseding the original promotion-of-commerce rationale for the rule. Dodge, Breaking the Public Law Taboo, 43 Harv. Int'l L.J. 161, 178 (2002); . . . . The early English cases rest on a far different foundation from that on which the revenue rule came to rest. They thus say little about whether the wire fraud statute derogated from the revenue rule in its mid-20th-century form.

3

Granted, this criminal prosecution "enforces" Canadian revenue law in an attenuated sense, but not in a sense that clearly would contravene the revenue rule. From its earliest days, the revenue rule never proscribed all enforcement of foreign revenue law. For example, at the same time they were enforcing domestic contracts that had the purpose of violating foreign revenue law, English courts also considered void foreign contracts that lacked tax stamps required under foreign revenue law. See *Alves v. Hodgson*, 7 T.R. 241, 243, 101 Eng. Rep. 953, 955 (K.B.1797); *Clegg v. Levy*, 3 Camp. 166, 167, 170 Eng. Rep. 1343 (N.P. 1812). Like the present prosecution, cases voiding foreign contracts under foreign law no doubt "enforced" foreign revenue law in the sense that they encouraged the payment of foreign taxes; yet they fell outside the revenue rule's scope. The line the revenue rule draws between impermissible and permissible "enforcement" of foreign revenue law has therefore always been unclear.

The uncertainty persisted in American courts that recognized the revenue rule. In one of the earliest appearances of the revenue rule in America, the Supreme Court of New Hampshire entertained an action that required extensive recognition of a sister State's revenue laws. *Henry v. Sargeant*, 13 N.H. 321 (1843). There, the plaintiff sought damages, alleging that a Vermont selectman had imposed an illegal tax on him. The court found that the revenue rule did not bar the action, though the suit required the court to enforce the revenue laws of Vermont.

Likewise, in *In re Hollins*, [citation omitted], the court held that an estate executor could satisfy foreign taxes due on a decedent's estate out of property of the estate, notwithstanding a legatee's argument that the revenue rule barred authorizing such payments. The court explained:

> "While it is doubtless true that this court will not aid a foreign country in the enforcement of its revenue laws, it will not refuse to direct a just and equitable administration of that part of an estate within its jurisdiction merely because such direction would result in the enforcement of such revenue laws."

These cases demonstrate that the extent to which the revenue rule barred indirect recognition of foreign revenue laws was unsettled as of 1952. Following the reasoning of *In re Hollins*, for instance, Congress might well have thought that courts would enforce the wire fraud statute, even if doing so might incidentally recognize Canadian revenue law. The uncertainty highlights that "[i]ndirect enforcement is ... easier to describe than to define," and "it is sometimes difficult to draw the line between an issue involving merely recognition of a foreign law and indirect enforcement of it." 1 A. Dicey & J. Morris, Conflict of Laws 90 (L. Collins gen. ed. 13th ed.2000). Even if the present prosecution is analogous to the indirect enforcement cases on which petitioners rely, those cases do not yield a rule sufficiently well established to narrow the wire fraud statute in the context of this criminal prosecution.

B

Having concluded that revenue rule jurisprudence is no clear bar to this prosecution, we next turn to whether the purposes of the revenue rule, as articulated in the relevant authorities, suggest differently. They do not.

First, this prosecution poses little risk of causing the principal evil against which the revenue rule was traditionally thought to guard: judicial evaluation of the policy-laden enactments of other sovereigns. See, *e.g., Moore v. Mitchell,* 30 F.2d 600, 604 (2d Cir 1929) (L.Hand, J., concurring). As Judge Hand put it, allowing courts to enforce another country's revenue laws was thought to be a delicate inquiry

> "when it concerns the relations between the foreign state and its own citizens .... To pass upon the provisions for the public order of another state is, or at any rate should be, beyond the powers of a court; it involves the relations between the states themselves, with which courts are incompetent to deal, and which are intrusted to other authorities." *Ibid.*

The present prosecution creates little risk of causing international friction through judicial evaluation of the policies of foreign sovereigns. This action was brought by the Executive to enforce a statute passed by Congress. In our system of government, the Executive is "the sole organ of the federal government in the field of international relations," and has ample authority and competence to manage "the relations between the foreign state and its own citizens" and to avoid "embarass[ing] its neighbor[s]," *Moore, supra,* at 604 (L.Hand, J., concurring). True, a prosecution like this one requires a court to recognize foreign law to determine whether the defendant violated U. S. law. But we may assume that by electing to bring this prosecution, the Executive has assessed this prosecution's impact on this Nation's relationship with Canada, and concluded that it poses little danger of causing international friction. We know of no common-law court that has applied the revenue rule to bar an action accompanied by such a safeguard, and neither petitioners nor the dissent directs us to any. The greater danger, in fact, would lie in our judging this prosecution barred based on the foreign policy concerns animating the revenue rule, concerns that we have "neither aptitude, facilities nor responsibility" to evaluate. *Ibid.*

More broadly, petitioners argue that the revenue rule avoids giving domestic effect to politically sensitive and controversial policy decisions embodied in foreign revenue laws, regardless of whether courts need pass judgment on such laws. See *Banco Nacional de Cuba v. Sabbatino,* 376 U.S. 398, 448, 84 S.Ct. 923, 11 L.Ed.2d 804 (1964) (White, J., dissenting) ("[C]ourts customarily refuse to enforce the revenue and penal laws of a foreign state, since no country has an obligation to further the governmental interests of a foreign sovereign"). This worries us little here. The present prosecution, if authorized by the wire fraud statute, embodies the policy choice of the two political branches of our Government-Congress and the Executive-to free the interstate wires from fraudulent use, irrespective of the object of the fraud. Such a reading of the wire fraud statute gives effect to that considered policy choice. It therefore poses no risk of advancing the policies of Canada illegitimately.

Still a final revenue rule rationale petitioners urge is the concern that courts lack the competence to examine the validity of unfamiliar foreign tax schemes. See, *e.g.,* Leflar 218. Foreign law, of course, posed no unmanageable complexity in this case. The District Court had before it uncontroverted testimony of a Government witness that petitioners' scheme aimed at violating Canadian tax law.

It is so ordered.

FINAL NOTE

The cases in this Chapter go a long way toward shaping the way courts will act in revenue law recognition cases. The Revenue Rule is not what it once was, but it is still affecting international custom, national law, and the interpretation of those laws. A good understanding (if that is possible) of the development and modern analog of the Revenue Rule is necessary to further study of law and international business.

It ought not surprise anyone that there are other areas of law where the Revenue Rule has founds application. As we have already seen, if a foreign law is characterized as *politici juris,* i.e. "public laws", Mansfield's rule has potential application in areas beyond the field of taxation and into the field of business regulation. (One definition - offered by Prof Andreas Lowenfeld to the class I took in law school - is that "public law" is "the kind of law other countries don't want to enforce").

Business regulation takes many forms. The effectiveness of one nation's attempt to regulate international business is likely to depend on the level of recognition will be given by other countries to that regulatory scheme. Even when the regulatory schemes are the same- like the tax laws in *Government of India v. Taylor* - a clash of sovereigns is certainly possible.

Since every country regulates (just as every country taxes), it might be expected that the lessons learned in this chapter can be applied to areas of law like employment law, securities law, environmental law, and competition law, i.e. antitrust law.

Unfortunately, the answers to these problems, and these clashes of policy, will not come easily. The next chapter explores one such set of problems - antitrust law - in depth.

MULTIPLE CHOICE REVIEW QUESTIONS

1. Lord Mansfield's "Revenue Rule"

    a. derives from a rule previously applicable to penal laws

    b. dates from a time when "smuggling and freedom ganged together"

    c. involved the question of how a French court would view an English law regulating, i.e taxing, English commerce

    d. all of the above

2. The Law Lords' decision in *Government of India v. Taylor*:

    a. was based on the validity of the system of Indian taxation

    b. was based on the observation by Lord Somervell that tax gathering is an "administrative act"

    c. is best understood in terms of assigning the question of recognition to the appropriate branch of government

    d. All of the above

3. The result in *Regazzoni*:

    a. is a reflection of the continued influence of Lord Mansfield

    b. was based on principles of comity

    c. would have been the same regardless of whether the Indian law was "against morals"

    d. is consistent with the policies that underlay *Boucher v. Lawson*

4. When the New York Court of Appeals (in *Banco Frances e Brasilero v. John Doe*) wrote that "the modern analog of the revenue rule is justifiable neither precedentially or analytically", it was:

    a. referring to the decision in *Government of India v. Taylor*

    b. reversing its holding in *Banco do Brasil v. Israel*

    c. adopting an approach based on comity

    d. basing its decision wholly on the Treaty at Bretton Woods

5. In *Pasquantino*, the U.S. was:

   a. applying the revenue rule

   b. assisting the Canadian Government in collecting its taxes

   c. applying principles of comity

   d. applying US law to US conduct

IDEAS FOR RESEARCH AND FURTHER LEARNING

1. What types of tax treaties has the U.S. entered into? How many such treaties are there? What are the issues when such treaties are negotiated?

2. The revenue rule's origins in penal law have led to the existence of the concept of extradition? What are the issues associated with extradition? What treaties exist? Aside from cases involving murderers and terrorists, what are some interesting historical incidents involving extradition for economic crimes? For tax evasion?

3. The Earl of Mansfield, born William Murray, was part of a long line of great English jurists. Read about some others, such as Glanvil, Bracton, Hale, Coke, Pound and Blackstone. Can you identify the influence of these judges on law today?

4. The (English) Commonwealth of Nations is mentioned in several of the cases. What is it? Why was it created, and what is its status today? How does it differ from the European Union, NAFTA, or the Russian Federation?

CHAPTER 6

Jurisdiction to Prescribe - The Antitrust Example

Having viewed the development of law in the area of penal and revenue laws, we turn to a related area: regulation of business. As was suggested toward the end of the last chapter, the existence of the "revenue rule" was to infect this area of law as well.

Legal regulation of business conduct cuts across a wide variety of subjects, and includes (a) laws governing employment and labor; (b) laws affecting the issuance of and transactions in securities, such as stocks and bonds; and (c) environmental issues. There can be no doubt that most laws of this type are public laws (*politici juris*), because in making and trying to enforce such laws, the nation so acting is expressing its own public policy about the way business may (or must) behave.

In these three areas of law, it is not unusual to encounter the occasional case or dispute which raises issues concerning the applicability of the laws of one nation to activities that take place outside that nations borders. But there is one area of "economic law" where these disputes seem to erupt with greater frequency and vitriol, and where interesting lessons can be learned about the choice of law issue in the area of public law. That area is "antitrust law", what the Europeans call "competition law".

Over the last century, there have been a significant number of cases involving attempts by the United States to apply its antitrust laws to conduct occurring outside its borders. Some of these cases have been private law suits, others governmental prosecutions. In some instances, the cases have resulted in law suits outside the United States seeking to flout U.S. law; in others, there has been significant diplomatic fallout. We will look at several such cases and incidents in this Chapter.

AN ANTITRUST PRIMER

The United States first enacted antitrust legislation in 1889 in the form of the Sherman Act. While there have been other antitrust statutes passed since that time, the Sherman Act remains the central focus of the law. The main part Sherman Act consists of two sentences: the first (section 1) makes illegal "contracts, combinations and conspiracies in restraint of trade" and the second (section 2) prohibits "monopolization and attempts to monopolize". In economic terms, section 1 prohibits cartel-like behavior; section 2 is directed at anticompetitive use or acquisition of monopoly power. These laws have become central tenets of our legal and socio-economic system, having been described, by various U.S. courts at various times as the "magna carta of free enterprise".

Over the course of its history, U.S. antitrust enforcement has waxed and waned with the political forces of populism vs. pro-business conservatism. Even with these fluctuations in governmental policy and enforcement, U.S. antitrust law has, until the recent advent of strong competition policy in the European Union, been more vigorous and pro-active than the laws of other countries, especially England and Japan. While many of these countries (including Japan) have an antitrust law, it is rarely enforced with the vigor that such laws are enforced in the United States.

I. APPLICATION OF THE U.S. ANTITRUST LAWS TO CONDUCT TAKING PLACE ABROAD; "TERRITORIAILITY" v. THE "EFFECTS" DOCTRINE

One of the first cases involving antitrust law as applied to conduct taking place outside the U.S. was <u>American Banana v. United Fruit</u>. In that case, the upstart American Banana sued the giant United Fruit Co. in a U.S. court alleging that United Fruit had conspired with others in Costa Rica and Panama to prevent American Banana from gaining a toehold into the business of importing tropical fruits into the U.S.

The United States Supreme Court ruled that the case should be dismissed because U.S. law is "territorial", <u>i.e.</u> it does not apply outside our territory. The now-famous opinion was penned by Oliver Wendell Holmes, the legendary U.S. jurist. The following is the key excerpt from his opinion:

> . . . No doubt in regions subject to no sovereign, like the high seas, or to no law that civilized countries would recognize as adequate, such countries may treat some relations between their citizens as governed by their own law, . . . But the general and almost universal rule is that the character of an act as lawful must be determined wholly by the law

of the country where the act is done. . . . For another jurisdiction, if it should happen to lay hold of the actor, to treat him according to its own notions rather than those of the place where he did the acts, not only would be unjust, but would be an interference with the authority of another sovereign, contrary to the comity of nations, which the other state concerned might justly resent. . . .

American Banana Co. v. United Fruit Co., 213 U.S. 347, 29 S. Ct. 51, 53 L. Ed. 826 (1909).

Holmes' decision seems rooted in Holman v. Johnson and the revenue rule, since he states that "the character of an act as lawful must be determined wholly by the law of the country where the act is done." Holmes, however, also considers the concept of comity, but his view of comity is somewhat different from that we saw in cases like Reggazoni and Banco Frances e Brasiliero v. John Doe. According to Holmes, if another jurisdiction (here, the U.S.) "should happen to lay hold of the actor" (what does that mean?), it would be "unjust" for that country to apply its own laws, rather than the law of the place where the acts were done. Why is that? To what injustice does Holmes refer?

Injustice aside, Holmes tells us that application of U.S. law in this instance "would [also] be an interference with the authority of another sovereign, contrary to the comity of nations, which the other state concerned might justly resent." What does he mean by that? Did that view figure in the "revenue rule"? Would Costa Rica really think it intrusive if a U.S. court applied U.S. law to a U.S. company, even as to conduct which occurred in Costa Rica? How about to Costa Rican company acting in the U.S.? How about to a Costa Rican company acting in Costa Rica in a way which affects the United States' economy?

The law articulated by Holmes would not remain the law of the United States for long. Within just a few years, in United States v. Sisal Sales Corp., the Supreme Court distanced itself from American Banana, although it did not reverse the earlier case. In Sisal, the Supreme Court found that the illegal agreement had been made in the United States amongst U.S. nationals, and was intended to control both "internal and external" trade. The actual illegal conduct, however, took place abroad, implicating the rule of American Banana. The Court in Sisal did not say that such a violation could exist "regardless of where the parties acted" - for that proposition, the law would have to wait a few more years, as the next case demonstrates.

UNITED STATES
v.
ALUMINUM CO. OF AMERICA [ALCOA]

148 F.2d 416 (2d Cir. 1945)

HAND, J.

This appeal comes to us by virtue of a certificate of the Supreme Court, under the amendment of 1944 to §29 of 15 U.S.C.A. The action was brought under §4 of that title, praying the district court to adjudge that the defendant, Aluminum Company of America, was monopolizing interstate and foreign commerce, particularly in the manufacture and sale of "virgin" aluminum ingot, and that it be dissolved; and further to adjudge that that company and the defendant, Aluminum Limited, had entered into a conspiracy in restraint of such commerce. . . .

At the date of judgment there were fifty-one defendants who had been served and against whom the action was pending. We may divide these, as the district judge did, into four classes: Aluminum Company of America, with its wholly owned subsidiaries, directors, officers and shareholders. (For convenience we shall speak of these defendants collectively as "Alcoa," that being the name by which the company has become almost universally known.) Next, Aluminum Limited, with its directors, officers and shareholders. (For the same reason we shall speak of this group as "Limited" [this was a Canadian firm].) . . .

...We conclude that "Alcoa" was not a party, to the "Alliance," and did not joint in any violation of §l of the Act, so far as concerned foreign commerce.

Whether "Limited" itself violated that section depends upon the character of the "Alliance." It was a Swiss corporation, created in pursuance of an agreement entered into on July 3, 1931, the signatories to which were a French corporation, two German, one Swiss, a British, and "Limited." The original agreement, or "cartel," provided for the formation of a corporation in Switzerland which should issue shares, to be taken up by the signatories. This corporation was from time to time to fix a quota of production for each share, and each shareholder was to be limited to the quantity measured by the number of shares it held, but was free to sell at any price it chose. The corporation fixed a price every year at which it would take off any shareholder's hands any part of its quota which it did not sell. No shareholder was to "buy, borrow, fabricate or sell" aluminum produced by anyone not a shareholder except with the consent of the board of governors, but that must not be "unreasonably withheld." Nothing was said as to whether the arrangement extended to sales in the United States; but Article X, known as the "Conversion Clause," provided that any shareholder might exceed his quota to the extent that he converted into aluminum in the United States or Canada any ores delivered to him in either of those countries by persons situated in the United States. This was confessedly put in to allow "Limited" to receive bauxite or alumina from "Alcoa," to smelt it into aluminum and to deliver the aluminum to "Alcoa." . . .

The agreement of 1936 abandoned the system of unconditional quotas, and substituted a system of royalties. Each shareholder was to have a fixed free quota for every share it held, but as its production exceeded the sum of its quotas, it was to pay a royalty, graduated progressively in proportion to the excess; and these royalties the "Alliance" divided among the shareholders in proportion to their shares. . . . Although this agreement, like its predecessor, was silent as to imports into the United States, when that question arose during its preparation, as it did, all the shareholders agreed that such imports should be included in the quotas. The German companies were exempted from royalties-for obvious reasons-and that, it would seem, for practical purposes put them out of the "cartel" for the future, for it was scarcely possible that a German producer would be unable to dispose of all its production, at least within any future period that would be provided for. The shareholders continued this agreement unchanged until the end of March, 1938, by which time it had become plain that, at least for the time being, it was no longer of service to anyone. Nothing was, however, done to end it, although the German shareholders of course became enemies of the French, British and Canadian shareholders in 1939. The "Alliance" itself has apparently never been dissolved; and indeed it appeared on the "Proclaimed List of Blocked Nationals" of September 13, 1944.

Did either the agreement of 1931 or that of 1936 violate §l of the Act? The answer does not depend upon whether we shall recognize as a source of liability a liability imposed by another state. On the contrary we are concerned only with whether Congress chose to attach liability to the conduct outside the United States of persons not in allegiance to it. That being so, the only question open is whether Congress intended to impose the liability, and whether our own Constitution permitted it to do so: as a court of the United State§, we cannot look beyond our own law. Nevertheless, it is quite true that we are not to read general words, such as those in this Act, without regard to the limitations customarily observed by nations upon the exercise of their powers; limitations which generally correspond to those fixed by the "Conflict of Laws." We should not impute to Congress an intent to punish all whom its courts can catch, for conduct which has no consequences within the United States. American Banana Co. v. United Fruit Co., 213 U.S. 347, 357, 29 S. Ct. 51 1, 53 L. Ed. 826, 16 Ann. Cas. 1047; ... On the other hand, it is settled law -as "Limited" itself agrees-that any state may impose liabilities, even upon persons not within its allegiance, for conduct outside its borders that has consequences within its borders which the state reprehends; and these liabilities other states will ordinarily recognize. . . .

Two situations are possible. There may be agreements made beyond our borders not intended to affect imports, which do affect them, or which affect exports. Almost any limitation of the supply of goods in Europe, for example, or in South America, may have repercussions in the United States if there is trade between the two. Yet when one considers the international complications likely to arise from an effort in this country to treat such agreements as unlawful, it is safe to assume that Congress certainly did not intend the Act to cover them. Such agreements may on the other hand intend to include imports into the United States, and yet it may appear that they have had no effect upon them. That situation might be thought to fall within the doctrine that intent may be a substitute for performance in the case of a contract made within the United States; or it might be thought to fall within the doctrine that a statute should not be interpreted to cover acts abroad which have no consequence here. We shall not choose between these alternatives; but for argument we shall assume that the Act does not cover agreements, even though intended to affect imports or exports, unless its performance is shown actually to have had some effect upon them. Where both conditions are satisfied, the situation certainly falls within such decisions as United States v. Pacific & Artic R. & Navigation Co., 228 U.S. 87, 33 S. Ct. 443, 57 L. Ed. 742; Thomsen v. Cayser, 243 U.S. 66, 37 S. Ct. 353, 61 L. Ed. 597, Ann. Cas. 1917D, 322 and United States v. Sisal Sales Corporation, 274 U.S. 268, 47 S. Ct. 592, 71 L. Ed. 1042. . . .

Both agreements would clearly have been unlawful, had they been made within the United States; and it follows from what we have just said that both were unlawful, though made abroad, if they were intended to affect imports and did affect them. . . .

. . . We shall dispose of the matter therefore upon the assumption that, although the shareholders intended to restrict imports, it does not appear whether in fact they did so. Upon our hypothesis the plaintiff would therefore fail, if it carried the burden of proof upon this issue as upon others. We think, however, that, after the intent to affect imports was proved, the burden of proof shifted to "Limited." In the first place a depressant upon production which applies generally may be assumed, ceteris paribus, to distribute its effect evenly upon all markets. Again, when the parties took the trouble specifically to make the depressant apply to a given market, there is reason to suppose that then, expected that it would have some effect, which it could have only by lessening what would otherwise have been imported. If the motive they introduced was overbalanced in all instances by motives which induced the shareholders to import, if the United States market became so attractive that the royalties did not count at all and their expectations were in fact defeated, they to whom the facts were more accessible than to the plaintiff ought to prove it, for a prima facie case had been made. Moreover, there is an especial propriety in demanding this of "Limited," because it was "Limited" which procured the inclusion in the agreement of 1936 of imports in the quotas.

There remains only the question whether this assumed restriction had any influence upon prices. [citation omitted] To that Socony-Vacuum Oil Co. v. United States, 310 U.S. 150, 60 S. Ct. 811, 84 L. Ed. 129, is an entire answer. It will be remembered that, when the defendants in that case protested that the prosecution had not proved that the "distress" gasoline had affected prices, the court answered that that was not necessary, because an agreement to withdraw any substantial part of the supply from a market would, if carried out, have some effect upon prices, and was as unlawful as an agreement expressly to fix prices. The underlying doctrine was that all factors which contribute to determine prices, must be kept free to operate unhampered by agreements. For these reasons we think that the agreement of 1936 violated § I of the Act. . . .

NOTES AND QUESTIONS

1. The <u>ALCOA</u> case is famous in U.S. antitrust law for several reasons in the domestic antitrust arena, but we deal here with the portion of the decision addressing the conduct of a foreign defendant, Aluminum Limited, which was Canadian. While Limited was at one time a subsidiary of ALCOA, by the time of the events complained of, Limited had become a separate company. Limited, which had offices in the U.S. (and thus was exposed to our "judicial jurisdiction"), was charged membership in the Alliance, an international cartel which controlled a portion of the trade in Aluminum.

    A. Judge Hand begins his analysis by asking whether there has been a violation of the Sherman Act. "The answer," he says, "does not depend upon whether we shall recognize as a source of liability a liability imposed by another state." What does he mean by that? Is he casting aside comity altogether? Or is he merely saying that this is an issue of U.S., not Canadian, law? Is that what he is saying when he writes "[a]s a court of the United States, we cannot look beyond our own law"? Is that sentence in any way rooted in the "revenue rule"?

    B. Hand responds to his own query by stating that "[t]he only question open is whether Congress intended to impose the liability." Can that be so? What about Justice Holmes' warning that any attempt to apply the Sherman Act to conduct taking place abroad would violate principles of comity, be unjust, and might cause resentment on the part of the country where the act occurred? Aren't the things on Holmes' list valid areas to be concerned about? Is Hand disagreeing with Holmes, or is he simply saying that these concerns are just not within the province of the judiciary? Isn't that, after all,

345

the point Hand was making in <u>Moore v. Mitchell</u> (the U.S. case cited by Lord Keith in <u>Government of India v. Taylor</u>)? Even that observation, however, is of little utility, since be does go on to say that such considerations can go into the analysis extent that the judiciary is charged with interpretting legislative intent, when he writes: "We are [nevertheless] not to read general words, such as those in this Act, without regard to the limitations customarily observed by nations upon the exercise of their powers". Put another way, is Hand saying that the comity question lies, in the first instance, with the lawmakers in Congress, and then, with the courts?

2.   Having described the judicial role as being restricted to the task of interpreting Congressional intent, Judge Hand nevertheless demonstrates that the judiciary nevertheless wields some latitude in matters of this kind:

> "Nevertheless, it is quite true that we are not to read general words, such as those in this Act, without regard to the limitations customarily observed by nations upon the exercise of their powers; limitations which generally correspond to those fixed by the "Conflict of Laws." We should not impute to Congress an intent to punish all whom its courts can catch, for conduct which has no consequences within the United States. [citing <u>American Banana</u>]. On the other hand, it is settled law -as "Limited" itself agrees - that any state may impose liabilities, even upon persons not within its allegiance, for conduct outside its borders that has consequences within its borders which the state reprehends; and these liabilities other states will ordinarily recognize. . . ."

A.   This paragraph, much reviled in Britain and other parts of the world for its seeming arrogance, forms the basis for an important American doctrine associated with jurisdiction to prescribe. It is called the "effects doctrine", and it owes it birth to Judge Learned Hand.

B.   How is it that this key passage, which starts out humbly - referring to "limitations customarily observed by nations upon the exercise of their powers," and contains a warning that "we should not impute to Congress an intent to punish all whom its courts can catch" - became a lightning rod against imperialistic U.S. assertions of "extraterritorial jurisdiction"?

C.   This criticism exists because foreign courts have focused on Hand's next sentence - that "it is settled law . . . that any state may impose liabilities, even upon persons not within its allegiance, for conduct outside its borders that has consequences within its borders which the state reprehends; and these liabilities other states will ordinarily recognize. . . ." Do you think it is "settled law"? Or is it like beginning a sentence "with all due respect"?

3.   Obviously, Learned Hand's view of the world is markedly different from that of Justice Holmes. Holmes' theory of "territoriality" is at polar extremes with Hand's "effects" test.

   A.   Again, what about Holmes' warning that other states will resent the intrusion caused by Hand's approach? Hand seems to take for granted the other country's compliance with U.S. will. Have things changed so much by 1945? Perhaps things have not yet changed, but Hand is ahead of his time, anticipating cases like Reggazzoni and Banco Frances e Brasiliero v. John Doe, where one country recognized another country's public laws. Or perhaps these things will not change as much as Hand and the U.S. would like them to.

   B.   Does it bother you that, 36 years earlier, the U.S. declined to apply its law to U.S. citizens acting abroad, yet in 1945, that same law would be applied to a foreign citizen acting outside the United States? Isn't the case for comity even stronger here than in American Banana? Why isn't comity extended? It is, after all, presumably not a one-way street.

   C.   What does Hand mean by not imputing to Congress "an intent to punish all whom our courts can catch"? Is he referring to jurisdiction to prescribe, or jurisdiction to adjudicate? If he is referring to the latter, has Hand helped you to understand the relationship between these subjects?

4.   As suggested at the outset, Learned Hand's "effects doctrine" was the subject of a great deal of criticism abroad. But in the United States, the decision was viewed as a logical (if bold) extension of Sisal, and a sign (from a leading American jurist sitting in an especially important case) that the approach of American Banana was dead. The repercusions of that death, and the ascendency of the effects doctrine in the U.S. would be felt very profoundly in the next case, which is in fact a series of cases growing out of an attempt, by a U.S. court, to apply the effects doctrine. The results are amusing, if not enlightening.

II. A CONFLICT OF THE LAWS?

UNITED STATES
v.
IMPERIAL CHEMICAL INDUSTRIES, LTD.

105 F. Supp. 215 (S.D.N.Y. 1952)

RYAN, J.

. . .

We have found that the patents and processes agreements "did, in operation, result in restraints of United States trade." DuPont agreed to restrict its use of United States patents by undertaking not to ship products manufactured under these patents to the territory assigned exclusively to ICI. To make this restriction effective, duPont was also required to impose like limitations on the shipments of anyone whom it might license under its United States patents. Insofar as shipments to Great Britain were concerned, the restrictions imposed by agreement were further implemented by the granting to ICI of exclusive licenses under the British counterparts of the United States patents. Thus, the exclusionary right under the British patents was applied against imports from the United States, and the basic understanding by which ICI recognized the United States as the exclusive territory of duPont was in turn observed by the granting of an exclusive license to duPont in the United States. This kept the patented products manufactured in the United States out of the market of Great Britain, and the like products manufactured in Great Britain out of the United States.

The agreement between ICI and duPont also brought about a situation by which the United States patents of both were placed in the hands of duPont. This was a pooling of patents for a purpose in restraint of foreign trade. This use of patent rights was condemned in United States v. Line Material Co., 1948, 333 U.S. 287, 3117 68 S. Ct. 550, 92 L. Ed. 701, when employed as a means to effect price fixing arrangements. Line Material was, like the instant suit, brought under Section I and neither monopoly nor domination was charged. We have held that when patents are pooled to carry out a division of territories, it is equally as unlawful as when they are unified to effect price fixing.

The remedy of compulsory licensing is not to be restricted to monopoly situations. An effect of compulsory licensing is to grant to the public a right to use the patented invention and thus remove an impediment to competition. The wrong it is designed to correct arises from the misuse of lawful patent rights pursuant to an unlawful agreement. Such misuse creates an extension of the patent monopoly. Here, we have had proof of a wrong-unlawful restraints on our trade-accomplished by agreement between ICI and duPont. It was made possible of performance by the voluntary abstention from trade by one in the exclusive territory of the other, and the restrictive provisions **in** patent licenses and in technology exchanged. We may hope to compel an abandonment of limitations in the exchange of patents and technology which are used to violate the anti-trust laws only by decreeing that ICI and duPont grant to all others what they have heretofore granted to each other. It may be that the decree will permit them to make better and more profitable terms for the additional grants than they have heretofore demanded *inter sese*. . . .

. . . We are also concerned with increasing the possibility of competition between ICI, duPont and others who might desire to enter the field. The unquestionable right of ICI to determine whether or not it will manufacture under its American patents, to select its licenses, and to determine whether licenses granted shall be exclusive or non-exclusive, has been exercised to implement the allotment of territories. Compulsory licensing will be a cure and not a punishment for this.

It has been contended on duPont's behalf that compulsory licensing should not be decreed because it would not "cause duPont to export and would not affect in any way the result of past failure on the part of duPont to export." Perhaps this is so, and it leads us to observe that neither would a simple injunctive provision in the decree produce this result. But compulsory licensing will enable others to manufacture and put them in a position where they will be able to export. The application of this remedy might serve as an impetus to a sincere desire on duPont's part to enter the export field on an active and competitive basis.

The provisions for fixation of reasonable royalties will follow substantially the provisions in anti-trust suits in which similar relief has been decreed. . . . The royalties are to be determined by the court, when agreement has not been privately reached, on petition from the applicant and on proof submitted by the applicant and the defendant involved.

The Government does not seek a decree directing ICI to grant compulsory licenses of its British patents. The Government requests that ICI be required to grant immunity under its foreign patents which correspond to the United States patents which we have made subject to compulsory licensing. . . . We have had testimony offered on behalf of ICI by an expert in British law that a provision for granting immunities is contrary to British public policy and that a British court will not enforce such a provision in the judgment of a court of a foreign jurisdiction. As to this, we observe that, acting on the basis of our jurisdiction in personam, we are merely directing ICI to refrain from asserting rights which it may have in Britain, since the enforcement of those rights will serve to continue the effects of wrongful acts it has committed within the United States affecting the foreign trade of the United States.

We are not unmindful that under British law there are restrictions upon exports from the United States by reason of the existence of the British patents owned by ICI. The exclusion of unlicensed imports and the prohibition of unlicensed sales is enforceable because of the legal rights which attach to a British patent.

We accept as correct the statements in the brief of ICI that: "Under United States law if a product is patented, sale into the United States of that product constitutes clear infringement of the rights of the American patentee. Such sale will therefore subject the vendor to a suit for infringement even though his acquisition of the patented article abroad (and his use and sale of it there) may be wholly lawful. Boesch v. Graff, 1890, 133 U.S. 697, 1 0 S. Ct. 378, 33 L. Ed. 787. This is true even though the vendor may hold the foreign patent on the article in question....

We accept as correct the statements in the brief of ICI:

> In the British Empire the law is even more stringent. The owner of a British patent may bar the importation of any product patented in Great Britain and also any product made by any process where the process is patented under British law. It is clear that a patent on a process essential to the production of a product is infringed by sale of an imported product made abroad by that process. Von Heyden v. Neustadt, 1880, 14 Ch. D. 230; United Horse Nail Co. v. Stewart and Co., 1885, 2 R.P.C. 122, 133-134; Saccharin Corp., Ltd. v. AngloContinental Chemical Works, Ltd., 1900, 17 R.P.C. 307, 318-319; Terrell, The Law and Practice Relating to Letters Patent for Inventions (London, 1934), pp. 1 73-177.

> There is no requirement under American law which required duPont to license ICI under its United States patents or ICI to license duPont under its British patents. To the extent that each retained the right under the laws of its respective country to assert patents against imports, this resulted in no limitation upon such imports which in any way exceeded the limitation that would have existed had there been no agreement at all.

But as we have heretofore observed these lawful rights were employed as means to accomplish the unlawful purpose of their underlying agreement.

While it is true that these rights exist independent of any provision in the patents and processes agreements, they were granted to ICI by the disclosure or assignment of inventions by duPont pursuant to the terms of these agreements. Inventions were also licensed by ICI to duPont for its exclusive use and exploitation in the United States in accordance with the agreements. In the first instance the patents were employed to restrain duPont's exports to Great Britain, in plain violation of American anti-trust laws; in the second instance, the patents were used as a means to prevent ICI exports to the United States and placed a restraint upon the foreign trade of Great Britain, in violation of her declared policy, if not her laws. It does not seem presumptuous for this court to make a direction to a foreign defendant-corporation over which it has jurisdiction to take steps to remedy and correct a situation, which is unlawful both here and in the foreign jurisdiction in which it is domiciled. Two evils have resulted from the one understanding of ICI and duPont-restraints upon the foreign trade and commerce of the United States as well as on that of Great Britain. It is not an intrusion on the authority of a foreign sovereign for this court to direct that steps be taken to remove the harmful effects on the trade of the United States.

We recognize that substantial legal questions may be raised with respect to our power to decree as to duPont's foreign patents as well as those issued to ICI. Here, we deal with the regulation of the exercise of rights granted by a foreign sovereign to a domestic corporate defendant and to a foreign corporate defendant. Our power so to regulate is limited and depends upon jurisdiction *in personam;* the effectiveness of the exercise of that power depends upon the recognition which will be given to our judgment as a matter of comity by the courts of the foreign sovereign which has granted the patents in question.

Where we have required ICI to grant immunity under British patents which are the counterpart of duPont's United States patents, the payment of reasonable royalty upon imports of articles manufactured under them into Great Britain shall be paid to ICI.

Full recognition is hereby given to the inherent property rights granted by the British patent to exclude from Great Britain merchandise covered by the patent. Since a license under the corresponding United States patent conveys no right to ship into Great Britain articles manufactured in the United States under the patent, no royalty shall be collectible by duPont upon such items as are destined for export to Great Britain. . . .

The history of the basic British nylon patents reveals a studied and continued purpose on the part of ICI and duPont to remove these patents from within the scope of any decree which might ultimately be made by this court.... These British patents were issued to duPont. By the agreement of March 30, 1939, ICI received an exclusive license under them; in January, 1940, ICI granted irrevocable and exclusive rights to make nylon yarn from nylon polymer (which is manufactured by ICI) to British Nylon Spinners, Ltd. (BNS). ICI has a stock interest of 50% in BNS, the remaining 50% is held by Courtaulds, Inc. BNS is in the business of manufacturing and distributing nylon yarn. Not content with this arrangement and with the deliberate purpose to "materially reduce the risk of any loss of rights" as a result of this suit . . . . duPont pursuant to the nylon agreement of 1946 assigned the basic British nylon patents to ICI. It is now urged that we may not decree with reference to these British patents so as to direct ICI to remove restrictions on imports into Great Britain of nylon polymer or nylon yarn from the United States. It is argued that the sum total of all these agreements is not to create by itself any restrictions against American imports, and that those which exist arise from the right to be free from competition which is inherent in the British patents and cannot possibly be repugnant to the American anti-trust laws.

BNS is not before this court; although they were knowing participants in acts designed to thwart the granting of full relief, we may not direct our decree to them. The lack of majority stock ownership in ICI likewise prevents control of the future acts of BNS by this means; however, we are not without some remedy still available.

Objection is raised by ICI that we are without power to decree that the British nylon patents may not be asserted to prevent the importation of nylon polymer and nylon yarn into Great Britain because BNS has rights which exist independent of those possessed by ICI. This overlooks the circumstances under which BNS acquired its rights to these patents by licenses from ICI. . . . Throughout all these negotiations it appears that BNS was advised of the dealings between ICI and duPont concerning the British nylon patents. Both ICI and duPont are parties to the instant suit; they were advised in fact and realized that the further use and control of the rights pertaining to the British nylon patents were subject to a decree of this court to be entered in this suit. We find that in fact Courtaulds and BNS were also fully advised of this situation. The first, or "manufacturing sub-license" which BNS received granted to it no greater rights than had been acquired by ICI; it was subject to the same infirmities as existed against ICI. The second license granted after the assignment of the patents to ICI did not come to BNS as an innocent party. BNS, again, knew exactly what it was receiving; its rights are wholly subject to the inherent vices of the agreements through which they were acquired. We have found them to be tainted with the illegality of the unlawful conspiracy; of this probability BNS was informed. The circumstances surrounding the execution of the assignment to ICI in December, 1946, makes this clear (Op. 198, Ex. 708). It is also recorded that on October 17, 1946, "Courtaulds appreciated the difficulty in which all parties were placed consequent upon the American litigation and were, therefore, willing to accede to a modification of the duPont/ I.C.I. Nylon License Agreement.". . . On October 28, 1946, Courtaulds undertook to "take all steps in their power to secure that British Nylon Spinners also raise no objection to the conclusion by ICI of the new agreement ....))

We do not hesitate therefore to decree that the British nylon patents may not be asserted by ICI to prevent the importation of nylon polymer and of nylon yarn into Great Britain. What credit may be given to such an injunctive provision by the courts of Great Britain in a suit brought by BNS to restrain such importations we do not venture to predict. We feel that the possibility that the English courts in an equity suit will not give effect to such a provision in our decree should not deter us from including it.

In any event it appears that BNS would have the right under Section 63 of the Patents Act of 1949, as the exclusive licensee to bring suit for infringement against an importer of yarn and staple fiber. There would then be a speedy determination of the effectiveness of the immunity provision of the decree with reference to these products. If the British courts were not to give credit to this provision, no injury would have been done; if the holding of the British courts were to the contrary, a remedy available would not have been needlessly abandoned. . . .

NOTE

Judge Ryan's opinion produced quite a reaction in the English courts, where BNS brought suit to enjoin ICI's compliance with the U.S. court's order. BNS obtained a preliminary injunction against ICI's compliance. ICI, hardly a willing participant but nevertheless feeling compelled by Judge Ryan's order (and the fact that he had judicial jurisdiction over them), appealed. The following is an excerpt of the British Court of Appeals' decision denying ICI's appeal seeking dismissal of the injunction. At a later trial on the merits, the British court ruled that ICI was bound by British law to perform its contract with BNS and not act to permit DuPont to import nylon into England. See British Nylon Spinners, Ltd. v. Imperial Chem. Indus., Ltd., [1954] All E.R. 88.

BRITISH NYLON SPINNERS, LTD.
v.
IMPERIAL CHEMICAL INDUSTRIES, LTD.

[1952] 2 A.E.R. 780

SIR RAYMOND EVERSHED, M.R.

The agreement of December 31, 1946, was an agreement whereby the defendant company acquired outright from duPont de Nemours the patents (among others) which are specified in the schedule to the order, and one of the terms of the final judgment of the district judge, was that this agreement was thereby cancelled and terminated. That, however, was not all, for in a later part of the same judgment, Imperial Chemical Industries, Ltd. (the defendant company) was forbidden to make, among other things, "and, disposition of foreign patents" (i.e., patents foreign to the United States of America and including the patents now in suit) unless it required, as a condition of the grant, that the grantee agreed in writing to hold its licence subject to certain rights of immunity, viz., the rights of American manufacturers of these nylon products freely to import and vend in the United Kingdom articles manufactured in accordance with the patents or with comparable patents. The effect of any such condition, if insisted on, would, obviously, be to derogate in a most serious way from the value of the exclusive licences which the defendant company was under contract to grant to the plaintiff company. Further, if the defendant company were to re-assign these various patents to duPont de Nemours, as directed by the judgment of the district judge, it would, in fact, disable itself altogether thenceforward from granting licences in the terms which it had contracted to grant. The present proceedings have, therefore, been brought by the plaintiff company, in effect, to enforce what it claims to be its contractual rights under the contract of March, 1947, and by way of interim relief (seeing that the ninety days specified in the order of the district judge, are about to expire) the plaintiff company seeks to restrain the defendant company from executing an assignment in obedience to that order. Upjohn, J., granted an injunction, pending the trial, restraining the defendant company from so doing.

This is an interlocutory matter, and, therefore, it is inappropriate for the court to say more about the case or its merits than is necessary to make clear the grounds of the conclusion which it reaches. It is plain from what I have said that there is here a question of what is sometimes called the comity which subsists between civilised nations. In other words, it involves the extent to which the courts of one country will pay regard and give effect to the decisions and orders of another country. I certainly should be the last to indicate any lack of respect for any decision of the district courts of the United States, but I think that in this case there is raised a somewhat serious question whether the order, in the form that it takes, does not assert an extraterritorial jurisdiction which the courts of this country cannot recognise, notwithstanding any such comity. Applied conversely, I conceive that the American courts would likewise be slow (to say the least) to recognise an assertion on the part of the British courts of jurisdiction extending, in effect, to the business affairs of persons and corporations in the United States. In a judgment which the district judge delivered in May, 1952 (the second of his opinions in the proceedings to which I have referred), it is plain that the learned judge carefully considered this matter, and, indeed, as Upjohn, J., pointed out, expressed his own doubts whether, in giving effect, as he felt it his duty to do, to the implications of the Sherman Act, he might not be going beyond the normally recognised limits of territorial jurisdiction. But he said: "It is not an intrusion on the authority of a foreign sovereign for this court to direct that steps be taken to remove the harmful effects on the trade of the United States."

If by that passage the learned judge intended to say (as it seems to me that he did) that it was not an intrusion on the authority of a foreign sovereign to make directions addressed to that foreign sovereign, or to its courts, or to nationals of that foreign power, effective to remove (as he says) "harmful effects on the trade of the United States", I am bound to say that, as at present advised, I find myself unable to agree with it. Questions affecting the trade of one country may well be matters proper to be considered by the government of another country. Tariffs are sometimes imposed by one country which obviously affect the trade of another country, and the imposition of such tariffs, as it seems to me, is a matter for the government of the particular country which imposes them. And if that observation of the learned judge were conversely applied to directions designed to remove harmful effects on the trade, say, of Great Britain or British nationals in America, I should be surprised to find that it was accepted as not being an intrusion on the rights and sovereign authority of the United States. On the other hand, there is no doubt that it is competent for the courts of a particular country, in a suit between persons who are either nationals or subjects of that country or are otherwise subject to its jurisdiction, to make orders in personam against one such party, directing it, for example, to do something or to refrain from doing something in another country affecting the other party to the action. As a general proposition, that would not be open to doubt, but the plaintiff in this case is neither a subject nor a national of the United States, nor (unlike the defendant company) was it a party to the proceedings before the district judge, nor is it otherwise subject to his jurisdiction.

What the precise relationship, commercially or otherwise, is between the plaintiff company and the defendant company we have not at this stage of the proceedings considered, and I proceed on the assumption (and I am not to be taken as hinting that the contrary is the fact) that the plaintiff is an independent trade corporation and entitled to be treated as independent of the defendant company. Being so independent, it has beyond question, according to the laws of England, certain rights, certain choses in action, by virtue of the contract of 1947, which the courts of this country, in exercise of the laws which they claim to be entitled to administer, will in this country protect and enforce. Broadly speaking, the contract of March, 1947, being an English contract, made between English nationals and to be performed in England, the right which the plaintiff company has may be described as its right, under the contract, to have it performed and, if necessary, to have an order made by the courts of this country for its specific performance. That is a right, or, in other words, a species of property (seeing, particularly, that it is related to patents) which is English in character and is subject to the jurisdiction of the English courts, and it seems to me that the plaintiff company has, at least, established a prima facie case for saying that it is not competent for the courts of the

United States, or of any other country, to interfere with those rights or to make orders, the observance of which by our courts would require that our courts should not exercise the jurisdiction which they have and which it is their duty to exercise in regard to those rights.

I think, however, that the matter goes somewhat further. I have said that the subject-matter of the contract of December, 1946, is a number of English and Commonwealth patents. An English patent is a species of English property of the nature of a chose in action and peculiar in character. By English law it confers on its proprietor certain monopoly rights, exercisable in England. A person who has an enforceable right to a licence under an English patent appears, therefore, to me to have, at least, some kind of proprietary interest which it is the duty of our courts to protect. And, certainly, so far as the English patents are concerned, it seems to me, with all deference to the judgment of the district judge, to be an assertion of an extra-territorial jurisdiction which we do not recognise for the American courts to make orders which would destroy or qualify those statutory rights belonging to an English national who is not subject to the jurisdiction of the American courts.

As regards the patents other than the English patents, viz., Australian, Indian, New Zealand, South African, Irish or other patents, a possible distinction can, of course, be drawn, since the patents in those countries are a species of property in those countries, and an effective right to use those patents would, if necessary, have to be asserted in those countries. But no special point has been made before us as regards the Australian and other non-English patents, and, for present purposes, I do not understand that it is suggested, if the injunction goes as regards the English patents, that it should not go to the full extent of the patents specified in the schedule to the order of Upjohn, J. We must, in the absence of some evidence to the contrary, assume that the law in these other countries is the same as it is here, and, apart from what I might call the particular rights quoad the particular non-English patents, there remains the general contractual right which relates to all the patents and is derived from the English contract of March, 1947.

I think it undesirable that I should say more, except to re-affirm the proposition that the courts of this country will, in the natural course, pay great respect and attention to the superior courts of the United States of America, but I conceive that it is none the less the proper province of English courts, when their jurisdiction is invoked, not to refrain from exercising that jurisdiction if they think that it is their duty so to do for the protection of rights which are peculiarly subject to their protection. In so saying, I do not conceive that I am offending in any way against the principles of comity which apply between the two countries, and, like Upjohn, J., I take some comfort from the doubts which the district judge himself entertained about the extent to which his order might go, if carried to its logical conclusion.

DENNING, L.J.

I agree. It would be a serious matter if there was a conflict between the orders of the courts of the United States and the orders of the courts of this country. The writ of the United States does not run in this country, and, if due regard is had to the comity of nations, it will not seek to run here. But, as I read this judgment of the United States court, there is a saving clause which prevents any conflict, because, although the defendant company has been ordered to do certain acts by the United States court, nevertheless there is a provision which says that nothing in the judgment shall operate against the company for action taken in complying with the law of any foreign government or instrumentality thereof to which the defendant company is for the time being subject. In view of that saving clause I hope that there will be no conflict between the orders. I agree that the appeal should be dismissed.

ROMER, L.J.: I also agree.

Appeal dismissed.

NOTE

Placed between the conflicting orders of two sovereigns, ICI petitioned in the U.S. courts for a grant of immunity under duPont's nylon patents, which would have permitted ICI to import its nylon into the U.S. In the following decision Judge Ryan denied the petition.

UNITED STATES
v.
IMPERIAL CHEMICAL INDUSTRIES, LTD. (II)

1954 Trade Cases (C.C.H.) ¶67,739

RYAN, J....

ICI moves for an order directing duPont to grant to ICI pursuant to the provisions of Article IX-4 of the judgment entered herein "an unrestricted, nonexclusive, royalty-free immunity under any existing nylon patent . . . to import into the United States of America, . . . nylon filaments and bristles ... and nylon flakes and molding powders, which shall have been lawfully manufactured outside the United States."

By Article IX-4 of the judgment, it was decreed that "to the extent they have the legal right to do so, duPont and ICI shall: ... (b) grant to any person (including ICI and duPont) making written request therefor, in consideration of a reasonable royalty, an unrestricted, non-exclusive immunity under any existing or new patent to import into the United States any common chemical product lawfully manufactured outside the United States; . . . "

DuPont has refused to grant the request of ICI for immunities on the first two groups of the nylon products so scheduled. It has predicated this refusal upon the fact that ICI, by reason of its prior assignment to BNS of British nylon patents covering nylon yarn (group 3 of the scheduled nylon products) is presently unable to grant like immunities to duPont for the importation of nylon yarn into Great Britain.

DuPont urges in support of its refusal that the immunities grant directed by Article IX-4 is intended to be reciprocal and indivisible with respect to the three groups of products flowing from the several basic nylon patents. It contends that since it has not obtained immunities from ICI on all three groups of nylon common chemical products in their entirety, it should not be directed to grant to ICI immunities on the first two groups. Its position is that the immunities contemplated by the judgment were intended to embrace "whole patents" rather than "products."

On the other hand, ICI urges that the provision for immunities was intended to apply to the separate common chemical products rather than to "whole patents" or all the products produced under a given basic patent. It contends, therefore, that it rightly requested and should receive immunities from duPont on the first two groups only, and it points out that it has made this limited request since it may grant reciprocal immunities to duPont only on these two groups. ICI argues that to interpret Article IX-4 as providing for the grant of immunities only if the recipient itself has the legal right to grant complete immunities under a particular patent (as duPont would read it), is to take all meaning from the phrase "to the extent that it has the legal right to do so."

ICI SUPPORTED BY GOVERNMENT

The Government's position is substantially in accord with that taken by ICI. The Government contends that since a purpose of the judgment was to remove obstacles to free trade between the United States and Great Britain, opportunity is here presented to encourage such trade as to some nylon products, although not as to all, and that the present disability of ICI to grant immunities with respect to one group of nylon products-yarn-only, should not result in the continuance of restrictions on United States' commerce in the nylon products embraced in the other groups. It agrees with ICI that the request now made by the latter is consistent with the provisions of Article IX-4.

PURPOSE OF JUDGMENT TO FACILITATE TRADE

A purpose of the judgment was to encourage and facilitate trade between Great Britain and the United States. The provisions of the article in question dealing with the importation and exportation of various products flowing from the several basic nylon patents were intended to accomplish this end. The grants were intended, however, to be reciprocal and to embrace immunities on patents and their use in their entirety and not on products produced under a particular patent. Unless duPont is as free to export to Great Britain as ICI is to export to the United States, the granting of royalty-free immunities to ICI to export to this country without such a corresponding grant to duPont with respect to Great Britain would not be carrying out the broad purpose of the judgment; such a result was not contemplated or intended by Article IX or any article of the judgment.

It is no answer to say that nevertheless obstacles to free trade between these two countries would be removed by the granting of immunities on some of the nylon products. This does not justify splitting up and dividing products based on the same patents-a step which would be neither just nor equitable, nor in conformity with the purpose of the Article.

It is possible, as ICI and the Government point out, that BNS may by enforcing its claim under the assignment of British nylon patents from ICI, forever foreclose ICI from granting duPont immunities on nylon yarn. Such a course of action, if pursued by BNS, would permanently bar the exchange of reciprocal immunities on all nylon products, thus limiting the coverage of the immunity provisions and narrowing the original, broad purpose of Article IX-4 of the judgment. That this regrettable situation might develop was not entirely unforeseen at the time of the drafting of these provisions of the judgment. It was with this in mind that reassignment of the British nylon patents to duPont by ICI was decreed by an *in personam* direction, revoking an assignment which it was found had been made in 1946 with a purpose on the part of both duPont and ICI, and in which BNS participated, to thwart any adverse judgment which might be entered.

IMMUNITY APPLIES TO ALL NYLON GROUPS

The fact that now ICI finds itself able, and that it is willing, to grant duPont reciprocal immunities on two groups of nylon products is without significance in view of the interpretation here given to the immunities provisions of Article IX. The broad immunity covering all nylon common chemical products under basic nylon patents in their entirety contemplated by the judgment will not now be read so as to apply to some and not all of these products. Until ICI can grant duPont complete reciprocal immunities on all three groups of nylon products, it may not require immunities to be granted by duPont on these two groups.

III. A COMPROMISE APPROACH

TIMBERLANE LUMBER CO.
v.
BANK OF AMERICA

United States Court of Appeals.
For the ninth Circuit
549 F.2d 597
Decided December 27, 1976

CHOY, Circuit Judge:

Four separate actions, arising from the same series of events, were dismissed by the same district court and are consolidated here on appeal. The principal action is Timberlane Lumber Co. v. Bank of America (Timberlane action), an antitrust suit alleging violations of sections 1 and 2 of the Sherman Act (15 U.S.C. §§ 1, 2) and the Wilson Tariff Act (15 U.S.C. § 8). This action raises important questions concerning the application of American antitrust laws to activities in another country, including actions of foreign government officials. The district court dismissed the Timberlane action under the act of state doctrine and for lack of subject matter jurisdiction. The other three are diversity tort suits brought by employees of one of the Timberlane plaintiffs for individual injuries allegedly suffered in the course of the extended anti-Timberlane drama. Having dismissed the Timberlane action, the district court dismissed these three suits on the ground of forum non conveniens. We reverse the Timberlane dismissal, vacate the dismissals in the other three cases, and remand.

I. THE TIMBERLANE ACTION

The basic allegation of the Timberlane plaintiffs is that officials of the Bank of America and others located in both the United States and Honduras conspired to prevent Timberlane, through its Honduras subsidiaries, from milling lumber in Honduras and exporting it to the United States, thus maintaining control of the Honduran lumber export business in the hands of a few select individuals financed and controlled by the Bank. The intent and result of the conspiracy, they contend, was to interfere with the exportation to the United States, including Puerto Rico, of Honduran lumber for sale or use there by the plaintiffs, thus directly and substantially affecting the foreign commerce of the United States.

* * *

Facts as Alleged

The conspiracy sketched by Timberlane actually started before the plaintiffs entered the scene. At that time, the Lima family operated a lumber mill in Honduras, competing with Lamas and Casanova, in both of which the Bank had significant financial interests. The Lima enterprise was also indebted to the Bank. By 1971, however, the Lima business was in financial trouble. Timberlane alleges that driving Lima under was the first step in the conspiracy which eventually crippled Timberlane's efforts, but the particulars do not matter for this appeal. What does matter is that various interests in the Lima assets, including its milling plant, passed to Lima's creditors: Casanova, the Bank, and the group of Lima employees who had not been paid the wages and severance pay due them. Under Honduran law, the employees' claim had priority.

Enter Timberlane, with a long history in the lumber business, in search of alternative sources of lumber for delivery to its distribution system on the East Coast of the United States. After study, it decided to try Honduras. In 1971, Danli was formed, tracts of forest land were acquired, plans for a modern log processing plant prepared, and equipment purchased and assembled for shipment from the United States to Danli in Honduras. Timberlane became aware that the Lima plant might be available and began negotiating for its acquisition. Maya was formed, purchased the Lima employees' interest in the machinery and equipment in January 1972, despite opposition from the conspirators, and re-activated the Lima mill.

Realizing that they were faced with better-financed and more-vigorous competition from Timberlane and its Honduran subsidiaries, the defendants and others extended the anti-Lima conspiracy to disrupt Timberlane's efforts. The primary weapons employed by the conspirators were the claim still held by the Bank in the remaining assets of the Lima enterprise under the all-inclusive mortgage Lima had been forced to sign and another claim held by Casanova. Maya made a substantial cash offer for the Bank's interest in an effort to clear its title, but the Bank refused to sell. Instead, the Bank surreptitiously conveyed the mortgage to Casanova for questionable consideration, Casanova paying nothing and agreeing only to pay the Bank a portion of what it collected. Casanova immediately assigned the Bank's claim and its own on similar terms to Caminals, who promptly set out to disrupt the Timberlane operation.

Caminals is characterized as the "front man" in the campaign to drive Timberlane out of Honduras, with the Bank and other defendants intending and carrying responsibility for his actions. Having acquired the claims of Casanova and the Bank, Caminals went to court to enforce them, ignoring throughout Timberlane's offers to purchase or settle them. Under the laws of Honduras, an "embargo" on property is a court-ordered attachment, registered with the Public Registry, which precludes the sale of that property without a court order. Honduran law provides, upon embargo, that the court appoint a judicial officer, called an "interventor" to ensure against any diminution in the value of the property. In order to paralyze the Timberlane operation, Caminals obtained embargoes against Maya and Danli. Acting through the interventor, since accused of being on the payroll of the Bank, guards and troops were used to cripple and, for a time, completely shut down Timberlane's milling operation. The harassment took other forms as well: the conspirators caused the manager of Timberlane's Honduras operations, Gordon Sloan Smith, to be falsely arrested and imprisoned and were responsible for the publication of several defamatory articles about Timberlane in the Honduran press.

As a result of the conspiracy, Timberlane's complaint claimed damages then estimated in excess of $5,000,000. Plaintiffs also allege that there has been a direct and substantial effect on United States foreign commerce, and that defendants intended the results of the conspiracy, including the impact on United States commerce.

Extraterritorial Reach of the United States Antitrust Laws

There is no doubt that American antitrust laws extend over some conduct in other nations. There was language in the first Supreme Court case in point, American Banana Co. v. United Fruit Co., 213 U.S. 347, 29 S. Ct. 511, 53 L. Ed. 826 (1909), casting doubt on the extension of the Sherman Act to acts outside United States territory. But subsequent cases have limited American Banana to its particular facts, and the Sherman Act - and with it other antitrust laws - has been applied to extraterritorial conduct. See, e.g., Continental Ore Co. v. Union Carbide & Carbon Corp., 370 U.S. 690, 82 S.Ct. 1404, 8 L. Ed. 2d 777 (1962); United States v. Sisal Sales Corp., 274 U.S. 268, 47 S. Ct. 592, 71 L. Ed. 1042 (1927); United States v. Aluminum Co. of America, 148 F.2d 416, (2d Cir. 1945) (the "Alcoa" case). The act may encompass the foreign activities of aliens as well as American citizens. Alcoa, supra; Swiss Watch, 1963 Trade Cases P 70,600; United States v. General Electric Co., 82 F. Supp. 753 (D.N.J.1949), judgment implementing decree, 115 F. Supp. 835 (D.N.J.1953).

That American law covers some conduct beyond this nation's borders does not mean that it embraces all, however. Extraterritorial application is understandably a matter of concern for the other countries involved. Those nations have sometimes resented and protested, as excessive intrusions into their own spheres, broad assertions of authority by American courts. See A. Neale, The Antitrust Laws of the United States of America 365-72 (2d ed. 1970); Assn. of the Bar of the City of New York, National Security and Foreign Policy in the Application of American Antitrust Laws to Commerce with Foreign Nations 7-18 (1957); Zwarensteyn, The Foreign Reach of the American Antitrust Laws, 3 Am.Bus.L.J. 163, 165-69 (1965). Our courts have recognized this concern and have, at times, responded to it, even if not always enough to satisfy all the foreign critics. See Alcoa, 148 F.2d at 443. In any event, it is evident that at some point the interests of the United States are too weak and the foreign harmony incentive for restraint too strong to justify an extraterritorial assertion of jurisdiction.

What that point is or how it is determined is not defined by international law. Miller, Extraterritorial Effects of Trade Regulation, 111 U.Pa.L.Rev. 1092, 1094 (1963). Nor does the Sherman Act limit itself. In the domestic field the Sherman Act extends to the full reach of the commerce power. To define it somewhat more modestly in the foreign commerce area courts have generally, and logically, fallen back on a narrower construction of congressional intent, such as expressed in Judge Learned Hand's oft-cited opinion in Alcoa, 148 F.2d at 443:

The only question open is whether Congress intended to impose the liability and whether our own Constitution permitted it to do so: as a court of the United States we cannot look beyond our own law. Nevertheless, it is quite true that we are not to read general words, such as those in this Act, without regard to the limitations customarily observed by nations upon the exercise of their powers; limitations which generally correspond to those fixed by the "Conflict of Laws." We should not impute to Congress an intent to punish all whom its courts can catch, for conduct which has no consequences within the United States.

It is the effect on American foreign commerce which is usually cited to support extraterritorial jurisdiction. Alcoa set the course, when Judge Hand declared, id.:

It is settled law . . . that any state may impose liabilities, even upon persons not within its allegiance, for conduct outside its borders that has consequences within its borders which the state reprehends; and these liabilities other states will ordinarily recognize.

Despite its description as "settled law," Alcoa's assertion has been roundly disputed by many foreign commentators as being in conflict with international law, comity, and good judgment. Nonetheless, American courts have firmly concluded that there is some extraterritorial jurisdiction under the Sherman Act.

Even among American courts and commentators, however, there is no consensus on how far the jurisdiction should extend. The district court here concluded that a "direct and substantial effect" on United States foreign commerce was a prerequisite, without stating whether other factors were relevant or considered. The same formula was employed, to some extent, by the district courts in the Swiss Watch case, 1963 Trade Cases P $ 70,600, in

United States v. R. P. Oldham Co., 152 F. Supp. 818, 822 (N.D.Cal.1957), and in General Electric, 82 F. Supp. at 891. n17 It has been identified and advocated by several commentators. See, e.g., W. Fugate, Foreign Commerce and the Antitrust Laws 30, 174 (2d ed. 1973); J. Van Cise, Understanding the Antitrust Laws 204 (1973 ed.). Similarly, see Report of the Attorney General's National Committee to Study the Antitrust Laws 76 (1955) ("substantial anticompetitive effects"); Restatement (Second) of the Foreign Relations Law of the United States Restatement § 18.[1] The "direct" and "substantial" requirements come from (b)(ii) and (iii). Comment a to this section specifically indicates, however, that this rule applies only to aliens, since United States citizens may be bound by nationality, and only where there has been no significant conduct within the United States, since otherwise territorial jurisdiction could be asserted.

Few cases have discussed the nature of the effect required for jurisdiction, perhaps because most of the litigated cases have involved relatively obvious offenses and rather significant and apparent effects on competition within the United States. Id.; P. Areeda, Antitrust Analysis 129 n.455 (1974). It is probably in part because the standard has not often been put to a real test that it seems so poorly defined. William Fugate, who has identified the "direct and substantial" standard as the rule, has described the meaning of that phrase as being "quite broad." W. Fugate, supra, at 174. What the threshold of significance is, however, has not been identified. Nor is it quite clear what the "direct-indirect" distinction is supposed to mean.

* * *

The effects test by itself is incomplete because it fails to consider the other nation's interests. Nor does it expressly take into account the full nature of the relationship between the actors and this country. Whether the alleged offender is an American citizen, for instance, may make a big difference; applying American laws to American citizens raises fewer problems than application to foreigners. As was observed in Pacific Seafarers, Inc. v. Pacific Far East Line, Inc., 131 U.S.App.D.C. 226, 404 F.2d 804, 815 (1968), cert. denied, 393 U.S. 1093, 89 S. Ct. 872, 21 L. Ed. 2d 784 (1969):

---

1. Restatement § 18 reads:

A state has jurisdiction to prescribe a rule of law attaching legal consequences to conduct that occurs outside its territory and causes an effect within its territory, if either
(a) the conduct and its effect are generally recognized as constituent elements of a crime or tort under the law of states that have reasonably developed legal systems, or
(b)(i) the conduct and its effect are constituent elements of activity to which the rule applies; (ii) the effect within the territory is substantial; (iii) it occurs as a direct and foreseeable result of the conduct outside the territory; and (iv) the rule is not inconsistent with the principles of justice generally recognized by states that have reasonably developed legal systems.

> If . . . [American antitrust] policy cannot extend to the full sweep of American foreign commerce because of the international complications involved, then surely the test which determines whether United States law is applicable must focus on the nexus between the parties and their practices and the United States, not on the mechanical circumstances of effect on commodity exports or imports.

American courts have, in fact, often displayed a regard for comity and the prerogatives of other nations and considered their interests as well as other parts of the factual circumstances, even when professing to apply an effectstest. To some degree, the requirement for a "substantial" effect may silently incorporate these additional considerations, with "substantial" as a flexible standard that varies with other factors. The intent requirement suggested by Alcoa, 148 F.2d at 443-44, is one example of an attempt to broaden the court's perspective, as is drawing a distinction between American citizens and non-citizens.

The failure to articulate these other elements in addition to the standard effects analysis is costly, however, for it is more likely that they will be overlooked or slighted in interpretating past decisions and reaching new ones. Placing emphasis on the qualification that effects be "substantial" is also risky, for the term has a meaning in the interstate antitrust context which does not encompass all the factors relevant to the foreign trade case.

Indeed, that "substantial effects" element of interstate antitrust analysis may well be responsible for the use of an effects test for foreign commerce. The Sherman Act reaches restraints directly intended to limit the flow of interstate trade or whose sole impact is on interstate commerce, but it also reaches "wholly local business restraints" if the particular restraint "substantially and adversely affects interstate commerce." Such a test is necessary in the interstate context to separate the restraints which fall within the federal ambit under the interstate commerce clause from those which, as purely intrastate burdens, remain the province of the states. Since, however, no comparable constitutional problem exists in defining the scope of congressional power to regulate foreign commerce, it may be unwise blindly to apply the "substantiality" test to the international setting. Only respect for the role of the executive and for international notions of comity and fairness limit that constitutional grant.

A tripartite analysis seems to be indicated. As acknowledged above, the antitrust laws require in the first instance that there be some effect - actual or intended - on American foreign commerce before the federal courts may legitimately exercise subject matter jurisdiction under those statutes. Second, a greater showing of burden or restraint may be necessary to demonstrate that the effect is sufficiently large to present a cognizable injury to the plaintiffs and, therefore, a civil violation of the antitrust laws. Third, there is the additional question which is unique to the international setting of whether the interests of, and links to, the United States - including the magnitude of the effect on American foreign commerce - are sufficiently strong, vis-a-vis those of other nations, to justify an assertion of extraterritorial authority.

It is this final issue which is both obscured by undue reliance on the "substantiality" test and complicated to resolve. An effect on United States commerce, although necessary to the exercise of jurisdiction under the antitrust laws, is alone not a sufficient basis on which to determine whether American authority should be asserted in a given case as a matter of international comity and fairness. In some cases, the application of the direct and substantial test in the international context might open the door too widely by sanctioning jurisdiction over an action when these considerations would indicate dismissal.

At other times, it may fail in the other direction, dismissing a case for which comity and fairness do not require forbearance, thus closing the jurisdictional door too tightly - for the Sherman Act does reach some restraints which do not have both a direct and substantial effect on the foreign commerce of the United States. A more comprehensive inquiry is necessary. We believe that the field of conflict of laws presents the proper approach, as was suggested, if not specifically employed, in Alcoa in expressing the basic limitation on application of American laws:

> We are not to read general words, such as those in this Act, without regard to the limitations customarily observed by nations upon the exercise of their powers; limitations which generally correspond to those fixed by the "Conflict of Laws."

148 F.2d at 443. The same idea is reflected in Restatement (Second) of Foreign Relations Law of The United States § 40:

> Where two states have jurisdiction to prescribe and enforce rules of law and the rules they may prescribe require inconsistent conduct upon the part of a person, each state is required by international law to consider, in good faith, moderating the exercise of its enforcement jurisdiction . . . .

The act of state doctrine discussed earlier demonstrates that the judiciary is sometimes cognizant of the possible foreign implications of its action. Similar awareness should be extended to the general problems of extraterritoriality. Such acuity is especially required in private suits, like this one, for in these cases there is no opportunity for the executive branch to weigh the foreign relations impact, nor any statement implicit in the filing of the suit that that consideration has been out-weighed.

What we prefer is an evaluation and balancing of the relevant considerations in each case - in the words of Kingman Brewster, a "jurisdictional rule of reason." Balancing of the foreign interests involved was the approach taken by the Supreme Court in Continental Ore Co. v. Union Carbide & Carbon Corp., 370 U.S. 690, 82 S. Ct. 1404, 8 L. Ed. 2d 777 (1962), where the involvement of the Canadian government in the alleged monopolization was held not to require dismissal. The Court stressed that there was no indication that the Canadian authorities approved or would have approved of the monopolization, meaning that the Canadian interest, if any, was slight and was outweighed by the American interest in condemning the restraint. Similarly, see Lauritzen v. Larsen, 345 U.S. 571, 73 S. Ct. 921, 97 L. Ed. 1254 (1953), where the Court used a like approach in declining to apply the Jones Act to a Danish seaman, injured in Havana on a Danish ship, although he had signed on to the ship in New York.

The elements to be weighed include the degree of conflict with foreign law or policy, the nationality or allegiance of the parties and the locations or principal places of business or corporations, the extent to which enforcement by either state can be expected to achieve compliance, the relative significance of effects on the United States as compared with those elsewhere, the extent to which there is explicit purpose to harm or affect American commerce, the foreseeability of such effect, and the relative importance to the violations charged of conduct within the United States as compared with conduct abroad.[2] A court evaluating these factors should identify the potential degree of conflict if American authority is asserted. A difference in law or policy is one likely sore spot, though one which may not always be present. Nationality is another;

---

2. Foreign Relations Law Restatement @ 40 states that a court should act in the light of such factors as

    (a) vital national interests of each of the states,

(b)   the extent and the nature of the hardship that inconsistent enforcement actions would impose upon the person,

(c)   the extent to which the required conduct is to take place in the territory of the other state,

(d)   the nationality of the person, and

(e)   the extent to which enforcement by action of either state can reasonably be expected to achieve compliance with the rule prescribed by that state.

President (then Professor) Brewster lists the variables of:

(a)   the relative significance to the violations charged of conduct within the United States as compared with conduct abroad;

(b)   the extent to which there is explicit purpose to harm or affect American consumers or Americans' business opportunities;

(c)   the relative seriousness of effects on the United States compared with those abroad;

(d)   the nationality or allegiance of the parties or in the case of business associations, their corporate location, and the fairness of applying our law to them;

(e)   the degree of conflict with foreign laws and policies, and

(f)   the extent to which conflict can be avoided without serious impairment of the interests of the United States or the foreign country.

    K. Brewster, supra at 446.

though foreign governments may have some concern for the treatment of American citizens and business residing there, they primarily care about their own nationals. Having assessed the conflict, the court should then determine whether in the face of it the contacts and interests of the United States are sufficient to support the exercise of extraterritorial jurisdiction.

We conclude, then, that the problem should be approached in three parts: Does the alleged restraint affect, or was it intended to affect, the foreign commerce of the United States? Is it of such a type and magnitude so as to be cognizable as a violation of the Sherman Act? As a matter of international comity and fairness, should the extraterritorial jurisdiction of the United States be asserted to cover it? The district court's judgment found only that the restraint involved in the instant suit did not produce a direct and substantial effect on American foreign commerce. That holding does not satisfy any of these inquiries.

The Sherman Act is not limited to trade restraints which have both a direct and substantial effect on our foreign commerce. Timberlane has alleged that the complained of activities were intended to, and did, affect the export of lumber from Honduras to the United States - the flow of United States foreign commerce, and as such they are within the jurisdiction of the federal courts under the Sherman Act. Moreover, the magnitude of the effect alleged would appear to be sufficient to state a claim.

The comity question is more complicated. From Timberlane's complaint it is evident that there are grounds for concern as to at least a few of the defendants, for some are identified as foreign citizens: Laureano Gutierrez Falla, Michael Casanova and the Casanova firms, of Honduras, and Patrick Byrne, of Canada. Moreover, it is clear that most of the activity took place in Honduras, though the conspiracy may have been directed from San Francisco, and that the most direct economic effect was probably on Honduras. However, there has been no indication of any conflict with the law or policy of the Honduran government, nor any comprehensive analysis of the relative connections and interests of Honduras and the United States. Under these circumstances, the dismissal by the district court cannot be sustained on jurisdictional grounds.

We, therefore, reverse and remand the Timberlane action.

NOTES AND QUESTIONS

1. The Court in Timberlane tries hard to address a primary weakness of the opinions in ALCOA and ICI(1): the perception that the United States was being legally imperialistic in insisting on the unfetered right to export U.S. law into a foreign country.

a. Following the lead of legal scholars such as Professor Kingman Brewster (the reference to "President" is that he was President of Yale, not the U.S.) and the authors of the so-called Restatement of Foreign Relations Law, a structured analysis is developed to demonstrate how reasonable the U.S. will be before it applies U.S. antitrust law to conduct which took place abroad. The (not unreasonable) hope is that if the U.S. is reasonable in the first instance, it is more likely that the foreign jurisdiction will be reasonable (if cooperation is needed) or at least it will not be offended by the U.S. action.

b. Note that in the first stage of the analysis, the court rejects the notion that a "**substantial** effect" be required for U.S. law to apply in cases such as this. The "substantiality screen", as it has been called, was developed as a way for a court to temper the apparent harshness of the straight effects test. Why did the court rejected a substantiality screen? Do you think that a better approach to the problem? After all, it certainly is simpler. Or do you agree with the Judge Choy that a structured, detailed analysis of state interests is more conducive to developing and encouraging the "rule of law".

c. From what you have read, do you think this approach is likely to work? Will the United States finally be successful in getting the rest of the world to accept a limited form of the "effects doctrine"? Or do you think the world (including the British) will be unappreciative, cynical or simply unmoved by the new approach? Do you think other courts in the U.S. (including the Supreme Court) will adopt this new "comity balancing" approach?

d. What do you think Judges Learned Hand or Sylvester Ryan would think of this approach? Would they think that the U.S. is being too soft, not sufficiently advancing U.S. interests? Or would they say that's what they meant all along, that they were misunderstood by the Europeans who thought them arrogant and intrusive?

2. The seven factors articulated by the court are directed at determining which state or nation has the predominant interest in prescribing the rules governing the legality of the conduct which took place.

a. This type of "interest analysis" is not unknown to ordinary U.S. choice-of-law analysis - since the 1960s it has largely supplanted the traditional talismanic "place of the contract"/"place of the wrong" regime that remains the law in England today. What is the U.S. court saying by applying normal choice-of-law rules to the problem at hand?

b.   The comity balancing approach of <u>Timberlane</u> has been criticized as being too uncertain, producing a lack of predictability in the law. Businesses, the criticism continues, will be unable to determine what rules govern their conduct abroad. Do you agree with that criticism? Or do you think that even with this broad, multi-factor test, a little judicial experience and a few more published decision will be sufficient guidance for business?

c.   Do you think courts are equipped to conduct the type of balancing required by Judge Choy? Or do you think that the decisions about when to apply U.S. law to conduct that takes place abroad are too judgmental, too political, or too sensitive to foreign policy concerns to expect judges to make? Note that the Restatement talks about "vital concerns"; another court adopting the approach has raised as a factor "foreign policy concerns". See <u>Mannington Mills, Inc. v. Congoleum Corp.</u>, 595 F.2d 1287, 1294-1298 (CA3 1979). Are these determinations courts should make?

3.   Interestingly, on remand, the lower court determined that U.S. antitrust laws should not apply to the conduct which took place in Honduras. The court looked primarily to the fact that exports of Honduran lumber to the U.S. accounted for less than 1% of the U.S. lumber market, while such exports constituted a far larger share of Honduras' own lumber business. Based on this evaluation (along with the other factors, which split evenly), the court dismissed the action, ruling that U.S. antitrust law did not apply.

*   *   *

At the same time the <u>Timberlane</u> litigation was proceeding through the courts, other courts in the U.S. were struggling with similar issues. A somewhat atypical example follows. While the decision is lengthy, it is very instructive because the Judge presents a highly articulate case for the effects doctrine. Equally important, the judge also (1) defines the problem we have been studying in a new way that makes understanding it easier and (2) he rejects the comity balancing approach in favor of something different.

IV. ANOTHER CONFLICT

LAKER AIRWAYS LIMITED
v.
SABENA

United States Court of Appeals.
For the District of Columbia Circuit

731 F.2d 909
March 6, 1984

WILKEY, Circuit Judge:

We review today the limits of a federal court's power to conserve its adjudicatory authority over a case properly filed with the court when, instead of actively raising all defensive claims in the federal court, the named defendants initiate suits in foreign tribunals for the sole purpose of terminating the federal court's adjudication of the litigation. Three months after Laker Airways, Ltd. ("Laker") filed an antitrust action in United States District Court for the District of Columbia against several defendants, including domestic, British, and other foreign airlines, the foreign airlines filed suits in the High Court of Justice of the United Kingdom seeking an injunction forbidding Laker from prosecuting its American antitrust action against the foreign defendants. After the High Court of Justice entered interim injunctions against Laker, the Court of Appeal issued a permanent injunction ordering Laker to take action to dismiss its suit against the British airlines. In the meantime, Laker responded by requesting injunctive relief in the United States District Court, arguing that a restraining order was necessary to prevent the remaining American defendants and the additional foreign defendants Laker had named in a subsequent antitrust claim from duplicating the foreign defendants' successful request for an English injunction compelling Laker to dismiss its suit against the defendants.

If these defendants had been permitted to file foreign injunctive actions, the United States District Court would have been effectively stripped of control over the claims — based on United States law — which it was in the process of adjudicating. Faced with no alternative but acquiescence in the termination of this jurisdiction by a foreign court's order, United States District Judge Harold H. Greene granted Laker's motion for a preliminary injunction restraining the remaining defendants from taking part in the foreign action designed to prevent the district court from hearing Laker's antitrust claims.

Two of the defendants enjoined from taking part in the English proceeding, KLM Royal Dutch Airlines ("KLM") and Societe Anonyme Belge d'Exploitation de la Navigation Aerienne ("Sabena") now contend on appeal that the court abused its discretion. Their arguments are essentially two-fold: first, that the injunction tramples Britain's rights to regulate the access of its nationals to judicial remedies; second, that the injunction contravenes the principles of international comity which ordinarily compel deference to foreign judgments and which virtually always proscribe any interference with foreign judicial proceedings.

Our review of the limited available facts strongly suggests that both the United States and Great Britain share concurrent prescriptive jurisdiction over the transactions giving rise to Laker's claim. Ordinarily anti-suit injunctions are not properly invoked to preempt parallel proceedings on the same in personam claim in foreign tribunals. However, KLM and Sabena do not qualify under this general rule because the foreign action they seek to join is interdictory and not parallel. It was instituted by the foreign defendants for the sole purpose of terminating the United States claim. The only conceivable benefit that KLM and Sabena would reap if the district court's injunction were overturned would be the right to attack the pending United States action in a foreign court. This would permit the appellants to avoid potential liability under the United States laws to which their business operations and treaty obligations have long subjected them. In these circumstances there is ample precedent justifying the defensive use of an anti-suit injunction.

The injunction does not transgress either the principles of international comity or nationality-based prescriptive jurisdiction on which KLM and Sabena rely. Limitations on the application of comity dating from the origins of the doctrine recognize that a domestic forum is not compelled to acquiesce in pre- or post-judgment conduct by litigants which frustrates the significant policies of the domestic forum. Accession to a demand for comity predicated on the coercive effects of a foreign judgment usurping legitimately concurrent prescriptive jurisdiction is unlikely to foster the processes of accommodation and cooperation which form the basis for a genuine system of international comity. Similarly, the mere fact of Laker's British juridical status simply does not erase all other legitimate bases of concurrent jurisdiction, as appellants suggest. Thus, the appellants' arguments that the district court abused its discretion fall well short of their mark.

The claims raised by KLM and Sabena do pose serious issues regarding the Judiciary's role in accommodating the conflicting implementation of concurrent prescriptive jurisdiction. We have necessarily inquired into the source of the conflict facing the courts of the United States and United Kingdom, and probed the extent to which the judicial processes may effectively be employed to resolve conflicts like the present one. Given the inherent limitations on the Judiciary's ability to adjust national priorities in light of directly contradictory foreign policies, there is little the Judiciary may do directly to resolve the conflict.

Although the flash point of the controversy has been the anti-suit injunctions, the real powder keg is the strongly mandated legislative policies which each national court is bound to implement. Thus, it is unlikely that the underlying controversy would be defused regardless of the action we take today.

Because the principles of comity and concurrent jurisdiction clearly authorize the use of a defensive preliminary injunction designed to permit the United States claim to go forward free of foreign interference, we affirm the decision of the district court.

I. BACKGROUND

This case raises especially troublesome issues on two different fronts. It represents a head-on collision between the diametrically opposed antitrust policies of the United States and United Kingdom, and is perhaps the most pronounced example in recent years of the problems raised by the concurrent jurisdiction held by several states over transactions substantially affecting   several states' interests. These problems are all the more intractable because of the vehicles involved in the collision: anti-suit injunctions designed to preempt the parties' access to the courts of foreign jurisdictions. The intersection of these issues confronts us with the Herculean task of accommodating conflicting, mutually inconsistent national regulatory policies while minimizing the amount of interference with the judicial processes of other nations that our courts will permit. Resolution of this appeal thus requires a clear grasp of both the underlying factual background of Laker's antitrust claims and the complex sequence of litigation and counterlitigation in which those claims have been asserted by Laker and attacked by the foreign defendants.

A. Laker's Antitrust Claims

Laker Airways, Ltd. was founded as a charter airline in 1966. It began charter operations between the United States and United Kingdom in 1970. As early as 1971 it sought to branch out into scheduled transatlantic air service. Laker hoped to gain a sizeable share of the transatlantic market by offering only basic air passage with little or no in-flight amenities and non-essential services. Flying at a reduced cost would enable Laker to set rates much lower than those then charged by existing transatlantic air carriers.

Laker's potential competitors allegedly resisted the entry of this new carrier, delaying the commencement of Laker's novel economy service for several years. However, by 1977 Laker obtained the necessary authorizations from the United States and British governments and inaugurated its low cost transatlantic airline service between London and New York.

The prices for scheduled transatlantic air service are substantially controlled by the International Air Transport Association ("IATA"), a trade organization of the world's largest air carriers. The IATA meets annually to establish fixed fares for air carriage, which are implemented after authorization by national governments of the individual carriers. Laker's fares were approximately one-third of the competing fares offered by other transatlantic carriers which were predominately set under the auspices of the IATA. The airline members of IATA allegedly perceived Laker's operations as a threat to their system of cartelized prices. The new competition not only jeopardized the established markets of those carriers operating between the United Kingdom and the United States — such as British Airways and British Caledonian Airways — but also affected the demand for services provided by airlines flying direct routes between points in Continental Europe and the United States — such as Swiss Air Transport ("Swissair"), Lufthansa German Airlines ("Lufthansa"), KLM, and Sabena — since some passengers allegedly found it cheaper to fly through London on Laker Airways, rather than direct on the other European transatlantic carriers. During meetings of the IATA in July and August 1977 the IATA airlines allegedly agreed to set rates at a predatory level to drive Laker out of business.

Notwithstanding this asserted predatory scheme, up until 1981 Laker managed to operate at a profit. At its zenith, Laker was carrying one out of every seven scheduled air passengers between the United States and England.

However, during 1981 Laker's financial condition rapidly deteriorated. In mid 1981 the pound sterling declined precipitously. A large segment of Laker's revenues was in pounds, but most of its debts, such as those on its United States financed fleet of DC-10 aircraft, and expenses were in dollars. Already weakened by the asserted predatory pricing scheme, Laker ran into repayment difficulties. Fearing financial collapse, it sought to have its repayment obligations refinanced.

At this point several airlines allegedly conspired to set even lower predatory prices. In October 1981 Pan American Airlines, Trans World Airlines, and British Airways dropped their fares for their full service flights to equal those charged by Laker for its no-frills service. They also allegedly paid high secret commissions to travel agents to divert potential customers from Laker. These activities further restricted Laker's income, exacerbating its perilous economic condition. At IATA meetings in December 1981 at Geneva, Switzerland, and in January 1982 at Hollywood, Florida, the IATA airlines allegedly laid plans to fix higher fares in the spring and summer of 1982 after Laker had been driven out of business.

IATA members also interfered with Laker's attempt to reschedule its financial obligations. After Laker arranged a refinancing agreement, KLM, Sabena, and other IATA airlines allegedly pressured Laker's lenders to withhold the financing which had previously been promised. As a result of these alleged conspiracies, Laker was forced into liquidation under Jersey law in early February 1982.

B. Litigation History

In the aftermath of these asserted conspiracies, Laker, through its liquidator, commenced an action in United States District Court for the District of Columbia to recover for the injuries sustained by the airline as a result of the alleged predatory pricing and unlawful interference with its refinancing arrangements. Laker's complaint filed on 24 November 1982, Civil Action No. 82-3362, alleged two counts: (1) violation of United States antitrust laws, and (2) a common law intentional tort. Named as defendants were four American corporations, Pan American World Airways, Trans World Airlines, McDonnell Douglas Corp., and McDonnell Douglas Finance Corp., as well as four foreign airlines, British Airways, British Caledonian Airways, Lufthansa, and Swissair.

. . . The four foreign defendants in No. 82-3362 initiated a similar suit in the High Court of Justice. Their writs filed on 21 January 1983 sought (1) a declaration that the four foreign defendants were not engaged in any unlawful combination or conspiracy, and (2) an injunction prohibiting Laker from taking any action in United States courts to redress an alleged violation by the defendants of United States antitrust laws. The writs specifically sought to compel Laker to dismiss its suit against the foreign defendants in No. 82-3362 and to prohibit Laker from instituting any other proceedings in any non-English forum to redress any alleged violation of English or other laws prohibiting intentional or unlawful commercial injury.

Shortly thereafter Justice Parker issued an interlocutory injunction preventing Laker from taking any action in the United States courts or elsewhere to interfere with the proceedings the defendants were commencing in the High Court of Justice.

On 24 January 1983, to avoid being enjoined from continuing to sue the four United States defendants, Laker sought a temporary restraining order from the United States District Court preventing the American defendants from instituting similar preemptive proceedings in England. The order was granted the same day, and later extended pending a hearing on Laker's motion for a preliminary injunction.

Approximately three weeks later, on 15 February 1983, Laker commenced in the district court a second antitrust suit, Civil Action No. 83-0416. Appellants KLM and Sabena were named as defendants. A temporary restraining order was also entered against the appellants, preventing them from taking any action in a foreign court that would have impaired the district court's jurisdiction. This order was extended pending a hearing on Laker's motion for a preliminary injunction.

On 2 March 1983, the British defendants in No. 82-3362 successfully petitioned Justice Parker of the High Court of Justice to grant a second interim injunction against Laker preventing Laker from taking "any further steps" to prosecute its United States claim against the British airlines. Although the injunction was only designed to preserve the status quo pending a ruling by the High Court of Justice on the merits of the British airlines' suit seeking dismissal of No. 82-3362, the injunction prevented Laker from filing any discovery or other motions against British Airways and British Caledonian.

At a hearing held five days later, Laker's motion for a preliminary injunction against the four American defendants, KLM, and Sabena was considered by the United States District Court. By order of 7 March 1983 and memorandum opinion dated 9 March 1983, the district court granted a preliminary injunction. The terms of the injunction were designed only to "protect the jurisdiction of [the district court] over these proceedings" to the extent necessary to preserve "the rights of the plaintiff under the laws of the United States." The injunction prevented the defendants from taking any action before a foreign court or governmental authority that would interfere with the district court's jurisdiction over the matters alleged in the complaint. In its memorandum opinion, the court made it clear that it would consider further narrowing the terms of the injunction at the request of any party as long as it would not leave the defendants "free to secure orders which would interfere with the litigation pending" before the district court.

KLM Royal Dutch Airlines and Sabena Belgian World Airlines, joined by amici curiae Swissair and Lufthansa, now appeal the 7 March 1983 order and 9 March 1983 memorandum of the district court which enjoined KLM and Sabena from seeking an injunction against Laker's antitrust suit in the English courts. However, during the pendency of this appeal, the process of litigation and counterlitigation has continued in the United States and English courts.

On 29 March 1983, Justice Parker vacated his 2 March 1983 injunction against Laker's prosecution of its antitrust suit against the foreign defendants in No.83-3362. This interim injunction was then reinstated pending appeal.

In April and May 1983 Laker continued its efforts to proceed in its United States antitrust actions while defending itself against the proceedings in the High Court of Justice which were designed to terminate its United States claims. On 26 April 1983 Laker issued a summons in the High Court of Justice seeking a dismissal or stay of the suits initiated by Lufthansa and Swissair. Laker also moved in the High Court of Justice for a discharge of the injunction granted on 21 January 1983.

In a judgment read by Justice Parker on 20 May 1983, the High Court of Justice held that the injunctive relief requested by the British airlines was not justified and terminated claims for relief filed by British Caledonian and British Airways. Justice Parker held that the application of American antitrust laws to companies carrying on business in the United States was not contrary to British sovereignty or the terms of the Bermuda II Treaty, at least while the dormant terms of the British Protection of Trading Interests Act had not been invoked. The judgment did recognize that a determination by the English Secretary of State that Britain's trading interests were negatively implicated by the United States antitrust action could change the result. However, at this point, before any intervention by the British Executive, the British court was willing to hold that Laker could not be prohibited from proceeding with its antitrust claims against British Airways and British Caledonian. The original interim injunctions were maintained pending an appeal to the Court of Appeal by British Airways and British Caledonian.

The complexion of the controversy changed dramatically the next month when the British Government invoked the provisions of the British Protection of Trading Interests Act ("Act"). Upon a determination that measures taken to regulate international trade outside the United Kingdom "threaten to damage the trading interests of the United Kingdom," the Act authorizes the English Secretary of State to require that any person conducting business in the United Kingdom disobey all foreign orders and cease all compliance with the foreign judicial or regulatory provisions designated by the Secretary of State. The Act authorizes the Secretary of State to prevent United Kingdom courts from complying with requests for document production issued by foreign tribunals, and forbids enforcement of treble damage awards or antitrust judgments specified by the Secretary of State. On 27 June 1983 the Secretary of State for Trade and Industry cited his powers under the Act and issued an order and general directions prohibiting persons who carry on business in the United Kingdom, with the exception of American air carriers designated under the Bermuda II Treaty, from complying with "United States antitrust measures" in the district court arising out of any (1) "agreement or arrangement (whether legally enforceable or not) to which a UK designated airline is a party," or (2) "any act done by a UK designated airline" that relates to the provision of air carriage under the Bermuda II Treaty.

Laker applied for judicial review of the validity of the order and directions. The Court of Appeal considered this application with the appeals by British Airways and British Caledonian of Justice Parker's judgment of 20 May 1983.

On 26 July 1983 the Court of Appeal announced its judgment that the order and directions were well within the power of the Secretary of State to issue, and hence valid. Because the order and directions of the British Executive prevented the British airline from complying with any requirements imposed by the United States District Court and prohibited the airlines from relying on their own commercial documents located within the United Kingdom to defend themselves against Laker's charges, the Court of Appeal concluded that the United States District Court action was "wholly untriable" and could only result in a "total denial of justice to" the British airlines. As a result, the

Court of Appeal held that Laker must be permanently enjoined from proceeding with its United States antitrust claims against British Airways and British Caledonian.

After a hearing following judgment, the Court of Appeal granted an injunction (1) restraining Laker from taking any steps against British Airways and British Caledonian in the United States action, and (2) directing Laker to use its best efforts to have British Airways and British Caledonian dismissed from the United States action. The second aspect of the injunction was stayed pending appeal to the House of Lords. Subsequently, on 21 October 1983 Laker's summons to dismiss or stay the Lufthansa and Swissair action issued on 26 April 1983 was also adjourned pending the outcome of Laker's appeal.

C. Current Appeal in this Court

As the litigation now stands, British Airways and British Caledonian have obtained an injunction by the English Court of Appeal restraining Laker from prosecuting its civil antitrust claim against them. Swissair and Lufthansa have applied for similar relief, but their applications are still pending. However, they are apparently protected by the interim injunctions that prevent Laker from taking any action in United States courts to thwart their 21 January 1983 claim for relief. KLM and Sabena are restrained by the United States District Court from joining the English proceedings.

Supported by amici curiae Swissair and Lufthansa, KLM and Sabena challenge the United States District Court's preliminary injunction on appeal to this court. They claim that the injunction was unnecessary to protect the district court's jurisdiction and violates their right to take part in the "parallel" actions commenced in the English courts. Denial of this opportunity, they assert, flouts international principles of comity. Moreover, they charge that the district court ignored Britain's "paramount right" to apply British law to Laker, which is a British subject. Appellants and amici request that we overturn the district court's injunction as a clear abuse of discretion.

II. ANALYSIS

This appeal is the direct result of a clash between two governments asserting jurisdiction to prescribe law over a single series of transactions. The district court's injunction is defended by Laker as necessary to protect the court's jurisdiction. If there is no justification for the court's exercise of jurisdiction, the injunctive relief should necessarily fail. Similarly, if the United Kingdom courts would lack jurisdiction over a claim filed by Sabena and KLM, the district court should be under no obligation to defer to the actions of those foreign tribunals. A true conflict arises only if the national jurisdictions overlap. We must therefore begin our analysis with a review of the recognized bases supporting prescriptive jurisdiction, and then examine whether the alleged facts of this case satisfy those requirements.

A. Bases of Concurrent Prescriptive Jurisdiction: Territoriality and Nationality

1. Overview

Territoriality and nationality are the two fundamental jurisdictional bases on which courts of the United States and United Kingdom rely to assert control over the controversy between Laker and the antitrust defendants.

The prerogative of a nation to control and regulate activities within its boundaries is an essential, definitional element of sovereignty. Every country has a right to dictate laws governing the conduct of its inhabitants. Consequently, the territoriality base of jurisdiction is universally recognized. It is the most pervasive and basic principle underlying the exercise by nations of prescriptive regulatory power. It is the customary basis of the application of law in virtually every country.

In the context of remedial legislation, prohibition of effects is usually indivisible from regulation of causes. Consequently, the principles underlying territorial jurisdiction occasionally permit a state to address conduct causing harmful effects across national borders. Territoriality-based jurisdiction thus allows states to regulate the conduct or status of individuals or property physically situated within the territory, even if the effects of the conduct are felt outside the territory. Conversely, conduct outside the territorial boundary which has or is intended to have a substantial effect within the territory may also be regulated by the state.

Just as the locus of the regulated conduct or harm provides a basis of jurisdiction, the identity of the actor may also confer jurisdiction upon a regulating country. The citizenship of an individual or nationality of a corporation has long been a recognized basis which will support the exercise of jurisdiction by a state over persons. Under this head of jurisdiction a state has jurisdiction to prescribe law governing the conduct of its nationals whether the conduct takes place inside or outside the territory of the state.

Because two or more states may have legitimate interests in prescribing governing law over a particular controversy, these jurisdictional bases are not mutually exclusive. For example, when the national of one state causes substantial effects in another state, both states may potentially have jurisdiction to prescribe governing law. n24 Thus, under international law, territoriality and nationality often give rise to concurrent jurisdiction. A court faced with assertions of conflicting or inconsistent prescriptive power under facially concurrent jurisdiction must first examine the sufficiency of jurisdictional contacts under each base of jurisdiction to determine whether either claim of jurisdiction is unfounded. If both claims to jurisdiction are legitimately exercised, avenues of conflict resolution must be considered before jurisdiction to prescribe can go forward.

2. United States Jurisdictional Base

The prescriptive application of United States antitrust law to the alleged conspiracies between KLM, Sabena, and the other antitrust defendants is founded upon the harmful effects occurring within the territory of the United States as a direct result of the alleged wrongdoing. Before we examine the nature of those effects and consider whether they support the prescriptive jurisdiction over the claimed conspiracies, we wish to make it clear that this aspect of territorial jurisdiction is entirely consistent with nationally and internationally recognized limits on sovereign authority.

It has long been settled law that a country can regulate conduct occurring outside its territory which causes harmful results within its territory. The traditional example of this principle is that of the transnational homicide: when a malefactor in State A shoots a victim across the border in State B, State B can proscribe the harmful conduct. To take a more likely example, embezzlement or unauthorized access to computerized financial accounts can certainly be controlled by the territory where the accounts are located, even though the thief operates by telephone from a distant territory. Other examples are easily multiplied.

Even if invisible, the radiating consequences of anti-competitive activities cause economic injuries no less tangible than the harmful effects of assassins' bullets or thieves' telephonic impulses. Thus, legislation to protect domestic economic interests can legitimately reach conduct occurring outside the legislating territory intended to damage the protected interests within the territory. As long as the territorial effects are not so inconsequential as to exceed the bounds of reasonableness imposed by international law, prescriptive jurisdiction is legitimately exercised.

The territorial effects doctrine is not an extraterritorial assertion of jurisdiction. Jurisdiction exists only when significant effects were intended within the prescribing territory. Prescriptive jurisdiction is activated only when there is personal jurisdiction, often referred to as "jurisdiction to adjudicate." A foreign corporation doing business within the United States reasonably expects that its United States operations will be regulated by United States law. The only extraterritoriality about the transactions reached under the territorial effects doctrine is that not all of the causative factors producing the proscribed result may have occurred within the territory. Although some of the business decisions affecting United States operations may be made outside the forum state, the entire transaction is not   ordinarily immunized.

Certainly the doctrine of territorial sovereignty is not such an artificial limit on the vindication of legitimate sovereign interests that the injured state confronts the wrong side of a one-way glass, powerless to counteract harmful effects originating outside its boundaries which easily pierce its "sovereign" walls, while its own regulatory efforts are reflected back in its face. Unless one admits that there are certain vital interests than can be affected with impunity by careful selection of the decision-making forum, with the result that a country may be forced to rely entirely on the good offices of a foreign state for vindication of the forum's interests — even when vindication of the forum state's interests would contradict the foreign state's own policies — then availability of territorial effects jurisdiction must be recognized. For these reasons

territorial effects jurisdiction has been implemented by several European forums. Indeed, the British have vigorously legislated on this principle in the Protection of Trading Interests Act.

a. *Territorial Contacts Justifying Application of United States Antitrust Law.*

The circumstances of this litigation suggest numerous American interests that would be vindicated if Laker is permitted to proceed with its antitrust claim. Although some of the alleged anti-competitive actions occurred within the United States, most   of the conspiratorial acts took place in other countries. This distinction, however, has no overriding significance, since the economic consequences of the alleged actions gravely impair significant American interests. If the only interest involved were that of Laker, a British corporation, then it may very well be that United States jurisdiction to prescribe would not exist. However, Laker is in liquidation.

 Therefore its interests are only nominal compared to those claiming through it. A primary objective of antitrust laws is to preserve competition, and thus ultimately protect the interests of American consumers. For decades, a great percentage of passengers on North Atlantic air routes has been United States citizens. The greatest impact of a predatory pricing conspiracy would be to raise fares for United States passengers. No other single nation has nearly the same interest in consumer protection on the particular combination of routes involved in Laker's antitrust claims. Application of antitrust laws would thus directly benefit American consumers.

Because Laker is currently being liquidated, the claims of its creditors are even more directly at stake than consumer interests. Laker is now little more than a corporate conduit through which its assets, including any damages owed Laker, will pass to its creditors. Its antitrust action is primarily an effort to satisfy its creditors, who ultimately bear the brunt of the injury allegedly inflicted upon Laker.

381

Although the precipitous actions of the British airline defendants prevented the district court from conducting a thorough inquiry into the underlying facts relevant to this aspect of the litigation, the facts indicate that Laker's principal creditors are Americans. Laker's fleet of American manufactured DC-10 aircraft was largely financed by banks and other lending institutions in the United States. Moreover, a substantial portion of its total debt obligations are likely to have been American, since the bulk of the debts and expenses were payable in American dollars. The actions of the alleged conspirators destroyed the ability of Laker to repay these American creditors; any antitrust recovery will therefore benefit these United States interests.

In addition to the protection of American consumers' and creditors' interests, the United States has a substantial interest in regulating the conduct of business within the United States. The landing rights granted to appellants are permits to do business in this country. Foreign airlines fly in the United States on the prerequisite of obeying United States law. They have offices and employees within the United States, and conduct substantial operations here. By engaging in this commercial business they subject themselves to the in personam jurisdiction of the host country's courts. They waive either expressly or implicitly other objections that might otherwise be raised in defense. A major reason for this subjection to business regulation is to place foreign corporations generally in the same position as domestic businesses. Thus, United States creditors are entitled to, and do, rely on their ability to enforce their claims against foreign corporations like the appellants.

b. Adequacy of United States Territorial Interests

[The Court determined that] significant and long standing American economic interests would be vindicated through a successful antitrust action by Laker.

3. British Jurisdictional Base

Some of the British jurisdictional contacts are territorial. The plaintiff did business on routes between the United States and United Kingdom. A number of the purported conspiratorial acts took place in Great Britain. The conspiracy allegedly caused bankruptcy of a corporation operating in Great Britain.

However, the primary base of jurisdiction is the British nationality of the parties involved in the transactions cited in Laker's complaint. Laker itself is incorporated under Jersey law, and is thus a British national for purposes of, this litigation. Two of the named defendants, British Airways and British Caledonian, are also incorporated under British law. In addition, the conspiracy may also tangentially implicate the activities of other British entities such as the Bank of England and the Civil Aviation Authority.

Regulating the activities of businesses incorporated within a state is one of the oldest and most established examples of prescriptive jurisdiction. We cannot say that these nationality-based jurisdictional contacts would be insufficient to support British jurisdiction over a claim filed by KLM or Sabena, especially when the conspiracy charged does have territorial contacts with the United Kingdom. Thus, existence of British jurisdiction to prescribe is not seriously challenged by Laker.

4. Concurrent Jurisdiction

The sufficiency of jurisdictional contacts with both the United States and England results in concurrent jurisdiction to prescribe. Both forums may legitimately exercise this power to regulate the events that allegedly transpired as a result of the asserted conspiracy.

Concurrent jurisdiction does not necessarily entail conflicting jurisdiction. The mere existence of dual grounds of prescriptive jurisdiction does not oust either one of the regulating forums. Thus, each forum is ordinarily free to proceed to a judgment.

In the current situation, appellants charge that the district court abused its discretion by forbidding them from joining the "parallel" proceeding in the English courts. They argue that this result is compelled both by principles of comity and by respect for a country's paramount interest in controlling the remedies available to its nationals. Before we can fully consider the extent of appellants' rights based on comity and Laker's nationality to participate in the English

proceedings, we examine whether the district court's injunction contravenes the well-established limits on the use of in personam injunctions against litigation in foreign jurisdictions.

B. Propriety of the Antisuit Injunction

It is well settled that English and American courts have power to control the conduct of persons subject to their jurisdiction to the extent of forbidding them from suing in foreign jurisdictions. However, the fundamental corollary to concurrent jurisdiction must ordinarily be respected: parallel proceedings on the same in personam claim should ordinarily be allowed to proceed simultaneously, at least until a judgment is reached in one which can be pled as res judicata in the other. The mere filing of a suit in one forum does not cut off the preexisting right of an independent forum to regulate matters subject to its prescriptive jurisdiction. For this reason, injunctions restraining litigants from proceeding in courts of independent countries are rarely issued.

A second reason cautioning against exercise of the power is avoiding the impedance of the foreign jurisdiction. Injunctions operate only on the parties within the personal jurisdiction of the courts. However, they effectively restrict the foreign court's ability to exercise its jurisdiction. If the foreign court reacts with a similar injunction, no party may be able to obtain any remedy. Thus, only in the most compelling circumstances does a court have discretion to issue an anti-suit injunction.

There are no precise rules governing the appropriateness of anti-suit injunctions. The equitable circumstances surrounding each request for an injunction must be carefully examined to determine whether, in light of the principles outlined above, the injunction is required to prevent an irreparable miscarriage of justice. Injunctions are most often necessary to protect the jurisdiction of the enjoining court, or to prevent the litigant's evasion of the important public policies of the forum. We consider the applicability of each category in turn.

i. Protection of Jurisdiction

Courts have a duty to protect their legitimately conferred jurisdiction to the extent necessary to provide full justice to litigants. Thus, when the action of a litigant in another forum threatens to paralyze the jurisdiction of the court, the court may consider the effectiveness and propriety of issuing an injunction against the litigant's participation in the foreign proceedings.

However, when a party requests the issuance of an injunction to protect the court's jurisdiction before a judgment has been reached, the rules are [un]clear. Some courts issue the injunction when the parties and issues are identical in both actions, justifying the injunction as necessary to prevent duplicative and, therefore, "vexatious" litigation. However, this rationale is prima facie inconsistent with the rule permitting parallel proceedings in concurrent in personam actions. The policies underlying this rule — avoiding hardship to parties and promoting the economies of consolidated litigation — are more properly considered in a motion for dismissal for forum non conveniens. They do not outweigh the important principles of comity that compel deference and mutual respect for concurrent foreign proceedings. Thus, the better rule is that duplication of parties and issues alone is not sufficient to justify issuance of an anti-suit injunction.

Similarly, the possibility of an "embarrassing race to judgment" or potentially inconsistent adjudications does not outweigh the respect and deference owed to independent foreign proceedings. The parallel proceeding rule applies only until a judgment is reached in one of the actions. After that point, the second forum is usually obliged to respect the prior adjudication of the matter. n61 If the rules regarding enforcement of foreign judgments are followed there will seldom be a case where parties reach inconsistent judgments.

There is little, if any, evidence of courts sacrificing procedural or substantive justice in an effort to "race" to a prior judgment. To the extent this slight risk exists it is outweighed by the more important policies favoring respect for concurrent proceedings. In any event, most forums need not fear that their crucial policies would be trampled if a foreign judgment is reached first, since violation of domestic public policy may justify not enforcing the foreign judgment.

The logical reciprocal of the parallel proceeding rule proves that there must be circumstances in which an anti-suit injunction is necessary to conserve the court's ability to reach a judgment. Just as the parallel proceeding rule counsels against interference with a foreign court's exercise of concurrent jurisdiction, it authorizes the domestic court to resist the attempts of a foreign court to interfere with an in personam action before the domestic court. When the availability of an action in the domestic courts is necessary to a full and fair adjudication of the plaintiff's claims, a court should preserve that forum. Thus, where the foreign proceeding is not following a parallel track but attempts to carve out exclusive jurisdiction over concurrent actions, an injunction may be necessary to avoid the possibility of losing validly invoked jurisdiction. This would be particularly true if the foreign forum did not offer the remedy sought in the domestic forum.

The district court's injunction was clearly proper under these principles. As far as could be determined by the initial pleadings and papers filed, jurisdiction to prescribe was properly exercised. Consequently, the court's ability to render a just and final judgment had to be protected, absent clear evidence that the foreign action could fully consider the litigant's claims.

Appellants characterize the district court's injunction as an improper attempt to reserve to the district court's exclusive jurisdiction an action that should be allowed to proceed simultaneously in parallel forums. Actually, the reverse is true. The English action was initiated for the purpose of reserving exclusive prescriptive jurisdiction to the English courts, even though the English courts do not and can not pretend to offer the plaintiffs here the remedies afforded by the American antitrust laws.

Although concurrently authorized by overlapping principles of prescriptive jurisdiction, the British and American actions are not parallel proceedings in the sense the term is normally used. This is not a situation where two courts are proceeding to separate judgments simultaneously under one cause of action. Rather, the sole purpose of the English proceedings is to terminate the American action. The writs filed in the High Court of Justice sought to paralyze or halt the proceedings before the United States District Court. Although they also sought a determination that the defendants had not engaged in any unlawful conduct, the clear thrust of the requested relief was the termination of the United States antitrust claim. Appellants conceded at oral argument that they are not interested in concurrent proceedings in the courts of the United Kingdom — they want only the abandonment or dismissal of the American action against them. Further proof of this is Judge Greene's offer to draft the injunction more narrowly to permit certain proceedings that were not inconsistent with the unhindered continuation of the United States antitrust action. That no suggestions were made by the appellants to narrow the injunction indicates that they are only interested in interfering with the antitrust action, and not in adjudicating the existence of an unlawful conspiracy under British law.

Judge Greene faced the stark choice of either protecting or relinquishing his jurisdiction. Midland Bank had previously obtained a preemptive interim injunction against Laker's naming it as a defendant in a United States antitrust action. Subsequently all of the foreign defendants in No. 82-3362 appeared in the High Court of Justice without notice to either Laker or the United States District Court and obtained interim protection. The remaining defendants, although domestic corporations, had to be restrained from attempting to follow the same path. It was equally clear that appellants also intended to seek English injunctive relief. Due to the lack of any prior notice by the four foreign defendants, the district court was threatened with a potential fait accompli by the appellants which would have virtually eliminated the court's effective jurisdiction over Laker's facially valid claim. Given the tensions between the parties, it is likely that the threat worsened every day. Thus, there was nothing improper in the district court's decision to enjoin appellants from seeking to participate in the English proceedings solely designed to rob the court of its jurisdiction.

ii. Evasion of Important Public Policies

Antisuit injunctions are also justified when necessary to prevent litigants' evasion of the forum's important public policies. This principle is similar to the rule that a foreign judgment not entitled to full faith and credit under the Constitution will not be enforced within the United States when contrary to the crucial public policies of the forum in which enforcement is requested. Both rules recognize that a state is not required to give effect to foreign judicial proceedings grounded on policies which do violence to its own fundamental interests.

The standard for refusing to enforce judgments on public policy grounds is strict; defendants are rarely able to block judgments on these grounds. Enjoining participation in a foreign lawsuit in order to preempt a potential judgment is a much greater interference with an independent country's judicial processes. It follows that an anti-suit injunction will issue to preclude participation in the litigation only when the strongest equitable factors favor its use. Both the importance to the forum of the law allegedly evaded, and the identity of the potentially evading party are relevant.

In this situation, the district court's injunction properly prevented appellants from attempting to escape application of the antitrust laws to their conduct of business here in the United States. KLM and Sabena seek to evade culpability under statutes of admitted economic

importance to the United States which are specifically applicable to their activities in the United States, and upon which Laker may have legitimately relied.

Whatever the merits of the British defendants' claims based upon the Bermuda II Treaty, KLM and Sabena have no claim to antitrust immunity under their air service treaties. In fact, far from conferring any immunity, their treaties contain express language subjecting them to the jurisdiction of the United States over predatory pricing and abuse of monopoly power. . . .

[W]e find it offensive that KLM and Sabena attempt to ride on the coattails of the British airlines under the Bermuda II Treaty and the British Protection of Trading Interest Act, which were respectively intended to regulate British air carriage and to protect primarily the economic interests of British domestic corporations. We do not see how a suit by a British corporation against Dutch and Belgian corporations involving anticompetitive activities allegedly taken by the defendants to protect their United States-Dutch and United States-Belgain air markets adversely implicates British trading interests.

iii. Effect of the English Injunctions

The district court's injunction was within its discretion even though the United Kingdom courts have issued in personam injunctions stopping Laker from proceeding against British Airways and British Caledonian. Long experience derived from this country's federal system teaches that a forum state may, but need not, stay its own proceedings in response to an anti-suit injunction against a party before the court. This is consistent with the general rule permitting concurrent proceedings on transitory causes of action. In extreme cases it may even be necessary to issue a counterinjunction to thwart another state's attempt to assert exclusive jurisdiction over a matter legitimately subject to concurrent jurisdiction.

C. Paramount Nationality

We turn now to the appellants' argument that Laker's nationality requires the United States District Court to defer to the njunctions issued by the courts of the United Kingdom.

KLM and Sabena do not dispute the power of the United States District Court to issue the injunction. They contend rather that the district court abused its discretion by issuing an anti-suit injunction instead of relinquishing its jurisdiction, staying its proceedings, or adopting some other vehicle of conflict resolution. Appellants are therefore in the contradictory position of supporting the right of English courts to issue an anti-suit injunction, but opposing the United States District Court's issuance of the same kind of injunction. The only way appellants can differentiate between the two injunctions is to focus on the nationality of Laker.

The similarity of the injunctions is underscored by the way Sabena phrased the issue posed by this case: "which sovereign, the United States or Great Britain, has the right to determine whether British law permits Laker to conduct private treble damage actions in the United States." As counsel for Sabena recognized at oral argument, whether British law permits or proscribes certain activities is primarily a matter for the British courts to determine. On parity of reasoning the availability of treble damage actions in United States courts is a question of United States law. Appellants' case thus hinges entirely on the consequences attending the existence in one court of nationality-based jurisdiction over Laker.

Appellants attempt to prioritize the authority of the courts to proceed in cases of concurrent jurisdiction by arguing that the nationality of the plaintiff gives the plaintiff's state an inherent advantage which displaces all other jurisdictional bases. They label this principle "paramount nationality," and present this as the theory of conflict resolution to be used when concurrent jurisdiction is present: "assuming that two or more states exercise jurisdiction over Laker's allegations, the state with jurisdiction over its national must have the paramount right to determine whether and, if so, where litigation by that national may go forward."

We are asked to recognize an entirely novel rule. Although a court has power to enjoin its nationals from suing in foreign jurisdictions, it does not follow that the United States courts must recognize an absolute right of the British government to regulate the remedies that the United States may wish to create for British nationals in United States courts. The purported principle of paramount nationality is entirely unknown in national and international law. Territoriality, not nationality, is the customary and preferred base of jurisdiction. Moreover, no rule of international law or national law precludes an exercise of jurisdiction solely because another state has jurisdiction. In fact, international law recognizes that a state with a territorial basis for its prescriptive jurisdiction may establish laws intended to prevent compliance with legislation established under authority of nationality-based jurisdiction.

All proposed methods of avoiding conflicts stemming from concurrent jurisdiction indicate that nationality of the parties is only one factor to consider, not the paramount or controlling factor. Appellants have not cited any cases where the principle has been followed as a method of choosing between competing claims of jurisdiction, despite the numerous occasions when the principle could have been decisive. As this paucity of case law implies, significant adverse consequences would attend the adoption of this rule, and we decline to do so.

The rationale behind the claim of paramount nationality seems to be that particularly important foreign sovereign prerogatives are infringed when a foreign national sues in domestic courts against the wishes of a foreign state. However, this argument ignores the stronger policy interests of the domestic forum. If a country has a right to regulate the conduct of its nationals, then a fortiori it has the power to regulate the activities of its very governmental organizations, such as its courts, which it establishes and maintains for the purpose of furthering its own public policies.

United States courts must control the access to their forums. No foreign court can supersede the right and obligation of the United States courts to decide whether Congress has created a remedy for those injured by trade practices adversely affecting United States interests. Our courts are not required to stand by while Britain attempts to close a courthouse door that Congress, under its territorial jurisdiction, has opened to foreign corporations. Under the nationality base of jurisdiction, Britain can punish its corporations for walking through that courthouse door, but it cannot close the American door. Thus, although British courts can sanction their citizens for resorting to United States antitrust remedies, United States courts are not required to cut off the availability of the remedy.

The position advanced by appellant would require United States courts to defer to British policy when there is no statement by Congress that it does not wish the courts to provide the remedy. Appellants' argument that there is no absolute duty to exercise jurisdiction has no merit in this context. It is based on abstention and forum non conveniens cases, which in turn are premised on the availability of a second forum that can fully resolve the plaintiff's claims. In this case, the English Court of Appeal has admitted that there is no other forum for Laker's claims.

Besides lacking any basis in national or international law, and besides ignoring important domestic interests, the paramount nationality rule would generate more interference than it would resolve. Legislation based on nationality tends to encourage chauvinism and discrimination without enhancing international comity. The paramount nationality rule would be no exception. Foreign plaintiffs in our courts could routinely face public policy challenges in their domestic courts, while our courts would be required to stay proceedings pending foreign authorization. On the other hand, as the district court noted, United States courts could use corporate nationality as a pretext to interject themselves in foreign proceedings involving United States corporations and subsidiaries.

The paramount nationality rule would also be impractical to administer. It would be difficult or impossible to determine when the nationality of a corporation is sufficiently strong that legitimate territorial contacts should be nullified. There are at least five competing methods of determining nationality of a corporation. Multiple countries could simultaneously assert controlling jurisdiction over one "national" corporation based, for example, on shareholder nationality, state of incorporation, or other corporate links to a particular forum. There would be no paramount nation in this situation. The conflicts associated with concurrent jurisdiction would continue to confront the courts.

Finally, KLM and Sabena are not British nationals. Thus, their claims are fundamentally different from those advanced by British Airways and British Caledonian. Nothing gives KLM or Sabena a supreme right to vindicate the British national interests that may be implicated by Laker's suits. Sabena, at least, is specifically entitled to the protection of United States antitrust laws under its air services agreement. KLM no doubt would expect the same protection. No rule of paramount nationality should free them from obligation under United States antitrust laws and at the same time protect them from other corporations' violations. Contrary to appellants' arguments, Laker's nationality is clearly an insufficient basis to reverse the district court.

D. International Comity

Appellants and amici curiae [other European airlines] argue strenuously that the district court's injunction violates the crucial principles of comity that regulate and moderate the social and economic intercourse between independent nations. We approach their claims seriously, recognizing that comity serves our international system like the mortar which cements together a brick house. No one would willingly permit the mortar to crumble or be chipped away for fear of compromising the entire structure.

"Comity" summarizes in a brief word a complex and elusive concept — the degree of deference that a domestic forum must pay to the act of a foreign government not otherwise binding on the forum. Since comity varies according to the factual circumstances surrounding each claim for its recognition, the absolute boundaries of the duties it imposes are inherently uncertain. However, the central precept of comity teaches that, when possible, the decisions of foreign tribunals should be given effect in domestic courts, since recognition fosters international cooperation and encourages reciprocity, thereby promoting predictability and stability through satisfaction of mutual expectations. The interests of both forums are advanced — the foreign court because its laws and policies have been vindicated; the domestic country because international cooperation and ties have been strengthened. The rule of law is also encouraged, which benefits all nations.

Comity is a necessary outgrowth of our international system of politically independent, socio-economically interdependent nation states. As surely as people, products and problems move freely among adjoining countries, so national interests cross territorial borders. But no nation can expect its laws to reach further than its jurisdiction to prescribe, adjudicate, and enforce. Every nation must often rely on other countries to help it achieve its regulatory expectations. Thus, comity compels national courts to act at all times to increase the international legal ties that advance the rule of law within and among nations.

However, there are limitations to the application of comity. When the foreign act is inherently inconsistent with the policies underlying comity, domestic recognition could tend either to legitimize the aberration or to encourage retaliation, undercutting the realization of the goals served by comity. No nation is under an unremitting obligation to enforce foreign interests which are fundamentally prejudicial to those of the domestic forum. Thus, from the earliest times, authorities have recognized that the obligation of comity expires when the strong public policies of the forum are vitiated by the foreign act. Case law on the subject is extensive and recognizes the current validity of this exception to comity.

Opinions vary as to the degree of prejudice to public policy which should be tolerated before comity will not be followed, but by any definition the injunctions of the United Kingdom courts are not entitled to comity. This is because the action before the United Kingdom courts is specifically intended to interfere with and terminate Laker's United States antitrust suit.

The district court's anti-suit injunction was purely defensive — it seeks only to preserve the district court's ability to arrive at a final judgment adjudicating Laker's claims under United States law. This judgment would neither make any statement nor imply any views about the wisdom of British antitrust policy. In contrast, the English injunction is purely offensive — it is not designed to protect English jurisdiction, or to allow English courts to proceed to a judgment on the defendant's potential liability under English anticompetitive law free of foreign interference. Rather, the English injunction seeks only to quash the practical power of the United States courts to adjudicate claims under United States law against defendants admittedly subject to the courts' adjudicatory jurisdiction. The Court of Appeal itself recognized that there is no other forum available for resolution of Laker's claims.

It is often argued before United States courts that the application of United States antitrust laws to foreign nationals violates principles of comity. Those pleas are legitimately considered. n106 In conducting this inquiry, a court must necessarily examine whether the antitrust laws were clearly intended to reach the injury charged in the complaint. n107 If so, allowing the defendant's conduct to go unregulated could amount to an unjustified evasion of United States law injuring significant domestic interests. This is one context in which comity would not be extended to a foreign act. On the other hand, if the anticompetitive aspect of the alleged injury is not appreciable; the contacts with the United States are attenuated; and the actions of foreign governments

391

denote the existence of strong foreign interests, then comity may suggest a lack of Congressional intent to regulate the alleged conduct. In this context, comity may have a strong bearing on whether application of United States antitrust laws should go forward.

However, the appellants' plea to comity is fundamentally different. KLM and Sabena contend that comity compels us to recognize a decision by a foreign government that this court shall not apply its own laws to corporations doing business in this country. Thus, the violation of public policy vitiating comity is not that the evasion of United States antitrust law might injure United States interests, but rather that United States judicial functions have been usurped, destroying the autonomy of the courts. Under the position advanced by appellants, the United States District Court would no longer be free to rule that comity prevented the United States from exercising prescriptive jurisdiction over the defendants, since that determination would be made as of right by a separate forum.

In this latter context we cannot rule that the district court abused its discretion to protect its jurisdiction. Between the state courts, the Full Faith and Credit Clause has not been held to compel recognition of an anti-suit injunction. A fortiori, the principles of comity do not prevent proceeding in the face of a foreign injunction.

Comity ordinarily requires that courts of a separate sovereign not interfere with concurrent proceedings based on the same transitory claim, at least until a judgment is reached in one action, allowing res judicata to be pled in defense. The appeal to the recognition of comity by the American court in order to permit the critical issues to be adjudicated in England, which is the plea made by appellants here, thus comes based on a very strange predicate. Since the action seeking to determine Laker's right to recover for anticompetitive injuries was first instituted in the United States, the initial opportunity to exercise comity, if this were called for, was put to the United Kingdom courts. No recognition or acceptance of comity was made in those courts. The appellants' claims of comity now asserted in United States courts come burdened with the failure of the British to recognize comity.

Although reciprocity may no longer be an absolute prerequisite to comity, certainly our law has not departed so far from common sense that it is reversible error for a court not to capitulate to a foreign judgment based on a statute like the British Protection of Trading Interests Act, designed to prevent the court from resolving legitimate claims placed before it. We cannot forget that the foreign injunction which creates an issue of comity or forbearance was generated by the English Executive's deliberate interference with a proceeding which had been ongoing in the American courts for over six months. Deference to the English courts is now asked in a situation in which all the English courts are doing is supporting and acquiescing in the action taken by their executive. There never would have been any situation in which comity or forbearance would have become an issue if some of the defendants involved in the American suit had not gone into the English courts to generate interference with the American courts.

There is simply no visible reason why the British Executive, followed by the British courts, should bar Laker's assertion of a legitimate cause of action in the American courts, except that the British government is intent upon frustrating the antitrust policies of the elective branches of the American government. The effort of the British therefore is not to see that justice is done anywhere, either in the United States or British courts, but to frustrate the enforcement of American law in American courts against companies doing business in America. Absent a clear treaty concluded by the United States Executive Branch, this simply cannot be agreed to by the courts of the United States.

Nothing in the British Executive order and directions suggests that they are entitled to comity. The order and directions purport to counteract United States regulation of international trade outside its territorial jurisdiction. The Protection of Trading Interests Act and the order govern "any person in the United Kingdom who carries on business there." They forbid any person in the United Kingdom from furnishing "any commercial document in the United Kingdom," or "any commercial information [apparently regardless of location] which relates to the said Department of Justice investigation or the grand jury or the District Court proceedings." Even United States airlines would be swept within these broad directives, but for the directions' specific exclusion of United States carriers.

The English Executive has thus issued an order to every airline in the world doing business in England to refuse to submit to the jurisdiction of the American court and not to submit any documents from England pursuant to an order of the American court. If the exercise of "extraterritorial" jurisdiction under United States antitrust laws can ever be described as arrogant, the order and directions issued by the British Government certainly bear the same characteristic. United States antitrust laws are enforced where there is an impact in the United States, but only after an adjudication in the United States courts of a violation. Here the English Executive has presumed to bar foreigners from complying with orders of an American court before there is an adjudication by a court on the merits of the dispute.

Moreover, since oral argument before this court, the English Secretary of State has interpreted the order and directions to bar the furnishing of any "commercial information," even that located exclusively within United States territory. On the basis of this interpretation the British Government has refused to permit Laker's use of commercial information contained in documents situated in the United States to respond to interrogatories propounded by Trans World Airlines. The orders thus interfere with any attempt by Laker to use any commercial information, whether located in the United Kingdom or the United States, to proceed against any of the defendants, whether British or American.

This development completely undermines the appellants' strongest argument in favor of the application of comity — namely, that all United States interests protected under the antitrust laws could be adequately enforced through means other than a treble damage suit, such as a civil or criminal action brought by the Government, or a creditors' class action. Since the British Government is refusing to permit Laker to proceed with its suit even insofar as it relates to American defendants, it is clear that it would prevent Laker's participation in any proceeding designed to vindicate United States interests allegedly harmed as a result of injuries suffered by Laker and its customers. Thus, Laker would be hampered in assisting the plaintiffs in any alternative action. Without crucial information provided by the injured party, Laker, any other suit would be procedurally doomed to failure, regardless of its merits. Therefore, comity can not be extended on the grounds that the British directions protect solely British interests while permitting the United States to vindicate its own policies; the truth, the reality, is far different.

If we are guided by the ethical imperative that everyone should act as if his actions were universalized, then the actions of the British Executive in this particular matter scarcely meet the standard of Kant. For, if the United States and a few other countries with major airlines enacted and enforced legislation like the Protection of Trading Interests Act, the result would be unfettered chaos brought about by unresolvable conflicts of jurisdiction the world over. If we were to forbid every American airline and every foreign airline doing business in the United States from producing documents in response to the summons of an English court, or a French court, or a German court, and the French and the German governments were to enact and enforce similar legislation, there could be no complete resolution of any legal dispute involving airlines around the world. The operations of the airlines would be snarled in a criss-cross of overlapping and tangled restrictions to the extent that no airline could be certain of its legal obligations anywhere. Thus, even the practical consequences that would flow from a grant of comity counsel against deferring to the British injunctions triggered by the Protection of Trading Interests Act.

There is nothing in the nature of the parties which suggests comity should be exercised. Laker appears before the court as a voluntary plaintiff, under no compulsion to sue. Laker prosecutes its action here subject to sanctions that may be issued against it in the United Kingdom. Thus, there is no suggestion that comity should be exercised to avoid hardship to a party who might otherwise be caught between the inconsistent imperatives of two forums.

No facts have been presented here suggesting that the antitrust suit adversely affects the operations of foreign governments. Laker is a privately owned airline. To the extent KLM and Sabena are governmentally owned, they are non-British. The ownership of these airlines implicates no significant interests of Britain as a state. The parties have not seriously asserted otherwise.

Similarly, the parties have not invoked either the sovereign immunity doctrine or the act of state doctrine, which insulate from review those foreign governmental actions which are not compatible with judicial scrutiny in our domestic courts. That neither of these doctrines even arguably would apply here is further evidence that no significant British or other governmental interest would be violated by Laker's suit.

Although unlikely, it may subsequently be shown that there was sufficient foreign governmental involvement that enforcement of United States antitrust laws is not appropriate. In that event, any of several other well-established principles could be invoked in favor of the defendant. However, these are hurdles that are more appropriately cleared at later stages in the proceeding when the facts are fully developed.

Now a word about the position of our dissenting colleague. We submit that the dissent relies on a skewed view of comity, ignoring the significant prejudice to the administration of justice in our courts under United States laws in order to accommodate the strongly asserted views of the British Executive and Judiciary. However laudatory the impulse to adjust and compromise, we are unable to plunge ahead as the dissent advocates. The path to "the seemly accommodation of . . . competing national interests" eked out by the dissent turns comity into quicksand, snares the district court in the very pitfalls which it attempted to avoid, and leads the parties and the district court to a result so vague and ill-defined that it cannot possibly solve the problems raised by the actions of the two governments. This position is neither legally tenable nor pragmatically dictated by the extraordinary circumstances of this litigation.

The interpretation of international comity propounded by the dissent is a weak reed indeed under the aggravated facts of this case; it does not rest upon any legal precedent, and ignores the previously recognized limits on the doctrine. The central authority quoted, Hilton v. Guyot, recognizes that comity never obligates a national forum to ignore "the rights of its own citizens or of other persons who are under the protection of its laws." Laker's United States creditors and consumers are entitled to the protection of United States antitrust laws. Furthermore, although not a United States citizen, as a corporation operating within the United States, Laker qualifies as an "other person" entitled to the protection of United States law. Heretofore comity has never been thought to require mandatory deferral to a foreign action primarily intended to cut off these domestic interests.

There are weighty reasons why the absence of any current expression of affirmative United States interest should not be fatal to Laker's antitrust action. The American Executive has been in contact with the British Executive seeking to iron out differences under the Bermuda II Treaty. It may very well be that since the State Department is seized with the responsibility for negotiations with the British it has advised the Antitrust Division that it would be inappropriate for that division to take an adversary position in the ongoing private civil suit at this time.

The sensitive status of current negotiations may even preclude the Department of State from actively participating in this litigation. Significantly, the British Government is not involved in this litigation either, presumably confining itself to consultation and to the creation and interpretation of the executive orders giving rise to the controversy. This counsels against inviting the Executive to present the views of the United States on remand. Unless and until the views of the American Executive are made known, the absence of any Executive expression of United States sovereign or other interests should not be a bar to proceeding with Laker's suit, or to the protection of jurisdiction to hear the claim.

F. Judicial Reconciliation of Conflicting Assertions of Jurisdiction

We recognize that the district court's injunction, precipitated as it was by preemptive interim injunctions in the High Court of Justice, unfortunately will not resolve the deadlock currently facing the parties to this litigation. We have searched for some satisfactory avenue, open to an American court, which would permit the frictionless vindication of the interests of both Britain and the United States. However, there is none, for the British legislation defines the British interest solely in terms of preventing realization of United States interests. The laws are therefore contradictory and mutually inconsistent.

i. Nature of the Conflict

The conflict faced here is not caused by the courts of the two countries. Rather, its sources are the fundamentally opposed national policies toward prohibition of anticompetitive business activity. These policies originate in the legislative and executive decisions of the respective counties.

Congress has specifically authorized treble damage actions by foreign corporations to redress injuries to United States foreign commerce. Equally significant, Congress has designed the private action as a major component in the enforcement mechanism. The treble damage aspect of private recoveries is the centerpiece of that enforcement mechanism.

We find no indication in either the statutory scheme or prior judicial precedent that jurisdiction should not be exercised. Legitimate United States interests in protecting consumers, providing for vindicating creditors' rights, and regulating economic consequences of those doing substantial business in our country are all advanced under the congressionally prescribed scheme. These are more than sufficient jurisdictional contracts under United States v. Aluminum Co. of America and subsequent case law to support the exercise of prescriptive jurisdiction in this case. Congress has been aware of the decades-long controversy accompanying the recurrent assertion of jurisdiction over foreign anticompetitive acts and effects in the United States dating back nearly forty years but has, with limited exceptions, not yet chosen to limit the laws' application or disapprove of the consistent statutory interpretation reached by the courts. Thus, aside from the unprecedented foreign challenge to the application of the antitrust laws, there is noting in either the facts alleged in the complaint or the circumstances of the litigation which suggests jurisdiction should not be exercised in Laker's suit.

The English courts have indicated that they, too, have acted out of the need to implement their mandatory legislative policy, and not out of any ill will towards our courts or the substantive law we are bound to follow. Although the injunctive relief sought by British Airways and British Caledonian set the stage for a direct conflict of jurisdiction, until action by the political branches of the English Government the English courts remained largely acquiescent to Laker's invocation of United States jurisdiction. Justice Parker's well reasoned judgment initially denied the injunctive relief sought by British Airways and British Caledonian. That judgment was rendered even after the district court issued the injunction under appeal here.

However, the government of the United Kingdom is now and has historically been opposed to most aspects of United States antitrust policy insofar as it affects business enterprises based in the United Kingdom. The British Government objects to the scope of the prescriptive jurisdiction invoked to apply the antitrust laws; the substantive content of those laws, which is much more aggressive than British regulation of restrictive practices; and the procedural vehicles used in the litigation of the antitrust laws, including private treble damage actions, and the widespread use of pretrial discovery. These policies have been most recently and forcefully expressed in the Protection of Trading Interests Act.

The nature of the direct conflict between the political-economic policies of the two countries is put into focus by considering whether the British Government would have been likely to attempt to stop Laker from suing in United States courts if Laker brought a suit other than an antitrust action. If Laker had sued the American defendants for fraud, or on a contract claim for failure of performance, the British would not have been at all interested in intervening, irrespective of the financial condition of Laker at the time it brought the suit. The indifference would not lessen whether British Airways and British Caledonian were included in the group sued by Laker in the United States court. It is the hated application of United States antitrust laws to conduct involving British corporations that has triggered the involvement of the British Government, and ultimately, the British courts.

Under the provisions of the Protection of Trading Interests Act, after Justice Parker refused relief, the English Secretary of State issued an order and directions prohibiting all those carrying on business in the United Kingdom, with the exception of United States designated air carriers, from complying with United States antitrust measures arising out of the provision of air carriage by United Kingdom designated airlines under the terms of the Bermuda II Treaty.

Because these directions reflected the firm conclusion of the British Executive Branch that British trading interests were being threatened by Laker's antitrust claim, they presented an entirely different situation to the Court of Appeal than that which Justice Parker had faced. The restrictions placed on the British airlines by these orders "fundamentally altered" the perceived ability of the Court of Appeal to permit concurrent actions. Because the directions of the British Executive blocked British Caledonian and British Airways from complying with Laker's discovery requests, the court concluded that the British airlines could not thereafter adequately defend themselves. According to the Court of Appeal, this rendered Laker's claim "wholly untriable" and was therefore "decisive."

Thus, to a large extent the conflict of jurisdiction is one generated by the political branches of the governments. There is simply no room for accommodation here if the courts of each country faithfully carry out the laws which they are entrusted to enforce. The Master of the Rolls expressed hope that "the courts of the two countries will . . . never be in conflict. The conflict, if there be conflict, will be purely one between the laws of the two countries, for which neither court is responsible." We echo that hope.

ii. Judicial Interest Balancing

Even as the political branches of the respective countries have set in motion the legislative policies which have collided in this litigation, they have deprived courts of the ability meaningfully to resolve the problem. The American and English courts are obligated to attempt to reconcile two contradictory laws, each supported by recognized prescriptive jurisdiction, one of which is specifically designed to cancel out the other.

The suggestion has been made that this court should engage in some form of interest balancing, permitting only a "reasonable" assertion of prescriptive jurisdiction to be implemented. However, this approach is unsuitable when courts are forced to choose between a domestic law which is designed to protect domestic interests, and a foreign law which is calculated to thwart the implementation of the domestic law in order to protect foreign interests allegedly threatened by the objectives of the domestic law. Interest balancing in this context is hobbled by two primary problems: (1) there are substantial limitations on the court's ability to conduct a neutral balancing of the competing interests, and (2) the adoption of interest balancing is unlikely to achieve its goal of promoting international comity.

a. Defects in the Balancing Process

Most proposals for interest balancing consist of a long list of national contacts to be evaluated and weighed against those of the foreign country. These interests may be relevant to the desirability of allocating jurisdiction to a particular national forum. However, their usefulness breaks down when a court is faced with the task of selecting one forum's prescriptive jurisdiction over that of another.

Many of the contacts to be balanced are already evaluated when assessing the existence of a sufficient basis for exercising prescriptive jurisdiction. Other factors, such as "the extent to which another state may have an interest in regulating the activity," and "the likelihood of conflict with regulation by other states" n146 are essentially neutral in deciding between competing assertions of jurisdiction. Pursuing these inquiries only leads to the obvious conclusion that jurisdiction could be exercised or that there is a conflict, but does not suggest the best avenue of conflict resolution. These types of factors are not useful in resolving the controversy.

Those contacts which do purport to provide a basis for distinguishing between competing bases of jurisdiction, and which are thus crucial to the balancing process, generally incorporate purely political factors which the court is neither qualified to evaluate comparatively nor capable of properly balancing. One such proposed consideration is "the degree to which the desirability of such regulation [of restrictive practices] is generally accepted." We doubt whether the legitimacy of an exercise of jurisdiction should be measured by the substantive content of the prescribed law. Moreover, although more and more states are following the United States in regulating restrictive practices, and even exercising jurisdiction based on effects within territory, the differing English and American assessment of the desirability of antitrust law is at the core of the conflict. An English or American court cannot refuse to enforce a law its political branches have already determined is desirable and necessary.

The court is also handicapped in any evaluation of "the existence of justified expectations that might be protected or hurt by the regulation in question." In this litigation, whether the reliance of Laker and its creditors on United States antitrust laws is justified depends upon whether one accepts the desirability of United States anti-trust law. Whether the defendants could justifiably have relied on the inapplicability of United States law to their conduct alleged to have caused substantial effects in the United States is based on the same impermissible inquiry. The desirability of applying ambiguous legislation to a particular transaction may imply the presence or absence of legislative intent. However, once a decision is made that the political branches intended to rely on a legitimate base of prescriptive jurisdiction to regulate activities affecting foreign commerce within the domestic forum, the desirability of the law is no longer an issue for the courts.

The "importance of regulation to the regulating state" is another factor on which the court cannot rely to choose between two competing, mutually inconsistent legislative policies. We are in no position to adjudicate the relative importance of antitrust regulation or nonregulation to the United States and the United Kingdom. It is the crucial importance of these policies which has created the conflict. A proclamation by judicial fiat that one interest is less "important" than the other will not erase a real conflict.

Given the inherent limitations of the Judiciary, which must weigh these issues in the limited context of adversarial litigation, we seriously doubt whether we could adequately chart the competing problems and priorities that inevitably define the scope of any nation's interest in a legislated remedy. This court is ill-equipped to "balance the vital national interests of the United States and the [United Kingdom] to determine which interests predominate." When one state exercises its jurisdiction and another, in protection of its own interests, attempts to quash the first exercise of jurisdiction "it is simply impossible to judicially 'balance' these totally contradictory and mutually negating actions."

Besides the difficulty of properly weighing the crucial elements of any interest balancing formula, one other defect in the balancing process prompts our reluctance to adopt this analysis in the context of preservation of jurisdiction. Procedurally, this kind of balancing would be difficult, since it would ordinarily involve drawn-out discovery and requests for submissions by political branches. There was no time for this process in the present case. Either jurisdiction was protected or it was lost. It is unlikely that the employment of a hasty and poorly informed balancing process would have materially aided the district court's evaluation of the exigencies and equities of Laker's request for relief.

b. Promotion of International Comity

We might be more willing to tackle the problems associated with the balancing of competing, mutually inconsistent national interests if we could be assured that our efforts would strengthen the bonds of international comity. However, the usefulness and wisdom of interest balancing to assess the most "reasonable" exercise of prescriptive jurisdiction has not been affirmatively demonstrated. This approach has not gained more than a temporary foothold in domestic law. Courts are increasingly refusing to adopt the approach. Scholarly criticism has intensified. Additionally, there is no evidence that interest balancing represents a rule of international law. Thus, there is no mandatory rule requiring its adoption here, since Congress cannot be said to have implicitly legislated subject to these international constraints.

If promotion of international comity is measured by the number of times United States jurisdiction has been declined under the "reasonableness" interest balancing approach, then it has been a failure. Implementation of this analysis has not resulted in a significant number of conflict resolutions favoring a foreign jurisdiction. A pragmatic assessment of those decisions adopting an interest balancing approach indicates none where United States jurisdiction was declined when there was more than a de minimis United States interest. Most cases in which use of the process was advocated arose before a direct conflict occurred when the balancing could be employed without impairing the court's jurisdiction to determine jurisdiction. When push comes to shove, the domestic forum is rarely unseated.

Despite the real obligation of courts to apply international law and foster comity, domestic courts do not sit as internationally constituted tribunals. Domestic courts are created by national constitutions and statutes to enforce primarily national laws. The courts of most developed countries follow international law only to the extent it is not overridden by national law. Thus, courts inherently find it difficult neutrally to balance competing foreign interests. When there is any doubt, national interests will tend to be favored over foreign interests. n162 This partially explains why there have been few times when courts have found foreign interests to prevail.

The inherent noncorrelation between the interest balancing formula and the economic realities of modern commerce is an additional reason which may underlie the reluctance of most courts to strike a balance in favor of nonapplication of domestic law. An assertion of prescriptive jurisdiction should ultimately be based on shared assessments that jurisdiction is reasonable. Thus, international law prohibits the assertion of prescriptive jurisdiction unsupported by reasonable links between the forum and the controversy.

However, it does not necessarily follow, as the use of interest balancing as a method of choosing between competing jurisdictions assumes, that there is a line of reasonableness which separates jurisdiction to prescribe into neatly adjoining compartments of national jurisdiction. There is no principle of international law which abolishes concurrent jurisdiction. Since prescriptive jurisdiction is based on well recognized state contacts with controversies, the reality of our interlocked international economic network guarantees that overlapping, concurrent jurisdiction will often be present. There is, therefore, no rule of international law holding that a "more reasonable" assertion of jurisdiction mandatorily n168 displaces a "less reasonable" assertion of jurisdiction as long as both are, in fact, consistent with the limitations on jurisdiction imposed by international law. That is the situation faced in this case: the territoriality and nationality bases of jurisdiction of the United Kingdom and the United States are both unimpeached.

In our federal system of parallel sovereign courts, several lines of cases recognize that prescriptive jurisdiction is often shared among several forums. Those forums may participate in interforum compacts that provide a basis for allocating jurisdiction to one forum over another. Similarly, the problems associated with overlapping bases of national taxation in international law are directly addressed by numerous bilateral and multilateral treaties rather than a judicially developed rule of exclusive jurisdiction grounded in a prioritization of the relative reasonableness of links between the state and the taxed entity. Because we see no neutral principles on which to distinguish judicially the reasonableness of the concurrent, mutually inconsistent exercises of jurisdiction in this case, we decline to adopt such a rule here.

iii. Political Compromise

The district court could capitulate to the British attacking law, at the cost of losing its jurisdiction to implement the substantive policies established by Congress. Alternatively it can act to preserve its jurisdiction, running the risk that counterinjunctions or other sanctions will eventually preclude Laker from achieving any remedy, if it is ultimately entitled to one under United States law. In either case the policies of both countries are likely to be frustrated at the cost of substantial prejudice to the litigants' rights.

We unhesitatingly conclude that United States jurisdiction to prescribe its antitrust laws must go forward and was therefore properly protected by the district court. Despite the contrary assertions of the British government, there is no indication in this case that the limits of international law are exceeded by either country's exercise of prescriptive jurisdiction. But even so, application of national law may go forward despite a conflict with international law. Both Britain and the United States recognize this rule. It follows a fortiori that national laws do not evaporate when counteracted by the legislation of another sovereign.

Although, in the interest of amicable relations, we might be tempted to defuse unilaterally the confrontation by jettisoning our jurisdiction, we could not, for this is not our proper judicial role. The problem in this case is essentially a political one, arising from the vast difference in the political-economic theories of the two governments which has existed for many years. Both nations have jurisdiction to prescribe and adjudicate. Both have asserted that jurisdiction. However, this conflict alone does not place the court in a position to initiate a political compromise based on its decision that United States laws should not be enforced when a foreign jurisdiction, contrary to the domestic court's statutory duty, attempts to eradicate the domestic jurisdiction. Judges are not politicians. The courts are not organs of political compromise. It is impossible in this case, with all the good will manifested by the English Justices and ourselves, to negotiate an extraordinarily long arms-length agreement on the respective impact of our countries' policies regulating anti-competitive business practices.

It is permissible for courts to disengage when judicial scrutiny would implicate inherently unreviewable actions, such as conduct falling within the act of state or sovereign immunity doctrines. But both institutional limitations on the judicial process and Constitutional restrictions on the exercise of judicial power make it unacceptable for the Judiciary to seize the political initiative and determine that legitimate application of American laws must evaporate when challenged by a foreign jurisdiction.

Unilateral abandonment by the Judiciary of legitimately prescribed national law in response to foreign counter-legislation would not materially advance the principles of comity and international accommodation which must form the foundation of any international system comprised of coequal nation states. The British Government's invocation of the Protection of Trading Interest Act to foreclose any proceeding in a non-English forum brought to recover damages for trade injuries caused by unlawful conspiracies is a naked attempt exclusively to reserve by confrontation an area of prescriptive jurisdiction shared concurrently by other nations. This assertion of interdictory jurisdiction propels into the courts a controversy whose eventual termination is restricted to two unsatisfactory alternatives: (1) either one state or the other will eventually capitulate, sacrificing its legitimate interests, or (2) a deadlock will occur to the eventual frustration of both the states' and the litigants' interests. The underlying goal of the legislation is apparently to compel the United States to cede its claims to regulate those aspects of its domestic economy deemed objectionable by the United Kingdom. However, the possibility of a cooperative, mutually profitable compromise by all affected countries is greatly restricted. Granting recognition to this form of coercion will only retard the growth of international mechanisms necessary to resolve satisfactorily the problems generated when radically divergent national policies intersect in an area of concurrent jurisdiction.

Rather than legitimizing the interference and stultifying effects that would follow widespread acceptance of interdictory jurisdiction, we prefer to permit Laker's suit, based as it is on well recognized prescriptive jurisdiction, to go forward as free as possible from the interference caused by foreign antisuit injunctions.

III. CONCLUSION

The conflict in jurisdiction we confront today has been precipitated by the attempts of another country to insulate its own business entities from the necessity of complying with legislation of our country designed to protect this country's domestic policies. At the root of the conflict are the fundamentally opposed policies of the United States and Great Britain regarding the desirability, scope, and implementation of legislation controlling anticompetitive and restrictive business practices.

No conceivable judicial disposition of this appeal would remove that underlying conflict. Because of the potential deadlock that appears to be developing, the ultimate question is not whether conflicting assertions of national interest must be reconciled, but the proper forum of reconciliation. The resources of the Judiciary are inherently limited when faced with an affirmative decision by the political branches of the government to prescribe specific policies. Absent an explicit directive from Congress, this court has neither the authority nor the institutional resources to weigh the policy and political factors that must be evaluated when resolving competing claims of jurisdiction. In contrast, diplomatic and executive channels are, by definition, designed to exchange, negotiate, and reconcile the problems which accompany the realization of national interests within the sphere of international association. These forums should and, we hope, will be utilized to avoid or resolve conflicts caused by contradictory assertions of concurrent prescriptive jurisdiction.

However, in the absence of some emanation from the Executive Branch, Laker's suit may go forward against appellants. Laker seeks to recover for injuries it allegedly sustained as a result of the defendants' conduct in violation of United States antitrust laws. The complaint alleges a conspiracy to drive out of business a corporation permitted by United States treaty to operate within the United States and conducting substantial business here. If Laker's allegations are proved, the intended and actual effect in the United States are   clear since Laker, which was carrying up to one out of every seven transatlantic passengers, was subsequently forced into liquidation. Resolution of Laker's lawsuit would further the interests protected under United States law, since American creditors' interests in open forums, and consumers' interests in free competition may be vindicated.

Under these circumstances, judicial precedent construing the prescriptive jurisdiction of the United States antitrust laws unequivocally holds that the antitrust laws unequivocally holds that the antitrust laws should be applied. That jurisdiction is well within the bounds of reason imposed by international law. Because the factual circumstances of this case made a preliminary injunction imperative to preserve the court's jurisdiction, and because that injunction is not proscribed by the principles of international comity, the district court acted within its discretion.

The decision of the district court is therefore Affirmed.

STARR, Circuit Judge, dissenting:

It is with reluctance that I am constrained to dissent, for there is much in the majority's thorough opinion with which I fully agree. The majority's opinion demonstrates persuasively that the jurisdictional basis for Laker's action in the United States District Court is firmly established under settled principles of United States and international law. Judge Wilkey's scholarly analysis further demonstrates that it is not at all unusual for a court vested with jurisdiction to issue appropriate orders to vindicate that jurisdiction, even when such orders arrest the prosecution of actions in the courts of another sovereign.

But it is my judgment that principles of comity among the courts of the international community counsel strongly against the injunction in the form issued here. The concept of comity of nations, a "blend of courtesy and expedience," was defined by the Supreme Court in Hilton v. Guyot as: the recognition which one nation allows within its territory to the legislative, executive or judicial acts of another nation, having due regard both to international duty and convenience, and to the rights of its own citizens or of other persons who are under the protection of its laws.

The difficulty in applying this open-ended idea stems from the fact that "'comity,' in the legal sense, is neither a matter of absolute obligation, on the one hand, nor of mere courtesy and good will, upon the other." Few hard-and-fast rules or talismanic tests are to be found. Nonetheless, it is clear that under appropriate circumstances, United States courts will invoke the principle of comity in recognition of the interests of another sovereign.

In light of these principles, it is important to note that this is, at bottom, a private antitrust action filed in a United States court by a foreign litigant against, among others, four United States corporate defendants. This is plainly not an action informed with a public interest beyond that implicated by any private litigant enforcing admittedly important congressionally granted rights. Not only is the instant action not brought by the United States to vindicate sovereign United States interests, but no evidence has been manifested of any sovereign United States interest in the present suit. For whatever reason, and I do not pretend to powers of divination as to why, the Executive has been silent as to what, if any, public interests are touched by Laker's antitrust suit.

In stark contrast, it is clear beyond cavil that the British Executive is emphatically interested in this suit brought by a British subject in United States courts. This sovereign interest articulated by representatives of Her Majesty's government, premised upon British disaffection for the operation and reach of United States antitrust laws, is one that I cannot in conscience reasonably discount. After all, Laker is a British subject which carried on its operations as a heavily regulated air carrier under United Kingdom law. Its routes, to and from the United States were established under the umbrella of the Bermuda II Treaty between the United Kingdom and the United States. The United Kingdom thus possesses a clear governmental interest in the activities of a now defunct but once heavily regulated British concern.

To be sure, Laker's status as a British subject, without more, does not mean that United States courts must unalterably bow to the rulings of British courts in actions filed after the instant suit was in progress. The majority has indeed persuasively demonstrated that no principle of "paramount nationality" is recognized in international law. But I am persuaded that it is not at all incompatible with our oath of office for United States judges to recognize the practical reality that the United Kingdom may in fact ultimately have power to prevent Laker's maintaining any United States antitrust action. And the exercise of such a power should not automatically, without benefit of the views of either the British or United States Executive, be deemed violative of United States public policy.

I would favor vacating the present injunction and remanding the case to the District Court for consideration of narrowing its order.

I would further suggest that in the exercise of its sound discretion the District Court invite the Executive to present the views of the United States. Those views might well have an important bearing upon the extent of the sovereign interests of the United States, if any, in this action.

A tempest has been brewing for some time among the nations as to the reach of this countries antitrust laws, and today's decision strikes a strong blow in favor of what will be viewed by many of our friends and allies as a rather parochial American outlook. But whether that blow is well conceived, it is, with all respect, at tension with the orderly operation of our two nations' respective judicial systems. As both the majority and the District Court recognize, it is serious business to issue an injunction against proceedings in a sister nation. This is most keenly true with respect to a nation from which we inherited so much of our legal system. Inasmuch as only extraordinary reasons justify the issuance of such an injunction, I would remand the case to the District Court for further proceedings aimed at narrowing the

injunction, consistent with the principles of comity that inform the seemly accommodation of sharply divergent and competing national interests.

NOTES AND QUESTIONS

1. The legal battle described in <u>Laker</u> holds special interest because it demonstrates the lengths countries (and litigants) will go to vindicate their interests. In that regard, note at the outset that Justice Parker, after due deliberation, decided not to grant any injunction against the U.S. proceeding because he concluded it didn't violate British interests. The British Executive branch then intervened, invoking the provisions of the British "blocking statute", the Protection of Trading Interests Act. The

day for "comity" was thus short-lived, as it was this act, which especially irked Judge Wilkie: "We cannot forget that the foreign injunction which creates an issue of comity or forbearance was generated by the English Executive's deliberate interference with a proceeding which had been ongoing in the American courts for over six months," he wrote. Like Judge Ryan, however, Judge Wilkie is left powerless to do anything about the British carriers, because they successfully enjoined Laker from suing them, and there is nothing Judge Wilkie can do. But, like Judge Ryan in ICI, Judge Wilkie does get in some last licks to demonstrate American resolve - he enjoins the other (continental) carriers from joining in the British action. Interestingly, the case settled within a few months of Judge Wilkie's decision.

2. Judge Wilkie presents an especially lucid analysis of "jurisdiction to prescribe" and the justification for the effects test. He writes:

> It has long been settled law that a country can regulate conduct occurring outside its territory which causes harmful results within its territory. The traditional example of this principle is that of the transnational homicide: when a malefactor in State A shoots a victim across the border in State B, State B can proscribe the harmful conduct. To take a more likely example, embezzlement or unauthorized access to computerized financial accounts can certainly be controlled by the territory where the accounts are located, even though the thief operates by telephone from a distant territory. Other examples are easily multiplied.

> Even if invisible, the radiating consequences of anti -competitive activities cause economic injuries no less tangible than the harmful effects of assassins' bullets or thieves' telephonic impulses. . . .

> The territorial effects doctrine is not an extraterritorial assertion of jurisdiction. Jurisdiction exists only when significant effects were intended within the prescribing territory. Prescriptive jurisdiction is activated only when there is personal jurisdiction, often referred to as "jurisdiction to adjudicate." A foreign corporation doing business within the United States reasonably expects that its United States operations will be regulated by United States law. The only extraterritoriality about the transactions reached under the territorial effects doctrine is that not all of the causative factors producing the proscribed result may have occurred within the territory. Although some of the business decisions affecting United States operations may be made outside the forum state, the entire transaction is not ordinarily immunized.

> Certainly the doctrine of territorial sovereignty is not such an artificial limit on the vindication of legitimate sovereign interests that the injured

state confronts the wrong side of a one-way glass, powerless to counteract harmful effects originating outside its boundaries which easily pierce its "sovereign" walls, while its own regulatory efforts are reflected back in its face. Unless one admits that there are certain vital interests than can be affected with impunity by careful selection of the decision-making forum, with the result that a country may be forced to rely entirely on the good offices of a foreign state for vindication of the forum's interests — even when vindication of the forum state's interests would contradict the foreign state's own policies — then availability of territorial effects jurisdiction must be recognized."

A. Judge Wilkie's metaphor about the one-way glass seems especially appropriate in a global business environment. The effects, he says, easily pierce our borders and sovereign walls, yet our laws are reflected back. Put another way (as he does), in the modern business world, it is (and should be) largely irrelevant to the law from where the causative acts emanated - the issue **must be** "where are the effects felt?", else lawlessness is easily achieved, and, as Judge Wilkie states, enforcement becomes dependent on the "good offices" of the foreign state.

B. Judge Wilkie obviously does not want to commit our important interests to such "good offices", which seem never to be open to our public law (especially antitrust law) in any event. How do you think the British would respond? Would they say that their good offices are open for assassins and embezzlers, but not for those charged with price fixing and cartelizing behavior? If so, is it that the British favor anticompetitive practices, or simply that they disfavor our law?

3. Just as Judge Wilkie works to establish the "legitimacy" of U.S. interests in prescribing regulations affecting its trade, he recognizes the legitimacy of the British interest in doing the same, especially as it regards their citizens and subjects. The issue, he says, is how to resolve the conflict caused by this "concurrent jurisdiction to prescribe".

A. Judge Wilkie declines to adopt the theory of "paramount nationality" which was advanced by the defendants. Do you think such a prioritization makes sense in a modern, global business environment?

B. Judge Wilkie also rejects the comity balancing approach, saying (1) that courts cannot meaningfully balance factors that are too political for judicial resolution, that it belongs to the legislative and\or executive branches, and (2) that the attempt to appear reasonable through the comity balancing approach is not likely to achieve reasonableness in return. Which of these is the better rationale? Even if these rationales are sound, what is the alternative? It appears to be more all out legal war, like in this case. That may, however, be better than the alternative - surrender.

C.   What, then, is Judge Wilkie's approach to solving the "concurrent jurisdiction" dilemma? Comity, he says, means I won't interfere with your proceedings, and you shouldn't interfere with mine. The first to final judgment will gain international respect under the established rule that F2 will normally respect F1's judgments. There are, of course, some wrinkles:

   i.   The Protection of Trading Interests Act renders a treble damage judgment unenforceable in England. All antitrust judgments are automatically trebled. Of course, the judgment is still good in the U.S. and in countries that will recognize it, which is good enough, at least, when dealing with large international enterprises like Sabena and KLM.

   ii. This rule encourages a "race to final judgment". "There is little, if any, evidence of courts sacrificing procedural or substantive justice in an effort to "race" to a prior judgment," Judge Wilkie says. "To the extent this slight risk exists it is outweighed by the more important policies favoring respect for concurrent proceedings." Assuming he is right, the first court to act will vindicate its policies, with the other left out. To make that more palatable, Judge Wilkie goes on to allow that "most forums need not fear that their crucial policies would be trampled if a foreign judgment is reached first, since violation of domestic public policy may justify not enforcing the foreign judgment." If there were no injunctions, he opines, the interests of comity would thus be served from both ends. The British courts, if left alone, would defeat even that opportunity for comity, and that is why Judge Wilkie justifies his own antisuit injunction.

4.   Judge Starr (recently of "Whitewater" fame) is critical of Judge Wilkie, calling his approach "parochial." What does he mean? He says that the United States really has no over-riding interest in applying our antitrust laws. He points out, for example, that this a private law suit brought by a foreign entity against, inter alia, four U.S. corporations (Boeing, McDonald Douglas and Laker's U.S. banks). What difference should that make? He also points out that this not a government prosecution, and that the U.S. Executive has not indicated how U.S. interests are involved. By contrast, he says, the British Executive has stated that the issues relate to that country's vital interests. Thus, while he agrees with "much in the majority's decision" (such as the basic effects test, and the rejection of paramount nationality), he would have acted in a more narrow fashion that Judge Wilkie. What, exactly, would he have the lower court do? Do you think if the court had followed Judge Starr's approach, greater comity would have been achieved in this case? In future cases?

409

5. After review, do you find Judge Wilkie's <u>Laker</u> opinion as confrontational as it seemed on first reading? Is it simply a practical defense to an unusual legal battle, or is it instructive in general about how to handle garden variety jurisdiction to prescribe cases, like <u>American Banana</u> or <u>Timberlane</u>? Does it shed any light on the wisdom of Hand and Ryan, and does it help you to understand the issues in those cases and cases of that kind? Finally, what does it tell you about what portends for the next battle of this kind? Will the British be more reasonable? Will the U.S. take a middle of the road, reasonableness approach. Stay tuned, ladies and gentlemen!

* * *

V. THE SUPREME COURT FINALLY SPEAKS

HARTFORD FIRE INSURANCE CO., ET AL.
v.
CALIFORNIA

Supreme Court of the United States
509 U.S. 764
Decided: June 28, 1993

JUSTICE SOUTER announced the judgment of the Court and delivered the opinion of the Court with respect to Parts I, III, and IV. . . .

The Sherman Act makes every contract, combination, or conspiracy in unreasonable restraint of interstate or foreign commerce illegal. 26 Stat. 209, as amended, 15 U.S.C. § 1. These consolidated cases present questions about the application of that Act to the insurance industry, both here and abroad. The plaintiffs (respondents here) allege that both domestic and foreign defendants (petitioners here) violated the Sherman Act by engaging in various conspiracies to affect the American insurance market. A group of domestic defendants argues that the McCarran-Ferguson Act, 59 Stat. 33, as amended, 15 U.S.C. § 1011 et seq., precludes application of the Sherman Act to the conduct alleged; a group of foreign defendants argues that the principle of international comity requires the District Court to refrain from exercising jurisdiction over certain claims against it. We hold that most of the domestic defendants' alleged conduct is not immunized from antitrust liability by the McCarran-Ferguson Act, and that, even assuming it applies, the principle of international comity does not preclude District Court jurisdiction over the foreign conduct alleged.

I

The two petitions before us stem from consolidated litigation comprising the complaints of 19 States and many private plaintiffs alleging that the defendants, members of the insurance industry, conspired in violation of § 1 of the Sherman Act to restrict the terms of coverage of commercial general liability (CGL) insurance available in the United States. Because the cases come to us on motions to dismiss, we take the allegations of the complaints as true.

A

According to the complaints, the object of the conspiracies was to force certain primary insurers (insurers who sell insurance directly to consumers) to change the terms of their standard CGL insurance policies to conform with the policies the defendant insurers wanted to sell. The defendants wanted four changes.

First, CGL insurance has traditionally been sold in the United States on an "occurrence" basis, through a policy obligating the insurer "to pay or defend claims, whenever made, resulting from an accident or 'injurious exposure to conditions' that occurred during the [specific time] period the policy was in effect." App. 22 (Cal. Complaint P 52). In place of this traditional "occurrence" trigger of coverage, the defendants wanted a "claims-made" trigger, obligating the insurer to pay or defend only those claims made during the policy period. Such a policy has the distinct advantage for the insurer that when the policy period ends without a claim having been made, the insurer can be certain that the policy will not expose it to any further liability. Second, the defendants wanted the "claims-made" policy to have a "retroactive date" provision, which would further restrict coverage to claims based on incidents that occurred after a certain date. Such a provision eliminates the risk that an insurer, by issuing a claims-made policy, would assume liability arising from incidents that occurred before the policy's effective date, but remained undiscovered or caused no immediate harm. Third, CGL insurance has traditionally covered "sudden and accidental" pollution; the defendants wanted to eliminate that coverage. Finally, CGL insurance has traditionally provided that the insurer would bear the legal costs of defending covered claims against the insured without regard to the policy's stated limits of coverage; the defendants wanted legal defense costs to be counted against the stated limits (providing a "legal defense cost cap"). To understand how the defendants are alleged to have pressured the targeted primary insurers to make these changes, one must be aware of two important features of the insurance industry. First, most primary insurers rely on certain outside support services for the type of insurance coverage they wish to sell.

Defendant Insurance Services Office, Inc. (ISO), an association of approximately 1,400 domestic property and casualty insurers (including the primary insurer defendants, Hartford Fire Insurance Company, Allstate Insurance Company, CIGNA Corporation, and Aetna Casualty and Surety Company), is the almost exclusive source of support services in this country for CGL insurance. See id., at 19 (Cal. Complaint P 38). ISO develops standard policy forms and files or lodges them with each State's insurance regulators; most CGL insurance written in the United States is written on these forms. Ibid. (Cal. Complaint P 39); id., at 74 (Conn. Complaint P 50). All of the "traditional" features of CGL insurance relevant to this case were embodied in the ISO standard CGL insurance form that had been in use since 1973 (1973 ISO CGL form). Id., at 22 (Cal. Complaint P P 51-54); id., at 75 (Conn. Complaint P P 56-58). For each of its standard policy forms, ISO also supplies actuarial and rating information: it collects, aggregates, interprets, and distributes data on the premiums charged, claims filed and paid, and defense costs expended with respect to each form, id., at 19 (Cal. Complaint P 39); id., at 74 (Conn. Complaint P P 51-52), and on the basis of this data it predicts future loss trends and calculates advisory premium rates. Id., at 19 (Cal. Complaint P 39); id., at 74 (Conn. Complaint P 53). Most ISO members cannot afford to continue to use a form if ISO withdraws these support services. See id., at 32-33 (Cal. Complaint P P 97, 99).

Second, primary insurers themselves usually purchase insurance to cover a portion of the risk they assume from the consumer. This so-called "reinsurance" may serve at least two purposes, protecting the primary insurer from catastrophic loss, and allowing the primary insurer to sell more insurance than its own financial capacity might otherwise permit. Id., at 17 (Cal. Complaint P 29). Thus, "the availability of reinsurance affects the ability and willingness of primary insurers to provide insurance to their customers." Id., at 18 (Cal. Complaint P 34); id., at 63 (Conn. Complaint P 4(p)). Insurers who sell reinsurance themselves often purchase insurance to cover part of the risk they assume from the primary insurer; such "retrocessional reinsurance" does for reinsurers what reinsurance does for primary insurers. See ibid. (Conn. Complaint P 4(r)). Many of the defendants here are reinsurers or reinsurance brokers, or play some other specialized role in the reinsurance business; defendant Reinsurance Association of America (RAA) is a trade association of domestic reinsurers.

B

The prehistory of events claimed to give rise to liability starts in 1977, when ISO began the process of revising its 1973 CGL form. Id., at 22 (Cal. Complaint P 55). For the first time, it proposed two CGL forms (1984 ISO CGL forms), one the traditional "occurrence" type, the other "with a new 'claims-made' trigger." Id., at 22-23 (Cal. Complaint P 56). The "claims-made" form did not have a retroactive date provision, however, and both 1984 forms covered "'sudden and accidental' pollution" damage and provided for unlimited coverage of legal defense costs by the insurer. Id., at 23 (Cal. Complaint P P 59-60). Within the ISO, defendant Hartford Fire Insurance Company objected to the proposed 1984 forms; it desired elimination of the "occurrence" form, a retroactive date provision on the "claims-made" form, elimination of sudden and accidental pollution coverage, and a legal defense cost cap. Defendant Allstate Insurance Company also expressed its desire for a retroactive date provision on the "claims-made" form. Id., at 24 (Cal. Complaint P 61). Majorities in the relevant ISO committees, however, supported the proposed 1984 CGL forms and rejected the changes proposed by Hartford and Allstate. In December 1983, the ISO Board of Directors approved the proposed 1984 forms, and ISO filed or lodged the forms with state regulators in March 1984. Ibid. (Cal. Complaint P 62).

Dissatisfied with this state of affairs, the defendants began to take other steps to force a change in the terms of coverage of CGL insurance generally available, steps that, the plaintiffs allege, implemented a series of conspiracies in violation of § 1 of the Sherman Act. The plaintiffs recount these steps as a number of separate episodes corresponding to different Claims for Relief in their complaints; because it will become important to distinguish among these counts and the acts and defendants associated with them, we will note these correspondences.

The first four Claims for Relief of the California Complaint, id., at 36-43 (Cal. Complaint P P 111-130), and the Second Claim for Relief of the Connecticut Complaint, id., at 90-92 (Conn. Complaint P P 120-124), charge the four domestic primary insurer defendants and varying groups of domestic and foreign reinsurers, brokers, and associations with conspiracies to manipulate the ISO CGL forms. In March 1984, primary insurer Hartford persuaded General Reinsurance Corporation (General Re), the largest American reinsurer, to take steps either to procure desired changes in the ISO CGL forms, or "failing that, [to] 'derail' the entire ISO CGL forms program." Id., at 24 (Cal. Complaint P 64). General Re took up the matter with its trade association, RAA, which created a special committee that met and agreed to "boycott" the 1984 ISO CGL forms unless a retroactive-date provision was added to the claims-made form, and a pollution exclusion and defense cost cap were added to both forms. Id., at 24-25 (Cal. Complaint P P 65-66). RAA then sent a letter to ISO "announcing that its members would not provide reinsurance for coverages written on the 1984 CGL forms," id., at 25 (Cal. Complaint P 67), and Hartford and General Re enlisted a domestic reinsurance broker to give a speech to the ISO Board of Directors, in which he stated that no reinsurers would "break ranks" to reinsure the 1984 ISO CGL forms. Ibid. (Cal. Complaint P 68).

The four primary insurer defendants (Hartford, Aetna, CIGNA, and Allstate) also encouraged key actors in the London reinsurance market, an important provider of reinsurance for North American risks, to withhold reinsurance for coverages written on the 1984 ISO CGL forms. Id., at 25-26 (Cal. Complaint P P 69-70). As a consequence, many London-based underwriters, syndicates, brokers, and reinsurance companies informed ISO of their intention to withhold reinsurance on the 1984 forms, id., at 26-27 (Cal. Complaint P P 71-75), and at least some of them told ISO that they would withhold reinsurance until ISO incorporated all four desired changes, see supra, at 3-4, into the ISO CGL forms. App. 26 (Cal. Complaint P 74).

For the first time ever, ISO invited representatives of the domestic and foreign reinsurance markets to speak at an ISO Executive Committee meeting. Id., at 27-28 (Cal. Complaint P 78). At that meeting, the reinsurers "presented their agreed upon positions that there would be changes in the CGL forms or no reinsurance." Id., at 29 (Cal. Complaint P 82). The ISO Executive Committee then voted to include a retroactive-date provision in the claims-made form, and to exclude all pollution coverage from both new forms. (But it neither eliminated the occurrence form, nor added a legal defense cost cap.) The 1984 ISO CGL forms were then withdrawn from the marketplace, and replaced with forms (1986 ISO CGL forms) containing the new provisions. Ibid. (Cal. Complaint P 84).

After ISO got regulatory approval of the 1986 forms in most States where approval was needed, it eliminated its support services for the 1973 CGL form, thus rendering it impossible for most ISO members to continue to use the form. Id., at 32-33 (Cal. Complaint P P 97, 99).

The Fifth Claim for Relief of the California Complaint, id., at 43-44 (Cal. Complaint P P 131-135), and the virtually identical Third Claim for Relief of the Connecticut Complaint, id., at 92-94 (Conn. Complaint P P 125-129), charge a conspiracy among a group of London reinsurers and brokers to coerce primary insurers in the United States to offer CGL coverage only on a claims-made basis. The reinsurers collectively refused to write new reinsurance contracts for, or to renew long-standing contracts with, "primary . . . insurers unless they were prepared to switch from the occurrence to the claims-made form," id., at 30 (Cal. Complaint P 88); they also amended their reinsurance contracts to cover only claims made before a "'sunset date,'" thus eliminating reinsurance for claims made on occurrence policies after that date. Id., at 31 (Cal. Complaint P P 90-92).

The Sixth Claim for Relief of the California Complaint, id., at 45-46 (Cal. Complaint P P 136-140), and the nearly identical Fourth Claim for Relief of the Connecticut Complaint, id., at 94-95 (Conn. Complaint P P 130-134), charge another conspiracy among a somewhat different group of London reinsurers to withhold reinsurance for pollution coverage. The London reinsurers met and agreed that all reinsurance contracts covering North American casualty risks, including CGL risks, would be written with a complete exclusion for pollution liability coverage. Id., at 32 (Cal. Complaint P P 94-95). In accordance with this agreement, the parties have in fact excluded pollution liability coverage from CGL reinsurance contracts since at least late 1985. Ibid. (Cal. Complaint P94).

The Seventh Claim for Relief in the California Complaint, id., at 46-47 (Cal. Complaint P P 141-145), and the closely similar Sixth Claim for Relief in the Connecticut Complaint, id., at 97-98 (Conn. Complaint P P 140-144), charge a group of domestic primary insurers, foreign reinsurers, and the ISO with conspiring to restrain trade in the markets for "excess" and "umbrella" insurance by drafting model forms and policy language for these types of insurance, which are not normally offered on a regulated basis. Id., at 33 (Cal. Complaint P 101). The ISO Executive Committee eventually released standard language for both "occurrence" and "claims-made" umbrella and excess policies; that language included a retroactive date in the claims-made version, and an absolute pollution exclusion and a legal defense cost cap in both versions. Id., at 34 (Cal. Complaint P 105).

Finally, the Eighth Claim for Relief of the California Complaint, id., at 47-49 (Cal. Complaint P P 146-150), and its counterpart in the Fifth Claim for relief of the Connecticut complaint, id., at 95-97 (Conn. Complaint P P 135-139), charge a group of London and domestic retrocessional reinsurers with conspiring to withhold retrocessional reinsurance for North American seepage, pollution, and property contamination risks. Those retrocessional reinsurers signed, and have implemented, an agreement to use their "'best endeavors'" to ensure that they would provide such reinsurance for North American risks "'only . . . where the original business includes a seepage and pollution exclusion wherever legal and applicable.'" Id., at 35 (Cal. Complaint P 108).

C

Nineteen States and a number of private plaintiffs filed 36 complaints against the insurers involved in this course of events, charging that the conspiracies described above violated § 1 of the Sherman Act, 15 U.S.C. § 1. After the actions had been consolidated for litigation in the Northern District of California, the defendants moved to dismiss for failure to state

cause of action, or, in the alternative, for summary judgment. The District Court granted the motions to dismiss. In re Insurance Antitrust Litigation, 723 F. Supp. 464 (1989). It held that the conduct alleged fell within the grant of antitrust immunity contained in § 2(b) of the McCarran-Ferguson Act, 15 U.S.C. § 1012(b), because it amounted to "the business of insurance" and was "regulated by State law" within the meaning of that section; none of the conduct, in the District Court's view, amounted to a "boycott" within the meaning of the § 3(b) exception to that grant of immunity. 15 U.S.C. § 1013(b). The District Court also dismissed the three claims that named only certain London-based defendants, invoking international comity and applying the

Ninth Circuit's decision in Timberlane Lumber Co. v. Bank of America, N. T. & S. A., 549 F.2d 597 (CA9 1976).

The Court of Appeals reversed. In re Insurance Antitrust Litigation, 938 F.2d 919 (CA9 1991). Although it held the conduct involved to be "the business of insurance" within the meaning of § 2(b), it concluded that the defendants could not claim McCarran-Ferguson Act antitrust immunity for two independent reasons. First, it held, the foreign reinsurers were beyond the regulatory jurisdiction of the States; because their activities could not be "regulated by State law" within the meaning of § 2(b), they did not fall within that section's grant of immunity. Although the domestic insurers were "regulated by State law," the court held, they forfeited their § 2(b) exemption when they conspired with the nonexempt foreign reinsurers. Second, the Court of Appeals held that, even if the conduct alleged fell within the scope of § 2(b), it also fell within the § 3(b) exception for "acts of boycott, coercion, or intimidation." Finally, as to the three claims brought solely against foreign defendants, the court applied its Timberlane analysis, but concluded that the principle of international comity was no bar to exercising Sherman Act jurisdiction.

We granted certiorari . . . to address the application of the Sherman Act to the foreign conduct at issue. n9 506 U.S. (1992). We now affirm in part, reverse in part, and remand.

II

[The Court rejected the argument, made by both the U.S. insurers and the foreign reinsurers that the McCarron-Fergusson Act (a part of U.S. antitrust law) exempted them from antitrust law]

III

[W]e take up the question presented by No. 91-1128, whether certain claims against the London reinsurers should have been dismissed as improper applications of the Sherman Act to foreign conduct. The Fifth Claim for Relief of the California Complaint alleges a violation of § 1 of the Sherman Act by certain London reinsurers who conspired to coerce primary insurers in the United States to offer CGL coverage on a claims-made basis, thereby making "occurrence CGL coverage . . . unavailable in the State of California for many risks." App. 43-44 (Cal. Complaint P P 131-135). The Sixth Claim for Relief of the California Complaint alleges that the London reinsurers violated § 1 by a conspiracy to limit coverage of pollution risks in North America, thereby rendering "pollution liability coverage . . . almost entirely unavailable for the vast majority of casualty insurance purchasers in the State of California." Id., at 45-46 (Cal. Complaint P P 136-140). The Eighth Claim for Relief of the California Complaint alleges a further § 1 violation by the London reinsurers who, along with domestic retrocessional reinsurers, conspired to limit coverage of seepage, pollution, and property contamination risks in North America, thereby eliminating such coverage in the State of California. Id., at 47-48 (Cal. Complaint P P 146-150).

At the outset, we note that the District Court undoubtedly had jurisdiction of these Sherman Act claims, as the London reinsurers apparently concede. See Tr. of Oral Arg. 37 ("Our position is not that the Sherman Act does not apply in the sense that a minimal basis for the exercise of jurisdiction doesn't exist here. Our position is that there are certain circumstances, and that this is one of them, in which the interests of another State are sufficient that the exercise of that jurisdiction should be restrained"). Although the proposition was perhaps not always free from doubt, see American Banana Co. v. United Fruit Co., 213 U.S. 347, 53 L. Ed. 826, 29 S. Ct. 511 (1909), it is well established by now that the Sherman Act applies to foreign conduct that was meant to produce and did in fact produce some substantial effect in the United States. See Matsushita Elec. Industrial Co. v. Zenith Radio Corp., 475 U.S. 574, 582, 89 L. Ed. 2d 538, 106 S. Ct. 1348, n. 6 (1986); United States v. Aluminum Co. of America, 148 F.2d 416, 444 (CA2 1945) (L. Hand, J.); Restatement (Third) of Foreign Relations Law of the United States § 415, and Reporters' Note 3 (1987) (hereinafter Restatement (Third) Foreign Relations Law); 1 P. Areeda & D. Turner, Antitrust Law P 236 (1978); cf. Continental Ore Co. v. Union Carbide & Carbon Corp., 370 U.S. 690, 704, 8 L. Ed. 2d 777, 82 S. Ct. 1404 (1962); Steele v. Bulova Watch Co., 344 U.S. 280, 288, 97 L. Ed. 319, 73 S. Ct. 252 (1952); United States v. Sisal Sales Corp., 274 U.S. 268, 275-276, 71 L. Ed. 1042, 47 S. Ct. 592 (1927). Such is the conduct alleged here: that the London reinsurers engaged in unlawful conspiracies to affect the market for insurance in the United States and that their conduct in fact produced substantial effect. See 938 F.2d, at 933.

According to the London reinsurers, the District Court should have declined to exercise such jurisdiction under the principle of international comity. The Court of Appeals agreed that courts should look to that principle in deciding whether to exercise jurisdiction under the Sherman Act. Id., at 932. This availed the London reinsurers nothing, however. To be sure, the Court of Appeals believed that "application of [American] antitrust laws to the London reinsurance market 'would lead to significant conflict with English law and policy,'" and that "such a conflict, unless outweighed by other factors, would by itself be reason to decline exercise of jurisdiction." Id., at 933 (citation omitted). But other factors, in the court's view, including the London reinsurers' express purpose to affect United States commerce and the substantial nature of the effect produced, outweighed the supposed conflict and required the exercise of jurisdiction in this case. Id., at 934.[3]

When it enacted the Foreign Trade Antitrust Improvements Act of 1982 (FTAIA), 96 Stat. 1246, 15 U.S.C. § 6a, Congress expressed no view on the question whether a court with Sherman Act jurisdiction should ever decline to exercise such jurisdiction on grounds of international comity. See H. R. Rep. No. 97-686, p. 13 (1982) ("If a court determines that the requirements for subject matter jurisdiction are met, [the FTAIA] would have no effect on the court['s] ability to employ notions of comity . . . or otherwise to take account of the international character of the transaction") (citing Timberlane). We need not decide that question here, however, for even assuming that in a proper case a court may decline to exercise Sherman Act jurisdiction over foreign conduct (or, as JUSTICE SCALIA would put it, may conclude by the employment of comity analysis in the first instance that there is no jurisdiction), international comity would not counsel against exercising jurisdiction in the circumstances alleged here.

The only substantial question in this case is whether "there is in fact a true conflict between domestic and foreign law." Societe Nationale Industrielle Aerospatiale v. United States District Court, 482 U.S. 522, 555, 96 L. Ed. 2d 461, 107 S. Ct. 2542 (1987) (BLACKMUN, J., concurring in part and dissenting in part). The London reinsurers contend that applying the Act to their conduct would conflict significantly with British law, and the British Government, appearing before us as amicus curiae, concurs. See Brief for Petitioners in No. 91-1128, pp. 22-27; Brief for Government of United Kingdom of Great Britain and Northern Ireland as Amicus Curiae 10-14. They assert that Parliament has established a comprehensive regulatory regime over the London reinsurance market and that the conduct alleged here was perfectly consistent with British law and policy. But this is not to state a conflict. "The fact that conduct is lawful in the state in which it took place will not, of itself, bar application of the United States antitrust laws," even where the foreign state has a strong policy to permit or encourage such conduct. Restatement (Third)

---

3. JUSTICE SCALIA contends that comity concerns figure into the prior analysis whether jurisdiction exists under the Sherman Act. Post, at 19-20. This contention is inconsistent with the general understanding that the Sherman Act covers foreign conduct producing a substantial intended effect in the United States, and that concerns of comity come into play, if at all, only after a court has determined that the acts complained of are subject to Sherman Act jurisdiction. See United States v. Aluminum Co. of America, 148 F.2d 416, 444 (CA2 1945) ("It follows from what we have . . . said that [the agreements at issue] were unlawful [under the Sherman Act], though made abroad, if they were intended to affect imports and did affect them"); Mannington Mills, Inc. v. Congoleum Corp., 595 F.2d 1287, 1294 (CA3 1979) (once court determines that jurisdiction exists under the Sherman Act, question remains whether comity precludes its exercise); H.R.Rep. No. 97-686, supra, at 13. But cf. Timberlane Lumber Co. v. Bank of America, N.T. & S.A., 549 F.2d 597, 613 (CA9 1976); I J. Atwood & K. Brewster, Antitrust and American Business Abroad 166 (1981). In any event, the parties conceded jurisdiction at oral argument, see supra, at 28-29, and we see no need to address this contention here.

Foreign Relations Law § 415, Comment j; see Continental Ore Co., supra, at 706-707. No conflict exists, for these purposes, "where a person subject to regulation by two states can comply with the laws of both." Restatement (Third) Foreign Relations Law § 403, Comment e.[4] Since the London reinsurers do not argue that British law requires them to act in some fashion prohibited by the law of the United States, see Reply Brief for Petitioners in No. 91-1128, pp. 7-8, or claim that their compliance with the laws of both countries is otherwise impossible, we see no conflict with British law. See Restatement (Third) Foreign Relations Law § 403, Comment e, § 415, Comment j. We have no need in this case to address other considerations that might inform a decision to refrain from the exercise of jurisdiction on grounds of international comity.

IV

The judgment of the Court of Appeals is affirmed in part and reversed in part, and the case is remanded for further proceedings consistent with this opinion.

It is so ordered.

JUSTICE SCALIA delivered . . . a dissenting opinion with respect to Part III, in which JUSTICE O'CONNOR, JUSTICE KENNEDY, and JUSTICE THOMAS have joined.

. . . I dissent from the Court's ruling concerning the extraterritorial application of the Sherman Act. . . .

The petitioners in No. 91-1128, various British corporations and other British subjects, argue that certain of the claims against them constitute an inappropriate extraterritorial application of the Sherman Act. It is important to distinguish two distinct questions raised by this petition: whether the District Court had jurisdiction, and whether the Sherman Act reaches the extraterritorial conduct alleged here. On the first question, I believe that the District Court had subject-matter jurisdiction over the Sherman Act claims against all the defendants (personal jurisdiction is not contested). The respondents asserted nonfrivolous claims under the Sherman Act, and 28 U.S.C. § 1331 vests district courts with subject-matter jurisdiction over cases "arising under" federal statutes. As precedents such as Lauritzen v. Larsen, 345 U.S. 571, 97 L. Ed. 1254, 73 S. Ct. 921 (1953), make clear, that is sufficient to establish the District Court's jurisdiction over these claims. Lauritzen involved a Jones Act claim brought by a foreign sailor against a foreign

---

4. JUSTICE SCALIA says that we put the cart before the horse in citing this authority, for he argues it may be apposite only after a determination that jurisdiction over the foreign acts is reasonable. Post, at 23-24. But whatever the order of cart and horse, conflict in this sense is the only substantial issue before the Court.

shipowner. The shipowner contested the District Court's jurisdiction, see id., at 573, apparently on the grounds that the Jones Act did not govern the dispute between the foreign parties to the action. Though ultimately agreeing with the shipowner that the Jones Act did not apply, see discussion infra, at 18, the Court held that the District Court had jurisdiction.

"As frequently happens, a contention that there is some barrier to granting plaintiff's claim is cast in terms of an exception to jurisdiction of subject matter. A cause of action under our law was asserted here, and the court had power to determine whether it was or was not founded in law and in fact." 345 U.S., at 575.

The second question — the extraterritorial reach of the Sherman Act — has nothing to do with the jurisdiction of the courts. It is a question of substantive law turning on whether, in enacting the Sherman Act, Congress asserted regulatory power over the challenged conduct. See EEOC v. Arabian American Oil Co., 499 U.S. 244, (1991) (Aramco) (slip op., at 2) ("It is our task to determine whether Congress intended the protections of Title VII to apply to United States citizens employed by American employers outside of the United States"). If a plaintiff fails to prevail on this issue, the court does not dismiss the claim for want of subject-matter jurisdiction — want of power to adjudicate; rather, it decides the claim, ruling on the merits that the plaintiff has failed to state a cause of action under the relevant statute. See Romero, supra, at 384 (holding no claim available under the Jones Act); American Banana Co. v. United Fruit Co., 213 U.S. 347, 359, 53 L. Ed. 826, 29 S. Ct. 511 (1909) (holding that complaint based upon foreign conduct "alleges no case under the [Sherman Act]").

There is, however, a type of "jurisdiction" relevant to determining the extraterritorial reach of a statute; it is known as "legislative jurisdiction," Aramco, supra, at (slip op., at 8), Restatement (First) Conflict of Laws § 60 (1934), or "jurisdiction to prescribe," 1 Restatement (Third) of Foreign Relations Law of the United States 235 (1987) (hereinafter Restatement (Third)). This refers to "the authority of a state to make its law applicable to persons or activities," and is quite a separate matter from "jurisdiction to adjudicate," see id., at 231. There is no doubt, of course, that Congress possesses legislative jurisdiction over the acts alleged in this complaint: Congress has broad power under Article I, § 8, cl. 3 "to regulate Commerce with foreign Nations," and this Court has repeatedly upheld its power to make laws applicable to persons or activities beyond our territorial boundaries where United States interests are affected. But the question in this case is whether, and to what extent, Congress has exercised that undoubted legislative jurisdiction in enacting the Sherman Act.

Two canons of statutory construction are relevant in this inquiry. The first is the "long-standing principle of American law 'that legislation of Congress, unless a contrary intent appears, is meant to apply only within the territorial jurisdiction of the United States.'" Aramco, supra, at (slip op., at 3) (quoting Foley Bros., Inc. v. Filardo, 336 U.S. 281, 285, 93 L. Ed. 680, 69 S. Ct. 575 (1949)). Applying that canon in Aramco, we held that the version of Title VII of the Civil Rights Act of 1964 then in force, 42 U.S.C. §§ 2000e-2000e-17 (1988 ed.), did not extend outside the territory of the United States even though the statute contained broad provisions extending its prohibitions to, for example, "'any activity, business, or industry in commerce.'" Id., at (slip op., at 4) (quoting 42 U.S.C. § 2000e(h)). We held such "boilerplate language" to be an insufficient indication to override the presumption against extraterritoriality. Id., at (slip op., at 5); see also id., at - (slip op., at 6-8). The Sherman Act contains similar "boilerplate language," and if the question were not governed by precedent, it would be worth considering whether that presumption controls the outcome here. We have, however, found the presumption to be overcome with respect to our antitrust laws; it is now well established that the Sherman Act applies extraterritorially. See Matsushita Elec. Industrial Co. v. Zenith Radio Corp., 475 U.S. 574, 582, 89 L. Ed. 2d 538, 106 S. Ct. 1348, n. 6 (1986); Continental Ore Co. v. Union Carbide & Carbon Corp., 370 U.S. 690, 704, 8 L. Ed. 2d 777, 82 S. Ct. 1404 (1962); see also United States v. Aluminum Co. of America, 148 F.2d 416 (CA2 1945). But if the presumption against extraterritoriality has been overcome or is otherwise inapplicable, a second canon of statutory construction becomes relevant: "An act of congress ought never to be construed to violate the law of nations if any other possible construction remains." Murray v. The Charming Betsy, 6 U.S. 64, 2 Cranch 64, 118, 2 L. Ed. 208 (1804) (Marshall, C. J.). This canon is "wholly independent" of the presumption against extraterritoriality. Aramco, 499 U.S., at (Marshall, J., dissenting)(slip op., at 4). It is relevant to determining the substantive reach of a statute because "the law of nations," or customary international law, includes limitations on a nation's exercise of its jurisdiction to prescribe. See Restatement (Third) §§ 401-416. Though it clearly has constitutional authority to do so, Congress is generally presumed not to have exceeded those customary international-law limits on jurisdiction to prescribe.

Consistent with that presumption, this and other courts have frequently recognized that, even where the presumption against extraterritoriality does not apply, statutes should not be interpreted to regulate foreign persons or conduct if that regulation would conflict with principles of international law. For example, in Romero v. International Terminal Operating Co., 358 U.S. 354, 3 L. Ed. 2d 368, 79 S. Ct. 468 (1959), the plaintiff, a Spanish sailor who had been injured while working aboard a Spanish-flag and Spanish-owned vessel, filed a Jones Act claim against his Spanish employer. The presumption against extraterritorial application of federal statutes was inapplicable to the case, as the actionable tort had occurred in American waters. See id., at 383. The Court nonetheless stated that, "in the absence of contrary congressional direction," it would apply "principles of choice of law that are consonant with the needs of a general federal maritime law and with due recognition of our self-regarding respect for the relevant interests of foreign nations in the regulation of maritime commerce as part of the legitimate concern of the international community." Id., at 382-383. "The controlling considerations" in this choice-of-law analysis were "the interacting interests of the United States and of foreign countries." Id., at 383.

Romero referred to, and followed, the choice-of-law analysis set forth in Lauritzen v. Larsen, 345 U.S. 571, 97 L. Ed. 1254, 73 S. Ct. 921 (1953). As previously mentioned, Lauritzen also involved a Jones Act claim brought by a foreign sailor against a foreign employer. The Lauritzen Court recognized the basic problem: "If [the Jones Act were] read literally, Congress has conferred an American right of action which requires nothing more than that plaintiff be 'any seaman who shall suffer personal injury in the course of his employment.'" Id., at 576. The solution it adopted was to construe the statute "to apply only to areas and transactions in which American law would be considered operative under prevalent doctrines of international law." Id., at 577 (emphasis added). To support application of international law to limit the facial breadth of the statute, the Court relied upon — of course — Chief Justice Marshall's statement in The Charming Betsy quoted supra, at 16. It then set forth "several factors which, alone or in combination, are generally conceded to influence choice of law to govern a tort claim." 345 U.S., at 583; see id., at 583-593 (discussing factors).

Lauritzen, Romero, and McCulloch were maritime cases, but we have recognized the principle that the scope of generally worded statutes must be construed in light of international law in other areas as well. [citations omitted]. More specifically, the principle was expressed in United States v. Aluminum Co. of America, 148 F.2d 416 (CA2 1945), the decision that established the extraterritorial reach of the Sherman Act. In his opinion for the court, Judge Learned Hand cautioned "we are not to read general words, such as those in [the Sherman] Act, without regard to the limitations customarily observed by nations upon the exercise of their powers; limitations which generally correspond to those fixed by the 'Conflict of Laws.'"

More recent lower court precedent has also tempered the extraterritorial application of the Sherman Act with considerations of "international comity." See Timberlane Lumber Co. v. Bank of America, N.T & S.A., 549 F.2d 597, 608-615 (CA9 1976); Mannington Mills, Inc. v. Congoleum Corp., 595 F.2d 1287, 1294-1298 (CA3 1979); Montreal Trading Ltd. v. Amax Inc., 661 F.2d 864, 869-871 (CA10 1981); Laker Airways v. Sabena, Belgian World Airlines, 235 U.S. App. D. C. 207, 236, 731 F.2d 909, and n. 109, 731 F.2d 909, 938, and n. 109 (1984); see also Pacific Seafarers, Inc. v. Pacific Far East Line, Inc., 131 U.S. App. D. C. 226, 236, 404 F.2d 804, and n. 31, 404 F.2d 804, 814, and n. 31 (1968). The "comity" they refer to is not the comity of courts, whereby judges decline to exercise jurisdiction over matters more appropriately adjudged elsewhere, but rather what might be termed "prescriptive comity": the respect sovereign nations afford each other by limiting the reach of their laws. That comity is exercised by legislatures when they enact laws, and courts assume it has been exercised when they come to interpreting the scope of laws their legislatures have enacted. It is a traditional component of choice-of-law theory. See J. Story, Commentaries on the Conflict of Laws § 38 (1834) (distinguishing between the "comity of the courts" and the "comity of nations," and defining the latter as "the true foundation and extent of the obligation of the laws of one nation within the territories of another"). Comity in this sense includes the choice-of-law principles that, "in the absence of contrary congressional direction," are assumed to be incorporated into our substantive laws having extraterritorial reach. Romero, supra, at 382-383; see also Lauritzen, supra, at 578-579; Hilton v. Guyot, 159 U.S. 113, 162-166, 40 L. Ed. 95, 16 S. Ct. 139 (1895). Considering comity in this way is just part of determining whether the Sherman Act prohibits the conduct at issue.

In sum, the practice of using international law to limit the extraterritorial reach of statutes is firmly established in our jurisprudence. In proceeding to apply that practice to the present case, I shall rely on the Restatement (Third) of Foreign Relations Law for the relevant principles of international law. Its standards appear fairly supported in the decisions of this Court construing international choice-of-law principles (Lauritzen, Romero, and McCulloch) and in the decisions of other federal courts, especially Timberlane. Whether the Restatement precisely reflects international law in every detail matters little here, as I believe this case would be resolved the same way under virtually any conceivable test that takes account of foreign regulatory interests.

Under the Restatement, a nation having some "basis" for jurisdiction to prescribe law should nonetheless refrain from exercising that jurisdiction "with respect to a person or activity having connections with another state when the exercise of such jurisdiction is unreasonable." Restatement (Third) § 403(1). The "reasonableness" inquiry turns on a number of factors including, but not limited to: "the extent to which the activity takes place within the territory [of the regulating state]," id., § 403(2)(a); "the connections, such as nationality, residence, or economic activity, between the regulating state and the person principally responsible for the activity to be regulated," id., § 403(2)(b); "the character of the activity to be regulated, the importance of regulation to the regulating state, the extent to which other states regulate such activities, and the degree to which the desirability of such regulation is generally accepted," id., § 403(2)(c); "the extent to which another state may have an interest in regulating the activity," id., § 403(2)(g); and "the likelihood of conflict with regulation by another state," id., § 403(2)(h). Rarely would these factors point more clearly against application of United States law. The activity relevant to the counts at issue here took place primarily in the United Kingdom, and the defendants in these counts are British corporations and British subjects having their principal place of business or residence outside the United States. Great Britain has established a comprehensive regulatory scheme governing the

423

London reinsurance markets, and clearly has a heavy "interest in regulating the activity," id., § 403(2)(g). See 935 F.2d, at 932-933; In re Insurance Antitrust Litigation, 723 F. Supp. 464, 487-488 (ND Cal. 1989); see also J. Butler & R. Merkin, Reinsurance Law A.1.1-02 (1992). Finally, § 2(b) of the McCarran-Ferguson Act allows state regulatory statutes to override the Sherman Act in the insurance field, subject only to the narrow "boycott" exception set forth in § 3(b) — suggesting that "the importance of regulation to the [United States]," id., § 403(2)(c), is slight. Considering these factors, I think it unimaginable that an assertion of legislative jurisdiction by the United States would be considered reasonable, and therefore it is inappropriate to assume, in the absence of statutory indication to the contrary, that Congress has made such an assertion.

It is evident from what I have said that the Court's comity analysis, which proceeds as though the issue is whether the courts should "decline to exercise . . . jurisdiction," ante, at 31, rather than whether the Sherman Act covers this conduct, is simply misdirected. I do not at all agree, moreover, with the Court's conclusion that the issue of the substantive scope of the Sherman Act is not in the case. See ante, at 29, n. 22; ante, at 30, n. 24. To be sure, the parties did not make a clear distinction between adjudicative jurisdiction and the scope of the statute. Parties often do not, as we have observed (and have declined to punish with procedural default) before. See the excerpt from Lauritzen quoted supra, at 14; see also Romero, 358 U.S., at 359. It is not realistic, and also not helpful, to pretend that the only really relevant issue in this case is not before us. In any event, if one erroneously chooses, as the Court does, to make adjudicative jurisdiction (or, more precisely, abstention) the vehicle for taking account of the needs of rescriptive comity, the Court still gets it wrong. It concludes that no "true conflict" counseling nonapplication of United States law (or rather, as it thinks, United States judicial jurisdiction) exists unless compliance with United States law would constitute a violation of another country's law. Ante, at 31-32. That breathtakingly broad proposition, which contradicts the many cases discussed earlier, will bring the Sherman Act and other laws into sharp and unnecessary conflict with the legitimate interests of other countries — particularly our closest trading partners.

In the sense in which the term "conflict" was used in Lauritzen, 345 U.S., at 582, 592, and is generally understood in the field of conflicts of laws, there is clearly a conflict in this case. The petitioners here, like the defendant in Lauritzen, were not compelled by any foreign law to take their allegedly wrongful actions, but that no more precludes a conflict-of-laws analysis here than it did there. See id., at 575-576 (detailing the differences between foreign and United States law). Where applicable foreign and domestic law provide different substantive rules of decision to govern the parties' dispute, a conflict-of-laws analysis is necessary. See generally R. Weintraub, Commentary on Conflict of Laws 2-3 (1980); Restatement (First) of Conflict of Laws § 1, Comment c and Illustrations (1934).

Literally the only support that the Court adduces for its position is § 403 of the Restatement (Third) of Foreign Relations Law — or more precisely Comment e to that provision, which states:

> "Subsection (3) [which says that a state should defer to another state if that state's interest is clearly greater] applies only when one state requires what another prohibits, or where compliance with the regulations of two states exercising jurisdiction consistently with this section is otherwise impossible. It does not apply where a person subject to regulation by two states can comply with the laws of both . . . ."

The Court has completely misinterpreted this provision. Subsection (3) of § 403 (requiring one State to defer to another in the limited circumstances just described) comes into play only after subsection (1) of § 403 has been complied with — i.e., after it has been determined that the exercise of jurisdiction by both of the two states is not "unreasonable." That prior question is answered by applying the factors (inter alia) set forth in subsection (2) of § 403, that is, precisely the factors that I have discussed in text and that the Court rejects.

I would reverse the judgment of the Court of Appeals on this issue, and remand to the District Court with instructions to dismiss for failure to state a claim on the three counts at issue in No. 91-1128.

NOTES AND QUESTIONS

1. Hartford Fire is a departure from the comity-influenced Restatement and the Timberlane approach. Why did the Court decline to adopt Brewster's jurisdictional rule of reason? How did the Court avoid the issue of conflicting regulatory schemes?

    A. Note that the Court traces the history of, and invokes, the effects doctrine; the territoriality approach is rejected. What does that portend for the future of the revenue rule?

    B. The majority seems to quickly dispense with issues of intrusion and conflict, reducing the entire subject to a paragraph. Is that a wise treatment? Do you think the British will think it an adequate justification for application of US law?

2.   The decision states that, in this case, there is no need to consider comity because there is no "conflict of laws"

   A.   What is the Court's definition of conflict? What is Justice Scalia's definition?

      i.   Which of these definitions would you have given before you read this case?

      ii.   Re-read Judge Ryan's decision in ICI (1). Is it the same as that of the majority, or of Justice Scalia?

   B.   If considerations of comity do not underlie this decision, what policy justifies the Supreme Court's decision to (essentially) ignore the British regulatory scheme? Think about the differences in policy between Boucher v. Lawson(17th century) and Regazzoni v. Sethia(20th century). What analogies can be drawn?

3.   What do you think will be the reaction to this decision? Will the British reinsurers pull out of the U.S.? Or will they try some other legal device? What might that device be? (Hint: consider Judge Ryan's statement that:

> Our power so to regulate is limited and depends upon jurisdiction in personam; the effectiveness of the exercise of that power depends upon the recognition which will be given to our judgment as a matter of comity by the courts of the foreign sovereign . . .

What could a foreign corporation do to avoid "the power to regulate"?

* * *

IV. AFTER *HARTFORD FIRE*

UNITED STATES OF AMERICA
V.
NIPPON PAPER INDUSTRIES CO., LTD.

United States Court of Appeals for the First Circuit
March 17, 1997
109 F3d 1

SELYA, Circuit Judge.

This case raises an important, hitherto unanswered question. In it, the United States attempts to convict a foreign corporation under the Sherman Act, a federal antitrust statute, alleging that price-fixing activities which took place entirely in Japan are prosecutable because they were intended to have, and did in fact have, substantial effects in this country. The district court, declaring that a criminal antitrust prosecution could not be based on wholly extraterritorial conduct, dismissed the indictment. See *United States v. Nippon Paper Indus. Co.*, 944 F. Supp. 55 (D. Mass. 1996). We reverse.

I. JUST THE FAX

Since the district court granted the defendant's motion to dismiss for failure to state a prosecutable offense, we draw our account of the pertinent events from the well-pleaded facts in the indictment itself.

In 1995, a federal grand jury handed up an indictment naming as a defendant Nippon Paper Industries Co., Ltd. (NPI), a Japanese manufacturer of facsimile paper. The indictment alleges that in 1990 NPI and certain unnamed coconspirators held a number of meetings in Japan which culminated in an agreement to fix the price of thermal fax paper throughout North America. NPI and other manufacturers who were privy to the scheme purportedly accomplished their objective by selling the paper in Japan to unaffiliated trading houses on condition that the latter charge specified (inflated) prices for the paper when they resold it in North America. The trading houses then shipped and sold the paper to their subsidiaries in the United States who in turn sold it to American consumers at swollen prices. The indictment further relates that, in 1990 alone, NPI sold thermal fax paper worth approximately $ 6,100,000 for eventual import into the United States; and that in order to ensure the success of the venture, NPI monitored the paper trail and confirmed that the prices charged to end users were those that it had arranged. These activities, the indictment posits, had a substantial adverse effect on commerce in the United States and unreasonably restrained trade in violation of Section One of the Sherman Act, 15 U.S.C. § 1 (1994).

427

NPI moved to dismiss because, inter alia, if the conduct attributed to NPI occurred at all, it took place entirely in Japan, and, thus, the indictment failed to allege an offense under Section One of the Sherman Act. The government opposed this initiative on two grounds. First, it claimed that the law deserved a less grudging reading and that, properly read, Section One of the Sherman Act applied criminally to wholly foreign conduct as long as that conduct produced substantial and intended effects within the United States. Second, it claimed that the indictment, too, deserved a less grudging reading and that, properly read, the bill alleged a vertical conspiracy in restraint of trade that involved overt acts by certain coconspirators within the United States. Accepting a restrictive reading of both the statute and the indictment, the district court dismissed the case. See United States v. NPI, 944 F. Supp. 55 at 64-66. This appeal followed.

II. ANALYSIS

We begin — and end — with the overriding legal question. Because this question is one of statutory construction, we review de novo the holding that Section One of the Sherman Act does not cover wholly extraterritorial conduct in the criminal context.

Our analysis proceeds in moieties. We first present the historical context in which this important question arises. We move next to the specifics of the case.

A. An Historical Perspective.

Our law has long presumed that "legislation of Congress, unless a contrary intent appears, is meant to apply only within the territorial jurisdiction of the United States. *EEOC v. Arabian American Oil Co.*, 499 U.S. 244, 248, 113 L. Ed. 2d 274, 111 S. Ct. 1227 (1991) (citation omitted). In this context, the Supreme Court has charged inquiring courts with determining whether Congress has clearly expressed an affirmative desire to apply particular laws to conduct that occurs beyond the borders of the United States.

The earliest Supreme Court case which undertook a comparable task in respect to Section One of the Sherman Act determined thatthe presumption against extraterritoriality had not been overcome. In *American Banana Co. v. United Fruit Co.*, 213 U.S. 347, 53 L. Ed. 826, 29 S. Ct. 511 (1909), the Court considered the application of the Sherman Act in a civil action concerning conduct which occurred entirely in Central America and which had no discernible effect on imports to the United States. Starting with what Justice Holmes termed "the general and almost universal rule" holding "that the character of an act as lawful or unlawful must be determined wholly by the law of the country where the act is done," id. at 356, and the ancillary proposition that, in cases of doubt, a statute should be "confined in its operation and effect to the territorial limits over which the lawmaker has general and legitimate power, 11 id. at 357, the Court held that the defendant's actions abroad were not proscribed by the Sherman Act.

Our jurisprudence is precedent-based, but it is not static. By 1945, a different court saw a very similar problem in a somewhat softer light. In *United States v. Aluminum Co. of Am.*, 148 F.2d 416 (2d Cir. 1945) (Alcoa), the Second Circuit, sitting as a court of last resort, see 15 U.S.C. @ 29 (authorizing designation of a court of appeals as a court of last resort for certain antitrust cases), mulled a civil action brought under Section One against a Canadian corporation for acts committed entirely abroad which, the government averred, had produced substantial anticompetitive effects within the United States. The Alcoa court read American Banana narrowly; that case, Judge Learned Hand wrote, stood only for the principle that "we should not impute to Congress an intent to punish all whom its courts can catch, for conduct which has no consequences within the United States." 148 F.2d at 443. But a sovereign ordinarily can impose liability for conduct outside its borders that produces consequences within them, and while considerations of comity argue against applying Section One to situations in which no effect within the United States has been shown — the American Banana scenario — the statute, properly interpreted, does proscribe extraterritorial acts which were "intended to affect imports the United States] and did affect them." Id. at 444. On the facts of Alcoa, therefore, the presumption against extraterritoriality had been overcome, and the Sherman Act had been violated. See id. at 444-45.

Any perceived tension between American Banana and Alcoa was eased by the Supreme Court in its most recent exploration of the Sheman Act's extraterritorial reach. In *Hartford Fire Ins. Co. v. California*, 509 U.S. 764, 125 L. Ed.2d 612, 113 S. Ct. 2891 (1993), the Justices endorsed Alcoa's core holding, permitting civil antitrust claims under Section One to go forward despite the fact that the actions which allegedly violated Section One occurred entirely on British soil. While noting American Banana's initial disagreement with this proposition, the Hartford Fire Court deemed it "well established by now that the Sherman Act applies to foreign conduct that was meant to produce and did in fact produce some substantial effect in the United States." 509 U.S. 764 at 796. The conduct alleged, a London-based conspiracy to alter the American insurance market, met that benchmark.[5] See id.

To sum up, the case law now conclusively establishes that civil antitrust actions predicated on wholly foreign conduct which has an intended and substantial

---

5. As NPI reminds us, four Justices dissented in Hartford Fire. This is cold comfort, however, for the dissenters expressed complete agreement with the majority's view on extraterritoriality. See Hartford Fire, 509 U.S. at 814 (Scalia, J., dissenting). By the same token, NPI's attempt to distinguish Hartford Fire on the ground that the defendants there conceded the United States, jurisdiction over their conduct fails for two reasons. In the first place, the assertion is no more than a play on words. The majority opinion in Hartford Fire stated that the district court "undoubtedly" had jurisdiction over the civil claims, "as the London reinsurers apparently concede." Id. at 795. It is obvious, therefore, that jurisdiction did not depend on the concession; to the contrary, jurisdiction would "undoubtedly" have existed in any event. In the second place, one of the London defendants did not join in this apparent concession, but the Court nonetheless held that defendant's foreign conduct to be within the Sherman Act's proscriptive ambit because it was part of a scheme which "was intended to and did in fact produce a substantial effect on the American insurance market." Id. at 795 n.21.

effect in the United States come within Section One's jurisdictional reach. In arriving at this conclusion, we take no view of the government's asseveration that the Foreign Trade Antitrust Improvements Act of 1982 (FTAIA) 15 U.S.C. § 6a (1994), makes manifest Congress' intent to apply the Sherman Act extraterritorially. The FTAIA is inelegantly phrased and the court in *Hartford Fire* declined to place any weight on it. See *Hartford Fire*, 509 U.S. at 796 n.23. We emulate this example and do not rest our ultimate conclusion about Section One's scope upon the FTAIA.

B. The Merits.

Were this a civil case, our journey would be complete. But here the United States essays a criminal prosecution for solely extraterritorial conduct rather than a civil action. This is largely uncharted terrain; we are aware of no authority directly on point, and the parties have cited none.

Be that as it may, one datum sticks out like a sore thumb: in both criminal and civil cases, the claim that Section One applies extraterritorially is based on the same language in the same section of the same statute: "Every contract, combination in the form of trust or otherwise, or conspiracy, in restraint of trade or commerce among the several States, or with foreign nations, is declared to be illegal." 15 U.S.C. § 1. Words may sometimes be chameleons, possessing different shades of meaning in different contexts, see, e.g., *Hanover Ins. Co. v. United States*, 880 F.2d 1503, 1504 (1st Cir. 1989), cert. denied, 493 U.S. 1023, 107 L. Ed. 2d 745, 110 S. Ct. 726 (1990), but common sense suggests that courts should interpret the same language in the same section of the same statute uniformly, regardless of whether the impetus for interpretation is criminal or civil.

Common sense is usually a good barometer of statutory meaning. Here, however, we need not rely on common sense alone; accepted canons of statutory construction point in the same direction. It is a fundamental interpretive principle that identical words or terms used in different parts of the same act are intended to have the same meaning. [citations omitted]. This principle — which the Court recently called "the basic canon of statutory construction, *Estate of Cowart v. Nicklos Drilling Co.*, 505 U.S. 469, 479, 120 L. Ed. 2d 379, 112 S. Ct. 2589 (1992) — operates not only when particular phrases appear in different sections of the same act, but also when they appear in different paragraphs or sentences of a single section. See *Russo v. Texaco, Inc.*, 808 F.2d 221, 227 (2d Cir. 1986) ("It is a settled principle of statutory construction that when the same word or phrase is used in the same section of an act more than once, and the meaning is clear as used in one place, it will be construed to have the same meaning in the next place." (citations and internal quotation marks omitted); *United States v. Gertz*, 249 F.2d 662, 665 (9th Cir. 1957) (similar). It follows, therefore, that if the language upon which the indictment rests were the same as the language upon which civil liability rests but appeared in a different section of the Sherman Act, or in a different part of the same section, we would be under great pressure to follow the lead of the *Hartford Fire* Court and construe the two iterations of the language identically. Where, as here, the tie binds more tightly — that is, the text under consideration is not merely a duplicate appearing somewhere else in the statute, but is the original phrase in the original setting — the pressure escalates and the case for reading the language in a manner consonant with a prior Supreme Court interpretation is irresistible. [citation omitted].

. . . The words of Section One have not changed since the *Hartford Fire* Court found that they clearly evince Congress, intent to apply the Sherman Act extraterritorially in civil actions, and it would be disingenuous for us to pretend that the words had lost their clarity simply because this is a criminal proceeding. Thus, unless some special circumstance obtains in this case, there is no principled way in which we can uphold the order of dismissal.

NPI and its amicus, the Government of Japan, urge that special reasons exist for measuring Section One's reach differently in a criminal context. We have reviewed their exhortations and found them hollow. We discuss the five most promising theses below. The rest do not require comment.

1. Lack of Precedent. NPI and its amicus make much of the fact that this appears to be the first criminal case in which the United States endeavors to extend Section One to wholly foreign conduct. We are not impressed. There is a first time for everything, and the absence of earlier criminal actions is probably more a demonstration of the increasingly global nature of our economy than proof that Section One cannot cover wholly foreign conduct in the criminal milieu.

Moreover, this argument overstates the lack of precedent. There is, for example, solid authority for applying a state's criminal statute to conduct occurring entirely outside the state's borders. See *Strassheim v. Daily*, 221 U.S. 280, 285, 55 L. Ed. 735, 31 S. Ct. 558 (1911) (Holmes, J.) ("Acts done outside a jurisdiction, but intended to produce and producing detrimental effects within it, justify a State in punishing the cause of the harm as if he had been present at the effect, if the State should succeed in getting him within its power.") . It is not much of a stretch to apply this same principle internationally, especially in a shrinking world. See, *e.g., Chua Han Mow v. United States*, 730 F.2d 1308, 1311-12 (9th Cir. 1984) (applying Strassheim principle to conduct in Malaysia involving drugs intended for distribution in the United States), *cert. denied*, 470 U.S. 1031, 84 L. Ed. 2d 790, 105 S. Ct. 1403 (1985) *United States v. Hayes*, 653 F. 2d 8, 11 (lst Cir. 1981) (similar) *cf.* John Donne, Devotions Upon Emergent Occasions, no. 17 (1624) (warning that "no man is an island, entire of itself; every man is a piece of the continent, a part of the main").

431

2. Difference in Strength of Presumption. The lower court and NPI both cite *United States v. Bowman*, 260 U.S. 94, 67 L. Ed. 149, 43 S. Ct. 39 (1922), for the proposition that the presumption against extraterritoriality operates with greater force in the criminal arena than in civil litigation. This misreads the opinion. To be sure, the *Bowman* Court, dealing with a charged conspiracy to defraud, warned that if the criminal law "is to be extended to include those committed outside of the strict territorial jurisdiction, it is natural for Congress to say so in the statute, and failure to do so will negative the purpose of Congress in this regard." Id. at 98. But this pronouncement merely restated the presumption against extraterritoriality previously established in civil cases like *American Banana*, 213 U.S. at 357. The *Bowman* Court nowhere suggested that a different, more resilient presumption arises in criminal cases. . . . There is simply no comparable tradition or rationale for drawing a criminal/civil distinction with regard to extraterritoriality, and neither NPI nor its amicus have alluded to any case which does so.

3. The Restatement. NPI and the district court, 944 F. Supp. at 65, both sing the praises of the Restatement (Third) of Foreign Relations Law (1987), claiming that it supports a distinction between civil and criminal cases on the issue of extraterritoriality. The passage to which they pin their hopes states:

> In the case of regulatory statutes that may give rise to both civil and criminal liability, such as the United States antitrust and securities laws, the presence of substantial foreign elements will ordinarily weigh against application of criminal law. In such cases, legislative intent to subject conduct outside the state's territory to its criminal law should be found only on the basis of express statement or clear implication.

Id. at 403 cmt. f. We believe that this statement merely reaffirms the classic presumption against extraterritoriality — no more, no less. After all, nothing in the text of the Restatement proper contradicts the government's interpretation of Section One. See, e.g., id. at §402(l)(c) (explaining that, subject only to a general requirement of reasonableness, a state has Jurisdiction to proscribe "conduct outside its territory that has or is intended to have substantial ef f ect within its territory") ; id. at §415 (2) ("Any agreement in restraint of United States trade that is made outside of the United States. . . subject to the jurisdiction to prescribe of the United States, if a principal purpose of the conduct or agreement is to interfere with the commerce of the United States, and the agreement or conduct has some effect on that commerce."). What is more, other comments indicate that a country's decision to prosecute wholly foreign conduct is discretionary. See, e.g., id. at § 403 rep. n.8.

4. The Rule of Lenity. The next arrow which NPI yanks from its quiver is the rule of lenity. The rule itself is venerable; it provides that, in the course of interpreting statutes in criminal cases, a reviewing court should resolve ambiguities affecting a statute's scope in the defendant's favor. [citations omitted] But the rule of lenity is inapposite unless a statutory ambiguity looms, and a statute is not ambiguous for this purpose simply because some courts or commentators have questioned its proper interpretation.[6]307-13 (1993). [citations omitted] Rather, "the rule of lenity applies only if, after seizing everything from which aid can be derived, court] can make no more than a guess as to what Congress intended." *Reno*, 115 S. Ct. at 2029 (citations, internal quotation marks, and certain brackets omitted) ; accord United States v. O'Neil, 11 F.3d 292, 301 n.10 (lst Cir. 1993) (describing the rule of lenity as "a background principle that properly comes into play when, at the end of a thorough inquiry, the meaning of a criminal statute remains obscure,,) . Put bluntly, the rule of lenity cannot be used to create ambiguity when the meaning of a law, even if not readily apparent, is, upon inquiry, reasonably clear.

That ends the matter of lenity. In view of the fact that the Supreme Court deems it "well established" that Section One of the Sherman Act applies to wholly foreign conduct, *Hartford Fire*, 509 U.S. at 796, we effectively are foreclosed from trying to tease an ambiguity out of Section One relative to its extraterritorial application. Accordingly, the rule of lenity plays no part in the instant case.

5. Comity. International comity is a doctrine that counsels voluntary forbearance when a sovereign which has a legitimate claim to jurisdiction concludes that a second sovereign also has a legitimate claim to jurisdiction under principles of international law. See Harold G. Maier, Extraterritorial Jurisdiction at a Crossroads: An Intersection Between Public and Private International Law, 76 A. J. Intl l L. 280, 281 n.1 (1982). Comity is more an aspiration than a fixed rule, more a matter of grace than a matter of obligation. In all events, its growth in the antitrust sphere has been stunted by Hartford Fire, in which the Court suggested that comity concerns would operate to defeat the exercise of jurisdiction only in those few cases in which the law of the foreign sovereign required a defendant to act in a manner incompatible with the Sherman Act or in which full compliance with both statutory schemes was impossible. See *Hartford Fire*, 509 U.S. at 798-99; see also Kenneth W. Dam, Extraterritoriality in an Age of Globalization: The Hartford Fire Case, 1993 Sup. Ct. Rev. 289, 306-07 (1993) . Accordingly, the *Hartford Fire* Court gave short shrift to the defendants' entreaty that the conduct leading to antitrust liability was perfectly legal in the United Kingdom. See *Hartford Fire*, 509 U.S. at 798-99.

---

6. Leaving aside the lower court's decision in this case, no reported opinion has questioned the applicability of Hartford Fire's exercise in statutory construction to the precincts patrolled by the criminal law. Nevertheless, Hartford Fire's rendition of the statute has drawn criticism from the academy. See, e.g., Kenneth W. Dam, Extraterritoriality in an Age of Globalization: The Hartford Fire Case, 1993 Sup.Ct.Rev. 289.

In this case the defendant's comity-based argument is even more attenuated. The conduct with which NPI is charged is illegal under both Japanese and American laws, thereby alleviating any founded concern about NPI being whipsawed between separate sovereigns. And, moreover, to the extent that comity is informed by general principles of reasonableness, see Restatement (Third) of Foreign Relations Law § 403, the indictment lodged against NPI is well within the pale. In it, the government charges that the defendant orchestrated a conspiracy with the object of rigging prices in the United States. If the government can prove these charges, we see no tenable reason why principles of comity should shield NPI from prosecution. We live in an age of international commerce, where decisions reached in one corner of the world can reverberate around the globe in less time than it takes to tell the tale. Thus, a ruling in NPI's favor would create perverse incentives for those who would use nefarious means to influence markets in the United States, rewarding them for erecting as many territorial firewalls as possible between cause and effect.

We need go no further. *Hartford Fire* definitively establishes that Section One of the Sherman Act applies to wholly foreign conduct which has an intended and substantial effect in the United States. We are bound to accept that holding. Under settled principles of statutory construction, we also are bound to apply it by interpreting Section One the same way in a criminal case. The combined force of these commitments requires that we accept the government's cardinal argument, reverse the order of the district court, reinstate the indictment, and remand for further proceedings.

Reversed and remanded.

LYNCH, Circuit Judge (concurring).

. . . courts must be careful to determine whether this construction of Section One's criminal reach conforms with principles, of international law. "It has been a maxim of statutory construction since the decision in Murray v. The Charming Betsy, 6 U.S. 64, 2 Cranch 64, 118, 2 L. Ed. 208 (1804), that 'an act of congress ought never to be construed to violate the law of nations, if any other possible construction remains.'" Weinberger v. Rossi, 456 U.S. 25, 32, 71 L. Ed. 2d 715, 102 S. Ct. 1510 (1982).

In the Alcoa case, Judge Learned Hand found this canon of construction relevant to determining the substantive reach of the Sherman Act, observing that "we are not to read general words Section One] . . . without regard to the limitations customarily observed by nations upon the exercise of their powers, *United States v. Aluminum Co. of Am.*, 148 F.2d 416, 443 (2d Cir. 1945); see also *Hartford Fire,* 509 U.S. at 814-15 (Scalia, J., dissenting).

The task of construing Section One in this context is not the usual one of determining congressional intent by parsing the language or legislative history of the statute. The broad, general language of the federal antitrust laws and their unilluminating legislative history place a special interpretive responsibility upon the judiciary. The Supreme Court has called the Sherman Act a "charter of freedom" for the courts, with "a generality and adaptability comparable to that found . . . in constitutional provisions." *Appalachian Coals, Inc. v. United States*, 288 U.S. 344, 359-60, 77 L. Ed. 825, 53 S. Ct. 471 (1933). As Professors Areeda and Turner have said, the federal courts have been invested "with a jurisdiction to create and develop an 'antitrust law' in the manner of the common law courts. [citation omitted]. The courts are aided in this task by canons of statutory construction, such as the presumption against violating international law, which serve as both guides and limits in the absence of more explicit indicia of congressional intent.

Here, we are asked to determine the substantive content of Section One's inexact jurisdictional provision, "commerce . . . with foreign nations.,' 15 U.S. C.§ 1. Because of the "compunctions against the creation of crimes by judges rather than by legislators," II Areeda & Hovenkamp, Antitrust Law P 311b, at 33 (1995 rev. ed.), the constitution-like aspects of the antitrust laws must be handled particularly carefully in criminal prosecutions.

As the antitrust laws give the federal enforcement agencies a relatively blank check, the development of antitrust law has been largely shaped by the cases that the executive branch chooses - or does not choose - to bring. Accordingly it has been said that:

> novel interpretations or great departures have seldom, if ever, occurred in criminal cases, which prosecutors have usually reserved for defendants whose knowing behavior would be generally recognized as appropriate for criminal sanctions. Id. at 34.

This case does present a new interpretation. We are told this is the first instance in which the executive branch has chosen to interpret the criminal provisions of the Sherman Act as reaching conduct wholly committed outside of this country's borders.

Changing economic conditions, as well as different political agendas, mean that antitrust policies may change from administration to administration. The present administration has promulgated new Antitrust Enforcement Guidelines for International operations which "focus primarily on situations in which the Sherman Act will grant jurisdiction and when the United States will exercise that jurisdiction" internationally. Brockbank, The 1995 International Antitrust Guidelines: The Reach of U.S. Antitrust Law Continues to Expand, 2 J. Int'l Legal Stud. 1, 22 (1996) . The new Guidelines reflect a stronger enforcement stance than earlier versions of the Guidelines, and have been described as a "warning to foreign governments and enterprises that the enforcement] Agencies intend to actively pursue restraints on trade occurring abroad that adversely affect American markets or damage American exporting opportunities." Id. at 21. The instant case is likely a result of this policy.

It is with this context in mind that we must determine if the exercise of jurisdiction occasioned by the decision of the executive branch of the United States is proper in this case. While courts, including this one, speak of determining congressional intent when interpreting statutes, the meaning of the antitrust laws has emerged through the relationship among all three branches of government. In this criminal case, it is our responsibility to ensure that the executives interpretation of the Sherman Act does not conflict with other legal principles, including principles of international law.

That question requires examination beyond the language of Section One of the Sherman Act. It is, of course, generally true that, as a principle of statutory interpretation, the same language should be read the same way in all contexts to which the language applies. But this is not invariably true. New content is sometimes ascribed to statutory terms depending upon context. Cf. *Robinson v. Shell Oil Co.*, 117 S. Ct. 843, 847, 136 L. Ed. 2d 808 (1997)(depending on context, statutory term may have different meanings in different sections of single statute); 3 Sutherland, Statutory Construction @ 60.04 (5th ed. 1995) (statutes with both remedial and penal provisions may be construed liberally in remedial context and strictly in penal context). As NPI and the Government of Japan point out, the Supreme Court has held that Section One of the Sherman Act, which defines both criminal and civil violations with one general phrase,' "should be construed as including intent as an element" of a criminal violation. [citation omitted]. Where Congress intends that our laws conform with international law, and where international law suggests that criminal enforcement and civil enforcement be viewed differently, it is at least conceivable that different content could be ascribed to the same language depending on whether the context is civil or criminal. It is then worth asking about the effect of the international law which Congress presumably also meant to respect.

The content of international law is determined "by reference 'to the customs and usages of civilized nations, and, as evidence of these, to the works of jurists and commentators. *Hilao v. Marcos*, 103 F.3d 789, 794 (9th Cir. 1996) (quoting *The Paquete Habana*, 175 U.S. 677, 700, 44 L. Ed. 320, 20 S. Ct. 290 (1900)); see also *Kadic v. Karadzic*, 70 F.3d 232 (2d Cir. 1995) . The Restatement (Third) of the Foreign Relations Law of the United.States restates international law, as derived from customary international law and from international agreements to which the United States is a party, as it applies to the United States. See Restatement (Third) of the Foreign Relations Law of the United States §§1, 101 (1987) Restatement] . The United States courts have treated the Restatement as an illuminating outline of central principles of international law. See Hartford Fire, 509 U.S. at 799 (citing Restatement); Hartford Fire, 509 U.S. at 818 (Scalia, J., dissenting)("I shall rely on the Restatement (Third) of Foreign Relations Law for the relevant principles of international law. Its standards appear fairly supported in the decisions of this Court construing international choice-of-law principles . . . and in the decisions of other federal courts. . . "); In re *Maxwell Communications Corp.*, 93 F.3d 1036, 1047-48 (2d Cir. 1996).

The Restatement articulates principles, derived from international law, for determining when the United States may properly exercise regulatory (or prescriptive) jurisdiction over activities or persons connected with another state. It serves as a useful guide to evaluating the international interests at stake. Sections 402 and 403 articulate general principles. See Restatement §§ 402, 403. Section 415 applies these principles to "Jurisdiction to Regulate Anti-Competitive Activities." Id. §415.

Application of the [Restatement] principles to the indictment at issue here leads to the conclusion that the exercise of jurisdiction is reasonable in this case. Here, raising prices in the United States and Canada was not only a purpose of the alleged conspiracy, it was the purpose, thus satisfying Section 415's "principal purpose" requirement. Moreover, Section 415's requirement of "some effect" on United States markets is amply met here. The indictment alleges that NPI sold $ 6.1 million of fax paper into the United States during 1990, approximately the period covered by the charged conspiracy. In 1990, total sales of fax paper in North America were approximately $ 100 million. NPI's price increases thus affected a not insignificant share of the United States market.

These same factors weigh heavily in the Section 403 reasonableness analysis. Because only North American markets were targeted, the United States' interest in combatting this activity appears to be greater than the Japanese interest, which may only be the general interest of a state in having its industries comport with foreign legal norms. Japan has no interest in protecting Japanese consumers in this case as they were unaffected by the alleged conspiracy. The United States, in contrast, has a strong interest in protecting United States consumers, who were affected by the increase in prices. In this situation, it may be that only the United States has sufficient incentive to pursue the alleged wrongdoers, thereby providing the necessary deterrent to similar anticompetitive behavior. In another case, where the consumers of the situs nation were injured as well, that state's interest in regulating anticompetitive conduct might be stronger than it is here.

Other Section 403 factors also counsel in favor of the exercise of jurisdiction here. The effects on United States markets were foreseeable and direct. The

Government of Japan acknowledges that antitrust regulation is part of the international legal system, and NPI does not really assert that it has justified expectations that were hurt by the regulation.[7] The only factor counseling against finding that the United States' antitrust laws apply to this conduct is the fact that the situs of the conduct was Japan and that the principals were Japanese corporations. This consideration is inherent in the nature of jurisdiction based on effects of conduct, where the situs of the conduct is, by definition, always a foreign country. This alone does not tip the balance against jurisdiction.

For these reasons, I agree with the majority that the district court erred in dismissing the indictment.

NOTES AND QUESTIONS

1. Nippon Paper was a criminal antitrust prosecution of a foreign firm, based on foreign activity that caused an effect in the US. Should Mansfield's revenue rule apply? If so, why? What would Oliver Wendell Holmes say?

2. What happened to comity? Is the US guilty of being disrespectful of Japanese interests, or is Japan being disrespectful of important US interests? The answer might depend on from which of the border you view the case. Is there a neutral view of comity? Or is it always a question of whose ox is being gored?

3. What about the reverse situation from the cases we've been looking at? Are there comity considerations if US firms "cartelize" to harm consumers in foreign countries? In the next (and last) case, the Supreme Court addresses that question in a case where it is stipulated there is no effect in the US. Could it be that even the US has discovered the limits of comity? If so, what are they, and when do they apply?

---

7. While criminal prosecution may come as a surprise, NPI should have known that civil antitrust liability could include treble damages. A corporation found guilty of a criminal violation of Section One is subject to a fine not exceeding $ 10 million. See 15 U.S.C. sec. 2. Treble damages obviously do not include a similar cap.

F. HOFFMANN-La ROCHE LTD.
v.
EMPAGRAN S.A.

US Supreme Court
June 14, 2004
572 U.S. 155

Justice Breyer delivered the opinion of the Court.

The Foreign Trade Antitrust Improvements Act of 1982 (FTAIA) excludes from the Sherman Act's reach much anticompetitive conduct that causes only foreign injury. It does so by setting forth a general rule stating that the Sherman Act "shall not apply to conduct involving trade or commerce ... with foreign nations." It then creates exceptions to the general rule, applicable where (roughly speaking) that conduct significantly harms imports, domestic commerce, or American exporters.

We here focus upon anticompetitive price-fixing activity that . . . causes foreign injury. . .

. . . [T]his case involves vitamin sellers around the world that agreed to fix prices, leading to higher vitamin prices in the United States and independently leading to higher vitamin prices in other countries such as Ecuador. We conclude that, in this scenario, a purchaser in the United States could bring a Sherman Act claim under the FTAIA based on domestic injury, but a purchaser in Ecuador could not bring a Sherman Act claim based on foreign harm.

I

The plaintiffs in this case originally filed a class-action suit on behalf of foreign and domestic purchasers of vitamins under, inter alia, §1 of the Sherman Act §§4 and 16 of the Clayton Act. Their complaint alleged that petitioners, foreign and domestic vitamin manufacturers and distributors, had engaged in a price-fixing conspiracy, raising the price of vitamin products to customers in the United States and to customers in foreign countries.

As relevant here, petitioners moved to dismiss the suit as to the foreign purchasers (the respondents here), five foreign vitamin distributors located in Ukraine, Australia, Ecuador, and Panama, each of which bought vitamins from petitioners for delivery outside the United States. Respondents have never asserted that they purchased any vitamins in the United States or in transactions in United States commerce, and the question presented assumes that the relevant "transactions occurr[ed] entirely outside U.S. commerce." The District Court dismissed their claims. [The Court of Appeals reversed.] . . .

439

We granted certiorari . . .

II

The FTAIA seeks to make clear to American exporters (and to firms doing business abroad) that the Sherman Act does not prevent them from entering into business arrangements (say, joint-selling arrangements), however anticompetitive, as long as those arrangements adversely affect only foreign markets. See H. R. Rep. No. 97—686, pp. 1—3, 9—10 (1982) (hereinafter House Report). It does so by removing from the Sherman Act's reach, (1) export activities and (2) other commercial activities taking place abroad, unless those activities adversely affect domestic commerce, imports to the United States, or exporting activities of one engaged in such activities within the United States.

* * *

IV

We turn now to the basic question presented, that of the [FTAIA's] application. Because the underlying antitrust action is complex, potentially raising questions not directly at issue here, we reemphasize that we base our decision upon the following: The price-fixing conduct significantly and adversely affects both customers outside the United States and customers within the United States, but the adverse foreign effect is independent of any adverse domestic effect. In these circumstances, we find that the FTAIA . . . appl[ies] (and thus the Sherman Act does not apply) for two main reasons.

First, this Court ordinarily construes ambiguous statutes to avoid unreasonable interference with the sovereign authority of other nations. See, e.g., *McCulloch v. Sociedad Nacional de Marineros de Honduras*, 372 U.S. 10, 20—22 (1963) (application of National Labor Relations Act to foreign-flag vessels); *Romero v. International Terminal Operating Co.*, 358 U.S. 354, 382—383 (1959) (application of Jones Act in maritime case); *Lauritzen v. Larsen*, 345 U.S. 571, 578 (1953) (same). This rule of construction reflects principles of customary international law–law that (we must assume) Congress ordinarily seeks to follow. See Restatement (Third) of Foreign Relations Law of the United States §§403(1), 403(2) (1986) (hereinafter Restatement) (limiting the unreasonable exercise of prescriptive jurisdiction with respect to a person or activity having connections with another State); *Murray v. Schooner Charming Betsy*, 2 Cranch 64, 118 (1804) ("[A]n act of Congress ought never to be construed to violate the law of nations if any other possible construction remains"); *Hartford Fire*

Insurance Co. v. California, 509 U.S. 764, 817 (1993) (Scalia, J., dissenting) (identifying rule of construction as derived from the principle of "prescriptive comity").

This rule of statutory construction cautions courts to assume that legislators take account of the legitimate sovereign interests of other nations when they write American laws. It thereby helps the potentially conflicting laws of different nations work together in harmony–a harmony particularly needed in today's highly interdependent commercial world.

No one denies that America's antitrust laws, when applied to foreign conduct, can interfere with a foreign nation's ability independently to regulate its own commercial affairs. But our courts have long held that application of our antitrust laws to foreign anticompetitive conduct is nonetheless reasonable, and hence consistent with principles of prescriptive comity, insofar as they reflect a legislative effort to redress domestic antitrust injury that foreign anticompetitive conduct has caused. See United States v. Aluminum Co. of America, 148 F.2d 416, 443–444 (CA2 1945) (L. Hand, J.); 1 P. Areeda & D. Turner, Antitrust Law ¶236 (1978).

But why is it reasonable to apply those laws to foreign conduct insofar as that conduct causes independent foreign harm and that foreign harm alone gives rise to the plaintiff's claim? Like the former case, application of those laws creates a serious risk of interference with a foreign nation's ability independently to regulate its own commercial affairs. But, unlike the former case, the justification for that interference seems insubstantial. See Restatement §403(2) (determining reasonableness on basis of such factors as connections with regulating nation, harm to that nation's interests, extent to which other nations regulate, and the potential for conflict). Why should American law supplant, for example, Canada's or Great Britain's or Japan's own determination about how best to protect Canadian or British or Japanese customers from anticompetitive conduct engaged in significant part by Canadian or British or Japanese or other foreign companies?

We recognize that principles of comity provide Congress greater leeway when it seeks to control through legislation the actions of American companies, see Restatement §402; and some of the anticompetitive price-fixing conduct alleged here took place in America. But the higher foreign prices of which the foreign plaintiffs here complain are not the consequence of any domestic anticompetitive conduct that Congress sought to forbid, for Congress did not seek to forbid any such conduct insofar as it is here relevant, i.e., insofar as it is intertwined with foreign conduct that causes independent foreign harm. Rather Congress sought to release domestic (and foreign) anticompetitive conduct from Sherman Act constraints when that conduct causes foreign harm. Congress, of course, did make an exception where that conduct also causes domestic harm. See House Report 13 (concerns about American firms' participation in international cartels addressed through "domestic injury" exception). But any independent domestic harm the foreign conduct causes here has, by definition, little or nothing to do with the matter.

We thus repeat the basic question: Why is it reasonable to apply this law to conduct that is significantly foreign insofar as that conduct causes independent foreign harm and that foreign harm alone gives rise to the plaintiff's claim? We can find no good answer to the question.

. . . Respondents reply that many nations have adopted antitrust laws similar to our own, to the point where the practical likelihood of interference with the relevant interests of other nations is minimal. Leaving price fixing to the side, however, this Court has found to the contrary. See, *e.g.*, *Hartford Fire*, 509 U.S. at 797—799 (noting that the alleged conduct in the London reinsurance market, while illegal under United States antitrust laws, was assumed to be perfectly consistent with British law and policy); see also, e.g., 2 W. Fugate, Foreign Commerce and the Antitrust Laws §16.6 (5th ed. 1996) (noting differences between European Union and United States law on vertical restraints).

Regardless, even where nations agree about primary conduct, say price fixing, they disagree dramatically about appropriate remedies. The application, for example, of American private treble-damages remedies to anticompetitive conduct taking place abroad has generated considerable controversy. See, e.g., 2 ABA Section of Antitrust Law, Antitrust Law Developments 1208—1209 (5th ed. 2002). And several foreign nations have filed briefs here arguing that to apply our remedies would unjustifiably permit their citizens to bypass their own less generous remedial schemes, thereby upsetting a balance of competing considerations that their own domestic antitrust laws embody. E.g., Brief for Federal Republic of Germany et al. as Amici Curiae 2 (setting forth German interest "in seeing that German companies are not subject to the extraterritorial reach of the United States' antitrust laws by private foreign plaintiffs–whose injuries were sustained in transactions entirely outside United States commerce– seeking treble damages in private lawsuits against German companies"); Brief for Government of Canada as Amicus Curiae 14 ("treble damages remedy would supersede" Canada's "national policy decision"); Brief for Government of Japan as Amicus Curiae 10 (finding "particularly troublesome" the potential "interfere[nce] with Japanese governmental regulation of the Japanese market").

These briefs add that a decision permitting independently injured foreign plaintiffs to pursue private treble-damages remedies would undermine foreign nations' own antitrust enforcement policies by diminishing foreign firms' incentive to cooperate with antitrust authorities in return for prosecutorial amnesty. Brief for Federal Republic of Germany et al. as Amici Curiae 28—30; Brief for Government of Canada as Amicus Curiae 11—14. See also Brief for

United States as Amicus Curiae 19—21 (arguing the same in respect to American antitrust enforcement).

Respondents alternatively argue that comity does not demand an interpretation of the FTAIA that would exclude independent foreign injury cases across the board. Rather, courts can take (and sometimes have taken) account of comity considerations case by case, abstaining where comity considerations so dictate. *Cf., e.g., Hartford Fire, supra,* at 797, n. 24; *United States v. Nippon Paper Industries Co.,* 109 F.3d 1, 8 (CA1 1997); *Mannington Mills, Inc. v. Congoleum Corp.,* 595 F.2d 1287, 1294—1295 (CA3 1979).

In our view, however, this approach is too complex to prove workable. The Sherman Act covers many different kinds of anticompetitive agreements. Courts would have to examine how foreign law, compared with American law, treats not only price fixing but also, say, information-sharing agreements, patent-licensing price conditions, territorial product resale limitations, and various forms of joint venture, in respect to both primary conduct and remedy. The legally and economically technical nature of that enterprise means lengthier proceedings, appeals, and more proceedings–to the point where procedural costs and delays could themselves threaten interference with a foreign nation's ability to maintain the integrity of its own antitrust enforcement system. Even in this relatively simple price-fixing case, for example, competing briefs tell us (1) that potential treble-damage liability would help enforce widespread anti-price-fixing norms (through added deterrence) and (2) the opposite, namely that such liability would hinder antitrust enforcement (by reducing incentives to enter amnesty programs). Compare, e.g., Brief for Certain Professors of Economics as Amici Curiae 2—4 with Brief for United States as Amicus Curiae 19—21. How could a court seriously interested in resolving so empirical a matter–a matter potentially related to impact on foreign interests–do so simply and expeditiously?

We conclude that principles of prescriptive comity counsel against the Court of Appeals' interpretation of the FTAIA. Where foreign anticompetitive conduct plays a significant role and where foreign injury is independent of domestic effects, Congress might have hoped that America's antitrust laws, so fundamental a component of our own economic system, would commend themselves to other nations as well. But, if America's antitrust policies could not win their own way in the international marketplace for such ideas, Congress, we must assume, would not have tried to impose them, in an act of legal imperialism, through legislative fiat.

Second, the FTAIA's language and history suggest that Congress designed the FTAIA to clarify, perhaps to limit, but not to expand in any significant way, the Sherman Act's scope as applied to foreign commerce. See House Report 2—3. And we have found no significant indica-tion that at the time Congress wrote this statute courts would have thought the Sherman Act applicable in these circumstances.

V

. . .

For these reasons, we conclude that petitioners' reading of the statute's language is correct. That reading furthers the statute's basic purposes, it properly reflects considerations of comity, and it is consistent with Sherman Act history.

VI

We have assumed that the anticompetitive conduct here independently caused foreign injury; that is, the conduct's domestic effects did not help to bring about that foreign injury. Respondents argue, in the alternative, that the foreign injury was not independent. Rather, they say, the anticompetitive conduct's domestic effects were linked to that foreign harm. Respondents contend that, because vitamins are fungible and readily transportable, without an adverse domestic effect (i.e., higher prices in the United States), the sellers could not have maintained their international price-fixing arrangement and respondents would not have suffered their foreign injury. They add that this "but for" condition is sufficient to bring the price-fixing conduct within the scope of the FTAIA's exception.

The Court of Appeals, however, did not address this argument, 315 F.3d, at 341, and, for that reason, neither shall we. Respondents remain free to ask the Court of Appeals to consider the claim. . . .

For these reasons, the judgment of the Court of Appeals is vacated, and the case is remanded for further proceedings consistent with this opinion.

It is so ordered.

MULTIPLE CHOICE REVIEW QUESTION

1. The Rule of Territoriality:

   a. does not apply on the high seas

   b. is an example of the Revenue Rule applied to antitrust law

   c. is the same as the effects doctrine

   d. is currently the law in the United States

2. The effects doctrine:

   a. is accepted as the law everywhere except in England

   b. is the same as the purposeful availment principle

   c. was rejected in Hartford Fire Insurance

   d. none of the above

3. The "Comity Balancing" approach:

   a. is the law in the 9th and 3rd Circuits

   b. has its roots in academia

   c. is the law when there is no effect in the U.S.

   d. is based on the Revenue Rule

4. According to the US Supreme Court, a "conflict" of laws exists only if:

   a. the laws of the foreign country are repugnant to the U.S.

   b. the laws of the foreign are materially different from those in the U.S.

   c. the laws of the foreign country permit conduct prohibited in the U.S.

   d. the laws of the foreign country compel conduct that is prohibited in the U.S.

445

5. Which of the following quotations most accurately describes the current state of US law:

a. "The character of an act as lawful in determined wholly by the law of the place where the act was done."

b. "One country never takes notice of the revenue laws of another."

c. "it is settled law . . . that any state may impose liabilities, even upon persons not within its allegiance, for conduct outside its borders that has consequences within its borders which the state reprehends; and these liabilities other states will ordinarily recognize."

d. "it is well established by now that the Sherman Act applies to foreign conduct that was meant to produce and did in fact produce some substantial effect in the United States."

PROBLEMS FOR ANALYSIS

PROBLEM 1

In March 2002, an English businessman named Robert Fallwell met, in London, with the chairman and officers of Leasco, Inc., an American corporation based in New York. Mr. Fallwell owned and controlled Pergamon Press, a British firm, and Fallwell had invited Leasco to London to discuss a plan for a joint venture in Europe. While in London, Leasco politely declined the offer, but the parties kept talking.

A second meeting took place in Bermuda, and the discussion turned to the acquisition of Pergamon by Leasco. There were several transatlantic telephone calls between Fallwell in London and Leasco in New York. In the calls and meetings, Fallwell made false and misleading representations to Leasco concerning Pergamon's assets, sales, and earnings, and he e-mailed Leasco false and misleading financial statements.

Eventually an agreement was signed - in London - whereby Leasco offered to buy all the outstanding shares of Pergamon at 6 Euro. per share.

Soon thereafter, Fallwell told Leasco's chairman that there was a rumor going around London of a (hostile) counter-takeover bid, and he urged Leasco to begin buying Pergamon's stock on the London Stock Exchange (where it was publicly traded). Leasco, fearing that the deal will be blown, purchased 38% of Pergamon's shares on the London Stock Exchange at prices above 7 Euro.

Leasco later found out that if there was a counter-takeover rumor, Fallwell started it, and that Fallwell had been selling while Leasco was buying. Trading in Pergamon's stock was suspended by the London Stock Exchange, and the Exchange began an investigation, which is continuing.

Leasco sued Fallwell in New York for violation of the Federal (U.S.) Securities Act which makes illegal the use of deceptive practices in the purchase or sale of securities. Fallwell was served in London with the Summons & Complaint.

(A)   Assume that Fallwell makes a motion to dismiss the NY proceeding for lack of in personam jurisdiction. What result do you think the New York court would reach?

(B)   Assume that all the allegations are true, and, that if the allegations are proven, a violation of the Federal Securities Act would exist. How would you expect a judge to rule on a motion by Fallwell that the U.S. Securities Act does not apply to him or to this transaction.

PROBLEM 2

CasinoWorld is an Antiguan corporation offering casino-type wagering on the Internet. CasinoWorld operates exclusively in Antigua, where it employs computer programmers, operators, data-entry and customer-service employees. CasinoWorld is owned by a Canadian Corporation licensed by the nation of Antigua to offer real-space and on-line gaming. CasinoWorld knows that many, if not most, of its customers live in the United States.

Internet gaming is illegal in the United States under the (US) federal "Wire Wager Act". The Act makes illegal the transmission of gambling information on wires or other electronic transmissions across state lines. The Act has criminal penalties, including fines, prison for offenders, and, relevant here, forfeiture of assets used in gaming in violation of the Act.

Customers of CasinoWorld use their credit cards to establish accounts at the CasinoWorld's "virtual casino"; when the account is established, CasinoWorld debits the credit card account for a pre-agreed limit (e.g. $500). The customer then is given that amount of "Antiguan dollars" with which to gamble. If the customer wins, the customer's credit card account is credited for the winnings when the customer decides to "cash out". If the customer loses money equal to the pre-agreed limit, the customer must re-submit the credit card and the process begins again.

On March 2, 2006, the United States Attorney for New York (i.e. "the feds") obtained an order directed to Citibank and Chase Manhattan Bank freezing, and seeking the turnover and forfeiture, of all moneys charged by U.S. customers of CasinoWorld but not yet remitted to CasinoWorld. The Order affects $3 million (U.S.) In moneys at Citi and Chase yet to be remitted to CasinoWorld.

The U.S. Attorney is arguing that the Wire Wager Act governs CasinoWorld's activities, and the moneys should be forfeit. CasinoWorld wants its money. What arguments would you expect CasinoWorld to make? How do you think a U.S. court would rule on a motion by CasinoWorld to vacate the freeze order?

IDEAS FOR RESEARCH AND FURTHER LEARNING

1. US Antitrust law has clashed with the laws of other countries in many situations that became newsworthy, and in which the resolution was interesting. Conduct research into "*HAPAG* and the creation of the Federal Maritime Commission"; the "Lightbulb Conspiracy" cases; or "*the Swiss Watchmaker's Case*". What lessons can we learn from those cases? How do they fit into the legal regime developed here?

2. Microsoft received a dismissal of the US' antitrust charges relating to their monopoly position and practices. The European Union found Microsoft liable for violating their antitrust laws. Read the history of this litigation, and see what happens when the shoe is on the other foot.

3. International treaties cover some areas of (public) law that differ from country to country. The treaties governing protection of Intellectual Property, e.g. exist to harmonize national differences and (try to) present a single international regulatory system. The Universal Copyright Convention, The Berne Convention, Trademark Law Treaty, and the Patent Cooperation Treaty are among them. What are the issues? How are they harmonized? What role does the World Intellectual Property Organization ("WIPO") play?

4. The (British) Protection of Trading Interests Act is the blocking statute involved in the *Laker* case. Swiss banking secrecy laws are another such statute. How do they work? How has the US asserted its "jurisdiction" in cases where those laws are involved?

5. The Foreign Corrupt Practices Act is US law that governs US companies and their subsidiaries when acting abroad. What is the history of the statute? What types of activities are covered? What lessons does the Act teach regarding the regulation of international business by the US?

TABLE OF CASES

W

Y